EVER, DIRK
THE BOGARDE LETTERS

'Don't think that this is a letter. It is only a small eruption of a disease called friendship.'
(Jean Renoir to Janine Bazin, 12/6/74)

'Letters, I think, unless they are brilliant, can be a bit of a bore. And mine are not brilliant. Amusing, perhaps, light, and loving but they aint Intellectual!'
(Dirk Bogarde to Dilys Powell, 25/3/89)

'Good correspondence, like music, does nice things for the spirit, as you obviously discovered long ago.'
(Robert L. Palmer to Dirk Bogarde, 23/5/91)

'Letters are, after all, fragments of autobiography.'
(Richard Mangan, Introduction to *Gielgud's Letters*, Weidenfeld & Nicolson, 2004)

John Coldstream, Literary Editor of the *Daily Telegraph* from 1991 to 1999, is the author of *Dirk Bogarde: The Authorised Biography* (2004). He also edited *For the Time Being* (1998), a collection of Bogarde's journalism. With his wife, Sue, he 'divides his time' between West Sussex and London.

EVER, DIRK

THE BOGARDE LETTERS

SELECTED AND EDITED BY

JOHN COLDSTREAM

PHOENIX

A PHOENIX PAPERBACK

First published in Great Britain in 2008
by Weidenfeld & Nicolson
This paperback edition published in 2009
by Phoenix,
an imprint of Orion Books Ltd,
Orion House, 5 Upper St Martin's Lane,
London WC2H 9EA

An Hachette UK Company

1 3 5 7 9 10 8 6 4 2

A CIP catalogue record for this book
is available from the British Library.

ISBN 978-0-7538-2589-1

Typeset by Input Data Services Ltd, Bridgwater, Somerset

Printed and bound in the UK
by CPI Mackays, Chatham, Kent

The Orion Publishing Group's policy is to use papers
that are natural, renewable and recyclable products and
made from wood grown in sustainable forests. The logging
and manufacturing processes are expected to conform to
the environmental regulations of the country of origin.

www.orionbooks.co.uk

To the Van den Bogaerdes –
for their trust, encouragement
and laughter

CONTENTS

List of Illustrations xi

Introduction 1

Dramatis Personae 13

Nicknames 17

Selected References 18

Chronology 20

PART ONE:

THE CONTINENTAL YEARS 25

PART TWO:

THE LONDON YEARS 417

Dirk's Out-takes 597

Acknowledgements 608

Index 611

LIST OF ILLUSTRATIONS

Section One

With Kathleen Tynan and Tony[2] · With Jack ('Tony') Jones[1] · 'Mrs X' – Dorothy Gordon[3] · Jill Melford at Villa Berti[1] · With Eduardo and Antonia Boluda[1] · Joseph and Patricia Losey[4] · With Ian Holm and Bee Gilbert[1] · With Ann Skinner and Arnold Schulkes[5] · With Visconti[6] · At the NFT[7] · Dilys Powell[8] · With Penelope Mortimer[1] · With Ava Gardner[1] · With Margaret Van den Bogaerde[1] · The house on the hill[1] · Clermont by Tony Forwood[1] · The drawing-room[1] · The 'cockpit'[1] · The terraces[1] · With Daphne Fielding[1] · With Norah Smallwood[1] · Julie Harris and Julie Harris[9]

Section Two

On the set of *Providence* with Gielgud, Burstyn and Warner[10] · With Fassbinder[1] · Tom Stoppard[1] · With Elton John[1] · On location for *The Patricia Neal Story*[1] · With Natalie Wood[1] · Charlotte Rampling and Jean-Michel Jarre[1] · Painting the 'Hippo-Pool'[1] · The pool and the Drummer[1] · Glenda Jackson with Tony[1] · With John Huston and Isabelle Huppert at Cannes[11] · Dirk's Presidential notes[1] · Jacques Henri Lartigue[1] · At St Andrews University[12] · Olga Horstig-Primuz and her clients[13] · Patricia Kavanagh and Julian Barnes[14] · Brian McFarlane[17] · Susan Owens[16] · David Frankham[15] · With Daisy and Labo[1] · With Bendo[1] · Mowing the terraces and making piccalilli[1] · Patrolling his acres[1]

Section Three

With Princess Anne[18] · On stage in the early 1990s[1] · With Bertrand Tavernier and Jane Birkin[19] · Hélène Bordes[21] · With Peter Ustinov and Jacques Chirac[20] · Christine and Alain de Pauw[22] · Dominique Lambilliotte[20] · John Osborne[23] · With Eileen Atkins[24] · Bacchus[1] · At King's School, Rochester[25] · *Carte de séjour*[1] · Filming *Dirk Bogarde – By Myself*[26] · The portrait: David Tindle's pencil drawing[27], pre-study[28] and finished canvas[29] · As Sydney Carton, by Ulric Van den Bogaerde[30, 31] · Tableau for Sybil Burton[32] · With Tony[1]

Endpapers

(front) At work in the Studio, Clermont, July 1978, by David Steen[33]
(back) Dirk, by his near-neighbour, Jacques Henri Lartigue[34]

The line-drawings in the text are by Dirk Bogarde.

The editor and the publishers are grateful to the following for permission to reproduce the photographs listed above:

1 Dirk Bogarde Estate
2 Lichfield Studios
3 Carol Gordon
4 Patricia Losey
5 Ann Skinner
6 Mario Tursi
7 Brian Baxter/BFI
8 Ivor Powell/Colin Thomas/BFI
9 Julie Harris/Impact Photos Inc
10 Action Films
11 Festival du Film, Cannes
12 University of St Andrews
13 Véra de Ladoucette
14 Patricia Kavanagh
15 David Frankham
16 Susan Owens
17 Brian McFarlane
18 Doug McKenzie/Professional Photographic Services
19 UGC Cinemas
20 Dominique Lambilliotte
21 Hélène Bordes
22 Christine de Pauw
23 Jane Bown/National Portrait Gallery
24 BBC
25 Vernon Stratford/Chatham Standard
26 Paul Joyce/Lucida Productions
27 David Tindle/Jenny Arthur
28 David Tindle/Redfern Gallery
29 David Tindle/National Portrait Gallery
30 Audrey Carr
31 Kenneth J. Westwood Collection
32 Jean Selfe
33 Alpha Photographic Press Agency
34 J.H. Lartigue/Ministère de la Culture, France/AAJHL

While every effort has been made to trace copyright holders, if any have been inadvertently overlooked, the publishers will be happy to acknowledge them in future editions.

INTRODUCTION

'It is an astonishing thing to me to find that I am really not
a bit happy unless I am writing. Even a letter will do.'
– Dirk Bogarde to Norah Smallwood

In the last of his passports Derek Van den Bogaerde, otherwise Dirk
Bogarde, described himself simply as 'Actor'. Which is odd, because
from the late 1970s his success in a second, parallel, profession – that
of Writer – gave him just as much pride and fulfilment, if not more.
Novelist, poet, essayist, reporter, editor, scriptwriter, critic, auto-
biographer – in his time Dirk was all of these, and a diarist too. In
1986 he put his own early journals, along with much else, to the torch.
However, for the best part of his forty-year companionship with
Anthony Forwood the latter kept for them both a Diary, which began
as little more than a patchy record of visitors and appointments, but
became a daily rumination. On the few occasions when misfortune
befell Tony in the form of hospitalisation, or digital damage in a
gardening accident, Dirk would take over. The evident commitment
and relish with which he did so was all the more remarkable considering that he would have already spent much of the day crouched at
his desk, releasing through one of successive hard-pressed typewriters a
torrent of words.

Some who write for publication – nowadays especially – are not
necessarily driven by an inexplicable interior force. Dirk was. It would
be safe to say that he satisfied more than most the definition of the
'born writer'. This much-used, and often misused, expression applies
in truth only to those continuously in the grip of a compulsion. Those
such as the 2007 Nobel Laureate, Doris Lessing, for whom writing is
'a bloody neurosis'; and the late John Updike and Anthony Burgess,
whose affliction has been diagnosed by their fellow-novelist Martin
Amis as 'pressure on the cortex, facility in the best sense'. No one

would ever have described Dirk's written work, least of all in the original, as that of the conscious belletrist. However, with the simplicity of his language, his directness, his vigour, his skill at making 'a connection' – as he did so effectively in the Cinema – he more than compensated for what one might call politely his lapses in literary convention. In every one of the forms where he put words on paper he displayed the priceless gift of the compelling conversationalist. With no effort he made his reader – whether of a 250-page novel, a twenty-seven-line poem or a five-line scribbled note – his confidant.

Perhaps the most convincing symptom of the *need* to write, rather than merely to record, to reply, or to fulfil a commission, is found in the unsolicited, unprompted letter. Dirk was a prolific correspondent – not only in the astonishing quantity of notepaper and card that he consigned over the years to postboxes in various countries, but also in the length at which he wrote. Misspelt, eccentrically punctuated and paragraphed, his letters became essays. Yes, his hand was all over the place and often indecipherable: he admitted as much, often enough. But that was not the main reason why he typed even many of his postcards. More urgent was the need to cram the maximum number of words on to every available surface because he had so much to say. It was not uncommon for one of his letters to fill three sides of A4 paper, the typing single-spaced, the margins and paragraphing almost non-existent; and even then a fourth side might be invaded by that unruly script, offering a piece of unfinished or overlooked business as a P.S. There is a real likelihood, too, that such an epistle would be rattled off on a day when progress was being made with a novel or a new volume of autobiography. Sometimes when that progress was stumbling, and the wastepaper basket beginning to fill with crumpled drafts, he would pause and hammer out an 800-word letter in the same way that other writers might drift to the kitchen, make a cup of coffee and listen absent-mindedly to the news from the outside world or from the hearth. Dirk, by contrast, had to 'talk'. When he wrote, the shyness which beset him in public – and in overcoming which he could sometimes appear almost unrecognisable to those who knew him privately – lay dormant. In the safety and sanctuary of any room that he commandeered as an office, and above all in the studio he made from a former olive store at his farmhouse in Provence, he felt ultimately free to speak as he wished. 'I have done quite enough talking,' he says as he reaches the foot of a tightly packed second page;

but you can sense the reluctance to stop. And fortunately the other parties to these conversations recognised the quality of what he had to say, and the way he said it, to the extent that they kept his side of the exchange. It is thanks first to the foresight and then to the generosity of some of those confidants that his circle of 'listeners' can now be widened.

Few examples survive from Dirk's early life, but scraps from the young teenager's wretched exile in Glasgow indicated the strength of his prose, the vividness of his description and the fertility of his imagination. Some of his letters home were illustrated, flamboyantly so: to his sister Elizabeth ('Lu', 'LuLu') he sent pictorial puzzles for her to solve, and, at one point, a fairy tale painted on playing-card-sized pieces of art paper and posted episodically like a magazine serial. During his Army training in various parts of Britain he kept in contact by mail with a girlfriend, Nerine Cox – indeed he did so, on and off, for the rest of his life. When he joined the Allied Forces liberating Europe in 1944 he began the first of his several copious, extra-familial correspondences. This was with Jack ('Tony') Jones, the dashing Naval officer who had captured Dirk's heart the previous year and who, I believe, was his only serious love until the relationship with Tony Forwood took hold after the war. It is evident from various asides that Dirk's letters to Jack from Europe, India and Java were not only many in number but also explicit in their affection. Years later, Dirk sought his assurance that none survived and was told that all those before 1954 had been destroyed. The significance of the date is unclear, except for the fact that the Home Secretary had begun to crack down hard with prosecutions for breaches of the laws on homosexuality, especially by the prominent. It was the year of the Montagu/Wildeblood/Pitt-Rivers trial and of Alan Turing's suicide. It was also the year in which Dirk became the most popular British screen actor, thanks to *Doctor in the House*. Then again, Dirk had by that time been living with Forwood – as he most often referred to him among friends and strangers alike; or 'Tote' among their closest familiars – for six years; and it is my further belief that Dirk was 'monogamous'. So it is highly unlikely that there was much communication between him and Jack. Certainly, by 1949 they had gone their separate ways, and seldom, if ever, met again. The desultory correspondence which resumed when Dirk became a published author – a development that gave the extremely well-read Jones equal measures of satisfaction and amusement – is of little merit; it emits the unmistakable sound of Dirk's teeth being gritted and ground while he responds as cordially as possible to someone who represented a period in his life which he both wanted and, because of his subsequent, almost immediate, celebrity, needed to bury. In the modest, but significant, archive left by Dirk there is no trace of Jack Jones's existence; even a postcard liberated by the latter during his exploits in the D-Day landings, and pinned to the wall of Dirk's studio, was safely unsigned.

The bulk of Dirk's wartime letters home does not survive. As with the childhood correspondence, the few exceptions were drawn upon heavily for *Dirk Bogarde: The Authorised Biography* and are not repeated here. Likewise, two long, self-analytical letters which he wrote from Java to Dorothy Fells, an Army wife who contributed to the 23rd Indian Division newspaper, have already been quoted *in extenso*. His own commitment to *The Fighting Cock*, which he edited for a few months in 1946, probably reduced his mail from that theatre; apart from snapshots, some 'captioned' on the reverse, there is nothing in his family's papers. There is, too, a dearth of material from the immediate post-war years. This is explained, in part anyway, by the fact that Dirk's working life took him over. It must be borne in mind that within a year of his demobilisation he was in front of the cameras for *Esther Waters* as its leading player – a status, 'above the title', which he would maintain in the industry for four decades. Under his obligations to the Rank Organisation he was preparing for, and making, three or more films a year. Such correspondence as he was producing emerged mainly via loyal secretaries – principally Val Geeves and, later, Peggy Croft. Inevitably, this filter, while helpful to formal presentation, led to a dulling of impact. However good he was at giving dictation, the result could never be as effective as if he had struck the keys himself.

For all the above reasons, therefore, this selection is confined to the second half of Dirk's adult life. The years from 1969 to the mid-1990s yielded a crop of great, at times astonishing, abundance – much of it, unlike that from the earlier period, preserved.

The main cause of Dirk's increased productivity was simple. The opportunities for satisfying film work in England had been drying up, and on 1 March 1969 he and Tony set off for the Continent, where they would remain until 1987. In that time he made just nine films, two of them for television. For those eighteen years they were without a secretary, and even afterwards Dirk would employ one only on rare occasions, and briefly, to see him through a crisis. There was another persuasive factor. In those days the telephone in both Italy and France was primitive, unreliable and expensive. The call, either for business or for social purposes, was no longer quite the simple matter it had once been. However, armed with his typewriter and unbound by any of the strictures imposed by secretarial help, he was free to 'talk' whenever, and at whatever length, he wished. Quite apart from the cost and telephonic hazard of trying to converse with subscribers in Britain, he had by this time an obligation across the Atlantic which, were he to have pursued the traffic by any means other than mail, would have reduced him to near-penury.

In the spring of 1967 he had received a letter, franked in America, from a total stranger, Dorothy Gordon. A friend of hers had sent a copy of a magazine containing a photograph of Dirk at his house, Adam's Farm, on the Kent and Sussex border. Mrs Gordon had lived there before the war, and was curious to know how it had fared in the intervening thirty years. This was no fan letter; to those – except in cases where he guessed that the sender stalked the wilder shores of dottiness – he would reply with a crisp but polite note, or a signed photograph if one was requested. No, this was something way out of the ordinary, from a highly intelligent woman, a librarian at Yale University, who cared not a fig for Dirk's fame. With his reply, from the house in which they had a common interest, a 'conversation' began which lasted, at a fierce intensity, for three years, then dwindled somewhat during a further two, until Dorothy Gordon's death from cancer in 1972. Dirk had guessed almost from the beginning that she was mortally ill. He wrote to keep her intellectually stimulated. She, in turn, recognised that his flair on the written page needed to be disciplined sufficiently to move him towards being considered for publication as either a memoirist or a novelist. The result, in her case, was much solace at a desperate time; in Dirk's, five years later, it was *A Postillion Struck by Lightning*, the first of his fifteen books. 'FORCE memory!' she had exhorted him. And he did.

Their correspondence, the origins and progress of which Dirk described in *An Orderly Man*, is believed to have amounted to somewhere between 600 and a thousand pieces. Sometimes Dirk's cards would be held up by industrial trouble and would arrive together in a flock, to be dubbed by their recipient 'starlings'. The letters, in their airmail envelopes, were known as 'bluejays'. In quantity they humbled those between the American author Helene Hanff and the London bookseller Frank Doel. The latter correspondence was published in *84 Charing Cross Road* (André Deutsch, 1971); Dirk's, in 1989 by Chatto & Windus, as *A Particular Friendship*, with Dorothy Gordon disguised as 'Mrs X'. But there were differences between the two books. For a start, the Hanff–Doel exchanges were a dialogue; Dirk printed only his own letters, greatly edited and revised, and often with the help of the Diary, so some of the words in his monologues are, in fact, Tony's. Second, Hanff and Doel were in contact for almost twenty years, until the latter's death in December 1968. Third, Hanff and Doel wrote to each other with greater brevity. More telling than the differences, however, was the factor common to both of these transatlantic relationships, in which the distance seemed to heighten the affection. Hanff and Doel never met. Neither did Dirk and Dorothy Gordon. In fact they spoke only once, when Dirk telephoned her from a hotel room in New York. It was a disappointment, compromising one element of their hitherto cement-hard bond: mystery. Nevertheless, a quarter of a century after the last 'starling' fluttered into Dorothy Gordon's letter-box on the morning of her death, Dirk remembered their remarkable relationship as 'a kind of love affair without the carnality – strange but true'.

Although his letters and cards were returned to him after Dorothy Gordon's death, they, and hers, were consigned to the bonfire before Dirk left Provence. She makes little impression in the pages that follow, except as someone to whom Dirk refers with due appreciation. This book, therefore, is largely concerned with his other 'particular friendships', at least one of which was, in its way, as passionate. Norah Smallwood, who ran Chatto, opened the door to Dirk's new life as an author. She saw him, by chance, on a weekend television chat show, and said to her senior colleagues when they met on the Monday morning that 'if he writes as well as he talks, he might have a book in him'. Her shrewd judgement and her encouragement swiftly earned her the right to the title of Dirk's second 'Needlewoman'. 'I WANT to write,' he told her a few days after the publication of *A Postillion Struck by Lightning*. 'I WANT. I WANT. And it's all your fault.'

Who else, apart from Dirk's family, qualifies for that 'particular' billing? Some of his friends in the film business feature heavily in these pages, among them Bee Gilbert, who was not-quite-married to Ian Holm; Ann Skinner, who met Dirk while handling the continuity for

Darling; the actor David Frankham; the director Bertrand Tavernier; the critic Dilys Powell; and, primarily, Joseph Losey, with whom Dirk worked five times, and his wife Patricia. Losey is as much a subject of Dirk's letters as he is a recipient, and often he seems to be the object of disparagement – but there is no disguising the mutual respect and the affection that informed their productive, radical and exciting professional association. Theirs was, in its masculine way, another love affair. Luchino ('The Emperor') Visconti and Alain Resnais, two dominant figures from Dirk's European period in the 1970s, are less well represented than they deserve because there were few written exchanges with the former and those with the latter have not been traced. However, there is compensation from unexpected quarters – for example, Hélène Bordes, a French academic who sought Dirk's permission to write a paper on his first three volumes of autobiography. Norah Smallwood had died two weeks before, and he was despondent about the future of his own writing. The fortuitous timing of Mme Bordes's approach led not only to her being christened 'The Plank' but also, again, to a kind of love. They met eventually, just once, and happily. Then there was the writer Kathleen Tynan, who hit it off immediately with Dirk and Tony while assigned to cover the filming of *Justine.* And, perhaps most significant, there is Penelope Mortimer. Another successful writer, of novels and screenplays, she made contact with Dirk in the hope of producing a script that might bring him together with Bette Davis. This tantalising prospect never came even close to realisation, but a remarkable, interrupted, correspondence developed in which Dirk was at his most confessional.

There are other, less easily explicable 'friendships'. Two of those which I have been able to identify were with women in the north of England who have nothing whatever to do with either the film business or publishing. When she was ill the family of Susan Owens wrote in the hope that a message from Dirk would cheer her up; the subsequent twenty years' worth of his cards and letters filled two straining lever-arch files. Tina Tollitt was a schoolgirl who picked up a copy of *The Films of Dirk Bogarde,* by Margaret Hinxman and Susan d'Arcy, and found that 'something clicked', but 'not in a heartthrob sort of way'. She wrote to Dirk and so began a charming, occasional exchange, unfortunately now lost, in which he took on the role of a Dorothy Gordon or a Norah Smallwood. He was, in effect, Tina Tollitt's 'Needleman', urging her to write and advising her on whom to read.

As is apparent, most of the enduring contacts were with women, some of whom were high-achieving professionals, while others lived quieter, more obscure, lives. Some were equipped with a razor-sharp intellect, education at the highest level and the experience of the well travelled; others, with a more gentle wisdom. What they all had in common were, first, a neediness – it was said most astutely of Dirk that 'he needed to be needed'; and, second, a complete lack of dis-simulation, or what he would call bullshit. In their different ways they all spoke the same language as he did – direct, unfussy, blunt and, in several cases, very funny.

Proof of this can, fortunately, be found in the case of Penelope Mortimer, to whom Dirk once wrote with reference to the celebrated correspondence between Bernard Shaw and Mrs Patrick Campbell: 'We may not be the GBS and Mrs P of the seventies, but it might be simply lovely to try!' It was she who hit the nail most smartly on the head when she told him: 'I know you're a great believer in long distance and remote devotion.' To my delight I found I could hear both sides of their conversation, because Dirk kept her letters; and when his were returned to him he chose, uniquely, to add them to his manuscripts at the University of Boston. Perhaps in doing so he was giving a nod towards, if not exactly an invitation for, a volume such as this. He was far too aware of the literary value in his social writings not to predict that *A Particular Friendship* would one day need to be, not superseded, but succeeded; and with a much wider reach of source material.

Literary value is one thing; literacy value quite another. Poor Dirk. As mentioned at the outset, his letters are an orthographical, gram-matical and syntactical nightmare. In a 1974 letter to Penelope Mortimer, he writes of a recent visit from Losey: 'He said that he still liked me even though I used the worst grammer [*sic*] and wrote the worst spelling he had ever seen or heard.' It was ever thus. The 1931 Michaelmas term report from University College School on the ten-year-old Derek Van den Bogaerde pronounced his performance in English 'Terribly inaccurate'; by the Lent term in 1934 matters had not improved: 'Promise – in the way of oral work – is always so much better than performance of written work.' Half a century after those adjudications he wrote to Norah Smallwood: 'I should have been educated, really. I might have done awfully well . . .'. Because he was so conscious of his failings, and so often apologised for them, his letters are rendered here as he wrote them. Those dots, or ellipses, speckle the text like measles. They were his preferred punctuation; for him it was far too much of a chore to work out whether a full-stop, a colon, a semi-colon, a comma or a dash was the most appropriate. He also had a tendency to use an initial capital in mid-sentence, sometimes for emphasis; these too are preserved. For practical reasons his para-graphing, which varied with the years, has been somewhat formalised, as have the dates on which he wrote, except in those cases where he seems to be making a point of them. It is a pity, really, that practicalities also prevent reproduction in facsimile, à la Henry Root. As Ann Skinner observed: 'I think the *look* of Dirk's letters is very interesting because they do consist of a stream of thought (rather than consciousness).'

Hanging participles, dangling nominatives, split infinitives and other provokers of Fowler's frowns, were grist to Dirk's mill. The correct use of the apostrophe was as alien to him as Sanskrit; so dont, cant (for cannot), are'nt, were'nt, could'nt and should'nt proliferate. As for his spelling ... (those dots *are* catching) ... during the tran-scription process I could have sworn I heard sounds of anguish from the inner workings of sundry computers, where the checking pro-gramme has been worn to a frazzle: athmosphere, definatly, careing, embarress, hideious, excercise, immensley, infinate, shareing, valient, seldome, randome, whome, and many others recur throughout. They have been left alone, as have some misspelled names, such as Deitrich, which require no further identification or explanation, and appear as they should in the Index. In one or two cases, a word has become so mangled – primitavte – that it is given correctly. 'I'm typing terribly badly this afternoon,' he groaned in mid-letter to Penelope Mortimer. 'I am thinking too fast .. and thus all the letters on the machine get stuck together or go back to front ilek hist. Sorry.'

That his spelling, as opposed to his typing, should have been so bad is odd. Here was a man of wide knowledge and fierce intelligence, who made his mark in a profession where the script carries biblical weight. Dirk knew not only how to read scripts with attention to every nuance, but also how to amend them and, in one case, write an entire film. By that time he was ten years into a second, parallel, career where the drafts for his own books were corrected and returned to him from England by his dedicated typist, Sally Betts, before a proof stage, and sometimes bound proof copies, for his further attention. Surely he would have noted the basic alterations and stored them away in that receptive brain? Surely from his reading – which became very wide indeed, both in the classics and in modern biography, history and fiction – enough would have been absorbed to inform his own deployment of words? Surely he could simply have reached for the dictionary on the shelf a few inches away? No; to John Charlton, the patient and meticulous editor who worked at Norah Smallwood's right hand, Dirk admitted: 'I just "bash" along I fear, and things get left behind rather.' Added to which was a famous impatience; a desire to press on, to finish or to embark on something new; and, most probably, a touch of the dyslexia that runs in the family. All contributed to a carelessness for the detail which counts for little, if nothing, in speech. If we accept that to read Dirk's letters is to hear him talk, we should perhaps then ask ourselves how often we correct our utterances? In any case, to be exposed to his descriptive passages about the sun setting on his terrace in the hills above the Riviera; his startlingly original use of simile and metaphor; and, alas!, the odd droplet from his acid tongue about his fellow man – all tend to elicit forgiveness of his offences against strict usage.

In the Prologue to *A Particular Friendship*, composed in 1989, he confesses that while reading the edited letters to 'Mrs X' someone (a senior executive at Penguin Books) said that for the first time in his life he felt he *must* vote socialist. 'My arrogance and politics', wrote Dirk, 'apparently "got to him", although I am as political as a garden gnome.' Nevertheless Dirk decided not to make alterations of that kind because, after two decades of living abroad, he now saw himself as one who 'has had a lot of opinions altered and his life-style greatly changed. I hope for the better.' Such opinions ran counter to a literal interpretation of 'political correctness'. Those who monitor its present, much wider, meaning will probably experience the heebie-jeebies if they happen upon one or two observations in this volume. The very frankness which makes Dirk's writing so compelling might, like that of Philip Larkin and others before him, be his undoing. Even allowing for the passage of time – and, more important, the privacy of the medium – we can only wince at some of his asides about the blacks, the Asians and the Jews. Yet although he could make a crude generalisation, Dirk was neither truly a racist nor an anti-Semite. Despite his frequent use of the words 'detest' and 'loathe', and his unwillingness to step into a lift with the Japanese because of what he had seen and heard in the Far East during the war, he was not full of hate. Yes, he could be waspish, cutting, bilious, sometimes cruel. Yes, he was impatient with trivia, and fools were not suffered gladly. Yes, he could be hasty to judge: we see, for example, how dramatically his opinion of one of our foremost actresses changed from scorn to admiration once they had worked together. Yes, he could offend. But he was no bigot. On the contrary, he was an admirer of the 'great Tolerant', Voltaire. He had seen too much extreme prejudice to espouse it himself.

One further understanding is asked of the reader. At a very rough guess two million of Dirk's written words were considered for this selection. About half a million were transcribed, and, after extensive cutting, some 250,000 remain. An early decision was required about whether to allow the longer letters to run, or to pick nuggets. I chose the former, partly because many of the 'highlights' were used in *Dirk Bogarde: The Authorised Biography;* more important, because there is an advantage as well as an allure in being able to follow, to listen to, Dirk's train of thought as he flits from one subject to another. Inevitably this course had implications for the number of items which could reasonably be included, and in order to prevent an already long book from becoming one of those which are impossible to pick up rather than to put down, most of the letters from which I quoted at length in the *Life* are omitted. That volume, published in 2004, was criticised in some quarters as being too heavy to read in bed; but fortunately a paperback edition followed. Much, if not all, of the essential background to the correspondence presented here is given in the biography – for example, a detailed account of the controversy surrounding Dirk's portrayal of 'Boy' Browning in Richard Attenborough's film of *A Bridge Too Far,* and, at a less momentous but more grotesque level, the eye-witness testimony from the late Willis Hall of a hideous lunch chez Dirk and Tony at Drummer's Yard which he attended with Keith Waterhouse. To avoid duplication, therefore, explanatory linking passages have been kept to a minimum. Which means that – at the risk of my seeming to indulge in shameless auto-publicity – the context of these letters will be most easily understood if a copy of the earlier book is within reach.

Finally, the purpose of this volume is to complete a quartet, initiated by Dirk's Estate, and comprising otherwise the *Arena* television documentary, 'The Private Dirk Bogarde', first broadcast by the BBC on Boxing Day 2001; the authorised Life; and the official website, www.dirkbogarde.co.uk, which was launched on what would have been his eighty-sixth birthday in March 2007. It is not some opportunistic indulgence, but an attempt to give the last word to a formidable communicator; one who would receive envelopes addressed to 'Dirk Bogarde Esq, Legendary British Actor, Chelsea, London, England', 'Mr Dirk Bogarde, An apartment overlooking trees, A Short Walk from Harrods, London SW1' and 'Sir Dirk Bogarde, Author, (who lives) A Short Walk from Harrods'. Any response would be courteous, but would bring this epistolary equivalent of the cold-call to an abrupt end, and has no place in a distillation devoted almost entirely to the conversations he wished to sustain. Dirk apologised for the fact that the one he preserved as *A Particular Friendship* was 'edited by myself rather crudely, and unfinished as a book', adding that collections of letters 'can be tiresome, and monotonous'. I bore those adjectives in mind while preparing this fuller and much further-reaching selection, and hope that its readers will agree with John Byrne, the archivist who catalogued Dilys Powell's papers. He concluded: 'My impression is that Dirk Bogarde was incapable of writing an indifferent letter.' Or, indeed, of being dull in conversation. Here, if you like, is a final chance to eavesdrop.

John Coldstream
West Sussex 2008

DRAMATIS PERSONAE

Non-family recipients of Dirk's more significant correspondence, as featured to a greater or a lesser extent in this volume:

Eileen Atkins – Dirk's co-star in the BBC production of *The Vision* (1988), and morale-booster-in-chief when he was at his lowest ebb during Tony Forwood's final illness and in the aftermath of the latter's death.

Hélène Bordes – Former Maître de Conférences at Limoges University, whose study of Dirk's early autobiographies helped to free him from a 'block' at a crucial time in his writing career.

George Cukor (1899–1983) – Hollywood giant, who rescued two of Dirk's films, *Song Without End* and *Justine*, after mishaps befell their original directors.

Roald Dahl (1916–90) – Author and at one time near-neighbour, whose response to the stroke suffered by his wife was depicted powerfully in *The Patricia Neal Story* (1981), starring Dirk and Glenda Jackson.

Molly Daubeny – Widow of Sir Peter, the impresario who brought *Power Without Glory* into the West End in 1947.

Alain and Christine de Pauw – Belgian couple who in October 1986 bought from Dirk his beloved Le Haut Clermont, near Grasse.

Mary Dodd (née Forwood) – Cousin to Tony Forwood, occasional companion to Dirk and Tony on holidays in the 1950s, and dedicatee of *Jericho* (1992).

Rainer Werner Fassbinder (1945–82) – Prolific German director for whom in *Despair* (1978) Dirk gave what he felt was his finest performance, but whose editing damaged the film.

Daphne Fielding (1904–97) – Former wife of the 6th Marquess of

Bath (Henry Thynne); met Dirk in July 1956 when her second husband, Xan Fielding, was technical adviser on *Ill Met by Moonlight*. Dedicated her second volume of memoirs, *The Nearest Way Home* (Eyre & Spottiswoode, 1970), to Dirk.

David Frankham – Former BBC Radio employee, who interviewed Dirk in the early 1950s; since then he has lived and worked as an actor in the United States.

Bee Gilbert – Photographer, screenwriter and producer, who met Dirk and Tony on location for *The Fixer* (1969) when she was living with **Ian** (later Sir Ian) **Holm**. He is one of the few colleagues who has written at any length about Dirk (*Acting My Life*, Bantam Press, 2004).

Dorothy Gordon (1902–72) – Librarian at Yale University and the 'Mrs X' of Dirk's *A Particular Friendship*.

Laurence Harbottle – Solicitor to Dirk from the early 1950s until the latter's death.

Olga Horstig-Primuz (1912–2004) – Paris-based agent, who managed some of Dirk's work in France, notably *Providence*. They met in late 1954, when her client Brigitte Bardot was cast in *Doctor at Sea*.

Patricia (Pat) Kavanagh – Literary agent who handled all Dirk's books and journalism from 1983. Her husband **Julian Barnes** exchanged views with Dirk on matters horticultural and culinary.

Dominique Lambilliotte – Former editor at the Parisian publishing house Editions Fernand Nathan; with her Dirk established the last of his 'particular friendships'.

Joseph Losey (1909–84) – Director who worked with Dirk five times: *The Sleeping Tiger* (1954), *The Servant* (1963), *King and Country* (1964), *Modesty Blaise* (1966) and *Accident* (1967). His fourth wife, **Patricia** Tolusso (née Mohan), corresponded with Dirk in her own right.

Brian McFarlane – Honorary Associate Professor (in film and literature) at Monash University, Melbourne, who interviewed Dirk for *Sixty Voices* (British Film Institute, 1992), an 'oral history' of the British cinema.

Jill Melford – Actress, who met Dirk and Tony in 1962 while on holiday in the South of France with her husband, John Standing, who appeared in *Hot Enough for June* (1964). By helping Dirk after his return from France, she earned the sobriquet 'Swiss Army Knife'.

Penelope Mortimer (1918–99) – Novelist, screenwriter and memoirist, who approached Dirk in 1971 about a possible, unrealised, project with Bette Davis. Their intermittent correspondence over the next two decades found Dirk at his most self-revelatory.

John Osborne (1929–94) – Playwright, whose lethal autobiographies won favour with Dirk. The two never worked together, but began a somewhat eccentric correspondence in the 1990s. Osborne's fifth wife, **Helen** (née Dawson; 1939–2004), also wrote to Dirk.

Susan Owens – Cheshire housewife, with whom Dirk corresponded for twenty years.

Dilys Powell (1901–95) – Film critic of *The Sunday Times* from 1939 to 1976. Her contribution to a 1956 BBC radio profile of Dirk led to an occasional correspondence and a strong relationship rare between actor and critic – especially one involving this actor.

Nerine Selwood (née Cox) (1921–2003) – Friend, and almost exact contemporary, from Dirk's teenage years in East Sussex. Her father, Lionel Cox, founded the Newick Amateur Dramatic Society, in whose hall Dirk made his theatrical debut in 1938.

Ann Skinner – In charge of Continuity on *Darling* (1965), *Modesty Blaise* (1966) and *Sebastian* (1968). One of the few film-unit members with whom Dirk pursued a lasting friendship.

Norah Smallwood (1909–84) – Managing Director of Chatto & Windus, whose chance exposure to an edition of *The Russell Harty Show* in 1974 led to Dirk's second career, as a writer.

Tom Stoppard – Playwright, adapter of Nabokov's *Despair* for Fassbinder's film, and creator of the text for Dirk as narrator at Glyndebourne Festival Opera's 1993 concert performances of *Die Lustige Witwe (The Merry Widow)*.

Bertrand Tavernier – Director of Dirk's final film, *Daddy Nostalgie (These Foolish Things)*, shot in the South of France in 1989.

Kathleen Tynan (1937–95) – Writer, married to the critic, essayist and dramaturg Kenneth Tynan. She met Dirk and Tony in October

1968 while working with the photographer Patrick Lichfield on location for *Justine*.

Luchino Visconti (1906–76) – Director of *La caduta degli dei (The Damned)* (1970) and *Morte a Venezia (Death in Venice)* (1971). For Dirk he was 'The Emperor', while Losey was 'The King' and Tavernier 'The Genius'.

Members of Dirk's family who appear variously as featured players, in walk-on roles, or in passing mentions:

Ulric and Margaret (née Niven) Van den Bogaerde – parents

Elizabeth Goodings (née Van den Bogaerde) – sister

Gareth and Lucilla (née Dilke) Van den Bogaerde – brother and sister-in-law

Mark and Judy (née Roberts) Goodings – nephew and niece-by-marriage

Brock and Kim (née Barker) Van den Bogaerde – nephew and niece-by-marriage

Rupert Van den Bogaerde – nephew

Ulric Van den Bogaerde – nephew

Alice Van den Bogaerde – niece

Forrest McClellan – cousin, nephew to Margaret

NICKNAMES

The Atts – Richard and Sheila Attenborough

Boaty – Alice Lee Boatwright

Coz; Fat Friend – Tony Forwood

Fatso – Richard Burton *et al.*

Frankenstein – John Frankenheimer

(Mrs) Glum – Eileen Atkins

The Hippo Pool – Dirk's 'swimming-pool' at Clermont

HRH; Millionair – Ian Holm

Lady; Ladie – Successive domestic helps in both France and London

Lally – Ellen Holt (née Searle)

Lordie – Patrick Lichfield

Lu; (Auntie) LuLu; Tide – Elizabeth Goodings (née Van den Bogaerde)

Maud(e) – Jill Melford

Mrs X – Dorothy Gordon

Oscar's – The Cadogan Hotel, Chelsea

Plank (1); Planche; Mme de la Planche – Hélène Bordes

Plank (2) – Nicholas Shakespeare

Schles – John Schlesinger

Sno, Snowball, Snowflake – Bee Gilbert

Ully – Ulric Van den Bogaerde (Dirk's father)

SELECTED REFERENCES

BOOKS BY DIRK BOGARDE

A Postillion Struck by Lightning (Chatto & Windus, 1977; Phoenix paperback, 2006)

Snakes and Ladders (Chatto & Windus, 1978; Phoenix paperback, 2006)

*A Gentle Occupation** (Chatto & Windus, 1980)

*Voices in the Garden** (Chatto & Windus, 1981)

An Orderly Man (Chatto & Windus, 1983)

*West of Sunset** (Allen Lane, 1984)

Backcloth (Viking, 1986)

A Particular Friendship (Viking, 1989)

*Jericho** (Viking, 1992)

Great Meadow (Viking, 1992)

A Short Walk from Harrods (Viking, 1993)

*A Period of Adjustment** (Viking, 1994)

Cleared for Take-Off (Viking, 1995)

*Closing Ranks** (Viking, 1997)

For the Time Being: Collected Journalism (Viking, 1998)

*Novels

BOOKS ON DIRK BOGARDE

Dirk Bogarde: The Authorised Biography by John Coldstream (Weidenfeld & Nicolson, 2004; Phoenix paperback, 2005)

Dirk Bogarde: Rank Outsider by Sheridan Morley (Bloomsbury, 1996; updated paperback, 1999)

Dirk Bogarde: The Complete Career Illustrated by Robert Tanitch (Ebury Press, 1988)

The Films of Dirk Bogarde by Margaret Hinxman and Susan d'Arcy (Literary Services & Production, 1974)

OFFICIAL WEBSITE OF THE DIRK BOGARDE ESTATE

www.dirkbogarde.co.uk

CHRONOLOGY

1920   7 January – Marriage of Ulric Van den Bogaerde and Margaret Niven

1921   28 March – Born Derek Niven Van den Bogaerde, in West Hampstead

1924   2 April – Elizabeth Van den Bogaerde (sister) born

1931–4 Attends University College School, Hampstead

1931–3 Family rents cottage for holidays at Lullington, East Sussex

1933   19 July – Gareth Van den Bogaerde (brother) born

1934–7 Attends Allan Glen's School, Glasgow

1938–9 Attends Chelsea School of Art

1938   Makes stage debut in *Alf's Button* for Newick Amateur Dramatic Society

1939   Auditions for Old Vic School; makes screen debut as extra in *Come On George!*

1940   Makes London stage debut in *When We Are Married* at Q Theatre; West End debut in *Cornelius* (Westminster Theatre) June–Dec: member of repertory company at The Playhouse, Amersham Meets Anthony Forwood (b. 3 October 1915)

1941   *Diversion No. 2* (Wyndham's Theatre) Enlisted into Royal Corps of Signals as Signalman 2371461

1943   Commissioned as 2nd Lieutenant into Queen's Royal Regiment

1944   Appointed Intelligence Officer, 21 Army Group (Army Photographic Interpretation Section); seconded to 39 Wing, Royal Canadian Air Force for liberation of Europe

1945   Appointed Temporary Captain; exhibits paintings and drawings at the Batsford Gallery; posted to India with RAF; posted to Java

1946   Edits forces newspaper, *The Fighting Cock*; demobilised

1947   Makes television debut in *Rope*; plays Cliff in *Power Without Glory* at New Lindsey Theatre and in West End (Fortune Theatre); signs contract with Rank Organisation; first speaking role in *Dancing with Crime*; makes screen debut 'above the title' in *Esther Waters* (released 1948); rents 44 Chester Row, Belgravia

1948   Makes *Quartet* ('The Alien Corn'), *Once a Jolly Swagman* and *Dear Mr Prohack*
        For Better, For Worse (Q Theatre)

1949   Makes *Boys in Brown*, *The Blue Lamp* and *So Long at the Fair*
        Foxhole in the Parlor (New Lindsey Theatre) and *Sleep on My Shoulder* (Q)
        Buys Bendrose House, Amersham, from Forwood family

1950   *The Shaughraun* (Bedford Theatre) and *Point of Departure* (Duke of York's)
        Makes *The Woman in Question* and *Blackmailed*

1951   Makes *Hunted* and *Penny Princess*

1952   *The Vortex* (Lyric Hammersmith)
        Makes *The Gentle Gunman*, *Appointment in London* and *Desperate Moment*

1953   Makes *They Who Dare* and *Doctor in the House*

1954   Buys Beel House, Amersham
        Makes *The Sleeping Tiger*, *For Better, For Worse*, *The Sea Shall Not Have Them* and *Simba*; (26 March) *Doctor in the House* released

1955   Makes *Doctor at Sea* and *Cast a Dark Shadow*
        Returns to the stage in *Summertime* (Apollo)

1956   Makes *The Spanish Gardener*, *Ill Met by Moonlight* and *Doctor at Large*

1957   Makes *Campbell's Kingdom* and *A Tale of Two Cities*

1958   Makes *The Wind Cannot Read* and *The Doctor's Dilemma*
        Final stage appearance, in *Jezebel* (Oxford Playhouse and Theatre Royal Brighton)

1959   Makes *Libel*, *Song Without End* and *The Angel Wore Red* (*La sposa bella*)

1960   Makes *The Singer Not the Song*; *Lyrics for Lovers* (LP) released
        Buys Drummer's Yard, near Beaconsfield

1961   Makes *Victim* (playing Melville Farr) and *HMS Defiant*; leaves Rank

1962   Variety Club film actor of the year for 1961
        Makes *The Password Is Courage, We Joined the Navy* (cameo),
        I Could Go On Singing and *The Mind Benders*
        Buys Nore Farm, near Godalming
1963   Makes *The Servant, Doctor in Distress* and *Hot Enough for June*
1964   Variety Club Award for *The Servant*
        Makes *King and Country, The High Bright Sun* and *Darling*
1965   Makes *Modesty Blaise*
1966   Buys Adam's Farm, near Crowborough
        British Film Academy Award for *Darling*
        Makes *Accident* and *Our Mother's House*
1967   Makes *Sebastian* and *The Fixer*
1968   Makes *Oh! What a Lovely War* (cameo), *The Damned* (*La caduta degli dei*) and *Justine*
1969   1 March – Leaves the UK for Italy; leases Villa Berti, Labaro, near Rome
1970   Buys Le Haut Clermont, Châteauneuf de Grasse
        Makes *Death in Venice* (*Morte a Venezia*)
1971   Fiftieth birthday
1972   Makes *The Serpent*
1973   Makes *The Night Porter (Il portiere di notte)*
1975   Makes *Permission to Kill*
1976   Makes *Providence* and *A Bridge Too Far*
1977   24 March – *A Postillion Struck by Lightning* published
        Makes *Despair*
1978   *Snakes and Ladders* published
1980   *A Gentle Occupation* published
1981   Makes *The Patricia Neal Story*
        Voices in the Garden published
1982   Appointed Chevalier dans l'Ordre des Arts et des Lettres
1983   *An Orderly Man* published
1984   *West of Sunset* published
        President of Cannes Film Festival jury
1985   Hon. D.Litt., University of St Andrews
1986   Makes *May We Borrow Your Husband?* (also debut as scriptwriter)
        Backcloth published
        Sells Le Haut Clermont

1987   Returns to UK; rents 15 Moore Street, Chelsea
        Makes *The Vision* (BBC TV)
        Awarded BFI Fellowship
        Buys Queen Anne House, Dukes Lane, Kensington
1988   18 May – Anthony Forwood dies
        Honoured by BAFTA
        Moves to 2 Cadogan Gardens, Chelsea
1989   *A Particular Friendship* published
        Returns to Provence to make *Daddy Nostalgie (These Foolish Things)*
1990   Promoted to Commandeur dans l'Ordre des Arts et des Lettres
1992   Knighthood conferred
        Jericho and *Great Meadow* published
1993   Hon. D.Litt., University of Sussex
        A Short Walk from Harrods published
1994   *A Period of Adjustment* published
1995   *Cleared for Take-Off* published
1996   Has stroke following operation
1997   *Closing Ranks* published
1998   *For the Time Being* published
1999   8 May – Dies suddenly but peacefully at home in Chelsea

EDITOR'S NOTE

As explained in the Introduction, these letters are reproduced faithfully and at length, apart from cuts made for reasons of repetition, unfathomable sense, acute sensibility and actionable defamation. In the main, Dirk's abuses of syntax and punctuation, and his misspelling – as opposed to patent mistyping – are preserved. One or two ruffles, such as stray full-stops within bracketed asides and the inconsistent use of inverted commas, have been ironed out. Proper names which he has given wrongly are usually corrected either in the footnotes or in the Index. None the less, the reader's indulgence throughout is craved.

I
THE CONTINENTAL YEARS

I *n 1961, after fourteen years with the Rank Organisation, Dirk had*
severed his contractual ties and begun a brief period of challenging and
artistically satisfying work, notably with Joseph Losey. By the late 1960s,
however, such opportunities were scarce. A call from Luchino Visconti for
Dirk to co-star in The Damned *helped to convince him that his destiny lay*
in Europe. So, on 1 March 1969, he and Tony left England for the Continent
and an uncertain future. Ten days later they moved into a rented house in
the village of Labaro on the outskirts of Rome. They were joined by the
Spanish couple who had looked after them latterly in Sussex, Eduardo and
Antonia Boluda. From now on, Dirk had no secretarial help.

The following is the only letter from Dirk to Dorothy Gordon that is
known to have survived. It was typed on his favourite machine, an Adler.
A comparison with the version on pages 170–73 of A Particular Friendship
indicates how substantially he edited and revised the 'Mrs X' cor-
respondence for publication.

To Dorothy Gordon

Villa Berti
18 March 1969

You will have to excuse the paper and all the rest .... I am not nearly
sorted out enough to write a letter at all!

Everything is very Italian .... not enough blankets: two pitiful
table lamps, a few tin knives and forks and some ashtrays stolen at
various times from different Roman resturants .... the matresses
covered in pee stains (it was leased for a year to an American family
in the Embassy with six children .. maybe that accounts for the muck
left behind).

However, it is about twelve kilometers from Rome .. on a hill with
lovely views over the city dump and the neighbouring villages which
are now really suburbs of Rome .... but the mountains are there still
.... and the Pines smell devine, the Mimosa is tossing great golden
rain over the violets ... real Parm[a]s, with a scent in the rain like

nothing on earth .... there is a pool ... and I sleep in a small fourposter
with Bloomingdales stamped on the back! The Widow who owns the
place loved America so much that she bought all her wall paper and
curtain stuff from Maceys or Korvett ... and the Colonial Furniture
from Bloomingdales .... only the matresses alas, come from Rome.
Wire frames with a thin straw sack.

Eduardo and Antonia arrived pale and tired from Valencia on
Friday, and we all hastened home .... the dog I have adopted from a
local peasant, has a broken leg, naturally, and copious worms, naturally
... I'd fed him well before leaving for the airport ... and the result of
my lavishness was apparent in the air the moment the door was opened
... and even more apparent underfoot! A good omen? I was scurrying
about with shovels and earth and retching all over the garden for an
hour ... he is still with us, needless to say, but under strict supervision
... and later I'll take him into Rome and have the leg re-set and the
worms abated ... meanwhile he sits with me constantly .. with great
brown eyes .. and a golden coat .. a cross between a Whippet and a
hound .... God knows what. Named Labbo .... after the village!

After great heart searching, Candy[1] will <u>not</u> arrive in Italy. My sister

---

1. Dirk's mastiff, part of the family since 1961.

and her family of kids have tumbled in love .. and no one seems sure enough for me that she would survive the journey in a crate at her age .. 9 ... what is the possible pleasure of killing her off for my benifit? If she is happy and well where she is, and she is, and if she is deeply loved and spoiled, which she is, then it is kinder to her to remain in England ... also .. if she did come out here and for some reason or another I had to go back to England, she could not ... without six months in quarantine.

So ... our minds are all made up and there she stays .... Antonia blanched a little ... but has finally understood that it is kinder and wiser. And after all she has Labbo ... and he <u>does</u> bark ... Antonia is terrified, terrified, of the Mafia. As far as she is concerned they lurk under every cypress ... in every oleander ... on every balcony ... and they wait solely to get HER! .... maybe they do ... I'm not that brave myself.

What idiots we are .. not a word of Italian and running a not too small house. The Supermarket is fun ... I have never been able to visit one freely before ... now I take my list in one hand and a trolly in the other and wander among the rest of the perplexed 'housewives' studying prices and the freshness of the artichokes .... astonishing piles of things are bundled into the car ... detergents ... Tide ... Candles ... cutting board ... brush for hearth ... four colored cups ... dog biscuits . carrots and black olives ... six toilet rolls .... cheese and four dozen eggs ... Martell ... and a feather duster.

Really crazy, but fun .. except that I am living, for the first time in my life almost, on a limited capital with absolutely no income .... as a British citizen I am not allowed any foreign posessions of any sort .. and anything earned here goes straight to the Bank of E. Bugger it. It was only because the Italian Government 'froze' half my salary here that we are sitting up on the hill in Villa Berti ... and god knows how long that will last .... Candles burn ... Toilet rolls roll ... eggs become ommletts ... only the four colored cups MAY survive.

Adler is very battered about, poor love ... he's been all over and looks a bit worn and weary ... but he is happy at last to be on a desk again ... I had to rent the damn thing .. the desk: and side tables and arm chairs, and chests of drawers ... what on earth do the Italians do with their knickers and shirts and things I wonder.

The people at Adams, I hear from my gardener who still works there for them, are very happy, very ambitious and very rich ... the

gardens are going to look like Botanical ones from what I can gather
... and the whole house is being re decorated by one of the swankest
firms in London ... he had nearly all my furniture photographed and
COPIED! Can you imagine anything so Bizzar .. Fred, the gardener,
says that except for minor details the whole place is almost exactly as
it was .... it must have cost him thousands, silly sod. However the
house is being loved again, thats the main thing ... and after all one
only leases happiness ... one cant buy or keep it for ever ... thats not
allowed, I have found out ..... and my three or four years at Adams
were marvellous ... and strangely enough the death of Ricci[1] rather
started a little curtain to fall. Enough was enough .... as I told you,
it would have been sad to have had Adams haunted ... and had I
stayed there there is no question [but] that it would have been.

The sun this morning is high and the sky blue ... Antonia is on
her knees in the hall washing tiles ... Eduardo is doing the windows
and our Gardener, Tonino, a sort of gnome like fellow who plants
celery, peas and lettuce with the abandon of a drunken God ... Tonino
is tying up some of the vines which tumbled in the torrential rain of
last week .... I have moved on to another page and this will make the
letter heavy ... I must try and get some airmail paper in Rome ...
how does one ask for it I wonder? How does one ask for Worm Powder
too?

What a lot of problems to face .. and to follow ... now Antonia
has moved in here and is washing literally round my feet ... I think
she will be dead in a week at the way she['s] working .... oh dear!

The Widow Berti has arrived in a mink and sunglasses and rinsed
hair and is doing the inventory with a pale faced madonna holding a
note book and pencil ... I cant check myself, as everything is in rapid
Italian ... suppose a jug has a crack on the lip ... do they say so ...
or will I be charged when I leave? If there is a cigarette burn on the
oak table in the hall is it mine or the late Mr Ryans? What to do ...
what to do ... I think what to do is not to be a bloody fool at my age
and trip off into the unknown as if I were a boyscout or someone
intent on tracing the source of the Blue Nile .... which is what I feel
like I am doing. No: that is horrid american grammer: which is what
I Feel I am doing ...

1. Ricki Huston, fourth wife of John Huston, had died in a car crash in France on 29
January.

Tomorrow is a National Holiday we discovered from the postman
... so now to the village to get more bread, great round lumps with
glorious crusts, pommadoros[1] ... cheese and vino ... .

Among the bits and pieces left behind by the Ryans is a great pile
of books ... all of them dated about 1935 when Maureen Ryan signed
her scrawley name on every flyleaf .. among a bewilderingly catholic
aray of books I have found a few to read myself!

'Little Women' ... 'How To Landscape Your Home' by Malkin ...
'The American Twins of 1812' by Lucy Fitch Perkins ..... 'Adventures
With A Lamp' by Ruth Louise Partridge. Bet you aint got that set in
your little library with the stone and ivy!!

My favourite one really is simply called 'You Must Relax' ... in its
third edition by Machonichie ..... but I did find Leahmans[2] 'The
Weather In The Streets' which I have long adored, and something
called 'Fall Of Valour' which was an unlikely choice for this library
but interesting ... also some Dickens and Trollop and a few modern
novels which will be fine in the sun under the olives by the pool ... .
what I should be doing is reading my Italian grammer ... or even the
dictionary. But I dont think that I'll ever lick it ... it is a fearfully
'Grammery' language ... . I find English really almost as much as I
can bear to learn ... . But now I must get on with the rest of the jobs
... and this must be your 'ration' for a little while ... I really am so
terribly tired: it seems so silly ... but I really have been on the hop
since Budapest[3] ... and think how many things have happened to us
both since then

Is'nt it madenning ... I have'nt one single photograph of Adams ..
inside or out .. I suppose it is just as well ... what is over is the past.
and Nostalgia is a dangerous thing really ... .

My love to you ... excuse the mistake and corrections .. and the
nasty paper ... and don't get too grumpy with me ... I do my best!
Love D.

---

1. *Pomodori.*
2. Rosamond Lehmann.
3. Where he made *The Fixer* in late 1967, under the direction of John Frankenheimer.

To Joseph Losey

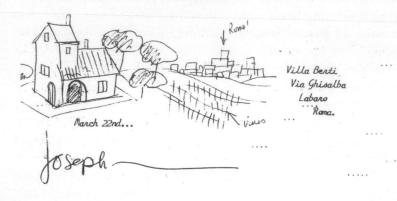

Villa Berti
Via Ghisalba
Labaro
Roma.

March 22nd...

Joseph ———

I had just written you a letter, and went down into the village to buy some bread and a pot to put geraniums in, when I passed the postman in his little 500. We stopped and he gave me your letter of the 19th .. and saved himself a journey up the hill.

We have just about settled down .. the <u>dust</u> is settled anyway ... and the villa, which is not a St Simieon .. or whatever the place is called that Hearst had in Calif ... is really a bit pretty ... it is well built ... on a hill among olives and pines and mimosa ... overlooking all the slums of Rome and the rubbish tips of Labaro and Porta Prima[1] ... but somehow living actually IN the place is better than those awful no-living places on the Appia Antica ... we are actually residents of the Commune da Roma, and we are finding it rather nice, thank you very much.

The blinding fact that none of us, Antonia and Eduardo or Tote or me (natch, me) can say more than 'Good Morning' or 'Thank you' or sometimes if put to it 'How much does this bolt of muslin cost?' does tend somewhat to delay matters ... but whatever else the Italian is, he is, anyway in the working class areas, or in the villages, amused, concerned, and patient as long as one is not a Yankee ... whome for some reason they dont seem to care for ... I suppose they have had a belt of Frankenheimer once.

We have so far managed to register with the police, cope with the Central Heating (Jokey at best, scalding at worst) buy all our grub in

1. Prima Porta.

supermarkets and deal with our gardener Antonino, who is as bent and sturdy as an Olive tree, as enduring and as incomprehensible .... but he is planting beans and garlic and lettuce and peas and radish and chick peas and Dhalias and pruning the vines ... and tells me that we must 'Tread' the grapes in October ... we can actually make our own wine from our own vines ... or am I being a little too A-Tree-Grows-In-Brooklynish?

Most days, if we dont go to the supermarket which is cheating because all the names and prices are written up for you .... we go to the stalls in Porta Prima and stagger back with wondrous bunches of artichokes, of parsley, of Broccoli ... and the first of the broad beans .. small as the nail of your little finger and as tender as a virgin nipple! [...] Hmmmmm.

Anyway, as you might be gathering, so far, so far, no regrets .. as long as the lolly holds out .. .. ..

The first night we moved in, T. and I, absolutely alone except for the Rolls and the Simca ... we felt a bit bereft! There was nothing much in the house ... it is a leasing villa, so apart from a bed in each bedroom, and a couple of chairs and a settee in the drawing-room, and a few ashtrays stolen from a resturant near Lake Garda ... there really was nothing much else .... and then a dog with a broken leg and worms came to visit .. and a cat with half a tail ... and with them some sort of life entered the closed-up feeling .... we lit a timid fire, lighted a candel and eat Libbys Bullybeef with a hunk of bread and a flask of Antinori .... and slept trembling together in a nasty little bed from Bloomingdales!! With one blanket! Furnished house in the Italian manner you gather .. .. .. However next morning, in torrenting rain, we surveyed our new villa and found it not unpromising ... we rented some furniture .. tables, chest of drawers, and a couple more chairs .. and for three days we washed floors, shoved beds about, humped chests and matresses, washed cupboards, and finally when Eduardo and Antonia arrived from Valencia we were on our way to being a household ... and then they pitched in, and now the brasses flash .. the floors gleam, the kitchen cooks and the sun has come out to bless us ... and Tonino is filling the pool ... and they have cut off the water for two days without telling us .. .. .. and we are going to have a veal stew for supper.

And I'm liking it all very much so far.

I am sad about 'Go Between'[1] .... I spent a lot of time with Julie[2] and did what I could to persuade her to do it ... she longs to work with you, and she liked the script .. and she KNOWS that she SHOULD do it, but it's that sodding Warren[3] .... and unless you offered him the part of Tom and let him play it bare assed, I cannot think that he'll let her do it ... as you say. Mia[4] I would think was utterly wrong .. too nurotic and angular and wild-beast-under-the-parlour-table stuff ..... Willie has'nt much of a part really ... one of the few faults I find with the script are that the parts are so terribly stripped down ... it's rather like painting mahogany wood white and fitting steel wheels to it all .... it's redolent of 'Accident' ... 'heat haze, she smiles, sweat runs, he looks, she smiles, heat haze' .... it was a little too un-rich for me .... I wanted a little more fruit in the pie ... and a little custard ... I did'nt give a tinkers Gob about anyone ... and when it was over I felt that a gentle wind had riffled past me .... that a whisper had been whispered ... that nothing very much had happened at all ..... except they cut the trees down at the end .... naturally I'm talking nonsense, you know that ... but it does, I feel sure, need to be a little more developed (I know Harold[5] DOESENT develope, dear) to make some of the parts really tempting ... however, thats me. And I [am] not much of a judge, except I do get worried a bit that Pinter may soon become an adjective.

and thats that. I'm allowed to talk to you like this because I love you almost as much as Patricia .. and know that I can get away with it as long as no one else hears what I say!

I am sad that she, incidentally, is still bedded ... but that is to be expected I fear ... I had eight or ten weeks[6] ... I forget which .. and then an awful long 'recovery' crawling about drinking tonic water and bitters and pretending I was enjoying it .... give her my deepest love .. or give her this letter to read if you cant be bothered ... and tell her she'll always find a bed, of sorts, at Villa Berti .... but no Candy; she is going to stay with my sister ... it's kinder and less of a wrench for her ... that flight is a bit hellish at her age and in freight, in a smallish

---

1. Losey had long wished to direct an adaptation of L. P. Hartley's 1953 novel.
2. Julie Christie.
3. Warren Beatty.
4. Mia Farrow.
5. Pinter, who had scripted *The Servant* and *Accident*.
6. Dirk had had hepatitis in 1955.

crate . . . . so the wormy dog is mine now, and a complete life is wiped out except for the clothes in the suitcase and a couple of photographs up on the wall.

I long to hear about Paris. Did you have power cuts? Or did you incite the Left Wing to burn down the Chateaux? You are so <u>difficult.</u> Like Resnais [. . .] By the way there is some sort of a film[1] out last month here, about Galleleo (cant spell it but I can spell CUSACK . . . whome to my horror plays the gentleman . .) When did that happen? And where were you. I expect that you knew all the time . . . . but I got a shock driving through Popolo and seeing the poster.

Secret C.[2] is on here . . . not a bad poster . . . rather better than the flick actually . . . but I did'nt see any reviews . . . how was it in Paris. I bet they liked it.

I do wish that you could come out for a bit here. Sit under the mimosa and watch the flies buzzing on the rubbish dumps and sip a very good Vodka and Pommedora Juice . . . strangely enough you are someone that I find I constantly miss . . . and as we really have'nt been THAT close all THAT number of years it is strange . . . . . but I am a loving soul, and there you are . . . .

As soon as your old troglodyte-wife-with-a-yellow-face is getting a little stronger, bundle her up, like in May or June . . . before the heat, and bring her to us . . . . we would love it beyond endurance, and get tins and tins of beans and pickled onions for you.

And write to me more fully next time . . dont sign off with a ghastly line like 'I Have No Idea What Next.' . . . . . . I felt quite weepy, and had another beer and came up here to write to you, tear up the first letter, and get this sent off to cheer u.

Love and deep affection to you both [. . .]
        What a Soppy letter –
        Love Dirk –

Dirk had sent a postcard to Losey, blaming for a delay in writing (a) the sun, (b) the 'dulling' wine, (c) the daily chores and (d) 'running a rest home for our English Chums, which is fun, expensive, exhausting, & quite <u>lovely</u> when they go!'

---

1. *Galileo*, starring Cyril Cusack, directed by Liliana Cavani. Losey had staged Brecht's *The Life of Galileo* (*Das Leben des Galilei*) in Hollywood and New York in 1947, and would finally realise a film version in 1974.
2. *Secret Ceremony*, directed by Losey, with Elizabeth Taylor and Mia Farrow.

To Joseph Losey   *Villa Berti*
                                                12 August 1969

Oh! My dearest boy!

What a miserable letter from you today dated the fifth. I really do feel that I should swiftly fly to your side and hit you between the eyes. So <u>much</u> self pity! You really are a sod.

My card was really not dismal ... or I dont remember that it was ... I have been and still am, touch wood, supremely happy here. I mind not working, of course, but that is by the way .... I wont do what I wont do ... and the crap that they have sent me in the last few months defies description .... re-makes of 'Accident' or of 'Knife In The Water' or very often, a terribly 'Nazi-Hates-Yanks??-Hates-The-World' kind of crap ..... so I just sit and POUR beer down my throat at lunch ... wine after, and swim and sleep and willingly write to you or anyone who writes to me, and enjoy it all! Hugely! I garden a lot ... not your idea of joy, I know, but useful therepy ... and I read a great deal .... and get pissed again in the velvet evenings and shop and market and wander about feeling happy and smug and on holiday ...... and really, thats about it! Lots of chums have come to stay ... from Bumble[1] on the one hand to David Baily and Penelope Tree on the other .... we are a cheap holiday, you must remember, with fifty quid and nowhere to go for our chums .... and we are only about fourty minutes from Fregene and the sea ... and twenty from Piazza del Popolo ... and Bologonaise .... if you cant manage Antonias cooking, which is super now that we are all in the Med. together!

Actually I buy myself large tins of ITALIAN baked beans in the supermarket and eat them from the tin .... constantly. I can also manage to get, if I am really very persistant, PICKLED ONIONS. The Farting can be heard at the Catholic church in Prima Porta.

Jean Smith[2] came to stay a week before the Edgartown Rumpus, and I bet that was her last happy holiday .... Gareth has been out ... Simone and the Trintignants (Yves was still stuck in Paris)[3] ....

---

1. Beatrice Dawson, costume designer.
2. Jean Kennedy Smith, sister to John and Robert Kennedy; later US Ambassador to Ireland. Their brother Edward had been involved one month earlier in the so-called 'Chappaquiddick Island Incident', near Edgartown, when Mary Jo Kopechne drowned.
3. Gareth Forwood; Simone Signoret and her husband Yves Montand; Jean-Louis Trintignant.

Visconti comes to swim ... and, I dont know ... it's all a bit nice really. We shall probably leave, with two cats and the dog and Antonia and Eduardo, for Jamacia in December for a few months ... unless something smashing happens film wise ... which I doubt. Visconti has a super idea which I wont tell you, because it'ud make you mad, and we could never get the lolly in England [...]

'Justine' has opened in N.Y. with odd notices ... the Studio has obviously panicked and cut hours of it, and it is the one thing the critics complain about! More time, rather than less ... Anouk [Aimée] is alright I gather, I'm 'overwhelming' (When have I not been) [Michael] York survives .. (well: time will tell) ... Anna Karina is 'Charming' .... the film is very distinguished, and the notices for [George] Cukor are super, thank God .... but the picture has been destroyed by the Zanuck-Berman set up ...... The N.Y. Times is superly good .... I await the rest with bated breath ... although 270,000 dollars still makes me feel warm, it aint the same as 'King And Country' for tuppence and three weeks ... however you have learned that little truth, I'll bet.

'Gotterdammerung' [*The Damned*], the Visconti thing, is staggering ... it is far too long ... by about almost half an hour ... but where to cut! The picture is tilted towards the boy[1] ... but then he did that with Delon[2] ... one understands ... but the sheer spectacle ... the detail ... the splendour of the high opera acting ... is unforgettable. It is not something that an American Audience in the Bahamas will readily cope with ... Brian Forbes might well be ill, after all he was running 'Chaillot'[3] (Pronounced; SHY-O O T.) According to the handouts ... at the same place, and I am sure they will all <u>love</u> that. But, Goodness! The camera work ... the playing ... the whole horror and beastliness of Germany in '33 is before you .... I would think you have seen the various spreads on the film in 'The Sunday Times' thing: and in Stern and various European papers ... it IS obscene, if cruelty is obscene, it <u>is</u> perverted, if fucking your mother is perversion, it IS unrelenting in its castigation of the People in Berlin and the Krupps and Thyssssins in general ... (I have to use too many letters to explain my dislike) and it wont make a sodding penny.

---

1. Helmut Berger.

2. Alain Delon, star of Visconti's *Rocco and His Brothers* (*Rocco e i suoi fratelli*) and *The Leopard* (*Il gattopardo*).

3. Bryan Forbes's *The Madwoman of Chaillot*, from the 1945 play by Jean Giraudoux.

Unless Warners cut it, and play it all for the Queer element, the incest and the tarts . . . not to mention the hero dressed as Marlene singing 'Ein richtiger Manne'.

Thats not me dear.

I really think that the most successful thing I have done in ten years or more is a one minute bit in 'Oh! What a Lovely War'[1] . . . which gets applauded every time. <u>Now why?</u> What was wrong with three hours in 'Accident' or two in 'The Servant' . . . . . are'nt people funny.

I have written a long recollection of Asquith[2] . . . . I was asked to, and was unable to refuse because I did know him well . . and was tremendously grateful, apart from other considerations, to him . . . and suddenly I remembered 'Go Between' . . . . When do you start? In spring, I hope. How is Mr [Robert] Shaw? Unhappy I hope. But doubt. The first time I ever met him was on a film of Asquiths, oddly enough, 'Libel' . . he had three lines as a Press Photographer . . . rather too many I thought at the time. But he was awfully worried about the tilt of his hat . . . and if his mackintosh was too short, or long, I forget which, it was a fearful bore anyway . . . and we nearly recast. Is'nt life odd again . . . . . and there goes the professional Welshman, Mr ~~Baker~~ Burton (!) – Freudian slip – [Stanley] Baker for Burton – both as tiresome as each other – being so tactless that I rather think he's lost his Knighthood . . . . tactless just before the Investiture thing[3] . . . in 'Life' Magazine . . . . . 'I am a patriotic Welshman and I care about our language . . . they cannot foist a foreign prince on our country.'

It's all cock anyway, but have you ever heard such rubbish? 'OUR' country . . when has he ever done more for it than cheer a Rugby Game or send a donation to Aberfan . . . . what Taxes has that little fellow with his Mammy-Wife ever paid, I'd like to know . . .

I better stop . . . the white wine has released far too much.

I hope you and Lady Patricia realise that this letter is written in a temperature of untold degrees, and only written for your amusement . . . . . probably better than the script you are shooting . . . but dont take it heavily and seriously . . . . You cant, can you, with my awful spelling.

Now what else. Rossella [Falk] is coming to supper this evening . . .

---

1. Directed by Richard Attenborough.
2. For R. J. Minney's '*Puffin' Asquith*' (Leslie Frewin, 1973).
3. The Investiture of the Prince of Wales was to take place at Caernarvon on 1 July.

we will give her fishcakes and beans. This, she thinks, is English Dinner ... and tells her friends ... Did I tell you we sat through THREE HOURS of 'Hedda Gabbler' with Miss Falk playing Hedda? A long bumsearing evening, but she really was'nt bad ... a pretentious production, and I only understood one word the whole night .. 'Certo.'

Which does'nt get you far.

Not with Ibsen in Italian, it does'nt.

It would be lovely if you could come to us for your holiday ... on the other hand it is possible that we could get to you in Sardeginia .... if I can leave the staff and house for some time .... but we dont have a lot of spare cash ... lira but not francs ... so the Colombe [d'Or] is dicey .... we were going up to stay with Simone [Signoret], but really .... I have a pool here, and my bar bills are far less expensive .... anyway: lets see. Keep me informed of your lobster-like movements and we'll do all we can to meet you .... but not until after September 18th. We are, as they say, booked 'solide' with expatriats until about then .... and just remember what I said ... I can get baked beans here ... fresh from the tin. (Chilled they'll give you a hard.) And if we try we can wrastle up some onions ... Antonia cooks like a dream on charcoal ... and the wine spills down from the vine ... actually you could both come and do a little pressing! We start to gather about mid September ...... gather the grapes I mean .... so, anyway [...] keep us informed.

Dont be too sad and depressed ... this might be the best film you ever did .... and if it aint stop whining and think of the lolly! I hear that you have bought 'next door' in Chelsea! Goodness ... what expansion ... and here I am wondering if I can get a small Monastary in Tuscany ... I can too, but they are huge. Want to come and see?

My devoted love to you both ... T. sends his, I know, but he is the new possesor of a super BMW 2800, white and black and terribly sexy and far too fucking fast for elderly fellows like me – and he's washing it –

I love you ... and miss you ... but thats your fault!

Warmest wishes to you both and much happiness.

<u>Dirk</u>

I have reached the end of this letter without any idea WHATSOEVER of your address. You dont put one and Patricia sends nervous postcards from airports with 'Tuesday' written on them. Would Tuesday, South Spain, reach you. I doubt it … I'll have to dial Robin.[1] What fun. Actually we CAN dial direct to London … but so can everyone else ….. so one never gets through. D –

To Joseph Losey
(Postcard)   *Villa Berti*
16 October 1969

Your letter made me feel sad! I'm fine! I have a film with Visconti in March. One with Resnais in June – & we are off to Tuscany to look at a house tomorrow. Life is'nt all that bad, Joe. It can, actually, be fun if you try! My love to you both – as ever. D.

Luchino Visconti had asked Dirk to play Gustav von Aschenbach in Death in Venice. *While waiting for production to start, Dirk had found, and begun the procedure to buy, Le Haut Clermont, a former farmhouse at Châteauneuf de Grasse.*

To Ann Skinner   *Villa Berti*
15 January 1970

Dearest Beloved AS.

What a smashing letter from N.Y. And it only took four days to get here! Quite a record considering that I am still getting Christmas Cards dated December 18th from places like Haywards Heath and Cowfold!

I am so happy that you liked 'Gotterdammerung' … (I cant bring myself to use the American title.) …. the blood and sweat and tears were terrible … and even though the old sod cut me to buggery in order to give the Boy more screen time … I am proud as proud that I am in it.

Is'nt it super too … that both 'Lovely War' and 'Damned' are on the N.Y. critics list of ten best! I mean thats a pretty good acheivement even if the customers dont call. Which in the case of the Visconti I am delighted to tell you that they do. Or are. And even in Italy we have started to make our Profits! And now all the battles rage because

---

1. Fox – Dirk's agent.

I have a modest 15% .... which I shall <u>never</u> ever see ... but I am bloody well going to fight for it somehow.

Returning to Viscontiville .... we were not dubbed, except in Italian, but Ingrid [Thulin] re dubbed herself and one other actor ... Helmut Griem, dubbed himself .... I must confess that the accents did'nt really bother me that much ... Visconti used German and English actors because he says, and I think he is right, that the Italians are only good singing in opera ..... as you recall from his other films, he tries not to use Italians if he can help it! [...] fortunatly I persuaded V. to import English actors from London .. and not use the Yanks here in Rome who do all the dubbing on every picture and sound exactly as if they were in the American Express Office.

Now I am sitting in a damp heap of wet, Rome, rain .. waiting to start work with V. on 'Death In Venice' ... which he has asked me to play. I feel a little sick at the idea, with nerves and terror, but long and long to do it .... we start shooting in mid March at the Lido in Venice ... and then exteriors there. After that I hope, only hope, to be able to move into my new house in Grasse what I'v bought myself at a VAST cost.[1] It is a small bergerie ... (with not enough space.) .. built in 1642 ... almost untoutched .. restored by a brilliant young painter who presently lives there with six small kids and a Maoist wife! It stands on the slope of a hill among twelve acres of giant olives .. and looks right down the plain to the bay of La Napoule. It is sheerest beauty .. and it is half an hour from Nice Airport ... and thirty minutes from Cannes ... and ten from Grasse. No swimming pool! I have to go up next week and sign the documents ... and then it is mine ... but I cant get the fellow out for three months from signiture ... on account of his smelly little children and Easter ... or something .... by which time I'll be up to me cod piece in Venice .... anyway; I must be calm. And you are welcome anytime you care provided that you dont mind sleeping in an olive tree ... we wont have a guest room for a year!

In order to do all this I have had to become a Non Resident of GB. A beastly feeling .... but essential .... and after all it really does'nt mean so much ... just that I can only stay for 100 days a year for the first four years .... but it does make you feel a tichy bit wobbley at first.

In the Autum I hope to do a rather super film with Damiani[2] ... one

---

1. He would pay 740,000 francs, roughly £56,000.
2. Damiano Damiani, who was planning a project titled *The Time of Your Life*.

of the greatest local Directors . . . . it's terribly funny and sad . . . . a sort
of 'Zorba' with me being a sort of [Alan] Bates . . . but much better! The
other gentleman is a tremendous star in Europe . . . a wild bull of a man
called Jean Pierre Volonte[1]. . . . and everyone is very frightened of him
. . . including me . . . . he has to chuck me in a harbour. And I cant swim.
I hope he grows to love me. I'll try to make him.

Then . . . if all that works out I am going into another Visconti!
Proust no less! Yippeee! It's almost as regular as Box and Thomas![2]
And a fucking sight more fun. Mind you the only thing that is FIRM
is D in V. and the house in Grasse . . and that is that. I am not at the
moment complaining. Do you remember the miseries of 'Sebastian'
and how I said never again for sheer lolly? And went and gave a
smashing perf. in 'Justine' which no one went to see and which I
loathed. So now it's for what money they can afford to pay me and
what I can afford to live on and who is the director and what is the
part . . . nothing else matters. I do wish I could work with Schles.[3] but
I dont think he terribly cares for my work . . . . and I long to work
with T. Harvey . . . and nearly did once . . . and hope the chance will
come again.[4] Super that he is settling down in N.Y . . . . . not so long
ago he was a timid and charming little director, floating about in the
sea in Venice . . . and I congratulated him on his 'little' film . . . . and
he said wistfully . . . . 'well . . . I dont think anything will happen for
me here . . . but I am just going to wait, and hope the lolly holds out,
until the last day.' And we all know what happened then![5] Is'nt life
funny?

Remember Lords and the hoses and the first Cont Sheets? . . and
Arnoldie[6] being devine as ever . . . . he writes occasionally . . . I have
asked him to come and do D in V [. . .]

---

1. Gian Maria Volontè, who had co-starred with Clint Eastwood in *A Fistful of Dollars*
(*Per un pugno di dollari*).
2. Betty Box and Ralph Thomas, the producer and director with whom Dirk made nine
films for Rank.
3. John Schlesinger. It was on his film *Darling* that Dirk first met AS, in charge of
continuity.
4. It did. Dirk would work with Anthony Harvey in 1981.
5. His success at the 1967 Film Festival with *Dutchman* was followed in 1969 by an Oscar
nomination for *The Lion in Winter*.
6. A sequence in *Darling* at Lord's cricket ground called for artificial rain, which resulted
in AS's continuity sheets being sodden. Arnold Schulkes, Dirk's stand-in since 1957, joined
the rescue mission by pegging the bedraggled papers to the hallowed, sun-drenched turf.

I must write some more, dull, letters ... I mean letters to dull
people .... and then go and finish my reading in St Peters ... doing
a rather super two hour documentary for NBC[1] with R. Richardson,
E. Evans, O Wells and me ... reading letters of Bonnie Prince Charlie
(I am) and a HUGE chunk of Childe Harolde[.] Which unnerves
me ... 4am in St Peters is an odd hour ... but your voice does'nt half
sound lovely! All my love and from Tote .... Dirk – XXX

To Joseph and Patricia Losey

Villa Berti
15 February 1970

Well ... actually we are still here at this Villa, which becomes increasingly miserable as the year goes on ... a year ago yesterday I left
England.[2] What a lot happens in such a very comparitavly small time
... small, anyway, as one gets older. I loved your two funny-grumpy-
slush-and students letters! I do think you were DOTTY to go and
try and teach the heathens.[3] Almost as useless as Aid To Biafra ...
however I suppose it got you out of the way of the Hickery-Dickery
taking place in your house in Chelsea ... let us hope that you also
managed to get some of them on your side in the Students Hall, Man
.. like it was for real, man, like you could get them to dig you and
PINTER at the same time.
    We have been sort of commuting, Wagon Lits Style, to and from
La Colombe for the last three months .... I have bought my house
near Grasse [...] Simone was a bit undecided about the idea that I
would become a immigrant, which I have had to do now, and buy
anything which she would approve ... however we did the whole deal
by ourselves ... (it cost me a fortune ... nearly 100,000 quid) and
when I took her over on Thursday all she could say was 'Ah! C'est
vrai! C'est vrai! C'est beau ..' or Belle ... I cant remember the gender.
I never, for that matter, have.
    Anyway I am ravished by it ... we have a good deal to do ....
throwing three large rooms on the ground floor into one ... building
another bathroom ... and another kitchen and flat for A. and E. ....

---

1. *Upon This Rock*, transmitted in 1973.
2. Dirk's personal chronology was, as usual, awry.
3. Losey had been Visiting Professor of Film and Drama at his alma mater, Dartmouth
College.

we shall not be able to move in until I have finished with Visconti
sometime, fingers crossed, in late June .... but the house is paid for,
signed and sealed, and I have total posession in six weeks ... when the
builders will move in with the architect.

Death In Venice starts April 1st outside the Hotel des Bains on the
Lido. Visconti is scouring Stockholm, Warsaw, and Budapest for his
Tadjio[1] .... he has left instructions to have the WHOLE of St Marks
re-dressed as it was in 1911 .... we are shooting in Panavision which has
added millions to the slender budget ... I have 18 changes ... and we
shoot also in the Tyrol and in Munich ... because the TRUE story of
DIV was that Mann, an old friend of Viscontis, was travelling on a train
from Venice to Munich in 1910 ... and in the compartment was a strange
being in full slap ... desperatly unhappy, his ~~died~~, dyed, hair streaky ..
his false eyelashes coming off in his tears. They spoke .... It was Gustave
Mahler .. and he had just fallen in hopeless love with a child of thirteen
in Venice ..... and so from there it went. So, although <u>we are not telling
anyone,</u> I am in fact playing Mahler ... and look rather like him with
the putty nose-job and the rimless Lennon-glasses .... long hair ... oh!
dear I am a sight at the moment ... So I rather fear that what my father
calls a 'slender little tale' will end up with fifteen weeks shooting and
then some, and so the house must wait ... because this comes very much
first ... although how I am going to manage on the piddling little salary
I dont know ... we are back to OUR days of the Servant again ... no
lolly and everything needed.

'The Damned' has been a sort of run-away success here and in the
States, and in little old Belgium where it took 800,000 dollars! It
opens tomorrow in Paris at the Opera, which is right and fitting
because that is what it is and how it was concieved, <u>as an opera</u> .. Your
chum Roude[2] sneaked in and saw it here in Rome and wrote a beastly
notice ... calling it very Grotesque and silly. (I gather he is Canadien
or something) .. may account for things ... also he saw it in Italian
and cant speak it ... so what WAS he about .... but, to be fair, I
think the vast majority of the British Press will think so too .... they
wont get it, I'm afraid.

Except Maggie Hinxman who spent three days here last week doing
an indepth thing on me, get that, for the Telegraph ... she adored it

1. Tadzio, the boy in Thomas Mann's story.
2. Richard Roud, critic.

... and got it's points ... but she did warn that a lot of her colleagues did'nt. We'll see .... if we ever get a release there.

[...] I hope that we can get into the house in July .. and settle there for a bit until a picture I want to make, very much, with Damiani starts ... in October ... a bit like 'Zorba' but MUCH better and without that terrible [Anthony] Quinn. Damiani wrote it as well ... so thats a bit of a help. If there is'nt a civil war here before then, and there is every chance that there will be next summer .... that should keep me busy for a while ... anyway until Prousts' 'Rememberance Of Things Past' which V. is signed to do in the late spring of '71 ... but now that I have spent me savings I have to get to work ... but not doing 'Doctors' again!

Angela and Robin [Fox] came down to the Colombe with us .. and A. and E. and the dog [...] and one day at lunch on the terrace, the sun blazing, the mimosa great golden plumes, the almond blossom drifting in the soft wind .. and the doves scattering in an arc of blue sky, Antonia said 'I think this is as near as I will ever get to Heaven.' which was rather nice [...]

In Italy, like everywhere else, films are at a terribly low ebb ... Laurentis[1] is closed and reopens as a Japanese Transistor and telly factory! Paradox ... Cinecitta is the only one left that is making anything .... and that only has one on the floor right now. But I dont think the really Good stuff will fade away ... so long as everyone takes fair cuts and shares ... your Greedy Guts Chums fairly did for us all, I fear ... and the folly of their ways washes on to us all ... One simply does'nt find greed attractive, without talent at any rate .... still, they were not the only ones .. the Zanucks and the rest all helped hard to kill. So now we all have to hang on by our back teeth and start from scratch again ... a new wind is blowing ... one does'nt want to be a dead leaf in a bad winter! Rather a green bud ... even at my age.

[...] I'll take a house in Venice for the duration of the film .... if I can afford to ... no Gritty Palaces now! Oh! dear! Oh! dear! Where are Box and Thomas and the RICH days? Well; they are making a new Doctor film with someone called Simon Dee .... wow!

We, that is you and I, have a week of Losey Bogarde films at the little Everyman[2] ... how a week I dont know, but I suppose they'll

---

1. The studio built by Dino De Laurentiis.
2. The independent cinema in Hampstead.

put 'Blaise' on in two halves .... Oddish notices for 'Birthday Party'[1]
today ... not tremendous ... except for Dandy Nicholls and Sydney
Tafler ... (Rightly, I should think) and other than the new Arthur
Shaeffer play,[2] not Peter, his brother, which opened on Thursday <u>to
the raves of all the world</u>, there is nothing much to tell you ..... the
Schaeffer play is called 'Sluth' ... and I was asked to do it with Keith
Baxter ..... Quale (Ugh) plays it now.

Raining and blowing a gale here ... but the violets are out, the
blossom is frothing ... lunch on the terrace ... and four eggs from
the chickens this afternoon ... Tony is downstairs reading a catalogue
of French Cookers and I am about to drop into the Cognac and
Soda ...

[...] Devoted love as ever ...
<u>Dirk</u>

To Joseph Losey   *Villa Berti*
                                              6 March 1970

[In red ink] <u>WARNING!</u>
This is supposed to be a funny letter – if <u>you</u> dont think so, ask Josh.

Dearest Josieposie ....

Of course you WOULD be distressed by the 'Telegraph' bit[3] ... I
<u>knew</u>, the very second I read it .... 'Watch it! Loseys going to be
pissed off about this one.' Well; I <u>loved</u> it ... and <u>approved</u> it, and was
terribly pleased to get the coverage .... things on which you did not
comment .. like us both trying to work for English Films and make
them go ... seem to have passed over your huge head .... the fact
that I did NOT say you were pissed out of your mind, and disgusting,
the night I walked off the set ... and took ALL the blame; you choose

---

1. William Friedkin's belatedly released film of Pinter's play, with Robert Shaw, Patrick
Magee, Sydney Tafler and Dandy Nichols.
2. The world première of Anthony Shaffer's *Sleuth*, at the St Martin's Theatre, starred
Anthony Quayle and Keith Baxter.
3. JL took exception to the interview with Margaret Hinxman (*The Sunday Telegraph*, 22
February), in which Dirk recalled an incident during the making of *Accident*. 'We'd been
waiting all night for a sunrise and I moved a prop, a child's tricycle ... Joe yelled at me
"Can't you ever learn to be disciplined?" It was the one thing he knew would hurt me
because I've prided myself on being professional above everything. Of course, he didn't
mean it.'

to ignore ... correctly, I suppose .... If one thinks one is God one must behave as God ... but I just honestly and calmly, do think that we have done all that we can together. I dont, honestly, see how we could work together again ..... we have said all there is to say as actor-director ...... and you decided, a while ago, to take another path my dear .. the one with the lolly and the lushness .... I have kept to my rather wobbley one; it has been a bit of a wrench ... but, after all, I had the lush one before Our Time, with Rank, I suppose .... so now it is refreshing to be free .... and to choose. It is frightning like shit .... but it is honour regained.

And remember about D in V .... I know that you have long wanted to make it. You told me until I was blue in the face .... but you never asked me to do it .... or offered me the chance, or remotely thought that I even could! Visconti, in May last year, did .... I was amazed and thrilled to my marrow .... he gave no excuses or reasons, except to say, in a rather grudging way, that I was 'like a dead pheasant ... hanging by the neck, and almost ready to drop.' the reference being, I hope, that I was RIPE. And also, that I do look like Mahler, and that I was 'one of the most perfect actors in the world today on the screen.'

You have never even said that I was more than passably good. To me anyway ... And from your interviews and books and all those itsy-bitseys you hand out to 'Isis' and papers of that ilk ... I was lucky to have you. Instead of the other way around, sweetie!!

You ARE a naughty fellow ... you know, full well that you are deeply loved by me ... and that you always will be. No matter what. But you are a solitary .... there is no helping you .... you eat love like candy and vomit it straight up again: like a dog.

It does'nt matter a scrap as long as your 'lovers' are patient, and have a sense, however wild, of humour .... but when you say that you are going to California to 'help Burton' get his Oscar, as if it were some noble deed ..... something in which you felt you should share .... so 'that my usefulness is not entirely gone.' Jeasus! What are you doing for the Welsh bastard? How can you help him get an Oscar for an indifferent performance that has already, sickeningly, been purchased by Hal Wallis?[1] Why lend yourself to that stuff?

---

1. Producer of *Anne of the Thousand Days*, for which Burton had been nominated as Best Actor. And the Oscar went to ... John Wayne.

And something else, Loseyposie . . . the Old Master . . . to whome you grudgingly accord the phrase 'very good' . . . . did not do 'L'Etranger'[1] for <u>Greediness</u> . . . he did'nt want to do the fucking thing at all . . . . (well, originally) but Mdm Camus put paid to that, and also the loyalty of his cheif actor . . . who pissed off at the last moment to another studio and left him with the alternative of a great and loving friend Mastrianni . . . . who <u>knew</u> that he was wrong . . and HATED the film . . . but offered to do it a few days before shooting to help Old Master out.

No one, least of all Visconti, wants to be reminded of that film . . . and you know yourself how tiresome writers widows can be. Or perhaps you dont?

The Mahler story is as old as God. I did'nt mean it to be a revalation to you . . I was just sharing an idea which I personally think exciting, simply, I suppose, because I love the Music and know well the story of the man . . . . however; does'nt matter.

Anyway . . . this is just to put you in the picture about a number of things. You whimper too often, you old sod . . . and you cant expect to pick up lumps of Cartier, and all the rest of the crap, with rotten scripts . . and wheather you like it or not they both were simply AWFUL! And dated. So come back to Europe and make a little bit of lovliness for tuppence. And screw the watches and the approbation of the Yacht Set. <u>They</u> really do say 'You are only as good as your last picture.' Perhaps you'll be lovely after 'Landscape'.[2]

And perhaps Shaw is JUST what you deserve. As far as I remember he only does two things really well . . shout above rain and wind and stand with his legs apart.

Now. To stop attacking you. We quit this horrid house, a year has been enough, and move to Venice on Wednesday . . . or to St Paul . . . . dont know which yet . . . we dont start to shoot at the Hotel des Bains until April 6th . . . . so I'll hang around until they need me. I went up to Venice last week and rented the Volpi house on the Guidecca . . an acre of garden, and a simple house with silence all around . . . . so we might be there in a week or so.

We shoot in Venice all the time . . . . dreading the start of the Season;

1 . Visconti's *Lo straniero* from Albert Camus's *l'Etranger*, with Marcello Mastroianni.
2 . *Figures in a Landscape*, an unhappy Losey project, starring Robert Shaw and Malcolm McDowell.

naturally Visconti wants the whole of the Piazza dressed as it was in
1911 . . . . . plus the vastly expensive boat . . . . we'll see. There are VAST
complications . . . . . not the least of whome is one José Ferrar[1] who
bought the rights years ago; and we all thought he was dead.

Not a bit of it . . . he is in Key Largo alive and well . . . and spitting
shit and hate. And refuses to sign a Quit notice.

So. I may just have to go back to Box and Thomas and be in one
of their Doctor Films as a 'Guest'. That'll take me down a peg or two
. . . . wont it?

Wet and cold here . . . and really hateful . . . . I have had two months
dentistry done in six days and am reeling from novacane and the bill
. . . . why does it always happen in a lump I wonder? Misfortune, I
mean.

[. . .] I have just read through the last two pages, and it seems as if
I were hitting the shit out of you. Well: I _am_ in a way . . . but you
know that I am the person who loves you most in all the world, save
for Patreeecia . . . . and I have the right, privatly, to say to you what I
feel. And it says something that I have bothered to write you all this
. . . . when I have a lot of other things to do, like have a drink . . . walk
the dog, and write to James Clark about a BBC Documentary they
want to make on me doing Mahler.

See how rotten I can be?

Incidentally I did 'This is Your Life' for Wendy Craig last week
. . . . . I thought I _had_ to after all the filthy things you have said about
her in print. So I did a lovely sick-making chat to her about how
SUPER she was in 'El Servo' . . . . and I must say I was pissing myself
at the thought of your poleaxed face, had you heard!

[. . .] Tote is off having a wheel changed on the new BMW . . .
which goes _much_ too fast . . . but does do Rome-Venice in $4\frac{1}{2}$ hours
flat . . . . and I mean flat.

I think that I told you that I took Simone and Yves up to the new
house and that they loved it . . . . which was a relief . . . . I cant wait for
April 6th . . . when I finally get posession, and start shooting on DIV!
What timing! Oy! Yoi! Do I ever do it well.

It is raining like hell . . . and I really must write a couple more bits
. . . . by the way [. . .] there is an odd little script with which I almost

---

1. The actor José Ferrer and the producer Joseph Besch had bought the rights in 1963
from Thomas Mann's estate.

fell in love [...] you might hate it ... it is called 'Thunder On The Left' ... was written by Christopher Morley about twenty five years ago,[1] and has been excellently lifted and re-set in England in '39. By ... dont faint, because I nearly did, Victor Lindon, or Lyndon[2] ..... for Willie, Vanessa,[3] self, Christie, and three or four other smashing parts ... it might be too much the same as 'Go Between' .... but it is interesting to read [...] And you dont need to play me .... Stanley [Baker] would do it quite lovely. With a little bit of help from his friends.

I'm being a bastard I know. But I do love you ... and Patreecia and her torn ligaments ... if you ever want to speak to me again am care of R. Fox.

I have never been <u>quite</u> so in limbo before!

Dirk –

On 1 April, in preparation for Death in Venice, *Dirk and Tony moved into Ca' Leone on the Giudecca. They made a brief visit to Rome for Dirk's costume fittings and make-up tests.*

To Joseph Losey   *Hotel Hassler, Rome*
                                       18 April 1970

Sad that my 'paranoid' letter caused you such anger – it <u>WAS</u> supposed to be funny (I even printed it red). However – accept, if you care to, my apologies – it is difficult for me to offer more.

My 'exile', as you quaintly call it, was not emotional, but very good business – I am enormously glad to be out of England, and I have a glorious house and ten acres of land and as soon as I can get there to live I shall be happier.

[...] Dont bother keeping this letter, or my dear American nit-wit, the last for 'whatever posterity' there might be – I can write ruder things – and funnier! – off to Venice again tomorrow for 3 months I hope (rented the Volpi house – super, if sodden) – love to Patricia & apologies for upsetting the bucolic peace of 'Pink Sands' – !

<u>Dirk</u>

---

1. Morley's novel was published by Doubleday, Page & Co. in 1925.
2. Victor Lyndon, associate producer of *Darling* and occasional screenwriter.
3. James (christened William) Fox and Vanessa Redgrave.

To Dilys Powell   *Ca' Leone*
                                              Giudecca 140
                                                   Venezia
                                       May 13th. at 3.05pm –

This is Boast Paper . . . . . but your letter, this morning, has tempted
me to write back to you . . . . as I can neither spell or punctuate, or use
this sodding little machine you are in for a 'bumpy read' . . . This is
the most enchanting little house. Built by one of the Volpies for a
mistress in about seventeen something, in an acre of garden facing out
to sea . . . it's on the <u>Other</u> side of the Guidecca . . . . looking towards
an infinity of little islands . . and then the tip of the beastly old Lido.

The mistresses all prospered here, I gather, and the last one is the
father of the present Count . . a sly looking little bastard, judging by
a pastel, sadly Stiltoned by damp, which hangs in the saloon. They
dont 'let' it . . . but lovely Visconti said I was ok and they repainted
the kitchen . . . pulled up the weeds, and let me in at a million Lire a
month . . . . considering that I am hardly being paid a million lira a
<u>year</u> for the film, I think they were molto generous. Odd people. Volpi
made a specific rule that there would be '<u>not photography in the house
or the garden.</u>'

I wonder why we are ALL classed as Burtons . . . it <u>is</u> a bore
sometimes. By the way . . . incase you panic . . . this letter is not an
invitation to a long course in letter exchange. As I oncex (I hate this
blasted machine.) told you in a postcard . . ours is NOT that sort of
friendship . . . we dont HAVE to write . . . it is just that sometimes it
is pleasant and lovely to 'touch' you. As you are able, unknowingly,
every week to touch me.

After our shy luncheon, which you pleaded <u>not</u> to have, but to
which you wonderfully 'gave in', with your funny plastic umbrella and
Claudette Colbert just across the room . . . . I am deeply aware of not
'pressing' things . . . but it is a titchy bit tough when one actually loves
a person, to always keep distance . . . . especially when one has to be a
very great deal 'decontracté' . . . of which I am well aware.

Anyway, the hell with all that . . . . I have made the point, I hope,
clear . . . Visconti is doing something magical . . . . we have absolutely
NO money at all . . . . Warners are 'behind' us, but would have preferd
'a little girl', instead of a little boy . . . . this was their own suggestion.
They thought it would be more 'youth oriented' . . (for Gods sake

dont tell anyone.) .. but there it is in a nutshell. Now they are bemused, and wonder how to sell a movie about 'This old fag who digs kiddies.'

One has, always, to catch ones breath and clench ones fists, and be nice to them . . . . . the Yanks I mean . . . but in ALL degrees they are dreadful. And I use the English word . . . . . one is full of DREAD for them & they are full of dread too – . . . from Cambodia to Kent[1] .. to the idiotic values, or non values, which they attach to Mann and 'DIV'.

But in any case we have completely stripped the [Hôtel] des Bains and re-done it for 1911 . . . it is ravishing. To make you blub, a bit. Great cartwheel hats, ablaze with ribbon and stuffed birds . . . persian carpets . . . brass bowls full of Hydrangias .. (Wrong spelling again) tables and basket work chairs . . . lamps with frilly shades .. palms . . . . waiters with white gloves . . . . 'smokings' . . . hobble skirts . . . children with lampshades for hats . . . The Merry Widow from the Orchestra . . . the clack of heels on parquet .. Nannies, and boys in sailor suits; drinks to be drunk through straws . . . . suddenly a daring Tango creeping in to the [repertoire] . . . laughter, and idle chatter . . . the dining room full of white chairs and gilded mirrors . . . (The original white chairs which we found on the local rubbish tip . . . all two hundred of them.) temps perdue . . . time recaptured. And odd. Shivers up ones spine when one sinks into a stuffed leather armchair and reads the 'Times' of June 11th, 1911 . . . to see pictures of the review at Spithead .. (what a huge Navy we had.) .. and on the opposite page a sad picture of the Prince of Wales with his Welsh Gear. What an odd, odd, feeling it is . . . . . almost . . . no, not almost, clearly a case of Priestly[2] . . . . . . I have been here before . . . . and in this room . . . this odd mahogany room with mirrors and art neauveau lamps.

And then a blackbird starts singing in the trees outside and the first ultamarine blush of the dawn, about to come, is heralded.

And 'Viejlia'[3] still scrapes on from the Orchestra .. to be followed, as the first blush of dawn hits the billowing curtains, and streaks across the floor, by the 'Blue Danube'.

I HAVE gone on a bit . . . . . but we are working at night at the

---

1. On 4 May National Guardsmen had killed four and wounded nine during a student demonstration at Kent State University.
2. At the beginning of his career Dirk had acted in two works by J. B. Priestley, master of the 'time play'.
3. Vilja – the forest fairy in *The Merry Widow*.

moment, as you gather ... and somehow night adds a timlessness to
it all ... and the women look SO beautiful. So elegant ... mincing
along on their heels ... fans clacking ... skirts a shimmer ... hats
brimming ... what we have <u>lost</u>. Oh! Dearie me .... not comfortable,
I agree, but that has never been a reason for correct behaviour, for
elegance ... for beauty even ..... but how much nicer it was then ...
just before the sky went dark, and 'the lamps went out.'

This machine is so foul ... and my spelling so awful .... that I
shall seal the letter with a kiss and clear off to bed for an hour or two
before I have to trail across to the Lido to be turned into (I hope) a
fiftytwo year old Jewish Genius with a 'hang up' (As Warners call it)
on kids. Male.

Seriously ... I am off to be Aschenbach* .... based as you know
on poor, sad, Mahler, who Mann met in a train from Vienna weeping
in the compartment, and with a squint wig and running mascara
.... and from the stumbled story came DIV.

We have gone back to Mahler .... and it is tough.

Now the ribbon has run out – <u>mercifully</u> for you! – excuse, if you
can, the utter lack of spelling – and <u>never, ever</u> – use an Olivetti 'made
in Spain' – they really dont work –

My love to you – for ever – as ever —
    <u>D.B.</u>

*Actually; Visconti has had me made up as Mann – whome he knew
well – So it's a pretty dreary evening – I <u>look</u> like Lloyd George!

*After completing his work on the film, Dirk and Tony moved into Le
Haut Clermont on 5 August. They were joined by the loyal Boludas.*

To Luchino Visconti

Clermont
19 September 1970

My dear Luchino:

I was tremendously happy to have your note, and the letter which
you so kindly enclosed, but distressed to hear that you are STILL
haveing battles with Warners.

What on earth do they want? I suppose we spent too much and
now the film is finished they refuse to help with extra expenses ...

well: DONT give in to them easily, they have a marvellous picture
and a bargain anyway.

I really do loath them . . . even Mr Katz[1] who is quite nice and who
I met here in the Colombe d'Or a few weeks ago . . . . but he said that
he thought the picture was a 'Masterpiece' but that we had spent too
much . . . . I told him that I thought that was perfectly reasonable for
a 'Masterpiece'.

My house is almost a home now! It has taken a long time to get
settled in . . . . Poverino[2] HATES it because there is no pee-pee to
smell, only rabbits and foxes and thyme and laurel . . . . . one can never
please truly common people. He would be much happier back in
Prima Porta.

Much of my furniture was badly smashed during the journey from
London . . and almost all my Meissen china . . . . however the pictures
were safe, and look very fine on the white walls.

So far we are happy . . . . and things are going calmly. My Parents
are staying with me for two weeks . . . . . which is rather ghastly . . .
and the servants have to go back to Spain next week where the poor
girl has to have a (we hope) slight little operation . . . . so I shall be
washing the floors myself and cooking . . . which I hate.

It seems incredible to me that the film is over only by a few weeks
. . . I am very nostalgic for it and for Gustav . . . and always for you,
and I will never be able to thank you enough, ever, for your marvellous
kindness in offering me the Part, and then in helping me to do it . . .
I hope that I have done what you wanted. I can only tell you that I
did my best from my heart not only for myself and Mann . . . . but for
you as indeed I always will.

I know that you do not care to read long letters in English . . . so
I'll finish off. I will come to you in Rome when you need me; I MAY
start a film here in France at the end of October . . . but I want to be
very sure of the thing first after 'Death'.

Fellini had very indifferent notices[3] in London, as you may know,
they called him a 'Conjouror with nothing up his sleeve and too many
bad tricks . .' but most of all they were appalled by the terrible dubbing
and the voices . . . . . so do be careful with those dreadful Americans

---

1. Norman Katz, a vice-president of Warner Bros.
2. The nickname Dirk shared with Visconti for Labo.
3. For *Fellini Satyricon*.

in Death .... remember what you once told me .. 'We have all the guns on us!'.

My love and respect to you and my warmest affection always in all ways ...

      With love
        <u>Dirk</u>

To Patricia Losey   *Clermont*
September 25th. Friday.

Darling –

It was super to have your long letter ... and superer, if that is a word, to know that you have fallen in love (sic) with the country.[1] However; I feel that a couple of weeks in Febuary there would finally spell the end for Joe! Lonliness is corrupting in the <u>real</u> country unless you HAVE to go about the place doing things to keep warm, fed and occupied!

I know. I tried it for a long time ... however it does teach one tolerance, I found ... and peace of mind to a certain extent.

God knows that is what is needed all round these days.

We have rid ourselves of my parents after a L O N G two week visit. He was devine as ever pottering about painting, and smelling the air, and trying to 'capture' Cezannes' light on paper. But she sat in a heap, with tired legs, rather hating the whole thing and most of all me. As usual! I feel it so wretched that she is utterly incapable of enjoying a thing. Except the bar of the Colombe and a good flask of wine. And we all know what that leads to.

However off they went from Cannes on Monday and on Tuesday the Staff flew off to Valencia. Antonia had found a lump in her breast, poor darling, so ..... and we now sit in our bergerie on the hill 'doing' for ourselves. I loath it .... and very much hope that all goes well with Antonia for her sake as well as my selfish own. Floors to scrub, beds to make, food to prepare, eat and wash up .... windows and shutters to lock and open, and the fucking incinerator to relight every morning! However; here we are in a beautiful place, where I have always wanted to be, and that should jolly well be enough. And, in truth, it is [...] We are a bit primitave here ... only one loo so queues

---

1. The Loseys were on location in Norfolk for *The Go-Between*.

form in the morning like on airoplanes! The highest single cost here at
Clermont is the Liquor! As you can imagine there is quite a lot of glug-
glugging and it is lovely because the actual bottles are cheaper than with
you . . . . and the wine is absurdly cheap . . . and the beer from Strasbourg
cheap and potent. Meat is a real sod, and we cannot really afford to
have it more than once a week and then in a sort of stew . . which
does'nt bother me because I dont care for it all that much . . . . but the
local fish, vegetables and things are super and abundant.

A pause while we trailed the dustbins down to the end of the lane
. . . Friday is the day . . .

The Film with Visconti was amazing . . frightning and the most
exhausting I have ever done in my life . . . to walk the knife edge
between a sort of Peter O'-Tool-Chips performance with Granny-
Glasses and an elderly 'twitch' . . . and a performance which would
suggest a pre-senile man of fifty-one walking to his death, because his
legs would not very well carry him to the edge of the tomb without
reluctance . . . and because he actually could not see without his glasses
. . . . . . this was a very different thing. I hope that we have done it,
otherwise, as Visconti says, 'We are morto . . . perqui[1] all the guns are
at us with this'.

I had a letter from him this morning to say that he was just starting
to 'cut' . . . . he has been sitting in Ischia in the Palace refusing to see
anyone from Warners because he feels, rightly I think, that they are
all cheats [. . .] I rather think, but dont know, that we went over
budget by a bit . . . . we were slated at 1,500,000 and I think we almost
made it to two . . . and anything after 1,500,000 was supposed to be
covered by V. Personally . . . . . which I am sure he has refused. It is a
bargain picture whatever way they try to cut it . . . and trust the bloody
Yids to know that! Excepting Danny A.[2] there really are'nt any in the
Movies that I would trust round a corner.

However . . . there it is. The film is made . . the agonies . . . including
paying off Jose Ferrer 100,000 dollars to clear off (he had half the
rights we discovered the day we were to start shooting!) and the worry
about the boy[3] shooting up feet in days . . and staying up until seven
every morning doing the 'Frug' or something frightful with the kids

---

1. Presumably *perché* (because).
2. Daniel M. (Danny) Angel, producer of *King and Country*.
3. Björn Andresen.

on the Lido and arriving for shooting with hoops of black under each eye ... our 'pure' unblemished 'Canava Marble' falling to dust before our eyes; stuffed with Pot and pea nuts and chewing gum ...... what with all these agonies we made it. And it is done. Enough.

The boy, like Joe's Leo,[1] was sensational ... 15 years old playing 14 .. Swedish .. absolutely extraordinary. We worked together as if he had been in the business as long as I .. which is 36 years this June ... and he was as utterly professional as Sarah Miles[2] is not ... I mention no other names ... naturally.

But the strain was teriffic .... we finished shooting in a plum orchard in Bolzano at noon on August the 2nd .... and drove a packed car ... (Totes new, super white Maserati) plus dog to Cremona ... then to Nice .. and moved in the furniture and Staff the day after. Exceptionally tiresome .. especially as the heat was up in the ninties and we had not even seen the house really ready for us before then. It is really rather fine. We have done a hell of a lot to it; opened up walls and floors and closed doors and windows and generally transformed a stable, workroom and kitchen into a fifty foot room with a great terrace and windows out over the whole of the Provence countryside to the sea at La Napoule ... We really do rather adore it, and keep hoping that God, or the fates, will allow us a little time to stay here .... apart from the always present hazard of age and health there should be no real reason why not .... I dont have to work again for twenty years, which will take care of me anyway! And I am not all that eager to do so .... Joe and Visconti are terrible spoilers for one .... no one else quite hits the same mark.

The Resnais script ... due to start in January ... is extraordinary ... a Marienbad about de Sade. Original. Confusing. Brilliant and un commercial. We just will have to wait and see if anyone will give us the lolly. I dont mind working for nothing so long as the Katzes and the Hymes and the Shinklehubbers cut their salaries! But they bloody well dont! There they all are at the Colombe ... fat and bulging and spending our profits .. Ugh!

---

1. Dominic Guard, playing the eponymous go-between.
2. This swipe at one of the leading players from *The Servant* might owe something to the fact that at the time the film was shot, she was living with Dirk's co-star, the twenty-three-year-old James Fox. It seems especially vindictive given that in her own memoirs Miss Miles would record that 'Dirk, being an absolute professional, was good fun to work with and I learned a lot from him.' (*Serves Me Right*, Macmillan, 1994)

[...] Otherwise we sit and write and read and garden and play music and shop and eat and wander about hanging pictures and dusting books ..... and generally settling in for a Stay.

[...] The sun is beginning to dip over the big mountain to my left ... I have fed the dog ... mended a fuse and am now about to wander down to watch the workmen finish off my fencing ... ten square acres of it ... RATHER expensive ... but now the chasseurs cant just wander in and blast everything that moves to feathers and pulp!

My devoted love to you as ever and to Joe ... pass him the news you think he'd listen to, and tell him I'm delighted he's on the booze again .. he was a bit of a drag on Tonic and bitters, and I dont suppose a smoke did much difference to him!

I'm off for my 'jar' [...] I love you and miss you both.
<u>Dirk</u>.

To Joseph Losey   *Clermont*
                                              30 November 1970

Joseph –

A hurried note to say how smashing it was to hear you on Saturday. A lovely bit of a surprise while I was planting out a lady called Nelly Moser ... who I hope will smother the south wall with a 'palet of brilliant colours and enchanting blooms.' As the lable says ... by June.

I await with great intrest for the Mosley script[1] ... you are not too often pleased with the writing in scripts generally ... so your obvious enthusiasm for this is splendid. I forgot to ask you, and probably should'nt, where the backing was coming from, because if it is from Columbia you wont get me I fear! They loath my guts for some reason which I have never found out. Except that I <u>did</u> call Frankavitch[2] a 'fat white slug' to his face, and in public, which obviously cant have helped!

I gather today that Death In Venice opens in Febuary in London ... God knows after that I'll really have to retire .... but if they liked

1. Nicholas Mosley, author of the novel *Accident*, was writing the screenplay for *The Assassination of Trotsky*.
2. Mike Frankovich, whom Dirk would have encountered in the 1950s, when the former was head of Columbia's British operation.

'Scrooge', as they all seemed to do yesterday, ... they may like us!

Dont be too upset about 'Figures' ... you had a typically marvellous personal press ... and the Match reaction is marvellous as you know ... and it is a hell of a time to open a picture ... a month from Christmas ... have they played it in a good house? Or one of those barns? Anyway .. it has only added luster to your already burnished crown ... so why worry about the lolly, especially as you seem to have no problems in that direction for the next couple of movies.

My typing is getting simply dreadful ... I keep on missing out bits and pieces ... and I feel that the real reason is that I am keeping one eager eye on the clock to see when I can go down and get myself a bottle of Kronenberg.

Anyway this is just a note to say thank you for the call ... and I'll speak to you as soon as I get my hands on the script.

devotions to Patricia ...

And you. Dirk

To Luchino Visconti   *Clermont*
                                                  4 December 1970

My dear Luchino –

First of all please forgive me for typing this letter, and also for writing it in English.

Your long letter has just reached me today and filled me with sadness to know that you are so unhappy.[1]

I cannot comment on the piece in 'Vogue', because I have not read it ... but I can, and do, apologize for any distress that a friend of mine, Mrs Tynan, should have caused you. It is important to try and reply to your 'points' individually.

1. I have NEVER EVER said that I was 'miscast' in 'The Damned', as a matter of fact I dont think that I was! However it is perfectly true that other people DO think so, and have written it in the Press in America and in England, so I suppose that Mrs Tynan is entitled to quote them, if that is what she has done.

---

1. LV had taken exception to Kathleen Tynan's report from the *Death in Venice* location, published in the December issue of American *Vogue*.

2. I tell the story of our first meeting, in the Hassler, and it is intended to be a compliment to your magnetism and charme. I always say that I had no intention of playing Freidrich[1] because I knew that it was a poor part, but that after about five minutes of your concentrated charm I was quite unable to say 'no' ... and knew that I wanted to work with you <u>above all things</u>. This is true and I shall continue to say so.

3. I am often asked what I learned from you, and I always reply that this is a very difficult question. As an actor, perhaps nothing; possibly because I am too old to learn. But about the Cinema, and as a man, I think that I have learned very much from you .... but it would be very hard to express just exactly what it is. Later perhaps I will know. This is what I tell people.

4. Your direction of me as Freidrich. I dont know what has been written and possibly it is my fault for trying to explain something difficult, not very well. It is my attempt to explain the method of 'Shorthand' communication between Director and Actor. You used to say very little to me but I knew, or thought that I knew, what you wanted from me. Certainly at times you <u>did</u> use musical terms such as 'a little too much Lohengrin' or something equally amusing, and this would always indicate to me that I should give a little less or a little more. It is a very personal thing between an Actor and his Director; difficult to explain properly to people who do not exactly understand, but I am often asked this about you, about Losey, Cukor and Clayton.

5. I <u>cannot</u> believe that Mrs Tynan has deliberately written unkindly. I know well her total admiration, and indeed affection, for you. It is possible that I may have given her a wrong impression by talking too much about you, as one does about someone of whom one is deeply fond, and whom one admires as much as I do you. It is equally possible that her article may have suffered from bad editing (as so often happens) so that things have been condensed and appear out of their true context. Possibly she has tried to show some of your fallibilities to make you appear more of a human being than a Giant, and possibly she has miscalculated the effect ... but ... I really cannot say

---

1. Friedrich Bruckmann, Dirk's character in *The Damned*.

until I have read the thing, and I do not yet know how to get a copy of 'Vogue'.

That is that as far as I can explain.

Incidentally I do not <u>ever</u> remember recieving a letter from you about the many other things which I have said about you in the worlds Press ... and on Film. These remarks have prompted letters from people like Losey and Clayton and Schlesinger saying (in an amused way) it would have been marvellous if I had ever said that about them! I think that if you had read some of these items you would have been not too distressed. You must realise my deep feeling for you, my implicit trust in you and my enormous respect for your energies and brilliance. It is <u>so</u> easy to read only the trivial things and be hurt ... as hurt indeed as I have been by your remark that, au fond, I 'am like all other actors' in my shallowness.

I have said to the Press constantly that if I succeed in 'Death' it will be entirely due to you ... and if I fail it will be equally so, for I gave myself to you entirely to do as you chose. I cannot think of a higher compliment.

When I have read this wretched article in 'Vogue' I may be able to make some further comment; for the moment I can only apologise for having had you distressed by someone I trusted and to whome you have shown such great kindness.

With affection
<u>Dirk</u>

To Bee Gilbert and Ian Holm   *Clermont*
                                                 9 December 1970

Dearest, beloved, Sno and Ian ...

You ARE super chums. I mean about not being pissed off with us because we did'nt see you during the horrid five days we were in your Burg. It was really pretty foul; first Tote had a cyst problem, and so that meant Doctors and etc.. and us not being able to tell people exactly what we were up to on account of not wanting to worry anyone; also his Pa is dying-sort-of and is in a nasty little nursing home [...] and we had to trail to and from there and deal out cheer and keep the Matron charmed so that she does'nt pinch all Totes Pa's lolly ... she is a sort of Irish Bodkin-Adams-Type[1] ... with the full Dancing Eyes and Irish Sparkle and a firm determination to grab her elderly patients' money for a colour Telly set .... anyway ... then I had to spend two ghastly days, freezing, in the Furniture depositary in Victoria getting rid of all the stuff I have left from the Move. [...] In between I had to fit in the Lecture at the NFT,[2] which was sold out and great fun and very irreverant .... I showd clips from all my worst Movies and worst perfs ... and it made us all laugh very much indeed ... I did'nt realise that I go back such a long way! There I was looking like a half cooked featus at one point, and at another like a very poovey person in black leather making eyes at John Mills ... this last part brought down the house ... and I feared libel .... but as I only opened my eyes wide and looked at the audience with surprise and shock ... and never said a word, I think I'll escape. Perhaps not with Frankenstein[3] ... I was a bit forthright about him and his Tense Set Lark and they thought that was all a bit larky too ... apparently they had all seen the documentary on Grand Prix ... I have not ... but it made for a super happy, funny two and a half hours! Naturally I was whacked afterwards ... and we went back to the Connaught with an illassorted bunch of Audience ... the Tynans ... he dressd in some plastic Python with shoe buckles large enough to frame a Valesquez ... and she preggers but sweet [... E]veryone drank a great deal and some of them talked about me, so that was lovely. And really after that, we were so hating London, the cold, the bad tempers the garbage the prices and everything else, that as soon as Tote was thankfully put in the clear, and the old Pa was sorted out ... we grabbed the first flight to Paris and caught the Blue Train home without telling anyone ..... it was a lousy thing to do but we really wanted to get back as soon as possible because the Staff dont speak Frog and we were leaving them for the first time in a strange country. Anyway all was lovliness the next morning when we got off the train in Cannes Station in blinding sun ... went straight to the Market and bought lunch and drove through the golden countryside to the house.

Anyway here we are ... breakfast on the terrace every morning – in sweaters! ... and a log fire at night ... It's superly warm about mid

---

1. John Bodkin Adams, Eastbourne doctor and murderer.
2. Dirk was interviewed by Margaret Hinxman as part of the John Player Lecture series.
3. John Frankenheimer, director of *The Fixer*.

day and then the temperature dips a bit as the sun sets and one feels a nip and starts the fire and the record player and the brandy bottle and settles down with the daily (London) papers which arrive every evening at five.

We have just bought another fucking dog. A Boxer bitch with ricketts, called Daisy. She is supposed to be a wife and companion for our Roman Bastard, Labbo, but so far he has shown no great intrest, and one fears, like all Italian men, that faced with the Lady he'd rather have a feller. However we have only been en menage for four days; it's a bit early yet.

I SO agree with Ian about the Bread bit and loosing ones Pride. I did it for ages . . . and then broke away for a while to earn Self Pride for no Bread and felt poorer, but richer . . . if you know what I mean . . . and then came a time when I just had to get bread for Taxes and all, as you both well know, and that was dreadful . . . part of the misery of the 'Fixer' thing was that. I earned possibly 1,000 dollars a WORD in that load of crapperoo, and it paid an awful lot of taxes and so on, but made me feel physically ill to do. I dont think that it really works. Once one is out of the Wood, so to speak, and can steady oneself financially, <u>even a little</u>, Back To The Quality is the motto. Self respect, for a man, after a certain age is terribly important in Actors.

Does one want to be a Burton? An O'Tool? Or a Lesley Phillips!! Besides . . . the parts that dont pay well are usually the most interesting I find. I got pennies, literally, for 'Death In Venice' . . . we had to pay our own expenses even . . . but what a chance to act for the Cinema! It was worth paying to be in it . . . even if it is an unholy flop . . . . So, dear Ian, most respected Sir, and adored friend . . . play your hunch and piss off out of the Ratty-Land.[1] It does no good to ones soul . . . unless one happens to be K. Moore . . . and soulless.

I have just been asked to do a couple of movies . . . and me really trying to retire and pull out gradually . . . one is with Losey and is marvellous, obscure, and wild . . . and no lolly as usual . . . which is as it should be . . . the other is for America . . . . at least American financed . . . . and is a stunning support part a la Bibikov[2] . . . . but all QUITE different . . . and the lolly will keep me here for fifty years almost! I dont really want to do either . . . . they both happen in early spring

1. He was appearing in Terence Rattigan's *A Bequest to the Nation* at the Haymarket.
2. Dirk's role in *The Fixer*.

JUST when all the things one has done to the garden here start to
show ... and who wants to be in Shepperton during April and May,
when one could be here in the idle sun, tending the vines and seeing
that the sheep dont eat the wild tulips and hyacinths on the hill? ...
anyway, fate may intervean .. I cant spell a bloody word these days ...
intervene. Better.

Sno; I do hope you pass your 'A' Levels ... you ARE clever. If I had
to try now I'd end up in a home for retarded children in Lowestoft,
or somewhere ... thank the Lord they were'nt invented in my time.

Daisy has just wobbled up stairs to my room, here, and is scratching
herself all over. Love or a rash?

When we were in Rome a few weeks ago, doing some dubbing for
the Film, I met a Doctor [...] who told me some worrying news about
a mutual chum of ours. No names, no pack-drill. He was with us in
Budapest and Ian cleaned up the sick. If things are true, he apparently
did the window leap one evening ... but not with the full intention
of killing himself ... apparently if you REALLY want to do that you
dont jump feet first: but head first. Anyway ... I don't know if it is
true or not .. and one has not liked to ask before this. He was so
funny and charming in California ... I thought that things were going
to be better for him. If it's true it's rotten. If not do forget it.

Jolly indescreet of the Doctor anyway. And he told the story in a
lift full of Americans who goggled all the way up to the seventh floor.
                    Daisy has just been sick on my bed.

I have just finished Nancy Mitfords 'Fredrick'[1] ... smashing if one
can wade through the battles, which are as boring as they must have
been frightful ... and am about to start on the Speer[2] book ... thats
a great chunk of winter evening reading .. snug in bed while the mistral
tugs at the shutters and dogs howl in the village ... Breckenbridge[3] was
a nasty little book, I thought ... and it shocked me a bit too ... I
believe the film is unbelievable in it's horror ... and Mr Vidals comments would make Hell burn out. However he made a lot of Bread
from that little item, I can tell you. I dont know why I suddenly
remembered, in the middle of that line, about Bates having twins? Is

---

1. *Frederick the Great* (Hamish Hamilton).
2. *Inside the Third Reich* by Albert Speer (Weidenfeld & Nicolson).
3. An adaptation of Gore Vidal's novel *Myra Breckinridge*, written and directed by Mike
Sarne.

it true? Rather super for him, if he is happy and can afford the sods
.... did you manage to see 'Hamlet'?[1] Or will you?

Incidentally; if the Ratty does come off in Febuary .. and if you
felt a long week-end away would clear the heads and brains and things,
why not come to us for a stay? Not the most perfect month ... but
then it's better than Buda or Pest ... and the Mimosa is out and you
can have a double bed ... bath and loo along the corridor, and
every word heard through the walls .... farts, paper and all! But do
think about it ... it's only 1 Hr. and a half from London .... you
could be back in a flash ... and it is quite pretty, and we would
adore to see you again privatly, as it were ... and not in Connaught
Drawingrooms ..

It's high time that we did some Leaf-Catching again[2] ......
Love and devotions ...

Dirk.

To Luchino Visconti

Clermont
12 December 1970

My dear Luchino:

I have just recieved a copy of the Vogue article from New York and
must write to you without delay. I have also spoken to Mrs Tynan on
the telephone and told her of your anger. She is frightfully upset and
has not read the article herself which both she, and I, feel must have
been severly Edited.

The article, I dont honestly think, is all that good ..... but it is
really not all that bad. And it really is not unkind to you, nor does it
make you, as you said, 'look rediculous'. The one person who comes
out badly is myself! I sound like an opinionated, concieted, thankless,
Actor ... which I dont think I am and would hate to be. My interview
with Mrs Tynan was loyal to you and very devoted ... it was also self-
mocking, which does not emerg from this obviously condensed and
mutilated Article.

The other person who will be hurt and sad is Mrs Tynan herself ...
for I feel sure that this is not what she intended, and some idiot has
edited, and lost the sense of the article very badly.

---

1. Alan Bates, who co-starred with Dirk and IH in *The Fixer*, was playing the princely
Dane in Nottingham and had indeed fathered twins.
2. A reference to their spare time on location for *The Fixer*.

I think, Luchino, that perhaps you have not quite understood the 'Genre' of this kind of an article ... I assure you that it does not give an unfavourable impression ... it is not, for example, as wretched as 'Womans Wear Daily' which could have caused far more distress ..... and WHO reads Vogue except a few women in hairdressers?

However it obviously did distress you; and I can only repeat that Mrs Tynan was tremendously aware of her debt to you, and her affection and respect was immense. It is very sad that it should have all come to this.

With love and affection
Dirk

To Joseph Losey

Clermont
25 March 1971

Joseph –

You have just told me to write to you ... a letter of 'some sort'. So I am. At this moment. I have just, as I told you, written to Melissa Dearden[1] ... what a strange thing growing older is .... one looses hair, teeth and good friends ... time gallops. Oh dear! O shit!

Teeth. All mine fell out the week before I was due in London for DIV ... not all, exactly, just the key tooth which held in a VAST bridge of all sorts of delicious back teeth ... so now I trail over to Monte Carlo twice a week where the only dentist in ALL FUCKING FRANCE, would'nt you know, does the job that I have to have done. He is very chic, Baldheaded, from choice, golden bracelet, wife minus a gall-bladder .... and a faux Utrillo in the waiting room along with two colour snapshots of Grace and H.R.H. Rainier ... so we know what happens pricewise ... socially he's ok ... but God help the patients if H.R.H. Grace gets the jaw ache ... cancell all appointments. Anyway he costs a fortune ... has bad breath, but is rather good at the job and was trained at the University of Illinoise ... (is there an 'e'?) Apart from that, as they say, time drifts along in planting and weeding and reading and generally getting ready for the summer ... a long long time a-coming. We have had such rain and snow and shit as you'd not believe ... I should never have moved into the mountains,

---

1. The actress Melissa Stribling, whose husband Basil directed four of Dirk's films, including *The Blue Lamp* and *Victim*, and bought Beel House from him. Dearden had died in a car crash two days earlier.

after all we are nearly 2,000 feet high ... almost ski-ing country ... however the buds are all bursting out ... blossom on every tree ... the sky is clear and steady blue ... and it is really hot for lunch on the terrace.

I am so happy that you may be in Cannes[1] ... it's a bore being in competition with you, but rather fun too ... in a way .... I ought to have played Maggie Leightons part but you are always so stingy with me .... however we'll see what happens. Whatever <u>does</u> happen we'll all be close to each other for a while ... which is always pleasant. And we are so very near the Colombe .... incidentally I think that Simones' film with Gaban[2] is also entered ... we ought to be a happy little gathering.

[...] Does Trotsky go? You did'nt mention it today ... so I expect it's among the worries. So far I seem to be recieveing a lot of scripts about old Queers in love with butchers boys .... or schoolteachers in love with their Best Pupils ... <u>Oh Will</u> they <u>never</u> learn in the film business? I'm not REALLY Aschenbach .... just 'being' him for one film. I have given up smoking, entirely, which has made me difficult to live with and I eat quantities of sweets and goodies ..... but it has been nearly ten days since I had a 'ciggie' ... and considering I was a three pack a day boy I dont think thats too bad.

Hell on the friends .... but I decided that as I am about to be fifty, really and truly, on Sunday I'd better get a hold on myself and do something adult for a change. So we'll see .... I do feel better for it ... but depressed and miserable most of the time. Which is a fat lot of good.

Later.

Just fed the dogs and Tony is polishing the tiled floors downstairs ... a great black cloud has crept over the hills from Grasse .... and the day is almost spent. I long for my Brandy, but it's not six yet [...] I am busy reading Harold Actons Memoirs[3] ... know them? Fun and a little tedious .... but good in bed ... read a funny book called 'Soldier Erect'[4] ... which is bawdy but excellent ... and am just through with the Cocteau book[5] ... a bore. And so was he. On our

---

1. With *The Go-Between*.
2. *Le Chat*, with Jean Gabin.
3. Acton's *More Memoirs of an Aesthete* had recently been published by Methuen.
4. *A Soldier Erect* by Brian Aldiss (Weidenfeld & Nicolson).
5. *Cocteau* by Francis Steegmuller (Macmillan, 1970).

way back from the old Dentist yesterday we sat in the sun outside the
Welcome in Villefranch and had a beer in the sun on the harbour ...
it was so quiet and one found it difficult to remember all the magic
which had once been generated in that little hotel ... Nijinski ...
Diaghilev, Colette ... Bakst ... all lost now I suppose save for the
relics left behind.

I must put you down and go and get the evening papers ... pay off
the little Arab Gardner, Ahmet, who makes atrocious things in ciment
and stone and which I am always trying to cover with creepers ... and
get on with the evening.

Huge love to you both as always, and as you know,
    for always.
        Dirk
XXXX for Patreeecia

To the Loseys

Clermont
12 June 1971

My dearest Joe and Patricia:
    A delayed letter to thank you, once again, for my Olive Pot! And
also to say ... as if I had not done so already .. how super it was about
the GBween and the Palm d'Or.[1] I really did clap myself silly when
you wandered laconically onto the stage to Romey ... and a little,
only a little harder, for MY pappa .... he behaved a bit tiresomly I
fear during that nervous day ... but he can hardly be blamed because
we were ASSURED a month before in Rome that we had got the
palm ourselves! .. and that I was to 'Shut up' and not make a fuss
about being suddenly dubbed because although I could not win ...
or be in competition ... the film already HAD! So it came as a bit of
a shock to pappa to find that this was not quite the case! However ..
he saved face and got immense coverage in the glossies coming down
the stairs with Romey and I ... and off he went to buy up the Picasso
shop in Valauris before leaving for Rome .... and we are doing colossal
business in Paris .. Germany and Italy .... and the reviews are quite
dotty with praise and love, except for Nice-Matin who said it was the

1. Romy Schneider presented Losey with the Palme d'Or at Cannes for *The Go-Between*.
Visconti was given a special prize marking the twenty-fifth anniversary of the Festival, for
Death in Venice and for the rest of his *oeuvre*.

most boring thing she'd seen since measles . . . . or something.

Anyway . . . it piss'd with rain for a week after you all left . . . and then sudden Mistrals came and we had a few super days . . . and more rain . . and all the rose growers in Antibes were ruined because the hail smashed all the glasshouses . . . . and tore all the lettuce and early peas and so on. All disaster.

Now it really is lovely and glowing and we have made the hay . . carted and dumped it . . . . the pool is reduced to a trickle . . . . the sky aches with blue and I have just planted five mimosa trees . . . . three inches high. I suppose you could call that optomism!

Romey called the other night and is coming over for lunch this week . . . she naturally wants to talk about you . . . . so I shall be simply lovely about you and hope to God you dont let me down and treat her as you treated poor Jacquline Sassarde[1] who is still not out of shock! I met her at the airport the other week and she is still wincing at the memories . . . . rotten old sod you.

[. . .] Old Alice Bates[2] came up to the house for the day, just before you all left, and brought that rather agressive wife with him . . . she seems to spend her time looking over her shoulder to see if Alan is still there. As well she might. He is a nice fellow but as viril and sexual as a packet of Kleenex . . . . the main fault of GBween I felt . . . no sort of animal magnetism . . . . like Sean Connery has . . . . however obviously, as you said it was that or no lolly and in the end Leo and Maggie[3] will swamp them . . . and you and dear Carmen[4] will do all the rest very neatly!

I have to write about fifty more letters . . . this was just to send you my love again . . and my happiness for your success . . . do let me know, one day, how and when you get your showing . . . . it ought to be sometime in September . . . . not really before. A fat kiss to Patreecia . . . . and every love to you both . . . . . Dirk –

---

1. Jacqueline Sassard, whom Losey cast in *Accident*.
2. Alan Bates, star of Losey's *The Go-Between*.
3. Dominic Guard and Margaret Leighton.
4. Dillon, set designer.

To Bee Gilbert and Ian Holm   *Clermont*
                                                   30 June 1971

Darling Snowball and Millionair:

Mansions this time.[1] Ye Gods! What <u>did</u> they pay you on the
Rattigan thing! I cant imagine ... but seriously how super smashing
... as long as the Channel Tunnel is not running across the front lawn
in 1975 .... Lovely letter from you today. [...] Long article in this
months Show Mag (New York) by the Dreaded Frankenstein who
names every film he has ever made, and talks on a bit alarming about
most of them, with never a single mention of the 'Fixer'. Out of sight
out of mind. I wish he were. More often.

[...] I have so far said no ... I mean NO. to Somerset Maughm;
Trotsky: Chaucer: Randolph Churchill: Tarquemeda[2] (Spanish
Inquisition) and a Major in the Indian Army in 1888 ... they were not
dirty propositions .. Parts, if you know what I mean. My fat Friend[3]
is fair out of his bonce with worry .. whose to pay for the Maserati
when it next has a face lift? But, honestly, the absolute SHIT is
unbelievable ... and after being vastly spoiled by Visconti and Mann
I am not budging till I'm sure. Opened in N.Y last week [to] mixed
reviews .. all the male Critics say it is a film about a Sodomite ... the
Female ones have raved and we are packed out for weeks to come by
all the kids ... funny thing .. same as London, Rome and Paris and
Berlin ... all kids. I wonder why? Vastly intresting to really find out
... it's a sort of cult ... but why I cannot imagine. Enough that it is
... and thats lovely. Next Visconti is doing a story about the last two
days in the life of Ludwig of Bavaria ... with Helmut Berger and
Romy Schnieder as the Empress Elizabeth ... nothing for me unless I
play a castle on the lake ... and he has all those from the German
Government. Still not smoking ... weeeeeel. One or two with a beer
and a couple in the evenings with the Daily Telegraph (does'nt that
sound ghastly!) The fucking Daily Tel. It's not as bad as that though
... weather golden, still, blazing and the geraniums, you were right, a
blaze of red and white and night scented stock dotting the pots and
beds and everything now glorious and in full leaf ... alas! The hols.

---

1. Ian Holm had bought a 300-year-old house in Kent.
2. Torquemada.
3. Tony.

start tomorrow officially ... and for the next two months the roads, hotels, beaches and everything will be unbearable with burnt Frogs and G.B's and nasty Allemands and stuffy Dutch and the very commonest Americans. Question: How can an American BE common. <u>They are.</u> Essentially an Immigrant Race they remain such. We had two for dinner last night ... Jewish mother and daughter .. daughter with a Nose Job, Mother with bronchitis caught on the boat coming over. By talking I'll bet. Both on Microbiotic Food ... ghastly. Kind. Foolish. Blind. and fucking bores .... but [...] I had to be pleasant.

Tote is upstairs writing a long letter about Stocks and Shares ... I'm sitting here on the terrace in the late evening sun ... and the sea shimmers .. little white sails scud toward La Napoule ... the scent of wild broom and carnations make the hill smell like the Cosmetic Section of Boots Cash Thingummy ... but it is for real at least.

I'll go and fill up my glass of Fundador ... just about gone now ... and wish that we were in Corsica if thats where you will go .... funny how much one loves you both. Quite dotty. But it has lasted with firmness ever since Charlie Chan smashed up that wardrobe .... and it'll go on ...

my heart on a salver for you .. and a seemly hug to your mate .. always, anyway, my love.

<u>Dirk</u>
XXXX+300

P.S. Ghastly typing – sorry machine gone potty.
P.P.S. Daisy in the Nunnery. Got the curse bad – & Labbo in a heap of despair in the Studio – Dogs <u>do</u> fall in love! And I <u>cant</u> explain to him she'll be home in 2 weeks – Oh! now one knows what it means 'To live a dogs life' – poor sod.

To Ann Skinner   *Clermont*
July 27th. 110° in the sun –

This is hotter than Morocco! Christ! I really dont care for heat at this advanced age. It is only nine thirty am and already great dollops of sweat are plopping onto my lap ... I'm trying to keep them off the keys because it makes everything so slippery. And thats the scene here this morning ... cozadas¹ screaming in the olives ... crickets in the grass ... the dogs lie gasping under the vine trellis ... we have just heard the BBC telling us all about Lords .. (Fond memories of rain and flying continuity sheets) and the Astronauts on their dotty way to the Moon and something vague about another Coup ..... Gareth Forwood is here for a hol ... and lies moaning face upwards in the swimming hole ... and the whole of the Attenborough family, minus of course Pappa, decend for luncheon. They are very sweet but it means that I wont get a siesta this arvo .... and that makes me grotty if I have a beer too many before lunch. All I seem to be doing is grumbling ... and I really dont mean to at all. It's all lovliness as far as I am concerned.

Your smash-hit of a letter made me piss myself [...] You are simply doing a perfectly normal thing in falling in love with married men ..... who wants to start breaking them in, for Gods sake? let someone else do that for you ..... it's rather the same thing with Pipes .... my father never ever smoked a NEW pipe but gave it to our gardner to smoke about the place for a month or so until it was really ripe and then he stuck it on his stem, if you know what I mean, and smoked a perfectly cured pipe. Same with Married Fellows. Got it? No need to come to a Shrinker. I'm one.

I wrote to John about Sunday² ... it was tremendously exciting getting all the notices and finding each one better than the other .... I was as happy as if I had been in the bloody thing ... and he wrote a sweet note back and wondered, wistfully I thought, if I would like it .... well, I'm pretty sure that I will although I dont go a great bundle on Miss J's tits ... all nibbled and Russeled³ .... however I'll have a look when I come over in October .... I have to then, to chat with Business Gentlemen ... it's hopeless on telephones and in letters to get things straightened out .... so a trip to London is indicated I fear.

[...] You will know by now, dont we All, what the Press said about the Devils⁴ .. some people who have seen it literally had to leave the cinema for fear of throwing up! And if the porno has gone God help what is left ..... I do think he is a frightful man. I met the Vice Pres

---

1. Presumably cicadas.
2. Schlesinger's *Sunday, Bloody Sunday,* starring Peter Finch and Glenda Jackson.
3. In Ken Russell's *The Music Lovers* Glenda Jackson had been obliged to appear in sequences of intimacy with Richard Chamberlain.
4. Another Russell extravaganza, starring Oliver Reed and Vanessa Redgrave.

of Warners the other day and he was sickingly rubbing his hands with joy at the VAST takings .... all house records broken etc ... and poor little DIV dragged off and sent to Baker Strasser for a final week. Shit. [...]

They are still putting pressure on me to do Trotsky ... and I really dont want to one bit .... it is a difficult decision to make .... I worship Joe and so on, but I dont want to do anymore elderly gents ... this time wigged I imagine .... and the flight out to Mexico (if they do go there) would have me in fits before we'd passed Plymouth!

There are other things floating about in the pipeline ... but I am not very eager. I feel retired now .... a funny feeling and not one to thrill old Noldie Schulkes! [...] I have begged Joe to use him. He really is so fucking good on a Unit and splendid for moral .... seems a pity to stand in for Alice Bates and that awful Belgian Postman Max Schell .... however it's better than no work at all.

Did I tell you that Ronnie Neame had asked me to be in his film with Jackson about Isobella of Spain? Well he said he'd 'drop by' with a script five weeks ago .. so I reckon <u>thats</u> folded. Or at least perhaps the American Company said nix to me .... DIV has become a sort of 'Fag Movie' in the US and generally had v. awful notices which made us all sad .... they quite misunderstood the picture and the book too, for that matter ... they are a bloody awful country .... sorry: I forgot that you had an 'intrest' there!

Not much news left really lovie .... life is rather sedentary .. watering, haying, emptying the pool ... feeding a family ... preparing for constant guests on their way to or from somewhere .... The Holmes come out for a week at the end of August ... and between now and then we have a constant stream of onenight stands .... tough on the sheet situation and as there is only one loo and one bathroom and the water pressure here in July and August is so low that we cant get it up stairs ... life is fun but not luxurious!

Anyway .. one day it'll be <u>you</u> from your slum dwellings ... and I assure you no one will be happier to see you than us here at Clermont.

All my love .. postcards from the Rift Valley[1] ... watch your bum in Morocco ... and a great hug and kisses from ...

<u>Dirk</u>.

---

1. AS was on location in Africa for *Young Winston*.

To Joseph Losey

My dear Joe:

Thank you so much for calling the other evening and my apologies for not speaking myself. But you MUST remember that you are one hour ahead of us in Italy, and that I am invariably in bed by eleven with two shovvers[1] up the arse, and that we only have one telephone in the house and that is two floors down! So. Fat Friend had to do the talking.

Sorry about T.[2] I just was too late ... Witt[3] suggested, very firmly indeed that I read the new script ... I did'nt even know there was one ... I knew that Mosley was 'doing' something to that awful load of old codswallop I read with you in January, or whenever it was .... but I had no idea that the Black Script existed.

Instead of soppy old Chatto[4] giggling away about T. <u>still</u> not being cast it might have been more expedient, not to say intelligent, of her to suggest a look at a new script .... however she did'nt and Witt did .... but having got the thing to me in a matter of hours he then had to aquaint me with the fact that Fatso[5] was in the running .... so I pulled out [...] I simply was not going to wait about for Fatso to make up it's mind about billing and cooing.

Really no ones fault .... but sad for me finally because T. is now a very superior, and amusing, fellow .... (I wonder if Fatso knows this? And that he was witty and compassionate?) and you have, to say the least of it, an Interesting Cast ...

I hope so much that all goes well with you and all who sail upon your Craft ..... I would send you a foot or a toad or a fist or something .... but reckon my love will be enough ... it is certainly strong enough for us both!

Marvellous to have Patricia to ourselves for a whole evening ... and I trust that she reached Rome safely, if not accurately .... love to you all .... as ever.

<u>Dirk</u>

---

1. *Suppositoires.*
2. Relations between JL and Dirk had become strained, mainly over the uncertainties in casting the title role for *The Assassination of Trotsky*.
3. Peter Witt, agent.
4. Rosalind Chatto, agent to Losey.
5. Richard Burton, who duly played the role opposite Romy Schneider, with Alain Delon.

P.S. Mrs T. is a pretty super part too .... oh fuck!.

To Bee Gilbert and Ian Holm Clermont
11 November 1971

[A guest from the Home Counties . . .] all of sixty-seven with a red beard
and a blondish wig which never ever moved in a Mistral on the Pic des
Courmes, or snoring on a blue chesterfield, came to stay for a week.

A week of unbelievable hell . . . of cliche's . . . bon mots . . . boredome
and incessant chatter .... 'Do you remember the Wigwool-
Smothersons? He was the son of old Joshua Sproat who lived over at
Thurleigh Down and she was SIMPLY NOT our Class and was a
rather poor creature .. Hetty Blythson-Walters .... they came from
Tidworth and had a ripping house in the Kenya Highlands . . .'

Night after night after night . . . .

'Well .... their daughter, Amanda, is riding at the Horse Of The
Year Show on one of Douglass Bunns Horses! What about that!'

What about it?

We thought that by sticking her in the pub up the road we could
be rid of her for at least a couple of hours between say, five pm and
seven . . . have an early dinner and shove her home in a taxi until the
trip to Grasse next morning. Not a hope in hell. She arrived on the
steps of her Pension with a wig-box . . . a sweater in a Marks and
Sparks plastic bag .. a book .. and her slippers . . . ours for twelve
hours .... and so it was to be. We dragged her up and down the Gorge
de Loupe . . . 'Glorious! Oh! Gracious me! What a Pretty Spot.' . . .
trailed her round a glass factory . . . 'Not as good as the one I saw
with the Harvey-Kellers in Venice .. but of course that was the real
McCoy . . . you know!' . . . in and out of Monoprix . . . 'Littlewoods
in Twickenham are really JUST as good you know dear . . . not the
range of cheeses . . . but much the same value . . .' and in and out of
one hill top village after another . . . 'When I was with the Winston-
Bouveries in Nnnndobbigie up in the Kenya Highlands we saw many
of the native villages. Too pretty for words . . . but they did smell so
terribly [. . .]'

I took three tranqualisers per day .. and had chronic indegestion
and High Blood Pressure .... Tote struggled through but daily got to
look more and more like McMillan . . . his eyes hooped with boredom
and exhaustion .. We desperately went and bought a colour Telly to

try and shut her up. But it did'nt work. She had seen all the films before ... liked Morecombe and Wise and was'nt dead keen on the de Gaullists ... we read all the sunday papers from the Gardening advertising to the Rubber Wear For Play and Fun, through Anne Edwards and Jilly Coopers and the most detailed reviews of books on the Battle Of The Nile ... anything so that we could seem to be concentrating ... but it always ended with a polite cough and 'I KNOW that you are reading, but do you remember Kitty Hogs-heads awful time with the will and the codacil? Well the same thing happened again in a place near Axminster. It's in the "Telegraph" ... is'nt that EXTRAORDINARY?'

We bunged her on the plane on Tuesday red eyed with grief and age (we – not she!) ... we waved her across the tarmac and onto the plane .. even in the backlash of a Jet that sodding wig did'nt move ... and as far as we know she is safely home [...] but never again. Also it rained for three days of the eight .. and we were stuck with her in the house ... her mouth open snoring after lunch taking her 'little sleepybye' ... and the snores roaring down to Antibes.

Never take pity on anyone ever! Remember what I say! [...] God! Help me from the defeated ... I have learned my lesson.

This note is really to explain why we have not answered your letters and so on, and you can, I hope, readily see why now .... but time is a great healer, they say ... and soon we will be better and back to the typewriters again sensibly.

Autumn has hit us wallop! Mistral and rain .. torrential ... the garden golden and red, muddy and clear .. the sea silver and streaked with sullen golden lights .... our new Cow Shed is super and the fellers can have a real piss now with a door and a bowl and a wash place and a view over the pond ... and we have a colour telly too.

Coming for Christmas?

[...] Love in haste from your devoted and exhausted chum.

<u>Dirk.</u>

Daisy has got the runs and has just done it on the rush carpet in the Studio ... now to wash it down, and try not to heave, slurping it into last week's 'Nice Matin' .... Tote has gone out to wash a car.

Natch.

Love.

<u>D</u>

Since 1963 Edward Thompson, a director of Heinemann Educational Books, had tried spasmodically to persuade Dirk to write a work of non-fiction. Encouraged further by his correspondence with Dorothy Gordon, Dirk began in August to plan a memoir under the provisional title of A Movement Afoot, *inspired by a backstage expostulation reported to him some years earlier: 'My God! There is a movement afoot to take Dirk Bogarde Seriously!' (See page 192).*

To Edward Thompson

Clermont
27 November 1971

Edward:

Not a word have I put to paper . . . not a word. I am not like J.G[1] who seems to positivly ooze with energy and can write between acts of Shaw . . . . I just sit in a sort of heap, sipping beer, and thinking that I really ought to be clipping back the large white dasies before the evening frost catches me by surprise . . . . and I have no ready apologies. I just am too damned lazy. Also I have been reading a lot of recent 'Film Actors' books . . . . and 'Actors' too. Sybil Thorndikes one, by some lady called Spriggs, and Hildegard Kneffs[2] . . . and they all have a frightning sort of similarity. I think nothing would be achieved by my cashing in on the past . . . it really has been pretty well raked over you know: from the internal squabbles at the Rank Org . . . to 'getting the break' . . . to the improper, and bizaar, propositions from retured Colonels in the respectability (!) of Frimley Green . . . well; it has all been done . . . and too much pain could be caused to too many people still around.

So I must try another tack . . . and see what can be done. Hope you had a lovely grub-up with Kozintsev[3] . . . and I bet he was nice: you really have to be to be that good . . . . only poor actors/directors/Writers are nasty. The others have all achieved. No need to be unpleasant or unkind or rude. Pity the world is so full of the failed.

Golden sun here but last week was Artic and we feared for the garden again. But today is blue, warm and gentle . . . and I dont want

1. John Gielgud, whose *Stage Directions* (Heinemann, 1963) had been sent to Dirk by ET.
2. *Sybil Thorndike Casson* by Elizabeth Sprigge (Victor Gollancz); *The Gift Horse* by Hildegard Knef (André Deutsch).
3. Grigori Kozintsev, Russian director of *Hamlet* and *King Lear* in the 1960s.

to do a stroke of work ... but will have to sooner or later ... like opening a bottle of beer .... for myself.

Lazy sod.

Thanks for your letter of 'encouragement' ... I am really

a

   bit

      of

        a

          bore.

          <u>Dirk</u>

Penelope Mortimer, novelist and screenwriter, had offered to write a script for Bette Davis who she felt was being wasted on sub-Whatever Happened To Baby Jane? material. Miss Davis replied enthusiastically, saying her last remaining ambition was to act with Dirk Bogarde ...

To Penelope Mortimer
Clermont
1 December 1971

Dear Penelope Mortimer

Did you ever know that I tried desperately to buy 'Pumpkin' and then that chap Wolf[1] bought it for a 'friend' ... and finally when Jack Clayton sort of asked if I would like to play 'Jake' ... it was too late and I could'nt and Wolf did'nt want me anyway. So that was a sad saga.

Then this morning, under my mistral-stripped vine .. in the golden light, the postman came with three early Christmas cards, a Telephone bill and your letter.

What a smashing surprise! I dont mean the letter only .. that was very nice indeed, all that blue Basildon Bond ... but the idea about Miss D. It is so odd, you know, because a few weeks ago I got a perfectly ghastly script about God knows what ... except that she was going to do it. I could'nt believe it really ... it was so awful.

She was playing Aunt Cecelia who seemed to spend a great deal of her time running about the railway lines in Geneva .... and one of the conditions which she – B.D. – made was that I should be in it

---

1. James Woolf, producer of *The Pumpkin Eater*, adapted by Pinter from PM's novel (Hutchinson, 1962).

too! I was to play 'a suave man of the world with a Franco-Greek accent and a way with women.' Literal description. I also spent a great deal of time nipping about the railway lines myself . . . when I was'nt Feaverishly Unbuttoning Aunt Cecilias Neices Knickers . . . or that sort of thing. I go on at length about this quite horrid experience simply to tell you that she insisted on me: it was what you so rightly call Hammer/Horror and WE NEVER HAD A SCENE or even a SHOT together in the whole thing!

Well . . I found all that a bit odd . . . and said 'no' but had to say it with terrific tact for I was in fear that she might think that I was judging her judgement, if you know what I mean . . . However I dont think any offence was given, and as far as one can judge she's not doing it . . . . if your letter from her was dated Westport . . . (The rest[1] I don't believe either!)

But, seriously, it is a marvellous and flattering idea. God only knows how we could team . . . I'm not young any more . . . and not that old . . . it makes it tough but very interesting. Since 'Death In Venice' I am only asked ever to do senile old sex-perverts or schoolteachers in love with their nymphetts . . . or whatever they are called . . . so I have called a halt for the time . . . almost two years now . . . and prefer to sit up here on my hill and regret nothing . . . rather than make all that awful crap and regret it all.

I go on and on . . . you asked a simple question and the simple answer is that it would be splendour to work with her. There are'nt many of the Masters left. PTO

Sorry; I cant be bothered trailing up to the top of the house for the second sheet of blank paper . . so forgive my laziness and try and read this side too.

I feel, as you do, that you simply MUST see her before you even started such a project . . . because who is she really one wonders? How exciting to find out . . . and then to write her down, as it were . . . I think your plan is absolutely spot on . . . . goodness! Why does she do all that Aunt Cecelia Tripe . . . Lolly, lack of choice, or is she a bit bonkers? Who can tell until you find out. Good fortune to you.

Anyway the answer is Yes . . . a marvellous honour . . and a thrilling idea.

---

1 . Two Trees, One Crooked Mile, Westport.

Now you can start being 'scared' and 'overwhelmed' if you want to
... you said that you would if I said 'yes ..'
      I have.
            Dirk Bogarde

P.S. Someone has just dumped a pregnant doe Rabbit in a basket on
the doorstep here! Is this a record?
P.S. Perhaps she is a bit bonkers – I mean wanting to do a film with
me in which we never, ever, met! – I mean – why.

To Penelope Mortimer   *Clermont*
                                              7 December 1971

Penelope M –
      White Basildon Bond! Whatever next .... a pinkie bent over the
Royal Doulton? Brown sugar for your coffee ... or multicoloured? A
nodding Alsation in the back window of your Mini ... gracious me!
The mind is flooded with delights White Basildon Bond brings along
.... beech leaves and bluebells in a copper jug ... and how to arrange
them.
      One part glycerine to two parts water for three weeks and then
place them (your actual beech leaves that is to say.) under the carpet
for a month ... and frost them for a 'pleasing' look at Christmas. I
love that word 'Pleasing', dont you? .. its rather like 'acceptable': how
the bloody hell do THEY know?
      Anyway cut the piddle. I'm afraid that I have been rather rude ..
but in fun rude ... and you were so nice today on your W.B.B
admiring this lousy German Bastard which cant, as you see, keep to
it's spacing. But then the Germans never really could I suppose. (Here
we go again .. single line. Shit.)
      And your letter was lovely in the middle of Christmas Cards and a
glass of beer .. Christmas Cards. God ... they are worse than the
pinkie and the doulton bit.
      I am surprised, only a little, that the 'Pumpkin' bit 'amazed' you
... but then you probably never knew that I ached to direct 'Daddys'
Gone a Hunting'[1] either? Agents are shitty things for the most part

---

1. PM's third novel, published in 1958 by Michael Joseph, under her first married name,
Dimont.

.... however thats all past and no skin off your nose really. Who's got the one about the birdseed breast ....? I wonder.

I am sorry that my beloved Aschenbach 'gets in the way a bit ..' he really needent ... I was simply staggering about with a funny walk and a couple of twitches .. he's not me ... nor am I any part of him ... remotely. And whatever you saw up there on the screen in the Kensington Odeon is nothing to do with me on my hill here: and you <u>must</u> come and see me on it. Tonight the sun has died like an Emperor ... great scarlet arcs of silk ... saffron .. green ... crimson .. and the blaze of Venus to remind one of the absolute and infinite ... and along the lower rim of beauty lay the hard, harsh, line of the hills ...

Someone said the other evening that these were the most beautiful five minutes of the day ... and should be watched and not 'talked' through .... he was a shepherd in the field next to mine ... this evening I yelled to Marie and Henri[1] .. (Who look after me and are Frog and ancient ..) to come and watch the sky. And they stuck heads from windows ... and we watched. And no one 'talked' through it .... and suddenly it was night ... a Venus brilliant as [a] lighthouse. Oh! It is so good here .... you'll like it ... it's not a bit posh. Port Out Starboard Home ... a gloriously idiot relic word of the middleclasses from the Raj days ... anyway it is'nt ... perhaps you like posh. All that David Niven stuff down on the Coast ... pools and cocktails and those fake Bauerhaus chairs filled with friends of Grace and Ranier ... anyway thats as maybe ... the grub is ok and the chairs need a bit of a clean .. and I do polish me own floor because H. and M are a bit long in the tooth.

This has nothing to do with anything except it would be lovely to see you here covered, the two of us, in shyness and spikes .... possibly. Letters are so much easier.

Loscy, I think, would be marvellous with Madam[2] ... he likes working with fellows, you see, and although he has a terrible private record of ladies of all sorts, he does'nt terribly adore them on his Floor ... unless they are Signoret .. or Moreau .. or Taylor .. ballsey ladies if you see what I mean. So I reckon he'd go a bundle on Mum.

And, since you ask, I did'nt do Trotsky because it was a lousy script and it seemed to me a bit of a 'faux' to bash away at another old man

1. Danjoux, who had succeeded the Boludas as live-in help.
2. PM had asked Dirk how Losey might react to directing Bette Davis.

... I had just come out of the absolute haze created by Mann and Visconti ... and shook still at that time. I really did'nt want to do it all again so soon .... grannyglasses and a beard.

But I was sad as hell when I found the alternative casting ... poor Joe. Anyway they finished shooting last Friday ... and he seems happy and I'll be speaking to him again soon .. we are never altogether very far apart. We have been through too much together since 1950 ..... One does'nt loose sight of those things.

Rabbits were all still born ... and I gave her away this evening in her super home made hutch, smothered in last night's 'Daily Telegraph' and lettuce leaves. A nice little boy called Thomas[1] ... thinks she's 'belle' ... his mother, I fear, had a sort of rage glimmering in her eyes ... but I pretended not to notice. Children NEED animals, dont they?

Wonder how your letter went down at Crooked Mile? Rum.

Someone who worked with her ages ago said that it was like coming through Hell and he needed Intensive Care until a year ago ... he almost fell into his Moules at lunch when I mentioned her name .. and his wife is quite ill still.

Because you said so ... I'll be
        Dirk

P.S. Almost forgot – last week, in N.Y – on Telly, she was asked if she had a final ambition – & said 'Yes – to work with D.B' – Do you think it could still be The Change? D.B.

To Bee Gilbert and Ian Holm

Clermont
December 19th. [1971] Saturday.[2]

My dearest S & I –

Most nasty day. Henri and Marie went on their annual holiday (3 weeks!!) this morning at six am .. and the Housework has to start .. and I dont care one little bit for polishing .. laying fires, washing up and laying tables. I just want to sit in a heap, booze silently, and read old copies of 'Country Life'. Intently.

Fat Friend is now busy with a Hoover Polisher doing all the floors

---

1. The son of Léon Loschetter, architect at Clermont.
2. Saturday was, in fact, the 18th.

in the studio . . . so I cant hear the BBC and find out what is happening in Daccar or what the Gnomes are doing [. . .] We had a super frost this morning . . . white as icing sugar and all the vine whitewashed with silver glitter . . . it melted in the sun instantly . . . but it was a titchy reminder than our worst two months are ahead! I have, unlike old Jacko Holme, swept all my leaves away . . and pruned the fuschias and covered the dasies and geraniums in plastic french letters . . . which reminds me [. . .] I have had to hide those snaps[1] . . . supposing Marie were to find them?

Nick And Alexander[2] . . . called 'The Little Bleeder' locally . . . is a flopt, as we call it, in the U.S. too . . . so I dont think that you should feel a whiff of any kind of jealousy at all . . . . thats not going to help the Lady and Gentleman much I fear . . and the only awful thing about it all is that everytime a big movie takes a plunge and goes down like the Titanic . . . we all stand to loose jobs in the after wash, if you know what I mean by that? Malcom Mcdowell has had THE smash notices of the year in 'Clockwork Orange'. . and 'Time' magazine calls him 'the new Superstar . . .' Well . . . . I dont know. Will Success Spoil Mcdowell . . . . and to think that a film like 'Percy' made more money at the box office than any other film this year in Britain. Goodness me.

Appropos all that. Arthur Miller[3]. . (I always confuse him with the Dancing Gentleman who teaches people things in a hurry[4] . .) must have been a night of toil and tribulation . . . I have been there myself in the past. It is an anguishing decision to take . . . the only thing is, and this is terribly important, is to really know, I mean REALLY, know what one wants and . . . most important WHO one is. Personal life has always seemed to me to be the most important thing ever. Over career, personal success, fame, lolly, achievement . . . the only achievement I truthfully believe in is Personal Achievement . . life and the way that one is able to live it . . . I have never sacrificed anything to that. Really and truly. And if all in the world of the Theatre or

---

1. Evidently souvenirs of IH's last stay at Clermont and sun-seeking on the slope above the house, christened 'Titty-Brown Hill' and occasionally 'Brown Titty Hill', because its seclusion allowed naturism to thrive.
2. *Nicholas and Alexandra*, directed by Franklin Schaffner, with Michael Jayston and Janet Suzman in the title roles.
3. An offer of work for IH, declined.
4. Arthur Murray.

Cinema fails me now, as indeed it could, I would have no sense of failure at all .. because my life has been the Career I wanted and planned and worked to have. And, as far as I am concerned, that has been pretty bloody good . . . . but, if on the other hand, one wants more the successful theatre life, the fame and the fortune the heights and the lows which go with it . . . the lonliness . . the worry . . . the terrors of a failure, of growing too old, of loosing to a younger man, of chucking up a solid background of untold happiness . . . then if one wants all this I suppose a trip to America and all the filth that that entails . . . is what one should do . . . . and certainly it should be when one is twenty . . . or under . . but after? Personal choice. But I think that Life, and with that I also mean Love, comes first . . . . it's the only thing that one has in the final seconds . . . the knowledge that one has had time, and sense, to live, breath, love and enjoy the time one has been given . . .

I expect that all sounds a bit soppy me sitting on a hill in France and not being in a lovely lane near Cockshott! But I do KNOW, I have been there myself . . . and I have never been surer. For me, at any rate.

I think, to change the subject rapidly, that you had better switch off the Telly when that Tome Browns Thing[1] comes on . . . you might just start having fantasies, like Daisy . . . . she is, by the way, all beautifully unswelled . . by that I mean her Dorothy Perkins Bra is no longer needed, and apart from constantly mounting Labbo, who resents it in a bewildered sort of way, she is as normal as any Bitch today . . . but alas! Off to the Nunnery in a month . . . but this time, when she goes, I think we'll let Labbo have a weeks hols with her . . . Very likely the result will be tears, not to say Shaggy Dogs . . but they do like one another very much . . and I think that he can JUST reach her . . . which is useful . . . because they dont do what we do and lie about being Missionaries . . . . . Incidentally we found a Filthy Shop in Cannes the other day . . . full of erotica . . . Tote was livid that I would'nt go in but I had been reckergnized, as one say[s], and it's too much being asked ones opinion of Death In Venice and Thomas Mann while one is fingering through packets of ladies and ladies and gentlemen and gentlemen and ladies and goats and packets of Spanish Fly. So I refused. But we were rather intrigued to find a packet, no larger than a Kellogs Corn Flake Box which contained a proper life sized Lady you could 'inflate' . . . and who would 'Service you happily

---

1. A BBC adaptation of the Thomas Hughes novel.

..' and could be dressed in pants and bra. and sit beside you in your car! 'Surprise Your Neighbours!' the packet cried!

Surprise a good deal more than the neighbours I'd say ... and she was'nt a bit expensive. 89 francs 50: Well ... without the pump.

The Attenboroughs, you probably know by now, are our neighbours in the little house next door ... plus four hectars ... they had to pay through the nose ... within a few shillings of what I paid for this .... and they have everything to do ... water, light, loos re-building .... but they fell so deeply in love with it that nothing could disuade them [... T]heir happiness was super. And she has been here for a week or two at a time measuring, planning, cutting grass, and so on ... Better for us than building plots which it was almost about to become ... and I really could not afford the lolly .... so we have bought a million bamboo plants ... and as soon as it is certain, I'll be planting along the boundry like a Green Giant.

Really; Totes Hoover is boring the shit out of me ... it drones along like a bad actor playing Malvolio ... and so I'll stop now. You probably have'nt got this before Christmas .. but if you have ... I hope [it] is gloriously lovely and good [...] and that you have the greatest happiness in the year to come.

Of course you WILL ... IF you come back to Clermont and suffer the creaking board ... not to mention the creaking bed ... and all the other things which await you ... including the Cowshed .. the new diningroom floor ... great black and white tiles which make it look like a Vermeer interior a bit ... and of course Daisy and her probable family ... all looking for Ratty. Ratty, I may add, is Back! At least another Ratty ... just as silly as the last one.

[...] All love ... always ... as ever from Tote-The-Hoover

and

<u>Dirk</u>

To Penelope Mortimer   *Clermont*
January 21st. [1972] Friday. In The Morning. In bed –

Dear Tugger-Of-Heads. Please dont anymore ... you'll have nothing left on your head to put your hat on ... and then how shall I know you at the airport? (I'll be wearing a red velvet turban I bought in the Portabello Road. And Carrying 'The Statesman.') I mean, I dont think I have ever actually laid my eyes on you have I? Except for those

Dorothy Wilding snaps on your dustjackets. Know the problem? I
wish I could spell and punctuate like you do; it's lovely .... but I cant,
so you'll have to go dotty with the dots .... I'm ILL. (That should be
a New Paragraph.) Not seriously ill, I hope, an intestinal bug got, I
believe, from a left over chicken liver which Marie chopped into a
Rissotto last week and which sent me into a series of explosions and
convulsions from which I seem not able to recover. A week is enough
... so yesterday, wan, holloweyed, and aching in every limb ... and
the workmen retiling the bit of the roof immediatly over my bed ...
I called Dr Poteau who is from the Pas de Calais and does'nt care for
any shit ... Liquid Diet I'm on ... (forgive the unintended pun) ...
and desertspoons of charcoal and antibiotics and bottles and bottles
of a filthy tastless water called 'Contrex' which comes from a spring
in the Vosges where it could quite happily remain. And nothing to
drink like lovely Brandy or Champs or even a Kronenbourg. Fuck it;
it _is_ boring ... and I do feel mouldy. Not to say weak.

[...] It was lovely that you liked me in 'ICGOS'[1] ... JUST the
sort of fellow I would like to be if I could ... actually I am nearer
Barret in the 'Servant' which was why it was so easy to do him ....
people dont realise. Never mind. However I have'nt got a trilby hat
... so cant wear that ... but do have a certain moment when I can
generate white hot rage. (I remember, you see.) But would'nt do that
to you. Ever. But God! That [_ICGOS_] was a hell of a film. Five
attempts at suicide in the seven weeks we shot together ... and when
I had finished my work ... she left the movie and flew home to L.A.
And we had four more weeks to do ..... with a double ... and the
awful thing was that I loved her terribly. And she, alas, me .... but
thats another story. The very last scene in the thing, which runs eight
minutes, I wrote especially for her. We sat in her trailer for six hours
and rehearsed every line, tear, and move ... and Mr Neame had the
full grace to tell the Press that he had just put up a camera and 'let her
be Spontanious'. Shit!! I corrected that impression in public at a recent
NFT thing I had to do and showd the clip to 2,000 kids in an
audience who had hardly heard of her, and who, at the end, sat stunned
with silence, except for sobs and sniffling, and THEN the thunder
broke ... and I wished, oh! how much I wished, that she could have
been there to hear it. She always thought that 'she would be found

---

1 . _I Could Go On Singing_, with Judy Garland, directed by Ronald Neame.

out' for not being able to act ..... oh the secret miseries.

New paragraph. Why bore you with all that? It's all over and done
.. I suppose my beloved monster is not even dust now. Ah yes ....
possibly dust.

Alas no possibility of a 78 Show ... but goodness what a collection
you got! I remember, I remember ... L. and J.¹ singing 'My Baby
Went Away And She did'nt Say Why' on a punt in, of all Places,
Twickenham .. and my Father and Mother doing the charlston on
the lock at Boulters ... with their chums ... to 'Bye Bye Blackbird' ..
(I believe I was fishing for a dead roach) ... Summer days of infinate
happiness ... No 78 possibilities here but masses of Gertie and Bea
and Noel ... and Conversation Piece and 'Someday I'll Find you' ...
and Jessie Mathews and 'Evergreen' and, if you really like madness,
Melbas' Farewell at Covent Garden in 1926 and ~~Lillie Elsie~~ Gertie
Millar (!) singing 'Chalk Farm To Camberwell Green' ... so if we find
that we cant talk to each other we can put records on and cry for our
various memories. I know, almost by heart, the Noel bit ... is'nt that
odd ... and the final toast from 'Cavalcade' which still makes me blub
.... but then I blubbed at Katie Kendall too .... so.

My Americain lady² is miserable that I wont meet her or speak to
her ... on the phone I mean .. but that would destroy all ... this way
it is lovely and uncomplicated and we have glorious 'images' of each
other which would be shattered in seconds like Baccaret Glass. You
and I are different. We know too much about each other in a way ...
and of course simply NOTHING in another. But it's fun this way. I
mean if you had'nt had that idea about Miss D. you would'nt have
written, would you? And I would only know you as the lady whose
books I could never get to film .... 'Daddy's Gone' I think I loved
best .... and oddly I wanted to do a directing job on that ... not play
in it ... I just sort of felt the tug of odd recognitions which I felt sure
that I could film ... however. Another time, as they say. And dont, as
you say, be 'terrified' when we do meet ... pretend that you are coming
to 'do' an interview ... it wont seem so awful then .... I'll tell you all
about making 'Death In Venice' and how ill it made me ... and how
I did'nt do 'Sunday Bloody' and how I have been asked to play
opposite a Baby Elephant in a sickening bit of G. Durrell ... and how

1. PM had offered to bring some records, including one by Layton and Johnston.
2. Dorothy Gordon.

I make lampshades, cook coq au vin, Keep My Image   my Fathers
name ... my ambitions for the Future. And why I did'nt marry
Capucine. I mean, if you have all those things in your mind we can
get rid of a super little evening: you'll feel no pain, except when your
tape recorder goes on the blink ... they always do .... and I'll be
solicitious and help you to mend it and we'll smile a lot, and I'll offer
you Framboise on a walk round the Grounds to 'get' the feeling .....
oh! Penneylope ... you know the kind of crap!

     [...] I watched my Telly last night with a wan face ... and saw all
of 'The Dam Busters'[1] in French with the unspeakable Redgrave and
Two Inch Todd ... what a tatty film about a quite marvellous act.
Afterwards, as is the habit in France, there was a two hour discussion
with three survivors .. Barns Wallis ... and the German team. Who
clearly pointed out that the whole operation was a complete wast of
time ... it did'nt do a jot of good. Typical [...] I bet [Kenneth] Tynan
would'nt believe that ... as infact he did'nt believe a word I told him,
drunkenly, one night in Rome about Belsen ... with sheer and utter
disbelief he kept repeating .. 'I never read that ...' or 'It's not in the
Roper book'[2] or something like it ... and I nearly took a swipe at the
pink tinted stuttering wet lipped face but Kath was beside me nursing
her hepatitis .... so I did'nt.

     Pissing with rain outside .. they have finished the roof ... and I
hear Marie clambering up with my cup of vegetable boullion ....
horrid. I must go. And will contact you as soon as all is well ... or
plans have changed or not ....

     No 'ifs' ...

          but empty stomached love
          from
               D.D.D.[3]

     Forgive all the Faults – its this bug bit –
     Love
          D

---

1. Michael Anderson's 1955 film of the assault by 617 Squadron RAF on the Möhne and
Eder dams in the Ruhr, using the 'bouncing-bomb' invented by Barnes Wallis. It starred
Michael Redgrave, with whom Dirk had made *The Sea Shall Not Have Them* (1954), and
Richard Todd, with whom Dirk never acted.
2. Hugh Trevor-Roper (Lord Dacre), author of *The Last Days of Hitler* (Macmillan, 1947).
3. Dirk had described himself in an earlier letter as Dreadfully Dull.

To Penelope Mortimer   *Clermont*
                              January 26th ... 27th .. not sure [1972]

Christ! You found me out ... that letter about the Petersfield-Trip and
that Agonizing Decca.[1] God! I really thought that that had faded into
oblivion. [...] Me breathing heavily with a close mike and No
Rehearsal. Too awful to contemplate. I think it probably sold five
copies in ten years and is one of the Collectors Of Kitsch Editions, if
you know what I mean [...] You caught me with my knickers down
... and I cant help that really because I did'nt know that anyone was
going to open the door.

     Rome. Wowie! Rome was smash-ville ..... sometime ago I got a
book[2] ... least said soonest mended. So no title. Rather super book to
be made with Ken Russellll. I said 'No' to that but suggested J. Losey
would be super and that I would be happy, nay! most happy to do it
thus. Time passes. Rome arrives. Dinner with Losey and Patreecia, in
that aching palazzo-apartment. Candles gleaming ... spaghetti drying
in bowls ... Vodka brimming in chilled glasses ... various children
about, in Portugese and Italian ... no fire, the thing smokes, so a
Japanese lantern in the hearth and barbaric hides scattered all over the
bits and pieces. And a pretty Lasilo ... (or is it Lazilo)[3] portrait of the
owners (Duc de Grammont naturally. Funny how the left of left curl
up in the aristocratic houses.) late wife.

     Anyway. Dinner went on .. fitfully on account of children wanting
Italian 'Glasses of water' ... and vodka flowed .. not me ... I'm brandy
... and lots of talk about the 'Trotsky' film ... and the problems with
an Actor (?) and so on and then on to detailed examination of 'the
book' which I had sent for selection ... masterful talk. Brimming with
ideas and suggestions and feelings ... but, oddly (at least I felt oddly)
not a word about me.

     I never seemed to be in the subject at all. I thought it might be
forgetfulness .. or just that perhaps I should 'take it for granted' that
we were discussing 'my' subject. But alas! It was another Actor Mr
Losey had in mind. Not I. So the evening, from my point of view, not

---

1. PM (and her dog Chloe) had heard on the car radio a track from Dirk's regrettable LP,
Lyrics for Lovers, released by Decca in 1960.
2. Malcolm Lowry's *Under the Volcano*, eventually made by John Huston with Albert
Finney.
3. Philip de László, the Hungarian-born portraitist.

his ... he was supremely ignorant, I presume, of anything unusual
..... suddenly became a morseau Jokey. I realised that the Trotsky
Actor who had been so bitterly discussed was now in the 'book'! Huge
Box Office even if he cannot act .... so: home I went in the wet
Roman night ... to the telephone to the American Agent who had
'done' the deal .. with questions and controlled rage ... to find out
that he had known for five days that 'the Actor' was going to do it ..
and had never told me. So fired him there and then and hung up, and
lay back on the bed and wondered what in hell one did now. And so
gave an enormous dinner party next night for Losey and Patricia and
Romey Schnider and an actor called Helmut Greim .. (The Schofield
of W. Germany. I ask you!) and one or two others who were as pretty
or prettier ... and it cost a bomb, and it was all splendidly catered at
El Tula ... and Losey was in Agony because by this time he knew,
because I had told him, and could'nt quite place the Englishness of
the evening .. the good face and behaviour and the worldly-wise not-
talking-about-anything-nasty-at-dinner. The Americans from the Mid
West are still terrifyingly childish even after twenty years of European
Exposure.

   Anyway ... end of histoire. Kissed them all on the pavement and
sped off in the biggest black Mercedes you have ever, or I, seen! And
that ... really and truly .. is basta. Now I am sacking the English
Agents ... because they are Cunts too ... and wail and squeal and
never tell the truth. Why! Why in the name of God, cannot people
have the full courage to tell the truth, even if it is unpalatable? I dont
know. Anyway ... I got home yesterday with not a Roman Mushroom
insight ... a better gut than before ... and a bottle of champagne
inside me ... and found your letter about the Decca .. and the book.[1]
So to bed with that ... and the first two chapters rather gobbled up
... and loved! But anyway I DO KNOW your work ... so I'm not
one to hurl away from you with looks of wide eyed dislike or dis-belief
... and you see, you are funny. Horribly, flintily, sideswipingly, funny.
OH! God! One can see so clearly how some people wince and <u>dont</u>
think it's funny! So easily.

   [...] I protest! I was NOT bitchy about T.C.[2] I adore him and
have far too much respect for his work ... I just wish that he would

---

1. PM's latest novel, *The Home* (Hutchinson).
2. Tom Courtenay, who co-starred with Dirk in *King and Country*.

support Football less and himself more. Mai Zetterling.[1] Oh! Lor! ...
those years ago when she was a dainty, Miss Sweedish-Vice and we
did a play together ... grubby, tiresome ... rather marvellous in the
play I thought ... and then meeting her in L.A a couple of years ago
.. agressive, plump ... bursting out of tired brown leather with a face
like a pumpkin and an abrasive laugh and that poor husband[2] ...
Goodness me today. How we change.

Am I one up on you now? I think possibly yes ... a Roman Postcard
from me .. and this, and are you coming to play with me? I'v seen
your new 'Dorothy Wilding' with the short flecked hair ... and
anteater eagerness ... so you neede'nt wear the red hat or carry the
Statesman. What a silly letter this is. Unnerved by Decca. Apprehensive, Antibes.

To Penelope Mortimer   *Clermont*
                                              11 February 1972

Motram dear –

It rains. God! How it rains ... a flat grey light, a mist hanging
down to the grass like Miss Havershams Weddingdress ... ragged,
tattered, drifting ... still. Swallowing all before and behind it ...
dense. Miserable. And I have a depression, with a capital D, which
one (you) could carve with an axe. Just a depression. Depression. Too
wet to pick olives ... or prune the vine or start tidying up the
geraniums in the pots ... too wet to haul a mower over the terraces
... walls suddenly sag, and tumble into the sodden grass, spewing
tones of earth and stones into sullen heaps .. lying like giant marbles
lost from a far-away Giants game ... abandoned. Forgotten.

The pond is rushing water in great runnels ... tumbling in a sort
of foam which reminds me of a melted Milky-Way or a Mars Bar ...
and I loath it all.

It has rained since you left actually: not from sentiment or anything
... just because it is the rainy season, so they say, and you were lucky
to miss this part! At least there was a bit of sun to sip a Bloddy M. in
.. was'nt there?

[...] Gave Marie and Henri the two days off ... and now am

---

1. Dirk's co-star in *Point of Departure* and two of his early films.
2. The novelist David Hughes.

enraged to trail about the place and find all the silly little things which they have'nt done ... oh! shit! What the hell.

Pause. A telephone call from New York ... (The outside world does really exist.) to ask if they, the Agents, could represent me 'world wide'. Feeling as I do .. a bit like Margaret Drabble in a swamp, if you know what I mean, I said that I was un-saleable and had had enough misery. We talked for a length of time ... they paid the call natch .. and I said 'If you want me, find me something by tonight.' And rang offish ... We'll see.

Forwood has just dropped a gas cylinder on his already broken foot. Daisy was sick on a bone and I have cleaned it up with a bit of Nice Matin and stuck it on the fire ... where it sizzled in a filthy way.

It was nice to see you. Funny shaky-handed-lady ... wondering how to cope with utter strangers .. and voluable too ... and doing it marvellously easily. Clever you. I think you are so brave .. I'd hate to have to fly to Nice to see the other half of a rather unlikely combination ... and then flit off to Crooked Mile and see the other[1] .. and wonder if there is a joining ... and having to put up with the Motel and it's deathly still rubber tree and almost-too-punctual-breakfasts.

Next time you'll go into the village Pub .. much better for you and you'd like it .. but how was one to know? Perhaps you would rather have had the Crillon .. or a Caravan ... one had no idea ... books dont give you away any more than Acting for the screen does ... it's strange is'nt it? And lovely new discoveries are made .. gold is washed from mud they say ... it's a super feeling to have found myself a nugget.

[...] Should be writing to My Lady in Connecticut ... but cant really get down to facing the correctness of the letter ... it cant quite be like this one ... not for absolutely real ... sort of 'edited' ... although none the less warm. But she is a different Lady. I think. Have'nt ever met her .... but I just thought I'd bash off to you. Tar-ra.

D..

---

1. Himself and Bette Davis respectively.

To Penelope Mortimer   *Clermont*
                                         18 April 1972

If I have not written it is because there really has been practically no
time to do so .... I had both your letters, and was tremendously
happy that you liked Regina[1] so well.

She really seems to resemble that lady in 'All About Eve' ... and
perhaps your original idea, of saving her from crap-pictures, will bear
fruit and was as wise as one (sorry) thought it to be ..... so get on
with your 'touching job' ... what does she really mean by a 'changed
woman.' It seems sad to settle for the obvious ..... but it would
probably be more commercial. And that we need. Or rather she needs.
We need. I dont know .... Losey needs too, having just sat stunned
through the boredom of 'Trotsky' in the local flics last week. However
enough of that.

I have not written on account of my aged parents arrived for Easter,
against all the family warnings .. (Too old to travel alone ... past the
age .. you'll be sorry .. they will be much happier left to stay where
they are in Sussex ... etc.) Pappa is 80 ... she is 75 .... he has a blazing
desire to paint the 'light of Bonnard and Renoir' she has no ambition
of any sort apart from telling long, long stories of the past. [...]
Anyway; they arrived late at Nice having had to stand for an hour and
a half in a corridor at Heathrow being frisked in the privates for
grenades! I ask you! Our darling Irish at it again apparently ... so
exhausted they arrived an hour late and we drove to the little pub ...
not the one you stayed in ... the smaller one with a little loo and bidet
in the room actual! And happy they were   a super view .. sun ..
and dinner ahead. I said I'd call back to pick them up in an hour. And
I did. To find my Mamma in a heap on the floor of the lobby
surrounded by guests and a white faced Pappa and the owner with
bandaids and scissors ... she had crashed the flight of marble stairs
and cut her self and shocked herself ... and also had broken her
shoulder.

Oh la la! Pain .. doctors .. pain killers .. a ghastly ride in a taxi in
the night to a clinic miles away in the hills above bloody Nice x
rays ... and the serious pronouncement of an immediate operation in
the morning. Oh! Shit. However ... to cut it all short .. she stayed in

---

1. Bette Davis.

the clinic for a few days ... the operation was not needed, a quite marvellous specialist managed to [manipulate] the bones together ... and for two long weeks we ferried them about from the local clinic here in the village ... before she was strong enough to go home last Tuesday. The miseries of one false move on a dark step swerved the entire pattern of their lives for ever. For she will never really be able to manage with it again even though it has started to heal and she is safe back in the Sussex, I suppose, she should never have left. Pappa painted a bit . . she sat and moaned a bit . . strapped up like a maniac in a sort of straight jacket ... but was really awfully brave. So there was little time to write, nor was there any inclination ... after I put them on the plane I felt wretched . . when to see them again? And would he, who I adore, ever see Bonnards Light again? So off I went into the Rex and sat through 'Trotsky' . . and wondered at the awfulness of it ... of the performances not much to be said . . Burton plays the whole thing with the charm of a dead baby and the unctiousness of a Used Car Salesman . . Delon bites his nails and rolls on beds in an agony, I presume, of doubt ... and Miss Schnieder comes up with your original Irma Greese[1] Role ... with a scrubbed face and rimless glasses.

The audience . . there were eight of us present ... laughed a little here and there, and shuddered at the bullfight, which is ugly and badly shot with five bulls playing one ... and I breathed a sigh of relief that I had NOT changed my mind and done the thing ... I would have been better I feel ... but not better enough to save a foundering bit of Jo pretension ... if I counted ten mirror shots I counted ten hundred ... and the dialogue has to be heard to be disbelieved. End of page. End of letter. Hope the trip was fun.

Love Dirk –

Following a conversation in Cannes with Losey and lunch at Clermont with Dirk, Alexander Walker, film critic of the Evening Standard, *commented on the partial estrangement between actor and director who then exchanged letters. Dirk described the piece as 'Quite dotty'; Losey, 'unforgivable'.*

---

1. Irma Griese, infamous guard at Auschwitz.

To Joseph Losey   *Clermont*
                                                         10 June 1972

Joe:

Your letter of the sixth arrived with another little note from a Well
Wisher enclosing the 'Standard' clipping ... which made me sort of
throw up, inspite of many years of that sort of rage and disappointment. What a stupid old faggot. Yet another Press Chum off
the list ... and another proof that even the nicest and most intilligent
and helpful are at heart decietful and vain and inaccurate! Except
Dilys?

Sure I adore Visconti ... I always will ... and I love you too ...
even inspite of your small treacheries .... if one has worked 'soul to
soul' as it were with a Director as I have with you and Luchino you
just dont fall off the tree like dead fruit. But that would be too hard
for Walker to understand. Although, I suppose to be fair, he was trying
to 'bring us together' ... which was a wast of time and not his function.
We'll get together under our own time. And not before. When I said
to Patricia that 'I did'nt want to meet you' it was not that at all. I dont
in the least mind <u>meeting</u> you .. (the wound has healed somewhat
anyway now) .. but I just did'nt want, or could not face, rather, getting
cosy and jolly over a meal ... or jammed in the Bar with Pierots Super
Elixier .... time will take care of it ... so it was not as violent as it
may have sounded. Naturally it would not be reported as slightly as
this, second hand.

However. Glad about Proust.[1] Another tiresome rumour ... people
delight in handing on. There is such pleasure in pain these days. Odd.
Good about Galielo[2] if it happens, I know that you have long wanted
this. Saw a ghastly film with Cusack on the Telly and words failed me.
Marvellously shot. Thats all. Also saw 'Fellini Roma' on Tuesday which
sent me reeling with delight. Not a complete film perhaps, but what
a marvellous eye. Eye. I should say. And clever little Rotourno[3]. I do
believe, as I always have, that the Italians are the master movie makers
and have been since the first Ben Hur in 1910![4] Fellini's Rome is the

---

1. Losey was still hoping to direct *A la recherche du temps perdu*.
2. A possible stage production of Brecht's *Galileo* in Germany.
3. Giuseppe Rotunno, director of photography on *Fellini's Roma*.
4. The silent classic, directed by Fred Niblo and shot partly in Italy, had its première in
1925.

one that I know sure as hell ... even to include, wickedly, M. [Gore] Vidal! Clever old thing ... F. not V. you gather.

[...] I am reading terrible scripts still. Oh dear ... the last an adaptation of Garnets[1] 'Lady Into Fox' which I have long adored and wanted to make with Asquith[2] years ago ... this has been 'up dated' and reads like Disneys version of 'Rebecca' .. or a sort of Carl Forman[3] 'Born Free With Foxes.' When, if ever, will they learn ...

Good about 'Accident'.[4] You have not bettered it ... still. Bugger the pace. It is a masterpiece.

Love
    Dirk –

In October and November Dirk had made The Serpent *in Paris with the director Henri Verneuil. His co-stars were Henry Fonda and Yul Brynner. The character, Philip Boyle, he likened to Kim Philby.*

On 5 November Dirk's father died.

At the time of this letter, Dirk was preparing for the filming in Rome and Vienna of The Night Porter, *to be directed by Liliana Cavani with Charlotte Rampling his co-star.*

To Penelope Mortimer   *Clermont*
                                        7 January 1973

Pennylopey —

There is a fearfully boring mail strike here, so this may never get to you .. or else terribly late. It is the Sunday letter I promised you in a hastily scrawled P.C the other day. A sort of catalogue letter; there is so much to say and so much to catch up on.

The film in Paris was okish. Jokey a bit ... lots of spies and car crashes and so on ... founded on fact. Me as Kilby ... Fonda the head of the CIA and Brunner being a crashing bore both on and off the screen ... and one way and another it all seemed to work out alright finally. In the middle of all this, one Sunday morning bleary from the

---

1. David Garnett.
2. Anthony Asquith, who directed Dirk in *The Woman in Question, The Doctor's Dilemma* and *Libel.*
3. Carl Foreman, producer of *The Guns of Navarone* and indeed *Born Free.*
4. Losey had seen *Accident* on television and, although critical of his own work – mainly in pacing – had found it 'more than good'.

Blue Train, I staggered into the Lancaster at eight in the morning ordered some coffee and started to shave. Telephone. Pa was dead at six that morning and the family had frantically been trying to get me .... I was on the fucking train. What to do. Apart from the terrific shock (I absolutely worshipped him and he me.) I could'nt leave Paris. Could contact no one there on a Sunday ... and had the first of the 'set pieces' to start the next morning. Fortunatly, oddly, I had a very important business luncheon at Lipp that day which I attended in a sort of numb way ... drank a lot and was amusing and 'on'. Business was excellent. Back at the hotel ... walking slowly back through the silent Sunday streets ... the tears came finally, in the loo where it was sort of private ... and I sat on the bidet and blubbed like a five year old instead of a fiftyone year old. Next day they all were deeply sympathetic but there was no possible way to England until the next Saturday which was a 'day off' with location shooting at the Travellers Club on the Champs on the Sunday at eight o clock am. So Pa was shoved into the deep freeze and I finally, after a nightmare journey by boat, car, train, got to the Funeral and sang those dotty hymns and watched them bung him into a hole. Then back to the house for a vast reception for all the super people who had come to be there. He was tremendously loved. Anyhow there it was ... and for the next two weeks I had to commute between Paris and Haywards Heath and here .... burning [...] papers diaries and private papers ... sending batches of stuff to 'The Times' where he was for forty years ... batches to the Royal Photographic Society[1] ... oh. The weariness and sadness of it all. My sister did the burning of clothes and personal gear, his shaving brush and tooth brush ... silly things. Mother sat in black; mute, brave, and sipping white wine while her family ransacked her house. Ghastly. But inevitable. And then finally all over and back to Paris for the final scenes (in French, which terrified me more than I can tell you) and eventually home here to the comparative calm of the terrace and the hills ... now slightly dusted with the first snow.

To wait calmly for the film in Rome ... fittings started almost at once and again it was a matter of bashing down to Rome and standing for hours while they stuck pins everywhere and shoved me into boots and shirts and hats ... and then back, home for a breather and off to

---

1. Ulric was a Fellow of the RPS.

Rome again for the Makeup ... two days before Xmas .. with an entire family of eight arriving for the week! Had to. What do you do with a new widow on her first Christmas alone? So they all arrived ... nieces and nephews sisters and brothers. Mother in a rather nasty hat and a set smile .... beds slung into odd corners ... Staff sent away so we could use their rooms ... 'We'll all Give A Hand' ringing out ... clattering about ... sharing the two loos ... Tonys son[1] arriving in the middle of it all [... W]e got through it all without once mentioning Pa or NOT mentioning him ... all was smooth until Christmas night when there was a call from London from the nephew who stayed behind to say that he was in St Georges with a seven inch stab wound four inches below the heart. Jolly. He had got into some awful party in Islington and it broke up into a fight with some yobs who tried to gatecrash the thing. In the scuffel a knife flashed. Mark[2] in the hospital. So. Happy. Happy Christmas. However everyone kept their cool and we went on with the celebration including boxing day tea for seven children. Shit. Thats all for this time ... I move off to Rome or Vienna in two weeks to start the film there with Cavani .... until April. I'll let you know where I am when I know ... but as usual it is an Italian Epic ... I mean not an Epic but an Italian Film and there seems to never be anysense in them. I wish I were'nt going. I have suddenly found that I simply LOATH the acting bit .... after three years away .... its such balls ... and I want out. I think after the Cavani that'll be it as far as I am concerned.

Golden and glorious here today ... frost on the back paddock ... snow on the higher hills .... sun striking off the terrace and the bare vine .. Mistral stripped and spare.

I'll go to the airport and try and find a post box .... and send you an ocean of love as ever. Do write back sometimes .... I miss you too you see. Funny.

Incidentally, a great box arrived from Connecticut some time ago with ALL the letters I ever sent to my LADIE. Over 2,000 .... they are FRIGHTFUL ... and off they go to the fire. After the shock of reading a random few written between 60[3] and 72 I decided I was not much cop at the writing ... and the person who emerged from

---

1. Gareth (1945–2007), whose mother was Glynis Johns.
2. Goodings, Elizabeth's son.
3. The correspondence began in 1967.

the typed pages was a mixture of Shirley Temple, Doopey,[1] and Oswald Mosely . . . . . so off with their heads.

[. . .] Love terrifically
<u>Dirk</u>

To Bee Gilbert   *Clermont*
20 July 1973

Snow darling –

Gosh! We have been busy one way and another . . . and it seems to me that I, or one of us, owes you a hundred letters and things. It is just not possible to get the time now that we run the house entirely on our own . . we sacked those two old farts the moment I got back, a day too soon, from Vienna and found the house looking like Miss Havershams. They had obviously been sitting on their bums watching telly for three months . . . and apart from feeding the dogs . . had done nothing else. Not even watered £500 worth of new trees which we have had to plant on the East boundrey, under Brown Titty Hill, because the Gobbies next door are building a cathedral. Anyway. They went. And a nice daily lady from up the lane comes two hours a day with swift washing and sweeping strokes, and frightful varicose veins. And we manage marvellously. Eat when we want to . . play records ALL night . . . and have a splendid new guest suite. Naturally . . . which has been almost constantly in use since the Festival in May. Which, for a bit of a change, was fun. Everyone seemed to come and eat with us, or swim, it was blistering hot for the two weeks, and we had lovely days with Ingrid B[ergman] and Rex and his new wife[2] (bought a new house on the coast . .) Malcolm McDowell and his gang from O Lucky Man[3] . . . and countless Americans who seemed to be here for some vast junket for Warner Bros. I think, accuratly, we had a luncheon every single day for at least four or six . . . but as it was so smashing and hot we just had vast picnics with bottles and bottles of chilled wine. It was tiring washing up . . . . but usually I was so pissed that I did'nt realise it much at the time . . . after two weeks, however, I had RATHER a LIVER. And suckled myself on bottles

1. Dopey, from Disney's *Snow White and the Seven Dwarfs*.
2. Rex Harrison had married Elizabeth Harris, his fifth wife, in August 1971.
3. Directed by Lindsay Anderson.

of Vichey .... well, anyway ... these are some of the excuses for not having put pen to paper for so long. Incidentally we did not see [...] Frankenheimer .. who was here [...] and who got a GHASTLY reception and Press. Ho Ho. What Glee.

Losey was in saddish form because of 'Dolls House'¹.. but looked rather beautiful with very long white hair and a brown face ... rather like a Sioux Chief dressed by Cardin .... Malcolm M. I liked enormously but was not so terribly taken with his wife² who suddenly appeared on the terrace, as we were all greeting each other, and to my consternation I realised she was once called Mrs Someonelse ... so it was a bit confusing. However shortly after luncheon, about five o clock she pissed off with a migraine and we all relaxed. Ian is TER-RIBLY lucky that you dont have the same effect on people! Tell him that from me please ... also it is awfully good that you are not an American Intellectual On The Cinema. She practically killed every-thing each time she opened her mouth under those silly granny glasses they WILL wear to be Hep.

Anyway, that does'nt matter. It was all fun generally ... I'm busy saying NO to everything that might start before the winter. Most of it is shitty anyway .. and I have played them all before ... which is never tempting. Got one today which is a sort of Moscow-Darling. I suggested that what they really needed was Michael York and a good Score. It does'nt exactly make friends, that sort of line, but makes me laugh anyway. And apart from the fact that Forwood wears a worried Frown all is well. My lovely Swiss Gnome says that I am 'alright'. So why should I bother when I HATE the work now. Honestly ... during my fifth simulated orgasm on the film with Cavani in Rome ... I suddenly wondered what the hell I was doing at 53 with my back on the floor, my flies undone, being straddled by beloved Miss Rampling .. with an entire Italian Crew watching and eating pizza. Nothing I had ever done in Rank prepared me for that ... and it also hurt my elbows most damnably. So I have decided not to do anything else until I REALLY feel so dotty about it I cant resist. But the shit of it all ... the hotel rooms, early calls, hanging about, arguing about continuity,

1. Losey's *A Doll's House*, with Jane Fonda as Nora, was sold to television and suffered from poor distribution; it was released three months after another version, by Patrick Garland, starring Claire Bloom.
2. Margot Bennett, formerly married to the actor Keir Dullea.

avoiding Press ... faking Fucks .. BASTA! We have apparently out
Tangoed 'Tango' ... I cant say that makes me happy ... but it might
make some lolly. I ADORED Miss Cavani ... I used to hit her so that
she would cry .. so that I could cuddle her. Kinky? Betcha ... Love.
end of page. D.

OOOO (Hugs for Ian.) For you XXXXXXXXXXXXX and two
OO's

To Penelope Mortimer   *Clermont*
                                                     14 October 1973

A Patriotic Letter. Christ knows what has gone wrong with this silly
Ribbon. Me, most likely. Rather exhausted from recording, here at
the house, some of the 12 Record Shows I have agreed to do for R.
Attenborough.[1] God knows why. Except it is super Lollipops and I
was able to go and buy a wonderful great set of Gramaphone, disc
recorder, mikes and speakers .... the studio looks rather like the
bowels of a space-craft ... covered in wires mixed up with disgruntled
dogs and worried Daily Ladie who is Not Allowed To Dust. Done
three of the sods ... it IS hard work .. and they seem happy in London
and have put in an order for more and more. Fun sometimes ...
especially to hear old records played beautifully on this new, and
wildely expensive, machine ... hearing K. Kendall's voice again .. my
God Mum, Yvonne Arnaud playing the piano ... Karajan and all
Mahler ... however we will see what happens on the 4th. K. Tynan
said the title .. 'Do I Hear A Waltz ..' was 'too dreadfully, and
relentlessly, nostalgic.' ... well that is maybe. It is geared for late
afternoon listning for sort-ofish Mrs B's[2] and nice Students Studying
High Maths ..

What AM I saying?

Rain yesterday. Terrific. Garden sodden and the vine dropping
leaves like used kleenex. Dogs feet scattering the tiled floor like those
neolithic cave paintings ... splats of personality etched in mud. Labbos
delicate and graceful ... a prince of Dogs ... Daisy a sort of wild
splodge ... a bull-dyke of a dog. And me swabbing up all the time

---

1. Richard Attenborough, as chairman of Capital Radio, had prompted Dirk to make a
series of programmes playing his favourite music.
2. His mother and/or a character in one of PM's novels.

where they have missed Nice Matin and three week old copies of The Observer.

And a new war we have.[1] Oh shit. Not AGAIN. Surely? One looks with a vaguely apprehensive eye towards oil and petrol ... and vague thoughts of having to flee the house, and shoot the dogs, and make for Geneva; enter ones head. (And try not to stay there.) I sometimes DO feel a foreigner in a large, frontiered, Country .... and images of Polish friends fleeing the Russians in '44 cant but help stick in the head. I knew one Lady who had two hours to leave 800 years of life and family in her great Estate .. and having bid the staff to burn their livery, turned the horses loose, she herself clad in old ski-ing gear, filled two saddle bags with some food and family papers and a bit of jewellery, and rode like hell for the Yanks who were fiddling about somewhere in the German area .... she never saw her home again. Now why did I tell you that? Sunday sort of gloom ... except that it really is THE most glorious day after all that rain ... and the hills look like something out of a Drury Lane Production of 'The Sound Of Music' ... all glorious colours .. fretworked against the arc of the sky ... an incredible blue .. with the Mistral starting over the hills behind. Pretty. Oh yes. You can come when you want to. There is a pleasant guest suite now that I have sacked the Staff and turned their rooms into something reasonably un-smelly. I DO know what 'the smell in a Maids bedroom' means now. It was not a nasty Mitfordish remark. It was true. We have had the windows wide open to the air since May ... repainted the place .. washed all the blankets and the damn carpet ... cleaned everything in sight. And the odour of 'frustiness' and sweat has only just now gone. To return. Better to wait until I get a few more of these jobs out of the way ... Programms I mean ... I spend most of the time wandering about wondering what to say about Vivaldi ... or Ethel Shutta ... or how to be tactful about Golders Green ... Radio Audiences are so dreadfully sensitive ... I recently, on Telly, said that I was very happy to live here (I'm always being asked that; with the implication that I have either come to avoid VAST tax, or have burned the Union Jack in Grasse Market ... or both; cunts.) happy to live here because it was warm and un-Fallish ... but that sometimes it could look like Tunbridge Wells on a wet Sunday ... Whereupon the ENTIRE population of the sodding place

---

1. The Yom Kippur War.

wrote furious letters (D. Bogarde. France.) asking what was the matter with T.W. And I wrote back and said that if they <u>did'nt</u> know, they were living in bliss; and if they DID know they'd be somewhere else. Grumpy, touchy, lot ... well you know that yourself.

[...]

<u>Two Hours Later</u>

Had to stop there very quickly; telephone calls from family with one horror chasing in on top of the other .... News has been broken, to OUR Mrs B., that the rest of her life is going to be spent, very comfortably and at great bloody expense, in a pretty and small and near-to-the-family Nursing Home. Not an easy moment to arrive at. Not an easy thing, at seventy five, to accept. Deed done. Now for the letter .... tomorrow ... to explain from a distance (In My Case.) why. Why? She cried ... Where do I go ... what will I do?

Well ... she wont fall down as often [...] but, oh shit. How I have dreaded this day .. for so many years ... years and years .... anyway; we'll all (the kids that is) have to fork out here and there and make the next ten .. (I reckon a hundred for her) ... years comfortable and happy as possible.

Not that she'll ever be happy really. The day after her honeymoon, in 1919,[1] she was busily packing a bag to join the Jesse Lasky Players in Hollywood My Pappa, aged all of 27, said 'Me or It.' and so she stayed and I was born. And she has never, ever, forgotten, nor will she ever, her Resentment. As she calls it. Christ! A loving and loyal husband .. and a very sexy fellow to boot ... and five children[2] and nannies and so on ... and now sitting in a titchy, but pleasant, Nursing Home in Haywards Bloody Heath. [...]

Where are the morals? What, as Lotte Leynia says, Would You Do. Anyway done.

I dont know; one always wants so desperatly to be 'Grown Up' ... it is'nt all that cop, is it? Except for one or two moments of wild, and stupidly glorious, happiness, it was MUCH nicer being little Dirk ... with nothing more worrying than how my Lizards and Frogs were breeding (if they were.) or the results of my French and Maths Exams .... or were there worse things really? I dont know. Wanting,

---

1. The Van den Bogaerdes were married in 1920.
2. Dirk's penchant for exaggeration extends here even to the size of his own family: Ulric and Margaret had three children.

desperatly, to win a canary at the village Fair . . . . . I'd rather have those than worrying about the letter to that nursing home in Haywards Heath tomorrow. And I <u>liked</u> my war. So there we are . . . where are we? . . Oh! It is so confusing to be middleaged . . . so lovely to worry only about babies and Biba and if you are 'with it' or without whatever IT is . . . enough.

Back to your letter and your, as usual, questions. You cant see 'Night Porter' until it opens in Jan in Parigi . . . . and then you could come with Lilly [Cavani] and me. She hates me calling her Lilly . . . and it simply does'nt suit her one bit. Tom or Dick or Harry would do much better . . . but she is my personal person. My Lilly. Just as, idiotically, you are my Pennylopé. With the acute.

[. . .] Off to feed dogs and cut the last remaining grapes for the rather nasty Grape Jelly that my Daily Ladie makes . . . but why leave them to the wasps and fee-fies? . . Oh shit. This has gone on long enough.

A thoroughly rotten letter – as you said – 'there are writing days – and non-writing days'. This is one of the latter for me and, as recipient, for you too —

Love –

<u>Dirk</u>

With its American backers dismayed by The Night Porter, *Dirk had arranged a private and 'off-the-record' screening in London for four selected critics. Alexander Walker of the* Evening Standard *broke the embargo and the others felt obliged to follow – among them Dilys Powell, who wrote a brief and complimentary review in her column on Sunday 20 January.*

To Dilys Powell   *Clermont*
                                              24th January [1974]
                                              Thursday evening.

[. . .] Thank you so very much for Sunday. It was a rather marvellous day [. . .] And now, you may be amused to know, the film has been rushed back, at urgent request, to the States. There you are, you see. We now await their verdict . . . the bastards. I fear that it wont be dirty enough for them .... or even Pekenpaish-Violent.[1] They really DO like it spelled out in letters of fire.

No; I agree with you utterly. I dont think that the general public WILL go along with it ... but we did'nt make it for them anyway. It can only possibly work in a small cinema where people who care about the cinema itself ... I mean the Work of the cinema can see it ... it is not for general consumption. Whatever our rather nitwitted, but kind, producer thinks! I remember once when Visconti was asked by a rather bewildered and angry American Critic 'Why' he made 'Death', he replied very gently 'Bogarde and I made it for ourselves.' ... which was true, but rather naughty and not to be at all encouraged!

I dont think, and dont be cross with me for saying this, but I dont think one can really see the 'NP' thing unless you, or one rather, has been desperatly, solidly, passionately in love. Or unless one has been loved. That is, ultimatly, what it is about. At least Charlotte and Lilliane and I thought so ... we hacked and cut and clipped the ten other plots away from the original script and tried to get to the bottom of Love.

Patrick White says somewhere in 'The Eye Of The Storm' ..... 'there is no desecration where there is Love.' I rather think that he is right ..... Enough of that. You'll probably never see it again. But at least you DID see it ... it was real .... your presence made it so. For that, if for nothing else, my humblest gratitude.

Spring is being a bit dotty here in the hills .... it's deceptivly warm and birds and things are scuttering about the olives as if it were April. The violets are thick and blue under the walls, and the primulas are fat, rather vulgar, cushions in the softest green grass .... of course, as I well know in these hills, tomorrow it can snow .. we had five meters of the blasted stuff four years ago ... oranges tumbled into the drifts, and the dogs had hysterics of delight. And I must be in London on Sunday for a week .. oh! hell! ... to see ageing Mamma somewhere near Haywards Heath and deal with Family Problems generally ... then, happily and hopefully, back the next Sunday. To snow drifts!

It'll be the first trip for 18 months. I ought to feel excited .. but apart from a visit to nice Miss [Joy] Parker at Hatchards and a bit of a spend in Floris .. I dread it all.

---

1. Sam Peckinpah – director of *The Wild Bunch* and, more recently, *Straw Dogs* which in its violence made DP for the first time in her life feel 'concern for the future of the cinema'.

It would be different if you were coming with one. We might find a lovely book on Iran!' But I suppose you have them all anyway ... end of page .. but NOT end of love – from Dirk –

To Dilys Powell   *Clermont*
                                          7th February 1974
                                          Thursday afternoon.

They tell me that it is the Mistral which is blowing across my hill; but I think it is the other, and nastier, wind. The Tramontine. And I simply loath it. The trees are bending to the earth ... tall cypress like ostrich feathers at a dance ... the olives wrenching and rolling .. and slates ripping across the terrace like old leaves. And it makes me most dreadfully fretful. Like the fern[2] in Austria ... beastly feeling. Weak and worried and a sense of apprehension. Last December we had a smashing wind .. of 150 kms an hour .. plus awful forest fires .... houses burned like matchboxes, and trees flew through the air as if an angry child was demolishing his Noahs Ark. I dread that it will not die down until tomorrow ... and I hate it all shuttered in the cottage with the roof sagging and the awful roaring everywhere.

So, instead of pruning the big vine, or levelling off my pond ... which I should be doing, I am in here writing my mail. Well. Some of my mail. The ones I <u>want</u> to answer. It is my day for self indulgence.

[...] I am just back from London. First time in 18 months ... to see Mamma (in a pleasant, but naturally sad, House for Elderly widows.) Wretched to see her sitting in a tiny facimile of her own room at home ... her own bits and pieces, paintings, pots and jars, a bowl of hyacinths ... a television .. a window out over the sussex lanes ... but empty.

Got that over .. in a sort of jolly-sad way ... then other family affairs ... brothers and sisters and nieces and nephews and god alone knows what else. Suddenly one finds one has no friends anymore. Is'nt it odd? Having left England I am now desperatly out of touch. Actor friends are DREADFULLY dull and boring and egocentric and full

---

1. DP was married to the archaeologist Humfry Payne from 1926 until his death in 1936, and had a considerable knowledge of the Middle East.
2. Yes, the *tramontane* is notorious; the Föhn, a warm and dry wind from the northern Alps, less so.

of something called Valium! I dont know what is what, or who is who, on the Telly ... which seems to rule me out as a conversationalist more than not knowing what is on at the Court or the NFT .... which I do ... and I feel that they have all, or nearly all, stopped dead in 1967. A little older .. children have grown ... clothes a bit more, or less, Bibaish .. desperatly dull I though[t]. All of them. Except one nice lady who writes books and lives on about five quid a week with whom I lunched ... and Losey and his wife who are still 'alive' and live in a dotty, but delightful, house in Royal Avenue ... I was deeply grateful for a couple of their hours. Refreshment in a dimming, arid, desert of ageing acquantances! Very odd.

But perhaps it is me. No one knows much about olives or vines or just pottering about at the Market every morning. And few people seem to read much. At least I have all the books here. I mean the new ones as well as Trollop ... which was about the only name I heard in London all the time I was there! Because of a thing they are up to on the Telly. Really.

And apart from horrid news about Mines and Petrol and all the rest, and a rather 'It Is'nt Really Happening' sort of thing generally about the streets .... there was very little else. I longed and longed for the airport and the flight home. Which is strange. For I have a ghastly terror of planes and flying. (In the war .. for seven years with the RAF and the Canadian lot ... I had to fly here and there. And I was convinced that it was so horrid and beastly and unnatural that when the war was over it would never catch on. I said.)

Anyway home was a short two hours away ... bumping into fearful rain and storms ... the sea like molten metal .. the palms screaming and racketing ... but the whole place seemed, to me at any rate, golden and glorious. That first smell of France. Cigarettes and tea and coffee and the pines ... the dogs going bonkers with joy and fighting each other in a wild showing off of Welcome Home. Unlocking a week-closed house ... smell of time .... a clock stopped .... soot down the big chimney ... mail in a neat pile made by my bonne ... a cold meal set under a cloth .... cold chicken, a mixed salad of watercress, endive and the first chives ... bread from the village with a crust ... a plump Pont L'Eveque ....

And then ones own bed after the Connaught elegance ... ones own bathroom .. unpacking the loot ... Floris bits and pieces ... Veganine ... razor blades ... Marks and Sparks sweaters ... a bundle of new books from Hatchards ... Country Life and The Field and <u>all</u> the Sunday papers to last me the week.

And as evening fell the lights sparkled away along the coast ... the tower of the Cathedral at Grasse was like a stick of barley sugar in the dusk ... the owls and the lambs ... peace and silence otherwise. Who would want the other!

I do go on ... an essay of doubtful merit ... a note to start with to say how lovely it was to have your note ... and your love .. and, indeed, your treasured freindship.

Self indulgance has got the better of me. I'll pack it in now.

[...] I have no cat to chase across my machine ... Daisy and Labaro, the dogs, are convinced that cats are really rabbits ... but forgive my own mistakes, and accept all my love and gratitude ... and dont feel, in the least, obliged to reply. Ours is not THAT kind of friendship. As you know ... perhaps thats why we have preserved it so well .....

'The desperation of Love' ... you say about the 'NP' thing ... thats it. Thats exactly what it's all about. But few, alas, will realise the fact ... ah well ... better than Percy's Progress.[1] I think.

My love
<u>Dirk</u>

To Bee Gilbert   *Clermont*
                                                31 March 1974

Dearest Sno:

A delayed letter to thank you for your long and full-of-woes one! What a pity about the dog. However if that happens they seldome, if ever, get cured and the only thing is a merciful shot gun. Or a place in Kensington not near the Serpentine. Labbo is a bit like that too; a Pussy-Killer and a Chickie Killer. Got ten pullets in my garden in Rome and chumped them all up happily covered in gore and white feathers.

Even the old trick of tying a corpse round his neck till it rotted, had utterly no effect. He just had a chumble when he felt like it .. and

---

1. Sequel to *Percy*, an alleged comedy from – alas – the Box/Thomas team, about a penis transplant.

eventually the smell was so vile that we were reaching and hacking away without any change to the sodding dog.

Anyway, 'spect you have sorted that out by now. Buy an Angora Cat.

HRH[1] has had some rum notices for his Epic. Some were really jolly funny. Anyway no one BLAMES the lad. His reputation is still intact. After all everyone knows that sometimes an [actor] does need the lolly. The only thing which sickens me is the Great Unwashed who CARE for that more than 'Homecoming' or 'Richard III' . . . . its really chips with everything. I sometimes feel that we should'nt indulge their silly little brains . . . and force them to watch proper things, properly done. However thats another argument. I do LOATH their silly faces and their sillier minds. They deserve a twenty quid or pence loaf . . . and Wlsion[2] too.

We are just back, almost intact, from Parige after a three day stint there for 'Night Porter'. A rather exhausting trip as I had eight to ten sessions with the Press every day, plus the Telly and Radio, and all in Frog. Trying . . . but they were dreadfully polite and kind and terribly interested. Unlike our lot, who only want to know who you are fucking, if you are, and wheather it is true that you really make your own lampshades and breed tropical fish . . . in Paris one had to compare Molier with Albee . . . Renoir with Hockney, Guilt with Innocense . . . lust with love . . . Losey with Visconti or Clayton and that sort of thing. Stimulating and interesting for both questioner and Victim. All a bit Cahi[e]rs du Cinema . . . but whats wrong with that? Better than Roderick Mann in the Express . . which is generally about our level in England. The film itself seems to have both shocked, as we hoped, and moved and excited, also as we hoped. People are either smashed completely or sent mad with rage . . . anti-jewish (we did'nt know!) or pro-Facist . . (I had a faint feeling that I knew THAT one.) And because the film was made by a Communist everyone got very Political. No one found it vulgar or obscene . . . like the Italians who have swiftly banned it because of a scene with Charlotte ontop of me, instead of the tother way round!

Anyway we open on the 3rd in Paris . . . in ten movie houses . . . and then we shall know. There seems still no chance of it reaching

1. Ian Holm had made *Juggernaut*, a thriller directed by Richard Lester.
2. An attempt at the Prime Minister (Harold) Wilson, who was presiding in inflationary times.

England. And I suppose that if it did that Whitehouse[1] lot would have screaming fits and we'd all be arrested. It is odd. Nothing happens that does'nt happen between an ordinary man and woman in love ... and who enjoy sex ... but there you go. There is one shot of two soldiers buggering each other, very very graphically ... and to which the Italian censors have'nt even turned a hair ... yet because Charlotte straddles me ...... I give up.

Busy preparing for the summer here. Steps to the swimming pool .. all by my own little hands. And rather good. And a new path to the port d'entre ... and the terrace on the North is super and finished, covered in Dorothy Perkins and honeysuckle ... and the kitchen is stripped and ready for tiling and the fitted things ... we should be shipshape in a couple of weeks. At the moment it is sheer hell because Tote is cooking in the corridor outside your room .. and I am washing up down in the washhouse .... a bit bizaar. We have'nt a grill or an oven so everything has to be boiled or steamed ... and we cant fry anything on account of the stink in the corridor and all the fat getting into your new curtains and so on .... ah well! By the time we HAVE the bloody new kitchen I reckon we shall have decided to live on pills and save the fucking washing up.

So dont come for your 'spring' holiday until after the middle of April .. then we can do a bit of boasting I hope. It has been a tough, wet winter here ... and a very wet spring. First medium day today. Everything wondrous green. Blossom in cascades ... peach apple, plum and quince .. and the grass is starred with scillas and buttercups and pale anenomies and great spreads of wild narcissi and bee-orchis. The frogs are screaming away preparing for the Big Fuck ... and the Toads have already had theirs and littered the pond with ropes and ropes of jet beading! All very pretty and promising. And this arvo we have six dozen petunias to pose, as they say in France, and masses of others as well .. a blue and white garden we plan, with no reds or purples or suburban colours ... otherwise, apart from the washing up, there is nothing to tell you ... save that you are loved and missed. Beware of that Snap-Fetish. I started with a Brownie. Ended with a Hasslebladt and a VAST dark room, brown staind fingers and a humped back .. and huge enlargements, 20 x 16 and a quite incredible overdraft. So watch it Sno Beaton.

---

1. Mary Whitehouse, president of the National Viewers' and Listeners' Association.

Must write some more, dull, letters ... all love and things to you both ... and come and see us soon ... the Festival should be fun this year ... but I reccomend you miss THAT!

Let me know in good time to change beds and clean room ... and shoot the Collie.

Love as ever –
    Dirk

Guess what! The Fucking Fixer is on Telly this week – in the series 'Dossiers de L'Ecran' – V. highbrow! A load of shit in ANY language – the village is agog! D.

To Joseph Losey

Clermont
11 April 1974

Dearest Jo – Joe, Joseph – Josef – Josephine –[1]

Dont panic. I am not starting a correspondance ... and I dont want a job. So you are relieved on both counts. However I <u>do</u> have to reply to your superly funny letter and have not replied before only because of a plethora of House Guests and NO kitchen still ... If your long suffering secretary lady WILL read my local paper I cant see why she should get the 'hives' because her chum only talks of the Hoover on the phone. I mean; if you read Nice Matin, and copy, or clip out, little pieces about Dogs Shit then it has to be a limited mind. N.M. <u>never</u> prints anything about anything at all. Only things like 'Shocking Double Murder In Pegomas. Wine Presser Castrates Wifes Lover And Presses The Unfortunate Woman In Concrete.' ... or else little sagas about Doggies shitting in odd parts of Holland. Nevertheless she can spell better than I (can) and punctuate too.

Maybe she'd better take 'Playgirl' and help her chum out ... or else he MAY, possibly, have a Hoover Fixation ... all those tubes ... and little bits one fits on ... and all the sucking and blowing stuff ...... one never can tell. Cant she? Poor dear.

Now. Be sensible for Christs sake. (Me; not you). 'Night Porter' is a critical smash. That much we know. Save for that old queen on The Tribune ... and Match and Le Point. Everyone else is radient ... and what Cavani calls, happily, Sublime ... and they are too. I dont think

---

1. Dirk had been told that Losey now insisted on being addressed as 'Joseph'.

I have read notices like them for a very long time .. and in such vast detail. Our President died, unhappily, on the very day we opened .. but even so we had 6,400 entries ... up to 9,000 the next day .. then the day of Mourning .. and then we rocketted up to 11,000. I dare not count our blessings until the end of the second week ... which will be a fair old indication I think. We were also completely banned, as I said, in Italy ... mainly because of Charlotte's position as The Dominent Sex ... secondly because it was compounded by the fact that A WOMAN had also directed the thing. The Vatican Press came out FOR us by saying that the Bible said, in some remote passage, that it was OK for the Lady to do that[1] under very special circumstances. Anyway ... Moravia, Bertolucci, Visconti, Antonioni, the whole gang .. some thirty names, made a TREMENDOUS fuss everywhere .. and Lilly went to the Tribunial .. and we got it passed without cuts. Triumph. Especially dotty was the fact that 'Elle' had voted the thing film of the month by all it's <u>women</u> readers! Which made the Italian Lot look sick. We open there this Saturday with a tremendous flurry of political and social cries.

We will wait and see. I have refused to attend. I'm dubbed anyway .. and I dont give a tuppeny shit for that Insular Pininsula ... except for V. Naturally. Who started his big epic[2] on Monday. Which is very brave and wonderous indeed. I hope he finishes it ...

[...] Alexis Smith. (If you can remember who she was. Is.[3]) arrived from Malaga last week and stayed an exhausting five days. Exhausting only because she has more energy than Lotts Road and Battersea[4] rolled into one. But loving and dear and fun ... and full of all the chatter from a now, for me, distant, land .... funny it was too ... she is well and successful and wonderfully pretty and lithe looking. And a remarkable survivor.

We bunged her onto the six am. (AM mark you) flight to N.Y with a very sad feeling, inspite of her exhausting chatter and delight at everything ... twenty years counts for something. We had a marvellously happy meal chez the Rouxs[5] and Simone in the private

---

1. Be dominant, rather than direct films.
2. *Conversation Piece* (*Gruppo di famiglia in un interno*), starring Burt Lancaster and Helmut Berger.
3. Dirk's co-star in *The Sleeping Tiger*.
4. Lots Road, Chelsea, and Battersea power stations.
5. The Roux family, owners of La Colombe d'Or.

Parlour .. and Alexis was bowled over and thrilled ... everyone was utterly delightful to her. Anyway .... we also had poor old Maurice Evans in for drinks one night. He was staying in the village and wrote asking if we could meet. I had worked for his company 'Compass' in N.Y a couple of times[1] .. and we had'nt met. A lonely, ageing, old man whome, it would appear, no one wants anymore. Which is unpleasant. But life.

And what else? Ah yes. Master Wisemans script.[2] Came the other day. Difficult to say what I feel. I have only read up to page 71 so far. Rather busy out in me garden. It's ok I guess. I cant help feeling we have all been there before .. that Author with the Hampstead-Life .... the elevator in a grand hotel ... the wandering enigma of a Poet ... shades here of better things ... Darling .... Pumpkineater ... Accident ... none of it is very new, really .... and someone seems to have shares in Kentucky Chicken .. but that does'nt matter. Perhaps thats what they ate in richish houses in Hampstead in the early sixties ..... but thats quite flippant. As you well know. I suppose it was a very bad thing to do to read lumps of the Pinter Collection to Alexis the other night .... somehow he 'sticks' ... and other peoples dialogue reads like the advertisements in the 'Sunday Times' .... I think 'O.T.'[3] would be super ... but no one would go to see it ... I imagine they <u>will</u> go to see Master W's epic .... all that naked romping in the Hampstead Garden Suburb Garden ... and the fuck (?) in the lift and the bits and pieces here and there. Thats what they want, I suppose. That and comedy. And there aint a laugh in this one which is intended. I am sure you will have lots to do and lots to re-do ... I must get on and read the next 171 pages this evening.

Meanwhile I must finish this, and get back to my cimenting and do a bit of bullying in the New Kitchen. We are nearly ready for the Festival! What a lark! Shall you be here? I DO hope so ... really. It makes me feel very put together to see you both again. And this time, or that time, next time I mean, I shall have splendid <u>ice</u> for Mrs Loseyposey.

Incidentally you say that you would not 'advise' me to be involved in an 'epic' on Nietzsche[4] ... well; I never said it <u>was</u> an 'epic' .... and

1. Dirk had starred in television productions of *Little Moon of Alban* and *Blithe Spirit*.
2. *The Romantic Englishwoman*, based by Thomas Wiseman on his own novel.
3. Pinter's *Old Times*, as a film.
4. Cavani's current project was a film about Friedrich Nietzsche, eventually released as *Beyond Good and Evil* (*Al di là del bene e del male*).

I am comitted to Lilly as deeply as I was to you for 'Accident' Remember? So morally I cannot take your advice this time! And I rather gather that her finance is secure after the Paris showings .... she really has rocketted to the heights. And naturally thinks, by this time, that she did it all by herself! But thats ok .... it is very usual I find. And she is a very clever little girl to boot.

Here comes the rain again. Fuck. Love to Patricia and that languishing secretary ... and you have always had all mine anyway ....

Dirk.

P.P.S.

Tote reminds me that you may be grumpy, but also pleased, to know that in all the Press about the 'NP' thing, Lillys work is not exactly compared to yours, and Viscontis, but 'suggests' the 'mark' of you both ..... it has happened in most of the 'intellectual' ones ... reminders of, and they quote, 'The Servant' ... 'Rocco', 'Senso', and to my delighted irritation, moments from even, 'Secret Ceremony' ... a big load of cods-wallop if ever there was one. (Entirely personal, you understand.) But watching it in the Goetzs' home, on that great screen behind the Braques and Chagalls and all that and with Claudette Colbert and out of season cyclamen nodding into frame, it was quite hard to be ..... entirely ..... objective. Anyhow; thats what Tote said I had to say ... the press were favourably impressed that Lilly had found overtones of the 'masters' ..... she is behaving just as tiresomely as they did as well. But has evolved, as indeed she should, her 'own' style. And if she gives a nod or two in your two very splendid directions, all the better for that. Funny that you, and he, should become adjectives .... Viscontisim. ... Loseyism ... better, by far, than some of the other 'ism's.'

Agree?

D.

---

1. William Goetz, the independent Hollywood producer behind *Song Without End*, and his wife Edith; they were famed for the opulence of their lifestyle and lavish entertaining.

To Joseph Losey   *Clermont*
                                                                          14 April 1974

My dear Joe –

Haste reccomends me to write to you again so soon after my last
letter .... Just to say that I finished the 'Romantic' script the other
evening and find that I cannot really change my opinion much. It gets
better, of course, after page 71 ... but I still think, wistfully, that we
have all been there before somehow.

I mean, I <u>know,</u> that there are only seven basic stories .... or
permutations of them, but somehow this seems to me to be rather like
a fly in amber. It does'nt SAY anything terribly much .... and I think,
and it is your teaching, that a Movie SHOULD now adays. And if it
disturbes, again your own council to me, then there is a sound reason
for doing it. But I cannot, for the life of me, see what this does to
disturbe .... the enegmatic lodger-in-the-house ..... the fantasy wife
.... the Did He Did He Not Murder .... the Au Pair. (Do they
STILL exist outside a Betty Box Epic?) munching her way through
yet another cake ... (Close on the stamps to show it's Italian) or
perhaps close on the chocolate dripping mouth to show she is really
Gluttony As well as unusually sluttish, even for an Italian Au Pair!

Splendid part for Tits Jackson, if thats what she wants ... and
pretty dreary for Lewis[1] .. one of those Yearning Dullards full of
patience and very little guile. He has no range, no rage, no true
dimensions .... hard to flesh out. Even though I KNOW that that is
the Actors job. But somehow it is rather like hanging up a suit of
clothes on a nail .... not on a coat hanger, if you know what I mean.

And unless the Poet is of such blinding beauty and strangeness I
cant think WHAT you'd do with him. No use using Old Bates or
someone ... and the days of That Kind Of Terence Stamp are well
over. It seems to me, and I am so often terribly off key and wrong
about things, that this is a comfortable Movie of the sixties ... and
that a great many things have happened since then. Forgive me if I
irritate you ... I know that I often do .... but equally I am aware that
you know it is entirely a personal and private re action .. and for your
eyes alone. And ears. It was wonderfully good of you to send it to me
and to allow me to read it .... As you know I have only made three

---

1. Michael Caine would play Lewis Fielding, opposite Glenda Jackson.

Movies in about six years ... (The Serpant was hardly a movie ... it was bread.) so maybe I'm VERY off key. Anyway, for what it is worth, that's my opinion. Right or, probably, wrong.

Still raining here and Easter is upon us with dripping tourists in sodden camps and muddy trailers ... terribly sad to see people who have saved up for a whole year being reduced to misery by the will of God ... oh dear! Love, and love ...

Dirk –

To Joseph Losey

Clermont
3 May 1974

My dear Joe –

The Script[1] arrived as hoped for, and safely. And I waited to read it until I was absolutely uncluttered with other things.

I find it marvellous. I think the condensing job utterly incredible. I cannot comprehend how it was 'managed' .... and can only understand your joint grief that so much work, and dedication, should be so fearfully delayed.

Naturally it'll cost a billion-dillion. That is apparent from the very outset. The amount of cast ... costumes ... not to say locations and colours and things. What I find a little worrying is that it is almost impossible NOT to have read the books before comprehending the scenario. And here, possibly, may lie it's greatest fault ... if fault there be. I cannot see the Yank Orientals on the Coast having an idea as to what it is all about .... unless they had first driven themselves through all twelve volumes. And as it is unlikely that they can read anything heavier than the latest copy of 'Variety', or the Menu at the Racketts Club or the Polo Lounge, that is an awesome thought.

And not only the Orientals .... the audiences too ... will they know who is who? Or what is what? The significance of the trees ... or the towers ... or will they know that Marcel is Jewish, middle Class, and an onlooker at a vastly higher strata of life than his own? Do they know, do you think, the meaning of the Vermeer? Or who Swan was to the hero's life line? Oh! A million questions .... but ones not to be answered in letters. However they are, I feel sure, questions which An Audience will ask .. and grow restless without the answers ..... It is

---

1. Pinter's adaptation of *A la recherche du temps perdu*.

all, of course, too complex for surface letter-writing. Enough that you sent it and that it proved a feast indeed. And forced me back to the books ... and also to that excellent book on Proust by Samson ... or Sampson[1] ... which has been vastly entertaining and helpful while one digested the script. Oh dear! What a fucking pity it is .... and especially when one reads the utter crap which comes ones way these days. Luchino said, years ago, that there was nothing for me in Proust. He is right. But I'd be happy even to play a door-knob simply for the sake of the experience. For the Awe. For the love of the writer and his books. Enough. Thank you both for a splendid script. And for sharing it with me. I am truly grateful.

Are you, I wonder, sitting in Morocco now? It's raining here ... and cold, and the Italian Police have confiscated the Negative, Matrix, all prints at hand and apparently all of us, of the 'Night Porter' .... not for obscenity ... but for the Corruption of Minors .... since no one under 18 can see it anyway, one is bemused, as well as saddned. So much work chucked away .... second biggest money maker in France ... and a very real possibility that it will never see the light of day anywhere else.

I am sure that you were trying to be comforting when you said that Julie straddled that rather heavy actor in 'Dont Look Now' ..... but alas! our picture is not quite like that. It's rather like comparing 'Little Red Ridinghood' with 'L'Histoire d'O'[2] .... or Disney with Klimt .... never mind; as you and I have had to say so many times, 'We Did Make It.'

Whatever the hell they finally do with it now. [...]

My love always
        <u>Dirk</u>

To Penelope Mortimer   *Clermont*
                                              9 August 1974

We bake; we bake; the sky an aching, ashen white. No breeze even .... the earth hard and dry and bracken-coloured. And I dont terribly care for it this hot. It's been like this, as a matter of fact, since the Circus (the F. Festival) left in May .... and not a titchy peardrop of

1. William Sansom's pictorial biography, *Proust and His World* (Thames & Hudson, 1973).
2. See p. 128, note 3.

rain has fallen. Oh. A flurry of plipplops yesterday at breakfast on the terrace … and that was all. And so I am making a big thing of not watering-the-pots this evening and am playing hooky here with you. Writing at you rather, I suppose, than To you. And you dont need to fear a permanent contact … or that'll be dreadful … I mean, I'm not, actually, really 'catching'. I dont feel the least obligation to write back to you … appropos your 'only Sensible' friend. I just want to. A different thing altogether. And I dont expect a reply either. […]

I have <u>had</u> to re-read the Gide book which everyone wants me to film and I cannot, ever, see why. The Immoralist.[1] I thought that now, after ten years, I'd be a bit clearer. But I'm not. I do find Arab boys and Elderly .. or even young .. Gentlemen deadly tedious. I simply cannot take any of it seriously. So No to the Immoralist again …. and then I had a go at something on Pontius Pilate … quite good. Astonishing loot … but tiresome to have to trail about in a nighty all over the Gaza strip where, natch, they'll shoot. And so on […]

I think what you are doing[2] is marvellously good. I do really. I mean if thats what you want and if it makes you work … which it clearly does. I expect today must be Quite A Day there. With Nixon going and all that.[3] The woman in the village this morning who said that she sat up till two am (our time) to watch it live on Telly and, having loathed his guts for years, was suddenly surprised to find herself saddened … and gulped down her Olvaltine (can you believe it?) and went tearfully back to bed. But the Postmistress said 'He's gone thank God!' and that seems to be the general feeling among the Frogs. The humiliation of it all has gone quite deep. But as long as you are not weaving and marching about in a goodhumoured group under the sycamores …. thats ok … I suddenly had a clutch of fear. But you re assure me.

[… Y]ou remember my other sad Laidie[4] who died in Connecticut and to whome I wrote for eight years? Well I got all the letters back in the will .. you know that too … but what you dont know is that I found them last month up on the landing when I was doing some plastering things ….. this great box, bursting with letters and post-

1. André Gide's novel was first published in 1902 and in English in 1930.
2. PM was teaching and writing at Yaddo, New York State.
3. Richard Nixon had resigned as President of the United States.
4. Dorothy Gordon.

cards and faded, now, telegrams. They were all in chronological order too! From the first .... to the last postcard of this village church ... which arrived on the morning of the evening in which she died. Horridly it says .. 'Do anything you want with the blasted letters (mine) Send them to Yale or U.C.L.A or will them to the British Museum. I dont care. Writing later. In haste.'

Oh dear. So I started to read and it took three days to do so. Each letter, each card, each telegram ... a strange, moving, love affair. And clearly I <u>knew</u> that she was dying all the time ... well; from pretty early on .. and just wrote and wrote to her and invented a sort of person who really did not truthfully exist. The me of the letters is almost unbearably AWFUL! I cant believe that she was so diverted ... so adoring .. so amused. I thought He was poisonous! For a while I toyed with the idea of editing and publishing them, as she wanted to do herself .... but soon it dawned on me that this was a totally private thing, and to be read by no one other than ourselves. Talk about Giving Ones self away! Christ! This is the most awful load of tinkling, trilling, self conciet I have ever read in all my days.

So back into the landing cupboard. And Dorothy can lie in peace. So, for that matter, can her chum Bogarde. What a VERY NASTY EXPERIENCE it was to sit here for three days and read all that crap.

Which makes me feel that I have gone on here long enough as it is ... and you have other things to do.

[...] I'd better go down and do a bit of watering ... the sun is still high ... five fortyfive ... the hills are the colour of pumice stone ... the olives still, not moving. Nothing seems to breath. The dogs lie splosh in the shade. I must go ... otherwise you'll screw all this up. Soon as I'v had a 'go' at LD[1] I'll let you know. I am enormously curious now that you have filled me in on the background. How splendid to be an imobilised apology! Thats one thing you cant possibly be with me.

> who love you
> > or is it I who love you?
> > > anyway from
> > > > <u>Dirk</u>

---

1. PM had sent Dirk a copy of her new, highly autobiographical, novel – *Long Distance* (Allen Lane).

Next Day. 10 Aug.

I wanted, simply, to say that I started on LD and was delighted ... if at first a little unsteady on my local etc .... but am getting into Kafka?Land very spiritidly. And see you so startlingly clearly, as in a Follow Spot [...]

I have now to go and do another chore ... finish off a book by, is it ~~Ackroyd~~ ACKERLEY about 'My Father and Myself'[1] which some idiotic producer (stage) wants me to adapt for him as a play. Quite impossible I find. Also I rather detest the book and the writer .... If one wants to blow off Guardsmen ok. But I dont, honestly, want to know anything about it ... and I'm sure an audience wont either. And I am rather bored with premature ejaculations in elderly men from the BBC ..... oh dear! I want a lovely, funny, dear, gentle, pretty film about lovely people like Gable and Lombard ... or Colbert would do. Actually nearly got one off the floor last month ... 'Aide Memoire'. ... a frog play written for [Delphine] Seyrig ..... we wanted to do the script as a movie ... and actually your 'ex'[2] was approached to do the English thing ... translation ... but it came to nought. The exhibitors wanted Giradout or Bardot or Vitti[3] .... not Seyrig. Ah well.

    I'v bored you stiff again.

      caio.

      <u>Dirk.</u>

To Penelope Mortimer   *Clermont*
September 7th. '74. After lunch.

They have all gone at last. The summer really seems to be over. After all; it starts here in April .... and staggers on through the heat and the vine-shadows and clinking ice in glasses, dragging with it various people who seem to become part of ones life for a few weeks .... all running-into-each-other, as it were. A sort of blur of faces and laughter, and odours of old sun oil and Pastis.

For the last two weeks this house has been a clutter of sandy bathingsuits, towels with lumps of tar smeared across their anchors and capstans patterns, half eaten apples, empty packets of Rowantrees

---

1. J. R. Ackerley's 1968 memoir, published by The Bodley Head.
2. The barrister and playwright John Mortimer, PM's second husband.
3. Annie Girardot, Brigitte Bardot, Monica Vitti.

Clear Gums, record sleeves scattered about the rooms like old, and very tatty, confette ... covered with dirty faces and repellant names like 'The Prudent Nuns Group' or 'Blazing Hot With Kung Fung Ho.' Or something.[1]

[...] It tired me. But, worse than that, it shattered any illusions I ever had that YOUTH was fun, interesting and alive. Whats happened to them all? Draped in poor copies of Carol Lombard from Biba, listning only to the dreary throb of electric Guitars and boys with spotty faces and Neasden-Negro-Voices .... no one had <u>heard</u> of Pavlova ... or Cyprus, or Toulouse Lautrec, or Pipperade, or pickled mushrooms, or .. oh, sweet God ... anything.

However they'v gone. And thats why I'm so long in replying to your long, lovely, too humble, letter of the 24th. And the N.Y. Magazine .... which I <u>loved</u>. The story[2] I mean, and hope you got jolly well paid for it. [...] It sounds a titchy bit like Garlands Weaving Place ... even if you pretend it does'nt. Or is'nt. But then I begin to think that America must be all a bit like that ... The verdegris rot of California on one side .... the gleaming Colonial-Tidiness of the East Coast. All those ghastly little trees on Long Island ... the Freeways ... the bits of rock I feel sure they 'imported' to landscape the Fall Colors .... and in the very middle a sort of Squash of Yaddos and wheatlands and red Barns and Grandma Moses and elms in picket fences ..... I could'nt live there. God no. Nor could I die there. Thats one of my most uncomfortable nightmares. I dont honestly think that I could even bear to go back there ... it was bearable as long as I knew that the 'Queen Mary' or 'Elizabeth' or 'The France' or even the elderly 'Mauretania' was moored, weekly, off that benighted coastline ... but now.

And tomorrow, I believe, Evil Kneival (or something)[3] does a jump across the Canyon. Oh what a debased land it is. I cant believe that it was better before the 1880's before the center of Europe burst it's seams like a rotting bag, and hurled all those debased rag-pickers into the Free World. But perhaps it was better. I dont know. And have no real way of telling. But it is a very aquired taste I feel ... like Fernet Branca or Tripes a La Mode or salt with your porridge. Is'nt it? Or does one settle down there? I know people do. I have a dotty, and very, very,

---

1. The residue of young visitors.
2. PM's 'A Love Story' had been published by *The New Yorker* on 15 July.
3. Evel Knievel, the daredevil motorcyclist.

English cousin who went to L.A twenty years ago and got a job mending china for a couple of Queer Antique Gentlemen (Is there any other kind, I ask?) ... now in San Fransisco and adoring it all, she is the happiest of mortals and still desperatly English but utterly adjusted and has only come 'home' as she calls it once, and then to see the source of the Thames before 'they moved it away' ..... So if Maureen can do it ... I suppose it is possible.

[...] Of course you are right, sort-of, about me being 'only an actor' ... but we do have to use some of our experiences of life, just as you do, to 'write' our people. I mean Pinter does a great deal to make a person ... but it is up to the actor to flesh that person out with his own inner experience, his own knowledge of pain, of joy, or of despair. Sometimes and it happens so often, there is not even a 'shape' written by the writer to flesh out .... So we have to use all our old experiences to make the most impact. To move an audience, to disturbe, to hurt sometimes .... this is often NOT done by the playwrite .... the actor does it himself. So the idea of 'wearing a sort of suit' does'nt always work out. You get some damn drear 'clothes' that way. 'Death In Venice' was a good suit ... but had to be filled with my body ... or rather Aschenbachs body ... and I had to feed an audience all the essences of pain through LONLINESS that I could muster. The fact that I might have succeeded in some part was the way that younger people got the lonliness in one go. And were smashed that Aschenbach was having it too. It was the recognition of lonliness, and apartness, which won that film an audience of young people. An extraordinary experience was to watch it with a full house here in Cannes, for example; there were 3,000 people in the place. At the moment when Aschenbach decides, at the railway station, to return to the Lido .... a look and a timid smile only, 3,000 people stood up and cheered and cheered and applauded. Visconti and I were quite shattered. And very silent and very respectful. But we knew that together we had worked. Not Thomas Mann.

[. . .] I was thinking in bed the other night about starting something ... I dont write for only pleasure or luxury. It is also a dire necessity to me. I always have done ... published poet, I'll have you know ... Times Lit. Poetry Today and some anthologies yet! And not to mention all those fucking scripts ... however in bed I was thinking How To Start.

And I invented a slightly alcaholic sister for your Mrs B. And brought them back to one or others flat in Queens Gate after a cremation of a long-ago-school-friend at Golders Green. Widows, I suppose, Rose Lover with Canasta Lover ... or maybe she writes cookery books like nice Elizabeth David .... and then I got rather interested in the school-friend. Was it a she? Or could it have been a He? And when do we find out ... how long will it take to talk about someone without giving the sex away.

Oh dear God! What in the name of hell am I doing. Chattering at my plots for you? I thought it might have been fun if we had both used the same premise and seen what happened. Nothing I suppose. I think, actually, it sounds like a bad first act by Rattigan. Or even the Unspeakable Waugh. Enough. I'm sorry.

Later –

Sweet Christ! What a ghastly long drivel-thing. You said of your letter that it said something with every appearance of nothing. Quite untrue ... I mean, not untrue, but, oh shit .... anyway THIS load of old cobblers really says Nothing with every appearance of Something.

I'd better chuck it. I'v done the dogs dinner. Meat and last nights pasta ... fed them. Next is the Typhoo tea tips and flies-cemetary biscuits. And then it's the bit on the terrace; watering the starting-to-get-shabby pots. The day is golden and still. I can see the little white prick of Antibes Lighthouse right through the olives. The sea is like a blue tin tray.

By the way, when I did my Dover bit[1] I was'nt entirely, that is physically, alone. No. You are different there naturally. But I was alone inside. And it stayed like that for rather a long time. I mean the alone-inside bit. After all I was just fifty. Very settled in a pleasant English Life. Family and friends and safety all about me. Servants and dogs and horses and my onions to harvest and my Sweet peas to dig trenches for and nothing much to trouble me. I was different of course. But I realised that if I stayed comfortably like that I would be done and finished. And that a new life had to be made. The old one not just made-over, but chucked, completely ..... and started anew. Cold and frightning with no tongue save Sloan Square English. And fucking lonely mate too .... and in the move I fear a lot of the sweet Chums went down the plug hole with, as they say, the bathwater. And that all

---

1. An earlier letter, not printed here, referred to Dirk's departure from Britain in 1969 without mentioning Tony.

had to be reckoned with. Strangely, and one cannot see why it should matter, one has still not been forgiven.

[...] I'm off. I'v been terribly irritating. I cant write at all. But one thing I sure as Hell cant do is to write economically. I use words like a diarohea case uses paper ... rolls of it .... anyway: there we are. You in Yaddo in the under-water light (it seems) of your room ... the lilly pool ... the dull brasses ... the Dijon Mustard on pseudo-Gruyere. Ah! Maybe THATS what America seems like to me. Dijon Mustard on pseud-Gruyere. And it wont do at all, dear.

Off to do the Typhoo tips ... and the un-pseud Flies Cemeteries.
I really must try and spell one day.

Losey was up here last week for dinner with his vast son of 18. He said that he still liked me even though I used the worst grammer and wrote the worst spelling he had ever seen or ever heard. And I was really rather pleased. I mean that he still liked me inspite of that.

But I must try.

Dirk

The Great Dane[1] went back to England and died, happily, in Angmering On Sea at my sisters. Rome, and the heat, and a longing for England drove her away. But I stayed on. Still.

To the Loseys   *Clermont*
                                    3 November 1974

Dearest Joe & Patricia –

No; we never got to meet.[2] I never saw the splendours of your much envied sitting room or Studio. Or basement. And I did miss you. [...] I thought of you a lot, as you may well imagine ... but there really was not a great deal of time eventually. I have never worked so hard in my fucking life for a Film. I had hoped to be there only for two days and skip quietly off ... but after the disaster of the N.Y. Press I realised that I had to stay on and 'fight' for my two women .. Lilly and Charlotte. Both utterly destroyed by the N.Y bit ... and punchy with hate and bitterness.

1. Candy was not a Great Dane, but a mastiff. She never left England.
2. Dirk had been to London to promote *The Night Porter*, which had finally secured a UK release.

No way to handle a Press Deal in London! Anyway I stayed there with Flu and an abscess and had a ball. In so far as I did twelve interviews a day ... Radio, Telly and God alone knows what else. After ten years away from that kind of exposure I was a bit scared. However my personal reception at the Press Lunch was so moving and genuine that I got the courage to battle through and thoroughly enjoyed it! I have never had so much cover .. and sincerely doubt if a film has! God knows what I was on about ... but it seemed to work. And the Telly ... an hour each time ... was super. I think that might be my new career[1] ... except the lolly is lousy and the movies are a tiny bit more fun. If more effort.

So far 'Porter' has grossed four million bucks in Italy and just about as much in France. The N.Y. bit is so far smashing ... and we have broken all the records in London. And now the scripts are flopping in like dead leaves. And read like them too .... my money is superbely high. If I can get it! And the Zurlinei film[2] folded in Rome as I pulled out .... which makes me sad on the one hand for him and delighted, child like, for me on the other! To topple a 5 mill. Production (dollars) seems to me to be almost SampsonLike in it's splendour .....

[...] We are off to Vienna at the beginning of the year .... a simple Thriller[3] with CIA over tones .. undertones? Anyway. No problems. Simple Kids Stuff. I have HAD the Polemic and the sexuality and the Messages. All I want is to chase someone in a fast car with a revolver. And thats just what I'm going to do. A 'straight' Gabriel[4] ... for rather a lot of money. After that it appears that I dont stop until November. Next. Where did all my strong resoloutions go? The October War[5] dealt THEM a blow, love. Simone for supper last night [...] clutching a script in blank verse about (another) boys school and a teacher. I got her pissed and sent her home to the Colombe. With the script.

Had flu and an abscess all week .. and we have a mail strike ... hence the delay in writing to you .. to thank you for your wire ...

1. It was, but not in the way he imagined. The interview with Russell Harty broadcast on 25 October opened the door to Dirk's new life as an author.
2. *The Investigation*, which was to have been directed by Valerio Zurlini.
3. *Permission to Kill* (working title *Kickback*), to be directed by Cyril Frankel, with Ava Gardner.
4. Dirk's high-camp character in *Modesty Blaise*.
5. The Yom Kippur War.

and to tell you that I shall be on the 'set'[1] on the 24th and expect to be treted like an Emperor. Or something. [...]

I love you very much ... be careful of your knee and Mrs Losey ... and get the pizza ready for the 24th.

Does Pamela[2] eat Pizza I wonder? Perhaps I'll make her a cheese Sandwich. She liked them on 'Accident'.

Dirk –

Saw 'The Servant' on Telly. What a SMASHING movie it is. D.

After Dirk's interview with Russell Harty, Norah Smallwood instructed one of her senior editorial colleagues at Chatto & Windus, John Charlton, to ask Dirk whether he had ever considered writing about his life.

To John Charlton   Clermont
                                                6 December 1974

Dear Mr Charlton

I am terribly sorry for the delay in replying to your very kind letter of November the 1st. It arrived at the Connaught after I had got home here to a seven week Mail Strike, So I only finally recieved it today! Sorry. I do hope that you understood the situation. I must confess that I did'nt know it would be so bad .... seven weeks is a hell of a long time stuck up on a hillside without mail or telephones.

Anyway: it was kind, indeed, of you to speak, write, so warmly of the Television thing ... I suppose it was the Russel Harty one? I did so much that week that I felt as overexposed as a blank negative.

The facts are these. I am writing a series of Essays, if one can call them that, on some of the odder highlights during my career ... part of which I did use on the Russel Hary thing ... there are VAST problems about libel, of course, it is quite useless to try and fake this stuff ... it does'nt work. So I get a bit hung up from time to time with worry! Ken Tynan said 'write it and let the Publishers worry ..' well .... I dont know. Anyway I am going on with it slowly, and without much incentive. I <u>do</u> feel that books by Film Stars are beastly boring ... and the few recent ones which have thudded onto the market

---

1. Losey would be on location in Villefranche for *The Romantic Englishwoman*.
2. Pamela Davies, responsible for continuity on many Losey films.

prove my point. I am not a David Niven .... so that is out ... and I truthfully feel that what I have to say has all been said before and usually better. However if you want to discuss it I'd be delighted but I dont think anything I have to say is really much cop.

This is simply to answer your charming note as soon as possible so that you wont think that bad manners are also a part of my work ....

I shall be here until the end of the year ... then Vienna until mid March.

Yours sincerely
Dirk Bogarde.

To Dilys Powell   *Clermont*
                                                        6 January 1975

So thats¹ where you have been. I wondered rather. I always feel a titch bit uncomfortable when I see that Prouse is at it and not you.

Did you care for India I wonder? I had two years² there in the War. I quite liked it. Quite. Beautiful beyond description ... Agra and even dreadful Calcutta ... and the Taj Mahal is'nt REALLY like a biscuit tin as Noël always swore it was .... however eventually I was happy to leave it and go south to Java and Bali and Borneo. I rather hated the Raj bit, which still fitfully operated while I was there, and found, at twenty three, the poverty and the lepers and so on difficult to manage after a sheltered life in green, contented Sussex.

I have just stripped off the Christmas tree. A job I detest almost as much as dressing the bloody thing. Another year over .. another Christmas. A god-son plus devine young wife and eleven month old baby.³ Not so devine, for two weeks. Quand meme. And then a strange assortment of people for lunches and dinners and even blasted tea, with crumpets and English Christmas cake imported from Richmond, Surrey, for some reason. The French find it rather delightful. I cant think why. I cut millions of cucumber sandwiches and they ate them all up as if they had been caviar. However; I grumble. Not really. I just

1. The Delhi Festival; Derek Prouse had reviewed the films for *The Sunday Times* in her absence.
2. In truth, four months.
3. Tony's son, Gareth, with his wife Véronique and the infant Thomas Forwood.

have to cope without all those super servants of ones past. And if it had'nt been for the washing machine and a great deal of Persil I think I'd have gone spare before the endless weeks were over.

Tomorrow I leave for Vienna until March. A daunting situation. I hate leaving here. I hate leaving the dogs and things, and I hate the idea of flogging, yet again, through another Movie. This time, however, it is a nonsense movie. Nothing at all cereberal here. A dull, if long, part ... so that I shall not 'do too much'[1] .... and with Ava Gardner who is very dear and better than one would think as an actress ... and sundry others. I adore Vienna and really decided to do the film for that reason. It is being made entirely in the city and on the Lake at Gmunden. And financed totally by the Austrian Treasury. So that cant be too bad, can it? And since the October War one is not sitting back with the pittance saved from the past. Now I have to work again for my living ... which is something I had firmly decided not to do again in the Cinema of today. However, my dearest Dilys, all good plans end in compromise I find. So I start a sort of Thriller .... instead of doing 'Coeur de Chien'[2] ... or 'L'Histoir d'O'[3], both of which I was begged to do. I just feel like having a bit of a lark after NP. I CANT go on explaining about the films I make. This time I have simply had to rattle, very pleasurably, through Le Carrier's latest book instead of bashing away at dossiers on Prison Camps and the life histories of Himmler and Heydrich. MUCH easier! 'Coeur' might have been fun, but the prospect of ten weeks with a talking dog rather put me off! Working with children is a total delight ... but working with trained dogs or cats or any other beast is horrid. And they usually treat them quite dreadfully which makes me wildly angry and causes 'unpleasantness' on the set. So better I'm out and Von Sidow (I cant spell that at all!)[4] in. I think he'll be excellent while I camp away in snow boots up the length of the Kartnerstrasser and back .....

I am so glad that you are working hard and that you feel 'fractionally' better for doing so. It really is, I fear, the only cure ... one does get immersed, one does meet new people, and one does start new memories again. Splendid.

---

1. In her review of *The Serpent*, DP had noted: ' ... that fine actor Dirk Bogarde, given too little to do, is understandably inclined to do too much with it.'
2. *Cuore di cane*, directed by Alberto Lattuada.
3. *L'histoire d'O*, directed by Just Jaeckin and now regarded as an erotic classic.
4. Not bad: Max von Sydow.

Well .... I'm off. I have just seen the blasted Christmas cards still huddle unseasonably in a corner. This is sixth night .. or twelfth night I mean, so I had better have them down. My sister always said it means bad luck ... and I dont want that at this moment.

Always my love to you ... as you know ...

perhaps you'd like to come to Vienna? Snow and wine and some excellent Opera. I'll be at the Bristol Hotel if you make a wild decision. Of course you wont. But you could.

I do love you very much ...

<u>Dirk</u>.

To Dilys Powell   *Clermont*
                                        27 March 1975

Dearest Dilys —

Home I am since two weeks today. Sweetpeas tumble in wanton, fat, bundles ... tulips and anenomies (cant spell THEM!) and forget-menots and wallflowers ... and the first leaves on the waterlillies uncurling like little crimson handkerchiefs .... Pear, apples and the pomegranit in blossom. Odd after the ice of Gmunden and Vienna .. the stark trees the forced bunches of quick-to-wilt daffodils ... the everlasting pine trees and the feeling of the East so near. I got a bit pissed off with Vienna after eight weeks ... the constant bottled cabbage, sausages, bits of veal and the interminable Goulash with gherkins .... simply no fresh vegetabls anywhere. I cant think why. And the prices so high they made one cry in disbelief. So getting into my fat Air Austria plane was really a bit of a relief. I felt a titch bit guilty, for I have worked often in Vienna and DID love it very much. But perhaps I was younger ... and it was usually in summer or spring and not in the darkest months of the winter. However: the film was fun. Really. Freddy Young[1] lighting: a glorious professional of seventy four ... delicious, loving, adorable man. Ava G. was in fine form ... Dom Perignon at five am at the make-up session ... but warm, funny, and GOOD too! And suddenly decided that she got a kick out of acting for the first time. Which is a help.

She really is the last of the Great Stars. And it shows. Her work on the screen may not be up to the standards of, say, Miss Garbo ... or

---

1. Freddie Young, multiple-Oscar-winning cinematographer.

Ethel Barrymore! But none the less she is, by God, THERE! And is
still incredibly beautiful ... really a face of quite glorious planes, and
eyes so green that the lakes were dimmed by her. Enough of that. But
she was splendid to work with. It was almost like the Old Days of the
Cinema and so old fashioned, my dear, that it is almost classical today!
You know; the Master Shot and then the two Over The Shoulders bit
.... funny. A long way from Visconti and Losey and the beloved
under-rated Clayton. But fun actually. And for this idiot picture full
of C.I.A and bombs and chases through the airports .... that sort of
thing ... excellent. Yes I enjoyed it. Far more than 'Porter' and nearly
as much as 'Venice'! We'll see.

Sadly .. and for your private ear only, I have had, this week, to
decline the new Cavani script. God knows what will happen now ...
I also declined Histoir d'O as you know ... but I simply will not
engage in any more films where people piss into chamber pots, bugger
little boys in Railway Lavatories, or indulge in Threesome sex situations. I'm not shocked by any of this. God knows. But bored ridgid.
Or rigid ... thats the word. And if Nietzsche WAS as hoplessley
sexually disorientated, vomited so often, and made long and dreary
speeches which make, to me at any rate, no sense at all ... then he
must have been pretty dull as a chap. And where therefore the Glory
we hear so much about. Or do we.

Oh dear. It's all very complicated indeed. And sad for Lilliana I
fear. But she really must get these things out of her system. In some
ways she is a sort of Moravia thirty five years too late. And that
wont do. I think, if I must, and it seems that I must, work I'd be
better 'going back' to the jollier subjects. I adored 'Thats Entertainment'[1] here in Cannes last week ... and long, before I am too
old, to dance along a black glass floor with an ebony cane ... or
better still splash about in a rainy street. Oh goodness! What a
super perfect piece of total cinema that scene is, is'nt it? I was
curious, and delighted, by your sane and sensible, I feel sure,
reaction to the new Bogdanovitch[2] ... I long for it to come here.
I think I'll feel the same as you did.

Christ! That reminds me of the Festival soon. Utter misery of that
apart from loving chums desperate to get up here for a breather. Losey

---

1. A compilation of scenes from MGM musicals, including *Singing in the Rain*.
2. Peter Bogdanovich's *At Long Last Love*.

has two[1] this year! On the Same day too. Galelio[2] .... or however the
paper spelled it! and the 'Englishwoman' thing. So I shall have to be
in attendance for those I fear. I long to see the Brecht .. he thinks it's
the best film he's ever made. Topol included. Well ... Joe is frail
sometimes ... as we know. He seems to detest the other Epic ... and
does'nt care WHO sees it. Of course it might just turn out to be
super. You never can tell!

How good that your walls are no longer bare.[3] It's a loathsome
feeling ... waiting for the pickers to pick ... and then put back the
remainder. I had to do it a couple of years ago when my adored Pappa
died. Splitting the loot among the children. His papers and books and
diaries ... his silly little personal things cluttering up the drawers of
his desk ... hopeless feeling. Not even time for lumps in the throat.
The end of something. So desperatly final. Ah well .....

India. Yes. To be avoided. Except for lovely Jaipur and green parrots
in the trees ... and bowling along the Calcutta Trunk ... a gloriously
romantic name for a main road I always think. But the rest; the Society
.. the corruption ... the poverty .. the babies in the rubbish bins
along Connaught Circus. Difficult to come to terms with.

I'v gone on far too long ..... so I'll stop now. I fear, so often, that
I bore you ... or, worse still, put you under a feeling of obligation.
There is none, as you know. But I am a shy-child ... and someones
love, unasked for, can be irksome.

I'm off to plant out some pots for the terrace ... and paint a bit of
fence ... and potter about a bit.

With my devoted love
Dirk.

To Dilys Powell   *Clermont*
                                                        24 May 1975

Dilys my dear –
The Festival ended on Friday night when a youth chucked a bomb
at the Casino, blew himself up, and destroyed a resturant and the

---

1. *Galileo* and *The Romantic Englishwoman*.
2. In DP's *Sunday Times* review it was printed as *Galielo*.
3. Leonard Russell, DP's second husband, had asked her to give some of his pictures to friends.

lobby of the swank Ambassadeurs. He stated, in a note found, that he detested 'all Capitalists everywhere, and Hitler is back' ..... after attending two or three of the damned things one almost saw his demented point of view. What a business. What a sorry spectacle of ugly, sweating, over-dressed and jewelled people. I find it constantly depressing. Only this time I HAD to go down because of Losey who, grumbling to the last, had two films entered and out of a sense of loyalty, misplaced I fear! One went. And to Schlesingers thing.[1] Otherwise I saw very little of anything or anyone else. Loseys stuff is rather dissapointing I felt. 'English-Woman' is particularly sad. A remake of a sort of sub-'Accident' filled with mirror shots and staircases and overdecoration. And two pretty grim performances too I thought. The reception was down ... but they are very loyal to Losey here ... and he has had some rave reviews from the Intellectual Press which made him jolly happy. The Topol thing[2] was much better I thought ... except for Topol .... not bad but not right. One sees Laughton all the time. One cant. But one wishes one could. It was shown without sub-titles so the French were a bit lost and it was hardly noticed. Schlesingers film split everyone in two camps. The Haters and the Lovers. The Americans, sensitive, a little, to Siagon, were furious at the attack on their life .... the French thought it self-indulgent .... which it is ... but why not?

John just shrugged, and started plans for his next film in America and a new play at the National! Young enough not to care so much what anyone in this beastly town really thought.

Apart from that I had a run of 'refugees' up for meals ... a good deal of the laying of tables and washing up went on ... and putting new paper in the Loo and filling ice buckets ... but I'd do anything rather than go 'down' there. My new Producers, very young and keen and intilligent, came up to discus the Resnais subject .. to now be called, 'Providence' as a working Title.[3] I think, but am not positive until the contract is signed, that I have got Ellen Burstien[4] for my leading lady. Which makes me happy: I think. Better than [Liv] Ullman who seems not to 'transplant' very well from Bergman. I was

---

1. *The Day of the Locust* – like the two Loseys, shown 'out of competition'.
2. *Galileo.*
3. From a script by David Mercer.
4. Ellen Burstyn, who was starring in the Broadway hit *Same Time, Next Year*.

assured by a Lady from the New York Times that Burstein is a 'cow and a bitch and a hogger. You'll HATE her. And she crowds the screen and she's SO tall!'. Which filled me with awe and a certain misgiving.

Having chosen her myself, Alain went to N.Y to see her play, was totally captivated by her work, and asked her to join us. She has said yes with great enthusiasm and we hope the Agents and things will agree. What a rum profession this really is!

For your shell-like ears only. Or eyes, rather. No. Ones eyes cant be Shell like, can they? Sapphire?

For the moment peace reigns on this hill. The planes are all jammed today with the last of the Festival Group ... like the swallows in October who stay just a little too long .... and normalicy returns to Cannes and the telephone. Well .. practically.

Now I can get back to the scything of the meadows ... I hate this job at my age and in the heat ... and the ruthless weeding up of brambles and nettles which seem to spring from beneath ones feet as one walks. It is a bursting time ... June and May here. Everything rushes to a great tossing, green, foaming head .... and then July burns it all away ... and August turns it to a dusty, brown and red, desert. But the spring .. like the spring and early summer in Cyprus .. blazes. And must be coped with.

So I'm off to my little Arab .. who I see sitting in the shade of the well eating sardins with his fingers from a tin and swigging away at a jar of water.

My love ....
<u>Dirk</u> XXX

To Kathleen Tynan   *Clermont*
                                                19 June 1975

Dearest Kathleen –

I have a stinking cold and feel grumpy as hell.

We have had 'Vogue' and someone from Conde Nast (?) shooting the house, and me, for five sodding days. And they brought the cold all the way from sunny London. So I'm not exactly joyful. They left yesterday to go to St Trop to shoot someone else ... and I was jolly glad.

'Your Room' seems not to have been empty since the blasted old Festival .. and I'm wearing of emptying ashtrays, refilling the lavatory paper things, changing sheets and planning food. Young photographers seem to eat constantly .. ice cream and fresh strawberries and more ice cream and more strawberries .... and the place is covered in old Kodak packets, spent flash bulbs and oil marks, for some reason, all over your new white carpet. However, if you do come down to the Yacht in August, I'll have it cleaned ... or spray the bed, or something.

Today we have a rest before tomorrow, when Daph Fielding arrives for her trip .... and after that Family with tents on the lower terraces, guitars, pot, and the demented wails of Bob Dylan being 'Folk'. Oh well.

Glad my letter did'nt irritate you. I worried lest it should .. and that I was taking it all too seriously ... but I do happen to love you very much ... as I reckon even you have grown to realise ... and it seemed important to me to deal with your book[1] at length. I was just worried that really it was all a bit long ... my letter ... anyway at least you gathered it was loving. And how.

Charlotte is too full of angles. She has no curves. Marina has. I feel essentially .... Charlotte is also very male. Marina, it seemed to me, was utterly not. Marisa [Berenson] I have known since she was eight ... and liked, enormously, working with her .. but she is a terribly superficial sort of child .... anyone who can hang about with Berger and that faux Jet-Set-Blow-Up-Set has to be ... she is not at all my idea of your lady .... also she is as tall as the Piltdown Man[2] .... with about as big a head. Have you ever seen A. Calder Marshall? a 'lady' and, I think beautiful, and very, very clever .... not yet a Star, I suppose, but does that matter? A. stands for Anna. And I bet youve seen her and hated her ... but I know she is excellent. And feminine .... I'm not being much help ... oh dear!

The Resnais film fills me with awe ... and delight in equal amounts. It is not often one gets a film written especially for one but it is a bit daunting. And New England in winter seems to be a bit remote from just where I sit now ... but if you were there at the time that'ud be super. After you alienating the Director[3] of course. We must go on as

---

1. KT's novel, *The Summer Aeroplane*, was published in April. She sought Dirk's advice on casting the character of Marina for a projected film adaptation. Dirk's previous letter has not survived.

2. Evidently a confusion with the Long Man of Wilmington, the Downland figure in chalk near the Van den Bogaerdes' holiday cottage at Lullington.

3. A reference to KT's *Vogue* article on *Death in Venice* and Visconti's reaction.

we start, must'nt we . . . end of page but never end of love . . . .
Next day. Feeling less grotty.
That was a dreary letter I wrote yesterday . . . but I'm not going to re-
write it . . . just add a bit, because re-reading yours made me laugh
so much about Zetterling and your bloke. She IS a wild lady . . . and
terribly good at whips I hear. Her last husband finally slunk off to an
island with a gentle creature and she lives all alone, for the moment,
in a large ruin near Uzès with cows, goats, and a donkey. She nearly
killed a house guest once by leaving a ciggie burning in an armchair . . .
she really is as full of jollity as a cobra. And I do, actually, like the
silly bitch. I'v known her since she first came to England . . a little waif
with no tongue save her native Lap . . . and wide eyes and slim legs . . .
then we did Anhoile[1] together and got very involved. But I ducked. Ken
will have one hell of a job . . . but she is TERRIBLY bright at her job
. . . and her film on Van Gogh[2] was spiffing, I thought . . . was'nt so keen
on her Olympic efforr,[3] but that was different and less exciting for her.
And oddly enough I feel it might work. She and he – I mean –
    Except for the clash of ego and will which <u>will</u> go on . . . . but thats
not my saga.
    After I had finished writing your rotten letter yesterday, and was
sitting sulking under the blasted vine (We had a ghastly hot mistral
the day before and everything is burned to a crisp . .) the telephone
rang and I found that I had agreed to be in the film Attenborough is
making of the battle of Arnhem. I must be mad. I was there in fact
from the 2[o]th of Sept until the 23rd of Dec . . . and got wet, shit
scared, cold and hungry and recieved a lasting loathing of bridges and
rivers . . . . so what the hell I am doing at fifty four re-doing something
I was <u>forced</u> to do at twenty four leaves me bewildered somewhat.
    Anyway it means a bit of loot, and all kinds of jolly people are
saying 'yes' . . . like Steve McQ. & Shaun, or Sean, and Newman and
rotten old Redford[4] and so on . . . it's costing millions and may well
be the last Epic ever to be made! I have a sneaking feeling that it will
be . . before the last, or next, real one comes along. So one might as

1. Jean Anouilh's *Point of Departure*. The Swedish actress was involved in an unrealised
project with Kenneth Tynan.
2. *Vincent the Dutchman* (*Omnibus*, BBC, 1972).
3. *Visions of Eight – The Strongest*.
4. In the event Steve McQueen and Paul Newman said no; Sean Connery and Robert
Redford, yes.

well have a go, providing we are not all in some Camp somewhere being re-educated by your husbands Beautiful People .. which does'nt at all seem as remote as once it did. Now that I live in the Mediterranean Area I am a little more aware of the shadows lengthening than ever I was in Crowborough Heath . . . .

Well: Daph will be arriving shortly from Paris . . . and I'll have to go and lay up the table and put her roses in your room . . . and put on my Talking-Attractivly-to-Guests-Face. I have just missed having to do a 'great in-depth' thing for the Sunday Observer, we have lost the gentleman who was supposed to come along with his note book . . . so thats very super. I already have a wadge in something called Nova next month . . . and enough is as good as a feast. What more, I ask you, is there to be said about 'My Extraordinary Recod Of 30 Years'? Nothing. Except that, by the elastic of my knickers, I'm still here . . . . and that is simply a case of Survival. Nothing else really. Except confidence. And perhaps a little conciet?

Anyway . . . I'll piss off now. Leaving you with the simple suggestion that Charlotte is too angular .. is all angles and planes and no curves or rounds .. Marisa is like the Piltdown Man . . . and A. Calder Marshall is, as far as I am concerned, lovely and clever . . . though, of course, not a bit like you. If you, incidentally, got David put together a bit more, dont you think D. Sutherland would be excellent? He's splendid in the Schlesinger film[1] . . . he looks a bit weird in life, long fairish hair and lots of Celtic crosses round his neck with Lanvin suits . . . but he's excellent with his hair cut .. and there is also always my beloved Julie Christie? What about her. Much better than any of the others . . . and the nearest, in life, to Marina – Aim high – why not? If you aim low you only get the mud – not the Stars!

On that bit of profundity I'll leave you – gasping no doubt, but I hope filled with my affection?

Love

Dirk

P.S. What a super read one is having about the Lucan business[2] – a relief from Portugal. Poor fellow – what a Very Nasty Lady She is! D.

---

1. Donald Sutherland starred in *The Day of the Locust*.
2. An inquest was determining how the nanny to the family of the 7th Earl and the Countess of Lucan had died. Portugal was in political turmoil.

For some while Dirk had been estranged from his brother Gareth, the younger by twelve years; but at the end of June the latter, with his wife Lucilla, stayed for three nights at Clermont. On the day of their departure Dirk wrote to say: 'I regret very much the wasted years' and hoped that Gareth's five children would help to 'form us into a unit of a sort. Even if we have to be all lumped under the title of "The Bloody Bogaerds"!' On 20 July, Brock Van den Bogaerde, the sixteen-year-old second son, arrived at Clermont, his tent on his back, en route to family friends at Ramatuelle. Dirk walked down through the garden to meet him and said: 'You can pitch that there.' Brock replied: 'Haven't you got a room?' It was the start of a deep and lasting friendship both with his uncle and with Tony.

To Penelope Mortimer   *Clermont*
                                                  8 October 1975

No. No my darling frail-heart, you did'nt tell me about any sort of Accident[1] [...] What on earth happened? Well .... I dont REALLY want to know ... I mean about what did happen. But are you alright now? No; of course you are'nt. Why are you so WILLFUL and so totally boring. Goodness. I could strike you hard [...] I thought all was going supremely well, that Life had reached it's peak in the Suburbia Of America and that you were about to be happy. Well; happy for you that is. That is very badly punctuated. I mean happy for YOU in capital letters. Fuck what makes other people happy.

[...] Anyway ... now I sort of know. But did'nt. And I am writing terribly badly only because it is after luncheon and I had a good half bottle of champagne before. So.

Cool today. October reaches as far down south as here, and I rather hate it. All those bloody Fall colours and mist in the valley and the grapes going bad and the wasps drunk from the juices and lighting fires again. End of season. Loath it. Long for winter and the real cold and no nonsense about bare twigs and frost on the grass and the thin cold line of snow on the hill above me. That bit I dont mind. I hate this lingering farewell to Summer.

Like streamers and confetti at a sailing .... the ship slowly moving away and the pink and green and yellow paper ribbons parting slowly

---

1. PM had sustained a back injury from a motoring accident in April.

and swirling into the black water of the docks. Farewells prolonged are like death without euthenasia.

Before the hated Autumn arrived Alain arrived with Florence.[1] They came for a day from Garde Frenet where they were slumming away in [Jeanne] Moreau's house. He was looking very pale and terribly thin. Too thin .... I did'nt say anything. He spent the day eating peaches and wincing in pain from something he had 'done' to his leg by falling into a three meter ditch in the dark a few days before. Florence was in good form and pretty and eager. They brought lots of stills of perfectly hideous places which he has discovered in New Hampshire and Connecticut for the locations. He emphasised that he wanted a 'nowhere place' and by god, thats what he has found. I do see what he means, now, by having to trail all across the Atlantic instead of doing it all comfortably in Burgandy or East Grinstead or the Massif Central. New Hampshire is another world indeed. Half Arabic, half Burford, half nothing at all. So off we trail. Apparently not until the snows have melted ... April? It grows longer each time we speak. No script yet from Mercer[2] ... he is due to deliver this week. As I did not comprehend one single word of the Full Treatment do you think I'll understand a word of the written script? Is he so obtuse? Or is it me? Me. Most likely.

What of the rest of the summer [...] Well ... a sort of hotel for lost Brits and vague Americans ... and without staff a bore. But in some ways fun ... A mass of chums all the season, food and drink to get, beds to make and tables to lay. House And Gardens did the house from cellar to attic ... quite pretty [...] Then Vogue (Hommes) did me ... cover and five pages ... and one begins to wonder what else lovely age has in store? I did'nt do Histoir D'O, and lost three hundred thousand dollars for twelve days work ... but really got so up-tight with the script that I had to be grand. And cant afford not having that kind of loot ... but really: after 'Porter' enough is enough ... and I wont wag my private parts on anyones screen. Why should I?

Nursed the [Rex] Harrison Break Up. Never jolly. Always sad at that age too ... Nearly had Miss Davis for a week end .. remember thats where we came in? ... but she went to Spain instead .. opens

---

1. Resnais' wife, Florence Malraux.
2. David Mercer, writer of *Morgan – A Suitable Case for Treatment* (1966), had created the original screenplay for *Providence*.

tonight at Croydon and later at the Palladium in her Show. All Sold
Right Out since June. Lovely, lovely, for her . . . . and she looks postivly
smashing in the press. Even the English Press cant make her ordinary
like Marcia Wilson;[1] the Lady is bigger than life.

Went to stay, well to have lunch with, some rich Texans I dont
know but who do know a Cousin in San Fransisco, at their rented
house on Cap Ferrat. Dom Perignon and Orange Juice for breakfast
and Boarsin cheese on hamburgers. Three refrigerators making
nothing but ice cubes all day, and each child, there were ten, had a car
to itself and a large bus to take them to La Reserve where they dined
nightly in sneakers and tea shirts with 'Fuck Me I'm Gay' written on
the backs . . . and 'Fuck Me I'm Straight'. On the fronts. One wonders.

A nephew I had never met [. . . Brock] arrived with [. . .] a tent and
a water bottle, running shoes, hair down to his hips and a heavy accent
from Wandsworth Comprehensive. Sixteen. Six foot three. With a
copy of 'Private Lives' in his bum pocket. Idea being to erect the tent
for two days and borrow the loo. Idea never materialised. He stayed
three weeks . . . . and we had a ball. I had no idea that youth was so
much fun, so bright, so clever and so far in advance of what I ever was
at that age! I learned pretty quickly.

The 'Private Lives' bit was no bait to catch Uncle. He just adores
Gerties Voice and Noels and knew the record off by heart. So we set
to with 'Hay Feaver' and the rest and lots of records and he got totaly
smashed on 'A Chorous Line' and 'Chicago' and was last seen tap
dancing with Danny La Rue who has a house in the next village. And
who is, not surprisingly, a smashing gentleman [. . .]

I fear, and my poor brother fears, that RADA is probably the next
step . . . after he had got his O's and A's and been to Poland on a
Windjammer, which chore he starts today I gather. But it was fun . . .
and took care of three long weeks. Took him one day to luncheon at
Oonagh Oranmores at Cap D'Antibe . . . . 'We'll be just the family . .'
she cried on the phone, 'Do come and just as you are.' In jeans and
boots (It was pissing with rain) we set off.

A nineteen twenties luncheon party for thirty. On 'our own' my arse.
Butlers and maids, five courses; an ex-lover (queer) of Barbara Huttons,
his lover; Daphne Fielding in a chiffon poncho with sequin eye lids,

1. An odd conflation of the Prime Minister's wife, Mary Wilson, with his Private and
Political Secretary, Marcia Falkender.

all the Kindersleys from Lambourne dressed by Herbet Johnston, an
Indian Lady who wrote poetry and wore a sari and whome we all,
privatly hated and called Miss Bengaladash, and an Irish M.P who
hated the British and his wife who was so pissed at the Duck a l'Orange
Part, that she fell out of her chippendale onto the marble floor and
lay helpless while the footmen served the rest of the guests. It went on
until four, when everyone retired to the Saloon for coffee in silver
cups, and the Young Ones went and swam, in the rain, off the rocks,
dressed in lilac and yellow dressingowns. Brock . . . from Wandsworth,
was struck dead with silence . . . . and realised that Coward still lived
on in some of the wilder parts of the world !

And so the summer faded into the mellowness of todays October.
I am busy on 'my book' . . . Chatto and Thing want it . . . but seem to
become more and more silent with every new chapter. It's not about
the Cinema. About me and my sister in Sussex in 1930 . . . which
makes nostalgic reading for me but must make pretty icky reading for
Chatto who REALLY want another David Niven. Thankfully I am
not he. Him? So I expect the Slip any day now . . . however 70.000
words is quite good, is'nt it? Good for discipline anyway. When I
wrote to my old Nanny[1] and said that she was to be the star of the
story and that I was going to change all the names except her 'pet'
name, she wrote back from her Caravan at Steeple, and said that she
was very happy to hear the news, that it was about time I got away
from That Acting Business, and what else could I possibly call her
except her real name? 'I'm who I am, dear, whatever you do to change
me, I'm sure I'll come through all your fiction no matter what. So you
MUST use my name because I should'nt like to be fictionalised at all
after all those happy years: and after all I shall know.' So she's herself.
And that does'nt matter a whit to you . . . but it is fun for me . . . mind
you she may not be all that keen to be reminded that when she secretly
took us to see 'Rio Rita' at a Cinema (forbidden!) she threat[en]ed to
hit us on the head until we got a mastoid if we told anyone. No. She
might not care for that. But she said it. And it was not fictionalised at
all.

I have written too much bunk to you . . . you'll be reeling if you
have got this far . . . . I must go and do dogs dinners and logs and so

1. Ellen Searle (later, Holt), the redoubtable 'Lally', who would be the star of the first
half of Dirk's book, to be titled *A Postillion Struck by Lightning*.

on .... this is a luxury for me .. a bore for you ... Oh! Before I go. Losey called the other night from Paris. New Hampshire was Hell. Politically America had changed. He was lonely and misplaced. The kids did'nt know who he was and wanted to know how they did the effects in 'Jaws'. He has left London and is now in Paris ... could I find him a flat, house, villa? He was staying in Jean Marais apartment and it was purple velvet from wall to wall and ceiling to ceiling and he had a bad taste in paintings. Nothing changes, does it?

Have you seen the dreadful 'Romantic Englishwoman' with Glenda Sludge and Mike Myopic? Oh lor! .... nothing changes.

Dont write back. Just get well. And I'll come and see you with a Brie or pot of Paté or something .... I think you ought to come back to Europe.

I never really thought that you should have left .... .

Love
Dirk

A second appearance by Dirk on The Russell Harty Show, *to promote* Permission to Kill, *prompted Jack ('Tony') Jones to renew contact after many years. In a letter to a family member Dirk described the response printed here as 'cool'. He had, in today's jargon, moved on. With the exception of a single brief entry by Tony Forwood in the joint Diary, there is no trace of Jack Jones in Dirk's own archive.*

To Jack Jones   *Clermont*
                                                17 November 1975

Dear Jack —

I am terribly sorry that I was unable to call you while I was in London. Everything was tremendously hectic, as you can imagine, and I did not go down to see the family until the day before I returned, last Wednesday.

Your Telegram shocked me very much.[1] I had no idea, naturally, what had happened to you over these many years, but assumed that you were still comfortably installed at the Maltings[2] and that time had taken care of things generally.

---

1. Evidently a reference to JJ's increasingly poor health – the legacy of serious war wounds.
2. JJ's former home in Suffolk.

I seldome come to England now ... about three resentful times in ten years and so it is very easy to get completely out of touch. My father died three years ago, leaving a dreadful gap in our lives ... and then it was a matter of dealing with Mamma who is now happily, well .... happily enough ... installed in an hotel for Elderly people. The house now belongs to my brother in law .... and generally life has found itself quite altered.[1]

I am sad that you did not let me know what had happened to you, but then of course it was pretty hard for you to do so not knowing where I had got to. To be truthfull I did'nt know where I was until about 1969 ... travelling a good deal from one land to another and finally settling, very happily, in this old cottage high in the hills and a very long way from anyone else. I have practically severed all the old relationships with the Cinema in England, and work as seldome as I am able .... or as the French Tax Man allows.

I had had a cheering idea that I had saved enough to keep me going for a few years ... but like everyone else, the moment the bloody old Wogs crossed the canal[2] my slender savings dwindled to a very thin skin! And the death of Pappa caused a bit of a blow for he left nothing whatever to my Mother or, indeed, any of us! I cant imagine how he managed to keep himself and her for so long ... he was practically skint when he died, but had always told the children that he was 'perfectly alright!'. Which he jolly well was not.

So Mamma costs a bomb per week ... and I have now to go back to work again. I dislike it ... and am getting older and dont much care for the 'new face' I am forced to see on the screen ... however pride never gets anyone anywhere. So I better shut up. I'm off now to work in Italy until Febuary ... and then to America until June or July, which saddens me for I shall have to leave the land here to take care of its self .... and that it cannot do.

As I no longer have servants and gardeners and all that, it means just shutting the door and clearing off. The best laid plans of mice and men, they say ....

I have been back a week now from the hellish publicity business ... and the annual visit to the family. Which was pleasant but also

---

1. JJ was popular with the Van den Bogaerde family during his brief but intense relationship with Dirk.
2. A non-historian's reference to the Six-Day War (1967).

astonishing to see vast nephews and Neices and all kinds of stray kids littered about who seem, somehow, to belong to the family!

Do, if you can, let me know how things are. I am glad anyway that you are, as they say, happy.

I am sorry once again not to have called ... but there was not the time, and I am only now sorting out the log of unanswered letters and telegrams.

As ever
Dirk

To Dilys Powell   *Clermont*
                                                                26 November 1975

Dilys my dear –

How dear and kind of you. And HOW you reward me. I blush. But I am satisfied that you could see that I did try at least! Films like that, which are really efforts to assist, as in this case with 'Wein' Film, can be pretty groggy to do. The only thing one has to try is to give it every ounce of work and experience and try to make the obvious a little less obvious .... I always remember, years ago in Hollywood, on a film with the super Mr Cukor, leaving a room through two double doors ... all I had to do in the last shot before the lunch break. Cheerfully I crossed the great gilded room, opened the roccoco doors, and went into the 'hall', carefully closing the doors behind me.

Before anyone shouted 'cut' an hysterical voice shrieked 'What The Fuck Do You Think You Are Doing!'. Horrified I stuck my head into the room, camera still running, and faced an enraged, silent, glaring Cukor. I told him, humbly, what I was doing ... 'going out of the room, Mr Cukor.'

'Well for fucks sake make it INTERESTING!' ... he roared. And we re-shot. I never forgot. As I never forgot, in the early fifties, your perfectly valid complaint that I had never learned to 'command.' .... for both of you I have the greatest gratitude.

I stayed away from you, as you might realise, while I was in London recently to 'do' the publicity for this sad film ... and did 'chat' shows desperatly instead. But after Resnais ... an amazing, staggering, fearsome (for me) script by Mercer ... after Resnais I shall come and

---

1. *Permission to Kill* was made under the auspices of Austria's Wien Film.

see you, if I may .... we start shooting in Feb or March in nightmare-land which he has found in New Hampshire ... and I hope we shall be finished at the end of May.

Just off to the dentist, oh dear! I do so dislike lying flat on my back and having things 'done to me' .... and paying the bill afterwards!

Thank you my very dear, once again ...

With an ocean of love

<u>Dirk</u>

To Kathleen Tynan   *Clermont*
                                                28 December 1975

Dearest Kathleen –

I rushed you off a pretty predictable Impressionist Chrissy Card simply to say How Lovely about the film.[1] And now that the dust of this foul holiday session has somewhat settled, I want only to re-ieterate my pleasure. Unless, that is, it has folded, like so many others! Or unless, as is likely, you are a pale wraith lying in a darkened room after a shattering experience. Certainly the Set Up sounds rocky ... not to say bumpy ... but it would be glorious if you arrived at the end of it all as a sort of Lady Director! That really WOULD give me the greatest pleasure!

Actually, it is what you ought to be doing really ... with your beady eye and your swift assessment. And taste. However: it is a sodding job ... I would'nt do it for Brando's salary doubled.

The Mercer script is superb. Amazing, moving and totally, to me, incomprehensible! That is, I gather, what it is supposed to be .... it is a five-hander, Burstyn, Warner, Guilguid, Stritch and me. We start shooting, I hope to God, in New Hampshire on March 28th ... No! I lie! We WERE starting there but now we do the Paris Studio stuff first and New Thingummy in mid May. It is all so confusing I hardly know where I am. If you know what I mean. Ass from elbow sort of stuff [...] I ADORED Mr Mercer that day we met ... and find him as dear and warming and rich as a Teddy Bear. Which might seem odd to you but feels great to me. I mean I have to be frank with him and tell him that I dont know what the hell it is all about .. and he rather likes that ... because I dont think that HE really knows himself.

---

1. 'Trick or Treat' – a project duly abandoned after shooting had started.

It's all about a middle aged pre occupation with Death. As David is all of 44 I rather feel he is a bit ahead of Middle Age ... but there you are. I'm still struggling through lifes stormy waters at 55 looking for a raft or an Island.

Have'nt time for the Death pre occupation .... much too worried about the possibilities of a Change Of Life Saga which is supposed to smash one at this age of mine! After that ... Resnais and Mercer .. off, for a great deal of loot, to do a bit in Levine's Epic of Bang! Bang! Spot The Stars! about Arnhem ... a goodly company including Redford, Connery, Caine, [Gene] Hackman, Olivier, [Alan] Arkin, [Charles] Bronson ... well you KNOW the rest ... so it should be interesting if dull. And pay for the Resnais film as well!

We had a very solid middle-aged Christmas. I had a cold and washed out some sheets in the morning (Daily Lady on holiday for a month in Granada!) split logs in the afternoon, prepared the broccoli and potatoes for a small turkey T. insisted on buying for our Supper. It was more of a Moorhen than a Bird ... however it got stuffed and we ate it with me gasping and groaning and wallowing in Kleenex Man Size.

After that the fire, some Bendicks Mints, and Jean Renoir on the Telly and an early bed with Francis Donaldson.[1] How middle aged can one be? One wryly remembered together the staggering Christmases of Long Ago ... when eight servants flew about in white coats and Turkeys got carved for fifteen guests and trees were ladened with goodies from GTS, Peter Jones, Harrods, Halcyon Days and Orchids from Moyse[s] Stevens.

Fortunatly those days were had. Good they have gone!

I am staggering through My Book. 50.000 words at half time. New Part starting almost now [...] I had it all typed and corrected and that while I was in London by a nice lady in Hitchen[2] who said that she thought it was Very Good and Not Boring. She liked the last two chapters of the first half best. Perhaps I'm improving? But Shit! NOW I know what you went through ... research is lovely .. all those old books and maggers about 1931–32 .... names blazing into the present from the dusty pages of the past .... Ardath Cigarettes ... Binnie Hale ... Debenham And Freebodys ... Taxies with wire wheels ...

---

1. Frances Donaldson's *Edward VIII* (Weidenfeld & Nicolson, 1974).
2. Sally Betts, who would (re)type all but the last of Dirk's fifteen books.

Ralph Lynn ... Gunters ... and my first long pants from .. Burtons!
Ah well ... that part is fun, it's the putting it down on this sodding
machine I find the chore.

But I go on ... idiotically I suppose.

I must go and do something about lunch ... table to lay, potatoes
to peel ... that sort of thing. It does get in the way of 1931 terribly ...

Much, much love to you .. and great good fortune and happiness
in this next, curiously interesting, year!

Always my love
   Dirk

To Dilys Powell
(Postcard)

Limoges
13 *May 1976*

WELL – THE RESNAIS HAS STARTED. AND WITH IT THE
MAGIC, BECAUSE IT IS MAGIC: BACK, VERY MUCH, TO
THE 'MARIENBAD' STYLE. FRIGHTFULLY DEMANDING
INTELLECTUALLY AND PHYSICALLY! AND I HAVE
LITTLE OF EITHER THESE DAYS. BURSTYN DULL,
EXCELLENT, VERY 'METHOD' WHICH I FIND A LITTLE
TIRESOME – THE MOTIVATIONS OF RESNAIS DO NOT
BEAR DISCUSSIONS – AND MERCERS SCRIPT IS AS
COMPLEX AS 'THE TIMES' X-WORD. WITTIER POS-
SIBLY. JOHN G GLORIOUS – WARM, FUNNY, AND THRIL-
LED TO HAVE, AT LAST, HIS MOMENT-SUPREME IN THE
CINEMA. NO CAMEO, THIS! I ADORE RESNAIS – A
LITTLE SHADE OF MY ADORED MONSTER VISCONTI –
BUT ENTIRELY HIMSELF. STUBBORN, FIRM, JOYFUL,
PATIENT, BRILLIANT. IT COULD BE, MAY BE, PRE-
TENTIOUS CRAP – OTHERWISE SIMPLY HIS MAS-
TERPIECE. NOT BAD, REALLY. AS EVER, AS YOU KNOW,
MY LOVE. DIRK. XX.

*While Dirk and Tony were on location, Elizabeth and her family minded
the fort at Clermont. As on other occasions, her husband George brought
to bear his expertise in landscape gardening and tree surgery.*

---

1. On location for *Providence*. New Hampshire had been abandoned.

To Elizabeth Goodings   *La Chapelle St Martin*
                                           Par Nieul, Près Limoges
                                           [16] May 1976. Sunday.

My dearest Girl –

Another Sunday: another cold and wet and low-clouds and no sign
of a change. Goodness knows what happens next week ... we have
John G. coming back from London for eight days crucial work in the
gardens. A huge lunch party ... if it's dull we are finished! I dare not
contemplate it. Oh dear! This is a very odd count[r]y; some days
golden and hot, a few hours later freezing and foggy! Thats why
everything is so gloriously green and lush ... sheep everywhere, great
hedges, fat beech forests, rivers and streams and ponds ... it's so
beautiful, very like our old fashioned England before the war ... lots
of birds, frogs, and millions of beautiful wild flowers everywhere –
miles and miles of open countryside and neat little villages lost in
time. But oh! the damn weather. How I grumble. Yesterday we drove
down to a pleasant town called Uzeses [Uzerche] .... and had lunch
at the village hotel. Twenty years ago we stayed there with Ma and
Ully on our way to Spain to start the 'Spanish Gardner'. Had'nt
changed much ... red table cloths, little lamps and not too good
grub. Ully I remember liked the local wine, and dissapeared the next
morning JUST as we were about to start off for Barcelona ... the
longest haul of the trip ... looking for a special brand of cigarettes
which had not been made in France since 1917. We could have hit
him with a shovel. I found her[1] a p.c. of the pub and sent it off. She
wont remember, but might think she does ... anyway it was something
to say to her ... it is difficult to write to her as you know.

Today I have had to invite Ellen Burstyn and her friend Blossom
Plum (really her name!)[2] to lunch ... they are stuck in a beastly
modern hotel in the town, all plastic and nylon carpets, with a Telly
in the lounge bar and peeling paint. Their choice. They can call
America. From this hotel you can hardly call yourself. It depends who
is in the kitchen when you want to get through. And our nice little
girl, who was so pretty, fell down with an Epyleptic fit the other
morning and got carted off in a straight-jacket. Bought her some toilet

---

1. Their mother.
2. Not quite: Ellen Burstyn's companion was Blossom Plumb.

water yesterday ... but she was a bit brighter than the rest of the house. It's all very casually run by a young couple, very 'smart' ... she wears culottes and he wears a different half-belted jacket every evening and says that everything on the menu is 'Extraiordanary!' when it is mostly frozen or overcooked ... the house and furnishings are pretty ... but it is all a bit chi chi for me ... fresh flowers on the tables but no potatoes on the menue and too many sorts of sauces to disguise a bad chefs cooking ... anyway Burstyn better enjoy it. Later we might take them up the road to terrible Oradour.[1] They are both very full of 'progressivness and the moral language of Man' and all that crap. It might do them good to see just what man can do to man ... and only thirty years ago. I think Blossom will take a turn when she sees the village well into which they stuffed fifty of the men and boys that hot June day ... I said to Tote .. 'What'll we do if they come over queer and start sobbing?' and he said 'Let's sit in the car till we are ready. That'll teach them.' So perhaps we will! On the other hand they may be as saddened and moved as we were ... and now that I know all the story I act as a sort of guide. We have taken quite a few of the younger members of the Crew up there ... in their early twenties and mid twenties. I think it is important that that age should see something as frightful as this. The smell of ashes and burnt brick still hangs in the air ... the bullet holes are still in the doors which were not burned ... the skeletons of Singer Sewing machines, and clocks on the walls still ... the cooking pots in the fireplaces, the scorched refrigerators and twisted iron bedsteads ... everything that would not burn, still remain inside the shells of the houses ... and the gardens have been carefully preserved, the bushes trimmed, lawns cut, lilac heavy in blossom, trees all pruned. And totally deserted, silent except for the birds and the distant bleat of the sheep in the lush green fields which surround this hateful, sad, ruined little town.

Thats enough of that. Tote is trying to draw a version of our O.M.[2] Between us we have got it more or less right ... and I have now to copy it and send it off to Chatto. By the way I thought it might be a nice thing to do to give Lally the first 100 pounds I might get for the book ... dont you? And a percentage of the 'take' from then on in

---

1. Oradour-sur-Glane, the village preserved as the Nazis left it following their massacre of the inhabitants on 10 June 1944.
2. One of the cars Ulric owned during Dirk's childhood.

Kathleen Tynan – 'adorable, brilliant, maddening' –
with Dirk and Tony in a rare portrait, by Patrick Lichfield,
taken during the making of *Justine* in 1968.

With Jack ('Tony') Jones on wartime leave at the Van den Bogaerde family home in Clayton, Sussex.

(Below) Jill ('Maude') Melford at Villa Berti in 1969.

'Mrs X' – Dorothy Gordon, whom Dirk never met, but with whom he had 'a strange, moving, love affair'.

With the loyal Antonia and Eduardo Boluda, who followed Dirk and Tony to Rome and then to Provence.

'The King' and his consort: Joseph and Patricia Losey in Paris for the opening of *The Go-Between* (June 1971).

With Ian Holm (left) and Bee Gilbert on location for *The Fixer* in 1967.

With Ann Skinner and Dirk's faithful stand-in, Arnold Schulkes (right), at Lord's while shooting *Darling* on a sun-drenched day in September 1964. The story called for rain, with the result that hoses were deployed and the continuity script was soaked. Dirk led the rescue operation on the hallowed turf.

With 'The Emperor', Luchino Visconti, on location in 1970 for *Death in Venice*.

Dilys Powell in uncharacteristically flamboyant mode while launching a 1975 exhibition at the NFT devoted to her fellow critic, the late Richard Winnington.

'Sold out and great fun and very irreverant [sic]' – Dirk at the National Film Theatre, where he was interviewed by Margaret Hinxman in the John Player Lecture series on 8 November 1970.

On the terrace with the 'wise, funny, and often sharply bitter' Penelope Mortimer, who wrote of Dirk: 'Though he was older, more wizened than I had imagined, I loved him on sight.'

On location in 1975 for *Permission to Kill* with Ava Gardner – 'still incredibly beautiful [...] and eyes so green that the lakes were dimmed by her.'

Earliest days at Clermont: with his mother, Margaret Van den Bogaerde.

The house on the hill – 'a beautiful place, where I have always wanted to be.'

Not Van Gogh, but Tony: his idealised study of Clermont, painted on glass in 1971.

Le Haut Clermont

The drawing-room: once stabling, then the studios of an artist in stained-glass, finally transformed in 1970 by Dirk's architect, Léon Loschetter.

The 'cockpit', with Leonard Rosoman's 'The Wave, Amagansett' in pride of place.

The terraces in unfamiliar garb.

With Daphne Fielding at St Jean Cap Ferrat in August 1975. Twenty years later she told Dirk that 'the things I have loved most in my long and lucky life have been Reading, Riding, Rejoicing and Rogering. In that order. All that now remains is Reading.'

At work with Norah Smallwood – 'She was a titan! Nothing could escape her brilliant eye or the furious correcting of her right hand and pencil!'

Julie Harris meets Julie Harris. The costume designer and Dirk's almost exact contemporary (left) won an Oscar for her work on *Darling*. The actress co-starred in the 1964 NBC television production, *Little Moon of Alban*.

.... I feel she deserves it more than Ma at this time who at least has 'enough' .... Lally has simply nothing. So thats what I'll do ... if there is 100 pounds that is to say! I rather doubt it but you cant really tell.

After that I have to turn up a pair of slacks I bought yesterday in our local Nouvelle Galleries .... got my little 'housewife' with needles and thread and things and am not very sure HOW to turn things up without the stitches showing! Have a go. Things here are a third cheaper than on the Coast. Cognac is 30 Francs .. (at the Superette 38–42) and clothes and things are much cheaper in Monoprix and other shops ... just goes to show that the further south you go the more you have to pay ... even meals are cheaper ... and Kleenex!

I'm listening to BBC 2 at the moment ... we can get it here since there are no mountains between us and London ... and that awful Sunday Request Programme where the DJ screams 'Goodbyeeee' all the time. I think I'll go bonkers. And the slush they all want .. the favourite song seems to be something called 'The Queen Of The Mardi Gras' and it is as sicky as 'Happy Anniversary My Darling' which really makes you throw up! God! The trivial minds of most people ... it makes you sad. They are all Madame Martinez[1] ... key-rings and plastic ash trays ... some of the famous Limoge China on sale in the town is worse, by far, than the stuff in Vallauris .... ghastly! Crinoline ladies covered in spangles and gold, awful doggies, and cake stands made out of twisty gold wire and covered in china fruits and birds .. and of course they sell, Ducks on the wall .... where will it all end? Mediocraty everywhere.

Now I'd better stop this and let Tote use it for a letter to the Swiss Bank ... I do hope you are being sensible about your spending. The money in the bank is for you all to USE you know .... I have a terrible vision of you economising Uncle Dirks money by making one packet of fish fingers do for all .. and eating salade niceoise until you will all look like one. Do be good and eat properly, and use the wine in the cellar, if you can bear it, that was bottled for you ... and it'll only go 'off' if you dont use it ... not that it matters, but PLEASE enjoy yourselves in between painting out rooms and toiling in the garden!!! it is not your job! But I do love you for doing it! All my love as ever, for ever ..

Dirk XXXXXX and millions more –

---

1. The domestic help at Clermont.

To Elizabeth Goodings

La Chapelle St Martin
Sunday. 30 May [1976]

Darling one –

We are sweating a bit this week. Supposed to finish the whole Location before Thursday in the gardens of the Chateau[1]. .... this morning I awake to thick fog! Yesterday it was dull and rained ... what on earth will it be like tomorrow? I can see me sticking it out until the day before I have to go to Holland![2] Which means that I would'nt be back at Clermont until the middle of August at the earliest ... and my heart sinks. We have had enough of it already ... hotel rooms, resturants, washing the 'smalls' in the bathroom, and trying to find something to do on these interminable 'day off's' ..... However I am being a bit gloomy, probably because of the fog this morning. Anyway we HAVE to quit this hotel by Saturday morning ... he cant keep us longer; the summer bookings have started .... we should, if all went well, start up to Paris that day for the Lancaster ... but if the wether fucks things up we'll have to stay over until Tuesday at least because Monday is ANOTHER bloody holiday ... so is the Sat and the Sun ... so where we shall find a room at that time, in the middle of Whitsun, God alone knows. Anyway: maybe something lovely will happen. Like sunshine for five days and then we'll be off. But I have grave doubts.

Otherwise there is nothing to tell you since our gossip the other day. I am calling Leon,[3] I hope, this morning ... could'nt before. Lines jammed and etc ... we are really up in the hills here ... and the staff are overworked .... today we cant even have our table for lunch! They are booked out solid and the landlord, who left a very large bottle of cognac in my room yesterday with a very nice card saying how much they all admired my 'simplicity, kindness, and humility ...' I was rather toutched. And of course they have got it a bit wrong. Still: a nice gesture anyway. (Anyway he said he could'nt give us a table for 4.) So. We have to take John G. <u>out</u> to lunch, he is a bit fed up and lonely stuck in a terrible modern hotel in town ... so instead of having an elegant, comfortable, expensive, and not very good, meal

---

1. Le Château de Mont-Méry at Ambazac.
2. For the filming of Richard Attenborough's *A Bridge Too Far.*
3. Léon Loschetter.

here we have to drive him up to a lake some twenty miles away to a hotel which we have found and which is pleasant, on the lake, and not going to be crowded. It is a bit of a bore because he loves to reminisce all the time .. like Ma! And all about dead actors I either never saw or never wished to! 'Ah! dear Marie Tempest! I remember once at Juliet Duffs during the war, she lived at Henley you know, ravishing house, Oscar Whimper and Edith Wallop came to tea with Marie Tempest, who was married to Edgar Rudd . . .' etc etc etc .. and on and on they go, the stories, endlessly being repeated! You just have to sit there and listen. He HATES being interrupted and does not like anyone elses stories at all! A bit trying, and then you have to pick up the bill anyway. Not cheap. Never less than 300 francs a time!

We drove a couple of the young Crew members down to Perigaux [Périgueux] yesterday .. a lovely run even in drizzle . . . among miles and miles of walnut trees . . . this is the region for nut oil . . . . they use it always instead of olive oil . . . made from walnuts. It is sweet and delicious. So we bought a couple of litres . . . . if we ever get home to use it.

Had a long leasurly lunch at the Hotel du Parc, which has a star in the Michelin and cost a fortune. But the kids enjoyed it and we all got mildely wined and played idiotic word games in the car coming back and bought awful sweeties in a little village which were made of walnuts ... everything is made of walnuts and truffels in the Perigord. And then just had an omlette and atichikos for supper when we got back here, still too full to eat anything else. The Radio ... we can get BBC 2 for some reason, and a learn of the script and then to bed. Not very exciting ... and I envy everyone I see working in their gardens.

The BBC, talking of that, is doing a huge Homage to D.B sometime in August ... ten of my best films and a big interview in the Radio Times plus the cover in colour! Fame at last. Trouble is they want to come out on specific dates to do it all in Paris and I cant possibly say when I'll be free at this time. And they are panicking because their 'date line' is tight. Oh hell! There is always something.

[. . .] I must answer a few more letters which came in your bundle the other day, and send Ma another card full of drivel . . . and then get me jacket on and trail off to pick up John G. and a chap called Peter Arne who is quite pleasant but boring too! They all are! I really am OFF actors.

What about Sir Stanley Baker! And Dreaded John Mills![1] It makes
all the awards so cheap [...]

All love to you ... dont let Mark loose in the village! They may
lock him up with all that hair![2]

> Much love my little darling one, a big, big h[u]g as ever,
> my gratitude and thanks for all you are doing for me,
> I cant think how to repay you,
> But one day, you see, I will

Your devoted brother.

Dirk XXXXX

In June production of Providence *moved to studios in Paris. Dirk and
Tony settled into the Lancaster, the hotel which they favoured as the French
capital's answer to the Connaught.*

To Penelope Mortimer

Hotel Lancaster
30 June 1976

My dear –

The temperature is in the ninties .. flowers dead, airless, agonizing
on the set. Yesterday it was 125 and me in a neat double breasted St
Laurent, poor Burstyn in a vast cashmere robe. Death seemed not far
away and the floor felt like a rubber sponge beneath the feet. But we
are nearly at the end of this staggering, exciting, film.

[...] Enormously interested by your obvious interest in 'R'[3] ... I
think you are on splendid lines myself. Venice was simply an idea we
had ages ago, on one of the earlier projects of the thing, before Roeg
fucked it all up with Sutherlands cock and misty-dont-turn-round
shots[4] ... But DONT set a foot of it in America. I refuse to even set
foot on that blasted land.

---

1. John Mills and Stanley Baker were among those knighted in the controversial Resignation Honours dispensed by the Prime Minister, Harold Wilson, the names for which
were drawn up on the erroneously nicknamed 'Lavender List'.
2. Mark Goodings, at twenty-three, sported a coiffure redolent of the mid-1970s-aspirant-
rock-star.
3. PM had been commissioned to write the screenplay for a remake of *Rebecca*. Dirk had
been considered in the past for the role of Max de Winter; most recently, with the action
transferred from the West Country of Daphne du Maurier's novel to Venice.
4. Nicolas Roeg's acclaimed version of du Maurier's *Don't Look Now*, starring Donald
Sutherland and Julie Christie.

Directors are hellish. How cruel, wrong and unjust to blame Jack.[1] Unbankable is one of their excuse words like Powder Room. It really means that they dont like him. Gatsby was not the failure it was because of Jack but because the fucking Front Office blew it into some idiotic Product Selling Commercial. There was Gatsby Green, Gatsby Cuisines, Gatsby Sweaters, and even a Gatsby Hair Cut. They just had a foul cast and too much loot.

Losey is too long in the tooth anyway. I have just refused to do a 'bit' in his ill fated Proust! He sent all France and the U.S.A a carbon cable stating that he was now able to 'impliment' the production of PINTERS 'La Researche .. etc' and that he was 'sure there would be something for you in it. Please to telegraph immediate acceptance!' Those of us who recieved the cable in France politely, and regretfully in some instances, declined. He turned purple, I am told, and fled to do a Telly in Mexico. Proust has folded it's wings again and the dust has settled somewhat. Anyway: I cant think of a director ... no way can I.

There are too few. Schlesinger would camp it all up ... and Bog-danovitch has the style of a Macdonald Hamburger. Perhaps a lovely European? But I dont know and am too bushed to care right now.

Resnais, golden, steel, platinum, Resnais strides masterfully through his 'dream' brilliantly .. cooly, passionatly, calmly. What a superbe chap he is! This is a sort of marriage between us ... no words are wasted, all sign language .. exhilerating, lifting; one reels home to the hotel in the evenings amazed that one has been able to do things for him which no one ever botherd to ask for before .. (save Visconti) .. and this is harder, far harder, than 'Death In V.' And the Style demanded is immense ... partly Wilde .. partly Congrieve ... partly Sheridan and <u>lots</u> of Resnais! Very exciting indeed. I have not seen a foot but am told, as the Paris en dit, has it that it is the Event of the Season. I DO hope so. However drunken that red-plum-with-a-beard, Mercer, may be, he <u>can</u> write when he wants to ... and the film, amazingly for Resnais, is very, very funny ... black funny and not always comfortable funny, but funny! We'll see .... [...] I leave here, I think, by car for home on the 8th July .. and will have a merciful

1. *Rebecca*'s producer had told PM that Jack Clayton, director of *Our Mother's House* and *The Innocents*, was 'unbankable' following the failure of *The Great Gatsby*, starring Robert Redford and Mia Farrow.

five days at home before trailing up to Holland to play, is'nt it odd?
Browning (du Mauriers ex)[1] in 'A Bridge Too Far' which is costing 27
million dollars and is the most awful drag you can imagine. But the
loot is healthy ... the role nine days over four weeks ... and then I
needent work again until Alain starts again. He promised me he'd
have me again soon .. about March ... I want to play everything he
offers from a door handle to a spruce tree. We waited fourteen years
together. I think we both feel the wait was justified as well as the result.

Off now to the filthy Studio at Joinville ... by the Marne .. no air
conditioning and a set of such staggering proportions that it makes
Babylon in 'Intolerance' pale by comparison. No wonder the actors
did'nt get full salaries! The set must have cost the budget of ten movies
... and it is very very hot indeed in Mr Laurents dinner jackets [...]

Someone from Le Figaro is at the door ... I'll go and Parlez.

[...] devoted, if hot, love –
    Dirk XXXX.

P.S. What about my glorious S. MANGANO[2] for [Mrs] Danvers?

To Bee Gilbert   *Clermont*
                                              13 September 1976

Dearest Sno'

What a lovely long letter to cheer me up on my return, three days
ago, from a hellish week of looping in Paris. I got there to find that I
had to loop the entire fucking film[3] .. 200 loops. The sound engineers
were dreadful (from Telly natch) and the birds, dogs and airoplanes
which scattered across the locations screwd us up even more. However
clever old me, I broke the record at Billiancourt and did my lot in
three anguished days ..... it is a Mercer Script ... not Disney as you
know, so it had to be precisely as said originally. Well .. it is done now.
Am home again for a couple of weeks before returning to Old Father
Attenboroughs Disney-Arnhem. Which I dread. What a nonsense
that all is! Every 'Star' has a personal trailor with flush loo and a very

---

1. Lt-Gen. Sir Frederick 'Boy' Browning was Daphne du Maurier's late, not ex-, husband.
2. Silvana Mangano, Dirk's beautiful co-star from *Death in Venice*, who was married to
Dino De Laurentiis.
3. *Providence*, post-production on which was done at the Studios de Billancourt.

personal Servant to get the grub, water, towels, beer ... 450 Crew and 8 assistants ... three Units ... Arnold on one as 1st[1] ... untold tanks and planes ... millions of extras and a script written by a Brooklyn Jew called Goldman.[2] Almost unsayable. Odd, is'nt it? Shades of the dreaded 'Fixer' .... No one seems to care much about anything except getting it all done 'on schedule' ... so one take is often the norm. Ah well. It will make a bomb, with all those Stars how can it fail? Adored Sean C.[3] and worked very happily indeed with him ... and made a surprising new mate in Ryan O'Neil[4] who could not be nicer, jollier and brighter! That WAS a surprise. Tote says it was because he was so bloody respectful to me all the time .... but I just liked the bloke. And he's good too. And THAT was a surprise. Gene Hackman was a bit Methody and got cross if the camera operator was on the set while he was rehearsing .. but was very pleasant to me and quite good, not more, when it came to the Acting.

Mike Cain pulled the Movie Star bit a bit much .. the big cigar, black glasses and fat Cadillac ... but he was pleasant if dull and has to have the ugliest voice in the business .. and pop eyes. And that was a surprise too [...] I don't think I could go through it again for anything. Even the lolly. A woman from the New York Times ruefully mumbled that doing something as crappy for so much loot left 'a kind of stain.' I wonder if she was right. Holland was hell. Amsterdam dull with hippes and free sex and enormous dilldolls and rubber penis outside every shop ... plus those tatty ladies sitting in their windows offering a dose of clap at fifty guilders a throw ... toss? blow? .. I dont know. Apart from the van Goghs, Rembrants and the Vermeers it is all a lot of crappy horror .... We stayed in a 'dainty' little hotel in a wood where dinner started at six thirty pm and was off at eight forty five. THAT went down like a cup of cold sick as you may imagine. Especially as the prices were identicle to the Lancaster in Paris! However we had three weeks there and flew back on a beastly Caravelle, which bounced all the way to Nice .... and then off to Paris for the above mentioned chore.

---

1. Schulkes, who was first assistant director.
2. William – Oscar-winning screenwriter of *Butch Cassidy and the Sundance Kid* and *All the President's Men*.
3. Connery, who was playing Major-General Robert Urquhart, commander of 1st (British) Airborne Division at Arnhem.
4. Ryan O'Neal played Brigadier-General James Gavin.

'Providence' is a stunning experience! One of the most beautiful films I have ever seen . . . if not THE . . . I dont know what the hell it is all about . . . and feel that Mercers script is a lot of pretentious crap which we ALL play beautifully . . . . Johnnie G. steals the film, of course. But he is so smashing that one does'nt care . . and is only glad that such a fantastic performance should be honoured, at last, by the cinema. Burstyn is marvellous . . . the surprise is Stritch who is astonishing and hurts like hell . . . David [Warner] does his grovelling Saint Act excellently, if you can bear it, and I camp about in St Laurent quite effectivly. But no one knows what it is all about . . . and it wont make a nickle in comparison to the Disney-War up the road in Deventer, Holland. Thats always the way though, is'nt it? They are speaking of it in Paris in whispers as Resnais Masterpiece . . . but one never takes any notice of that. His best film ever, yes. The other I can not be sure about. Who can. It is impossible to be objective.

But I need a rest now. I have refused, during an hysterical weekend exchange, to replace Stephens¹ in 'A Little Night Music' and had the most lovely time doing it! It was SO super to say . . 'I'm sorry, I just dont <u>want</u> to do it . . . tell Miss Taylor I have a book to write.' I could have 'named your own price' (Which WAS a bit tempting . .) but I don't replace anyone – yet.

After the end of this month in Holland . . . . then to London for two short days to see my Mother . . . I come back to start work on my second book [. . .] 'Enter Demons . . .'² Which has to be done ready for the Autumn release next year. 'Postillion' (which looks very pretty but will probably bomb badly) comes out in March . . . just sent off the Cover design and an additional line drawing for the Title Page. It is all my own work, so to speak . . . so I'll really crumble when the Critics bash me this time. Oh well. I should'nt have stuck out my neck so far . . . .

My Sister and bro' in law were here for five months and sobbed at the parting. They can only now think of coming here to live for ever and sod England . . . . but it is a might harder to do than to say. I may be able to build them a little house up here on the hill and they could

---

1. Robert Stephens, who had been cast opposite Elizabeth Taylor in the screen adaptation of Sondheim's musical, directed by Hal Prince. Fired shortly after filming began because he and his co-star did not have 'the right chemistry', Stephens said: 'We're actors, not pharmacists.' Len Cariou stepped in.
2. A working title for *Snakes and Ladders*.

just look after the land and the house and me ... and guard things when I am off 'doing' the money earning ...... but how much longer will THAT last?

We have had, unlike you, a soaking summer ... everything green and lush ... while the great trees in the Luxumbourg Gardens are all dead. And now Tote is out mowing acres of white dasies and autumn crocus and I think I'd better go and help him ... regretfully. I am so lazy and full of reaction ... odd.

It WAS lovely to hear from you about you ... super about old neuro-Ian ... give him a bashing great kiss and tell him to keep brave, sane and far away from Frankenheimer. Thats what did it in the first place!

My electric typewriter ... for my 'book' you know .. is a sod .. it just has a will of it's own and the subtilty of a Combine Harvester with added weight .. and I am making more and more mistakes because I want a pre-lunch drink.

God bless you, pretty Sno ...
    all love as ever for ever ..
       as you
          know.
             Sno.
YoR
  Dirk

After thirty-seven years, Dilys Powell retired as film critic for The Sunday Times. *Dirk wrote an appreciation, published on 10 October.*

To Dilys Powell

Clermont
17 October 1976

My dear –

I am glad that you were pleased. Surprised, too, that the S.T. even printed it ... I was up to my eyes being one of Attenboroughs Wax-Figures at the time, and felt such a sense of grievous loss when I read your, typically, gentle 'bow out' at the end of the column. My own note to you was written on the back of a bouncing jeep in a rain-storm ... so maybe it was as incomprehensible as usual. But well meant. As you know. You would be SO gratified to see the stack of letters which I have recieved in this week appropos the letter. People, ordinary people for the most part, who loved you tremendously, and were as saddened as I. I only hope that some of them have written to you .... your face would have been alight with pleasure that the many years had not been <u>at all</u> in vain, and that they had given such enormous pleasure.

For my self I feel, in a strange way, a sense of almost relief. It has been very difficult, as you will imagine, to write to you as a very loving friend, which I am, while you were still a Critic. I was terrified of appearing to 'curry favour' ... although I know very well that this would never have occured to you ... but many things which I wanted to say to you had to be left unsaid because of Our Positions! Do you know what I mean? Awfully complicated really. That is why I was so desperatly tongue tied at our few meetings .... clumsy, idiotic, banal. The dreaded fear that one might, even unconsiosly, be influencing you in your work was abhorrent and frightening ... and consequently I was never able to say very much. Only generalities ... oh! shut up! I KNOW what I mean ... but it is impossible to explain. Now that you have no longer the responsibility of 'guiding' me, as you have done for so many years, I am free to say just what I jolly well like without fear of scorn or of favour! I feel a little lonely now .... who to help me? Certainly not your repellent Substitute![1] Alas! The standards are gone .... even Hobson,[2] for all his nonsense, was a Lover of our craft .... [David] Robinson on 'The Times' perhaps ... [Derek] Malcolm on 'The Guardian' .... I dont know. Anyway I did do the Resnais for you ... hoping for ultimate Command at last! And your approval can be written, or not written, just as you wish now, if and when you see it. However, just remember, and this is one thing I could NOT tell you before, if one can ever dedicate a picture, no .... a performance ... to any one person then Claud Langham in 'Providence' is, and was, completely dedicated to you. And you can do what you like about that! There! I have said something as dreadful as 'District Nurse!' (Do you remember 'Dear Octopus' by Dodie Smith?) I am getting boring .... so I'll shut up.

Terrific amount of garden work to do here after six months of neglect ... semi neglect that is ... acres of meadow to mow and keep down for the winter ... 'gourmands' round all the olive trees (350 of

---

1. DP was succeeded by Alan Brien.
2. Harold Hobson, theatre critic of *The Sunday Times* from 1947 to 1976.

the buggers) and the sad, withering stems of daisy, dahlia, and lavender ... the vine was stripped last week by the Daily Lady and her husband who make a fairly repellant wine from the 'tons' they cart away ... and all about the terrace late toads scramble for the flies and wasps among the fallen leavs and crushed fruit ... a big deal with broom and hose today in the golden sun, cooled now by the first fall of light snow up on the hills behind the house ....

Resnais leaves Paris today with a skeleton Crew for New England where he is to 'shoot' additional 'athmospheric' moments for 'Providence' of trees, bushes, roots, and vague, un-connected buildings. The Producers must be pleased with the very un-box office film it is ... for this will cost a pretty penny! Heaven knows WHAT he wants shots of New England for ... it is all a dream I suppose, the film, so he wants the flamboyance of the Fall colours to mix in with the summer at Limoges ... I do love him. And respect him. And cross fingers for him.

Dont think, for one second, that I am starting a Pen Pal situation ... with you I mean. I'm not. And you dont need to reply ever. Very tedious if you do ... feel forced to ... it is simply that I do absolutly adore you ... and now I am able to tell you. To your face.

Off to correct the 'proofs' of my book. Chatto are very demanding and bullying ... and I'm terrified. How DO you correct 'proofs' I wonder? The terrace will have to wait a little longer.

Always My Love
Dirk

To Lucilla Van den Bogaerde

Clermont
10 November 1976

Cilia love – et al[1] –

Well: said Tote after reading your delicious letter, They Seem To Have Got Off To A Slightly Shakey Start![2]

I did laugh though; not at that, but at your letter ... the sick bags in the hall ... What the fuck was Brock throwing Up for? Is he sensitive?

---

1. He means 'and all', of course.
2. Work opportunities had taken Dirk's brother and his family to Illinois for an indefinite period.

Poor loves ... Immigration is a bit of a wrench even, if as we all did, one <u>wants</u> to go ... for whatever reasons. And there is nowhere, to my mind, more foreign than America. I am less at ease there than in India, Greece; or even the darkest parts of Tibet! Which I visited in 1945 and thought I had hit Mars. Even that; prayer wheels, Lamas, Everest like a gigantic ice cream cornet, butter in the tea, lice all over the walls ... even that was more familiar than standing on the corner of 5th and 58th New York, where, the first time I arrived, I went into a total panic of homesickness and wanted 'out' as soon as I had landed. But it passed. Gradually. I loath America .. and dont awfully care for the race even tho' some-of-my-best-friends etc. But that is not the point at this moment.

Everything is bound to seem dreadfully strange just at first. But as soon as you get your house and the furniture arrives, and all the familiar feelings come back within the walls of your 'life' you'll be fine. I promise. You ARE both doing the right thing, of that there can be no possible doubt; taking Castor Oil is good for Constipation and some forms of sickness (or poisoning I mean) and tho' not at all pleasant is the RIGHT THING to do .... for that particular malady. Or maladies. Imagine your lives if you had stayed on in the U.K. Bugger a little job on Welsh Telly! Who wants it! It may not even be there in a year or so ... not Wales, but the Telly. England is slowly crumbling away into a sand heap of envy, spite, dislike, jealousy and apathy. I CANNOT think why. But it is ... and there is simply no point in you all hanging on for the Sunrise at your ages ... and at the ages of your children. You and G. have both given up SO much for your children that you might just as well go the whole hog and give up the rest. It will be marvellous for them. Even though, tragically, one knows, as in the past with other friends, they will all become Americans in the end.[1] Quicker than either of you.

It is an inevitable process ... and the mixture is not at all unattractive. The good British background marries well with the flip, whiz-kid innocence of most Americans. Especially in the Middle West. Which always reminds me, religiously, as well as climatically, of Mid-Lothian or the Black Country. But I'm told it is charming in the summer. You go to the Lake and have picnics and things. Or something. And join patchwork Clubs for company during the long winter evenings.

---

1. A prophecy robustly unfulfilled.

And you <u>will</u> make friends, you know … it seems impossible in an Hotel of course, but once you are in what they call, euphimistically, A Neiborhood, you will start to 'exist'. But do try it for a while … dont panic as I did and try to come back. Too soon: anyway. I know one girl who did the same as you; minus children. They went to New York, marginally more civilised. She cried for the first three years solidly. Her patient, very loving husband, did all that was possible to 'help' her .. but three sodden years passed before their First Leave back to the U.K. She was the original 'child Bride' suddenly … happiness, delight, joy. For two or three days. After one week of Hemel Hampstead and all the family, she begged her patient and loving husband to return to America IMMEDIATLY! NOTHING, and I use Capitals, would induce her to stay in Britain again. The rest of their leave they spent in France (some with us) in Italy and got the boat back from Genoa early .. so there.

No. I'm positive that, like Steve Sondhiem says, 'Your'R Gonna Be Alright.'

I bet by the time we meet again you'll be busy as a bee with your gold paint and rabbit glue,[1] your spaghetti parties, and there will be more painted crab shells up on the walls ..... bet you.

As for us here. Well. All is as before. We have just about settled back again after seven months away .... Tote had an aged Aunt to stay for two weeks ,.. agony. Recently widowd, ex-Sudan, totally bigoted, kind, tiresome. Church every Sunday (Cannes, naturally … Grasse has no English Church) and long discussion every evening round the fire about long-dead relations, of whome I had never heard, and details of everyones life in Khartoum and Cairo during the war. Unbelievably boring. But she had a simply lovely time … and actually got nicer as the days went on. We did'nt make any alterations in our lives … and she found that rather 'amusing'. But we were pretty tried [sic] after it all .. especially with poor old Tote trailing down to the Clinic in Nice three mornings a week (six am call) to have his bum pierced with some terrifying electronic 'ray' thing which is fearsome as well as undignified. It's getting better, thank the Lord .... another four weeks to go … and then, if all is well, we plan that delayed trip to London simply to see his father and for me to clap eyes on my wretched Charlstoning Mother. For the moment we are painting out

---

1. Lucilla Van den Bogaerde was, and is, a gilder and restorer.

the New Studio . . . we have converted the empty store shed at the end of the house into a proper Studio . . . tables, lamps, electric typewriter . . . paper and pencils . . . all the paraphanalia of a Proper Writer. I have another book to deliver to Chatto by March. However, if Mexico, and 'Under The Volcano',[1] DOES come off . . . . and it may . . . that'll have to be set aside. I shall have to be there mid-January-Febuary I think. Something to do with the weather and the fact that the Volcano claps on it's hat at the end of April until next January. Nature is irritating. And it is raining like hell here. So all the wallflowers, stocks, foxgloves and millions of tulip bulbs (all white this spring) are starting to rot because I cant get them in . . . . a small worry.

My book comes out in March. I'll send you a copy so that you can know how your husband arrived. Holt are publishing in America. I got a huge advance and a promise that they would not edit anything. And although I did'nt want it published there (they have screwd me so often in business I regret to say, the Film Chaps, not Publishers) I felt that since I was bound to make a cunt of myself in England in March I might just as well go the whole hog and be an International Cunt. So there we are.

Ages Later.

Stopped there to hear the mid day news from the poor old BBC. You really are well out! Healy[2] has now promised misery, extra taxes, and God alone knows what else, for the next two years. The next five or six, he said, would be grim. I cannot imagine what he thinks the last four were like. Then, much pleasanter news . . . . The Holt deal is definate, The Book Society have ordered a 'print' of 5,000 copies, and Penguin have bought the book. Modestly. But still . . . . I'm really rather pleased. Until those sneering Critics on that Sunday in March. Never mind. I did it. I made it. It's mine . . . cover, words, and 'sketches' . . . . . I think you have to have a bash, dont you? As you both have. It's so EASY to sit about and do fuck-nothing with your lives . . .

Welsh Telly! Perish the thought. When I left England seven years ago now, I was fifty . . and out of work. There was very little Capital left. All I had was Clermont. Could'nt really speak the language . . . and for a while it was very worrying, strange, even frightning. I was homesick, for an hour or two. Scared of getting ill and not being able

---

1. Dirk's interest in a film of the Malcolm Lowry novel had been revived.
2. Denis Healey, Chancellor of the Exchequer.

to drive ... of a million things. <u>But I was not alone</u>. And neither are you. Together is one thing. Alone is very much another. You can go-it together .. and there are a lot of you to be together with .... it is much tougher on your own. Remember that.

Now, my dear, wild horses and a million pounds, or dollars or whatever, would never, ever, get me back to that Fabled Realm. I'm French now. Taxes as well .... I'm happy, alive, and pushing along. Had I stayed behind .... God knows what would have happened. A Telly Series, perhaps ... a Tour of Shaw or Wilde, perhaps just 'No Sex Please, We're British.' ...... Thank Heavens I left.

So, I venture to think, will you all be. Love, end of page and enough lecture ...

Your very loving <u>Dirk</u> XXXXXX

On 1 February Dirk met Norah Smallwood. She handed him the first two bound copies of A Postillion Struck *by Lightning. The next day he recorded a further interview with Russell Harty.*

To Norah Smallwood

Clermont
5 February 1977

My dear Nora

I dont actually remember that you ever gave me permission to call you this, however I am presuming ... and you may rap my knuckles when next we meet ... Got home to find the mimosa in frothy bloom (filthy stuff: smells like a Maids' bedroom) and violets, wallflowers and toads mating like anything in the pond. But sun. And calm.

I hope that it was a useful week for you ... from the point of view of the 'jobs' I was able to do ... worked bloody hard, which must be a goodish sign? and got the whole of the Telly Programme to myself and the book. And plugged Chatto and everything like mad. Think it was alright. Enjoyed it ... usually a good sign with me ... and reeled onto the plane at filthy Heathrow with the nagging feeling that poor Lally might very well be splattered over peoples T. Shirts and Chocolate Wrappings in the near future!

Awful thought.

Sent Elizabeth a copy, which you gave me, of the book, in STRICT SECRECY, to be read only in the lavatory or somewhere ... and rather dread her voice when I will telephone on Sunday.

This is simply to 'thank you' for being so splendid, kind, warm and, I dare say it, loving. It made me feel tremendously 'safe'.

My most affectionate gratitude,

Dirk

Shall I bring you a bottle of olive oil in March? First pressing. Rather thick. But real? D.

To Elizabeth Goodings

Clermont
12 February 1977

Dearest darling Girl –

Well. That was the lovliest letter I have ever recieved in my life ... and I really do mean that. I have read it over at least five times! It is just about worn out.

Darling, thank you so much for being so dear and generous. Now that you have written I can tell you that I said to the Publishers at Lunch in London that if you read it ... or rather when you read it .. and I F you hated it or were upset by it or thought that it was beastly or vulgar to anyone, that I would insist that they [s]hould withdraw it!

That caused a bit of a stir, I can tell you! But they were very sweet and put it down to sort of First Night Nerves! Although they were secretly just as worried about your reaction, after that! as I was. That is why you got the first copy .. and why I was sitting biting my nails until I dared to call you on the Sunday!

What is so splendid about your letter is that you have written it in such an objective way ... when it must have been extremely difficult to BE objective. I know EXACTLY what you mean by a 'gentle writer'. It is precicely what I wanted to be. I wanted, very much, to write a book that I myself would enjoy reading ... do you know what I mean? I am sure that you do ... and for that reason I was very fastidious and tried not to hang onto things too long, a form of self indulgence in writing which I detest.

After eight Chapters of Lally and You and all, I realised that it had to change ... however delightful it was to 'remember' it could fast become 'sicky' ... The big difficulty, which I think and hope I have managed to overcome, was 'joining' the two styles ... writing as a boy of eleven and then as me at fifty six. Looking back .. but still keeping something of the First Part going. I think it has worked, and your approval of it seems to point to the fact that it 'gets better as it goes on' . . . which was the idea.

I dont think, or rather I hope I dont think! that Lally will mind . . or her children. I did, after all, offer to change her name at the very beginning . . but she wrote and said 'Lally I was and Lally I will be' . . (still have it) . . . so she cant be too distressed. I shall write to her when her book is on the way and gently explain one or two things to her . . . like Wimeraux[1] and so on . . . I think that what has so far captured the 'fancy' of the people who have read it . . . professional people on papers and so on . . is the time we had which is now lost forever. People have said, rather sweetly, 'We didn't know life was like that . . . we never had it ourselves' or on the other hand, as one young man said, 'I was sure that MY sister and I were the only people in the world to make Hikers Wine! We thought <u>we</u> did it first in 1950!' Recognition comes through so often . . . and they laugh too! Which is what I hoped for. I think Ma should be jolly pleased . . . and only wish that Ully could have read it because, as Russel Harty said before the programme the other day, 'It is clearly a loving memorial to your Father, isn't it?' and I had to admit that really it was . . . however he was always such an old stickler for the 'facts' that he might have been a bit disconcerted by the 'condensing' of time which I have had to do . . . and the leaving out of so many people. The O'Sheas . . , Prebble Rayner . . . Newbolds . . the Dowds[2] and so on . . . however it had to be done.

The thing which interests people so much, so far, is the way that Parents are shadowy at that age to children . . always there and loved, but distant . . . and then they start coming into ones life as one gets older. I think that bit works quite well . . . God alone knows what Scotland[3] will say. But since they refused to answer any of my questions . . as did Mamma I might add! I wrote them all, her included, a long, simple, questionair on the Nivens and got absolutely no answer from anyone. Sadie[4] said she couldnt comment, and would pass her letter on to Roey![5] It was the same letter to them both . . and very polite

1. The family took holidays at Wimereux in the early 1920s.
2. Friends and colleagues of Ulric and Margaret.
3. Margaret's family.
4. Sarah Niven, second of Margaret's three elder sisters, who with her husband William Murray gave lodgings to Derek for the first two of his 'Anthracite Years' in Glasgow (1934–7).
5. Neil Munro Niven, third eldest of Margaret's four brothers.

and asking for careful help. Not a word. So screw them. There is an AWFUL lot I HAVE'NT said about my little Scottish trip, I can tell you . . . .

The other thing, which is good, is that you and I have made such an, what is the word? impact, on people. As I told you, they speak of you, tremendously politely always, as just simply 'Elizabeth' . . . never 'your sister' . . . and Lally is the same. It felt rather funny the first time it happened, but I quickly realised that it was actually a compliment! And people have used the word 'vile' to me so often that even I roar with laughter now!

Anyway. There it is darling .. as you know with all my love and gratitude for the years we had together, and which, thank the dear Lord, we still are able to share in very much the same way . . . I mean we still behave, I know, like a couple of idiots even though we are into middle age . . . . our holidays here in France were very much like our times in Twickenham or Lullington . . . with the moods and every-thing. It is <u>marvelous</u> to have such a relationship.

The second book is almost sad, as Chatto said the other day (I have done the first four chapters) the war is suddenly over . . . you are talking of getting married, and I'm wondering wheather to go to that school at Windlesham which John Nelson[1] got me an interview to . . . as a prep-school teacher! It is all so dreadfully suddenly Grown Up . . . and in such a short time . . . but I think, and they do at Chatto, that Elizabeth and Dirk still 'come through' . . . and thats the part they all like the best! When you and I have a 'talk' .. naturally it is made-up from remembering . . . could'nt be anything else could it, but it has the feeling of Truth. And thats what makes the difference between a Real Book and one which is simply amusing to read.

Anyway .. we still have the dreaded critics to face . . . I must say I shall wish I had never started when they get at me with the choppers!

[. . .] Next week the BBC arrive to record, in the new studio, seven instalments for A Book At Bedtime! A bore .. but apparently wonderful publicity, especially BEFORE the book has been reviewed .. is'nt it odd? However Tote will have a hell of a lot of work to do .. because I shall be locked away all day for five days! Oh dear!

[. . .] The film – 'Providence' – is a TRIUMPH in Paris! Mar-vellous reviews and interviews and I am sailing with pleasure after the

---

1. A friend from Dirk's early Army days, now teaching at Woodcote House.

filthy things they wrote in New York ... they just dont know. So, darling, I'll be off and set the table and have a beer and start getting the Cannelonies out of the icebox for tonights supper ... and wash the lettuce and so on. And generally get back to earth .... thank you, dearest girl, for your super, marvellous, encouragement. I feel so much more able to face the critics and things with your sweetness and belief behind me.

Your ever devoted & loving bro'
    <u>Dirk</u> XXXXXX
These are hugs!
OOOOOOO

P.S. I just thought: after so many years of just being 'Dirk Bogardes Sister' ... you now REALLY ARE! And I hope that you will be as proud to be that as much as I am proud that you are.

To Dilys Powell
(Postcard)

Clermont
13 February 1977

No need for a reply to this; simply to tell you that 'your' film is a great success here in Paris. I dont think that I have ever been in a film which has culled such splendid reviews. Which is wonderous for Resnais, because he had a long time in the shadows. Now he is really, without doubt, the top ... I might, had he not been given the title by me already for ever ... remove Luchinos Emperors robe and drape it on the slightly bowed shoulders of Resnais! In N.Y, where it was unwisely opened before Paris, we were, naturally, butchered by Canby, Kael and Simon[1] ... but the rest flew to the attack and it is now a 'snob' success there ... what a lot they are. I have no way of knowing what you will feel about it ... some of it almost shocked me .. all of it amazed me .. the full architecture, for that is what it amounts to really, is staggering. It is so pleasing to be able to write to you like this! I would never have been able to in the past ... but IF it gets to London, and under the Delfonts and Cohens[2] I have fears it wont, ... I hope

---

1. Vincent Canby (*The New York Times*), Pauline Kael (*The New Yorker*), John Simon (*The New Leader*).
2. Lord (Bernard) Delfont and Nat Cohen, who ran the film division of EMI.

that your belief in the Cinema may be restored .. supposing that you ever lost belief! Which I very much doubt!

Much devoted love as ever ..

<u>Dirk</u>

Dirk had agreed to star opposite Andréa Ferréol in Despair, *adapted by Tom Stoppard from Nabokov's novel, for the German director Rainer Werner Fassbinder.*

To Lucilla Van den Bogaerde   *Clermont*
                                                   7 March 1977

<u>Keeping In Touch Letter.</u>

Cilla dear –

Rather a long silence from Chicago ... I suppose ice and fog and Bibles must be inhibiting, to say the least!

[...] It is no joke being in U.K now ... and even the weather has gone wrong-er than ever. Rain and floods for weeks ... and grey skies and when will it be Spring, and all that sort of thing. Here we are, oddly, basking in summer heat. A great big Lunch on the terrace on Saturday for Fassbinder, his Butcher Assistant chum (it takes all sorts!) and nice Tom Stoppard. We all sipped iced Ricards and watched the butter and paté melt slowly ... wallflowers, stocks, primulas, almond and white freesias ... all made it very un-German. I like Fassbinder very much. He'll be in N.Y. shortly I gather for a retrospective of his 30 films ... he is almost that age himself! Fattish .. like a red-haired buddah ... black leather jackets, boots, chain smoking, nicotined fingers, shrewd eyes, on-the-ball and how. I liked him immediatly. Shy though he, and I, was. So that is a big help. We start shooting in Munich on April 14th ... then Keil ... then Locarno ... then Berlin .. then Hamburg and Hamburg [sic]. I have asked him if I can look like an Egon Sheile drawing[1] .. and he was delighted! I had all my hair cut off in Cannes that morning to show him what it would be like. Well. It's like an elderly hedgehog. So there. And I'm stuck with it now. What I shall look like on the Telly in London when I have to

---

1. Not that it would have been much of a model. Dirk owned a Schiele drawing in pencil and watercolour: 'Mann am Bauch liegend, bekleidet' ('Man lying face down').

go and do the 'Tonight' show, 'Aquarius' and the rest I care not to think about. And anyway thats another thing I'm not relishing really ... the signing at Hatchards and all the brouhaha which seems to be building because of 'Postillion'. I expect you got your copy? The English have .... Lally despondant because I called her 'ignorant' ... I did'nt but she thinks I did ... Mamma deathly silent. Hating Lally and unable to remember anything. She gave the book to 'a lady down the hall who is very lonely' to read the day it arrived, and we all wonder if she ever bothered to get it back. Not enough about herself I fear. Everyone else v. kind ... and rumbles from Chatto pleasant so far. I read the fucking thing here in seven installments for Book at Bedtime. Awful chore. One BBC Sound Mixer called Harold .. who arrived with enough equipment to make a full length Movie ... a bossy [...] Lady Producer who, thankfully, got the runs on the second day and was kept weakly in her hotel up the road. But she wobbled back, alas! and made us do retake after retake 'You sound so DULL!' she kept crying, 'There's no LIFE' (no wonder) .. 'No EXCITEMENT!' In a desperate endeavour to be rid of them and their wires and plugs and tapes I did as she asked and feel sure that I must sound like an hysterical Governess with a class of autistic, black, two year olds. Joyce Grenfell would have done it MUCH better!

Well, it's all my fault anyway ... so I have only myself to blame.

What else? Oh yes ... Arthur Miller asked me to 'do' his new play,[1] with Bibi Andersson, in Washington on April 20th ... then open in N.Y. September. I was flattered but firm. Never the theater again, and never America if I can help it. Then a film in Cape Cod in the Summer with Lauren Bacall and so on ... and again no. I want to be here this summer .. and although the money is always vastly exciting from the States, most of it will go in Tax here anyway .. and why have a place like this if I'm only ever in it in the fucking winter?

'Under the Volcano' arrived yet again ... and a new script. Tote says it's better but still wont do ... so no Mexico in October. Perhaps I can really get down to the second book ... done the first 100.000 words and Chatto are pleased. So am I. I think I am getting better as I work on.

Lady, our daily that is, is bonking about with the Hoover ... and sniffing hard, a cold coming? Tote is busy outside sowing grass seed

---

1. *The Archbishop's Ceiling*. A more or less unholy disaster.

where the winter, and our nightly peeing in one place, has caught the lawn ... the sun is brilliant ... I'v trussed, and cleaned, a chicken for lunch, stuffed him with thyme all in flower, got the new totties in the old steamer and some fresh broccoli waits glossy green. I dont know why the Hell I got into all THAT! Probably because I am running out of steam ... I really need a beer. So I think I'll do just that and go down to the Saloon, as Lady calls it, reminding me of a cross-channel packet! and have one.

I hope that all is happy and well with the family ... and that the Bible Belt has belted up a bit. Are you down to 'work' of your own yet? I mean restoring, not washing Ulrics[1] knickers ...

A big kiss to you and to Gareth ... and to whoever else is about the porch or house in general ...

Much much love
Dirk.

To Tom Stoppard   *[Clermont]*
16 March 1977

Dear Tom –

Run out of letter paper so this[2] must do [...] I enclose some snapshots of your Luncheon with the Krauts. Not a fearfully glamorous party one thinks. However it may be useful one day for your 'book'.

I had a long read of 'T'[3] and was stunned that anyone in the world could learn so many words and say them! You are a bit difficult as an Author. And I though[t] Mercer was a bit hard! Goodness! He's Beatrix Potter in comparison. I do wish I'd seen it rather than read it ... but I always loose out on the few occasions I get to London. Maybe the English Play Society of Nice, run by the British Leigon, will do it one day ... when I am very old. But at least I'll be able to understand it since I have read it.

See you in Munich I expect ... glad you have done your writing .. did'nt think that you had much to do really. It [*Despair*] is all so well constructed.

---

1. Gareth and Lucilla's six-year-old son.
2. Notepaper from Résidence Roosendael, Arnhem – a souvenir of *A Bridge Too Far*.
3. TS had given Dirk a copy of his play *Travesties*.

Love to M.
Love to You ...
<u>Dirk</u>

Dirk had returned to London for the launching of A Postillion Struck
by Lightning. *The highlight of a triumphant week was his signing at
Hatchards in Piccadilly.*

To Norah Smallwood

Clermont
31 March 1977

My very dear Nora –
   Dont be silly dear; you cant get rid of me as easily as that! I'm for
'keeps' I fear ... how could I just fade away from a Family I cherish as
much as I do my own? And that is NOT being sentimental.
   Your dear, cherished, letter came this morning ,, my first day Up,
as they say, since I arrived back here with a sort of blazing throat and
high temperature and had caught, inevitably, a 'bug' .... but that,
even, was a delightful, if messy, souvenier of three quite extraordinary
days. I dont think, in all truth, that I have [ever] had such a time.
   Terror, and there was a great deal of it ... the dry mouth bit, the
palsey, and running to the loo ,, all before we bravely set off to
Hatchards .. and then very gradually it began to wear off and I really
started to enjoy myself. I could have gone on signing for hours. It was
the complete joy of the welcome which I recieved which so moved,
and humbled, me .... it was quite, quite unexpected. The kindness
of people there in the line astounded me and very nearly un-manned
me at times. To be still remembered, to be constantly thanked for the
pleasures, however small they might have been, that I had given people
over the many years, to be treated as almost a friend and not as a Film
Star was overwhelming. Someone wrote today and said that I must
have noticed her, I simply MUST have, because she was the woman
who left the shop six feet off the ground! I was able to assure her in
my note this morning that I was unable to recognise anyones levitation
since my own was so titanic! I was fifty feet above Piccadilly ... and
have'nt really touched base again yet!
   I told you at supper that it was probably the most important day
of my life .. and I hope that you believed me. For it was ... there have
been, of course, in the thirty or more years, days of splendour ... the

first showing of 'Death In Venice' here in Cannes to 3.000 roaring people with Visconti sitting beside me in silent tears, was one ... but Thursday last (was it so long ago?) was MY day ... not Visconti's, not Mann's ... this was all mine ... from cover to Fin. And the warmth, encouragement, and even pride which you all about me radiated simply filled my brimming cup to the point of spilling happiness such as I have never experienced before.

I dont give a fig about the Reviews ... except that they might harm sales for you of course ... but I do give a fig for your profits! At least, I pray, not your losses.

I am deeply stuck into Notes for 'Exits'¹ .. being in bed has been very, very useful ... cant remember when last I was! ... and all I long to do is get back here from Munich, Interlaken and ... can you believe it! Lubeck ... by June 20th so that I can push on with the next bit. It was with singular pride and pomp that I said 'no' to a very highly payed offer for some idiot film in July ... I told John [Charlton] to tell you, which I am sure he did, just as a joke ... I mean you dont HAVE to be burdened with any responsibilities ... but I want the time ... I WANT to write. I WANT. I WANT. And it's all your fault.

But you can just shove it back in Febuary if you dont like it ... and I'll try again.

Now; you have other writers and other books to worry about ... our little moment of time has passed for a while. So get on and be lovely to them, as you have been to me ... I'm 'launched' ... you broke the bottle across my bows and I'm off into a misty sea of self-discovery. I'll try to bring you back a worthy 'cargo' ....

Always, with the most devoted love –
    Dirk.

To Brock Van den Bogaerde   Clermont
                                                    14 April 1977

Brockalino –
    The boy is altering! Can it be Growing Up? How splendid .. and what a good, and funny, letter. Thanks. I dont expect you to write, as you know ... it is just a super bonus when you do.

---

1. 'Starting with Exits' was the latest working title for *Snakes and Ladders*.

See your point about the Americans. I cant bear them ... and never want to set foot in their immature, undiplomatic, plastic, mutilated land again. Nor will I. Made myself quite clear? Good. I do think, however, that they write super Musical Shows, make reasonable ice-cream, and sometimes make excellent Movies. It is not enough, I think, for The Greatest Nation In The World. However ... it takes all kinds, I suppose. And they do pay well. Usually.

I am just back from a four-day Publicity Stint in London .. and that was pretty tacky too ... Arabs and empty ice cream tubs at every bus stop ... the dirt and the shabbiness were not to be believed. Or the prices. For my four days at the Connaught the bill came to £2.000 .... minus the air fares. Shit. It is slowly but surely turning a bright shade of Pinky-Red ... and the resentment, the envy, the boredome is very trying to deal with. I stood for eight minutes (watched the airport clock) at a Tobacconists at Heathrow because I wanted one packet of ciggies ... not a whole Carton .. had about twenty minutes to get the flight. A fat lady, in uniform, was behind the counter talking to a thin lady standing beside me, also in uniform. They had a long chat about someone called Muriel and Hal ... angrily I waited. Eventually with many smiles she said 'Tat Ta ..' and the thin one left. Whereupon the fat one, tore a piece of paper in two and shoving a pencil at me demanded, without any apology or politeness at all ... 'Your Autograph.' I refused with ice white fury and said I wanted one packet of Kent. Which I got, from a glaring face of anger, and handed over my rotten Pence. Which she chucked on the floor! And that is syptomatic of England today.

A small thing ... but after eight years in France I am quite unused to that sort of behaviour. No wonder they are all striking everywhere. No one cares and Fuck You Charlie. Service is a dirty word ... pity. It was'nt like that once upon a time.

Off tomorrow to Germany ... Munich for Fassbinder and then on to Lubeck on the Baltic Sea ... which I look forward to as if it was pnumonia. We'll be there until June 20th. Lu and George, thank God, arrived here yesterday to look after things. G. pretty ill ... and almost crippled. Could'nt walk at the airport .. and was in bed in great pain until I got my local Doctor in who set him on a course of injections and pills ... and the man is alive again and can walk .. sit, almost bend ... he'll be fit as a fiddle in another day. And in England he had been simply told that his case was hopeless and 'to rest' .... Christ!

The difference in him today, and in Lu for that matter, is shattering. Hope is back ... and pain has finally gone ... we hope for a time at least.

Golden weather here .. hot and blue skies ... I shall hate leaving for the unfriendly north .. but the lolly is good, so ..... and Mamma, or Ginny [...] needs keeping. Ye Gods.

It would be SMASHING to see you in the summer ... anytime from July .. but you do remember, dont you, how dull it can be .. and since you dont drive, I suppose, you'll be a bit isolated ... and last time you came here you were little Dolly Starry Eyed .. that part of your life is over. So maybe you'd find it all dull and slow and too far from the tits .. However I would love to see you here ... as you know ... so it is over to you. I'll do the fare. You bring the Tent and ten bound copies of Colette ... or Wilde ... or even Austen!

And we wont play 'A Chorous Line' once ... or fucking old 'Chicago' ...

Tote is well and harassed, storing the BMW and so on away for the next two months ... Lu is ironing ... George lying naked in the sun ... and Daisy and Labbo lie in snoring heaps under the olives. I need a beer [...]

Glad the dancing¹ was useful ... and glad too that you are surprising yourself. Of <u>course</u> you have to <u>work</u> for it, nit. If I had <u>told</u> you that however you might not have tried so hard ... and so successfully ....

Your very fond Dirk –

To Tom Stoppard
(Postcard)

Lübeck
5 June 1977

I DO HOPE I WASN'T <u>TOO</u> DOPED WHEN YOU SO KINDLY CALLED! SUPPOSE I WAS. BUT I'M PRETTY WHACKED. OUT OF 32 DAYS SHOOTING I HAVE HAD ONLY <u>ONE</u> FREE! FASSBINDER HAS MADE IT THE STORY OF ONE MAN – AND FUCK THE REST! I DONT IN THE LEAST MIND AND FEEL LIKE A ONE MAN BAND –

---

1. With Dirk's encouragement, Brock had enrolled at the Dance Centre in London, where he worked with the choreographer Arlene Phillips.

R. DOTRICE, OR E. WILLIAMS, OR MAX WALL[1] EVEN! 2
MORE WEEKS TO GO. IT REALLY IS AN EXCEPTIONAL
FILM; BUT I HAVE NO IDEA HOW IT WILL ALL 'GO'
TOGETHER. FINISH HERMANS FACTORY TOMORROW
(ALL LILAC AND PINK!) AND ON TO THE MEETING
WITH FELIX.[2] THAT WILL FINISH THINGS. DID I TELL
YOU THAT WE <u>STARTED</u> THE SHOOTING WITH THE
VERY END? AND HAVE WORKED IT <u>ALL</u> BACKWARDS?
NO? WELL WE BLOODY WELL DID. MUCH LOVE TO
YOU BOTH. DB.

Late at night on 20 June, after the completion of shooting on Despair,
Fassbinder pushed a note of thanks under the door of Dirk's hotel room.

To Rainer Werner Fassbinder 	*Clermont*
24 June 1977

My dear Reiner –

Forgive me that I type this to you instead of writing to you in my
own hand ... you would never be able to read it I fear, and it is
important that you read what I want to say to you. After all, we have
never been able to 'speak' to each other, so I must take the chance of
writing.

Your abscence at the Farewell Party of course saddened me ... you
are the Boss and you were expected by us all ... however I did'nt
expect you myself, for I know you just a little bit now, and I knew
that you would perhaps not have the special kind of courage needed
for that sort of evening! However your letter gave me great happiness
as well as great sadness too. Paradox? Perhaps.

I suppose I have never worked ever with anyone before who had a
'Death Wish' ... and being a very adventerous, curious, believing
kind-of-person myself, I find it very difficult to understand. Although,
God knows, I do understand the athmosphere in Germany after only
three months stay ... it cannot be easy for a person of your age and

---

1. Roy Dotrice is, and Emlyn Williams and Max Wall were, famed for their solo
performances.
2. Two important sequences in *Despair*. Nabokov's protagonist, Hermann Hermann,
owned a chocolate factory.

generation to bear easily. But you must fight that terribly dangerous athmopsphere .. and push it aside ... You say in your letter to me that 'More likely there is more despair than anything else ..' I assume you mean Life? That is fundamentally NOT TRUE! Life is full of hope and promise.

A minor example, if you like, is our recent work together. Nabakov, the odd Mr Stoppard ... myself, Andrea ... all of us together, with you, under your controll, making a film of which we will all, I know, be tremendously proud. Sharing ideas and emotions among so many different ages and beliefs ... but all united under the splendid 'umbrella' of your particular form of Genius. And that is not too strong a word. Though often misapplied. In your case I dont think that it is. I did'nt actually 'learn' anything from you, I suppose ... that is not important ... but I hope that I was able to bring to <u>you</u> some of the learning or teaching which I have had from people like Cukor, Milestone, Clayton, Losey, Visconti and Resnais and the rest of them ... and to SHARE that learning with someone like you is quite wonderful. To see it used and re-used, as you did, to see you 'eat' literally, the training which I brought you, was magical for me. I was simply handing on the 'baton' in this extraordinary business of the Creative Cinema. And to see you take that 'baton' is HOPE, Reiner ... NOT ever despair! You must realise by now how devoted to you both Andrea and I were ... and how much we respected you and wanted to do our very, very best for you. At the beginning I admit it was far from easy and I was almost in despair myself! But we struggled on together, you and she and I, and I have no doubt whatsoever that we have made an extraordinary film together.

But we could not have done it without you ... is'nt that a hopeful sign? Surely? To recieve, and to give, love, and trust, in work as difficult as ours takes more than despair, my dear fellow.

I have probably bored you shitless by now, with all this. Anyway you can tear it all up and I will never know.

One thing more before I go ... you say in your letter that I have taught you Authority without Fear. I dont know if that is so .... But did you ever realise that that is exactly what you have NOT got? You have Authority <u>with</u> fear .... everyone, from Minx[1] down to the

---

1. Dieter Minx, production supervisor.

Publicity Frau was shit terrified of you. And your Authority. So if I have, by any chance, taught you what it is to have it WITHOUT fear, then for Gods sake use it soon! It will make your life slower, more irritating, and generally take longer. But it is well worth while winning. You create it wonderfully well for yourself . . . from your chain cap to your heavy boots . . . the too loud music the too fast car . . . the Death Wish I suppose . . . but I know, and you know, that all that junk really conceals a very pleasing 'soft center' as Herman used to say . . . but be careful of it. It can rebound in your face so damned easily. And with your blinding talent you really dont need too much. Just enough to keep the Front Office worried. But not too much.

The Cinema needs you very much. You have a tremendous amount to give it . . . there are marvellous people waiting to work with and for you . . . stay with us! There is so much for you to do, to give, so many roads for you to take . . . Life is not just one boring round of Clubs and Discos and Pills . . . and Pot. Use them, of course, for the relaxation you need from time to time . . . but not as often as you do. Dont live by them, or by the mindless people who exist in that world. They will only swamp you and kill you off far, far quicker than your own feelings of dissilusion or so-called Despair.

As you say at the closing of your letter . . . 'life is not, maybe, so sad like it seems' . . . . you are Fucking right, R.W.F! Life is bloody marvellous and you should be so damned grateful that you have the youth and the brilliance to storm it.

Now I'll stop. God knows what you will make of this. I dont know. But it comes with my warmest respect and affection, and gratitude, for all the kindness you have shown me in the last few weeks, and all the security which you gave me during, for me at least, a very difficult and bewildering (at times!) assignment. It is something I will never forget and a period of time which I would never have missed for anything. Thank you.

Remember; Despair comes when you have nothing. – you have everything – & everything to gain.

Affectionately

Dirk

PS. WHATEVER YOU DO, DO NOT DUBB THE CAST IN ENGLISH VOICES. IT WILL BE DISASTER. D.

To Dilys Powell   *Clermont*
                                          24 June 1977

Most dear Dilys –

I am simply silly with fatigue: three months with magic Fassbinder
and his Leather Gang, and all in German too .. (I mean they were ...
I just had to use a vague German Accent) .. but found it hard to
follow what was actually <u>wanted</u>, if you follow me.

Got home two days ago .. and am just thawing out. I am really too
old for this caper. Fourteen hours, sometimes twenty four depending
on the 'problems' ... a day, and hemmed into crummy hotels, smothered with gherkins and 'mixt salate' and everything fried or frozen
or dead or both. Oh To Be In France I kept wailing ... anyway: it was
a stupifying experience, marvellous and terrible and one I would
not have missed for anything. So I am really not complaining, just
collapsing. I have never ever worked with a man who has an in-built
Death Wish. And this I found a scrap trying. However living in
Germany, and very close all the time to the Eastern Border with
'Russia' ... makes one realise, drastically, that Youth there has it's
serious problems. The very obscenity of that Wall ... all 700 miles of
it ... shakes your head until what teeth you have rattle. They are so
terribly near. And all is so fearfully fragile across the mine-fields and
the wire. The hysteria of Berlin is one thing ... abnormal but copeable
with ... the sadness and horror of the countryside, the blocked in
windows, the savaged meadows sowen, sewen (?) with mines, the
Watch-towers .. the warnings at the end of gentle country lanes where
the roadsurface filters out into overgrown rank weeds and then the
startling horror of the anti-personel mines strung along on wooden
posts ... sun slanting, blackbirds singing .. wind in the un-cut hay.
And across the track of death, for that is what it is, a watching man
with binoculars. And all silent. No wonder Herr Fassbinder does'nt
believe in anything at all. After three months there I dont either. Now.

But your letter here to cheer me and worry me. What CAN you
mean about my being 'annoyed' with your wonderfully generous,
warm and loving review of my dotty book? I was only 'annoyed', and
NOT that anyway, that you had been so good and kind to me ... I
basked in your approbation and care. Everything I do, as I have told
you before so often, is done FOR you ... even if you dont care for
the result much ... it does'nt matter ... you are always, and always

will be, my steady councillor ... my balance. You may even have seen 'Your' film by now, 'Providence' ... and DETESTED it ... but I dont care. For whatever mistakes it might have it was all made for you ... and if I failed you ... simple! I try again!

[...] I have decided now to give the Movies a rest .... It all seems to be piling up on me once again, and it is not something that I like any more. I DETEST the work, I detest the job, and most of the time I detest the people. I started over thirty years ago ... and it is not one whit better. The fact that I have been chosen by Resnais, or Visconti, or Fassbinder helps tremendously ... of course ... but really, when all is said and done, it is what my Father always said. 'No job for a man.' .... it is'nt. So now I settle down, or hope to after I have got the hay in and the place cleaned up ... almost abandond since March ... into Volume 11, that looks like eleven, I mean 2 .... of 'Postillion' .... and then I can really say what I feel about the Movies!

I have been reading some of the Critics for 'A Bridge ..' .... what bothers me is that most of them are so young! Next, that so many of them appear to be right. 25 million on someone elses suffering seems excessive. I wonder if the Dutch cared for it? I did not. I was there at the time ... the only member of the entire Group who was. One day, standing miserably on an airstrip near Deventer a small, tubby, Dutch pilot came up to me and asked me if I had really been present in '44. I said that I had. 'Was it just like this?' he asked very quietly ... Trying to be loyal I said 'No; not quite ... not even just ... a bit.' He smiled and put his arm round my shoulder. 'I was fifteen, I was here ... too. A Boy Scout. It was'nt really like this at all, was it? This is just the Cinema ...?' I remember just smiling at the chap, rather helplessly ... 'It's just the Cinema' I repeated and we went our ways. He contented, I think. I irritated by the splendour being poured into something we had both seen 'for real' thirty two years before. I suppose it does'nt matter really ....

I must stop. This has bored you far too long and we have got a PACT.

[...] So much love –
Dirk

To Dilys Powell

Clermont
Wednesday: 6 July 1977

Dilys dear –

Dont for God's sake panic ... I'm not starting to break the Pact we made ... and I do not expect a reply to this. So there. And this machine, ages old, is'nt a bit Magic!¹ It is, I regret to say, German ... called an Adler, and I was deeply in love with it from the first moment I recieved a pleasant letter from some Agent in Hollywood. I did'nt do the Job for him, but did get the name of the machine. Better? Awful to believe in Magic.

I feel EXACTLY like you about the Germans. It IS a bother. I so liked many of them working there ... individuals on the Troup .. Make-Up, Hair, the adorable and brilliant Dagmar [Schauberger] in the wardrobe who designed all the magnificent, odd, Fassbinder-Nabakov costumes. (Berlin '29–30 again ..) but generally I found myself musing on people of MY age and just wondering what Daddy (or Mummy for that matter) did in the war. And then I felt hostile and uncomfortable. And guilty about feeling so crass and unforgiving. But under it all lay a deep compost of fear and distrust. The Japanese for me are as bad ... it was simply years before I could pull myself to even meet one during all those ghastly luncheons which Rank used to hold at Pinewood, and to which one was summonsed like a mechanical doll ... and I still cant travel in an Elevator with more than one! The voices terrify me still ... I only hear them through thick, glossy leaves, and in a sweat of steamy sweat [*sic*] ... lying trying not to breath.²

All this, of course, has to go into bloody Vol. II [...] Nora Smallwood the Devine insists on 'lots more war, dear' and I am as reluctant as a cat near a bath .. all claws out ... I so dislike other peoples wars .. in books ... and mine was not worse and no better than hundreds and hundreds of others .. well, in fact, better ... because I survived it intact. But Vol 2 is horridly difficult ... it is the leaving out of people which I find so difficult ... selection is frightfully tiresome and hurtful, of course, to people who tear out to read the

---

1. DP had asked Dirk to tell her about his typewriter – 'if it *is* a typewriter and not a form of magic'.
2. A received terror, of course; Dirk never fought in the jungles of Japanese-occupied territory. He consistently romanticised his military career and used others' experiences as his own.

index and find, angrily, that they are not included when they all 'did so much' for me. Oh bugger! Perhaps I'd be better employed with a novel.

That is no less difficult, I know ... but you can chumble up the facts and personalities and get away with all kinds of mischief ... In a Bio. it all has to be correct ... I'll jog on. It IS a bit hard what with the hay .. not all in yet .. and the bloody dogs grub .. and weeding the potager and deheading my miserable (because we are too high here, and the soil is sparse and full of limestone, which I gather Roses hate ... anyway Edith Piaf and Champes Elysees do ... bitterly) Roses. But I promised Nora and she is not one to be fobbed off for long .... 'Try and get this Cinema Thingamajig part over, and settle down, dear boy ... we dont want to wait all year ...' Awfully bossy. Very lovely. A glorious New Friend. How lucky one is ...

Resnais telephoned two days ago .. "Ow are you, Durk? 'Ow is your German Accent for Fassbinder? Is he really marvellous ... do you like 'im better than me?' He says that 'P' cant get a showing in England because no one will buy it ... they have, I dont know who, offered to 'take' it in and give the Company whatever percentage may come from whatever Profit. This they, the Frogs, rightly find un acceptable ... and Television wont buy it because it is full of four letter words .. and that wont do. John G. uses every one I think I know ... with a beauty and delicacy only he could muster ... someone here said that he made the nastiest words sound like Shakespear or Molier ... and he does. Are'nt they silly? So we just wait ... Resnais feels that something may happen in what he insists on calling The Fall ... he ADORES America ... without Television Sales. But I doubt it myself. And if it IS shown on the Box we are absolutely lost. It is the most un-television subject you can imagine. But it is still running in Paris ... and has now opened in most of the big University Cities of the U.S to much the same reviews as we had in Paris, Brussels and etc ... not a whimper along the lines of the irritating Miss Kael ... a clever journalist but a lousy Critic .. apparently she talked and coughed all the way through the Press Show in N.Y. in company with two elegant, tightly jeaned young fellows with braclets and ear-rings. When asked if she would care to see the film again, since she clearly could not have heard one single syllable, far less seen anything through the haze of smoke, she cried angrily .. 'I NEVER see a Movie twice!'. And that was that.

Another reason for chucking it all in very soon ... I feel, in my heart, that I have nothing new, vital, or exciting to do in my work. I am stale. So stop now. As I shall stop this over long note.

Glad about the flowers .. gladder about the cat[1] .. I bet it is a Siamese. And if I am right that barking hound will have his tail between his legs the next time you allow me to visit you ...

Dont reply, my dear .. we'll get into a 'thing' ... and thats exactly what we are not supposed to do.

<u>Always</u> my love
<u>Dirk</u>.

To Tom Stoppard   *Clermont*
                                                   8 July 1977

My dear Tom –

I am suddenly out of the haze ... two weeks home here, or a little over, and the world does'nt seem quite so frantic and awful as recently it did. I'm really writing to say how smashing it was to read all the splendid things about your last 'effort'[2] .... all that squeaking from the Dreadful [Bernard] Levin. That was magic ... and so were the others which I read. I had a bash, last Sunday, at trying to call you .... but after twelve duff tries I settled for another beer instead. But I did send loving thoughts, or whatever they are called, and dont suppose for one moment that they did the least bit of good.

I may be coming out of a haze ... but it appears that I have not yet re-mastered this sodding machine. Excuses upon excuses .... I am also writing to say that I am so tremendously grateful to you for the chance of doing 'Despair' ..... I hasten to add that while I would not have NOT done it ... and I mean that very sincerely ... I am not over anxious to repeat the trip again under the umbrella of Bavaria Films! A very unorganized lot, which amazed me slightly since we were always told the Krauts were so very organized in every form. Not true with Bavaria. And half the exhaustion and frustration on 'Despair' was due to them ... not to Fassbinder who was all I could have possibly wanted as a Director, and brilliant to boot. And nice. [R]eally

---

1. Dirk had sent a sheaf of flowers; DP had bought a cat.
2. TS's new play, *Every Good Boy Deserves Favour*, performed, with full orchestra, at the Royal Festival Hall.

nice. Under all the chains, leather, thigh boots and grannie-glasses a soft-center lies snuggled. And I found it and liked it enormously. Sadly the people who surround him are the most awful lot of scrubby, pot smoking, squealing little Leather Boys ... pretty tiresome; and dangerous too for I do think that they have a tremendous effect on Reiner who desperately needs love, as he calls it, and insists on rejecting it at the same time. Equally boring. However he is still pretty young .. and things can change rapidly. I hope that they will. Andrea Ferreol and I were really, when all is said and done, the only two really professional people on his Team of actors. The rest were hellish .... full of 'Method' .. full of 'pot' ... late, forgetting their lines, crying, sulking .. (lots of that went on ...) and generally behaving like a set of moronic infants in an Acting School. There really was'nt time, as I once did point out to Reiner, to learn all your splendid words, leap about the set like a mad Stag, progress towards madness in fifty different levels, AND teach his fucking Gang how to act. He was very concilatory about this ... and knew that it was damned tough for glorious Andrea and I .... and now that he really has, for the first time it appears, made a Professional Film with a large budget ... 2 million five hundredthou, I was told ... instead of shooting all Sunday Night in some celler with his mates ... which is how he made all the others (he only really comes to life at night) I think that he will want to go on .... he did re-act marvellously to the work we did for him ... and was bug eyed every day at Rushes ... and wrote a smashing letter at the end to thank one for all the things he had learned. The most important one seemed to be 'Authority without Fear' ..... I'm happy if I was able to show him that. For it is exactly the one thing which he lacks himself! He has Authority WITH fear. They were all shit scared of him from the head Dr Krapp to the smallest fag in the make-up rooms ... and no one, but no one, would say no to him. Except me. And he liked me for that.

Andrea and I never, ever, argued with him, or ever remotely let him feel that he was not absolutely right ... which he was most of the time. And whereas the rest of his Actors, so called, screamed, argued, insisted, stamped dear little booted feet, or got huffy, he sailed away with Lydia and Herman .. as he should. And we really were tremendously happy together. She is quite devine. Her Lydia is so moving, funny, and dreadfully sad ... her final crack-up is very tough to take ... You know all the time that Lydia and Herman desperately need

each other .. even though they are 'wrong' for each other ... and
everything <u>he</u> does, really, is for her, or for their life together in 'the
mountains.'

Klaus [Löwitsch], who plays Felix, was the other REAL pro. And
was superbe. OH! I DO hope you will approve. Did I tell you that
Nabakovs son came to see us? Very impressed by the 'seriousness' of it
all ... and by the 'feeling for my fathers work' which seemed to
emenate from the Set. I hope it did. We had a super script to start
with ... and I DO think it is the essence of the book ... though it
varies ... Fassbinder-wise ... a good deal. But I feel sure that he knew
what you wanted to say, and what Nabakov wanted to say ... and I
think that comes out clearly. It is not a cheap movie. I think it is a
very important one indeed. And thank you dear Tom, for your patience
and belief ... I shall long remember that evening at the Colombe d'Or
when you discovered that there were two actors for Felix and Herman!
And it is right, you know ... it really works so much better that way.

I heard today from Munich that there have already been two long
runnings of the film, and another takes place next week ... to see if
they can 'shorten' it ... he did, I regret to say, over-shoot dreadfully.
Alas! Something will have to go ... one sits nibbling finger nails
wondering just what they will be. Perhaps you'll be able to see it soon?
Do call me if and when you do ... Andrea is ill with worry that you
will be bewildered and not fully like what you see, but I really dont
think that you will. I think, and I can be most horribly wrong, that
you will be as proud of your first Real Film Script as we are proud of
the film. But I did promise that the least word from you would be
sent by telephone, Dove, airplane or courier to Andrea where ever she
may be at the time. She really BECAME Lydia ... as I rather exhaustedly became her husband. It was a very strange, exciting, bond. Oh!
the fun we all had with Chocky-Wocks and Goggle Moggle ....

One thing though, after 'Despair' I never want to LOOK at a box
of fucking chocolates ever again! Days we spent in factories, filled with
the rancid stink of margerine, peppermint substitute, violet creams,
vast vats of peled hazle, wall, and other nuts .... it was in our hair, in
our clothes, stuck to us like the smell of death does ... so, next time,
dear Tom, set the story in an open field! And we had a hell of a lot of
THEM too! And bloody lakes!

No really: I did love it all .... it was just tiring at the time ... now
I'd happily leap into one of my fifteen suits, slip my rings on my

fingers, and swagger out into the 'Berlin streets' .... to meet
Orlovious . . .

Nicer to meet you . . . and your scrumptious Doctor[1] . . will you
give her a kiss from me?

and a huge hug . . and once more,

congratulations . . . and love . .

Dirk

P.S. As a slight sample of how things were altered. Remember the final
scene in the village square, calling from the window to the crowds and
the police? Reiner thought it was all a bit too Richard Tauber . . . so
now the whole scene is played as a whispered soliliqy (cant spell it)
from Herman, crouched in the snow, surrounded by police. And it
works too. Bavaria had hysterics . . . the crowd cost a fortune, and all
got sent away without ever seeing the Camera! But I think you'll
approve . . , D.

To Jeremy Hutchinson[2]

Clermont
14 July 1977

Dear Mr Hutchinson –

I got back from my over-long trip to Germany, and have not
forgotten that I promised to write to you as soon as I was rested
and at 'peace' . . . which, if you dont count hay-making, weeding,
watering, raking and making enormous hay-stacks . . . I have twelve
acres of hillside . . . I suppose I am!

Really I was to write to tell you how happy your letter of May 15th
made me, and to see if I could find any more 'stuff' relating to the
Cottage during the late twenties early thirties.

There really is'nt much . . . an early picture postcard of the house
itself . . . as we first found it . . . . looking pretty scruffy . . . and what
you know as 'the end Papers' . . . a photograph which my father took
from a very small, and decidedly dangerous, airplane about '30 or '31.
Nothing else remains much except snapshots of people sitting under

---

1. TS's wife, Miriam.
2. Jeremy (later Lord) Hutchinson QC, had read *Postillion* and written – with considerable local knowledge – to congratulate Dirk, who replied briefly from Munich. This
more detailed letter is enjoyed to the fullest if copies of both *Postillion* and *Great Meadow*
are to hand.

trees ... and they would in no way interest you .. regrettably, I cant think why, no 'snaps' seem to have been taken of the Cottage itself. Which is why I had to do the small sketches, mostly from memory, some from ones my father did for me 'on the spot' so to speak some years before he died. They were not awfully good, so I sort of re-did them, using memory mostly.

In our day the cottage was very primitive indeed. As you have gathered. Lamps, privvy, pump ... the road from Lullington Court was a chalk road .. the path up to the cottage just a chalky track. Very slippery in the rain and dangerous with heavy baskets! Inside it was a warren of rooms each leading out of the other, as far as I remember .. and the North End was fearfully damp and rather gloomy ... we spent most of our time in the big room on the south looking down to Lullington Court and Littlington.

Lullington Court was a working Farm. Vast dairies with bowls of cream, and all kinds of milk, plus great blocks of yellow butter standing on slate slabs. It was very cool, covered in ivy, and sweet smelling. After the pig-sty, our favourite place ... apart from the great barn where the Stallion lived ... at the far corner of Great Meadow which was, I believe, converted into a chic house sometime just before the war. There was no one living nearer than the Axfords (as they were really called) at the Court .... I believe there are two cottages down at the bottom of the road now .. but they were not there in our time. Mrs Fluke lived in the pair of Victorian cottages at the bottom of Great Meadow opposite the Court, and Mrs Diplock, who sometimes came and 'did' for us, lived at the end of the garden behind the hedge where the pump was.

So we were pretty isolated ... there was, I remember, a bit of a ruined windmill up the lane towards Wilmington .. and a small quarry with some very creepy caves alongside. I was once told that ammunition was stored there during the '14, 18 war. But dont know if it was so.

The hole, through which my unfortunate mother fell, led to a strange tunnel, as I said in the book, and which is very likely still there today ... it was under the floor boards of what we called the 'hall' which led into the big room with the inglenook with it's two big built-in settles. Are they still there I wonder?

Did you know, I am sure that you do, that what is now called the Market Cross, or square, was originally called Waterloo Place? Because the cottages opposite the cross, at right angles to the Smugglers Inn, were used to station the miserable Troops who were later to fight in Waterloo ... the Market Cross was in a slightly different position, nearer to the Chestnut tree ... and rebuilt at least twice in our time because the Village Boys used to get a bit 'lit up' at Fair-time and tried, stupidly, to climb it. We were told of one who fell with the entire cross, and got a large piece through his lung ... but I expect that was just Mrs Fluke .... the Star was a family Inn .. not a lick of paint on The Dragon or the carvings along the facade. I remember the shock and horror everyone felt when it got 'taken over' and painted with bright cheap colours ... just down from the Star was an Ale Bar called 'The Steamer' ... it was closed just after we got there, I seem to recall ... and turned into cottages now called Steamer Cottages. There was not a tea shoppee or a gift shoppee for miles! And the only garage, well, there was'nt one really; just a big Shell Petrol Pump on the pavement outside Barkers .... Miss Barker once blew herself, and most of the shop, into the street one afternoon because she filled herself a can of petrol and took it into the kitchen to 'sponge down' some soiled clothing. By the open Range. We were very awed by the debris and the smell and the smoking timbers .. and poor Miss Barker (Baker?) being carted away to Seaford, in an ambulance.

None of this is in the least bit interesting ... I am being a bore; but oh goodness! I did so adore it all ... as I think I said in my card from somewhere, I never really ever went back. Once ... in the fifties ... for a brief, sad, trip around ... nothing was much as I remembered it. It was all so damned neat and tidy! The Court was very Homes And Gardens and Converted ... the Barn had great lawns around it ... many of the elms had vanished round the gully ... and round the church which was all neat too .. and the smother of trippers in the village saddened me more than anything. I did'nt come right up to the cottage ... peered over the hedge down by the Diplocks ex-cottage .. and it looked pretty and tended ... but I missed the rows of potatoes in the front beds! The currents ... the damson tree at the corner ... the rhubarb patch ... so I went away.

You must NEVER go back, must you?

[...] Forgive this 'book' of ill typed (and spelled) nonsense .. and thank you once again so much for such a very delightful letter.

Yours sincerely

Dirk Bogarde.

To Norah Smallwood   *Clermont*
                                              23 July 1977

Norah dear –

Goodness! You DO know how to make a chaps' heart thud!
With pleasure I hasten to add, not fear. Your telephone call was
cherished because I know that you dont really make long-distance
ones if you can send off a P.C of a Cream Puff ... and that evening
a P.C of a cream Puff would not have served to lift me from a spell
of gloom and despair ... (Nabakov clearly made an impact on me
...) However I set too with a stronger back next morning very
early, and bashed away and away, re-writing, re-forming, re-phrasing
and screwing up a great deal of the village typing paper. The result
of my labours is in your hands, or on your desk, now. Chapter 5.
The Clincher, really ... from this it must all truthfully 'stem'. I
mean the rest of the oeuvre.

And this morning. (NEVER begin a sentence with AND) your
splendid follow up letter arrived which, since I had just finished the
last corrections [...] came at an awfully good time. You are kind,
and generous to me. I am such a lucky fellow .. but it wont get in my
way ... I shall be very firm with myself and still re-rite (!) and all the
rest of it.

The Selection bit, you guessed, is MONSTROUS hard. A life of
some fifty six–seven years, pretty packed with things and people, is
frightfully difficult to 'Essence' without a faint odour of Cheating
coming in with the fabric. I shall have to leave so many people out:
so many things which happened, simply because there is either not
the time or the place, or because they would distress people ... even
those who did not know the facts about which I might write. This is
hellish. Yesterday, for example, I trailed miles in the blistering heat to
lunch with Rex Harrison and took with me a photo copy of a letter
which he wrote to me the day after Kay Kendall, who was my most
beloved friend ever perhaps, and certainly most missed, died of
Lukemia. It is a letter of such startling beauty, of such love, of such
pain, of such generosity and joy, of so very much that made his
adoration for Kate the triumph it was .... I wanted him to read it
and see if I could use, at least a fragment of it, in a forthcoming
chapter. She and he were so much a part of my life for over five years
that it would be totaly impossible NOT to use their story. But. Can

I? How much pain might it cause all the ladies who followed Kate, albeit after a decent interval?

I think the letter will distress him. He was to read it alone last night .. (there is yet another lady now ..) and would 'write to you old boy' but I dont think he will ... and if he does it'll be to say 'no'. So. I have to find another way around that. However that is only one example of the worries which face me ...

[...] I want, I feel, to back track, and go forward, like a Weaver in a way, so that past and present and the immediate moment are woven into a, possibly confusing, Jacobs Coat? Might this be wrong? Ah! You'll have to catch this feeling, and I think you only can, from this Clincher Chapter. But if you do hate it, stop me as soon as maybe with a telegram and say 'No!' .... I'll understand and try another form of 'style' ... but I have a secret feeling it MIGHT work .....

[...] I want to try and Investigate my theory of Acting ... to show, if I can, what the loss of privacy and annonimity meant to me and how much pain it caused. To re-call my Father and Elizabeth and Forwood as often as I can ... because they were always, and thank goodness in two instances still are, the keel to my boat.

Sometimes the sails as well! And I want to slip into the bits of the war which shocked me, or amused me, or altered me ... for the Growing Up Process is still taking place, and I think it is important to let it drift through the work.

And I have done quite enough talking. [...] So .... 'have a read' .. and tell me, if you can bear to, what you think ... because from now on in, that is to say from Chapter 6, I strike out on this route ..... I dont want to break all our necks at a crossroads!

With gratitude
& <u>much</u> love
<u>Dirk</u>.

To Ann Skinner   *Clermont*
                                              31 July 1977

Annie love –

What a super letter: at last. I thought you was dead, or something. Nearly are, working in Devon .. never mind. I am not too distressed about No Go With Prince Charles[1] .. he's really got awful little eyes .. I'll start collecting Views of Princess Risborough instead. Thanks for trying anyway.

[...] the Fassbinder Project [...] took me away for three long, facinating, but exhausting, months. I'm mad about Fassbinder. Very odd creature, simply brilliant; marvellous to work for and with, difficult; strange; granny glasses [...] caps with chains on them ... fast cars and 'Clock Work Orange Theme' on radio, cassette thing, every day, all day if it was'nt Callas in 'Tosca' or 'Norma'. At full blast. Wearying. But then he is awfully young too ... thirty in Berlin. We had a great party off the Kufurstendamm ... Tony was amazed at the beauty of the waitresses, 'the only really chic women I'v seen in Berlin .. or even Germany' he said confidentally. Save they were all fellows. Oh well .... But the film (Stoppard from Nabakovs novel Despair) was terrific, sets, costumes (mine was the biggest wardrobe since that God Awful 'Listz' and cost more!) and a devine leading Lady called Andrea Ferreol who was the Fat Lady in La Grande Bouffe ... but you probably never saw it. Anyway we were Hubby and Wife and made an astonishing pair. Funny, but I hope sad too ... I think I might have done some good work here. Perhaps some of my best. It remains to be seen naturally! I had to play with a German accent since I was the only Inglise in the film ... and it made us all a bit more harmonious. We made it in English, naturally ... he is breaking into the American Market.

Been through Aggers and Missers, as Connie Willis[2] used to say, with ABTF and [Richard Attenborough] got me into the shit over Browning, and I find it hard to forgive him .. since he refused to listen to my complaints that Browning, whome I knew, was not a cunt and never ever made the frightful balls up the film suggests. It all got a bit up-tight and I was on the point of returning my Fee (small in comparison to the Yanks) to Lady Browning for some Charity. Felt I could'nt take money for dishonouring a dead man. You know? However I got talked out of that since everyone said it would cause a scandal and so on. But I refused to have [Dickie] near me for a while, until I simmered down. Eventually, reluctantly, I did .. and we made a sort-of patch up. He and she were simply shattered by the effects on

1. AS had been unable to find a suitable postcard of the Heir to the Throne.
2. In charge of continuity on *A Bridge Too Far*.

the Critics and many of the Public who wrote bitterly complaining. I dont think he really thought it could <u>ever</u> happen to him. I actually DID feel a bit sorry for them, white, shaking [...] However; there you go.[1]

And it's not doing all that well I gather ... here or in the U.S and Bond and 'Star Wars' are scooping up the lolly. It was a silly, silly film to have made at such expense. Who CARES about that old war anyway. And a Fuck Up to boot! I am doubtful about 'Magic'[2] also ... thats all been done before, and [Dickie] is better with crowds than individual Actors; as I know. Anyway. Good luck and have a smashing time in L.A. I know just what you mean about wanting to work there. It's like, we used to say, 'not fucking the Maid' .... you really <u>must</u> work once in L.A. Even if you hate it [...]

Returning to your letter and a question you make about Fassbinder, he is now considered THE leading Director in German [sic] and in Europe. Of his age. And I agree. He is actually like a little edition, young yet, of Visconti ... the same feeling for actors, for texture, for light for timing ... and his Camera work is dizzying! We shot the whole thing on real locations all the time .. except for one stint in the Studios, with an Ari-Panavision. Fantastic! Talk about mobility! I was half dead with just getting to my marks on time! Let alone learning the fucking words ... the same with Resnais in 'Providence' all ten minute takes and at least fifteen to twenty Camera Marks ... the Dolly Pushers are all paid fortunes and deserve to be.

But I have decided to pull out again for a couple of years or so. I'm stale, and I think that my work is becoming 'mannered' ... and I am dead bored playing these 'suffering' men of fifty something ... be they Dons, Proffesors, Ageing Musicians or ex-Nazis ... or, like last time, refugee Chocolate Manufactures from St Petersburg! I want a lovely, elegant, sophisticated, comedy ... with a big grand piano and bowls of real sweet peas and wisteria .... and glass floors and marble pillars and all the crap. Surely there must be ONE before I hit sixty!

So the books take up my time now ... I really find it facinating but terribly hard work ... it takes me ages. I'm lucky if I get 1,800 words

---

1. A full account of this painful episode, which involved hostile letters in *The Times*, and of its repercussions – not least on the long friendship with Richard Attenborough – is given in Chapter 19 of *Dirk Bogarde: The Authorised Biography*.

2. Richard Attenborough's current project, starring Anthony Hopkins, on which AS was to be script consultant.

down a day ... sometimes it 'goes' well ... and at other times I just sit in a hump staring out the window here across the valley to the hills and feel glum.

[...] Now I really must clear off .... I hate not being in touch with you ... it has been a long time! Do you know I started thirty years ago on my first days work[1] [...] at Epsome, on August 12th! Goodness me today .... and you have 23 years. Where the hell did they go? The years ...

[...] All love as ever
    <u>Dirk</u>.

James Cairncross, a fellow actor, wrote to commend Postillion *and to explain that he had met Dirk twice: in the wings at Wyndham's Theatre in January 1941, when Dirk was appearing in* Diversion No.2, *and some twenty-five years later at the Oxford Playhouse where he (JC) was in a play for which Gareth Forwood, an assistant stage manager, had suddenly to 'go on', learning a scene at half an hour's notice.*

To James Cairncross   *Clermont*
                                              17 August 1977

Dear Mr Cairncross –

Oh dear! You make me blush.

And more than that I'll make <u>you</u> blush now. It was you, I believe, who said one evening at Farnham Rep. 'My God! There is a movement afoot to take Dirk Bogarde Seriously!'.[2] Everything is repeated, rightly or wrongly, but if this is rightly I love you for it; for it spurred me on to work like nothing else ever has! Honestly! And in Book Two, which I am now wading through (trying to avoid libel all the time) I am using it as a sort of Preface ... it worked. It was so valuable. And thank you.

I don't remember the Diversion bit ... I was too green and far too shy and timid and silly ... but I do remember how patient, if you insist that you were not 'kind', you were to my God Son ... Gareth

---

1. On *Esther Waters*.
2. JC confessed 'it is, alas! the kind of thing I might well have said in the old days'; however, the utterance is attributed firmly to another actor, Alfred Burke.

F. And I knew what bloody hell you must have gone through[1] .... we all do, dont we, we Actors. I DO wish that THEY knew. I mean 'civilians' and all that lot.

What a glamorous start to war you had. So much more warming than mine. Yvonne [Mitchell] found me this house ... lovely, laughing Yvonne .. and smashing James Donald ... how good he is, was ... (I am so out of touch I dont know if they still do it or are dead or something) .. Alec and Merula [Guinness] I have not clapped eyes on since the 'grand days' when I met them in Rome going to Mass. The Pope, alas, was 'off' that Christmas and Alec was v. cross. Mathew, are there two t's? Matthew[2] ... (looks better). Was about sixteen ....

Time, as J. Standing[3] might say, is a Fuck Pig. It goes so fast ... at this minute I have nephews lying all over the fields in the sun grumbling that there is not enough ice for the Ricarde, and that petrol is so expensive. They were not even thought of when you and I started on this worrying road to the Theater , , , and worse than that, Daddy was almost four. Christ.

I could hug your Mr Lavery[4] too. Absolutely right. But is'nt it hard to keep out of things? To live in solitude? To sit by the edge of evening and watch night come sweeping across the hills ... as it does here. And have no conversation anywhere ... only the early owl having a chitter in the big olive tree, second on the right ... and then to go up and start the night for oneself. Table laid, salad tossed, and, at this exact moment, the promise of Lady Curzon to follow, softly from the pages,[5] in the lamp light. I always thought she was merely a soup. It is so exciting to know that she was not.

Obsessional privacy. Terribly grand and difficult and tiresome for ones friends ... thank you so much for understanding; and shareing. And for the quote I treasure!

Yes: it is a lost world. But are'nt you glad that we had it?

With warmest wishes and gratitude ...

<u>Dirk Bogarde</u>

---

1. JC had referred to 'the deep hurts to the mind and spirit, which seem to have to go towards the making of an actor'.
2. The Guinnesses' son.
3. The actor John Standing, otherwise Sir John Leon.
4. JC had sent Dirk a *Guardian* article by Hugh Lavery which prompted (in JC) the thought that 'we natural solitaries should get together from time to time'.
5. Most probably *Mary Curzon* by Nigel Nicolson (Weidenfeld & Nicolson).

To Rainer Werner Fassbinder   *Clermont*
                                                        24 September 1977

Reiner –

Now I have had time to 'digest' the film.[1] And only now am I able
to write to you clearly about it. Forgive the delay ... but it is such a
difficult thing to discuss a film in which you have worked and with
which you have been 'so in love'.

I love the film. I am proud, immensley, of it, of you and of Andrea,
Klaus [Löwitsch] and even of my own work ... which I always find
impossible to judge or discuss. I am, like you, never really satisfied;
but this time I think that I can honestly say that you have enabled me
to do my best work for the Cinema. It is not perfect. But it is the best
I have done. Thank you.

Even though I saw it in black and white and in bad condition, I
was immediatly struck by the power it holds ... and I think you have
done a fantastic job in the editing. God knows what it would have
been like if it had been left to Reggie Beck ... who is brilliant for
some people[2] but not for you ... The clips the next day in colour,
however brief, made me realise the full value of the film, and I now
long to see it with sound and music and titles! Bring it to Nice when
it is done and let us run it at Victorine .. and have a HUGE party
afterwards. Before the Critics destroy us!

There is one extremely bad performance in the film which I feel
sure you could safely loose .. and just have voice over for ... that is
the shot of poor Ossie in the post office saying 'Your Pushkin Letter'
it is so BAD that everyone laughed, and it is not the place, or the
time, for laughter ... can you cut him out? DO TRY!

Stoppard called yesterday and I was happy to be able to make him
so happy ... he is now convinced that we have done a marvellous
film, and is very excited. I told him that he would be shocked here
and there the first time around, but that he would be immesurably
proud the second time ... I hope this is correct. For my part I am
tremendously happy that I was asked to be in it, and proud too ...
and I cannot thank you [enough] for such a marvellous chance and
experience. I once told you, early in the film, at Interlaken, that it was

---

1. Dirk had seen *Despair* at a dubbing theatre in Paris.
2. Reginald Beck, veteran film editor, noted for his long collaboration with Joseph Losey.

'paradise' working with you. I dont know if you remember? But it still is true. I will follow you to Alaska if you ask me . . . and even if you dont, be assured that you will always have my deepest respect, gratitude, and love . . .

Always
Dirk

P.S. Try NOT to open the film in New York first.
Have a Berlin or Paris opening first – anywhere in Europe. NOT the U.S. D.

To Ann Skinner   *Clermont*
                                                    18 October 1977

Annie love –

What a lovely letter and packet of 'goodies'.

[. . .] I'm in a sort of whirl myself . . . age stealing gently up . . . I have a nephew of 19 now living with me here in Europe to study French for four months.[1] Actually he originally came for a weeks holiday (from Chicago where Gareth, his father, now lives permanently) decided he liked Europe best, and we worked out an Educational Scheme which his father has agreed to me following. So I am now a Guardian . . . rather like something out of 'Jane Eyre'. Oh dear! My days are now filled with bleating questions like 'Have you had your Weetabix for breakfast?' 'Washed your socks?' 'Done your homework?' 'Written to Dad, Sarah, Rupert, etcetera.' Meanwhile he is working his ass off at the Berlitz in Cannes and rather loving it all. Thank God. The course costs over £2.000, much to my slack jawed horror, so it is just as well.

Life about the house has, naturally, had to change a bit. I am used now to nig-nogs screaming protest songs, Elton John doing something else, and I know, BY HEART, the theme from 'The Deep' and 'Star Wars' . . . and sing them mindlessly in my sleep . . . gone, for ever?, is Mozart, Franck, Mahler . . . . did someone say that the young kept one young? Must have made a mistake the cunts.

Seriously, though, it is all a lot of fun . . . and showing a young man who wants to learn about life is pretty thrilling. It was shattering for

---

1. Dirk had enrolled Brock at the Berlitz language school in Cannes.

me to realise that although he had actually graduated from his High
School in Chicago ... with top honours and a mortar board hat ..
(idiots) .. he knew not a word of French, had never heard of Napoleon,
and thought that St Moritz was a brand of cigarettes. So SOME-
THING had to be done, tactfully ..... starting out with Paris. The
fucking Louvre, Versailles and etcetera. He glutted .... so that was
encouraging enough to start off a European Education. And hence
the Uncle-Talk daily ....

[...] I'm battering along, inbetween feeding Weetabix, at the
second book ... got to deliver by Febuary. Last one opened in N.Y
last week with a rather good spread in the N.Y. Times ... but it
remains to be seen if anyone buys a copy. No Harold Robbins am
I. We 'open' in France in a good translation, next month ... very
distinguished cover ... a stormy sky with buttercups! And no 'snaps'
inside because they think it will appear to be 'more classical' without
them ... funny old things Frogs. 'Despair' is, I think cut and edited
[...] I think, with due modesty, it is my best work to date ...
you DO need young directors [...] 'Despair' is strange, sad, and
exciting cinema ... wonderfully shot; what H. Fassbinder can do
with a Camera would shame everyone else I have worked with
except perhaps Losey and Visconti ... he is nearer Fellini ... but
has a very individual style of his own. Tremendously exciting ....
and, by the way, the Krauts dont use a Script Girl! Odd and a bit
scary ... they have a lady who keeps track of footage, numbers and
etcetera ... and a Dialogue Director who's job it is to check Script
errors, and to write in moves ... all a bit confusing .. but it seemed
to work. No one does Continuity! Except you yourself that is, and
the Operator is responsible for that .... you can see them all at
Shepperton or Pinewood!

Anyway 'Despair' is my last for some time ... I really do not care
for it now, the Movies ... however with Brocks Weetabix and Fees
and Toe-Ointment, I have no doubt I'll be back sometime next year.
Ah well ... but like you, I feel the whole thing disenchanting ...
except that I DO get the chance to work with the young, and not the
halt and the lame .....

The dogs are barking ... someone must have come up the lane, so
I'd better hop off and see who, or what, it is ...

Golden hot days here now, after a mouldey summer ... off I go,
but with a big fat kiss to you as ever.

For ever! There!
Your loving mate
 <u>Dirk</u>.

To Norah Smallwood   *Clermont*
                                                    30 October 1977

Norah dear –

A note to say that I finished the book you sent from General Hackett,[1] and was'nt all that impressed. In spite, I hasten to add, of my weariness with the Christian Fellow personally! Jolly brave fellow, no doubt about that, but lots of others were also; one is not sent into a 'spin' [. . .]

However it WAS a saluatory bit of homework for me; I almost decided (did in fact) to chuck my present work after I had waded through that. Shoved the whole lot in a drawer and had a splendid two days holiday burning last summers weeds and bedding plants. However my nephew was playing an early Judy Garland record the other evening . . . and I remembered something she had said, and felt a bit encouraged and went and wrote it down and more or less started again. But I have'nt much heart for it . . . . what the devil is it all about eventually? Who cares? I am not capable of writing Intellectually about my work . . . since my work is totally instinctive most of the time . . . and a list of my boring films and all that can be done long after I am dead; by some ernest Student Of The Cinema who, I am sure, would handle it all far better than I. And I would'nt have to read it, either by then!

One thing I might do, later on, is write a nice bit of Porn; and send it to Briggs and Blond or whatever they are called . . . and then I need'nt worry any more.

Not a cheep from the U.S.A. so far! I feel that I was unhappily right . . . not their kind of book.[2] And I have'nt even had proofs from Paris yet . . . they start the thing November 15 . . . apparently without the cover I approved . . . I hear it is all pink and yellow now, and retitled.

---

1. *I Was a Stranger,* by Gen. Sir John Hackett (Chatto & Windus), who in *The Times* had condemned Dirk's portrayal of Browning in *A Bridge Too Far.*
2. *Postillion.*

I really dont give a damn. I should never have started this caper! Not at all what I thought it would be.

Anyway; thanks for Hackett ... I am <u>much</u> preferring the Indian book. 'The Golden Honyecomb'[1] ... Lally would have said it was a 'jolly good read.' And I agree ..

Love
<u>Dirk</u>

Its Sunday Morning – hence the errors – I'm head Cook and Bottle Washer today – my [daily] 'Lady' is capering about with pots of flowers in the local Cemetary. It's the Day of the Dead – feels like it too! <u>D</u>.

To Gareth and Lucilla Van den Bogaerde   *Clermont*
                                              20 November 1977
                                                Sunday, 11 am.

<u>Progress Report No. 7[2]</u>

After six days of Mistral we are now bathed in still sunny light: the garden a ruin, Brocks prodigious weekly-wash flutters on the line, and he is in his bed snoring, or whatever, after the hectic joys of whatever he did at His Club in Cannes last night. I think this time there was no problem with the damned accelerator cable ... and he was home about two thirtyish ... the porch light was out at three, when I got up for a pee ... we shall doubtless get the whole saga over the gigot at lunch.

Well; we are half way through; tomorrow starts the New Course, or the Second Half rather ... and he is apparently coping extremely well. This Club on Saturdays has been useful, at least there are pretty girls and he has to talk French to them even though the nicest one went to Birmingham U, for a couple of years ... but he understands Telly very well now ... really follows the thing from Kojak, to The Rivers Of The World and the Commercials for soap and 'softer than silk' lavatory paper. He sits in a heap with a thing screwd into his ear, which can only be described as a sort of posh Deaf Aid, not so much

---

1. Kamala Markandaya's *The Golden Honeycomb*, published by Chatto earlier in the year.
2. From October to Christmas Dirk sent bulletins to his brother and sister-in-law, monitoring Brock's progress at the Berlitz School.

to save us the interminable-harangue in French Dubbing, but also, as
he says, to get it drummed into his head. This seems to be working
excellently. And he has, this week end, to write his first essay ... he
has chosen the Dance as his subject because he feels that he can
write an amusing paper on the 'Bi-Sexuality in Ballet.' Which sounds
original if complicated! He is, I can see, determined to raise Mlle
Fouquetts eyebrows if it kills him. She is his Lady Teacher and most
of the effort seems to be to charm, or shock if the latter fails ... she is
a sort of Aunt Figure. And wont be either; maybe the Essay will help
to close the gap? Who can tell? I timidly suggested that a simpler
subject might be easier for him with a still somewhat, limited vocabulary .. but there was a wicked gleam and a curled lip ... and Mlle
Fouquet is going to get her deserts tomorrow. If he gets up today, that
is to say.

I venture to hope that Brock has learned a good deal more than
French, which after all was the main part of my excercise. He has
really behaved extraordinarily well and valiently; allowing himself
to be corrected on small points of behaviour which will be important
to him when he gets into that shitty outside world ... recieving
sensible, one prays, answers to every question he poises from
Dissidents to the State of Israel, the way to leave a table if a lady
is present, why to shake hands, easily, with EVERY Frenchman he
meets no matter who they are ... and so on. Trivia perhaps ... but
all of it is strength for him. He was, or did hold rather, the attitude
when he first came here that 'it did'nt matter any more in these
days' to either speak correctly or show any form of manners in
public. Especially among his own group. That has rather gone now;
he finds that his own group rather like his, what he calls, 'Old
Fashioned' manner, and he is delighted with the words he has
discovered! He has this amazing ability to retain everything he hears
or sees. Wish to God I had had it ... and he is out to get his share
of life; and how! Which is quite marvellous. One comes against so
many people of his age who conform to their own group-ideoligy
and close their minds to anything else unless it is sung to Folk
Music. Do you know what I mean? Not Brock. Now that we are
half way through not only the Course, but living together, I have
to confess that he is really a very parfait gentle knight ... although
he would probably scorn such a high falutin' title! No easy matter
to come out here and join us in an already well settled existance. I

imagine he must have felt a bit like I did when I was sent up to Glasgow to live with those sodding relatives for three years.

I only trust that he has never been made to suffer, and I use the word quite advisedly, as I did with those two well-meaning monsters.[1] We have discussed it at length and he assures me that it has never been like that; so much the better! And if he has been homesick, which he MUST have been from time to time, he has never once shown it or voiced it . . . a damned good effort.

He has always had a vast resovoir of charm; which has always been useful to him in general Company. Now he has developed another line . . . which is splendid; people _want_ to talk to him, to listen to him, and discuss a mass of small, and large, issues. It is very exciting to see the change! When he first met the Attenboroughs, for example, he disliked Dickie deeply . . . because he THOUGHT, inaccuratly as it happened, that he was being patronised . . now, since he feels he belongs here, and since Dickie is often in or out for a meal, he has quite reversed his opinions and is, I think, extremely fond of Dick. Who is equally fond of him and respects him tremendously. And as I pointed out to Brock . . . that cant be bad! Since D. is about the most influential fellow, at the moment anyway, in a number of lines . . . from Chelsea Footbal, Capitol Radio, the Cinema and Buckingham Palace! Anyway . . . it is all a wonderful change of attitude, and he has made two new, and lasting I know, friendships with people he really faintly despised before. It is rewarding all round.

[. . .] I really think I'd better get him up . . . this essay worries me a bit! He feels confident that he can 'dash it off' pretty easily . . . but I hae' me doots that it'll be that easy; especially if we have to plough all through Larousse for sexual, medical and balletic terms!

Off to the airport. Hope you get this next week . . .

Love to you both as always Dirk.

To George Cukor   *Clermont*
                                       7 January 1978

My dearest George –
    I am overwhelmed! Just what I longed to have arrived from you

---

1. William and Sarah Murray ('Uncle Murray' and 'Aunt Sadie').

this morning. A real Cukor Lecture and a suitably humble Student.[1]

Dearest George, how good of you ... and how infinatly generous of you to supply your own caption! I trust you will allow me to use it ... for how could I, a mere mortal Actor, hope to better the very succinct phrases which you use ... oh! I wish you had written your own book. You are MUCH funnier than Lambert[2] was ...

You were dear and kind to bother; and your very generous comments on my humble first attempt warmed my heart. I really was a bit amazed myself that it ever got to Press. Since I cannot spell or do that punctuation business. I have a splendid lady in Hitchen (Hertfordshire!) who does all that for me. She is named Sally and gets very cross indeed.

Was'nt it nice about Cathleen Nesbitt getting her award[3] ... rather like Gladys; too little and too late ... but still. We have all been gunning our idiotic P.M. to award Lynnie Lunt [Lynn Fontanne] a damehood .. but to no avail. I think they dont realise that she is a good old Enfield (Essex) girl ... and one of the greatest actresses of our time. But we did try ... a goodly number of us, by writing letters to the idiot at No. 10 .... however Isobel Baillie[4] got it ... we none of us know why. Madness. Lynn had the MOST fantastic reception here in London in the summer at some big Jubilee thing at Her Majesties ... Prince Charles gave her his box, and the entire Audience stood and roared an ovation for almost five minutes! She had taken them by surprise by her presence ... I have no doubt that they took her by surprise by the loving warmth of their welcome.

Forwood and I are well if exhausted from a huge family Christmas .. fourteen .. neices and nephews and a lot of rather awful, but nostalgic, Home Movies ... I have had my brothers middle son here from Chicago studying French. He leaves tomorrow after six months. I shall be sad but glad too. I can see him from the window at this moment wandering about saying goodbye to each and every olive tree. Chicago is a very different world. Ah well. He is eighteen, and I am sure will recover. Although there will be severe adjustments to make

---

1. Dirk had requested an image for inclusion in *Snakes and Ladders*. GC obliged, explaining that in the photograph he was doing his controlled best to teach the very rudiments of acting to a sulky and resisting Dirk. He added that Dirk had written 'a beautiful book'.
2. *On Cukor* by Gavin Lambert (W. H. Allen, 1972).
3. Cathleen Nesbitt had been made CBE.
4. The soprano was made a Dame in the New Year Honours.

when he gets to Princeton, or whatever University he gets into.

I must get on with the final pages of Volume 2 .. it has to be delivered by the end of this month, which is a bit of a strain. How I wish, <u>how I do,</u> that– we could do a film together from the very start ... we never had a chance, did we?[1] Not really ... and I long to be under your wing again ... perhaps one day I'll be Box Office in America ... you never know.

Meanwhile, my love, my gratitude, and my deepest affection as always ... and great happiness and health in this rather worrying new year.

Always,
<u>Dirk</u>

To Tom Stoppard   *Clermont*
                                              9 January 1978

Stoppard dear –

I am not starting a two-way letter chat thing; so have no fear ... this does'nt need an answer at all.

I was just a bit more cheerful on reciept of your, extremely vulgar, letter. Anita Eckberg! Really ... whatever next I ask myself.[2]

Anyway [...] you were more than kind to lift the veil of sadness which has enveloped me since well before Christmas. One hates to have made a 'lemon' of a job.[3]

The letter was doubly saddening when it came, for only a night before I had been on the telephone for hours and hours to Mrs Lovely Tynan who was in equal misery over what 'they had gone and done' to her script of 'Agatha' ... which was pretty dire. Far worse, I venture to guess, than anything we have done to yours. I mean, at least we did'nt bring on two other writers and start in from scratch .. even if we did fuck up your 'tempo' and 'trim' for vision as opposed to Play terms ... anyway, with the two of you in distress, and both loved, it

---

1. On their two collaborations, *Song Without End* and *Justine*, GC had been brought in to replace Charles Vidor (died) and Joseph Strick (fired).

2. TS had relayed to Dirk the then current story of an encounter between Miss Ekberg and a dwarf, who said: 'I really would love to fuck you.' To which the statuesque actress replied: 'All right. But if I ever get to hear about it ...'.

3. TS had written in December to say that he had seen the finished film of *Despair* and that they had a 'turkey' or 'lemon' on their hands.

was a cruel Christmas. I did'nt even dare read a motto from a single Cracker. So there. I presume that SOMEBODY must write those too? Oh . . it was a wretched time. However you have made me happier . . . I suppose by your keen generosity as much as anything? You may, of course, be dreadfully right eventually. We shall know by May.

One final remark on the English Voice. You are absolutely korreckt when you mention Romeo and Juliet and reading M. Nabakov . . . but it did sound utterly dreadful speaking my lovely, and noted, Sloan Square among a solid group of 'funny accents' which they were all, of neseccity, using. The only possible thing, and it was considered most carefully by us all, was that I should have to join them since I could not beat them and tended to sound rather like a refugee from Romford rather than Russia. So that is why we did that. And I spent a great deal of time learning the fucking accent with an Egyptian Expert on accents. Who was, oddly enough, brilliant and my first ever, after more than sixty movies. Voice Coach. He was, however, a garstly actor . . .

Anyway, dear Tom . . . ta. Pippip and all . . . and perhaps if you come to see us in May . . . which I suppose you'll not . . . you can either make a protest or pretend that you knew it all the time.

I had heard, some time ago in Munich, about the 'Lolita' thing . . . did you know that there is to be a Toe Ballet about it too? Nabakov Junior was very chuffed . . . and with the re-make of the film! He'll be rich . . . anyway I liked him because he liked the film . . . and said it carried out, truthfully, his fathers intentions. But that may have been a bit of flannel to persuade Andrea Ferreol into his Maseratti and his Art Deco flat. We shall never know.

My love to the lady in the conservatory . . . and love to you too. I had a very exhausting Christmas . . . fourteen family, lots of nostalgic Home Movies and everyone got flu by Boxing Day except me. I have never cut so many lemons, no pun intended, and boiled up quarts of Honey, in my life.

I'm going to have a rest now.

Dirk

Susan Owens, a mother-of-five from Cheshire, had been seriously ill with pneumonia, followed by Bell's palsy. Knowing she had been a fan of Dirk from the age of eight, and searching for a way to cheer her up, her family had written to him. His reply was the start of another remarkable,

*enduring and 'particular' friendship with someone whom he would meet
only occasionally, and then briefly, at book-signings. She asked his advice
on naming the family's new dog.*

To Susan Owens
(Postcard)   *[Clermont]*
                                                 28 January 1978

Right off I'd call her 'Daisy' – I like peoples names for dogs! My Boxer
is called that – and it becomes 'DAZE' for short! Or else 'Amber' or
perhaps 'Capucine' – (French for Nasturtium) & for short 'Capp' –
But really its up to you. What does she 'look' like? Perhaps just
'Annie' – 'Beth' – or even 'Mutt'!
    Yrs. D.B.

To Dilys Powell   *Clermont*
                                                 20 February 1978

Dilys dear –
    [...] It was very sweet of you to bother to alert me[1] .... but
honestly I am not sitting here twisting a handkerchief for your verdict
on 'P'! Just because I was a bit 'pushy' and dedicated (what a silly
word) it to you ... which I did with love and gratitude, does'nt mean
that you are to write and say just what you think immediatly. Or ever,
even. It's yours, if you know what I mean, and every frame was very
much made with an image of you in an audience. But that is not to
say that I ask your approbation ... or even that I suggest that you
like it! Lots of English people HATE the bugger. Pretentious, dull,
incomprehensible, cold and vulgar. I could go on ... Mrs Kael did
alas. And she, one gathers, is American. However <u>they</u> have no nuance
... so ...
    Actually John G. and I were jolly hard put to understand much of
what we said! 'Cant understand a word, dear!' he used to cry .. 'It
really does'nt make sense Alain ... I'll say it, but I have'nt the foggiest
notion of what it means.'
    Mind you, he actually claims that he does'nt understand half of
Shakespeare and had, or has, to get 'Dadie' Rylands in to explain

---

1. DP had written to say *Providence* was to play at the Academy Cinema in London.

things to him. I quite believe him and admire him all the more! Anyway, whatever else 'P' is or is not it IS a whacking great Memorial TO Johns work ... and Alain has said that. Takes a Frenchman to honour perhaps our greatest living Actor. So see it for his work, and Alains tribute to it ... and if you can cope, stay to the end ... not that you would do other ... but the end is very important and there is a rather interesting change of face and pace. It opens, by the way, after March ... April I think. It's all such a hell of a muddle. And really it is almost old hat by now. Alain is deep into his new script of 'Mon Oncle d'Amerique' and has seven coveted Oscars[1] ... so he is really perfectly happy. And we are released again all over Paris and the rest of the Country ... Anyway; dont fuss about it. You dont have to like it; I'm really not at all sure, now, that I do even! I much prefer 'Despair' ....

[...] Much love as ever ...
        Always Dirk

To Kathleen Tynan   *Clermont*
                                               3 March 1978

Kathleen love –

It was splendid to get your 'crazed' letter today. I think that you almost felt the way I WAS that night at the Connaught when I got so terribly pissed from total-exposure and exhaustion. Too well one knows the feeling ... and you still have the other 28.000 to do. Crikey! It's a long book.[2] Of course she was a long-lived lady I suppose.

But I am happy that the on-dit is good; of course it does'nt always follow that it will be right ... but it is FAR better than the other, very usual, way round. Incidentally, not my business at all, but I think you'd be dotty not to cash in <u>immediatly</u> and get onto another Script even if you do hate the idea. It's just the time to do it; while the chatter is good and your name used in daily conversation. When the thing comes out it MIGHT get a pasting and you'll not be asked so eagerly again. Do it now, and have something in hand for the success, or otherwise, of the first. Thats what I always did in the Great Days of

---

1. Or rather, the French equivalent, Césars, including those for best film and best director.
2. KT's *Agatha*, based on her screenplay, would be published by Weidenfeld & Nicolson in 1979.

my Cinema Work. Kept one ahead always, so that if one went off half-cock there was still another on the stocks as a second chance.

Know what I mean? Books dont make money, unless you are Ustinov, Jilly Cooper, or that blasted Edwardian Lady who did the Flower Diary[1] and should, as she did, have fallen into the Thames near Putney picking 'chestnut buds.' But normally speaking we dont make a bomb with your actual book. Scripts yes. And lots of residuals and things ... I know that you may well be feeling jaundiced at this moment 'in time' (will they ever learn to speak English in the States?) but would remind you that this whole enterprise of yours was yours alone from it's inception. And look what it has done for you already. If you have another idea lurking under that Alexandre-Wig[2] for a script set it down. Even in rough draft. I really would'nt let the chance you have now slip away so easily for a book or even an adaptation ... although thats not a bad idea either.

Lecture over. That part anyway.

I have, swank-pots, handed my oeuvre over to Chatto. Publishing October. I have doubts ... libel and so on ... so hard to write the truth about people who are still alive and prickley ... and even about oneself for that matter! I am far, far too long ... about 400 pages (book-wise) God knows how many words ... too many I venture to think. I now have to sit here and go through it all with a red plume and try to cut stuff. Repitition, over discription, adjectives and verbs. Hell. I'm quite bored with it already. Bits are good I think. Kate Kendall and Judy G ... Losey .. Cukor ... Visconti (the Star really) and some of the potted-war on which Chatto insisted. I had to do a whole extra fucking chapter, about 9.500 words, compressing four active years of battle. That is to say not training and all that stuff. Frightfully tiresome. I dont, as it happens, care to remember a good deal ... it was'nt all jolly ... and I dont, being me, remember Regiments or Divisions or even Ranks and names and numbers ... and so on. However a sort of pastiche has been acheived and is okish. I found, fortunatly, a small battered diary which I had studiously kept from D Day until the finali, for me, in Java .... very earnest, very 'young' (was twenty four at the time for God's sake!) and FULL of some strange

1. Edith Holden's 'Nature Notes' for 1906 were published in 1977 by Michael Joseph as *The Country Diary of an Edwardian Lady*.
2. KT was renowned for her luxuriant and entirely natural head of hair.

code which I cant, of course, now remember! However enough was there.

Anyway thats that ... for the moment ... after I have to do an immense index. And after that I'll start a novel. Easier than trying to write about oneself ... and far less boring. I have refused a mass of tedious Film Work ... I refuse to 'go back' to 'Justines' or any of that crap. And I am constantly being asked now to play parts which Alec G. or John G. dont want, or have now got a bit too old for. With dashing 'Stars' to support such as poor M. York, or McDowall or names I have never even heard of! Nothing really super seems to be employable these days ... they are deep into the Uglies. Oh for a Cary Grant instead of Mike Caine ... for Cooper instead of Pacino ... a sign of age I grant you ... but even T. Power was better than the homogonised sexlessness of York or Fawcett Major[1] ... she sounds like a Public School or some village in green Wiltshire. Is she?

So; The summer is, hopefully, free .... except that we are already taking the bookings for Your Room. It seems endless. It would be super to see you. But what a lot of decisions you appear to have to be making. Golly. It's the kids mainly I suppose. Education ... better come back. But not to England surely? And France may well be so far Left that Ken would be uncomfortable even. We rather wonder what will happen in two weeks time.[2] No one seems a bit sure here; mind you, Provence pretends that it is NOT France ... but the new Mayor of Grasse is Communist and busy erecting workers-flats for the Arabs and Portugese among all the elegant villas of the rich. So Provence aint that far away from France. I dont think I'd mind Communisim if it was'nt so spiteful, humourless, and repressive. Anyway I'll stick it here until, as might happen, they boot us out .... or off to the Gulag. I'll not go back to England. Although we are off for the Yearly Trip to Mummy next week ... and I really do dread it. Connaught not-withstanding. Taking the car so that we can fill the 'trunk' with Saxbys Pork pies, tinned tongue, Marks and Sparks goodies, Hatchards books and some other bits and pieces. Useful in a Camp.

Spain [...] is madly cheap and still very lux. Although the 'natives'

---

1. Farrah Fawcett-Majors (later, following divorce from the actor Lee Majors, trimmed to Farah Fawcett) – star of *Charlie's Angels* and, with Michael York, of *Logan's Run*.
2. Legislative elections, in which the Right would be returned with a much reduced majority.

are a bit restless now under Freedome .. and keep on striking during dinner in resturants and so on. They come back off strike for an excessive tip. [...] Good, of course, for Ken's Wheezes and so on ... and all that Flamenco and Charisma in the Bull Rings ... Do you think Hemmingway was a Dyke? I do.

'Providence' won seven 'Oscars'[1] and that was nice ... and Johnny G. got the N.Y Critics award which was even nicer ... and it may, we are not sure, open after all in London at the Academy. Unbelievable. It has been running, if you please, to packed houses in both Cape Town and Johnnesburg for a year, broken house records in Tokio ... and everywhere else. What CAN be the matter with London? I mean it may not be the best movie in the world ... nor the easiest to cope with .. (Mercer never is, I find) ... but it has some staggering work from John ... and it is proudly English in it's writing ... however pretensious, it IS true English and the words are used like jewels in a watch ..... Ah. Fuck 'em.

Cold and wet here. I collect Toads in bin-loads and daily dump them in a local stream. We have upset ecology by making a pond where there never, in all time, was one ... and toads, like eels, come back to where they were born. Which is very tedious of them indeed. Thirty pairs a day ... and if you ever thought sex was luducrous to watch take a gander at Toads doing it. You'd join a closed Order right away.

The nephew who was here for five months [...] is now back in Chicago and hell bent on returning as soon as he can. He just cant take it there. It's not that he misses his boudin blanc, his glass of wine, Coulommieres just au point, and sitting on the Croisette in the sun eating his oysters .... it's the total lack of apprehension, of awareness, of conversation without 'a lift' ... the lack of nuance ... the excesses of Drugs for every single 'turn on' and the ugliness of everything around him ... and the narrowness of the Bible Belt mind. And worse still, he finds, the total lust for money and power and everything haveing to be, as you say in your letter, a high Grosser. Success is all. And Money is success. Natch. But how refreshing to be able to be not-so-rich but expiriment. Anyway he's coming back to Europe and taking a job ... anything rather than spend four years in an American University.

---

1. See above, to Dilys Powell.

This letter is pretty 'all over the place'. Sorry ... I miss talking to you ... and miss you. Which is pleasant. But then I think you have always known that. At least I remember assuring you years ago. You were probably not as trusting then as you are today? Water under bridges ... but sometimes in life people really do mean what they say.

Good luck with 'Agatha' ... I mean the book ... and when you know a little what your plans must be, do let me know. A P.C does very well if there is'nt time for more. And there probably wont be .... but dont go away ...

My devoted love – D.

To Norah Smallwood   *Clermont*
                                                28 April 1978

My very dear Norah –

Although the sun is out, at last, and eight dozen petunias stand impatient for planting, not to mention white geraniums and a host of phlox Drummondi and a rather obscene looking root which, I am assured by Mmme Schnieder, is a Lotus with flowers as large as dinner plates and which must be shortly buried in the sludge of the pond ... inspite of all these temptations .. here I am at my little Electric and relying to your lovely, encouraging, letter of the 26th.

I'm better now. Thank you. It was all my own fault because I ate quantites of pomme de terre Grenobloise, two helps, which are vastly rich and fearfully dangerous for someone like myself who has almost no liver at all ... or rather a liver which must resemble, on close inspection, a shredded dish-cloth. Apparently all ones organs are very much concerned with each other, which is irritating ... and one scrumptious dinner can cause havoc all down the line. As it did with me. And so no booze, maddening, for ages .. and no cream, sauces, butter, fats, anything, in fact which is delicious to eat, for as long as I can stand it. And now I am reduced to the dullest diet of ham and salad or white fish BOILED, and hard cheese, and .... oh the hell with it all.

Glad the captions are alright [... A]nd two 'snaps' on the page are far better than three ... I always think a cluttered page is a cluttered page. I like to have a good look at things ... unless they are pictures of H. Nicholson or a bad car crash. Different, but both unpleasing in their ways. Oh! the 'neatness' and the chicken-bottom-mouth of Nicholson!

A 'rehearsal' by Dirk for his drawing of Clermont in Snakes and Ladders.

I really must stop! A diet of Leese Milne[1] is dangerous on an empty stomach. Finished him off, gladly, last night.

A scratchy, snobbish, little saga. Very well worth reading but a kind of Jennifers Diary written with acid. Clever fellow I admit. About Adams and Gibbons and Emeralds 'Ordinaries' ... now starting the Tolstoy.[2] So that'll be a bit of a rest from spite and self-pity.

Oh, I'm honest enough alright. Not ambigious much .. which has got me into all manner of trouble in the last fifty years or so. People,

1. James Lees-Milne, a fellow Chatto author, had recently published two volumes of wartime diaries, *Ancestral Voices* (1975) and *Prophesying Peace* (1977), and the previous month a novel, *Round the Clock*. He was now engaged on a two-volume biography of Harold Nicolson.

2. *Victims of Yalta* by Nikolai Tolstoy (Hodder & Stoughton).

in general, dont awfully like honesty. It has to be carefully administered
.. like small doses of cortisone. The side effects can be hideious! I
know only too well.

[...] I am glad, if surprised a little, that you like the idea for opus
3. I think it'll work myself. Calling it, provisionally, 'Postscript'.[1]
Which may not be any use ... and is not the prettiest of words .. but
I do have to have a title to work to. Do you know what I mean?

I <u>shall</u> be honest! But I must cut a lot of guff and emotional stuff
which is faintly sick-making read out of context. And a lot of stuff
which has been covered in Vols 1 and 2 already ... Grandfather in his
Chinese bed ... starting with Rank ... the family background ...
etcetera. But there is a mass of amusing, sad, curious stuff ... a long
letter I came across written after the filming of DIV in which I am
calmly convinced that I have 'fucked it up', not greatly, but 'just
enough to ruin the chance I had been given.' It is a curious letter,
written from the calmest of hearts, and not a little bit hysterical or
anything ... but exactly how I most privatly felt.[2] I was wrong-ish, as
it turned out, but it was a 'near miss' I feel.

Anyway: I'll have a go at things ... not immediatly of course, there
is much to do on 'Snakes' ... but it is seething about in my head like
a simmering casserole. Thats a condradiction of effects, is'nt it? A
casserole either simmers OR seeths. Well mine is doing both now ..
for the gestation period is upon me. I must just work out what to
eliminate from the point of view of things already written .. and
things which might be tiresome for her[3] family and friends, many of
whome, I gather still survive all over the place, and who knew, eventually, about this odd correspondance between a brilliant Lady Librarian and a Fillum Star. You can imagine Mr Leese Milne on that!

Now: this wont do. Writing away like I am ... and boring you ...
and irritating the petunias who wait with drooping leaves looking very
longingly at the beds already prepared. Rather like an invalide who
has been carried to a chair while the nurse re-makes the couch, and
plumps up the pillows. A longing to return. [...]

Love

<u>Dirk</u>.

---

1. It would eventually be *A Particular Friendship*.
2. This letter has, alas, not survived.
3. Dorothy Gordon.

To Kathleen Tynan   *Clermont*
                                                 14 June 1978

Dearest Kathleen –

I wonder where you are? I am sending this to the only address I
have for you .. knowing (or believing) that you are soon to vacate the
place. Where to then? [...]

The proofs[1] and a very glossy cover arrived a couple of days ago. I
started almost at once, and then had to give up and make lunch for
six ... that sort of time here as you may remember. I got as far as
chapter three only ... so for the moment I rest. Until I can get to bed
tonight or find a corner of the day into which I may drag both book
and body away from people wanting ice for drinks, towels for the
Hippo Pool, a trowel for the weeding or a stamp for a postcard.

Facinated how you have managed Truth-Fiction and have no idea
where the one begins or the other ends ... so far all VERY persuasive
indeed .. and a super Period athmosphere ... and a sort of Katy-did-
her-very-own Whodunnit, which is a splendid departure for Katy, and
very interesting indeed. Mind you, by the time I get to Chapter 11 or
so I may be as irritated as I usually am by Whodunnits. Even D. L
Sayers ones! But, seriously, so far so very, very excellent, economical,
swift, and holding.

The Festival (Film) was a sort of Nightmare as usual. A record
crowd of foul people ... and foul-er films. The main poster in the
town was one for something called 'The Stud'[2] which showed a ladys
bum with a fellows hand sliding into the crevis. Simple I suppose.

In the Carlton bar, the first afternoon I had to go down there, we
were slightly astonished, at three in the afternoon, to see a completely
naked lady standing at the bar swigging beer from a bottle and spilling
the foam into her pubic hair. To be utterly fair, she <u>was</u> wearing a
cowboy hat and a gun holster. Her name was Eadie Williams[3] I gather,
from the U.S, and she had recently buried an axe in her husbands
head. It was a noticed case. Everyone one hates most was there with
different wives, wigs and cigars ... Rank were advertising splendidly.

---

1. Of *Agatha*.
2. Starring Oliver Tobias and Joan Collins.
3. Edy Williams, formerly married to Russ Meyer and star of his *Beyond the Valley of the
Dolls*, was renowned for her exploits at successive Cannes Festivals. The reference to an
assault by axe is evidently an instance of Dirk confusing art with life.

'Apres dix annes de silence Le Gong De Ronk (sic) Sonnez Encore!!'
cried the banner headline.[1] The films ranged from 'The Wombles' to
another re-make of '39 Steps' .... we were spellbound. Especially an
Argentinian Distributor who asked me anxiously how he could be
expected to sell 'Tarka The Otter' and 'The Wombles' in Rosario ....

The Star Names were the ubiquitous M. York (plus wife) and
someone called Jenny Agutter ... which by all standards she should
change. It sure as Hell made for a glamorous line up. We entertained
a good deal .. had House Guests from Connecticut for two weeks ...
one being Mrs Cornelieus Ryan who is a new widow and busy writing
a book on her husbands last months which is to be called 'The Cancer
Tapes'[2] ... she made tinkling laughter on the terrace. A wild flurry of
escapees came up for supper and lunches .. Skolimowski[3] from
Warsaw, a grumpy Pole with considerable charm who patently looked
forward to his return there ... Givenchy with a cluster of nobles and
a sun-tan .. a tall Russian who MAY direct a film with Signoret and
myself in Spring, or even earlier, whose name I cant spell but the last
part is Kontchalovski[4] and who had a sparkling eye and too-tight jeans
.. (according to Capucine who was deeply suspicious because he was
wearing a Cartier watch and had delayed his trip home to Moscow to
have dinner with me. She was worried that he had no interpreter or
'watchdog' and sensed not all was 'well' somehow.) However he seemed
very pleasant and creative .. and was prettier, and much taller, than
Nureyev and seemed to be enjoying everything except Cannes.

Eventually everyone left and the town was fumigated and I went to
the dentist ... seem to spend a lot of my time there now ... and life
settled into it's natural Summer Orbit with London Pale Guests and
flagons of Cotes de Luberon which Ken would despise but which is
cheap and not quite what Kathleen Whitehorn insists on as 'plonk'.
Blazing sun for a time and rain today and folorn guests watching the
rain splatter the Hippo Pool and bow the Petunias. No watering
tonight! Hurrah!

My second effort comes out on October 5th ... just done the
damned Proofs .. hate that part .. and caption for the snapshots ..

---

1. Not exactly, unless Dirk was moonlighting as a sub-editor; but we follow his drift.
2. *A Private Battle* was published by Simon & Schuster under the joint authorship of
Cornelius Ryan (who wrote *A Bridge Too Far*) and Kathryn Morgan Ryan.
3. Jerzy Skolimowski, director of *The Shout*, starring Alan Bates.
4. Andrei Mikhalkov-Kontchalovski, a member of the 1978 Festival jury.

hate that too ... and Forwood has done, very generously, the Index. 500 names ... some 350 pages of book to wade through .. I think it is okish. Or should that be OKAYISH? Anyway the Book Society has ordered 12.000 already ... so I hope to make a little sale. I suppose the Garland-Kendall-Losey-Visconti bit will help.

I have to 'do' the whistle stop tour with it in England. Gone are the days of elegance when someone bought your book ... or did not ... now you have to go out and bash the shit out of them for their wretched six quid. If Ustinov could do it I suppose I can .. although, it must be faced, he is marginally funnier ... if you have'nt heard the patter before.

Spent a week in London (did I tell you?) in April. Ma's birthday and so on .. and Publishers. Connaught super. Bill astronomical. I did'nt get pissed this time but Tote practically passed out with a whacking great double abscess on a tooth ... and that was a dainty dance of cherchez the dentist at dawn. I HATED London. Dirty, sour, bad-tempered, expensive and doomed it seemed. I was deeply glad to get home. Bought a few bits and pieces at Acquescutam .. cant spell it .. and some soap and bath oils from Floris .. and Veganine and a mass of books from Hatchards and fled. Saw no one really but family. And missed none.

So here we all are, then. In the rain. And June almost half way through ... when will you come out to play? Or wont you? And what news of the Film anyway? Rumours in Cannes were rife ... family problems, Script problems, as you know only too well, and Production problems. All sounds deeply familiar and I only hope to God you got paid [...] I wonder what [J. Pierre[1]]'ll say when he discovers that as well as Veganine and grey flannels I also bought an IMMENSE Leonard Roserman[2] at the Fine Arts ..... well: I like it. It arrived in a crate last week and now hangs supreme in the cock-pit here. I wince a little at the price and open another flagon of cotes de Luberon. And better, this very minute, go and make some Earl Greys (plural did you know? Not in 'Agatha') and hope that no one will ask me to light the fire [...]

---

1. Jean-Pierre Aubert, who with Anton Troxler advised Dirk and Tony on their financial affairs.
2. Dirk bought Leonard Rosoman's 'The Wave, Amagansett' at the Fine Art Society for £1,400.

You are missed considerably ... actually it is true to say that T and I said flatly and honestly after the last lot departed that you are the only POSSIBLE person to share this house with. Even for a couple of weeks. And that is the highest accolade I can offer you. And it's true. So there.

And come and share the place again soon .. please? Who knows how many more summers we shall have on this pleasant terrace. Who can tell?

With devoted love –

As ever
    Dirk.

To Ann Skinner   *Clermont*
                                                21 November 1978

Annie dear –

It is always such joy to have a letter from you. Even if it is carping. I mean about the Index of 'Snakes' of course. But you see, well ... I mean if you <u>read</u> the sodding thing you'll discover just how impossible it was to avoid the Dreaded Baron.[1] She got me the job!

I DID try to mention every single loving name within the pages but Chatto and Windus got upright, naturally, and so I made it a bit shorter. The list I mean. However there is quite a lot left for you to play with ... and remember ... and a great deal written between the lines on account of Libel in England! I said some tough little things about some very tough little men: all out. Even had to call Judy's god-awful Agents by a jokey name instead of Leopold and Loeb: which is what they are and what she called them. No go. So you see it is quite a frustrating business writing your memoirs! However it has been a rollicking success so far. Second print within the first four weeks ... and according to the Bookseller it's been on the Top Ten for five weeks alongside the paperback of 'Postillion'. So thats alright. Kenny More secretly came out with his book[2] on the same day. Which shattered everyone in sight. In Publishing it is as henious a crime, and as daft, as us opening a couple of Movies on the same subject with many of

---

1. Zelda Barron, in charge of continuity on *Our Mother's House.*
2. Publication of *More or Less* (Hodder & Stoughton) coincided with that of *Snakes and Ladders.*

the same players on the same night in neighbouring cinemas. But for very differing Companies. However he has slipped a bit at the wayside I hear. (Seven people only turned up at Selfridges for a signed copy ... not much fun.)

I had a super Tour of the Provinces myself. Rather dreaded it but simply loved it once we were off ... British Rail to Birmingham, Bristol .. (Remember Bristol? 'When did you last read a book?'[1] Oxford and etcetera ... it was a glorious wallow in nostalgia for me. I had not been around those parts for many years and really DID think that no one would bother to come, or would remember, or even have heard of me.

The reverse was true. It was very moving indeed. Actually, in Birmingham, I did manage to controll a quite large lump in my throat and a suspiciously moist eye! Such warmth and kindness was totally unexpected. And no one blamed me for going abroad. They merely wistfully said 'Why dont we make those Movies any more ... we're sick to death of Telly' which I could heartily endorse.

After I got back from every Trip to the Connaught at eight something in the evening I just crashed down with a brandy and soda and had a baked potato and cold beef and watched an hour, nightly, of Telly ... and then went to bed like a good boy, to get my face un-crumpled for the next day. No good going off to the Provinces with a face like an old douche-bag. But the Telly I saw was ghastly! The Bruce Forsythe thing .. first show, saw Bette Middler and was spellbound, but apart from her ... Wow! Even lovely Ian Holm as J.M. Barry made me anxious to fully retire. And there was nothing much else in the whole ten days .... parlour games, dire Policiers, dreadful Lillie Langtry ... with all the nobility talking with voices from Cheam to Chester. Oh dear.

But of all the super things I discovered on my trips the MOST super was that I had bridged the Generation Gap unknowingly. While five hundred elderly ladies with shopping bags grabbed my hand and spoke wistfully of 'A Tale Of Two Cities' or 'The Wind Cannot Read' five hundred 'kids' in jeans and old scarves or tee shirts, banged away at me with tremendous questions about things like 'Despair' and 'Providence' and, most especially, 'Night Porter'. All VERY serious.

---

1. One of the questions asked by Dirk's character, the television presenter Robert Gold, on a real-life 'vox pop' in Bristol for *Darling*.

All super. Naturally 'Death In Venice' was THE movie, and I signed as many copies of the Penguin paperback and recordings of Mahler as I did my own effort. I was tremendously thrilled. I tell you all this only because you are about to embark, dangerously, into a world of Commercial Shits and you must have your courage strengthened! There is an audience for the kind of movies we try to make, you and I [. . .] but the only people who are'nt aware of this are the Distributors themselves . . . or the ghastly men who run Rank and EMI and the frail rest. It's all re-makes of old hits with new, and dreadful, 'stars'. I mean, alright, she's pretty . . but who is Jenny Agutter . . or the Dotrice girls all neat and tidy from Wimbledone . . or Someone Mckorkindale[1] . . . and of course all the 'Yorks' and 'Alice Bates' . . . . if you know what I mean! I love Alice. Think some of her work is splendid . . . most spurious [sic]. But why does no one ever use Felicity Kendal REALLY? Or Julie Covington? Helen Mirren? Tom Courtney? . . . ah shit. There are lots more . . . but they work in the Theater. In my day it was exciting. Even in your day too, at the beginning . . . Julie . . . where is another 'Julie' today? Maybe Felicity . . . where is there a Kay Kendall?
                              Enough.

Smashing news that you still go on with Pinter. I have read all the reviews for 'Betrayal' with mounting fury. Why do they disparage him so? Why do they constantly prove how little they actually know . . . and how out of touch they are with the Public! I love him so, that I twist with anger at the dumbness of the twats who review. Especially Madam [Bernard] Levin who is cloaking herself in the raiment of the old Masters, she thinks! like [James] Agate and even, I grudgingly agree, [Harold] Hobson . . . but it is false raiment. He was down here this summer on a Hol. I have never seen such affected nonsense in all my life! A timely reminder about Mr Tynan would'nt come amiss there . . . .

[. . .] Had Betty Box down for a week . . . . rather sad and heavy going. Her world has crashed around her it appears . . . and the effort now to try and start a movie is almost too much for her. I did my best to bully and bash, she is a bright woman and was a splendid Producer . . far better than Thomas was ever a Director. But she is worn out, disillusioned, lost . . . . hateful to see. And, what is far worse, out of touch. Oh dear. She said that you might be doing a film for him? If

---

1. Simon MacCorkindale.

so I can only hope it is to secure the roof or pay the Rates . . . there cant be any other reason I feel.

I must get back to Chapter 6 of my novel! Very hard work dear, wish I'd never started the sodding thing [. . .] I got a script from M[ichael] Winner last week. Honestly. It'll make a fortune. They fuck on the first two pages and rape each other on the fifth and sixth and two boys mastubate happily in a hedge on the tenth and eleventh . . . . . awash with sperm I swam towards the end to find out what I could possibly be playing. He was very nice about it . . . and just said, 'Well . . . perhaps next time?'

Must go. Thanks for super letter [. . .]

Great love & affection

    As ever –

        <u>Dirk</u>.

To Jean-Michel Jarre   *Clermont*
                                            28 November 1978

My dear Jean Michel –

    I am forced to write to you in English.

My French is enough to drive you to suicide and me to a form of hysteria.

Equinox[1] is sublime. I simply love it.

After five sessions, so far, it gets better and better.

After two or three moderate glasses of wine it becomes even more fun!

For that is what it all seems to me to be about. Fun.

The delight and gaiety is wildely infective.

Soothing, beautifully, the sadness which also lurks.

I hope to God that I am saying the right things for YOU.

I only know that I am saying the right things for ME.

A Tarentella! A Samba!

Mardi Gras.

Jamaica on a beach in the rain I remember well.

An accordian wistful in a sudden storm.

'Casque d'Or'.

Renoir.

---

1. The composer J-MJ, then married to Charlotte Rampling, had given Dirk a copy of his new LP, *Equinoxe*.

Matisse, Monet and even Manet too.

All the colours I see and you make me 'feel'.

The strange thing which is the Nostalgia of France.

Dieppe.

Roses, hot tar in the sun, coffee.

The rain drip drip dripping at the little Bal du village ... the passion and power and fun and hysteria of that snaking line through the streets of

New Orleans ..

And there are whispers of the sad ballrooms of Vienna.

There is SO much!

And that long, last, held moment . . . .

Sublime.

I dont know if any of these things are meant to be there.

I only know that in your music, they are for me.

You may be as Modern as The Pompidou Center, but you evoke total timlessness, memories, joys, undercutting sadness.

It is wonderfully Loving Music, wonderfully strong.

But perhaps most important of all,

Living.

 With great affection and admiration.

  Dirk.

To Penelope Mortimer   *Clermont*
                                                1 January 1979

P. dear –

 And so another one starts. God knows what this one will bring us all: but I hope it brings you happiness and health ... and anything else you need.

 I dont know where we got to, you and I.[1] Places. Drifting. Well, thats what friendships are about really, are'nt they? No need to be always 'in touch'. I knew you'd got back from America, and that you were alright after the scare thing[2] [...] and then there were 'Shorts' in some of the Sunday Colour Things and so I thought 'well,' I

---

1. If Dirk and PM had corresponded since December 1976, none of his letters from that period survives.

2. Suspected cancer.

thought, 'she still seems to be at it . . . and in form, so I suppose shes alive and well and earning her living.' And that was good.

And me? Oh I got fed up with the Acting . . . too old now for the early Calls, the bickering over money and so on, the Script Writers and the simply APPALING people who now run the Movies.

God knows they were pretty shitty in my earlier days . . . but Now!

This years Festival at Cannes finally convinced me that the gates of Hell had finally opened and filled the Carlton Hotel with it's entire contents. And so I crept up the hill here shivering with hate and rage and disgust and said no more.

And I 'rite'. Well, I try to. I like it. It is pleasanter to sit up here in the old olive store and be away from everyone and bash at this combine harvester of an electric T.riter. Very scary. But fun now I'm used-er to it. So far I've been terribly lucky . . . both books have done far better than I could have ever believed possible . . . and I rather like the Publishing Ladys and Gentlemen . . . well, the ones I know and have met so far. Did the 'Tour' with the last book all over England . . . Birmingham, Oxford . . . all University towns. Fun and moving at the same time. Harrods, on the other hand, was as funny as a babys funeral . . . millions of ugly people and a rude woman who said, in a v. loud voice, 'My God! Look what he's come to. Selling himself in Public!' . . . I was too. And rather enjoying it. In a ghastly way.

Now off on a novel.[1] Grave mistake I feel. Chapter seven and nothing much has happened. Chatto say all they need is a beginning and middle and an end. Bully for them. All I have at the moment is 90.000 words of beginning. I'll finish it . . . determined to . . . but may just slide it into that proverbial drawer and start something simple. With one lady in a chair in one room in one house. Oh! If only I was as clever as you! Or Caroline Blackwood . . . so spare, so economical . . so clear in plan. However: I have adjusted to the new work . . . like it greatly. Fret like fuck. Worry. Wander about splitting logs, washing the floors, laying tables, thinking one world away.

I am happy you are in your little cottage place . . . I hope you are happy too? Better than that College with the 'oddies'. One day write again . . . meanwhile great love . . . and be careful . . . and Happy, happy 1979 . . . . . .

Love D XX.

---

1. Dirk had put the third volume of non-fiction aside for the time being.

To Norah Smallwood   *Clermont*
                                                     14 January 1979

Norah dearest –

Not really a letter this: just a covering note [. . .] I discovered that
the Singnoret book[1] has sold over 600.000 copies .. which is not at
all bad. And splendid for her! She is quite astonished for, like myself,
she is not a proper writer and was totally taken by surprise. She earns
more for this book than for any film she ever made in her whole long
career. Odd. But it does go to show that you can sell books in France.

P. Hall and his little card[2] made me very happy indeed. Really
because I know, from experience, what a difficult critic he is .. and
how terribly demanding. I am still slightly astonished that he would
read my sort of stuff . . . and deeply gratified that he should bother to
write. He is not that sort of chap, and we dont keep in touch much. I
[. . .] only send it to you so that you can share my pleasure and
indulge in your own satisfaction a bit: for you did say, ages ago, that
you wanted the book to reflect the Time as much as the Film Actor.
Hall seems to have found that this could be so. Thats what made me
so happy. I am so thrilled that I have, perhaps, managed to achieve
what you originally wanted.

This machine has gone 'funny' today. It's the cold I think and the
keys are all stubborn and maddening. A bitter mistral and blazing sun
. . . cold, exhilarating, combination: but hell on the hands and feet
olive picking, which is in full swing now. I always had such a very
lyrical feeling about olives. Jolly peasants, great loaves of bread and
flasks of wine, beating the trees in the speckled shade of high summer
. . . Jesus preaching to his dim-wits under a gnarled trunk .. and eating
handfulls like pea-nuts. But none of it is like that at all. I had NO
idea they were culled in mid winter, that you crawled, blue with cold,
among prickly grass with numbed hands searching for the little black
fruit which closely resemble sheep droppings. A very dangerous hazard

---

1. Simone Signoret's memoirs, *La nostalgie n'est plus ce qu'elle était* (Editions du Seuil,
1976).
2. In a 'fan note' to Dirk, Peter Hall, who had directed him in *Summertime* and was now
running the National Theatre, wrote that *Postillion* and *Snakes* had 'made Christmas for
me. Beautifully written, extraordinarily observed. They are not only about <u>being</u> an actor:
I'll wager they will stand for ever as an important record of what has happened to this
country in this sad century.'

here, for the Shephard has been across the land ... ah well. We have about thirty kilos now. Enough to last until the middle of the summer. If one is careful.

[...] A copy of a very odd book from an unknown lady called Diggs-Jones, or the other way round, at Knopf. 'Birdy'[1] ... which she says she 'knows I will adore' [...] I dont think [...] that I <u>will</u> adore it.

It's all about a chap who wanted to be a bird. And full of that particular American Guilt which I really cannot stand.

Super review for it in this weeks Time. But not, I fear, my tass de thé. I wonder why she thought it was.

I struggle, between bouts of olive-picking and washing the kitchen floor, (Lady is still on her Hols in Spain) with your much detested Emmie ... and with Pullen and Clair[2] and all the others and wonder why I bother. I flee to Mrs Wolf from time to time to see how she coped .. with her people ... but she seems not to have had a great problem so far as I have got, and Mrs Dalloway rips along. 'I write and write and write' she boasts.

So do I Mrs Wolf. But not to the same effect.

So I turn to the Dotty Sitwells[3] and wonder who on earth could have ever invented Sir George and made him believable! What a very rum lot they were ... uneasy reading, but frightfully well written.

Trouble with Mrs W. is that she writes so beautifully that she brings tears to the eye .. and thats no good to a budding novelist ...

with the deepest love and affection ..

    As ever
    <u>Dirk</u>.

To Norah Smallwood   *Clermont*
                                            20 January 1979

Norah dear –

Got your copy of the corrected, or cut, book.[4] Cant quite work it all out ... most seem idiotic. Also your note from [Leonard] Rosoman.

---

1. By William Wharton (Random House NY).
2. Three of the characters from Dirk's novel-in-progress.
3. *Façades: Edith, Osbert and Sacheverell Sitwell* by John Pearson (Macmillan).
4. The French edition of *Snakes and Ladders*.

Sent him a p.c. and said Do Come and look ... I'll get down to the Frog Cuts in a minute. Probably have to call you before I do anything about it ...

Bit unhappy here today. Had to put poor old Daisy to sleep yesterday morning. V. sudden alas. Cancer, which we knew, but had hoped for a gentle six months .. however it started to race away and we had to make an immediate decision. Bloody.

Both holding her caressingly for the needle. Then a pretty filthy journey home from Grasse with an empty collar and the leash.

Snow not melted and the ground covered in the short hand of her pad-marks.

We spent a pretty glum day I fear. T. tremendously brave and v. quiet. I sort of in an ache. She arrived here with us as a very small puppy the summer we moved in. Part of the fabric of ones life here. Idiotic to mourn a dog. However one mourns for oneself really ...

In the night the thaw; the pad prints fade ... the toys, alas, all revealed. A favourite over-chewed ball, a veal bone ... I spent an age hurling everything I could find into the pond to avoid reminders: useless really ... crammed her bed into a shed, her food bowl into the dustbin ... Labbo, her not-over-loving husband aware of ones distress, stalking very quietly about, keeping near.

One biscuit now at tea, instead of two ....

So thats how I am this morning ..

Cope with the book business tomorrow.

Love, and love again,
    Dirk.

To Bryan Forbes   *Clermont*
                                        12 ~~Febua~~ *March. '79*

My Dear Bryan:

I have only just realised, see above, that for the last two weeks I have headed everything I have written in the wrong month. Thats typical. I live in clouds it would seem.

Thanks for letter and Bumph [...] since I choose not to live in England what happens there really does'nt affect me. Apart from driving me insane every time I hear the BBC World News. I dont suppose France will go along smoothly for ever ... signs that we crack as you have are already evident. But so far it is healthier and less mean-minded. I dont think we'll ever abandon our sick and infirm: and No Work For Much Pay seems to be peculiarly a British habit. However: we'll see.

How good about your book.[1] Seven months! Yea Gods! I have completed nine whacking chapters of a twelve chapter novel with about 100,000 words so far and that has taken me like forever. But I cant spell of course. And have to keep going back to Classical Dictionairies or M. Roget and all that.

And the Publishers, while deeply praising writing, construction, dialogue and description seem not to like my 'people' whome they describe as 'utterly unpleasant and disagreeable'.

Well: since it is all autobiographical and about an odd year I spent in Java in 1945 while they were having their Civil War there, I suppose that might just figure. However I have shoved it aside for a while to get the land here ready for our summer. Spring is upon us with mimosa and all manner of vulgar things in the grass ... including toads who copulate in a disgusting fashion. And I have a lot to do before the first onslaught of Guests which seems to co-incide with the Film Thing in May.

Lordy and Lady Nextdoor[2] were down recently in spanking form and I allowed myself to be taken OUT to dine. A thing I never normally do, I so detest restuarants and the last time we went off to one of Lordy's Two Stars In The Michelin I had deeply frozen Turbot and the runs all next day. So. But they mean well and I love them dearly. Give Best-Seller[3] a big kiss and when you are in the area next, and who can tell? come to supper here ... we do a rather good soja bean salad with prawns. Unfrozen!

Thanks again for info. Stuff it!

Love <u>Dirk</u>

---

1. BF's latest novel, *Familiar Strangers* (Hodder & Stoughton), based on the then rife speculation about the Philby, Burgess and Maclean affair and the identity of a 'Fourth Man', later revealed to be Anthony Blunt.
2. The Attenboroughs. BF and Richard Attenborough had founded the successful and provocative Beaver Films in 1959.
3. Nanette Newman had become a successful author.

To Norah Smallwood *Clermont*
21 March 1979

My very dear Norah –

A day of delights yesterday. Mixed ones.

First of all a fat, battered, packet from Watford full of red plastic worms (packing) and bulbs. Great excitement prevailed. They were shipped from Watford on the 15th January [...] However they look alright to me. Perhaps a titchy bit shrivelled but nothing which a good soil and some water wont cure. I am terribly tempted to put the Regale into the open ground, they would look so splendid ... but maybe I'll settle for a large pot. We'll see. At the moment it is raining so hard that it is impossible to do anything outside at all .. the land is flooded completely; my new bits of grass seed washed away for ever, beds of Night Scented Stock and Julien the same .. and the mildew begins. Gardening here is a savage business. And a risky one.

As you may remember!

But thank you, my dear, for such a fragrant thought ... and for such bother and care. Maddening for you, after so much thought and planning-with-Lanning[1] that they should arrive late. But at least they are now here and who can tell what May will bring? You may not see more than some wistful 'sprouts'. On the other hand you may reel with delight at the odour on a warm evening. If there is a warm evening in May!

I am beginning to doubt everything after these last five days of quite torrential rain and black cloud. Depressing to say the least.

Second delight Elizabeth. Who left her Family, my tiresome Mamma, her husband and everything, and came to spend both our birthdays here together.[2] Which'll be fun. If rather Elderly! She'll be here for two weeks [...]

A mixed delight was the arrival, the day before, of a baby Boxer dog.[3] Far, far too young. Six weeks. The house is rent with shrieks and wails and deep howls ... both ends of the beast function splendidly all over everything. 'A change of diet' we say cheerfully, hearts sinking with each lugged bucket of bleach and hot water and rags ... 'New

---

1. The bulbs were supplied by Lanning Roper.
2. 28 March and 2 April respectively.
3. Bendo – after their first house in Buckinghamshire.

surroundings of course' we say brightly . . . 'It'll soon settle down.'
When?

Hardly any sleep at nights . . . I should have bought a bloody Lion.
And all this to guard us from the wandering Arabs . . . civilisation.

An elderly woman up in Chateauneuf, walking in her daughters
garden last week to pick wild hyancinths, was caught by a savage
Alsation Dog belonging to the people next door, and quite literally,
eaten.

It has caused a huge furore in the village and the Press.

As well it might.

But we all have to have Guard Dogs now anyway. So even if they
eat us we simply have to manage somehow. Was'nt it LOVELY once
upon a time when there were arabs sitting in tents in the sand eating
dates?

Next day. 22nd March.

Stopped on the other side because suddenly the puppy was ill. Suddenly it was very ill. Vet-trips. Vomit, shivering, up all night . . . we
are well neigh . . . no: nigh dead [. . .] And this morning your letter
of the 19th [. . .] A big stack of letters, also, from 'Postillion' addicts.
There seem to be quite a comfortable number. They send dreadful
picture postcards of Alfriston, Lullington, Seaford etc . . . plus leather
book-marks with appropriate designs of Sussex. But the letters are
moving. And are not from children ever. One today from a Canadian
journalist who 'picked it up at Seattle airport thinking I'd have a good
laugh, a la David Niven, on my flight to New York: instead I found it
was a kind of kid's book, and I ended up in tears for my own lost
youth . . . it is a book I shall treasure all my days. In hard-back which
I got from New York as soon as we landed.' Anyway: that sort of thing
is most comforting: many complaints, incidentally, over the paperback
cover which people find 'misleading'. But it may not be a bad thing!
While 'Snakes' clearly appeals to people like Hall, Mercer, Resnais and
that ilk . . . and they have been deeply flattering I smugly admit . . it
is 'Postillion' which carries the banner. Nostalgia a bit. But as far as I
can see from the letters I get it is more a sense of loss . . loss of
simplicity . . loss of ease . . of safety . . of sureness in life.

As I said overleaf . . . it brings back to it's readers a time when the
arabs sat in the sand eating dates: instead of screaming for their bloody
democratic freedome. Whatever that means anyway.

Something I tried to convey, ineptly, in the aborted Novel . . . I saw it all happening in Java, this Native Emergence, when I was but a lad of 24 . . . . . it's still going on and I'm 58 any moment now.

I have shoved Miss Foto[1] into a drawer with her crowd. They can stay there for a while. Sadly it took me longer to realise than it took clever you, that it was'nt really very good. I think I got most dreadfully carried away in creative euphoria or whatever it is. Parts of it are frightfully good I think. Parts.

However it is set aside now. Marvellous experience for me . . after all I am still trying to teach myself how to write. Nothing has been lost except perhaps a possible book for you. But I think I must stick to the Autobio Bit . . . a little longer. Then cut my teeth on something less grand than a twelve-hander Novel.

I am in a difficult position really because of the modest success of the other two. First two. A first Novel is a brute. And they will all wait for me to fail at my first attempt. Rather as if I HAD gone and done my ruddy 'Hamlet' for Larry O. at Chichester.[2]

So I must take extra care and not just 'rush at things'.

So Vol 3 will start coiling about in my head. Has done already . . it wont follow the same rhythm as 'Snakes'. Less chronological I think. Although, naturally, progressive up to today . . . or the final shooting in Berlin of 'Despair' . . . . . that ought to be quite amusing. Me and the Youthful Marxist-Red Brigade Set all getting on splendidly together!

Talking of novels. I gave Elizabeth, last night, the glamorous Proof copy of 'The Passing Bells'[3] to pick through. There are some very splendid passages which make us ill with laughter. I once got Attenborough to read some of the best bits, including the Publishers Blurb, aloud after dinner one night. We were quite exhausted with laughter. And it is all, of course, deathly serious as you will know. Elizabeth, as indeed were Tony and I, was alas unable to read more than a bit here and there without stupification; and quickly took Iris M. off to bed.

But this is already a HUGE best-seller! How? Why?

800.000 dollars for the paperback rights before publication . . . .

---

1. Another character from the novel.

2. In late 1961 Laurence Olivier had invited Dirk to join his company for the first season of the Chichester Festival Theatre the following summer. After much deliberation, Dirk finally declined.

3. The opening volume in a First World War trilogy by Phillip Rock, published in the UK by Hodder & Stoughton.

something is wrong. And I must let you go … and go myself.
   With much affection
      <u>Dirk</u>.

P.S. I managed, very tactfully, to wriggle out of making any comment on 'The Passing Bells' for the British publishers – it was utterly impossible! <u>D</u>.

To Norah Smallwood   *Clermont*
                                                  27 June 1979

Dearest Norah –
   How wonderfully kind, and extravagant, of you to telephone me last night. I always feel so dreadfully guilty that it is 'your call' so to speak, and only hope that you dont put the money in the box yourself … since you have told me that all your trips out here have not been paid for by the Firm, and I cant imagine why not since, save for one private hol. they all had to 'do' with business … I get fussed at the expense. Goodness. Me! I am so sorry that I was out for the better part of the day; a most unusual thing. But I'd got sort-of summonsed to luncheon in St Maxime with Prince Bertil[1] and his pretty, funny, wife Princess Lillian who is English, and [an] old friend of Tony's from the early thirties and also of Kay Kendall. She had read 'Snakes' and loved it and wanted to 'talk about Kate again …' so we did. All morning.
   It was a long drive in great heat, Bendo gasping on the floor, and me in my only 'good' shirt and white trousers. And all of it a bit tedious frankly. Cold ham and salad and remembering manners.
   It's been a bit of a Royal week in a way. And thats odd too for me. The day before P. Alexandra (or is it 'ia'?) decided to come to tea. Staying secretly with a friend near here, had read 'Postillion' and longed to talk about it. That was rather pleasing. She was in a bit of a fuss and wanted to change from a tee shirt into a long frock for the event, was politely told not to, came and ate a vast amount of squashy shop-cake, many jam tarts, and was utterly adorable, funny and pretty as could be. It was a splendid afternoon and she was all for staying on to supper (cold ham pie, hot new potatoes with mint the idea of which

---

1. Of Sweden.

made her cry out with pleasure!) but had left her husband in Monaco on some boring business job, and the taxi fare from there is quite prohibitive ... so they went home at 7.30! having begged a mass of hollyhock seeds and four cakes of 'your' soap. She has promised to come back same time next year. Said the house was 'her sort of place'. What I particularly loved was her sincere concern for Lally! If poor old Lally ever knew that she had been the subject of a very long conversation with a Royal she'd have had a 'proper turn' I can tell you ... not to mention Elizabeth: who arrives tomorrow and has threatened to curtsey when we meet.

[...] John C. called a little after you did last night with his Title idea ... 'JUNGLE GREEN'[1] ... which I, truthfully, dont altogether like.

I was, I hope, very tactful. But he sounded a bit wistful.

It is a sort-of 'shock title'. I see <u>absolutely</u> what he means. 'Dirk Bogarde and "Jungle Green"!' Hard, crisp and very commercial I suppose. But it does sound to me rather like an Army Manual ... and is a sight too 'war-like' I think. After all the book, if book it is, is not about a war. It's about the people who are in a war. A comedy of manners rather than a 'saga of people in a war-torn Island, awash with blood, sweat and tears ... and sex!'

Oh dear, I can 'see' the blurb now. Dont lets have any of that stuff they did for the 'Passing Bells'!

I just think, and I do so hope that you do, that 'A Gentle Occupation' has a bit of style to it, is wonderfully ambiguous, and has a bitter connotation ... It can, on the one hand, apply to the Japanese Occupation, which was, to start with, gentle . it can apply to Miss Foto's whoring ... her intriguing and general use of her wiles and sex .. another Gentle Occupation ... or Nettles and Rooke searching her out, so to speak ... a sort of 'spy catch spy' business done in quiet serenity ... another Gentle Occupation ... it can equally apply to the supposed Gentle Occupation of the British Forces who thought that their war had ended four weeks before, and that they were off to a Treasure Island where all they had to do was herd the wretched Internees home and sit in the sun with a glass of gin and tonic.

I think it can apply to all kinds of things in the 'book' ... and I have promised John that I will slip the words into three or four

---

1. John Charlton's suggestion for the novel.

paragraphs throughout the 'book' to see if he can come to terms with it in the text.

[. . .] I look forward tremendously to getting my 'Corrections' in a few days and will apply myself dilligently. I have made a number of my own too . . . I find I use 'admonish' and 'serried' more than I use 'and' or even the dreaded 'really'! And I think it should be 'The Geneva Conventions' rather than 'The League Of Nations' . . . about prisoners of war . . . and there are many more to come. What a time I shall have. I shall also, if inspired, have a try at a suggested 'cover' . . . with little hope of success . . . but I do, terribly, lean towards 'Gentle O.' Not so commercial, but . . shall I say? 'Good taste?'

Well, anyway, I said it.

This is, as you gather, a private letter. It requires no kind of reply. As you know.

With my devoted love.

   <u>Dirk</u>.

To Norah Smallwood   *Clermont*
                                              7 July 1979

Norah my dear –

A personal letter. Needing no reply. Mainly in response to your lovely long one written in your wild hurricane under the duvett.

[. . .] I had a foul, well NOT really foul, but terribly full week . . Elizabeth and her tribe [. . .] and we had to feed eight daily for a week. They left for Como on the Sunday morning as a beloved cousin of Forwoods arrived, six exhausted hours late, from San Fransisco and took over the bedroom with a welter of long dinner dresses and Louis Viuton baggage . . she stayed five days, leaving yesterday morning for Monaco just as four hideious Americans arrived for luncheon. We did not know each other but were 'arranged' by a mutual friend who telephoned me from N.Y and begged me to entertain them since they had rented a house near Grasse . . . two ghastly children of eight with the mental intelligence of Bendo who terrified them into shrill squeals all day; as did the 'bugs' (butterflies) and 'snakes' (poor little lizards!) Awful.

In fareness I suppose the parents were'nt too bad really. If one had had the remotest chance of speaking with them.

It was difficult to hold any form of conversation with the two pale children clustered on their knees begging to "go home now" [. . .]

'You'll adore [the husband] . .' said my N.Y friend on the telephone . .
'he's wildley sophisticated and very, very intellectual . . he's just written
a book on "Decadence" . . .'

I was abashed.

And he brought the book, suitably inscribed. This is a habit which
begins to worry me. Is it correct manners for a writer to hand round
his books like cheese-biscuits? I've had no less than three in this last
ten days . . . . . . seems MOST odd.

The one relief in the tedium was Elton John who came for a drink
in a track suit and a Mercury cap . . with little green-felt wings on the
side. Wonderfully civilised, amusing, wise and interesting about his
recent, electrifying trip to Russia . . . which has been an amazing
success. And must have worried the Polit Bureau very much indeed
for it clearly proved that all Russian Youth manages to listen to the
forbidden radios of the West. Free Europe, BBC World, and the Voice
Of America. For although his audiences numbered many thousands
not one single record of his has even been allowed into the country.
When he left for the airport his car was followed all the way by
thousands of weeping young people . . . all the way mark you . . .
crying out 'Tell more people to come to us!' and throwing at him all
their most cherished possessions ranging from blue jeans to Biro pens
. . . . . . terribly depressing and sad. He was much moved. However he
managed to spend three days, all day, in the Hermitage and was
shattered by what he saw. An immensly pleasant, cultured, wise young
man. Odd for a Pop Singer. But of course he is a little more than that.

So that has been a tough ten days . . . . plus the Correcting!

[. . .] I wait, in some anxiety [Peter Cochrane's[1]] comments [. . .]
what pleases me tremendously, as far as I remember from your call,
was the fact that he 'recognised' this odd, awful, cruel non-war. So
few people know it happened, or if they do, have forgotten. I think I
am perhaps the only British person who has written it down.

Certainly the Dutch will have covered it I am sure of that . . . but
there were'nt many of us out there at that time.

It deserves, if only in fiction, to be remembered and recorded.

None of us who survived Europe and Burma wanted to do anything
about this local-war which was not our business. All we wanted, so

---

1. Peter Cochrane, DSO, MC, was 'vetting' the typescript of *A Gentle Occupation* for
military accuracy.

near to the time, was to get the hell home. Intact. Alive. I think I have made this clear enough in Rooke's last speech to the old General ... but a great many of us failed. And there they lie in the graveyards of South East Asia totally forgotten: dead a few weeks before Demob. For what good reason? Or bad?

Which brings me to a point. It is correct, I believe, to write to the persons or person to whome one wishes to 'dedicate' a book? Would you accept 'A Gentle Occupation?' I know that you have done so in the past, therfore perhaps you'd rather not. It might be embarressing for you .. I dont know .. however all I do know is that you are the only person to whome the book actually belongs. I shan't go into all the reasons, they'd weary you, and anyway I expect you can guess what they are yourself. [...] It would give me the greatest pleasure. But that is not the point.

[...] I shall rest up for a bit today ... Elizabeth and the family come back from Como on Monday; I gather, from a crackly telephone call the other evening, that it has not been a great deal of delight. Storms, lightning, low cloud, black skies over the lake and too many American tourists ... and Italy is now desperately dirty and seems to be falling down everywhere. At the Villa d'Este the gardens are slowly reverting to a wildreness. George was very distressed with his experts eye. But apparently the gardeners have downed tools and gone to strike for Fiat or protest for the Red Brigade.

Who wants to work for the rich anymore?

It's a sad world ....

I must be off.

I hope that I've not tired you .... I'll take down the sketch block and rough out yet another possibility for the cover. I've got a few ideas sculling about in this senile head of mine.

With very much love
  Dirk.
    XOXO.

P.S. Just had a note to say that the piece I did for the Guardian Travel Suppliment (on Jamaica)[1] has been accepted without cuts! Very

---

1. Eventually published as 'The Bay of the Little Lost Sheep' (The Guardian, 18 August 1979). Anthony Burgess and Paul Theroux were among the other writers commissioned for the series.

pleased. They are. And, can you believe it, are flying a photographer
all the way there to photograph the particular place of which I wrote.
About which I wrote.

Sounds wildly extravagant to me. But fun. He'll love the place!

Quite good company I'm with. A. Burgess and P. Theroux .... D̲.

To Ann Skinner   *Clermont*
                                              10 August 1979

Anne love –

Breathless, I am, from the splendour and wealth of your super-
super letter of the 1st ... arrived this morning. See how long it takes
from U.K?

[...] Self History. Well. Not a great deal here to report. The
Festival was even more ghastly than ever, and I stayed away inspite of
the fact that I DID rather long to see the 'Apoclypse' thing[1] and sundry
others ... it was a very good net of films, but deathly short on
Glamourous Ladies and Gentlemen. Everyone in filthy jeans and
sequins and stinking of pot. Or else corpulant Jews with cigars ... and
the Grades[2] did a tap routine on the Croisette for the press with straw
hats and cigars jammed into slurping lips ... not an edifying sight.
Rank spent £250.000 on promoting the same films they were promoting last year. IE. the Wombles and Micheal York in everything.
They had two stars present at every function. Herbert Lom and Jenny
Fishgutter. Where, oh where! are the Diana Dors all gone to ... I did
a huge Telly, 55 min. for ABC's show '20-20' which was fun .. talking
about acting, if you please. The bit in the Mail[3] was pinched out of
contex, naturally, from that ... so you can imagine how wrong it was.
I'm in the market for a comedy, and Woodey Allan is my last ambition
... but he, like John [Schlesinger], only works with Americans ...

Lots of jolly guests hit the terrace, now looking rather splendid
after ten, can you believe it? years ... ranging from Old Hollywood
in the amazing-still-shape of Alexis Smith and Ingrid B. to sundery
Royals [...]

The novel is finished and off to the printers. Publishing in March

---

1. Coppola's *Apocalypse Now.*
2. The brothers Lord (Lew) Grade and Lord (Bernard) Delfont.
3. A news story headlined 'I'm quitting films because I'm fed up with acting'.

under the ambigious title of 'A Gentle Occupation.' Naturally I'm a
bit pleased that it got 'took' right off … no fuss, no corrections, no
damned editing .. just my ghastly spelling and punctuation to put
right. It took fourteen weary months work .. and sometimes I was
near to tears: most times I was IN tears … however God leaned out
of heaven or something, and it was finished and delivered on time ..
and now I am at the 'cover' … a pretty thing of bamboo poles barbed
wire and butterflies … Dickie A. keeps wondering if 'there is a movie
in it' I keep replying that I [am] not absolutely sure that there is a
<u>novel</u> 'in it'. Anyway it would'nt be right for him I think. Not patriotic,
anti Ghandi (!)[1] and totally unsentimental. He is a good sort, really
… but he does seem to have so many irons in the fire that one wonders
if he has opened a forge. Probably has. Ghandi; as of last evening […]
it was firmly 'on' and he seemed to have spent most of the week
wrestling with his script-changes [. . .]

I rail away; and yet I got the best reviews of my life last month for
poor Fassbinders 'Despair' in N.Y. When the Critics are lovely the
sods are just glorious … what hypocrits we actors are! I have the idea
to get one line 'blown up' and pasted round the studio wall here: to
comfort me when I get to a 'block' in a chapter. 'One Of The Great
Screen Actors Of Our Time ..'[2] But I think it would look immodest.
Like telling you. I saw a good deal of 'AGATHA' .. which I did'nt
awfully care for I confess, but did think your director was rather fine.
And the sets and costumes, no joke intended, and the 'athmosphere'
were marvellous … and that awful, silly twit, Miss [Vanessa] Redgrave
once again managed to prove that she is probably the very finest actress
on the screen today. She leaves me stunned with her beauty and her
mind … how CAN she be so silly in private life?

I have just recorded, on cassett, an abridged version of the first half
of 'Snakes' … for Warner Bros.[3] Quite fun and exhausting too .. we
do the second half in January. But who really wants to HEAR a book
read to them? I mean, of course, apart from the blind and the physically
handicapped (which is why I did it really in the first place) but I cant

---

1. Richard Attenborough was about to realise his long-held ambition to film a life of
Gandhi.
2. Jack Kroll in *Newsweek* (12 March) described Dirk as 'one of the best movie actors ever,
at the peak of his talent'.
3. A double-cassette of Dirk reading from *Snakes and Ladders*, adapted by Evangeline
Banks and released by WEA. Many others would follow.

see someone slotting in Side Two at the Hogarth Roundabout or belting down the autoroute to Valence .. maybe I'm wrong. I hope so. There is a hefty royalty ... and now, while you bash away at glamourous old cinema I start, with some weariness I confess, Vol. 3 of the Bio. For this time next year. Seems a life sentence. But then I cheer myself up by remembering Visconti comes in again, a dotty Cavani, and extraordinary Resnais and the total and utter fantasy of working for my black-leather and studded booted Fassbinder who is one of the most exciting directors I have ever worked with in all my life ... and ten years of a very different life to set down on paper. This time I think the book has to be funny .... cross fingers!

Dearest Annie ... I must go. Dogs to feed, a beer to open, lunch to lay ... and the first tapes of the cassette to hear. They arrived at the same time as your letter .. and, guess what? Yes ... thats it ... Dickie wonders if 'it would be any use to Capitol Radio?' well ... thats up to them. But I'll ask him in after I've done a quick shufti myself, and see what he thinks ... I am sure his mind is swamped with dhoties and pupperdoms ..

Allloveasever –

Dirk XXX

To Kathleen Tynan   *Clermont*
                                                   11 October 1979

Dearest Kath –

I have just received your mammoth-thing on a post card which clearly states that you have not heard from this side for a long time. And thats maddening: because I wrote you a long letter in July [...] So I had better try and do a re-cap .. although by this time you may have got the wayward letter.

[...] A glorious, hot, rain-less summer ... we lived outside all the time and ate and drank vast quantities of food and wine, which seemed to cost the bloody earth. And did!

In the middle of all I had to finish off the novel ... which I managed to do by date-time, first of June ... and fell apart. After fourteen months it came as a shock to have nothing to do mentally. Apart from arranging beds and food and ice for peoples drinks. But I have no doubt you know that feeling well already?

However 'A Gentle Occupation' comes out in England in March

and in the U.S (Knopf . . . was'nt I lucky?) later. Probably summer. At the moment Plon are reading it, with a dictionary, for France . . . so I am very chuffed, and have let the healthy advances go to my head rather. Covering every single thing in the sitting room in heavy white cotton. At VAST expense but feel it is decidedly nescessary after ten years wear and tear. White I insist on. Virginal. The fact that we shall not be able to sit on it ever does'nt, at the moment, worry me. It looks ravishing .. very Siri Maughme[1] .. and is totally impractable with a huge log-burning iron stove and a boxer dog, Totes, which thinks itself to be a kitten and is, in full reality, a raging wild-stallion. Hopeless.

I went up to London for two days to see Mum and sign my contracts. And got bronchitis. From which I am slowly recovering. London was exceptionally seedy and sad and desperatly expensive. The Connaught, thank God, restores a little of what once was . . . at a price. Saw no one . . . it was a family 'do' really, and had to trail down to Sussex for a 'seperate tables' existance with my Mum, as I said, which was not exactly gay. Age, lonliness and slow death. If loneliness is terminal then my mother will be dead next week. But it is not, I gather, terminal. Lingering for ever and ever ..

And that was that. England, the part I saw in the car to Plumpton, was very pretty and smug and green and Brookish . . . but Brixton and Tooting were quite suddenly Port Antonio or Watts. Unattractive: but for the brilliance of the colours and the variety of the fruits in the street markets!

But it was not a London I ever knew. Even in the halcyon days . . . . and I was jolly glad to get back here and fold up with bronchitis.

I read your bit in the Observer (?) did you read mine in the Guardian?[2]

I think I'd quite like to go to Cuba. It is the new Soviet Russia for the Intellectuals. Rather as Stalin-Time was for the bright-eyed in the early thirties . . . or Spain was with the Franco Lot and Bull-fighting . . .

Now that I seem to be writing rather more frequently than filming I think I OUGHT to travel about a bit more and see things for myself. Sensible?

---

1. The designer; wife of Somerset Maugham for some ten tempestuous years.
2. 'The Bay of the Little Lost Sheep', op. cit.

But there is still such a lot of Europe I have'nt even set foot upon .. and before it becomes an ash basket I think I'll go and see things there. Here. I mean, of course.

Filming has faded away, thankfully. I really do detest it and the uglies who surround it ... the last thing I was asked to do .. a week or two ago .. was the 'Emperor Of Iran' or 'The Shah's S[t]ory' ... unbelievable.

A sort of 'Flight To Entebbe' thing. With Claudia Cardinale as the ruddy Empress .. I went through the whole thing in tight bandages, as far as I could see, and when they were finally removed, in the last ten minutes of the script, guess what? It was just me, all the time underneath.

I ask you.

And now that I seem to be making some loot from sitting up here on my arse and bashing away at this machine, I really, on the whole, prefer it all. I dont have to trail about from Hotel to Hotel ... or fuss about a ghastly script .. or the New Young Director .. or the New Young Leading Lady or, finally, the critics. I know we have critics for books .. but it is a bit different. A bit.

Attenborough is breathing fire about his forthcoming 'Ghandi' and I walk in dread that he'll ask me to read 'the first draft'. I know there is a middle aged clergyman lurking about in the pages which is 'a simply marvellous part, Dirkie' ... the idea of India, Jane Fonda, Jack Nicholson and Attenborough all beating it up for Ghandi makes me ill.

How to avoid reading and passing comment? Or accepting! By getting on with the second 'buke'. The second 'buke' is two chapters long and reads like sub Evelyn Waugh. So THAT wont do. I search desperately for an alternative plot .... thats the hardest part. Every time I think I have a perfectly super original idea I read a cross review for it in the Sunday Observer. And have to start again. Ah well ...

[...] Tote is well ... after HIS bout of 'flu. (The air up here is too rarefied I think.) .. and is busy writing <u>his</u> memoirs.[1] Having seen how I can make a bit of scratch from just sitting up here for the day he has reverted to his machine. At lunch time he arrives at the bar staggering, glassy eyed, and reaches a trembling hand out for the Campari ... it is beginning to dawn on him that it aint so easy!

---

1. An on–off enterprise, eventually abandoned – alas, for Tony was an engaging writer.

I have just corrected my 'proof' ... and finalised the cover, which I
did all by myself, as I always do ... and there it all is .. practically 400
pages of stuff waiting for the printer. I can rest up for a while: until
the thing goes off in March. And then the Tour! God help me. Knopf
want me to come out to the U.S and do a trip there. Cincinatti,
Pittsburg, Johnny Carson and the Today Show et all .... I DREAD
the idea. But am assured that you have to go and 'sell'. Well, I've been
doing that all my working life. So I suppose it wont be strange. Just
exhausting as one reaches Old Age.

I think I've said all there is to say on this dullish day ... rain and
low cloud and ham and mushrooms and eggs and baked beans for
lunch.

That do? Wish you were here to share them really. There is a lot of
chat we have'nt had. Anyway this is just a restoring-of-contact-type of
letter [...]

Do write. Fully. Not about your teeth, but about your travels and
your new house in Havana .....

You are missed, you know ... and loved. So be good and pen to
paper soon.   As ever, in every way –
        <u>Dirk</u>
        XXXXXX

To Norah Smallwood   *Clermont*
                                            18 October 1979

Norah dear –
    The rains have finally really stopped.
    Quite frightful tidal wave at Antibes and 12 or more people washed
away ... so you see I was not exagerrating. And the drive down to the
mail box has quite vanished ... or <u>not</u> vanished rather: it is a vast pile
of rubble and boulders at the far end, crushed against the gates.
However a dim-witted Arab has been digging a way out .. and I
managed to find your letter of the 16th with the G.G bit from the
Listener.[1]
    Enormously interesting. Deeply worrying.
    All those red lines. Silent admonishment?
    Adjectives.

---

1. NS had sent a Graham Greene cutting, marked-up for Dirk's attention.

Goodness I use them like carroway seeds in German cabbage ..

Adverbs I am not terribly sure about: mainly because I really did not know what a blasted Adverb was. I mean, I know now .. but cant imagine how many I use.

Of course that is why I love reading Waugh ... and Green for that matter. The utter simplicity. But who is going to tell me how to eradicate my adjectives? I rather love hunting them out. Thats the rub. I mean, I love hunting them out to USE! Not destroy or discard.

I suppose that will be one of the many knocks I'll get for 'Occupation'. It is stiff with adjectives, is'nt it? Even Forwood grumbled ...

But I really dont feel, at this moment, that I can write without them. I'll have to try. I re-read that first 'chapter' on the 'Thunder'[1] idea.

And, having spent the last few evenings reading Waugh, realised, to my distress, that it was the sub-subbest Waugh ever. So I have set it all aside in silent despair. Not destroyed it .. there _is_ something there .. but set it apart for a time. It wont do.

That is the grave trouble about reading while working. Influence.

During 'Occupation' I read only my newspapers and light stuff which could not, I thought, damage anything I was writing during the day.

But now that I am doing 'homework' ... and enjoying it .. as I told you in my last Express .. I realise my terrible shortcomings as a writer I am almost 'good Isis' or Student Stuff. Rather a brave, if idiotic thing to do ... to 'practice' as it were in public. But how else does one learn? And as long as one _does_ learn I suppose it is not so futile. I wrote, the other day, to a lady in Sussex who has been a sort-of pen friend, in the best sense of the word, for quite a while. She writes too, not badly. Thinks that 'Summer'[2] (Postillion) is the best writing on its level, childhood and the child mind, that she has ever read.

And I'd like to go on and do a full book, as you suggest, for children myself ... but it would not be about talking hedghogs or dancing mice. I'd do the Cottage-Great-Meadow thing again. I am constantly astonished to get letters from children who have had parts of the book read to them aloud in class at school. Really an awful lot. I cant

---

1. The working title of Dirk's new novel was 'Thunder at a Picnic'.
2. The first half of the first book. The second half was headed 'Winter'.

imagine just WHAT parts are selected by the rather sensible teachers
.. but the kids know that the book is, later on, too grown up for them.

Perhaps I should do something on that line. Lots of stuff in the
back of my mind. What do you think? Or dont you .. illustrated, of
course. Without people?

For the moment I am going on with Bio 3. The Orderly Man stuff.

It is amusing and helps me chuck off this ghastly post-nasel drip
which persists from my bronchitis-whatever-it-was.

It is an astonishing thing to me to find that I am really not a bit
happy unless I am writing. Even a letter will do.

As, poor you, have found.

And I must do something about my punctuation!

Learning!

And at my age.

Old dogs and new tricks.

Very difficult if one has the vocabulary of a switched-off Indian bus
conductor.

Oh! Very important news. On the day of the tidal wave in Antibes,
we braved the torrents and went, not there, but to Cannes and bought,
in a wild flurry of extravagance, two brass beds .. new not old, to
replace the ones in the Guest Room.

The worried shop keeper wondered what on earth I was doing
sitting on each bed in the shop trying to imagine if I could see out of
your window any better!

[...] I think you'll approve of them. Simple, rather like the ones in
the Paris Ritz .. not at all bobbles and knobs.

And every two days a white chair arrives and the sitting room begins
to glow. Daily Lady is in raptures. The dogs are in the kennels.

And I'm off to set up lunch. Liver and bacon, fresh broccoli and
the last of the new potatoes. To give me strength to clear up some of
the wreckage on the front terrace .... oh dear ..

With love, as ever,
<u>Dirk</u>.

To Norah Smallwood   *Clermont*
                                                    26 December 1979

Norah dearest –

Well: that part is over .. I mean The Day.

Perfectly horrid season I always think. Now we steam towards the great Fete of St Sylvester ... and when that is over I suppose the place goes slowly back to normal. At last.

[...] It rained dreadfully. All the time. Except for Christmas Eve which was golden, warm and full of promise. I went off and olive-d, and pruned five whacking great fig trees ... and coming up to the house to get the dogs supper saw a line of cloud creeping in from the West.

By nightfall the rain lashed the house like steel rods beating.

And so it remained; and still continues, and is cold and turns to snow on top of the ridge. [...] We did nothing much. There is nothing much to do on ones own thank God. A luncheon party earlier in the week for Jacques Lartigue and his wife,[1] and a novelist and his wife, who spoke perfect French fortunatly ... because although Jacques (85, but looking 15) and Florette speak faultless English they do not care to. So we stumbled about from one thing to another over an enormous fresh Loire Salmon and potato salad. Jacques is an extraordinary man, and incredibly young ... the youngest 85 I have ever met I think. Frightfully 'chic' white jacket from Lanvin, a pink silk shirt, impeccable white pants from Laurent ... and gay as a cricket.[2]

Brilliantly clever, he is the Pappa of French Photography .. and gave me the most ravishing calender which he had published, of his own pictures, but which were ordered only for the French President's personal Gifts ... so I got a spare. Enormous. Far too beautiful to use just in the Studio.

On Christmas Eve our annual party, tea, for our ex-Staff.[3] In their seventies and getting on a bit, as you might say. Cadbury's chocolate wafers, a large Fauchon Fruit Cake, Earl Greys tea ... presents to unwrap, dogs to pat and exclaim over, a fractured conversation in French about gall-stones, siatica, and a Roumanian neighbour of theirs who has diabetes but wont do anything about it, so Marie is terrified that she will find her flat on the floor in a coma one day. They left at six thirty and Tote drove them to Mass in Grasse Cathedral. The early house. Not midnight.

You see: nothing very exciting. Except that we had survived another

---

1. Jacques Henri Lartigue and his wife Florette lived in the next village.
2. In its conventional, un-hijacked meaning. Dirk never used the word otherwise.
3. Henri and Marie Danjoux.

Christmas Day. I was remembering the Christmas Days past. Inevitable at my age: from the earliest ones in Twickenham when I was, I suppose four or five ... to the glamourous ones in Rome, in Beverly Hills, in New York, in Paris. And friends arriving from, literally, all over the globe, at my expense, to join and celebrate together. Madness!

It was the stock-taking part that I did'nt care for this year.

The faces which are no longer about.

The marriages which have foundered.

The children who have now become adults and faded into their own life.

One is glad to have survived at least.

Added to this Daily Lady is still in Spain either with the corpse of her mother-in-law or a mended one. I dont know which. But I do know that eight bloody weeks without her is getting a bit boring. And I see no sign of a speedy return, for even if the old one did snuff it, or get better, they will surely stay there for the New Year.

I hate washing the kitchen floor, and I detest polishing, and I'm fed up with dusting! There is almost no clear time to come up here and get on with my work.

My Muse is pissed of: and sulks in the shadows. No sign of her coming out to play again until she is certain that I am there to stay.

[...] Reading, because I missed it when it first came out, the Evelyn Waugh Diaries[1] which I find interesting but irritating. As I suppose was he.

Tiresomly snobbish, and as far as I can tell constantly drunk.

However one cant quite put it down ... as I did with Mr Millar and his very long, but lazy, bit of writing.[2] Tote, on the other hand, rather likes it because he knew so many of the people mentioned from Rosa Lewis to Diana Cooper ... and it mentions many makes of motor cars too: which always goes well with Mr F. (I mean the Millar book.)

I think that this must be quite the dullest letter I have written for a long time. Symptomatic of this wet Holiday!

About a hundred and something cards to deal with. People write notes in them which cannot be totally ignored. A rather pleasing habit,

1. Penguin had published a revised edition of *Evelyn Waugh: Diaries 1911–1965*, edited by Michael Davie.

2. *Road to Resistance* by George Millar (The Bodley Head).

but at the same time annoying too . . because they must be replied to.

Then, aside from personal cards, masses from Fans of 'P' and 'S& L' . . which is heart warming indeed. I think that I shall have to get down to another book on the Lally-Sister-Cottage thing. Clearly this is the bit that has sold 'P'. It is a sort of nostalgia naturally. School Teachers, in America even, are reading bits to their Classes . . . but it has not appealed <u>because</u> it is a childrens book. I cant quite put my finger on it . . . it is having very much the same 'reaction effect' as 'Death In Venice' had . . . touching some silent chords somewhere in people. It is greatly interesting to me.

[. . .] This is, as you know, a NFR[1] letter . . . it is just me filling in a loose hour before starting up the lunch and laying the fire. We have to go and have a Christmas Tea with a vastly rich Jewish family in a HUGE apartment in Cannes. I really dread it but cant get out of it: ponsiettas everywhere, bowls of wilting Cyclamen, a plastic tree with all the lights on, and a marzipan cake with robbins. Really . . . .

Love, love,
<u>Dirk</u>.

To Norah Smallwood   *Clermont*
30 January 1980

Norah my very dear –

Absolutely real violets from just under the walnut tree where the grass is hazed with blue. I am delighted that you got them as soon as you seem to have done. Wilted, of course, but they were the first.

Stocks brilliant and smelling lovely, if you like the smell of stocks . . wild daffodils on the bank all out and jonquils too, and the first of the almond . . it was so warm on Thursday that we lunched outside.

We'll pay for this in Febuary, be sure of that.

[. . .] Into Lanvin for suit-looking. The prices were so utterly wild, six hundred pounds give or take a franc or two . . and so DULL and the athmosphere was so over elegant that I went away with murmured promises and went straight to a sort of Marks and Sparks shop in the middle of rue d'Antibes where I purchased TWO suits in English tweed for £70 each!

I bought two because they wont last long . . a week at most . . but

1. Not For Reply; a variant of NTBRT (Not To Be Replied To).

look very good with buttons altered, (I found the Palais des Boutons just up the road and bought two new sets ..) and a few minor, but essential, adjustments. I cant, of course, sit in the things .. but they look splendid standing up.

So I'll travel in old Huntsman and walk about in Marks and Sparks.

Since I never wear a suit from one years end to the other in the normal course of events it seemed foolish to spend so much money. I have'nt had a suit, a new one, since 1962 .. and I cant believe that the Booksellers will notice any difference anyway. And these are for the dreaded 'Promotion'[1] only.

I expect that by now [...] you will have had the MS pieces[2] [...] I read the first three pages yesterday and found them rather common. Oh dear [...] I have a frightful feeling that it is most wonderfully un-original.

Cliché after cliché tumbles from this machine, just as if I were writing mottos for Christmas Crackers.

I was perfectly pleased with it a week ago. Stuck it aside while I got on with unanswered mail and a desperately bad (cancelled now) piece for the 'Evening News' ... and lo and behold when I picked it up again only yesterday gloom came down like a Welsh mist .. a salutary thing to do: put something in the drawer so to speak and THEN look at it with a fresh but, in my case, jaundiced, eye. I dont mean that I have given in, as I confess I HAVE with the 'E.N' bit ... that simply was awful .. and after three or four brave attempts I came to the conclusion that writing a novel is quite one thing and writing a column for a newspaper is quite another. And one I have not yet mastered. Madness to go and do something mediocre and poor for a large scale readership. Even if they are all dummies and sitting in the Underground on the way home to Purley East.

So I have written a charming note of apology and admitted defeat.

Better to have no 'puff' in the Evening News than a damned poor one under my name.

[...] Had a long telephonic wrestle with Losey this week. Huffing and puffing about a script which he thinks 'brilliant' by Dennis Potter[3]

1. Of *A Gentle Occupation*.

2. Of the new novel.

3. *Blade on the Feather*, eventually made by Richard Loncraine for London Weekend Television, with Donald Pleasence and Denholm Elliott. Losey was also in negotiation with Graham Greene over his new novel, *Dr Fischer of Geneva or The Bomb Party*.

and wants me to do it with Alec Guinness and Tom Conti .. it is on it's way down by special Courier today and my heart sinks. I pray that I wont like it.

Alec called last night to ask if I had read it yet. Said no. Ah, he said worridly. Well, it's all very curious and brilliant and odd, but I confess I dont altogether understand it. I told him that I had NEVER understood any single script sent me by either Losey or Resnais but that it all came clear in the end. He sounded very fretful and very doubtful: but obviously intrigued. It keeps nagging in my mind, he said. Well .. thats not a bad thing for a script to do ... we'll see. It is to be made in some vast house in Derbyshire I gather in mid April for six weeks. QUITE the worst time for me to be away from here what with the garden the greenhouse and so on ... hell take it. But if it is good, and if they pay, then I must I suppose. And Cuckoo, Marcus and the rest must wait for me .. unless they go back to the drawer for a long rest ...

[...] I finished most of D. Cooper[1] and enjoyed it greatly .. but grew to so dislike Duff that he nearly choked me with anger. Prickly, pompous and jolly well self satisfied. I grew to link him, like a bookend, with Harold Nicholson ... and that is as tiresome a thing as I can do. And does'nt make for a good nights sleep after you have closed the book. Irritation makes one sweat with fury!

But she clearly did write a lot herself. What a job for an Editor THAT must have been ... but he, they, still failed to make it clear what on earth the golden lady saw in that bellicose little man.

And with that I'm off.

With greatest affection as ever.

<u>Dirk</u>.

---

1. Diana Cooper's *Autobiography*, comprising reissues of *The Rainbow Comes and Goes*, *The Light of Common Day* and *Trumpets from the Steep*, was published by Michael Russell in 1978.

To Jean Lion[1]

Clermont
29 March 1980

Dear Mrs Lion –

It is difficult to tell you of the intense pleasure your letter, and the splendid photographs, gave me today as all 'Nore' was suddenly once again before my eyes. A house I loved with a deep and lasting passion.

It seems so very long ago that it once was mine .. bought, indeed, from the rather un-likable Mrs Baker [. . .] I got the house away from her and her decorations. Lots of fake Louis, Royal Doulton and so on .. it took a small fortune to strip everything away. After I sold it, to a young couple who seemed extremely rich but who never, I understand, ever moved in, it all rather fell apart.

The gardens became a wilderness, the ponds silted up, the woods quite unkempt and the swimmingpool a ruin. I dont know if this is so .. it was gossip from local people. But it saddened me greatly that the house was neglected and unloved .. and that the gardens, on which I had spent a modest fortune (twelve gardeners in team three times a month!) had reverted to field and brush-wood.

How splendid it now looks again. Sad about the elms, but lovely that you left poor Sinuhe[2] where he is ... beside countless cats, two fat pekenese (which belonged to my Cook) and a small flock of birds of one sort or another. These had wooden place names which have long since rotted away ... but were smothered in bluebells and daffodils .. and set about with primroses. We always called it the Chestnut Walk and Cemetary Lane ... it led, does it still? to the little pools down among the azaleas .. both pools stocked with fish, one an enormous monster with scarlet fins; and toads.

The whole house was one, so to speak. Nore and East Nore .. which was then the guest wing and frightfully cold! I bought the two little cottages up in the woods and converted them into the Pheasantry as a possible 'retirement' home for myself .. but realised that living so close to a house which I had loved so well would be a foolish thing to

---

1. Jean Lion and her husband Jacques, the then owners of Nore, had sent photographs of the house which Dirk loved best of all his homes in England and which he and Tony had left in 1966 for Adam's Farm. A brief account of its previous occupants, including Brian Howard and Robert Godwin-Austen, is given – with references – in *Dirk Bogarde: The Authorised Biography.*
2. One of Dirk's and Tony's corgis; companion to Bogie.

do . . . so <u>that</u> became a secondary Guest House . . I found all the floor bricks and timbers up in the woods on the site of a long demolished woodmans cottage, and we humped them down in a jeep . . most of the beams came from the old bake house at Scaynes Hill![1] That was a hell of a journey . . . but the oven-bricks were glorious.

The little temple was, you are correct, brought over by Goodwin Austin, and when I found it, buried in brambles, it had a rather curious, and very detailed, phallic symbol standing erect in the very center!

So I am not absolutely certain that it was only spirits who went there to worship . . . there were four lion-dogs at each corner and a heavy round ball on the very top . . . lost in neglect I expect.

The carp pond, with the cherry, was a source of constant delight to my nephews and neices who used to fish there, the largest I ever landed, carp I mean, was about a six-pounder. We always let them go again . . and there were great fat eels there also.

I still have, to this day, a great sheaf of barley which I picked on my last day at Nore . . from the field below the swimming pool . . it still stands in a great luster jug in my present dining-room. A dusty, but nostalgic, reminder of England.

One curious thing, but not mentioned by you, was our Ghost.

We always used to think that it was Austin Goodwin himself . . but later came to believe that it was a more recent owner known to many of my guests but not personally to me. A rather sad and very tiresome fellow called Brian Howard (Brian Howard. Portrait of a Failure.) published by Blond in 1968 . . a good deal about Nore in this for it was then owned by his mother, Mary Chess.

However: he used to bash about up and down the big staircase, lock us into rooms, scatter records all over the drawing room . . OUT of their sleeves, and cut the heads off any large flower he fancied and stick them in the ashtrays . . the dogs loved him! They leapt and danced after him . . un nerving to many guests, I may add, but we all got perfectly used to him in time. He was more of a begnin poltagist (cant spell it!) than a ghost . . . although some people swore that there was an icy draft during his appearances. I never found this myself.

I am so happy that the house is now in such good hands and so well loved . . . happier too, because young people are once again running in it's gardens.

---

1. In Sussex.

Thank you for writing to tell me, and for the photographs .. I enclose one or two as it was in my time ..

I am sorry that I cannot tell you the second part of 'Snakes' will soon be out!' I have just turned it down .. such a wearying business and I have never heard that anyone, except yourself, has ever heard it! So ... my present work-table is heavy with unfinished business and I must sort myself out ... also the summer is upon us here on the hill, and the garden cries out for my spade, fork and clippers ..

I hope that you will continue to enjoy many more seasons at Nore, and that it will go on giving you the pleasure it so clearly does.

When I remember England up here on my limestone hills, I only really remember Nore. Thank you so much ..

Very sincerely
<u>Dirk Bogarde</u>

On his return to England to launch A Gentle Occupation *Dirk had visited his mother. She died, unexpectedly, two weeks later.*

To Norah Smallwood   *Clermont*
                                                          2 April 1980

Norah dearest –

When I was a very young Officer, I was once left to guard, all on my own, a very large empty hotel on the front at Worthing.

Acres of empty floors, endless corridors leading to infinity, silent rooms, dust .. a tap dripping in the deserted kitchens .. Nothing; not even a mouse. All about me silent, dead, no echoes of the past, of laughter, bells, music, knives and forks a-clatter, no rattle of the lifts .. only the distant sea soughing and my bedside clock tick-tocking as I tried to comfort myself, uselessly, with Wyndham Lewis and, I believe, 'Tarr'² ... an odd choice. Perhaps I found it in the silent library below?

All that preamble to say that in just such a state today .. for the bustle and hustle and mild hullabaloo is now over and an odd emptiness is all about me .. a letter from you, with two black feathers and full of generous delight.

---

1. JL had heard his first, abridged, recording on cassette (WEA).
2. Lewis's novel, published first in *The Egoist* in 1918, then by Chatto & Windus in 1928.

And the gloom, sort of, faded and I felt extremely happy.

Such a feeling, like the empty hotel, comes simply because for the last two months, about, I have been thinking and breathing 'the book', which I suppose is natural .. and really dreading the London Trip .. which was dotty in retrospect as it happend, but nasty at the time!

Now the book is off my head .. launched at least .. we can not tell yet if it founders: how I pray it does not.

As I said before, not only for myself .. but you and the Office and for your belief and all that … We'll see.

I should be out in the garden digging in my peat in the new bed I hacked out of reluctant turf last evening .. but the man who brings the peat, and the terre de brouyare,[1] and the pots for the seedlings and all manner of other things, has not yet arrived although he said faithfully he'd be here at the 'debut de l'apres midi' .. which at nearly three o'clock I think it must be. However: no sign.

And I cant do anything much until I have my blasted peat. So.

Vast piles of awful Fan Letters about the Parkinson Show and the other junk-stuff .. birthday cards galore, Pussies, Doggies, bunches of wild flowers in red ribbons and that wearying 'Hay-Waain' by Mr Constable: but all tremendously kind and loving .. and all of the senders have 'put our names down at the local library but there is a terrific waiting list already. Are'nt you lucky?'

Am I? I'd far rather the buggers bought the thing.

Golden day here. Hot in fact. Dogs pant, bees idle, trees glow with pale green buds and tiny leaves, wild garlic in frothy white clumps, pear, cherry and crab dazzling against the blue sky … and I'm trying to get a shape into the terrace for May …

The week has not been entirely empty however.

Sadly my Mamma died, very suddenly and without pain, on Saturday evening, so there has been too-ing and fro-ing trying to get me to England for the funeral tomorrow. No luck. Easter week and not a seat anywhere from Paris, Brussels, Zurich, Amsterdam or Geneva .. booked solid.

So Elizabeth and Gareth, my brother, are coping .. quite marvellously, and I sit here feeling guilty, of course, but resigned.

I was glad, indeed, of the London Trip for the main reason that I got down to see her that Sunday before I started 'work'.

---

1. *Terre de bruyère* (peat).

As I told you, I think, she looked so astonishingly beautiful and vivid that I knew, in a strange inner way, that she was actually dying.

I knew that she had made a supreme effort for me .. and was exhausted when I left. I knew, driving away from the pleasant house, that I would never see her again ... and I am certain that she knew it also.

However her happiness was that I was happy launching my book .. that I was busy and working ... she knew, more or less, about the reviews, and had, she said, started to read the thing herself .. but when I left, on the Sunday .. she was so proud that I had been on the Television and that the Telegraph had given me a cover.

Very important factors to an actress-mother!

So the week had it's double burden in a way .. I did my job and she got on with hers, and did it very neatly after supper, alone.

It was a full time.

And now I attempt to get back to the usual routine of work .. and it is really amazingly difficult ... Cuckoo wont come back, sulking away somewhere, and Marcus and Leni[1] are down on the beach .. where I left them ages ago .. my new people, on the yacht, being Italian are very impatient and tug my sleeve for attention .. glimmers of what must be done slip through into my fuddled head.

Once the peating is done, the planting out finished, the last of the daffodils deheaded and the final strands of toad-spawn netted, I shall come up here and sort them all out. But I shall have to re-read the whole pack once again. Thats wearying!

[...] Voila! Up the track comes M. Piedamento and his truck ... and off I go to peat and dig and plant .. and edge the borders with something called Golden Glory .. which is a sort-of alyssium and should last well until you arrive here in May.

Do hasten! So much to show you .. so much to say .. and the room is aired and beds made ready .. and gout-stool (is there an 'e'?) goute-stool standing sentinal in the archway. No 'e' –

And thank you for my swan feathers and for writing ...

    & your love –
      & mine as ever –
      <u>Dirk</u>
      XXX

---

1 . Three of the characters from Dirk's novel-in-progress.

To Jack Jones   *Clermont*
                                                                4 May 1980

Dear Jack –

I write in haste, (tomorrow starts the yearly Residents Rush .. the
Festival opens in Cannes and the first of the guests, my publisher Nora
Smallwood, arrives for ten days to be followed by a couple from
Connecticut ... to be followed by two more from London .. then my
brother and sister in law and on we go until, from where I sit now,
mid July ... and they'll continue until October!) So .. this, as I said,
in haste before I am embroiled in all the bed making and washing up,
to thank you for your splendid note about Mamma, and for the
photograph which was kind of you to send. I have a copy, but small,
and stuck in a fading album ... it was taken in June '45 .. while I was
on embarkation leave for India ...

How long ago it all was .. and how we have all changed.

The vivid lady in that photograph was finally a small, cross, sad old
lady with the same marvellous eyes and the same mouth ... but better
by far to remember her as she was then ... in her peak.

I've changed, God knows! Still as skinny .. and still have a trim
twenty eight waist .. and still wear, comfortably, a pair of breeches I
had made at a County Tailors in Lewes in 1939! Tight then, and tight
today .. if you stuck my head in a sack I look almost the same. But,
dear God! I need the sack ..

Thank you for offering to send a list of my errors in (AGO). But
honestly dont bother to take all that time. Not, I venture, MY fault.
I have two incredible Editors who alter all my spelling and all, nearly
all, my punctuation .. they edit for V. Wolf, V.S. Pritchett, I. Murdoch
and so on .. so they cant be TOO bad! And she, Nora, is the managing
Director of C. and W ... tough, brave, seventyish .. and adorable.
But tough! So any errors, apart from Printers Errors which I failed to
spot in the fifth reading of the sodding Proofs are not to be laid at my
door! So if you have complaints send 'em to Chatto and Windus ..
not me ... I do try; really.

I gather I am now No.1 on the Hit Parade. Which is comforting, if
true ... climbed over Carrier and Green[1] .. in four weeks. Many letters

---

1. John le Carré's *Smiley's People* (Hodder & Stoughton) and Graham Greene's *Dr Fischer
of Geneva.*

now from all kinds of people who were there at the same time, and many who remember it well ... including ex-POW's who are grateful that I 'remembered', because no one else, I gather, has!

Fortunatly all the characters are invented, and most of the events, so I wont be caught for libel! I hope ... we opened in the U.S on the 29th ... the American copy is tremendously elegant and the cover far better than mine .. paper and binding super: sad that we are so damned poor in England now and cant afford the 'style' we once had.

The next book .. if it ever gets finished .. will cost an extra quid already .. probably more, because of the Printers Union .. and the errors they make in the proofs defy belief! They dont deserve a raise of anything. If my Pappa could read his Times today he'd have passed out far sooner than he did, if you follow me! I get so fed up with trying to decipher the news, and re-placing lines and paragraphs, that I give up in anger ... and it costs a packet here .. which does'nt make me happier.

Grumble, grumble .. it's really because of the Guest Arriving that I feel disorientated and cross! Never fear: I'll enjoy them while they are here.

If I can afford them!

Must go ... this to thank you for your letter and the care you took with the 'snap' ... <u>do</u> burn all the rest of the junk you seem to have. I thought that you had? It is useless to me now, and all far far too long ago ... today, I think, thirtyfive years ago, I was sitting in a pine-wood outside Luneberg[1] waiting for Peace to be declared.

Peace! Ye Gods ...

We really need'nt have bothered, need we?

Yours
   <u>Dirk</u>.

To Kathleen Tynan   *Clermont*
                                    28 May 1980

Kath –

Boaty B.[2] is here .. on sudden and very unexpected impulse .. for

---

1. On 4 May 1945 Dirk's unit was some miles away, at Reinsehlen, near Soltau.
2. Alice Lee Boatwright, agent and friend of long standing.

a few days, and last night we all spoke glowingly of you, and that has sent me to my machina this morning.

Wondering really how you are after your sad little cryptic note of a few weeks ago ... Since I can only hazard a guess, and a bleak one at that, I had better wait news from you and rummage about to see what news, he said laughingly, I have on offer for you.

Not much as it turns out: and I'm too exhausted to invent any.

Very nasty Cannes Festival ended two days ago in torrential rain which did not stop for one single day during the whole two weeks ... sodden films, sodden Jury, sodden tempers.

I saw nothing .. nothing, apart from 'All That Jazz' that I really wanted to see, apart from the new Resnais[1] that is .. but we seemed to get the whole Cast up here trying to dry out, or wring hands, or sit in dejected heaps wrapped in thick wool and wellies. That sort of weather. And colder than you can believe.

On the Final Night I went down to award the Palme d'Or .. as usual a fuck up between Bob Fosse and Kurasawa[2] .. if that is how he is spelled from memory. Fosse declined to come for his award which insulted the audience and infuriated one Kirk Douglas, head of the Jury, who made extremely uncomplimentary remarks about said Fosse and won tremendous applause from the crowd. All v. embarressing, as Nanny would have said, and NOT to be repeated. I had a letter of apology, this am, from the organisers apologising for the 'debacle' due to TV and 'rival' gangs of hoologans. Whatever that means.

We had two extremely tiresome women staying with us .. from the state of Connecticut. One of them a writer who had just come from London where she was flogging her book on cancer. I refused to either read the thing or discuss it: which made her v. cross indeed. So she sat for eight days in the rain drinking strong black coffee, smoking up a heath fire, and swallowing glasses of Glenfiddich which made her extremely drunk in a very short time. Which I, personally, find boreing. Although I am well aware that I passed out once in your company not so long ago! But that was fear and exhaustion and elation compounded. Hope I am forgiven?

Meanwhile, with all this nonsense, work on Novel 2 has ground to

---

1. *Mon Oncle d'Amérique.*
2. Fosse and Akira Kurosawa shared the Palme d'Or for *All That Jazz* and *Kagemusha* respectively.

a miserable halt half way through. With a delivery date for September
... but it is impossible, as you will know, to try and cope with a
seething brain full of people and events when you have ice to fetch,
tables to lay, beds to make up or down, dustbins to empty and dogs
to feed ... and then try to 'glow' with conversation until everyone
wants to go to bed. Too late. The only pleasing guests, really of the
lot, were Nat Wood and her rather dull, but very nice, husband Bob
Wagner .. and Mark Cowley, who wrote 'The Boys In The Band' and
a super chap who runs Jo Allans[1] .. the resturant in London, not N.Y.
We drank a great deal too much wine .. laughed uproariously at Nats
ghastly stories of her trip to the Hermitage with P. Ustinov to 'do' a
Telly on the Impressionists ... which was sheer Waugh in it's horrors.

She, being Russian and speaking fluently, was in a far better, or
worse, position to know just what was going on, and how completely
they had been 'bugged' ... which was a startling realisation for two
refugees from Doheny![2]

[...] Boaty says [...] that you are the only woman in N.Y who
can make a grand entrance into a room with absolute silence and the
minimum of fuss .. and leave the 'whole fuckin' place stunned' ...
which is still a nice, and clever, thing to be able to do! [...] It is
comforting that one still has friends who come so far to hide away.
And seek comfort. Rare and rewarding ...

Tote hobbles about on a sort of arthritic-foot ... and gets fed up
because he cant work on the land. The grass is as high as that fucking
elephants eye already with all this rain .. and I can only manage a little
mowing on my own in between table-laying, washing lettuce, bouts.

So you see: not much news really. Almost none. But this was just
meant to be a Keep In Touch Letter [...]

Off to book a table for tomorrow at the Colombe. Boat has never,
oddly, been there and longs to. I ruefully count my small change from
the Housekeeping .. it wont go far tomorrow. But it'll at least save me
a washing up and a laying.

And for that I am deeply grateful. Even at 250 francs a head ...
sans the wine. I'm off ... pressing a kiss upon you ...

    With devoted love

    <u>Dirk</u>

---

1. Mart Crowley; Richard Polo, manager of Joe Allen in Covent Garden.
2. Daheny Drive, Hollywood.

To Norah Smallwood   *Clermont*
                                                        27 June 1980

Dearest Norah –

Pretty exhausted I am. Chapter 8 packed up and stuck into it's envelope for the mail tomorrow.

It seems to me, that with real hard-slog, six to eight hours per day, I can get one Chapter done in a full week. Saturday to Saturday. Without rushing, that is.

But I am not sure that I could keep it up over any great length of time. My eyes, at the end of the day .. about seven, have sunk into wells!

Poor little creature.

Australia:[1]

I really DO detest Australia. I dont care what they say, I dont think going there, at this stage, would sell sufficient books (which ones anyway?) to make the sheer hell of it worth while.

Amsterdam is one thing .. and not over exhausting. Bad enough, but not a killer. Australia would be. I would'nt do the trip in 'easy stages', it takes far too long ... I know! And it is the perepheral things which are so frightful. The Talk-Shows, the lunches, the bloody old Mayors, the Press in general and the wholesale swamping of ones privicy. Monstrous. I'm too old now. At thirty, maybe .. and even then I detested it all.

Provence Book. Well: thats a bit more interesting.[2]

Although God knows I am not the right chap to do it. I am most woefully ignorant of my history, my Arts, and all the other things which go up to the making of that kind of book. Durrell is a scholar. I am an amateur-actor-writer. There is a difference. It would take a hell of a lot of time. Travelling all over the place ... and at what seasons I ask? All? And who'se to look after my land and the damned house all that time I ask fretfully.

And what happens to Bio. 3 ... which I do want to tackle next.

However: let me get this present oeuvre off my shoulders, it is a strain to carry about with me all day ... and then I'll have a bit of a think. About Provence, I mean. Would it be a Travel Book? Or simply a 'lyrical set of essays about' things generally?

---

1. Dirk had been invited to go on a promotional tour to Australia.
2. A suggestion that Dirk write about Provence, in the vein of Lawrence Durrell.

You know all about me and my adjectives. Golly! What a risk ..

All those 'shimmering' 'glinting' 'satin smooth' 'veridian' seas ...
How could you BEAR it!

Had a short break yesterday afternoon. A fine, clear, warm day .. a
bit of a Mistral. Up to the Valley we went armed with baskets, boxes
and utensils for wrenching roots out of rocks.

Cowslip hunting. I am determined to try here, although I
KNOW the soil to be wrong. However I stood in the silence of
the hills yesterday surrounded with literally billions of the seeding
plants. Scooped out, very difficult, long roots, about eight clumps
... and then dug like a Jack Russel to fill three plastic bags with
the soil.

Extraordinary stuff. Lovely. Cocoa red-brown, moss, little shards of
limestone, pine cones, humus .. sweet smelling and unclinging.
Brought it all back and packed one big bowl with half a hillside, or so
it seemed, and the others (roots) I huddled about the edge of the pond
by the water channel. In pits filled with the earth from up top. They
looked a bit wilted after the trip back in the heat .. but are amazingly
perky and spiky today. I wonder if it'll work?

Also gathered (oh! how you would have cried out in wonder!) a
mass of wild flowers .. fat yellow renunculas, double buttercup things,
Ox eye dasies, clovers, Thrift, or is it Sea Pinks? Fat pink buttony
things on long sturdy stems? Meadow sweet, corn-cockles, Feverfew,
Angelica, Harebells, Scabious, Great Burnet and on and on .. never
seeming to repeat.

The fields up there were literally carpets of colour. One is reduced
to such a cliché ... none other will do. Stirred by the softest mistral ..
bending and waving .. swaying, rippling .. row upon row of blending
colour, with the great hills rising still and somber behind, and a sky as
clean as a scrubbed pan ... sparkling, winking .. not a cloud.

Summer has finally, finally, arrived. I am working as hard as I can
at the book, but have to get the hay raked ... not so awful if one does
it with a pitch fork I find .. pulling towards one and then pitching it
into big piles. But it has to be done ..

[...] One time .. I know it's impossible .. but one time .. you
really should chuck the May Visit and come in June. I know that it
would thrill you to the heart: it is so staggeringly calm and lovely;
before anyone sets foot up there with a haversack or a pair of walking
boots ... and leaves litter ...

Now I am off to get lunch ... I rather think Forwood has made a fish pie ... from yesterday's supper-Cod-Left-Over.

And it's steadily marching into the eighties ... oh well ...

As ever, my love,

Dirk

P.S. Naturally – naturally – I left the forks & trowels up on the hills – I can never do anything properly! Maddening really – I'd had the silly old fork ever since 1950! – fool. D.

Kenneth Tynan died on 26 July 1980

To Kathleen Tynan   *Clermont*
                                                      6 September 1980

Dearest Kathleen –

Dont know where you are at this moment; shant risk a letter to Beverly Hills ... so this can wait ... if it gets there, on your front door mat. Basement mat?

Thank you, in all your misery and 'bereftness' (what a word!) and hustle for writing. One tried to telephone you immediatly we heard the news on the BBC World Service (naturally) but got a very different lady from you in California who was sympathetic but said I was a 'digit' short. Which worried me a bit.

Then called London as usual for your number from lady secretary: and she'd gone too. So to the village and a telegram which may, or may not, have got there. Saga ends.

I dont believe in writing 'sorrow letters'. And I'd hate to read one. So this is'nt that sort of thing. But I might just as well say, here and now, how very much I have admired your strength and your love for K. and how much I know others have envied it.

It is something NOT given to us all. And once you have it nothing on God's earth, or in his Heaven come to that, ever quite matches it again. Ninteenth Centuary or not .. it smells very much of today to me. A rare, potent, thing. To be cherished in remembering, and to be grateful for having all your life.

I have a particular feeling, that is; it is particular to me only, that it is a 'once off' job. I dont think it happens again ... but I have no interest in the testing of such a theory.

It would help a deal if I could spell and punctuate ... but perhaps you are just skip reading this anyway. So it's not a matter of much concern.

I am sad that you have to go through all the mummery of a Memorial Service. They have become so singularly 'fashionable' ... and I have insisted [...] in my Will that there wont be any of that nonsense when I go ... on the other hand perhaps K. would have liked it. I am certain he'll have a hell of a house!

And you'll be reduced to sobs again, and smile bravely at Sir John G. or Larry and old Blowright.[1] But I suppose it is what one should do as a sign of respect ... even love I suppose? Just seems un-K.ish and v. expensive. A damned good dinner and a super bottle or two of his favourite wine ... now thats different. But not my business.

I am glad that you'll stay where you are (U.S wise) for the time, and gladder that you'll go to N.Y. I think Valium Land is fine.

But unconstructive now.

And as soon as all this nonsense is over you can get down to work for yourself and for the best things that K. could possibly have left in your care ... his children. Or, rather, your children.

And thats important and vastly comforting. You wont exactly be alone, you see. Ever. Or not AS alone.

Keep me in touch as to where you are and why ... Knopf have taken my second novel. (Romantic I fear) And I now languish after a years flogging ... awaiting the correcting-period and the cover-designs and all ... God knows what I think I am doing in the Literary World!

I do find it tremendously exciting and challenging ... and very worrying.

But the Movies are really a drag now. Locations, Scripts and ALL the players ... and in a pleasant way I like sitting up here in my own world at my own behest and on my own conditions inventing my own people and situations.

And of course, if all falls down, I only bring [sic] myself really ... not even the poor silly Publishers really. Although mine ARE rather terrific, and Mrs Smallwood extraordinary indeed and to be loved.

Going into Chatto and Windus today is rather like going into Dickens. Elderly people scuttle about, the wood crumbles, the paint

---

1. Joan Plowright, Lady Olivier.

falls from cracks, books lie stacked in odd piles, and the lift is worked by a rope and pulley.

But they publish some pretty erudite ladies and gentlemen . . . and I am utterly amazed that I am now allowed to be among them.

I'll stop this . . . it's boring me too . . .

To say only that one loves you. Deeply. And that you are to remember that . . . and act upon it when you need . . .

As ever – always –

Dirk.

To Norah Smallwood   *Clermont*
                                                    28 November 1980

My dear –

This really IS a NTBRT letter. Not even by very expensive telephone call disguised as 'business'.

[. . .] Crisp, clear, golden day today and the fig leaves scattering in shoals. The first touch of frost in the air and down they all clatter. But the recent rain has bogged the land badly . . and I cant dig or anything. I can only imagine what dreadful things this rain, torrential, has brought to poor ravaged Italy.[1]

All the people dead is one separate thing. But all the lost beauties in architecture and age is another. Naturally here our local paper is very angry. Most people in this area are Italian . . . . many have families who lived in the zone.

It's very saddening.

We felt nothing here oddly enough, although after the last quake in Algeria the whole house creaked and trembled and my bed, I was reading, shook so violently that the book fell from my hands. 'Whats that?' I stupidly yelled down the corridor to Mr F's room . . . 'Earthquake: I think' he said. The lights flickered, failed, went on. I opened the shutters. A clear, starry night. Very still. Except for a thousand dogs. Howling in the valley and from the hills. Odd. And that was all.

[. . .] My dotty lady from Bromley has started up long screeds again.[2] I am still, according to her, positivly bombarding her with

---

1. Southern Italy had been devastated by an earthquake; Florence, by flooding.

2. This correspondent, one of a few fans who carried their worship to the point of direct action, had been labelled 'Barmy Bromley' and seemed undeterred even by the rigour of Dirk's lawyer, Laurence Harbottle, who diagnosed her as suffering from 'Moon Troubles'.

secret messages in the 'Telegraph' and 'Times' ..... after very careful checking with her dates and the calander it is clear that this madness happens just before the full moon, and lasts until it wanes .... over a period, now, of three years. I am at a loss. Solicitors, threats of the Police, nothing puts her off.

And she is as mad as a snake ... but I imagine that her family, for she certainly has one and I know all their names, has not the least idea that she has this secret. How rum it is. Deeply boring too. But offending when she takes flights from London and arrives in Chateauneuf! I have told all the shop people and the Post Master that if a middle aged, very respectable looking, not to say almost affluent, English woman asks where I live they must immediatly send for a representative from Lady Yules Animal Sanctuary. She'd be happy there with all the bloody doggies and pussies, as she is predisposed to call them. I think I told you my last gift, in September, was a huge gift wrapped packet of hand picked Kentish Cob Nuts full of mould and earwigs.

I paid £1 Duty on the damn thing, and even Lady refused them for her ravenous Spanish litter.

You think you have problems, girl!

Dirk XXX

To Norah Smallwood   Clermont
                                                18 December 1980

Norah dear –

Quite mad to send that telegram by Express. You must have seen it was'nt, as you thought anyway, a chum or, thank God! The Menace![1]

But thank you anyway.

Two anyways.

It's that sort of morning.

What is funny, talking about Menaces, was that I got in the mail yesterday the very first 'Hate-Tape' I have ever received in my life.

Staggering.

I get quite a number of these things, ordinary tape cassettes which people send as presents. Usually greetings from them and their families, a bit of their favourite Music, (Nutcracker and Sylvia) or the Beatles. That sort of thing.

---

1. Undoubtedly 'Barmy Bromley'.

But this was different.

A lady (sic) who is, she tells us, 'a single parent family' .. with two sons, one fifteen (six O levels. The other 17, four A's) and who lives in [Sussex] saw fit to make a personal tape of her fury and rage after the TV Show¹ which, unhappily for me, she saw 'by accident, I was just getting the Take Away Chicken Maryland ready for supper that evening and YOU invaded my kitchen, Mr Bogarde.'

I, you will note, invaded <u>her</u> kitchen.

Then follows a continious, one hour exactly, stream of invective, fury, sneers, sarcasm, rage and envy. Above all envy.

Oh how sad it all is. How stunned one was to listen.

The bitterness, the warpdness, the snidery .. but oh! the envy.

Something I dont honestly remember that we were well known for in my day. I suppose we had such a vast Empire that we had no need to envy anyone?

But this, of course a sick creature, made one hide with horror.

The misunderstanding! She was convinced, for example, that when I spoke about wearing 'shoes' to try and 'find' the person I was playing that I was in fact insulting her personal feet!

'I looked down, and there I was in my muddy wellies .. I'd just been to feed the chickens, we are'nt all millionaires living off the money good, loyal, British people, have been forced to pay to see your work, as you call it, or buy your sneaky books . . . oh no! I have four Bantams, and I'd just been out to feed them, and thats why I was wearing my wellies. And you! So high and mighty about knowing people by their feet! What were you wearing may I ask?'

There is a long pause here. Then.

'Sneakers!' in tones of disgust and triumph.

And so it goes on. She finally ended up by saying that she too had a view from her house. When she sat on her 'loo seat', she was able to 'look right across the house, through my eldest sons bedroom door, to the channel. With my binoculars.'

How about that?

She works in [. . . a] Hospital .. and that 'gives you a real insight into true life.'

Well.

---

1. Dirk's interview with Elaine Grand on *After Noon Plus* (Thames Television, 4 December).

I suppose, if one ever saw the creature, she was, or would be, a perfectly ordinary 'normal' looking woman. She has been to France, she says, many times on holiday. Hates the French, though, because they are sneaky and underhand and let us down 'in our hour of need.' But she hates me far more!

Saluatory to hear I suppose. Shameful too. Hearing oaths used normally by Dockers .. twisted hate, fury, resentment.

God help the sons.

A thoroughly nice middleclass English woman [. . .] who can work a tape recorder, apparently, and is as vicious and ugly in mind as one could imagine.

I would'nt be a [patient] in her hands for anything. Think of the power she must weald!

I must go out and get some air: digging over the pond-bed and setting that to rights for summer. Five more roses. Tote chose them, so I dont honestly know <u>what</u> we'll have. Rasberrries I should'nt wonder.

Is it the New Year yet with you?

If it is, Happy one . . .

and love

<u>Dirk</u>

Saturday 20th.

I had sealed this missive yesterday, and was about to mail it off to you today, but by complete chance, turned the Hate Tape over as I was removing it from the machine . . . and found that there was more to come!

On the second side she had recorded I suppose about half an hour of the TV Programme . . . which sounded perfectly sensible to me, and not bad at all! I cant now recall what my last words were . . . something about hoping that I had been some use to somebody somewhere in earth in my life . . . then a nice swell of pretty music, and that was the end I thought. But NOT SO. She had her last word!

'Christ!' she said in a scornfull voice, 'Think your bloody God!'

So . . . however what was absolutely facinating was the fact that she had recorded me and herself OVER a tape which she had addressed to a brother [abroad] .. And so she went on for hours talking to him in EXACTLY the same way that she had addressed me!

Facinating.

'[——]'! she said severely. 'That was'nt a tarantula you found in your shower! Good grief! Not in your part of the world. Back to your books my boy . . .' and so on.

We still sit waiting for Labbo to Go. But he wont. Although his back legs are paralysed now. So I fear that Monday will have to be decision date.

I dread taking a life. But what else.

Delicious cards from you this morning . . . and a pile of hideious ones from ladies in merangue hats who send me bunnies and doggies and Dickens Inn's . . . . or even worse, Piccadilly in Snow.

Christ.

<u>D</u>.

To Norah Smallwood   *Clermont*
                                            27 December 1980

Norah –

. . . Then, quite suddenly, it was Christmas Eve and the Mail Box bulged.

Mr Beaton,[1] waspish, bright of eye, bringing, indeed as you said, many familiar faces . . alas! So many now no longer here.

But a splendid bit of nostalgia and a reminder to myself that I was'nt wrong.

Life <u>was</u>, once upon a time, Elegant.

And thank you. Very naughty indeed: but forgiven in gratitude.

And after Christmas Eve it was Christmas Day and so it went on.

I do rather hate it all. But suddenly this year did'nt!

I think because the week preceeding it was so bloody.

My little beast [Labo] could'nt make it in the end. We sat and watched him battle away and loose. His reproach, his apology, his shame when he peed himself and everywhere else, almost not to be born.

A gentleman, and he was that, of such impeccable manners . . I carried him about, he could no longer even stand, and finally we reached the Decision and it was done; well stage-managed I admit, in my arms in the patch of sunlight he used always to seek just beside my chair. He had no fear nor awareness. Only the very splendid Vet.

---

1. Probably *Self Portrait with Friends*, a composite edition of Cecil Beaton's diaries edited by Richard Buckle (Weidenfeld & Nicolson, 1979).

knew the grief; and simply left immediatly after without even a farewell
... which was tactful and kind.

And so Tote and I put him in his hole quite near the greenhouse,
under a flourishing bay, and shovelled in, together, not just the last of
a dog but fourteen years of our own lives. After that ... a minute or
two after .. we got back to wrapping the presents for the Dustmen,
the Mayors Wife, the lady who does the sheets and etc ... and so it
went on. Christmas Eve was a sort of mad charade; Labo in his grave,
and me off to the airport, at seven of the evening (!) to collect a script[1]
from a harrased couriour (cant spl.) courrior which I had to READ
before ten pm. Because at ten pm there was a call from California and
I had to make a decision. All this with turkey and all that rubbish
being prepared against the morrow, and Lady nowhere to be seen
since, with a blinding flash of happy beige teeth, she had announced
the night before that her husband had suddenly had a splendid idea
and they were all driving home to Alicante (!) for Christmas.

So you get the idea.

[...] The Script I had to read is curious and good. I have said Yes.
And leave for Hollywood, dear God!, on the 8th [...] Playing with
Glenda Jackson, which is the main bait, in the True Story of Roald
Dahl and his wife Patricia Neal. You'll not know about it I imagine,
but someone you know will ... so I'll not bore you with the details. I
have telephoned Roald and asked his permission to play him and he
has most warmly agreed. It seems to me, and to him, a perfectly
frightful thing that because a book was written about this part of
the[ir] lives, a tragic and fearful part, that a film of it can be made
without their permission. So they have co-operated wonderfully ...
and the Script has dignity and honour. But it still feels odd to 'play' a
man you know well and to re-enact a deeply personal period of his
life. We were neighbours for a while in Buckinghamshire ...

What about that for fiction? The last time we met was at that awful
Foyles luncheon[2] .... I never dreamed, as they say.

Well. Who would?

I suppose that I would'nt have touched the Cinema again if I had

---

1. A CBS production of *The Patricia Neal Story*, to be directed by Anthony Harvey. Dirk
was being enticed to play Roald Dahl. In their Buckinghamshire days, Dirk and Tony
lived not far from the Dahls' home, Gipsy House, and knew them socially.
2. In March, for *A Gentle Occupation*.

been able to make a living, even modest, from my writing. But now that the recession, or whatever it is called, has hit so hard, I have to go back to 'real work'. Mr F. pointed out, with great tact as you would imagine, that £10.000 today is worth only £1.700 in 'old' money terms and so that simply wont do. I want to hold onto Clermont for a bit longer. So: il faut . . . damnation.

And I really was getting along quite well with 'Lally'[1] . . . but she'll have to wait now [. . .] I'd FAR rather 'rite' than Film. And Hollywood! Oh God! I swore never to set foot there again.

I'm tired now. Cold too. Must go and light the fire and close the shutters. This with love, gratitude, and <u>always</u> . . . Devotion –

Dirk

To Patricia Neal and Roald Dahl   Clermont
                                          2 January 1981

My dear Pat & Roald –

I should have written to you both an age ago . . . well: a day or two at least.

But I would'nt until every single little 'wheel and deal' had been fixed on this Epic.

I trust no one in that distant Desert City . . . and swore never to return to it after the disasterous mess they made of Durrell's 'Justine', in which I was, sadly, involved.

However: as of this morning I am assured that all things are 'go' in their language. And so go I must. Because I greatly want to do your 'story'; if it must be called that.[2]

I am very contrite that I had to interrupt the Family Joys on Boxing Day . . . and a perfectly good game of billiards (and a goat?) to boot.

But I simply refused to take 'their' word that everything was okay .. and insisted that I first of all got your permissions.

That you both so generously, and warmly, gave them made me very proud.

I do not know Miss Jackson personally. An odd choice, at first glance, but after reading the script I knew a perfect one.

---

1. A new work-in-progress, which would be published twelve years later as *Great Meadow.*
2. *The Patricia Neal Story* told of RD's battle to keep his wife alive and motivated after her devastating stroke.

She has the integrity and guts: she has honour. She is not a bit shitty. And she is a bloody marvellous actress.

I can only do my best: I am too old, you know that, I am not a 'clone' by any means . . . nor do I intend to try to be.

Together, and with Tony Harvey who is pretty good, I am certain that whatever we manage to make of this thing we shall strive in any case to honour you and the valient fight you fought.

That's what it is all about, in the end. The Fight. And I think that it is extremely important to share it with others who may be, one day, faced with the same thing . . . or with those who say . . as so often one hears, 'Oh well . . it's no good. Thats that.'

That was'nt that.

Thats why I want to do it so much.

I cannot possibly hope to do more than re-represent what you went through with as much compassion and guts as possible.

I'll do my very damndest to make it possible for you not to be too furious! We'll fight too, if we have to, for you both.

Thats all: I only wanted to thank you, and assure you of my good faith and awareness of my responsibilities . . .

With love . .

Dirk

P.S. No old Fashioned roses up here! All limestone shale and dust alas! Just stuck in Mrs Herbet Stevens' and three Ophelia . . cross fingers.

To David Frankham   *Clermont*
                                                 14 March 1981

Dear David –

I'm bashing this off immediatly on reciept of your splendid 'snap' [. . .]

Your story, saga, of the RB thing[2] is so wonderfully, brutally, typical. I knew him 'socially' when he was married to Jean S . . . and that was

---

1. A climbing white rose famed for its vigour, stamina and fragrance. Dirk and RD shared a passion for gardening.
2. DF had a part in *Wrong Is Right*, starring Sean Connery and directed by Richard Brooks, who was married to Jean Simmons from 1960 to 1977.

a fairly horrendous time. He was every bit as loathsome and pretentious at home as he is on a Set. Once he screened, for the first time, a copy of 'Bullitt' (two 'T's?)[1] and I was invited along with Signoret and Montand and sundry other Europeans and at the end, as we sort of came out of the haze of splendour which was the movie, and having seen the now famous Car Chase for the first time, we were wide eyed and like a lot of kids in Disney Land. His only comment, as the lights came up in his over opulent screening room was 'Great television. Sorry you had to sit through crap like that.'

No one I know would work for him. How Sean gets by is his affair: but _he_ is a tough fellow to crack.

I was not, by the way, in a turmoil about the schedule of our unfinished epic.[2] Not that. Although 4.30 am was a bit early .. and half an hour for lunch not quite enough ... but we always got the first shot in the 'can' by 7.30 am .. and the Crew was fantastic and splendid and loyal and kind as could be. The main problem was our dreadful Producer[3] who, after the first days 'dailies' tried to fire everyone in sight. And then having said the script was 'twenty minutes too long by stop watch' (Why did'nt he know this long before?) insisted on inserting extra stuff which there simply was'nt the time to shoot!

The athmosphere on the Set was electric, with G. and I trying to hold it all together and to guard both lighting man, Villalobes[4] who is magic, and T. Harvey who is a bit hysterical, from being sacked overnight. It went on daily. The screams, literal, the yells, literal [...]! Amazing carry-on! One just stayed as calm as possible and worked. The Crew, plus the Teamsters, gave me loads of perfectly dreadful presents ... as a token of their gratitude for 'holding the place together' ... which was both touching and unexpected. I dont, in truth, know what to do with the stuff I was loaded with! A revolver which, when pressed, will light your cigar, beer mugs with hearts on them, a six-blade switch knife .. (they found it odd, but brave, that I actually WALKED from the Location House in Pasedena to the Shereton Hotel. All of five minutes down the road and in sight all the way from

1. Peter Yates's _Bullitt_ (yes, two 't's), starring Steve McQueen and Jacqueline Bissett, was released in 1968.
2. Work in Hollywood on _The Patricia Neal Story_ had been completed amid no little turmoil. The remainder of the film was to be shot elsewhere.
3. Lawrence (Larry) Schiller. Dirk would in due course revise his opinion.
4. Reynaldo Villalobos.

the Honey Waggon!) and a manicure set in plastic hide, plus a vast cowboy hat covered with feathers etc –

But it was extremely kind. And I was very moved indeed.

Glenda magical to work with. And the no-nonsense kind of lady I love.

We just bashed on together ... there are only a couple of small parts plus three, reasonably pleasant, children ... so it was not a chore from that point of view.

Having done the very first shot of the Movie on the first morning I suddenly realised that four years away from the business had in no way phased me at all. I was mainly concerned with the fact that I had ordered a bacon and egg sandwich and that it had'nt arrived.

It came later ... and only then did I realise that we had actually got the thing under way. But, Christ! What a way ...

What it amounts to is that we have shot, without loosing quality, two thirds of a Feature Movie (CBS Play Of The Week in the U.S. A Main Movie elsewhere.) in three weeks. Fourteen days to be precise.

Not bad; but it did need years of experience and all that Rep. stuff and banging about with Visconti and Resnais to 'manage'!

I saw the L.A. Times thing, and almost fainted with horror at the snap! Taken, we were assured, by THE greatest lady photographer in the world. Glenda murmured under her breath that the lady had one too many cameras and was clearly fussed and had lost her light meter. So we knew we'd get a stinker for a picture. We <u>did'nt</u> know that I'd look like Kenny Moore and she'd look like a simpering survivor from Belsen. Anyway.

The awful thing is that the English Part ... the final third, is now to be shot in Northern California .. because our Producer feels that he can keep a better eye on things, (he has subsuquently sacked the entire Crew ... only Harvey remains and the Cutter, Bernard Gribble) (from Ealing!) and also he insists that the British Crews are too slow and always go on strike. Which I cant deny. But how can we ever build Amersham High Street and Great Missenden north of San Fransisco? Well, of course, we cant ... and it'll all look like 'Mrs Miniver' ... but there you go.

He is convinced that G. and I will 'sweep the Emmies' .. which would be absolutely fine if we had a finished film. Which we have'nt!

The Parties, and there were'nt many because of dawn calls, were all as hellish as they ever are in H'wood, even those given by loved old mates. Underlying the whole thing was a new, for me, feeling of unease and fear. It was rather like going to parties in Rhodesia . . . . or India in 1850 . . .

The Blacks.

Three of my glamorous Hostesses showed me their tiny revolvers. My own agent wears a pretty gold pendant round her neck which is a gas-bomb . . . and most of the houses I went to 'visit with' had iron grills round the gardens . . . and mesh wire round the pools. My own Driver carried a gun in the palm of his hand, and had a switch knife on his belt. And we did, one dawn morning on the Pasedena run, get 'bumped' and 'nudged' by a clapped out old Chevvy, lightless, no plates, jammed with sullen black faces . . . I was told to take no notice; the doors of the limo were locked and we put on speed until we got to the City Limits . . . but it was'nt <u>fun</u>.

I would'nt live there for all the money in America. And Paris, the evening or morning, after I took off from International on Air France never looked so glorious, so free, so alive, so intense, so stimulating.

Ah well . . . the best part, apart from G. was the Concord to N.Y. It was a glory of gracious living, elegance, and quiet good manners . . . rather as travelling was in the days of the Boats. No fur fabric here! Sables! Two hours out of Paris we began the descent to N.Y. And I was slightly overcome in the Loo to realise that I was having a steady piss 65.000 feet above the world and at twice the speed of sound. Eight thirty am in N.Y and the first flight in . . . so no hassle there, and a full days work with my Publishers and bed at a reasonable hour. A little weak about the knees . . . naturally . . but otherwise perfectly normal. The TWA haul across your immense continent next day was much duller and more tireing . . maybe because of the in-flight Movie which, though I never listen to the things, flickers away maddeningly like an early, and bad, magic lantern. But it's all done now . . . home to getting the garden to rights after a month plus away . . . and off to London to award a prize at the Academy Awards Thing. God knows why . . but all expenses paid for three days and the Connaught rather calls me after a month of inedible food . . . all that cracked crab and those ghastly English Muffins! Not to mention Evian Water at 3.95 a bottle . . . which you <u>have</u> to drink in L.A because the chlorine, as you know, would melt a spoon!

So . . . thanks for super letter . . apologies for this ill typed missil . . I'm off now to finish correcting proofs of 'Occupation' in French! It's

in seven translations ... thank God I dont know Finnish or Israeli!
   As ever
      <u>Dirk</u>

To Norah Smallwood   *Clermont*
                                                   15 March 1981

Dearest Norah –
   N.R.N. means what it says.[1] And you go quite dotty and spend
£1.43 pence on ignoring the plea.
   So am I at this moment, for that matter. But that is my choice.
   [...] I had reason to return a fat bundle of Contract Papers to my
ex-Agents (now re-signed with) in H'wood yesterday. Cost me over
five pounds. The same packet of papers cost <u>them</u> three dollars to
send me five days before. Can my signature, on limitless pages, have
added to the weight I wonder? America is certainly cheaper ... What
I really mean is that just writing to each other now is in the same class
as all ~~luxurys~~. Should that be 'luxuries'. Looks better.
   I dont really know why you are 'facinated' by my going back to the
Set after four years. But your 'facination' has caused me to ponder on
it a bit.
   Not really so extraordinary: it is, I think, the same with painters
and musicians even ... surely with writers? A long pause to refresh
over-used parts of the mind, and then come back revived.
   I know that when I do I paint, better now than I did. Merely
because I dont do it often. And I could'nt paint properly; ever. I was
what you could call 'effective' only. Not enough.
   Acting is such a different thing to so many different types of people.
   I was aware, somewhere in my gut, that my work after thirty plus
years, was becoming mannered and stale. So I chucked it in for four
years and changed course, a little, by writing. There were times, I'll
confess, when I said to Forwood, just before we embarked on this last
peculiar project .. 'I wonder if I can still do it?' and he only remarked
that I'd have to have a shot at it to see, and that it was a fearful waste
of years of work to give it all up in one fell swoop.
   And then I was off: and the to-do about leaving the house, the
sudden alteration in my pattern of living, the speed, apart from

---

1. No Reply Needed.

Concorde! and utter difference to my life style here, was so intense that I had no time to think. I did'nt even bother to take the Script with me! I was so certain that there would be another, quite different one, waiting for me in N.Y. And, of course, there was!

So, rather like a captive duck being hurled into a pond after years of the security of a hen-run in a farm yard ... I merely swam.

It's so simple. Really. No great metamorphises take place I dont think. I know, before I start, after reading the script, who I am going to be and how. As you know already, I get the 'frocks' and shoes right first.

Shoes I hunted down here in Cannes ... before I left. A good pair of slim semi-brogue, black. With laces. 'Good Women' shoes my mother used to call them with certain dislike. And then I rummaged about in old cupboards and found a pile of 'cardies', old sweaters gone at the elbow, Vyella Shirts with discreet checks in beige and brown, and a hacking jacket made for me by Huntsmans, patched and shabby, but still a quite marvellous cut, which was made for me for the first film I ever did in 1947! And it STILL works today. Oh! And old knitted ties ...

So there was Roald Dahl's wardrobe at anyrate. And exactly what he wears today. And then. Of course I could'nt, and would'nt try to LOOK like him. I am not playing his clone. Merely re representing one amazingly brave thing in his life. So I had a bit of a tumble with a rather dotty hairdresser in L.A and we got a kind of 'Donnish' look of hair to fall across eyebrow, and changed partings .. and there I was: a rather tweedy, baggy, thin, ageing, narrow shoed, school teacher. Or writer. Either will do. And did. And thus I was armoured. So the battle to 'be' commenced. And with the right script it is not so hard.

Of course: that is all vastly simplified. But confidence has a lot to do with everything one does. And I have plenty of confidence about acting! God knows, after more than sixty major films, plus Theater, I should. And like a wine in a bottle in the cellar: one matures.

The only thing is that the Year has to be right.

And I know that my 'year' was a very good one indeed.

There is no conciet in this: it is merely a statement of fact.

The thing I simply adore is 'being' another person. Trying to use his mannerisms, finding what he'd do in a given crisis, how he'd move, walk, use his hands ... if he would perhaps have a particular 'tick' in distress ... tiny things which when added together give the audience the illusion that I am someone else. I dont always get this together fully. Sometimes I do.

After a few days of shooting in the awfulness of the Hospital in Los Angeles where most of the work was filmed, the Surgeon, a very civilised, charming man, who had actually performed the operation on Patricia Neal and who had gone through all the things WE were all so busy re creating, and who had agreed to be Technical Adviser on the Set, came up to me one day very quietly and said: 'It's quite strange for me. I knew Dahl intimatly during those weeks here .. you dont look a little bit like him, you know that. But you ARE him. You behave exactly as he did then .. same calmness, angularity in his walk; he only ever showed his distress in his hands. As you do. Behind his back.'

Of course I was pleased. And when I got home here I called Dahl on the telephone and told him, not braggingly .. just to possibly put him at ease. After all if someone he knew so well and admired so deeply, had been impressed at all, it was something. Dahl's reply was very typical.

'Of course you'd behave like me' he said. 'We are both English and we are both Gentlemen. Something the Yanks dont understand yet.'

Oh well . . .

There was a devine actress, Mildred Dunnock, who was also playing herself in the film. She had been, still is, Patricia's surrogate 'mother' and adores her. She agreed to play herself because the script was 'accurate', and she loved Pat so much she wanted to support her in some way. She is now eighty. Then, when it[1] happened, she was fifteen years younger . . . after she had finished her work and was going back to N.Y where she lives, she said, in her very quiet voice, 'You know Dirk, it's a strange thing. I have hated Roald for fifteen years because I did'nt understand what he was doing to Pat: why he was being so abominably cruel, so heartless . . . . apparently. But now I know why. And now I know how magnificent he was. I am deeply shamed.'

So that was good. And the odd thing is that I had no idea, at all, of his behaviour .. at that time. Or what he did. I only did what I would have hoped to do given the same set of appalling circumstances.

So you see: acting is a very different matter for a great many people. What is important to know about cinema-acting, mine anyway, is that

---

1. The stroke.

it must NEVER BE ACTING. And I cant really explain that. Miss Jackson, surely a plain girl, with feet like a goat-herd, hands like a bricklayer, bad teeth; has an inner magnificence I have only ever seen matched by Edith Evans. Her transformation, before ones eyes, to a really glorious, vibrant, living creature like Patricia Neal was absolutely staggering. And Pats own daughter [Tessa], now aged 23, who saw a good deal of the stuff we shot was literally overwhelmed, as she said, by seeing 'my own mother on the screen'. And she is a young woman not given to kindness or compliments I gather.

So . . . I dont know how it is done. Soul? Or magic? Very certainly NOT tricks.

A long letter this. Sorry. Your fault. And it answers nothing you asked! [. . .] but you do see it merits no reply as I shall call you tomorrow, Monday, anyway.

Much love
    Dirk

Dirk was awaiting the resumption of shooting on The Patricia Neal Story. *To add to the uncertainty, labour disputes involving both the directors' and writers' guilds had hit Hollywood.*

To Kathleen Tynan   *Clermont*
                                                    20 April 1981

Kathleen –

It's been Easter. Or rather, it still is I think. I sit here, the housework done; Lady is off genuflecting somewhere as a true Catholic, and await the rain, which threatens, and four guests from Up the Hill who are coming in for a pre-lunch drink. Which means pissed washer-up and 'caught' spring greens. And so this is haitus-period.

What better way of filling the time until they arrive for their bloody Dry Martini's than writing to you?

Did you know that they were invented in the Savoy Bar? Martini's?

Like Peach Melba and etcetera .. marvellous: my store of useless information.   Do be impressed.

[. . .] Our Epic staggers from the improbable to the impossible. Telephone calls every two days, from one side of the Camp or the other. Lies, half lies, mucky-truths. Which are worse to deal with than the rest. I dont know where to start believeing. And DREAD the idea of shooting Amersham High Street in Vancouver. The newest idea. Glenda, after a sticky start in her play,[1] has licked them into shape and is a success. So that's sad. I mean lovely for her but sad for me .. because if she had 'come on over' sooner we might have had a bit more time to work. As it is we must finish it all by midnight June 30th. So that the Directors can have their strike. Your lot are wallowing in one right now. What's to become of us all, I ask? Anyway: from the moment that Miss Jacksons final curtain falls at The Court, she has just eight days to get her ass to wherever it is and shoot the final third.

No way, you say? Ah ha! You dont know how fast we work. At fourteen hours per day we might manage. Might.

So I cant really settle to do anything 'proper' like riting. You must know the impotence of that feeling very well. I am to bash off at Bio.3 I am now instructed by my Publishers, unless 'there is some novel you'd like to write.' I mean, God! Do they think I have a hundred stored away in my too-small head? So Bio 3 it is. First chapter okay. Title goodish I think, 'An Orderly Man' .... it is, you'll guess, ironic. And a lot, a hell of a lot, has happened in the decade plus since we first rode bumpily up this old drive ... it's the losses which are so fearful. When you start counting. The faces which have gone. The faces which are lost to one. And laughter.

It was sickening, for me anyway, that one did not know you were in Londres when the razz-matazz was on for the Awards.[2] A sorry affair indeed; the whole business. The British simply cant organise a sale at Harrods: so how they are expected to organise a vast Oscar Thing with 3.000 people and far too many boring prizes I dont know. And one loo MILES away, to which one was allowed to hurry in the Commercial Breaks. Standing clutching your private parts in a huddle of people including Maurice Denham, Denholm Elliot, David Attenborough and Tony Snowdon and so on is not, at the time, amusing.

I rather had a mild attack of Fan Lust when I found myself crushed, a bit later, against Miss Gloria Swanson while we waited to 'present' the pressies. She's fairly formidable. The chic'est creature present: black and gold sequins, a long black glove on one hand holding a Baccarat rose. Calm, cool; Star. Eighty two. I thought of Ken and

---

1. Andrew Davies's *Rose* at the Cort Theatre in New York.
2. The BAFTA Awards, at which Dirk presented the prize for Best Film.

Louise Brooks.[1] Knew the feeling of sheer admiration. The rest, from Zhandra Rhodes (sp?) dressed in magenta punk, hair and all, and swaying under a homemade Calder mobile, was pretty miss-able. And by 'punk' I dont mean pink.

Tony Snow was actually very pleasing. I embraced him, somewhat to his vague astonishement because he had'nt got his glasses on and we have'nt met as chums since [...] oh .. sixty two or so. And he had'nt changed. Older; but we all are, but a survivor. As we all are. Thank God.

[...] I did a Duty while I was at the Connaught. Tea with Kathleen Sutherland. She lives there now since Graham died. In vast comfort, with, as she said, 'enough money, Dirk dear, to live out two lifetimes. And I dont even want what is left of this without G. I asked my devine Doctor what would happen if I took all my sleeping pills in one go with a bottle of Krug and he said I'd be hellishly sick, feel AWFUL, and that he'd never give me another pill ever again. So I sit here drinking champers, flirting with the waiters and waiting to die. Is'nt it boring of me?'

Small, vivid, black haired, extreme chic. Seventy something. Cucumber sandwiches and Earl Greys; lot of cigarette smoking and remembering G. at The Chelsea Poly where I was his student for some time and she taught Fashion. She was, at that time, Editor of London Vogue. And very intimidating. And totaly ignored me. Which she continued to do until she saw 'Death In Venice' and decided I'd made the Social Grade: for luncheons only.

But, because I worshipped Graham as a man, and because he gave me such deep awareness of colour and shape at a very early age, I was seventeen, I sort of feel I have to put up with this slightly silly, desperatly sad, widow.

And it IS a contact with a fantastic past. At the moment she is helping to prepare a gigantic retrospective, next year, of his work at the Tate. So at least the waiters are not so fussed. Most of them are squealing little fellows anyway, but I suppose that does'nt matter.

Apart from that, and two rather delicious, and wildely expensive, supper parties which I gave, nothing much more in a long week-end. But the supper parties were super because no one was over thirty one.

---

1. Kenneth Tynan wrote a now-famous profile, 'The Girl in the Black Helmet', for *The New Yorker* in 1979.

And they all came dressed as if we were playing charades and had gone through the Dressing Up box. Andrew Birkin[1] lost a whole tooth eating his asparagus and made a great tarrididdle, handing it round to us all to weight the thing, and Nicholas Bowlby, late of The Times, had just bought a fantastic motor bike on which he and his lady[2] are driving down here for a long hol. in July. We laughed, all of us, so much; argued, thumped tables, gobbled scotch salmon, and drank a good deal of a rather excellent wine ... and Bridget Holm said was it alright to smoke a 'ciggie', and I wondered, happily, if the Connaught would ever be quite the same again. I think people thought there was a grass-fire in Hyde Park. Well: there was a grass fire alright. But at our table.

I have made a perfectly shocking decision. Out with the Old on with the New. It works, it is fun, expensive, and rotten for the Old. But I wont be bored any more. And nor, my darling girl, will you. I'm off ... with kisses galore. Hiatus Letter Ends.

Love <u>Dirk</u> – XXX

To Norah Smallwood   *Clermont*
                                                        25 April 1981

Norah dearest –

I've just mucked up the big mower: hit a huge olive root hidden in the grass. Angry and hot I have pushed the damned thing into the garage. Done most of the big field behind the house: but hate leaving a job half done. Although the buttercups and thingummies are prettier than the close cropped field I have now left to dry in the sun. Rain for days .. a wind today .. spring. They say.

I loved your letter, as I always do, and this one even more because it was clearly written with a split twig dipped in your patrician blood. Or, to be more honest, a running-out felt pen. That made it MUCH more fun to read. The last few lines, in a clearly borrowed pen, were almost dull they were so clear.

[...] I am back at reading up diaries and letters for '70 ... in process of starting to get the shape of Chapter 2[3] roughed. a tedious business.

---

1. Screenwriter, brother of Jane Birkin; by then involved with Bee Gilbert.
2. Rosalind Bell, of Chatto & Windus, who handled the publicity for Dirk's books.
3. Of what would be *An Orderly Man*.

Irritating too .. re-reading stuff written when 'younger'. I was 49.

That irritates me now.

I'm doing my best not to strangle Vita and Violet and hit Harold on anything possible with something hard.[1] I cant, simply cant, reconcile them with the two people who gave me such enchantment! She with her delicious bits on Gardening in the Sunday paper, he with his wit and care of words, and his creation, with her, of the now rather over-trodden Sissinghurst. And how on earth did I revel in Violets clever, funny, book? I hate them all at present!

So 'The Shooting Party'[2] is a glorious escape. And HOW good! How clean and spare. How many layers in that simple, deceptivly so, writing.

What a lot to learn.

Which brings me to the odd enclosure which I thought might, perhaps, just interest you. In between chatter to Chatto[3] and dropping stitches. I dont know the child.[4] Never set eyes on her. She wrote first, I think, when she was about 14. Obviously from a working-class family: north. Her handwriting, then, was tiny and scribbled. But it electrified me for one reason. She clearly loved, and cared for, words .. knew how to use them, and wrote to me simply to tell me of her daily life.

I cant think why. No Film Fan gush. Nothing of that sort.

From a child of that age, living in a council house in Bury, with not much more than a loving family who all worked to support her, she has always seemed absolutely determined to 'get out'. But how I wonder. At first I set her off on a programme of books to read .. she did'nt know any. So we started off gently .. and then she progressed towards, and into, Austen, Brontë and so on. Predictable; but not bad thinking.

And twice a year a letter came: with comments, a chunk of Journal, often very funny and recorded perfectly calmly. The handwriting got better, the spelling, and so on .. and gradually a 'form' started to take shape in her.

I shall now have to write to her, after a silence of about a year, and make more comments. But I am foxed as to know how to budge her

---

1. *Harold Nicolson: A Biography* by James Lees-Milne, (Chatto & Windus, 2 vols, 1980 and 1981), detailing his relationships with Vita Sackville-West and Violet Trefusis.
2. Isabel Colegate's novel, published by Hamish Hamilton (1980).
3. NS's cat, not her colleagues.
4. Tina Tollitt, who was now eighteen.

on a bit further ... it seems such a waste to me. I feel that there is a potential there [...]

<u>Monday. 27th.</u>

A pause. Rain and guests are a poor combination. And now a bitter mistral blows from the snow fields [...]

Funny letter from Debbo Devonshire to whome I wrote a Fan Letter having caught, quite by accident, a 're-peat' or whatever they call them of a programme she and her sisters did about Nancy M[itford] when in London last. She, I thought, was vastly moving and her voice filled me with magic. So I wrote. And she says now she feels a 'proper person' having had a real Fan Letter from me. She's a dreadful fibber, but I do like her greatly. She once swore to me that she had NEVER dined in a private suite in an hotel in her life after supper once at the Connaught: she even went as far as to suggest that she had never even set foot in such a rakish thing as .. an hotel! Come on now! But she did rather long to meet Judy Garland, it was years ago, and did. And came with Lucien Froyd or Freude or however the man spells it ... and they sat in a sort of stupified silence, adoring Judy. She was in full evening dress. V. grubby slipper satin, with the Devonshire emerald clasp on her pearls held in place by a bit of twisty elastic. Great fun, and ravishingly pretty ... oh well ..

Our Elections yesterday. First part. Torrential rain and a moderate vote. Maddening how people fear wet feet but not the Communists.

Neck and neck result this morning. And the run-off in ten days time [...]

Now I must write to Miss Tollitt and encourage. Perhaps there is a very modest, but established Publishing Firm in Manchester who would give her a chance? I could suggest that ... it is so wretched to offer no hope. Or concrete suggestion ..

I was v. pleased [with] the clipping from The Bookseller[1] [...] it warmed my chilling heart a little. A leaf fire to frozen hands!

Off .. and DONT reply. In split twigs or thin blood ... blue, of course.

Devoted love.
    <u>Dirk</u>.

Shooting on The Patricia Neal Story *was finally completed in the Home*

---

1. In which Eric Hiscock previewed *Voices in the Garden*, describing the novel as 'lovely'.

Counties. Anthony Page had taken over direction from Anthony Harvey.

To Roald Dahl

Clermont
5 July 1981

My dear Roald –

I seem to have spent the week since I got back from damp old Angleterre writing 'thank you' letters as well as carting hills of hay about, and trying to sort out the wreckage of the rose garden (a mistral and torrential rain while I was away) and cope with the dead heading!

I am certain you know the problems.

Anyhow: this is to thank you, very sincerely, for coming down to the locations and, most particularly, for the marvellous 'stuff' you gave Page to salt into the [Robert] Anderson Script. They have been of the very greatest use, and we have used them wherever possible.

Time, of course, was our enemy.

Schiller behaved, for all his odious gluttony! extremely well .. and the terrifying clash of personalities in the U.S was not repeated in England for one second.

At one moment I saw him on the top of a vast rostrum swinging the camera about like billyho.

'You realise that Schiller is busy directing your shots?' I said in a modest voice to Mr Page who was busily eating a fat sausage roll.

'Oh yes!' he said cheerfully, 'You see he does so LOVE it!'

Which was a VERY different reaction to what would have happened in Hollywood where the whole thing would have ground to a halt while complaints of 'interfearance' were screamed at various Agents and the Screen Directors Guild!

All in all it was a happy time in England, and I do think that we have managed, at least, to honour both you and Pat ... which was something I promised.

Naturally neither of us are 'like' you ... and we do not seek to portray you, as you realised, but we did try to re-represent what you attempted: and suceeded in doing. I hope that you will think so too.

It was an enormous honour to be allowed to 'play' you; I hope, very much that I have not let you down.

With warmest wishes and thanks,

As ever
<u>Dirk</u>.

To Roald Dahl

Clermont
29 July 1981

Dear Roald –

This is to await your arrival from the awful U.S.A.

And to thank you for sending me 'DANNY',[1] which I have 'gobbled' almost as greedily as you your frais du bois and Schiller his cream and roast beef.

Shall we ever forget that sight?

Later, in the same day, I found him outside a shop in Aldbury with a vast twin-cornet ice-cream, PLUS a greasy cardboard box of sodden potato chips. French fries he called them. Hmmmm.

I found the book enormous fun, and moving and exciting .. but you know all that anyway! I honestly, hand on heart, cant see a movie there, however 'little', as you call it. But obviously, with the clang and clamour of people barking in your ears to make it, I have to be rong spells rong: as my Nanny said.

I shudder, I may add, at the thought of what the Movie People would do to all those ruddy pheasants ... cant ALL be stuffed!

As you will note I cant type. Nor do I have such a luxury as a Secretary. Handwriting absolutely nil. So please excuse errors as they come and merely say 'Poor fellow ..'

Royal Wedding[2] today and stuck I was watching on my titchy Soney. Very moving, very pretty, splendid as always those things are in England, with a splendour unmatched anywhere else on earth. The behaviour of the, incredibly vast, crowd was greatly heartlifting, proving, once again, that there is'nt much wrong with the people, but a very great deal with the idiots they have to elect to govern them.

Pleasant, so far, rumbles about our film from the dreadful desert City. But one has long since learned to take all that with the pinch of proverbial salt. And pepper.

I never thanked you, or if I did not enough, for the marvellous help you accorded me during the English Shoot. Cutting that Ivy Leagued

---

1. RD had sent a copy of *Danny the Champion of the World*. After what he called the 'cock-up' with the screen version of *Charlie and the Chocolate Factory*, he had turned down many requests from potential producers of *Danny*, but thought that Dirk might consider it if he ever wanted to make a 'little' film. RD predicted they would have fun – and money.
2. The marriage of Charles, Prince of Wales, to Lady Diana Spencer.

gentlemans icy script, over blown and over written, was a joy. When you reduced one whole block of black letters, half a page about, to one succint, brilliant, word 'Instinct!' I hugged myself with glee, and laughed loud at the surprise on everyones faces as I scored my fat red pen through the rubbish! Thank you: thank you.

Out now to water; the evening chore. My garden sere and bleached .. yours I hope not too rampant since you have been away.

My roses are faded almost to white, and spill like fallen cards in the heat.

Thank you again: love to you both as always . . .

Ever

Dirk

To Norah Smallwood   *Clermont*
                                                          29 September 1981

Dearest Norah –

A NTBRT letter this: written simply because I have wrenched the remains of the petunias from their pots, cleared a few beds of debris and sodden leaves, and cant be bothered to do anything else for a minute or two. And you need not even read this: which makes the excercise absolutely relaxing for me!

Day of torrential storms; really very, very bad in the valley and, you'll be delighted to know, at St Paul de Vence, where EVERYONE had to leave their rooms, or beds rather, and gather in the diningroom because the roof seems to have fallen in. Or something. Anyway: that bad.

Mr F. was shaken out of his bed by thunder, and the garden is now ruins of autumnal-tints. The russety-muck you so feel romantic. Some people! Happily, for me, we are hill-perched, and we had no landslides, as others have, nor mud ... four feet thick everywhere inside the house. So I am very grateful indeed. And, apart from being struck by lightning, which would have sent you scampering in a second, we are more or less ship-shape.

Is that the phrase? Or with all this mud and flood about us is it too, perhaps, apposite?

I am trying, extremely hard, to set my Parents on the written page.

Awfully difficult. Practically impossible in fact. How can one be so far removed from them as to be dispassionate? As well as tactful . . .

I'm not awfully enjoying it I confess.

But we drive on slowly. And I rip out page after page reminding myself constantly that it is MY blasted Bio. and not theirs that (which?) I am writing. Trouble is that without the parents there would not be a son. I have inherited so much from both; supressed rigourously, that which I feel came from Mamma as far as I can, and polished up the fragments from my secretive Pappa for personal use. Difficult I am certain you'll agree. Anyway, as soon as this 'hump' is flattened, or bridge crossed, I'll be in freer waters.

Not that THAT makes it easier! Bio's bore me witless .. The past, as far as I am concerned, is very much the past.

Fearful interlude this morning. I made a shameful record many years ago called 'Lyrics For Lovers'. I did NOT sing the damned songs .. but spoke them to a 'tinkling piano'. Someone, I am told, played one of them on his morning show on BBC 2, I imagine as a bit of a send-up ... and the BBC are so innundated with requests for the rest that Decca (as was[1]) has now asked me if I mind them re-issuing the thing.

Well: I dont <u>mind</u>. What the hell. I'm an Entertainer first and last I hope ... and although I am some little way towards shame about the way I did the thing, under rehearsed etc, I know that it is yukky and sentimental, but equally know that there HAS to be a revival of sentiment soon, so why not give the patient the medicin it requests?

But it's all the past.

So long ago ... but in those days we did'nt have Thatchers and Benns[2] and newspapers closing about our heads daily, it would seem. We did'nt even know all that much about weapons and Aldermaston ... although a scattered lot of people, led I rather think by Idiot Foot,[3] trudged along the main roads protesting.

And a fat lot of good that did.

I really do think that if someone put on 'The White Horse Inn'[4] again it would be a 'smash'. And all those beady eyed young ladies and gentlemen on the smart papers could writhe and press for 'Godot'. Or something.

---

1. And is, even today, although no longer independent.
2. Tony (Anthony Wedgwood) Benn, formerly Viscount Stansgate.
3. Michael, by now leader of the Labour Party in opposition.
4. The 1931 musical comedy which ran at the London Coliseum for 651 performances.

Timid letters on pale blue Basildon Bond, and worse, are beginning to flop into the mail box saying that they think 'Voices', in their phrase, 'just lovely.'

So thats one achievement! My Old Fans are not yet dead it seems .. and if they think that the thing is 'lovely' who am I to say 'What a lot of fat fools . . .'

I only wish they'd stop putting their names on the library lists! One blasted woman has been waiting eighteen months for 'Snakes and Ladders.'

Meanwhile .. apart from filliting my parents bones and wrenching up the leggy petunias, I struggle with A. Burgess and his vast volume.[1] I must confess to amazement at achievement but am weary with the result.

And I detest books which muddle up the 'real' people with the fictional ones. He's pretty tiresome about that.

I was impressed, but left ice, by Miss Spaak[2] . . . brilliant, sharp, simple . But who will care?

It's something to consider today alas.

[. . .] Miserable, wretched news about The Sunday Times and now the Times too[3] .. David Bailey (photographer of great renown and VERY nice as well as being brilliant) was here yesterday to do photographs. For The Times.

Big stuff: but I had to warn him that we may never see the light of day.

He went on anyway, clicking . . . but it is foul for us all. [. . .] David, who was just settling into a pretty super position with The Times (did you see his excellent 'snap' of Freddy Ashton among his box trees?) now looks to loose it. If he does he says he'll clear off to New York.

Where else, for Heavens sake, should he go? They'll use him there.

But I HATE the drain on brilliance which no one seems to care about in Britain now.

The sun is growing pale, the hills soft, the evening is on it's way. We have lost the hour too: same time, for a while, as you.

---

1. Anthony Burgess's *Earthly Powers* (Hutchinson).
2. Muriel Spark's *Loitering with Intent* (The Bodley Head).
3. As industrial relations worsened after Rupert Murdoch's acquisition earlier in the year of *The Times* and the *Sunday Times*, both newspapers had failed to appear in the previous two days.

But shortly, if you dont fall over a conker in the Auvergne, you'll be here by a crackling fire. That'll be VERY nice.

I'm off now to get some kindling for tonights bonfire ... and have another silent wrestle with my parents.

I bet they're laughing.

With love

   Dirk

To Roald Dahl   *Clermont*

18 October 1981

Dear Roald –

You may never get this: or if you do it'll be late because we are riding out the storm of a whopping great Mail Strike, which is why your splendid letter of the 7th only got here yesterday at five (!) in the evening.

Funny, is'nt it, how Socialism always seems to induce strikes right away?

The French are getting quite worried and wonder, among themselves, if they have really done the right thing this time.[1] I wonder too.

Gruesome tales you have to tell of the Epic and all the tarrididdle that goes with it.

I have ABSOLUTELY NO intention of going out to flog my book.[2]

It's died the death there anyway, as far as I can gather. Poor old Knopf. So there is no point in flogging away at a maggoty horse ...

They don't have any irony or satire, the Americans. You have to spell it all out loud and clear, pubic hair and all.

Glenda telephoned yesterday to say that she had been left a message while out at work (filming in Cricklewood. Is it possible ... ?) that Pat has now seen the film and is 'excited'.

Which we both feel is hardly the right word, really.

I expect, by now, you'll know all the truth and facts.

But it is not anything that I want to contemplate: trolling over

1. François Mitterrand had been elected President of France in May.
2. RD had reported a suggestion from Procter & Gamble, who were backing the film, that Dirk would combine an appearance at the proposed Kennedy Center screening with promotion for *Voices in the Garden*.

there and junketing. I am pretty CERTAIN that Glenda feels the same: but you know actresses, as you say, as well as I!

But I am all for keeping strictly away.

I have to come to London next week to meet Higgins[1] of The Times and do a TV Talk thing: I feel it is justifiable because the book got sent off on it's own, without any help from me, and has done well enough for me to support it now ... if thats what they want. Chatto do anyway .. so. Then Paris for the French Edition which will be harder because I cant speak French and they are SO bloody intellectual that I get dreadfully confused. However it gets me out of, or rather it just delays, clearing up the debris of summer in the garden and digging over the beds. I'm getting old now: I really think I'll slosh cement over everything and plant strawberries in pots, or something.

Goodness yes! Writing is a sod.[2] You DO have to squeeze the tube so hard now. I mean I do. One is too aware of the mistakes .... it was much easier at first 'try'! I am now so desperate about cliché, adjectives and adverbs and, with Fowler glowering at me from the shelf, I am quite straight-jacketed. It'll pass, I hope .. but it's wretched. [...]

Just put my splendid (EXHAUSTING) Norah Smallwood of Chatto on a London plane .. after a week here, which was fun but draining. I hope I have that energy at 70. So I'll now wander off and see if I can find anything that yells out for dead-heading. It's a fairly calm job, after all.

Thanks so much for writing: if you get any really horrifying news will you let me know? I don't trust the Soapflake People any more than the rest [...]

Ever – Dirk –

---

1. John Higgins, Arts Editor.
2. RD had encouraged Dirk by saying that the more one writes the more self-critical one becomes. It is, he added, a fearsomely difficult occupation for a good writer and 'a piece of cake' for a bad one.

To Norah Smallwood   *Clermont*
                                         22 November 1981

Dearest Norah –

I was so bloody angry after your call on Friday[1] that, instead of bashing on with Bio 3, we went off up to the hills and walked a rather surprised, but delighted, Bendo. Quite unaware of the business which had got him such a treat.

Nothing to be said about it all now. Anger has cooled a bit and it is 'all over and done with' . . I suppose some other poor person is being readied for the knives next time around . . .

What a perfectly filthy world we seem to inhabit now, when all grace, all decency, all honour is sacrificed for a tuppeny, two penny?, bit of paper.

What amazes me, and always will, is that there are people who actually read the damned thing.

Of course you wont forget the savaging: for a while. I know that very well from personal experience; but I try not to let it show.

Like you.

But the pain lingers; the cruelty, the un-justness hurts.

The thing, apart from the dispicable cruelty to you, that bothers me a great deal is that it's an inside job, so to speak.

There must be a mole, as they call it, comfortably snuffling along in the Publishing Garden. That is always terribly alarming.

At least this filthy thing has brought to your notice just how much you are respected and loved. I am perfectly certain, in your tight Scots way, that you knew that anyway. But it is, or surely it must be? very pleasing to have it literally brought before you, as it has been, in so many different ways and from so many different people.

Even if you had to suffer such distress before such a manifestation of affection could take a physical form.

---

1. Seemingly prompted by the submission of *Voices in the Garden* for the 1981 Booker Prize, *Private Eye* carried a story in its issue of 20 November about the wind of change blowing through Chatto & Windus. Carmen Callil, founder of Virago, was, the magazine alleged, waiting in the wings to replace NS whom it described as 'an aggressive old battleaxe, more noted for reducing her secretaries and staff to tears than caring for her authors'. Ironically, Dirk had been a shareholder in the satirical organ since the 1960s.

This is a very ill-written letter: but it is only one other to stick on the pile of wrath.

With my love, as ever –

Dirk

To Kathleen Tynan   *Clermont*
                                                        31 December 1981

Kathleen –

Got you loud and clear. And with a measure of relief.

I mean, one KNEW you were'nt dead, because there would have been an Obit in The Times, but one wasn'nt certain where you had finally got to, or even if you had reached N.Y.

Well now one knows.

[...] Whats on here? Nothing terrifically important really.

Book, 'Voices' hit the 36,000 mark which, during a recession, is not so bad ... and better than Muriel Spaak by a long chalk. Now being 'done' by the BBC, but I dont want to know.

Into Bio 3, a toughie, because the last twelve years are a haze.

Also writing another chunk of 'childhood' because the first effort was so successful that it has now become a 'standard' and is used in the L.C.C. Schools for some kind of exam. Fame?

Glenda and I did our nuts in the Epic and it really aint that bad ... it's Telly, not Movie, but considering we shot the whole fucking thing in 20 days, and on location with children, seems to me a minor miracle.

I bought a HUGE Video Thingummy which plays all three kinds of tapes and so, on Christmas Night, we had a packed house and My World (of a kind) Premier of the thing here. First time I'd seen it.

I'm a sucker for sweeping Theme music and Cadallics and all that jazz so I quite enjoyed myself. Especially as no one smoked, went for a pee or even coughed. Gratifying.

Unless they were asleep.

We had a full house [...] Glorious, blazing, weather. Lots of Perrier Jouet on the terrace and not a trace of Noel to be seen [...] now we gird our loins for New Years Eve this evening. Oh dearie me ...

I went and opened, or helped to open, a new Theater[1] for Princess Grace in Monaco; could'nt quite resist shareing the honour of being Godparent to it with Edwige Feuillier ... and Valentina Cortese as the Italian one. Tremendous nonsense. But glamorous, if you think that Tel Aviv's inhabitants are. We had two thirds present dripping in sable and gold. I said to Edwige that it seemed the very least bit frivolous to be opening a, to all intents and purposes, Toy Theater in a Toy Principality while Poland got wrenched to bits. But she, with her great sagacity and French sense pointed out that we could'nt really HELP Poland by NOT opening the thing and so we had better do our duty as professionals.

So we did.

And Valentina gave us her 'Day For Night' act which was won-derous. She in white chiffon and diamonds doing a GIGANTIC piece from some bloody Italian Poet with a crouching Lady Prompter in the wings.

Happy evening. Grace not as boring as one might think but deadly Royal. Caroline looking like a Vermont Co-ed escapee, the Prince fat and bored. But we supped until four am .. and I promised to go back one day. What for? Goodness ...

We heard the news of Natalie Wood's death[2] on the BBC World Service and went into a state of dis belief. She was an adored chum.

Called L.A immediatly and found that they had only just heard the news themselves (time change and all) .. so that was a bit of a fuck up for us all, and this week at the Colombe I felt a desperate wrench of sadness when I saw that the stool, on which she always sat in the bar, was vacent ... they were coming here for this week.

The sky is sullen with low cloud: far across the winter valley the sun gleams copper on the sea: I have a table to lay for eight .. and logs to split and tea to make.

I'm nagged by the thought: so I'd better stop this insane letter and get my arse up and out.

We are well: though you did'nt ask ... and life drifts comfortably

---

1. The renovated Théâtre des Beaux-Arts, reopened on 17 December at a gala 'starring' Edwige Feuillère, Valentina Cortese and Dirk.
2. Natalie Wood had drowned in suspicious circumstances while on a yacht off the coast of California.

past with sudden bursts of alarming excitement, but I, like you, have a living to earn so I simply have to get down to things properly once this bloody Carnival Time is over.

Roald Dahl wrote last week and said he was just starting a book. 'Fucking hard, is'nt it? To start?' he said.

And it is ... I am about to stop now. A blank sheet of paper faces me [...]

All love, always, and happiness in this daunting New Year ...

Your devoted
Dirk.

To Molly Daubeny *Clermont*
8 February 1982

Molly dearest —

How absolutely dear of you to write to me about 'VOICES', I am so glad that it gave you pleasure.

I find that writing is a fearful chore! And it's so difficult when you are in the middle of a 'tough' part, to be invited to lunch or something like that, when you know that everything will melt away! And people are wonderfully unaware that writing is a hell of a job; and always say 'Oh! Well you can always pick it up when you get home ... do come!'

Point is, you cant 'pick the bloody thing up' when you get home. It has usually fled! And holding on to people whome you have invented is terribly hard ... Cuckoo faded away from my grasp as often as she could if I was'nt terribly careful!

All this I am sure you know about: writing is, like the Arts of other kinds, every bit as demanding.

Saw, by the way, [Peter] Brook's version of 'The Cherry Orchard' (did you see it: I forget?) which was one of the most magical, moving and glorious two and a half hours I have ever had at a Theater!

I never knew, from English Productions, how gloriously Russian and amazingly human it was. Not dour and wistful; alive, brimming with laughter and life. Which, of course, made the sound of the axe on the trees at the very end all the more dreadful.

It is re-opening next year. Do, if you did'nt, go and see it!

I hear that Thomas Courtney[1] is now the Toast Of Broadway .. so that must be good.

At the moment we have a sort of false-spring. Almond is out, the mimosa (which I detest!) everywhere, violets, and the daffodils are all in bud ... I suppose we'll cop it with a terrible snowfall in a week or so. March, like many a girl, can be capricious and very dangerous!

[...] do please try and make a rendezvous (here!) in the not too distant future.

Your devoted

Dirk

In July, Dirk and Tony flew to London for the latter to see a specialist recommended by Norah Smallwood, as Forwood was showing early symptoms of Parkinsonism.

To Norah Smallwood

Clermont
21 July 1982

Dearest Norah –

I ought to be struggling with all this mail which has arrived since 'Death' was shown on the TV.

A mass of it .. all wonderfully kind, understanding of the film, and amazed that they had never seen it AS a film.

Silly buggers.

Perhaps if some of them had gone to the Cinema to see it (and a lot did of course) we might have run longer, I might have got paid, and everything might have been different; anyway: better late than never.

But I am <u>not</u> struggling away with the little mountain of Basildon Bonds and nasty floral-pieces, or even the elegant University ones.

Suspicious elderly Dons who were, naturally, sympathetic and so on ..

It's too hot.

Ninety in the shade at ten o clock in the morning ... and a hopeless wait until seven in the evening. Impossible to do a simple thing during

---

1. Tom Courtenay, a good friend of MD and Dirk's co-star in *King and Country*, was appearing to acclaim in Ronald Harwood's *The Dresser*.

that time .. the sweat runs, most unattractively, and one does'nt want
to eat or drink much .. anything .. and the land is brown and cracked
and the big willow, all of fifty feet high, is dying for lack of water .. a
sorry sight.

We got home, after a hellish time at Heathrow jammed with
screaming children and frantic parents and lost luggage. Thank God
we packed just enough to carry it on board ourselves ... next time
you really must try and do the same. It is astonishing that it is possible
to pack clothes for a week in London (or longer, I feared ..) and still
not wear them all! Easier for a woman: those light clothes you seem
to be able to crunchle up and stuff into corners: like a pair of socks.

Anyway everything was splendidly looked after here, the house full
of young, plus six month baby which Bendo ADORED, and offered
his ball to at the drop of a wail ... Lady (Mmme Martinez) had
skiddled off again to Spain where her mother this time is not dying,
but having a leg cut off. Very boring indeed.

So I suppose we've lost her until the end of the summer, because
she is bound to run her Holiday into the scheme of amputation.

I much prefer my Young anyway: cleaner, jolly, and prettier ...
Christine[1] said, this morning, that she was 'sorry' to have to tell me
that she had washed all the casseroles, marmites, and the shelves on
which the plates are stacked ... she had also washed out all the preserve
cupboards ... the hint was that the Spanish were'nt really 'propre'.
Anyway those who live in caves in Grenada, drive a BMW, and have
mothers who have to loose a leg now and again. It really is too tiresome.

Forwood is rapidly regaining the ground he was in great danger of
loosing. After six months of dire depression and weakness, and a
miserably ageing kind of malady, wrongly diagnosed and treated, you
can only imagine how deeply grateful I am to you. But enough of
that. It was done, and done in time; and Forwood is now back in 'his
skin' again ... and that is how it should have been ages ago; but I
really feared that he had either HAD a mild stroke or was building
up to advanced senility ... far too young.

You can see from my unusually bad typing (even for me) that the
shock has not yet worn off! Contained anxiety exhausts: as you know.

---

1. Marie-Christine, daughter of Marc Isoardi, the stonemason, and his wife Bruna, who
grappled weekly with the Clermont washing. She (M-C) had dog-and-house-sat while
Dirk and Tony were away.

It was simply lovely working with you in your new Office. I like it MUCH better than the last one[1] [...] WE have no place in the scheme of things now, in William IV Street ... This is a greater, deeper, grief for you than it could possibly be for me, but I am certain that you must go your way now. You built the Firm .. with [Ian] Parsons [...] but that particular Firm has gone, or is going; as surely as the tide erodes a sandcastle left on the evening beach ... no good trying to go back and mediate, no good going back without trust. And that you can no longer have.

I have'nt. And I'm Baby Bumbling in this affair ... so God knows where you think that you might find a shred of honour there now.

Writing to you like this is, I am aware, gross impertanance ... but I have always spoken out: very often got myself into trouble for so doing .. but this time I simply insist that you are no longer humiliated.

And remember that you will not be supported in anything, by anyone there, because everyone is too frightened of loosing their jobs and they all feel that they must brush themselves down and try to please Teacher.

At their peril if they fail ... for Teacher has a lot of Favourites all waiting in the wings: you wait and see.

And there is a lot of steam in you yet, Mrs S. It is a pity to waste a scrap of it .. you are sorely needed by many; so attend to us!

[...] I want to sharpen my writing .. reading John Mortimers autobio.[2] has been a good lesson. He does do it well: even though I find his drinking and wenching boring, and his plain-ness off putting. He has a splendid wit, even though he is a little over aware of it and often writes irritatingly. But it is useful to read. [...]

In the village this morning the lady in the paper shop handed me a copy of NICE MATIN wordlessly, looking at me searchingly through her glittery spectacles.

A colour photograph of dead horses and wrecked cars ... a giant headline about Terror In London. We looked at each other silently. She shook her head, and pressed my hand, which I thought exceptionally moving ... and went to serve another customer.

We heard, on the BBC, yesterday evening about the appalling

---

1. NS had been 'sidelined'.
2. *Clinging to the Wreckage* (Weidenfeld & Nicolson).

business[1]... but what can one do? What can one do? The cruelty, the mindless evil of it, produces only helpless oaths. I think that I hate the Irish now more than I ever did before. I understand [a friend] who said that she cant even bear to listen to her husbands chauffeur, who has been in their employ for twenty years, talking. The very cadence of his voice makes her rage. I felt like that with poor Patrick Campbell[2] ... and would not, discreetly, have him here after one ghastly business ... and tried not to speak to him in the village, unless forced. Idiotic. But I hated the cadence too.

This is a very disjointed letter. I keep pausing for air! And there is none even up here in the olive store ... blinding is the word for the sun, and white for the sky; and where John [Charlton] is going to have his holiday the temperature has been over 100 for a month, they are slaughtering cattle all over Italy, and the river Po is so shallow that you can walk across it ... as he sits permanently in the shade under a hat he might not suffer: but he will know what 'blinding' means when it is applied to light.

[...] I loved, as I have said, being with you in the coral office .. I think, nay! I <u>know</u> that it is the only way one can possibly work on a book. Arguing, persuading, giving in, grumbling, laughing, fitting things into place, building the thing together. When you were staying here in May it was ALMOST the same, but I had other pressures which would not go completely away: but I think that we managed pretty well, dont you?

Now I must take my sticky body into the fire-heat, and start preparing luncheon: which I shall not want to eat.

And after that, wash up.

After that prepare Bendo's grub. He lies dead, covered in flies, a hot dog if ever there was one. So he gets bathed .. and then I'll come back here and start answering the Mail. It'll cost a small fortune ....

A stoat ran up the tree beyond the window, just now ... I have never seen one so near to the house before, and an adder slid across the step of the long room door ... the intense heat has brought all kinds of strange creatures close to the house where, I suppose, the need for water makes them less timid.

---

1. The IRA had murdered four members of the Household Cavalry, and seven of their horses, in Hyde Park.
2. Lord Glenavy, the Irish peer and humorist.

I could do without the adder, though.

And the bloody stoat is after my blackbirds ... I had hoped that they had nested and reared and gone. Probably not, alas.

I must go and give you peace . . . .

and always my love –

Dirk.

P.S. Reading through the TS, yet again, I was uncomfortably aware that perhaps I had not, really, given you enough of a 'part' in my 'play'. This was entirely due to the fact that I was constantly anxious that you should not be embarressed. Mrs D.W.G[1] was as fastidious and correct as you .. hence 'Mrs X' and devious ways of concealing her.

Anyway I do think that I have honoured you as best I could under the circumstances [...] But I could have been more personal ... good manners held my hand away. Oh dear! Never explain never complain .. I know. But it did cross my mind that I might have fudged the issue by over-care and protectivness.

Tant pis! It's done now. Next time maybe ... watch out!

Love D.

To Norah Smallwood

Clermont
26 July 1982

Norah dearest –

Spoken to Madam Attenborough about the negatives and she is taking steps to have the one you want ... the walk into the sunset, so to speak, sent to you.[2]

[...] I am going to buy a single bore gun.[3] It sounds rather as if one was a White Farmer somewhere in the Bush. But that is rather what it has come to. Apparently we are swamped with a vast amount of maghrébins ... I am not, as you will realise only too well, sure of the spelling.[4]

These are lay-about Arabs between the ages of 13 and 20 ... the

---

1. Dorothy Gordon, whom Dirk was acknowledging fully in *An Orderly Man* as an 'incredible influence' on his writing, while keeping her identity secret.
2. A photograph by Sheila Attenborough of Dirk's retreating form was used on the jacket of *An Orderly Man*.
3. The Attenboroughs had been burgled.
4. Spot on.

translation of the word in English would be, literally, Street Arabs ..
and they do boring, messy, break in's ... and a gun is wise up here on
the hill (Oh! John! The House On The Hill.[1] Rebecca of Sunnybrook
Farm!) with the nearest Police Station five long kilometers away.

One shot, of small calibre, in the backside is quite sufficient.

So I'm off to buy a gun.

It's a bore. I hate shooting anything, and could quite easily get the
bastard in the head as the bum. Still: standing beside my chair or
beside the bed, seems comforting to have it there.

[...] Grey cloud has cooled us suddenly, there was a half moon
last night, and the air is there for one to breath again. It really has
been foul. The garden is a miserable sight. Brown, covered in ugly
thistles and all the lavander is dying off from lack of water. We are
rationed now, so I can only water the pots and things nearest the
house, and the wisteria is dying off ... I am told by M. Marc (who
seems to know) that it is 'finished'.

Perhaps he's right. Two viscious mistrals put paid to it at the start
of the season, and now the drought has finally sealed it's fate.

Oh well ..

I must go and feed Bendo.

My love, in haste ..

    Always

      Dirk.

P.S [...] I rather think that your next title[2] will be – 'West Of
Sunset' – (Sunset Boulevard). It may change, but thats what I'm
working to. So you'd better like it. For the moment. D

To Norah Smallwood

Clermont
19 August 1982

Norah – darling this is a NTBRT –

If I were to tell you that I have just seen a snake, as thick as my
forearm, attempting to devour a toad as large as a saucer, you would
not, I imagine, believe me.

---

1. John Charlton had suggested something of the sort when Dirk was seeking a title for
the new book.
2. A new novel-in-progress.

But I have. The snake I think, hope, is a grass-snake, all of a meter long, white-silver with glorious navy blue diamonds on his skin.

If this was not a grass-snake then we have problems.

There was no possibility that he could have engorged the toad, at least I dont think so, because it really was a very large creature, and putting up a fearfull struggle with it's head in the snake's mouth!

Amazing how one is diverted on a hot afternoon.

I tore off and got a camera (Country Life?) and took some astonishing snapshots which, I feel certain, you will not want to see. Pity.

But in my 'business' I irritated the snake who dropped the toad and shot back into his lair: just under the stone seat beneath the lime tree. The [toad] wandered blearily, and a little bloodily, away. Rather as if it had had an encounter at William IV Street; but was later found to be sitting perfectly happily in the sump which is the overflow for the swimming-hole.

Forwood was aghast at this encounter, and fled. Which just goes to show what cowards people are. I was rivitted: mind you, had it been an animal and not a reptile I'd have felt a great deal more distressed .. but a bloody old toad does'nt come high on my list of adorable-creatures. She's still sitting in the sump as I write; and Forwood has fed her some worms.

Are we all going mad?

A week of Kathleen Tynan (and lover) and assorted agonies and a hundred-weight of baggage might account for my feebleness.

Kathleen is adorable, brilliant, maddening, stubborn and pig-headed.

And I am devoted to her. She also comes in a most attractive size and a very pretty colour. Blond, bronze, green eyed.

Having been married to Tynan she is not expected to be a frump nor a dumb-blond, and is neither. But she does rattle me.

A telephone call, JUST as I was making certain the terrace lights were out and the doors secure, from Nice station with an anguished plea for a bed. So a cold supper is discovered and laid upon the table, beds made up and lights switched back on, and the Sunday Times sadly put aside. I had made plans to read the Book Section in my bed. And eventually they arrive, in a Taxi from Nice, with too much baggage and not enough money.

We settle down. It's alright really. I just <u>keep</u> telling myself. And the conversation is'nt half bad, and spirited.

Lover leaves for Paris in the Morning, Kathleen stays on to 'work on her book'. (History of K. Tynan.) The days are reasonably pleasant because she is working, and so I am able to work too: but there are drinks to get, food to find, so on. Irritating, but essential. She was so incredibly kind to Forwood and I during our stay in California that we simply had no alternative but to repay the debt. Although I know she would not consider it as such. She is far too loving of one.

But oh! The problems she throws at ones feet! How DO people survive? No money, two children, a vast flat in New York, a house in Thurlo Square, Kens debts to pay off, Publishers screaming for stuff, and advancing large sums of money against the book which is not yet written and wont be for another two years. By which time no one will remember who K. Tynan was!

She begged, every evening, sitting out on the terrace, for assistance and advice. All of which we liberally bestowed upon her; all of which she, of course, rejected.

I told her that she should write the story of her own life with Ken .. and leave the History until later. No way.

So she is wading through a thousand incomprehensible diaries, journals, and stuff. Interviewing people from his past, his school-days, his not-altogether-savoury family and so on.

It seems to me an awful amount of work to expend on a brilliant, but not amazing, Critic. Perhaps because I disliked him I am biased.

Anyway after five days of comparative peace, off she went to Barcelona to take the children (10–14) to their first real Bullfight. VERY Ken! She took them by train, sat up all the way there and all the way back, arrived here exhausted but satisfied that she had been a good Mother, that the children had adored the corrida (more shades of Ken!) and that she could now go back to work.

Which she did. She had left every single diary of Ken's in your walk-in cupboard, which was massed with papers and documents of every size and colour and which Lady was busting to 'tidy'. I was quite nervous.

So she left this morning for London, leaving the children with some long suffering people who 'have children' on the coast. And she was tearful and miserable, and it was blistering hot, and she suddenly looked dreadfully small, alone and a mess. Oh dear. But thank God for American publishers who pay enormous advances. Otherwise I cannot imagine what she would do. And they'll have to be patient publishers too.

As she went off so [my financial advisers] arrived [...] I was excercised, rather, because we have, as you probably know, a Wealth Tax being slammed on us in October by this tiresome Government. But they are confident that I'm not rich enough to worry: and that the house has no 'signs of wealth'. Viz. No grand piano, Butler, Swimming pool, Stables, Yacht, etc etc.

I can, they instructed me, also have a man to come and do the main bulk of the mowing and land-work generally. Forwood no longer can do very much: nor do I want him to. So that was a hell of a relief! But I have to find the man. Difficult today. They seemed quite pleased with my work as an earning-writer, and that pleased me!

But when I consider what has to be done to Clermont, just to maintain it as it is, no more, my heart, I confess, quails. The roof will cost at least £10.000. The rising damp not far off that sum. The problem being the depth of the walls. They cant stick their machinery or whatever it is through them. The front door is falling off, and the whole place should be painted out from head to foot. Or whatever the term is. Attic to cellar.

And that, at so much per square meter, is prohibitive. And it's no good asking ME to do the bloody job. I hate painting rooms, cant paint a ceiling, and I have to work up here. Otherwise ...

Re-reading the first few pages of the TS of 'AOM' yesterday I was sad to think that all that joy and glory of discovery, of making this house a house, has to be heavily paid for! Naturally, one always pays in life. That seems to be the rule. But that first year I really thought I'd be able to make it work. Maybe I will too: and of course in those days we did'nt know about Arabs and oil and Rising Costs and all the rest of it. Why is one eternally idiotic!

It's almost six pm. The air is just beginning to cool. A tiny zephyr trembles among the vine which is heavy now, and thick with grapes ... I must go and look at the toad in the sump.

Tomorrow I'll get back to work. The excitements are over .. including our luncheon yesterday for the Jarre's.[1] It's now back to work .. and I must stop this rabbiting on.

This, to divert you – & with my love – <u>Dirk</u>.

---

1. Charlotte Rampling and her husband Jean-Michel Jarre.

To Susan Owens
(Postcard) *Clermont*
22 November 1982

A week in London practically broke my bank![1] How do people afford
to live in England now? Silly question. Lots do, including my family.
Glad my note cleared your problems. Life is NOT all skittles, books
and land. There are human factors too: even for people as apparently
removed from 'life' as me! You'll find out when you get 'AOM' .. it's
all written down there for you to read!

Anyway: London cleared up a few problems for me, and gave me a
few more! [...] Thanks for your congratulations.[2] It means a Horse-
man, but Knight is okay ... the next rank is Commandeur .. and
thats VERY grand! Back home to damp, falling leaves, and rotting
grapes .. and a lot of work on the new book .. so I'll clear off for a
while; as long as you dont think I'm sulking .... all the best as ever ..
DB

To Nerine Selwood *Clermont*
23 November 1982

Nair dear

I have had to bash this[3] off in a hurry because your 'reminder' letter
reached me only this morning, and that does'nt give us much time! I
have written a piece, which I hope will do, as a letter to you, so that
you can read whatever part of it out you want.

There is no point in bleating on for too long, so many things

---

1. Tony had undergone more tests.
2. On 17 September Dirk had received by post from Jack Lang, the French Minister of
Culture, the document confirming his appointment as Chevalier dans l'Ordre des Arts et
des Lettres. He had been asked two years earlier whether he would be 'minded' to accept
such an honour, had replied in the affirmative, but heard no more until now.
3. A reminiscence of Dirk's time with the Newick Amateur Dramatic Society, which NS
duly read from the stage at the fiftieth anniversary of its headquarters, the Derek Hall –
built by her father Lionel Cox and named not after Dirk but after her brother. Humphrey
Jenkins, a pillar of the NADS as both director and actor, had invited Dirk to be its
president. He accepted diffidently, feeling that, although when he lived in Britain he had
'been President of a hundred things, from the Essex University Film Club to a Charity
for ageing ponies!', the thousand-mile distance meant he could nowadays be no more
than 'just a name on the letter-paper'. He did better than that.

happened in the Hall, so many people were a part of our lives, so many things a part of them also.

So I have, as you'll see, just stuck to essentials ... I dont think people want beating over the head at a celebratory evening!

[...] warmest wishes for a splendid, moving, evening on the 4th ...

Love as ever

Dirk

Nair dear –

The first time I ever trod upon a stage was this one: up there at the back. Stage right.

It was not a sensational beginning which your father offered me: but it WAS a beginning. I was a naked slave in 'Alf's Button' and all that was required of me was to stand perfectly still, for rather a long time, in an archway wearing a fez, a curly stuck-on moustache, a weskit, and a pair of transparent, saggy, orange bloomers.

The transparency caused a certain amount of trouble, which we managed in the end to overcome, but I never got over the cold. The stage was freezing, and I had been firmly instructed 'Not To Move a Muscle.' Harder to do than I thought under the circumstances. I 'acted' standing still with commendable effect.

That must have been in 1938 and I was seventeen.

But I had made a start. You have to do it somehow, and that was the way for me and I knew, without a shadow of doubt, baggy transparent bloomers and all, that I had found my metier. It seems a very long time ago now.

After that I rather think we did a Christmas pantomime, 'Babes In The Wood,' as far as I remember I was in it, neither a Babe nor a Robber but a Wicked Uncle. I remember that I did help to do some of the scenery, which was very useful for future work, and wound up the old portable gramaphone for 'God Save The King' at the end.

Nineteen Thirty Eight brought my supreme moment of triumph when your father suggested, in a round about way, that we might do 'Journey's End' which would be a very 'timely' play. It was timely alright, because we were on the brink of another war at the moment.

Naturally the Ladies in the Company got fearfully huffy because there was no part for them in 'Journeys' End' – but things were sorted out, the male members made sure of that, and we started rehearsals and I was asked to do the scenery once again. This time it was easier, a dug-out, mud, wooden boxes and beds, and I painted everything on huge sheets of brown wrapping paper. It was very effective – I thought. But with the war news growing ever more desperate it was thought more prudent to cancel rehearsals and we all got on with digging slit-trenches, fitting gas-masks, and filling sand-bags. As far as I was concerned my great moment in a great play had gone for ever.

But it had not. In the September Mr Chamberlain waved that idiotic piece of white paper and we all really believed there would never be a war in our time. Rehearsals started again, and 'Journey's End' opened and was a triumph. People were greatly moved to see a play about something they had just managed to avoid, a desperate war.

The following September it started. And the world, and this place, this hall, this village, none of them was to be quite the same again.

But there were wonderful times here: the Saturday Dance, swooping about in 'The Valeta,' avoiding the plainer girls during the 'Paul Jones,' whirling about in the last Waltz which was always 'Goodbye Sweetheart,' and during which your father wisely lowered the lights from time to time so that kisses could be sneaked before we all put on hats and coats and cycled to our homes in the area. In those happy days this village was still very much a village. Freelands stores faced The Bull across the green, and we all knew each other and exactly what we were all up to. Gossip was simple, un-malicious, deeply interesting, and about the most daring thing anyone had to do was to catch the 'bus to Haywards Heath or Lewes.

But I had had my very first crack at acting in the role of 'Raleigh' in 'Journey's End' and I knew that nothing would deflect me from my path as an Actor. And nothing did. Not even the war which took us by shocked surprise that hot September Sunday. However, it was a long time before I could settle down and just do my job: I had another job to do for those six years and it was a long time before I came back to the hall here, or the village. I wonder, this evening, how many of you sitting out there came to the old Dances? How many of you played Robins in paper beaks and wings with little red breasts for 'Babes In The Wood,' how many of you laughed and applauded 'Alf's Button?' How many of you will say 'Ah! They were the happy days then, war or no war, we managed, we laughed, we danced, we had a lot of fun, and we worked for it.'

And how many of you know, as I do, that we had the best of it all, the very best, and that those far off days will never come again?

Were'nt we really very lucky?

Love from Dirk

To Bee Gilbert

Dearest Sno –

Oh my goodness yes! 'Raw' as an egg you were.[1] And none the worse for that. Feather boas, pink velvet hats, frilly black frocks and black stockings, and eating your hair in handfuls .. I so well remember my 'suite' at the Gellert .. and I. breaking up a wardrobe, and me suggesting we all went off to Vienna, wondering, deeply, if it would work or if I. would be difficult or you would hate schnitzels and kaffee mit schlag. And it was all a wonder: was'nt it?

Catching the last leaves of the autumn as they blew across the mountain field outside Semmering .. seeing that great stag, remember? near the little caff we had a veal steak and chips at. Or did we have bangers?

Whatever it was, it was all a splendour and the years have not staled the memory even though, alas! we are getting older and older. Well ... not THAT old, but older. Fuck it. [...] Last year was a bugger of a year for us: things got very grotty and Tote was un-well and got treated with the wrong drugs for the wrong symptons and got iller, and I whizzed him to and from London a couple of times, and we got that sorted out. And now he's better, thank God, but it was an ugly time and Clermont started a little slide. However it all perked up, as I say, and the slide halted. But one had been warned that growing older was a fact to be faced, not a fact to try to overlook.

I wrote all the time, in a desperate sort of way to kill panic, and found it a vastly useful occupation. The new autobio. comes out in March .. and there is a novel three quarters finished .. which I'll have to lay aside while I do my piece with Miss Jackson[2] whom I deeply love.

---

1. Finding *Voices in the Garden* while replacing a book on her shelves, BG had written nostalgically about the early days of her friendship with Dirk and Tony, formed when she and Ian Holm (I.) joined them on location for *The Fixer* in Budapest.

2. Dirk and Glenda Jackson had agreed to appear in a Granada Television adaptation of Arnold Bennett's *Buried Alive*, to be directed by Mike Hodges.

We arrive sometime after this letter may reach you. That is to say about the 25th. At the Konnot. Until mid-March. a funny film. I dont know if it will work, but hope to God it does! Arnold Bennet was Father of it, and so it is not what you might call 'new'. But we are making it like 'new' Movies . . and new Scripting. There is not a whiff of Ealing or Rank about it anywhere. I've battled and struggled and I've won! That part anyway. And G.J likes it and has graciously consented to join me. We had a whale of a time in Hollywood on the 'Pat Neal Story' which no one saw when it was chucked onto British TV on New Years Fucking Night! What about that for planning? A lovely story about brain-tumors is JUST the thing to send you off to trample people to death in Trafalgar Square. Except they were all there anyway.

But we so enjoyed the experience of being actors together that we did all we could to find a subject. And G. found this. So . . . we are financed; we have been given Westminster Abbey to shoot in; and I like everyone connected with the thing because they all fit my RULE. No one old or middle-aged! Remember? And these are all about nine or thirteen.

I am most amused about the film Andrew is making.[1] I am [. . .] certain that [he] will do something very odd with it: he's good with children, as I know.

'Wind In The Willows'[2] sounds fun. Can I be Mole, please?

Delphine Seyrig[3] is a smashing actress and the biggest pain in the arse I have met in a hundred years. So watch out. She is a soppy, affected, very up-tight Feminist Movement Lady and can pick quarrels like chocolates from a box . . . but she is super at her job. And speaks, as you probably know, faultless English. When I last worked with her, on 'Accident' with Losey, she was less of a pain in the neck as a woman. But the years have baked her hard. I expect she'll be lovely to you, and you'll wonder what I was bleating about. She may have changed. Ladies, I find, often do: according to the man in their lives . . . . chamelions.

I think I have spelled that rong, dont you? But you'll get the drift.

---

1. Andrew Birkin wrote and directed an adaptation of Ian McEwan's 1978 novel, *The Cement Garden* (Jonathan Cape).
2. Another Andrew Birkin project – this time unrealised.
3. BG was trying to set up a Sylvia Plath play in Paris, with Delphine Seyrig.

Here, I mean in France, things are going a little bit wonky with the
Socialists and everyone is depressed, even the ones who were dotty
enough to vote them in, houses are'nt selling, the Rich are leaving,
and the big Hotels and Restaurants are in a mild state of panic. The
yacht harbours have emptied because of the huge Wealth Tax, but
everyone has just moved down the coast to San Remo and the Italians
are rubbing their hands with glee. However I must'nt knock them too
hard, the Mitterand Lot, because in their infinate wisdome they have
seen fit to honour me with the Chevalier de l'Ordre des Art et des
Lettres! Can you believe it? Not the Legion d'Honneur, but I aint
complaining, and I long to wear my little button-hole ribbon and my
medal one day. A signal honour for a foreigner: and very funny when
you remember, as you now must do, that I cant spell or write very
much more than would fill a baggage lable! However .. it all goes to
show that if you <u>try</u>, you <u>get</u> . . . . . something.

My sister was enraptured when I told her; because she is horse
mad and thinks that the award has something to do with horses and
so on.

Much nicer, I thought, than winning anything at all at BAFTA!

Anyway, anyway .. this is going on too long and it's all waffle.

Yes, please, I think it would be lovely to come and eat at your place.

I am going to find the Konot a bit of a strain since a ham sandwich
costs eight quid . . . so what I'll do is give you a tellyphone call as soon
as I have got in to London and as soon as the Fillum people have
made up their minds what to do with me as far as make-up and hair
and wardrobe are concerned . . . I <u>want</u> to look like Stanley Spencer ..
but I am not sure if I shall manage it or not. We'll see.

And then we'll have a meeting. But no wine, alas! I'm not allowed
it, I'm on a regime for the film and sip well-watered whisky.

[. . .] I'm off. Call you when I get there. I am so glad 'Voices'
caught your eye the other day . . . . was'nt that a bit of luck?

Love love
    <u>Dirk</u>.

To Penelope Mortimer   *Clermont*
                                                    14 January 1983

Penny-lopey –
    Well: you really are a bit rotten. After a hundred years sleep you

suddenly open a Lillywhites box[1] and decide to rite me a letter. And stuff it with hinty-bits of blame for desertion!

Who stopped first, answer me? You or I? I know. Yew.

Super to hear from you again. Really. I am a little amazed myself that we did write to each other for so many years ... you beat needlewoman 1[2] by about four years .. I found all your letters, while researching for 'O.M.', all snug and crackly, fresh as paint, full of worry, illness, distress about this and that. And fun! So much fun! Especially in the American ones .. the College and all.

But I have them all. Treasured.

I dont know why one drifts away .. it's strange. I am a timid soul, and sometimes my timidity gets wobbly and I sense things wrongly. I sort of felt that I was perhaps getting to be a drag. So stopped .. but was still there, if you know what I mean. And you probably dont.

I DISTINCTLY remember [J and C[3]] here and writing to you about them.

Very clearly indeed. So perhaps you lost that one in the scuffle in the Lillywhites box? That, I think was my last effort ... it got no response; that I can find, (you were AWFUL about yearing letters. Christ!) so I just thought, oh well, I thought, she's sitting in her Post Office[4] and gardening away and thats that for the time being.

And I was right, was'nt I? For the time being. For today brings me your letter of December 30th ... for some unexplained reason it only made this place today ... perhaps you forgot to mail it?

Anyway: one did'nt dare write letters to an un-caring Post Office.

And my first book came out in '77 .. I had two under my belt by the time I had got to '79 ... when your letters from me seem to stop, so I reckon you got that bit rong spells rong. You are tiresome.

Anyway, it's not done to write to real Professionals. About books .. I'm not that yet: another six vols and maybe. Novice, is what I am, and trying v. hard. I sit with Fowler and Roget and God Knows What Else, and try to avoid 'adverbs' and 'adjectives' and dreadful 'paradigms'. Although I dont really know what any of them are, truthfully. My first needlewoman, dead now, was tough. Norah

1. PM had kept Dirk's letters in a box from the sporting-goods store.
2. Dorothy Gordon.
3. John Bennett and PM's daughter Caroline.
4. PM's present address was The Old Post Office in a Gloucestershire village.

Smallwood tougher, but loving and careing and wanting me to get things rite spells rite.

So I did pay heed. And never got Edited! Was'nt that good . . . well, just a bit here and there, minor cuts, libel clauses (Christ! It's difficult to write about the recent past and avoid libel, anyway in my acting job.)

But no one carved me into chunks, altered my construction; or took offense at my spelling . . . much. Spelling drove them dotty. But thats not much of a problem, is it really?

You ask if it is happier, writing, than acting. Well: it is, in a way.

But much, much harder for me. Acting I know a good deal about .. after more than forty years I should. Writing is a new land, un-walked, full of strange paths through the peat, heather and bogs of despair. I'm having to teach myself to write. It's difficult. I think that people like you were born with pens, or quills, or whatever, in your mouths . . . unlike silver spoons .. and so it was your heritage. And it shows in the pristine beauty of your work.

But I bang about in despair. Trying to be a Writer and not a Film Star Who, Surprise! Surprise! Writes.

Thats not the idea at all.

Everything in 'O.M.' is true, I mean about the writing, so I need'nt go into all that here. I found that the winters on the hill here were boringly tedious. No land to tend (goody, goody) and I did'nt fancy pulling rugs or tapestry or painting bad canvases . . . so I wrote a bit.

And there we go. Went, rather. It's fun. The best part is knowing that your work, for it IS work, gets to such extraordinary places and brings pleasure. The Australian Outback, Kuwait, a Camp in the upper Himalayas, the Red-Eye-Special from L.A to N.Y . . . all manner of odd places my books go. And people write. The best thing of all. And I write back.

Only cards. But I acknowledge them all.

All this, of course, you know. Yourself. But it was absolutely new to me and deeply gratifying. Can you imagine a soldier in Lebanon (Israeli) with a paperback of a book of mine in his tank? And writing to thank me for reminding him of . . . childhood! Moving and amazing. And a reason for trying to write as well as you possibly can, and hook the Israeli Soldier by the lapel and say 'This bit will fill in the boredome, the fear, or the loneliness . . .' Thats EXTRA!

Never got that with Movies, really. Nothing so personal. A book is more personal than a film because, as one lady in Queensland wrote,

'You are beside my bed ... and if I cant sleep, or get the fidgets (sic) I read a bit of you ..' Well you cant just run a Movie, even on Video, without getting out of bed, can you?

So. I'm off to London, dread City [...] It'll be a six week shoot.[1] Boring really. But I'll miss the cold of Febuary here and most of the olive crop (which is a fuck-pig of a chore.) .. back to finish off novel 3, which is three quarters through. Irritating to lay it aside, but perhaps it is not a bad idea to rest it for a while and develop another part of my mind.

Not that I have much to develop. But whats left of it needs a shake-up.

[...] I have ratted on long enough. Off I go to do the fucking sprouts. (Kitchen) and then over to see chums who have just moved into a most unsuitable house in the next village. She wants advice on what to plant in her garden. As her only adventure in this direction has ever been an Impatiens in a pot on her kitchen window I'm in for a wearying arvo.

Thank you for taking down the Lillywhite box. Stuff this in with the others. You can fill the gap that way ... '79 83 ... and happiness, health, and no white-fly in 1983 ... and write again one day. But not here till after March. Then I'll be clearing out the pond weed, cutting back the waterlilly, planting a new willow in place of the big one which died in last summers fearsome drought ... and finishing off the buke.

Ciao!

With love

Dirk XX.

To Bee Gilbert   *Clermont*
                                                                    1 May 1983

Sno – oh! Sno – You were'nt roistering about in four poster beds in Shepton Mallet by any chance were you?

I discovered a cosy hotel in 'Country Life' today ... which bore many of the distinguishing marks of your lecherous, vino-filled, day or two. Moments after getting your letter, undated (naturally) but love-filled.

And thank you.

---

1. In the event it was a no-week shoot; *Buried Alive* was cancelled at a late stage.

And so here we are on May 1st .. raining. I don't know why I always think it MUST be a sunny day with May blossom frothing in the hedges and cowslips and ladies washing their faces in the dew: I always feel quite sure it will be like this: for the life of me I can not imagine why for it never has been in all my sixty two years.

Never mind. Maybe one day it will be. At the moment we must accept that it is the Workers Day, that tanks and guns will be on display, that the Students in Paris will rip up the cobbles and lob them at everyone in sight . . . and that it will, inevitably, rain.

And that was a long and wasted sentence if ever I saw one.

Tote is getting well quite quickly.[1] Up days and down days, naturally, but with a bit of careful arrangement we manage more up's than downs .. which is a great moral builder. He is putting on weight, moderatly, has a good colour and one crosses fingers for his first Medical in London on the 8th . . . tomorrow week to be exact. If that is all well, then we are on a good road, and he wont have to have another check for six months. So one waits.

I have managed, by doing my bleedin' nut, to finish off my third novel .. 'West of Sunset' [. . .] it has been useful therepy for me. I cant just sit about or look at the grass growing on the terraces in despair. Knowing that only I now can mow them, alas! What ever Tote's state of health we have to make some very serious decisions soon. And the mere thought of Holmes paying all that loot for a mews in fucking Holland Park[2] has dampened my soaring ideas, considerably! I want a dear little cottage, mit garten, in the Sloan Square area. Or near enough to Hatchards by foot! Fat chance of that, I know. We'll have to lease something anyway. No more buying.

I don't want the Finchley Road or Bayswater .. and I wont go an inch towards Highgate or Kentish Town! Cor'

I went to dine, when we were last in London, with Business People, who had a house in Kentish Town . . . it took HOURS to get there on a Sunday night. No taxi would take me, because they all said the fare back was 'dicey', so I hired a bloody car, and with a three hour wait (while I ate awful food cooked before my eyes by my Hostess in her kitch Kitchen) it cost me seventy quid! So no Kentish Town ta'

---

1. Dirk and Tony had spent February and March in London while the latter underwent an operation for bowel cancer.
2. Ian Holm's new London 'pad'.

A 'stunning experience' – working on Alain Resnais' *Providence* in 1976, with John Gielgud, Ellen Burstyn and David Warner.

With Fassbinder at Clermont in May 1977 to discuss *Despair* ...

... and, ironing out the 'bumps', its screenwriter Tom Stoppard.

The 'wonderfully civilised, amusing, wise and interesting' Elton John returns to Clermont in June 1980 with a copy of his latest album, *'21 at 33'*.

On location for *The Patricia Neal Story* in 1981.

With one of his most 'pleasing guests', the ill-fated Natalie Wood.

'Beloved' Charlotte Rampling, on assignment at Clermont for *Elle* magazine, and her husband Jean-Michel Jarre.

'It looks as if I am painting a backcloth; not the Hippo-Pool' – Dirk prepares *le bassin* for the summer of 1984. The former irrigation-tank was christened in honour of an ample guest who made a spectacular entrance.

The waters await.

'The no-nonsense kind of lady I love' – Glenda Jackson, with Tony.

The climax of the 1984 Cannes Film Festival: John Huston receives his *hommage* while President Dirk's 'adorable, sensible, grown-up' juror Isabelle Huppert looks on.

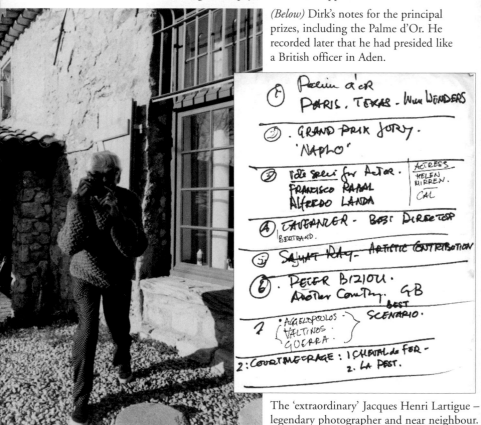

(*Below*) Dirk's notes for the principal prizes, including the Palme d'Or. He recorded later that he had presided like a British officer in Aden.

The 'extraordinary' Jacques Henri Lartigue – legendary photographer and near neighbour.

Waiting for his Doctorate: the man of letters at St Andrews University, 4 July 1985.

Olga Horstig-Primuz celebrates the publication of her memoirs in 1990. (Left to right, standing) Guy Tréjan, Claudine Auger, Gérard Oury, Michèle Morgan, Dirk; (seated) Charlotte Rampling, Françoise Christophe, 'Mamma Olga', Edwige Feuillère, Alain Delon. Absent, alas, was the most fêted of her stable, Brigitte Bardot, whose casting in *Doctor at Sea* (1955) initiated the enduring friendship between super-agent and Dirk.

Dirk's literary agent, Pat Kavanagh, with her husband, Julian Barnes, who shared his passion for gardening.

Left to right: Brian McFarlane, historian and inquisitor; Susan Owens meets her faithful correspondent as he signs copies of *Backcloth* at Hatchards, Piccadilly, in September 1986; an Englishman abroad – David Frankham at home in America.

'Part of the fabric of one's life here' – Daisy and Labo, and *below:* by the hearth, with Daisy's successor, Bendo.

Mowing the terraces and, in a virtually unprecedented burst of culinary initiative, making piccalilli

Following page: Patrolling his acres.

... even if the houses are quite pretty: if you like Pooter Land or Posey Simmonds People.

Anyway: anyway.

I'm sorry A. did'nt win an Oscar. I did'nt know, as a matter of fact, that he had a Nomination[1] .. but really: the whole thing is such a 'fix' .. I DO know that personally. And with Mighty Columbia behind it all there was little chance of anyone but Brother Gandhi,[2] or whatever, scooping the pool. The Atts are down here this week resting up after the Press Attack which did, I admit, seem harsh. And shook them both greatly. But left them pretty rich. So who's careing?

I never saw the Epic; read it, and that was enough for me, and don't think that I will. It's not my kind of fillum, and I'm not in favour of the little man anyhow. Gandhi, I mean. I was in India during Congress Riots and I hated his bloody, cunning, little guts then. At twenty four. So I am not about to start liking what he did, and did NOT do, at this advanced age.

But I sobbed myself to a fit during 'ET' ... and adored 'The Heat And The Dust'.[3] It takes all kinds, dunnit?

Saturday looms: Saturday means that the Festival opens in Cannes and that on the Opening Night I, with ten others, will be presented with a present for 'contribution to the eclat of the Festival for so many years' (which ACTUALLY means that we never won a prize) and also for 'our contribution to the Art of the Cinema.' Well: I don't mind. Sophia Lauren, Liza Minelli, Michel Morgan, Vittoria Gassman,[4] Glenda Jackson and so on ... a nice, honourable, Line Up. It'll be ghastly but possibly a bit amusing. We'll see.

[...] I hear feet on the gravel and Bendo (boxer fart-face) barking and that means the Attenboroughs are arriving for their Sunday May Day beer.

So I'll go ... if I can make my way through the rain ... and get the ice-box opened. Thanks for super loving letter: I'm so depressed about Holland Park I think I'll have a look at Twickenham.

Great love, a hug to Andrew [...]

<u>Dirk</u>

---

1. Andrew Birkin had written, produced and directed the live-action short film, *Sredni Vashtar*.
2. Richard Attenborough's *Gandhi* had won eight Academy Awards.
3. Directed by Steven Spielberg and (*Heat and Dust*) by James Ivory respectively.
4. More precisely: Sophia Loren, Liza Minnelli, Michèle Morgan, Vittorio Gassman.

To Norah Smallwood

Clermont
15 May 1983

Norah dearest –

And how it rains! A fine mist, which sends the grasses soaring and the weeds a-seeding.

The snowball tree, just outside my Studio door, is a mass of giant white blooms, the Super Star blazes in the fine downpour, the roses in the potager, all of thirteen or so years old, flourish madly just because, this year, I did NOT prune them. They are swamped with huge heads of bloom. Champes Elysee, Toscanni, Whisky Mac and the rest. Edith Piaf has quite taken leave of her senses and riots in a most abandoned way, her deep crimson petals glowing among the yellow-gold of the splurge. Which I have not yet weeded out!

I have just put in the forty quids worth of petunias (white) and begonias, (white and pink) and Forwood has retired to the big room with a motor paper, yesterdays Times, and a mug of tea.

And I am here to write to you.

The week [...] in London [...] has jumbled my brains a little. I am not certain where, or even who, I am ... but this will doubtless pass. The success of the week for Forwood was wonderfully relieving naturally. And I am anxious not to see another Waiting Room in Harley, Weymouth, or any other street for quite some time.

We went round to Edward VII after Mr Todd's[1] verdict, to say Thank you to the Ward sisters and nurses, and to show off the well-again patient. It was greatly appreciated. I dont think that many people bother to do that sort of thing once they are 'healed'. It is such a simple thing to do and causes much pleasure. Sad. And so here we are. The Festival still continues, inspite of the rain and generally ghastly muck-ups which go on. The new Festival Building is as hideious as you can possibly imagine and is already named The Bunker by the unhappy Cannoise who now have to face a monolithic, windowless, pink block right beside the Old Port where once the elegant, graceful, Casino stood. Designed, I am sad to say, by an English Architect who can only have been the same man who designed the Barbican![2] It is

---

1. Ian Todd, the surgeon who had operated on Tony in March.
2. Le Palais des Festivals et des Congrès was designed by Bennett & Druet; the Barbican Centre for the Arts, by Chamberlin, Powell & Bon.

loathesome in the extreme. Now covered with spray-bomb graffiti calling for the Downfall of the Government, Higher Wages For Nurses and Doctors, and Various Wails from the Students. Actually it looks prettier than it did thus decorated.

Until you read the inscriptions: which depress.

We have been through all this in dear Mr Wilson's time . . . it is sad to see the same thing happening again in a country which I so love and to which I fled to avoid the plague which now besets us here. If ONLY they had listened to me! I kept telling them not to vote for the Socialists . . . . but they paid no heed. Silly fools. However I am told that the Miners in the North love it all: so that must be that. The prolateriat must win.

I see that Attenborough has answered, in no uncertain terms, that rather silly bashing from Rushardie . . . or however he is spelled . . and it is quite clear that Attenborough has read the book, which got the fellow the Booker award,[1] and does'nt think it up to much! But I DO wish that they'd stop using the bloody film as if it was a political event [. . .]

Olga telephoned me this morning to say that my reception at the Opening Night of the Festival was the longest and warmest of any others! And there were a line of very Big Stars present. I realised, while it was happening, that a tremendous wave of warmth and affection was sweeping towards me . . . and I was moved, finally, to tears. In so far as I could barely speak my thanks when I was handed my, quite repellant, award! Not bad considering that I have not made a film for over six . . or is it five actually? years.

Never mind. I got it. And a most moving tribute from Michele Morgan who, apparently, was as moved and surprised as I, so that she forgot her words and just embraced me!

I tell you this because I know that it will please you. But we shall keep it quiet together. I was particularly happy that Forwood was attending in the wings while it all took place. He has helped me so greatly over the many years of struggle, and my reward that night was as much his as it was mine. So that was pleasing.

The next morning we left for London and Mr Todd . . . our mouths dry, and that fearful uncertainty masked properly.

---

1. Salman Rushdie's *Midnight's Children* (Jonathan Cape) won the Booker Prize in 1981. The author had criticised Richard Attenborough's film, *Gandhi.*

Probably why, today, I feel utterly drained. The stress, for the moment anyway, is relaxing [...]

The Japanese Film with Bowie (L.V.d. Posts book)[1] has not been well recieved here I gather, principally because of Bowie who worries people by his oddity. Hamaphrodite, I believe.[2] And I'm buggered if I can spell that!

But the Japanese emerge well, and it is, apparently, brilliantly shot. But that, as we know, is not enough. However Cannes is a capricious Town ... perhaps it'll fare better with the British Press. Although they are'nt what you might call reliable either.

Having taken a long, slow, look around the terraces, it has been decided to let things be as they are and then get a team in to do the lot at the end of May and once again in September ... I cant face it all alone ... and it really has got out of hand because of the two winter months I spent in London when I should, by rights, have been bustling away keeping things under control.

I suppose a house in London will be bearable. One must make it so.

But I do insist on a small garden .. even if it is only sixty by ten! A house we saw in Kensington, which was pleasant and had just what I would need, plus LARGE garden, and facing south ... was up for £850.000 for a long lease. So ...... I'll have to lower my sights!

And go and set the fire and sweep up the muck on the terrace which planting out 100 white petunias has made.

But this to you with my love ... as ever.

I'm mulling about with an idea for a further 'Bio! Not chronological as much as episodic .. possibly to be called 'Something I Forgot ..'[3] but we'll think of that later!

Meanwhile great love,
    from your very
      devoted
        <u>Dirk</u> XXX

---

1. *Merry Christmas Mr Lawrence*, starring David Bowie; directed by Nagisa Oshima and based on Laurens van der Post's *The Seed and the Sower* (Hogarth Press, 1963).
2. Doubtless Dirk meant androgynous.
3. Which would evolve into *Backcloth*.

To Susan Owens   *Clermont*
                                                    21 May 1983

Dear Mrs O –

Your letter of the 13th has just arrived and given me great pleasure. Pleasure because things seem not to be quite as terrible as they did when you last wrote.[1]

I think that Faith, which really CAN move mountains of trouble, is extraordinary, and even though I have no 'real' religeon I do know that the power of prayer can work. I've been through a bit of that business myself!

I think it is amazing that your husband has progressed so far and so well in such a very short time. Naturally he has'nt done it all on his own: he's had your help and sensible-point-of-view to lean on and to encourage him. That is the most important part of the 'cure' possible. The encouraging. A stroke-victim is prone to appalling bouts of depression and lonliness, and it is this which is perhaps the hardest thing to overcome for the family: as well as for the victim. But encouragement helps a hell of a lot. And you MUST remember, and so must he, that he is not a cabbage sitting in a heap.

Even buttoning up a shirt, his trousers, tying his shoes, any little idiotic thing can be done and must be done, and is a tremendous step towards getting the brain sorted out.

I think that if he finds the newspaper difficult, as he will .. even I do! it is not a bad idea to start him off with reading by the use of very simple, large printed, childrens books. This may sound a bit cissy, and he might resent it, but it would be interesting to see if, with larger print and simple words, he can hold a sentence and discover that the 'print is not running all over the page' ... this kind of therepy is very basic and simple, but if he manages just to make one simple line sit still on the page he'll gain a great deal of courage to read more, bit by bit.

It wont be easy for you of course. Patience is one of the toughest requirements ... and it wears one out pretty quickly.

Buy a packet of 'Smarties' one day, spill them on a saucer, make him try to put the red ones together, the blue ones, so on ... that sounds silly too: but it is not. It is FORCING the mind-muscles to

---

1. SO's husband had had a stroke.

function when they would far rather relax and become inert. Any little game of this kind can be a big help. But it takes time, and it takes a lot of patience. Long conversations will exhaust him just because he has to listen to them. But short, firm, determined speech, with a question placed which he has to answer will stimulate a sluggish brain.

What you have to remember is that, as I was told in America when we were doing the research on the Neal Story, if the brain has been damaged severely all it really wants to do is give up and sleep, and that is the WORST thing that could happen.

So, when you are able, or if the kids can take turns, small, silly little games like the one with Smarties or reading or asking questions like 'What colour is this sweater?' or 'Look for the green pencil among all these' stimulate the mind, as I have said.

I know what a haul it is going to be for you, I equally know that if you have anything to do with things it wont be a failure.

Recently I had a difficult experience with someone who was taken gravely ill. Operations, drip-feeds, plasma, all the rest. But that person began to fight back and finally was able to leave hospital. The Nurses, as always, were simply wonderful and so indeed was the Matron, but her remark was perhaps the best of all.

When my friend thanked her and the Staff for pulling him through she said, very firmly, 'Listen. We only did a <u>bit</u> of the work. You did the rest for yourself by your own willpower. We know that there are people who come into this Hospital and immediatly start to give up. We knew, from the very first day you got here, that you were not one of those, and so you would have a fighting chance because you would go in fighting. Remember that!'

It seems a very good bit of advice to offer you at this moment.

Dont let your husband give in, feel that he is useless, unwanted, a burden. Get him to fight back and he'll win out. I'm positive.

Glad, to turn to other things, that you enjoyed the Lecture[1] ... it was quite fun really. Two and a half hours with a very warm and affectionate audience. I enjoyed myself a lot. Now I dont want to make you unhappy! But in 'SIMBA' I never once left Pinewood Studios! It was all made on the Floor with a lot of backprojection! So

---

1. The televised recording of a Guardian Lecture – more accurately, an interview with Tony Bilbow, followed by audience questions – which Dirk had given at the National Film Theatre during the visit to London in February.

I have seen as much of Africa as you have! The Magic of the Movies I suppose.

Glad that 'Night Porter' was alright. I think that it is a jolly good Movie ... based on a true fact as it happens ... Max was really a man to pity more than hate. But a mixed up fellow for sure!

[...] I wont go on any longer: people coming in for a drink in half an hour, so I had better go and wash down the garden chairs.

It rained last night fairly heavily, the wind came from North Africa, so EVERYTHING is covered in a fine coating of red sand! Somehow the stuff is sucked up into the clouds and comes racing across to fall on us in the rain. It's a rite booger!

Courage, remember!

& my very best wishes

Dirk Bogarde.

To Joanna Lumley

(Postcard)
Clermont
1 July 1983

Dear Miss Lumley –

I have to type this because I really do want you to be able to read it! I have received a number of Happy-Fannie letters recently which have been anxious to let me know that you were on the BBC (with Maria Aitken?)[1] and that you said very many 'really nice things' about me! So insistant have the letters been, and so pleased, that I feel compelled to write and thank you!

Forgive me: but in an age when being clobbered is the fashion it is so super to know that someone like you, far away on the BBC, bothered to speak kindly of one.

But it was reeely nice of you! And thank you very, very sincerely ...

Dirk Bogarde

---

1. JL had taken part in a BBC2 programme hosted by Maria Aitken called *Private Lives*. In her memoirs, *No Room for Secrets* (Michael Joseph, 2004), JL describes Dirk as 'my hero', adding: 'I'd only become an actor because I admired Dirk Bogarde so and felt I looked like him. In interviews I always said I thought he was the bee's knees.'

To Norah Smallwood

Norah dearest –

It was such joy hearing your voice again, even though it crackled and barked, from time to time, and to know that you were safely back again after your trip into the Twentieth Century.[1]

It is so irritating to me that, as you said, people have remarked that you probably did'nt 'hear from Dirk B . . now' . . . rather as if you and I had had a Publishing Relationship and that I had discarded you the very moment that you left Chatto.

It's like the little note that Visconti sent me after I had gone up to Lake Como to see him on my way home from Munich.[2]

' . . . to come all this way to see me, now that I am no longer of any use to you.'

I think that that remark, although I understood why he had written it[,] in my heart, hurt me more than any other he had ever made, or anyone had ever made!

Did he, I wondered, really think that my admiration, my awe, my respect, for him was simply founded on his 'use' to me?

It was an alien feeling for him: one that he found hard to understand in the sometimes ugly world in which he lived when people DID only love him for his 'usefulness' or 'influence'.

But it was not, and could never have been, that with me.

As it is with you.

As you know, I trust by now . . . (for it has been written down by me to you often enough) . . . I simply love you.

I love you, respect, admire extravagantly, and depend, still, on you.

Even though Chatto (with it's purple painted doors) is light miles from us both now. People would ADORE to think that I had cleared off. Why are people so rotten! So un-understanding.

Enough! I get so furious. And it's really a waste of time and effort. One knows ones own heart. That must be enough.

Now [. . .] this is for your eyes only, three weeks ago we sold Clermont.

---

1. NS had been to the United States.
2. In 1972.

But: four days later, so distressed were we both, in particular T, that I withdrew it from the Market!

A perfectly enchanting young couple, Belgian, two small children, saw the house, loved it instantly, asked no single question, accepted to the last sou the asking price and went away showering me with gratitude.

Oh Lord! You may imagine my distress four days later when I had to say the deal was 'off'. And theirs, alas!

But it just could'nt be done. I dont know why ... T. was clearly deeply sad and I feared that he might become ill again. Is'nt it strange to love a place so deeply, solidly?

[...] One day, of course, Clermont will have to be sold. We shall not be able to cope with the land or, for that matter, the house.

But not at the moment. We stay.

I think I'll have two months in the winter in either London or New York. A madness, but a winter here is too harsh now: and I have learned, because I have had to, a short-cut to Instant Terrace Gardening which does'nt cost the earth, and one has cut down here and there. I get a Team in to mow the terraces which we can no longer manage ... or wish to manage!

And they are expensive!

But so is a house in Parsons Green! God forbid!

Dutch elm is rife again, the trees which I had injected last year have, alas! not survived the malady ... and blaze like scarlet torches among the olives. It is really bloody. I have lost over sixty. Not great Stoke Poges Elms ... but pleasant young trees anyway. Otherwise we are in fair nick: T. manages a bit of mowing, which is very rewarding to see ... and I bustle about watering things and dead-heading and all the rest. We manage. In October we come over for his second, important, 'check' ... and if that is good, and I pray and think that it will be both at the same time, we shall adress ourselves to the autumn when I have to go to Paris to do a whopping big Television Show from The Louvre. Rather in the style and manner of [Kenneth] Clark's 'Civilisation'. I hasten to add that I do not mean that I shall be near that brilliant mans work! The programme will try to be like that. I am speaking about 'The Golden Age Of Flemish Art' (which I honestly dont really care all that much for!) Rembrandt etc etc .. and Greek Art in the Mediterranian Basin ... (A lot of pots and dusty bits of terracotta) But I think it will be fun ... I hope it will be! And to have the Louvre entirely to oneself from six pm until mid-night (the only time we may work there) sounds fairly tempting. We'll see ...

It has already got a vast distribution from America to Japan .. and the money is pretty decent. So ..

An odd letter the other day, from South Africa, from a pleasant lady who once worked, or rather her father and mother did, in the service of Mrs X in Sussex! And it was <u>she</u> who sent the fatal womans magazine to New Haven! Thereby giving me a first chance at 'writing'. Is'nt it odd?

Apparently Mrs D.W. Gordon .. her real name as you know, wrote to thank her for the marvellous friendship which she had enjoyed by that simple action. And then there was silence. This letter simply asked if anything unpleasing (an odd word!) had happened to Mrs Gordon, and could I write and say what? The woman retired from service, and England, some years ago and went to live with a daughter in South Africa ... she had not read 'AOM' only 'Snakes' .. so I told her that the full story was available in her nearest book-store. I hope it is!

And that is about that. I'm writing very badly today ... hangover I fear. And must presently go and lay up the table [...] We are having a huge gigot and a tremendous bowl of Ratatouie and new totties in mint.[1] Jealous? It's a bit silly really, because the heat is belting up off the land, and we'd be better off with cottage cheese and apples. Cheaper too!

My love to you: I am so happy that you are back ... there was a feeling of emptiness around ... although I <u>knew</u> that you were having a splendid(ish) time I had no one to beef off at!

You thanked me, in your letter before you left for the U.S, for 'my love and loyalty ..' magpieing MY line with which I was about to finish this letter.

So I shall simply re-tread it!

Thank you for YOUR love: and loyalty.

Always –

<u>Dirk</u> XXXX

---

1. Not for themselves alone: Dirk and Tony had guests.

To Norah Smallwood   *Clermont*
                        October 15th. (Note new type!) 1983

Norah love –

Finally the old machine conked out .. well, half the letters began
to fall out like old teeth, and so I searched about for a new machine
here with an English 'clavier'. Impossible to find.

Eventually the shop-keeper said that he could order me a new, and
very daunting, 'Brother'. (Japanese. Need I say.) This arrived just
before we left for England and looked absolutely terrifying.

Bells rang, lights flashed, it was enormous and had just about every
key you could imagine: none of which, apart from the alphabet, did I
need.

But.

There is always a BUT in France.

The type is set on a very sophisticated circular thing called a Daisy!
And we could not find an English Daisy to fit the keyboard. So ..
undaunted .. I came to London and after all the Medical Chores,
went with a light heart and bought my English Daisies. Two. Costing
thirty quid!

In Grasse finally, filled with hope and excitement, I went off to the
shop and viewed yet again my amazing Japanese computer-typewriter
which I knew would take me all of a month to master.

Except that the English Daisy did'nt fit. Ah ha!

When one pressed the key for 'F' one got ç. And so on.

The machine had been assembled for Turkey!

As I am not a Turkish writer I bowed out at the loss of thirty quid,
but also, quite happily ... because the Japanese Monster cost over five
hundred pounds and was far more complicated than I could have
believed possible.

So: to Cannes. And in a good shop sad shakes of heads put paid to
my hopes of an English-bloody-Clavier! No way possible, and to order
one would take four months plus Customs, plus TVA.

I was just leaving, sadly, going down the stairs in fact, when I saw
this machine sitting like a yellow toad behind a mass of ones which
had come in for repair. It had, I instantly saw, an English Clavier!
Someone was summonsed and remembered, dimly, that there had
'been an error last year'. The result of the error is under my fingers
now. It cost me just three hundred pounds, is perfect, friendly,

un-fussy; no bells or lights ring and flash, and it's just an ordinary old type-writer without Daisies or anything more alarming than these two keys ¿ and ¡. Now what <u>do</u> they mean? I shall never use them, but they worry me sitting idle there.

This over-length tale is simply to demonstrate the machine. Yours is the first letter that has been written on it: it seemed fitting that you should get the first, dont you think? I write with the knowledge that the Mail Strike persists here, and we have had no foreign mail since our return .. and none since September 18th ... which is a hell of a long time to be isolated. I just hope that you will, one day, get this. It is a pastime as vague and uncertain as sending you a letter in a bottle and casting it off the beach at La Bocca.

[...] The morning mail has just arrived! A few battered letters from UK all dated 25th–26th September. But still NO MS from Sally. I'm getting very lost, because I depend on each chapter to fashion the next! Maddening. I have had a packet from Canada, however, with a cassette tape of a sermon at an Inter Church Conference somewhere. As far as I can gather from the sender, unknown to me naturally, he is worried that, from reading 'Snakes And Ladders' I have a suicidal nature. My choosing of the metaphor, that life is a series of doors, seems to worry him deeply! He's at great pains to offer me 'spiritual help'.

Oh dear. Nothing amusing in the mail today at all!

Can you imagine me sitting down and listening to a Sermon?

[...] On Monday week I 'do' a commentary for Thames Television on a rather remarkable, but distressing, documentary on Oskar Schindler ... you may recall the book 'Schindlers Ark'?[1] It's worth doing because I feel it important that the Young should realise just what happened to the Jews in the war. Even the Jews wont believe the appalling events. I have been asked to do it because of the Concentration Camp passages in 'AOM' .. anyway off I go to a studio in Monte Carlo: the programme is 'slated' for showing in early December. An odd time, I'd say, to put on such a depressing subject. What the Americans would call 'The Big Turn Off' programme!

Enough: you are weary I swear. And I am too. But I wanted to test this on you!

With devoted love always – Dirk –

---

1. Thomas Keneally's novel, published by Hodder & Stoughton, won the 1982 Booker Prize.

Amused, rather than sad; there was not one single copy of ANY of my books (in any form) in THREE seperate bookstalls at Heathrow on Friday! But <u>ROWS</u> of 'Lace'.[1] Ah well – D.

To Norah Smallwood   *Clermont*

Sunday. 20th November. '83 at 5 o clock –

Norah dearest –

Two solid hours work in the filthy old garden: a wilderness of dead leaves and dead summer-planting. Had all <u>that</u> out in a short time: the leaves are a hopeless job. They fall, with soft 'click clacks!', about ones shoulders as one sweeps. Boring business. We await a mistral to sweep them all away to the coast. We await rain too. None to speak of since summer. The soil as dry as old bones; the oaks are wilting. This, I am assured, is a NEW and awful desease   like Dutch Elm. The Government are supposed to be spraying from helicopters. But 'supposed' is the word. Meanwhile the trees die. Our great big one, at the top of the hill, perhaps five hundred years old, (certainly not less by the girth) started to die back in June . . everyone said it was nothing; a dry winter. But alas! by August it was fiery red, and is dead already. Right there on the top of the hill.

I went to work, after a few moments thinking hard, on the 'Sedum Bed' which, you may remember, you pruned back hard for me?

A row of ancient, but ugly, stones bordered the euphimistaclyy-ally named 'lawn'. (I say. I got into a bit of a mess with the above, did'nt I? Anyway. 10 for trying, I say.) So I have heaved all the stones out, ripped out the sedums, which were failing anyway after a second splitting-up, and levelled the whole place down . . . I'll sow grass seed there in Febuary.

It looks much better now. Tidy anyway. The old stones looked like a grinning mouth of rotten teeth and the couch-grass had invaded.

But all this activity did was to remind me, forcably, of Roald Dahl who, once a fanatical gardner, said: 'Anyone over sixty who digs and plants bloody things in the dirt needs his head testing. Get yerself a couple of boys, make 'em do it, and watch them from a deckchair . .'

He has a point I think.

---

1. Shirley Conran's novel, published by Sidgwick & Jackson in 1982, was not a contender for the Booker Prize.

What was excellent, on the other hand, was seeing Forwood lumping about with barrow loads of weed and sedum plants, and pulling up, with caution, the smaller stones. It was not so very long ago that I wondered, watching him hung about with Drip Feeds and Blood Things, if he'd ever move in a garden again.

See one: even.

So one was cheered. I have laid the fire, he's made himself a pot of tea and cut himself a chunk of cherry cake, and I've come up to the Studio to write to you ... because we are all, over that silly sedum bed, very much linked together. Not JUST because of the bed .. you do understand? But it became a modest symbol. And was pleasing to me. You were banging away in the shadows of my mind, trowl and secateurs in hand, the butterfly shirt .. and you were singing too: so there!

How I wish that I could be present at your Party on the 29th. How maddening to be so far, and so in thrall to Guardians and all that: not to mention the most expensive air-fare in the world ... But, in a way, apart from longing to be there to honour you, it is perhaps just as well that I am not.

After all, I'm a very new friend. The others present have known you for so much longer, the lucky creatures, and I'd probably have been a bit out of place. But I'll think of you that evening.

How you are loved!

What a wonderous reward you have for the years of loyalty, affection, teaching and learning that you have given to so many of us.

Better than a pocket-watch I'd say?

How little I thought, that evening when I 'did' the dreaded Russell Harty Show, that my whole life was about to be altered by a stranger from quite another world. And that through that stranger I would be permitted to set foot, all be it modestly, into that world. And that the stranger would shortly become so very dear to me.

Apart from 'that world'.

And that is far too many 'worlds' in three lines!

But this is a love-letter, so I can say just what I like, cant I?

No lovely J.C [John Charlton] to carp and wrestle with over : or ; or even ç!

I still cant imagine what ç is doing on an English Machine, can you? And already I seem to have lost the 'V', well almost ... because I have been writing a mass of biographical memories of Visconti for an American writer who is doing an enormous biography on him.

I've been setting some records right: the last biography written on him was by a most poisonous woman called Gaia Servadio, who had NEVER met him! And whose ugly book[1] distressed his family and his friends keenly .. I refused to read it; chicken that I am.

But this book is supposed to set things to rights .. I hope that it does. It is SO strange to me that now he is dead everyone has decided, what I knew from the moment I met and worked with him in 1966, that he is The Master . . . it would have pleased him better to have had that accolade while he was alive. He does'nt, did'nt, believe in Heaven and all that business!

I think that a good bit of 'Snakes And Ladders' will be quoted .. and parts about V. from 'AOM' .. Simon and Schuster are the US. Publishers.[2]

The writer sounds very sensible and wise. He knows, very well, what I used to call 'The Roman Gang'. They were the terribly grand people in Rome; Counts and Countesses, Princes and Princesses, and all manner of idiot people, who cried with delight at parties, to which I was on some occasions bidden. 'Ah, cher Luchino .. so sad. He is QUITE ruined professionally . . . no one will give him a single lira to make a film now. SO amusing . . .'

But they were happily wrong. Golly! He made them pay for those words when the time came! Delicious!

I think that this writer (Gordon Rogoff) is rather good when he writes of the Servadio book '. . . is quite awful. Not only because it is poorly written and full of gossip, but also because she has no capacity for pain, no sense of complexity, the dark and the light.' Which is what it is all about.

And now I see from my little window that it is dark already.

Time to light that fire I have laid, and set up the table for supper.

Cold lamb, baked potatoes and a bit of salad. Not as grand as a whole saddle and a souflee! Never mind ..

[. . .] So very much love –

Dirk
XOXOX.

---

1. *Luchino Visconti: A Biography* (Weidenfeld & Nicolson, 1981). Evidently Dirk assumed that because Visconti had died in 1976 the author and her subject could not have met.
2. The book did not materialise.

To Kathleen Tynan   *Clermont*
                                    30th (can you believe it!) Nov. '83.

Kathleen love –

God! How the time speeds away .. especially at this grim time of
year one is reminded. Christmas and all that hideious jollity.

Your long letter of the 20th got here, amazingly, because we have
had a foul MailStrike since September and everything is at odds and
sodds stage. If you know what I mean? Packets arrive, posted years
ago, along with something mailed the day before yesterday. Irritating.
Because one has to telephone people and say 'Your letter of the 20
September has just arrived ... I'd have <u>loved</u> to be present for my
"Hommage" in Strasbourg but alas ..' and so on. Boring. They 'did'
my hommage anyway, without me. Which was fine by me: I'm deadly
bored with 'Accident' and 'Portier de Nuite' et al. It's all SO long ago.
And I'm weary of being called a Legend. Can you imagine such rot?
Marlene, yes. Chaplin if you insist, certainly Garbo .. but pas moi.

[...] I have just come back from a hellish (because they WILL
talk so much) promotion of the translation, excellent I must admit,
of 'Voices In The G.' which has been most generously recieved ...
double colour spreads in 'Paris Match' 'Elle' and 'Figaro' and most
gratifying reviews suggesting, ever so timidley, that I was 'Proustian'.
Well: it's <u>balls</u> of course, but I dont terribly mind. The splendid thing
about Frog Critics and Interviewers is that they speak about the book!
No one askes if you are sixty five, homosexual, the price of your
apartment, or if you dye your hair. This I have had recently ... in
January actually .. as a constant battering in sweet old Angleterre. But
the French dont give a fig as long as there are lots of people in ones
book to tear apart. And thats fun! I began to argue and scold, and find
all kinds of extraordinary symbols in the bloody book which were
never in my mind at the time of writing! All good fun.

Paris, the Louvre part,[1] was pretty exhausting: five pm shoot until
one am and no where in the whole seven kilometers of corridors and
galleries to smoke, eat a sandwich, or, worst of all, have a pee. Worse for
the girls than for the fellers .. we could always piddle into an empty
Evian bottle behind the Winged Victory ... but the ladies writhed.

---

1. Where Dirk, Charlotte Rampling and others contributed to the Franco-Japanese
documentary, *Le plus grand musée du monde*.

Should one become absolutely desperate a Guardian, grumpy, was summonsed with huge key, and one trolled behind her, and a tiny torch (the whole building, except the 'shoot area' was in total darkness) for miles and by the time I got to the place, which she opened with a flourish and a clatter of metal, I'd forgotten what I'd come for and was utterly dried up. I wrote the text for Charlotte R. and myself, every morning, and she would telephone in from her fast, and glamorous Mercedes, as she was <u>driving</u>, and I'd read her the text. She was on her way into Town for her make-up and hair at fourish ... every time she hit a traffic block, she'd call in. Very glamorous, if inaccurate, Textwise, not driving-wise. She's very good at that!

'You just said Lyssipus .. right?'

'Right ..'

'And after that what?'

'The greatest copy done of an original Praxitele work ..'

'Spell.'

'P R A X ..'

'The lights have gone green. Call you back.'

That sort of caper. But we mugged it up, switched it about, and did the lot as impromptu. Not TERRIBLY Kenneth Clark, but better than the original text which was as worthy as a Bishops Gaiters .. and just as dull.

Tote had the dullest part of it all sitting alone in the Lancaster with his supper on a tray and watching DIRE TV. There was nowhere for him to sit in the Louvre, it was too far to walk anyway, and there was no point in hanging about all night.

So we did nothing amazingly interesting .. I worked all morning, did all my interviews in the afternoon until five and flogged off until one am. And got paid handsomly. Plus, on the last night, three hundred grams of Beluga and a couple of bottles of Laurent Perrier ... which was VERY nice.

It was mild, golden, and sunny all the time (three weeks) we were in Town .. and it really is the very best of Cities .. even though the poor Champes Elysees is now rather like Times Square or Oxford Street and there are as many traffic blocks as there are bloody Macdonalds ... but it still grabs one. And Sunday lunch at Fouquettes[1] is still Sunday lunch at Fouquettes .. and expensive. But who really

---

1. Fouquet's, on the Champs-Elysées.

cares? Sitting in the sun: the chestnut trees turning, the sky blue, the wine chilled, and people laughing and arguing and behaving. Very nice.

[...] I am glad that you have reached Chapter 4 ... thats terrific. Remember that Chapter Eight is the bastard: that's when you absolutely KNOW that you've written a load of shit! It's the 'Wobble Chapter'. But courage! It always happens apparently. I've now completed and had published six books ... the seventh is stirring uneasily in the darker recesses of my mind .. but I've been busy with the Louvre, and also doing a harrowing (because it is a harrowing film) commentary for a Thames TV Documentary on Schindler. Of the Ark Fame. [...] I must get back to work again, I hate not doing something. I was going to do a movie about Middletone Murray and Kathleen Mansfield.[1] But it was pretty awful: and he is such a piss-pot [...] So I bowed out [...]

Courage! And work hard, and huge amounts of love to you, as always ...

Ever, with love,
    Dirk XOXOX

To Dilys Powell
(Postcard)   *Clermont*
                                                25 January 1984

Dilys dear

I'm afraid that an idiot is born everyday! And I was one of them. This is just to amuse you and to tell you that at long last I have reached the age-of-dignity, at least in my beloved France! A Chevalier d'l'ordre des Arts et des Lettres and now, are you perfectly ready? I have been 'unanimously voted to be the President of the Jury at Cannes'! I MUST be barking mad. I LOATH Cannes more even than you do .. and detest all forms of Comittee or Jury-work .. and the very idea of having to sit through 18 films in ten days ~~appalls~~ me. (Appalls me, looks better!) However, since you have shared my career with me from the first tentative days in 1947 I thought it would amuse you to know that, as Visconti once insisted crossly, there are always heighs to scale! And bloody awful crosses to bear as well! 18 films in ten days! I reel.

---

1. John Middleton Murry and Katherine Mansfield.

One, I am assured, runs for four and a half hours.

Oh well .. Thank you, my dear Dilys for the sweet remarks about long-forgotten films (for me anyway) which seem to have resurfaced on the TV.[1] My sister assures me that they are 'much better than all that foreign stuff you did!' Ah well. One <u>tries</u>!

With great love. Dirk –

With Norah Smallwood's departure from Chatto & Windus, Dirk had acquired a new literary agent, Patricia Kavanagh, who sold West of Sunset *to Allen Lane, part of the Penguin group. All his subsequent books would be published under the group's Viking hardback and Penguin paperback imprints.*

To Pat Kavanagh

Clermont
28 January 1984

Pat –

Sweet Heaven! Why! I mean that quite literally. Just why?

Your letter of the 25th arrived this morning, along with a sodden copy of 'Country Life' (It's been raining for two days and the postman only has a 'bike. And cant be bothered to keep anything dry anyway) plus the local tax demand from Bar sur Loupe. Which sounds, perhaps, glamorous but is not. In the least.

And I read that you and your husband (I assume it is he? Unless it is your Daily or Secretary? I mean, you DO say <u>we</u>. So it must be.) sit and watch dead TV films!

Is it a sense of love and loyalty?

If it is there is no need for flagellation of this kind to prove it. I have a sort-of feeling that we all quite respect, like, care for, each other anyway.

Is it that you watch because J. has three TV sets running at the same time, and records what he really MUST see?[2]

Or is it that I was so bloody to you about green beans that you have entirely given up cooking and sit glued to the TV with a Mars bar and some old Ms? And that you are revengeful?

---

1. Since her retirement as film critic, DP had continued to work for *The Sunday Times*, previewing movies to be shown on television.
2. PK and her husband Julian Barnes, then television critic of *The Observer*, had watched *So Long at the Fair*.

Whatever it is, I implore you, dont do it any more!

I am, seriously, alarmed that I appear to be advancing towards the age of 'embalment'. The fly in amber. Petrified wood. Fossils. That sort of thing.

I dont even REMEMBER 'So Long At The Fair', except that it was a goodish little book written by Anthony Thorn (e?)[1] and is based on a true story.

So dont go back to Marseilles in a hurry.

What did I <u>do</u> to poor Jean Simmonds; languishing, I read, in 'Thorn Birds', which should'nt have happened to her at all: she is really rather nice. Was. I have'nt seen her for twenty four years!

I remember that we had to keep our hats on in bedroom scenes until that film .. when I absolutely refused to stalk about in a top hat and dressing gown. That MIGHT have altered the Breen Office Code.[2] I dont know.

But it was'nt worth sitting watching for that.

The 'quiff', as you call it so rudely, (some would call it 'Hair') was 'in fashion' then.

But I expect that you were spitting at your poor little black servants and stamping on their voodoo-dolls at that time.[3]

I think that I know what J. was doing ... up and down that Met. Line[4] ... but that is altogether different.

An appalling thought has just hit me, sitting here in bleary rain, and that is that perhaps you WERE NOT EVEN HERE ON EARTH THEN! Wow!

I really would'nt mind if I got a titchy residual from all this crap which rolls, weekly it seems, onto the Box at tea-time. But I dont.

Anymore than I get tuppence a year from a Library:[5] because I 'live abroad'. The people who write (the C&A ladies) cheerfully telling me that the 'list for "An Orderly Man" is still miles long. I think I may be lucky by July.' fill me with rage. Soppy farts. They think I'll be cheered up by the news that 'the book's obviously a success.'

God. The middle-mind.

---

1. Anthony Thorne adapted his own novel, published by Heinemann in 1947.
2. Joseph Breen, who as administrator of the Production Code in the USA was chief censor from 1934 to 1954.
3. PK was brought up in South Africa.
4. An allusion to Julian Barnes's first novel, *Metroland* (Jonathan Cape, 1980).
5. A reference to Public Lending Right.

My acid, but clever, French publisher, Mme Chabrier, called [...]
I HAD a vague hope that she was calling to say that 'Voices In The
Garden' was breaking all records in Montparnasse.

'Ah no!' she said. 'There is only a <u>tremor</u>.'

So you do get a bit dashed.

What is the good of being called, by the French Press, 'Proustian'
if no one buyes your buke.

[...] I am bashing away, very, very slowly, at 'Closing Ranks',[1] and
some of it is funny ... some of it good. . However there are another
nine [chapters] to go, goodness!

I am delighted that you have accepted to dine on the 28th .. not
my kind of deal: but if I can manage it we wont eat in a basement, a
celler, or the Gavroche .. I've suggested the Garrick: the Albert Hall:
or Derry and Toms Roof Garden. Or a sandwich at the Globe in
Covent Garden.

Fanny B.[2] is so burstingly pregnant that she really ought to be close
to a hospital. But I don't know any restuarants near St Thomases ...

I said that I'd bring a plastic bag.

'What for?' said Fanny.

'The afterbirth.' I suggested. She gave a little cry and has'nt spoken
to me since.

All this is rubbish. But no more rubbish than you and J. sitting
watching temps perdue .... and not very good temps at that.

I'm not, as you could be forgiven for thinking, pissed. It's just that
this machine got 'mended' in Grasse and has never recovered from the
shock, which is why the words get lumped together. Sorry.

[...] Thank you for [...] telling me that Penguin are 'so enthusiastic' about 'WOS' (They have'nt really said as much to me: but
then they are all in different departments now, and dont communicate
easily.)

I'd better go out and get a breath of fresh air: picking bloody olives
of which, I may say, we already have gathered over 600 kilos! Not bad
as an effort ... but bad on the knees and back.

Love

<u>Dirk</u>.

---

1. A new novel which would eventually see the light of day in 1997.
2. Fanny Blake, Dirk's editor at Penguin.

To Norah Smallwood

Clermont
14th March 1984
11.30 o'clock – pm

Norah dearest –

I have just telephoned the Hospital to make perfectly certain that you were there: and you are![1] So at least a form of contact has been established. A charming sounding girl (Sister?) gave me the low-down on you, and said that you were 'Cheerful' (a standard word, I find in Hospital life) and that you could <u>not</u> take incoming calls.

Now thats going to be a blow. I gather that you can call out but I cant call in, except to Sister. So, for the moment, it must stay like that. Heaven knows when this letter will arrive at your bedside, but I'll take a chance and write anyway ... I am stuck with 'writers block' on the final run to the finish of Chapter 3. Which is normal for me, but irritating.

And in any case I have a hell of a lot of work to do outside before we up-sticks and leave for London.[2]

I have cleared, dug and peated, the lower bed at the far end of the 'lawn' and bought thirty lavender plants, as I think I have already told you, from my pied-noir gardener down the lane. They were rather expensive, but very fine plants. Fat, bushy, and local. By that I mean they are the stock which they grow in the back-country for the scent people. Fat, tight, cushions. I dont think that they'll smother the weeds .. for a year or so .. but at least the bed wont look neglected and dreary this year. I left it alone, for obvious reasons, all last season .. there was'nt much time for gardening with the fate of the house rather hanging in the balance.

I am being as optimistic as possible this year: thinking positivly, I am assured, is far better than thinking negativly. But I <u>am</u> a negativly-Thinking person. When I think at all.

A relic, I fear, which I have inherited from my Ma.

[...] A great deal of bird seed (thrown over the bed during the very coldest period for my birds) has sprouted ... and I fear the Police may call and accuse me of growing cannabis! One never knows what is in those packets of seed. Whatever is growing is tough: and wont

---

1. Having an operation on her knee.
2. And the promotion of *West of Sunset*.

yank out easily. To my delight this year I have managed to convince a pair of thrushes and a couple of pairs of blackbirds, that it is wiser, and safer, to remain on my land rather than skitter off into the woods which are lethal with young idiots with double-bore rifles, who usually shoot each other, but quite often shoot a bird. And the hen pheasant, seldom seen except at early light, is now to be heard, and seen, scratching away in the thicket down by the cess-pool outlet! I think, from her industry, that she has a mate ... and I now spend my time trying to keep Bendo away from the area.

The pond is burgeoning with mating toads again, and I watch helplessly. The lillies have to be lifted and divided, but I cant face the idea just yet ... the water is glacial. I think I'll wait until we return, for that job. In any case my thigh-boots, which are essential to this operation, leak.

Five pm. Done it! Twenty four lavender plants stand witness to my labours. The thing was hell to do: kneeling on a slope, forking in yet more peat, cursing the oxalis which turned up with every trowel of earth .. sobbing with effort (I'm not young any more). So the sedum bed got short shift: I lifted a gathering of seedlings (California p.) and planted those in the bed under the terrace where they will get full sun and where, in a shorter time than one realises, you'll be suggesting, wistfully, that they were not a good idea.

Oh well.

I am reading the Nicholson Book (Milne)[1] .. somehow I never got around to it all that time ago. And I so dislike poor Nicholson that I stayed my hand each time it strayed. However, I got so damned bored with Nicholas Moseley .. or however he spells it .. Mosley? .. and his Mum and Dad,[2] that I pulled Nicholson off his shelf.

I am reading him, I confess, because Milne writes SO beautifully. With such ease and amusement. Rather like having the thing read to one, instead of reading it oneself. [...] I am not sure that I would have cared for the elegant life of Cimmie and Tom Mosley any more than I would care for Nicholsons. [...] I am not at all certain that Nicholas has done his parents a service. But I am certain that he has written with honour. More's the pity. [...] I always rather hope that

---

1. James Lees-Milne's *Harold Nicolson*, op. cit.
2. *The Rules of the Game: Sir Oswald and Lady Cynthia Mosley 1896–1933* and *Beyond the Pale: Sir Oswald Mosley and Family 1933–1980* (Secker & Warburg, 1982, 1983).

in retrospect people who have been so mis-treated in their lives for their beliefs, whatever they may be, might be seen to triumph in the end. Not so here.

I liked Nicholas M. very much when we were working on 'Accident', which as you know he wrote, and I am astonished to find that he is my age!

[...] Anyway I read on with Milne ... I just wish that he had not had to write about such a potty person. Forwood is reading, with certain interest for his own work the Edwina Mountbatten book[1] ... and she was no better than she should have been! But amazing in later life. I think the agony of NOT being 'the Queen' (after India) and having to bang about in a tiny house in Chester St must have been most irritating! And she showed it too.

I met him when I was in Java and he was the Supremo. He had a very odd collection of people with him. And I was not, as an ADC, deeply taken with his ADC who should have been wearing a crinoline. At least.

But he [Mountbatten] was enormously glamorous: and I was aware, even at the tender age of twenty four–five, that he had an amazingly mesmerising effect on the Lower Orders, or Other Ranks. However, it did'nt last for much longer than his visit. As soon as he had left the Island they soundly abused him for being a 'bleedin' aristo .. we'll get that lot out when we get back'.

That was, at that time, the most popular remark. And of course, to all intents and purposes, they did. Churchill went, Attlee came in .. and so on, in a slow, downward, spiral.

Someone locally has a friend in London who has 'taped' almost all of 'Jewels In The Crown',[2] and has been generous enough to loan them to me before sending them back. Forwood and I, bug eyed, hollow eyed, bleary eyed, unable to go to bed. Three or four episodes in a go .. NO commercials! Dame Peggy fills my heart with wonder and joy. How marvellous to watch such precision and care in a performance. The slightly 'off' accent, the busy walk, the inner despair and loneliness .. amazingly beautiful, because it is so true and so felt. We have, alas, finished our ration for the time being: maybe I can pick up the final chunk in London.

---

1. *Edwina* by Richard Hough (Weidenfeld & Nicolson, 1983).
2. The Granada Television adaptation of Paul Scott's *The Raj Quartet.* Directed by

[...] Oh dear. Foyles.[1] How I dread it. And it clashes, most dreadfully, with the service in the Abbey for Noel Coward, who, quite correctly, is being honoured with a plaque. So everyone will be there and no one but the merangue-hats will come to luncheon. Except Peter Hall. Who has accepted probably not realising the importance of the event down the road!

The sky is getting loomy-looking. Grumpy clouds drift in from Corsica, which is always a bad sign, and the bitter wind has dropped ... a three quarter moon tonight, so a weather change is due. I hope not snow. We are in danger until the 16th ... after that Spring OUGHT to be on it's way ... so they tell me.

[...] I'm off. My little owl is calling up above the top terrace: so thats where he is this year. His wife makes a very disagreeable sound. I'll wander up there, if my legs will take me after this afternoons labour, and spy out their nest: which will allow you to set this down and rest.

& remember that I love you greatly –
XXXX Dirk

To Dilys Powell   *Clermont*
                                                     27 April 1984

Dilys dear –

I think that the word you want is 'crock'! A cracked crock cant hold milk ... something like that: and I am steadily advancing towards that state myself! Flu is over .. just .. a really loathsome attack which caught quite a number of my 'retinue' who accompanied me on the 'Promotional'. One enchanting lady was v.v. ill and is only recovering now!

We think that we 'got it' in Oxford at Blackwells Literary Luncheon. Millions, it seemed, of vicars and merangue-hatted ladies sneezing cheerfully over the Dry Fly Sherry. Ghastly!

I was so sorry not to have had a longer moment with you at Foyles that day ... it was such a terrific birthday, and so splendidly fitting

---

Christopher Morahan, it starred Art Malik, Tim Pigott-Smith, Susan Wooldridge, Charles Dance and Peggy Ashcroft.

1. A Foyles Luncheon, his second, was to be held in Dirk's honour under the chairmanship of Peter Hall.

that so many of my dearest, and oldest, friends were there to share it.[1]
P. Hall DID read my obituary, which shattered me, but I just sat
there in deep embarrassment pretending that he was speaking about
someone quite other: that helped. Anyway: you did have E. [Edward]
Fox and he is a man of infinate manners and courtliness .. I also think
he is a splendid actor, so does he. But gets terribly frantic when his
younger brothers get the best parts! I cant say that I blame him.[2] We,
like you I gather from the family at home, have had the most glorious
weather: golden sun, shimmering sea, hazed mountains and a great
deal of work already to do on the land. Mainly weeding and cutting
the first hay! Amazingly summer just arrives here. A very short spring
of great beauty and bounty and then, wham! summer is upon us. So
flu has had to be overcome, it's silly to mope about in deep depression
in the middle of all this ravishing light and beauty. So up one gets
and staggers about with a hoe; or paint brush to tart-up the garden
furniture.

So far the new book is selling well and I'm number 2 on the Best
Seller list in the 'Bookseller' (Which sounds an odd sentence.) So I
dont complain, but do wish that a good film would emerge for me
before age really pulls me into Grandfather roles! But nothing seems
to be worth the doing: and I wont play bits and pieces after the
excellent roles I have once played. Pride? Maybe ... but I have set a
standard, for myself, and wont fall below it.

Ahead is the horror of the Festival. I cant imagine WHY I agreed
to be President. Maybe because it IS an honour and because I live in
France, and what the hell ... why not? I seldom see a Movie, I do hate
dubbed versions of things. So now I shall watch two a day in shaking
despair. Oh! The miseries of the Czheck, the Russian and the Bolivian
entries ... and those interminable Chinese bits! However my Jury is
distinguished and sounds as if it will really be serious ... and we have

---

1. In a note to Joanna Lumley, Dirk described the Foyles Luncheon as 'Perhaps the most
important, & certainly the most moving, 3 hours in my entire career.'
2. More hyperbole from Dirk. Of Edward Fox's two brothers only James was an actor.
Robert was already a successful producer. The previous year James Fox had published his
autobiography, *Comeback* (Hodder & Stoughton), recording his return to the screen after
ten years' work with a Christian organisation, the Navigators. Of his brother Edward he
wrote: 'Whenever we are together we have a huge laugh, although people like to make
something of our rivalry. There isn't much to it. I rather envy his range, and he may have
been jealous of my success, but we get on rather well.'

no idiot American writer to hinder us this year! They get so dreadfully drunk, cast the wrong vote, and insist that as America is spending so much money in the Town they HAVE to win the Palme d'Or. But this year things will, I hope, be different. We'll see!

[...] This letter is NOT for answering ... it is to thank you for your note, and to remind you that 'crocks' are all the same ... it comes to us all: and <u>very</u> boring it is!

I am now going to write off for your book, 'An Affair Of The Heart'[1] to the wonderous, if hefty, Miss Parker at Hatchards .. she manages to get me things here in days only ... and I'm just about ready for 'you'. I've finished, for the second time, Enid Bagnolds autobiography[2] ... and I am at a loss. You'll make it up for me ... as ever.

Your devoted <u>Dirk XXXXX</u>

To Norah Smallwood   *Clermont*
                                                      3 June 1984

Most dear Norah –

From the date above one would think, would'nt one, that the day was golden, that the sun beat down through the tender leaves of the vine, that lizards scurried across the hot tiles and the ice clinked softly in a tall glass of white wine?

Surely? The roses must be turning face-wards to the light, the pots and tubs must be garlanded with flowers.

But not so.

It rains. Torrentially.

Spills down the walls, courses down the drive, roars into the pond and sends the goldfish in tumbling, flapping, breaks of colour, into the cess-pit overflow.

All most romantic. June in the south of France.

Do you suppose it is because we have altered the balance of the weather by chucking all those dreadful satalites into the heavens? Or are we in for a New Age of dire summers? Yesterday I might have been persuaded that the weather had been as it always was, the first-weekend-in-June of so many idiotic songs of the 'twenties. When

---

1. A portrait of Greece by DP, originally published in 1958 by Hodder & Stoughton.
2. *Autobiography* (Heinemann, 1969).

Roses Are In Bloom, Tra Laa .. I painted most of the garden chairs, the table tops, the spindley little iron chairs which are so peculiarly French and have'nt altered since before Proust set them about in Swann's garden. And now they stand idle and drenched, the red dust from the Saraha speckeling the pristine surfaces ... for I painted carefully and with a new brush which did not leave hairs on the expensive plastic-based paint.

The wisteria blossom hangs wanly; wet handkerchiefs ... the splendour of Grandmere Jenny is all spilled open, the petals falling into the drooping fuchias below.

At least, thank God, I have not invited ten for luncheon!

That has been known to happen before: at least one has some frozen veal rissoles (rather scrumptious!) and spring greens and new potatoes for lunch. Which will be eaten by electric light in the dark dining room. No lobster salad! No crab mousse! No shrimps in 'sick sauce' and delicious gulls eggs .... not a summer lunch, just a nourishing 'Nursery' one. For a wet, cold beastly day in Kent or Westmorland or anywhere you like.

[...] Anyway: contact has been re-established. And you have no possible idea how important that is. I dont wish you to feel that you are burdened by your writer! Not at all .. but he is burdened by the need for your comforting voice and assurance. So there! Goodness! How I wish that you were still my Managing Director! That I could discuss, worry, fret about how to next go about a book. Being freelance, so to speak, has great advantages ... but equally it has disadvantages. One misses the closeness of ones Publisher? Editor? whatever role you played. The advice, the council, the rejection, even, of material ... it is all so greatly needed, and now, alas! I must find the way myself more or less.

A terrible moan, I agree. And selfish. But since (as) you started the ball rolling towards the hole marked 'WIN' I am fearful to tread on alone. Or should I say 'roll'; as I use the symbol of a ball?

This is, of course, just a momentary grab of nerves .. due to the inclement weather and the fact that the studio is dark and gloomy and the heater is up to Mark 2! It'll be alright soon .. I have got some ideas rolling about in my empty head, and I'll set them down on paper. Never fear.

The next 'buke' will be an ortobiographical-effort. There!

Novels are fun to write, in a way, but they dont, I think, sell as well as 'ortobios'. So I am going to persue that line .. there is, after all, a good deal that I have NOT written about ... and if old Compton M.[1] could mine his seam so thoroughly, then so can I. Although I am deeply aware of the difference in age and ability!

And L. v. d. P[2] has done much the same, I think.

Ones life is not tidily stacked, it is a sprawl of experience, so one can riffle about among the discarded bits and brush them up.

I am only writing all this down, presently, so that I gain courage. It is one thing to say, another to put into practice.

This week I am being made so acutely aware of June [6]th .. forty years ago.[3] The various Media-Machines are hotting up now, and reminding one of lost time. I can recall that day so vividly, so clearly, so sharply, it really is as if it had been yesterday, and I feel the same emotion now, as I did then. And not a whit older!

The appalling thing is looking at the photographs of men then and now! The unrecognisable faces of elderly gentlemen who, one feels, could NEVER have been 'boys'. One sees the wattles on ones own face! And one aches when one kneels for too long, as I know only too well. It was not yesterday .. but a long time ago. History in truth .. and so much since then has altered life. How pleasant it was before.

Never to come back.

A terribly gloomy letter indeed. All to be blamed, for I must lay blame! on the appalling weather beyond these two small windows.

Forwood has made a sensible, I think, suggestion. We shall drive down to the airport and get the Sunday Papers! What a treat that will be, huddled round the stove, in cashmere or woollen cardie, reading the exciting news about Strikes and [Arthur] Scargill.[4]

Enclosed a clipping from 'Jours de France'[5] ... not because it is the best, but because it is the <u>worst</u> ... a silly little paper with a vast circulation. But I thought that you might be amused to see what a twelve hour session with the jury did to me on the final day! I had exactly twenty five minutes to change into dinner jacket, to make my

---

1. Sir Compton Mackenzie, whose *My Life and Times*, published by Chatto & Windus between 1963 and 1971, ran to ten volumes, or 'Octaves'.
2. Laurens van der Post.
3. The D-Day anniversary.
4. The then leader of the National Union of Mineworkers and implacable foe of Margaret Thatcher.
5. Coverage of the Cannes Film Festival.

list of the 'winners', and to get onto the stage for a small audience, all over Europe (except, of course GB!) of fifty millions and break the tidings. We did it well. [Isabelle] Huppert, on my right, is the most adorable, sensible, grown-up, VERY brilliant, actress I have met in years. I immediatly made her Vice President of the Jury .. and it was an excellent idea. But we both look, as we were, absolutely exhausted. However: a job well and truthfully (unusual) done.

I'm off to the airport. Rain torrenting, mist thick, shall we ever get there I wonder?

With my love, and always my affection and respect.

Your devoted <u>Dirk</u> XXXXXX

To Kathleen Tynan

Clermont
9 June 1984

My dearest Kathleen –

[...] I'm glad that 'West of Sunset' was alright .. It is the most awful cheek for a foreigner to write about a city he knows as little, really, as I do. I shall probably get the chop when it comes out in the Fall on your side. L.A. Magazine (?) is printing a chunk in August, I think. But I am not certain if they are sending me up, or taking it straight!

Time enough for that!

Wim Wenders film, 'Paris, Texas'[1] is super. It has the typical lon-geurs which Wenders uses always, a kind of slow mastubation. But it is a wonderful foreigners-view of an America that too many Americans ignore or dont even see. And the performance from Karen Blacks child, Hunter [Carson], is not to be believed! He is absolutely magical. We tried hard to give him a special award at Cannes, but no such Prize exists ... stupidly.

It was quite fun, actually, Cannes. I was locked up hermetically in a very pleasant suite in the Majestic (on account of secrecy) when I was'nt at the Movies ... twenty four in twelve days, starting at eight fifteen am!

I got rather to like it all ... but some pretty crummy movies flashed over the screen I assure you! And if I have to look at another pubic-hair or another shot of a cow being slaughtered, a horse being drowned,

---

1. To which Dirk's jury gave the Palme d'Or.

a fat man having his orgasm, or however it is spelled, I'll choke. All that, I may add, jammed with Lesbian-Love scenes of extreme explicity, at cight of a morning is really not adorable.

However there were compensations: Wenders was one .. 'Another Country'[1] one other, and a modest, excellent little film about the Irish Business for which, to my delight (and astonishment) Helen Mirren won Best Actress, was splendidly done. Terribly moving, taut, and horrifying. It's called 'Cal',[2] and I don't suppose the Americans will ever see it . . . too many American Irish.

There was, as there always is, the usual Political Nonsense. I put paid to that!

I had a super jury: very adult and all successful, and not one dotty novelist on the list. American, Italian, Hungarian, Russian, French, etc. I got on terrifically well with the Russians[3] .. it is so sad that one can make warm friends in two weeks and forget the Sakharovs and all, simply because we are united as Film People. God! I detest bloody politicians. [...] They are disposable. But do appalling harm before dropping out.

I behaved rather like a British Officer dealing with the wogs in Aden! Snap, and a certain amount of table-banging. It worked splendidly.

We were, or rather I was, (as President) informed long before that we were to award prizes to 'commercial films and players, not to Art Subjects or players who are un-known generally This must be a Family Festival, not a political one.' So much for my personal brief; coupled with the vague suggestion, most delicately put, that John Huston had been PROMISED the Palme d'Or for 'Under The Volcano', Finney Best Actor, and Jacqueline Bissett, (not half bad, but not good enough) was to be best Actress.

Well: 'Volcano' stands or falls on the performance of the actor who plays 'Firman'.[4] And it fell. I regret to say that it only got two votes in all the sessions which I held (Secret ballots, so I never knew who had voted for what! which I think was quite bright of me. And I'm not given to brightness.)

Finally the Festival Organizers were appalled when we voted Best

1. Directed by Marek Kanievska, and adapted by Julian Mitchell from his own stage play; with Rupert Everett and Colin Firth.
2. Directed by Pat O'Connor, co-starring John Lynch.
3. The cinematographer Istvan Dosai and his interpreter.
4. The protagonist, Geoffrey Firmin, was played by Albert Finney.

Actor to two brilliant Spanish gentlemen.[1] And Helen Mirren sent
them into a sort of foaming fit! 'Who IS she!' they cried, 'What film
is she in?'

The final announcements, made by me, in frog, on the stage to an
audience of 3.000 on the final night, were recieved with cheers and
shouts of joy! They were quick to catch on that 25 million dollars does
not, nescessarily, mean a good film has been made. The reverse. Have
you seen 'The Bounty'[2] by any chance? We did ... oh dearie me, oh
dearie me ....

When I announced the Palme d'Or for Wenders I rather thought
that they would wreck the theater with their delight, and he was
exceptionally moved. And deserved it.

The U.S Majors slunk away in cold fury. I think it might be hard
to get them back next year, but that is not my problem! They dislike
being judged, they said, by 'a European jury'. Well: they bloody well
were this year: and found wanting.

The interesting thing is that the voting for 'Paris, Texas' was absolutely clear. Eight out of ten .. seven out of ten for Mirren, and nine
out of ten for the two Spaniards, Rabel and Landa ... both well into
their sixties and sheer magic. When we made the final announcement,
before leaving for the theater, to the Organizators, there was hell let
loose! They admitted, or one of them did to be fair, that Huston had
been promised that he'd win everything ... 'You have to award Huston
SOMETHING!' they, (he), yelled with a face crimson with rage. A
silence fell among us. There was nothing TO award. Then the spokes-
man said 'After all, be reasonable, he has had to come seven thousand
miles for this evening'. To which Stanley Donen, the U.S member of
the jury, said in his high, dry voice: 'You do not get a fuckin' Palme
d'Or for TRAVELLING!' Which ended the session neatly.

In the end we accorded him an 'Hommage' .. which was moving
and very spontanious ... the house stood to acclaim him. I insisted
that he got no ugly present, but just the applause and gratitude for his
long years of work from a live audience. I think he was pleased. I have
no way of telling.

Now I am back to laying the fucking table, splitting logs (it has

1. Alfredo Landa and Francisco Rabal, who shared the award as Best Actor for *Los Santos
Inocentes* (*The Holy Innocents*).

2. Directed by Roger Donaldson from a script by Robert Bolt; with Anthony Hopkins.

rained here for fifteen weeks solidly) and feeding the dog ...
Cinderella-Land.

[...] DO write soonish and let me know about August: but in any
case we will guard a case of Moet ... I got given presents at Cannes
and by the German TV Network who have done a three day 'in depth
interview' here. I cant think what for. But like the Moet! End of
paper – but not, ever, end of love –

<u>Dirk</u> XXXOX

*Joseph Losey died on Friday 22 June. Dirk was on the telephone, inquiring
after his friend's health, at the moment of death.*

To Patricia Losey

Clermont
22 June 1984

Patricia –

These letters are always bloody to write and nearly always trite.

I'm writing this only because today has been like a great black hole,
and I find it difficult to settle: rather like a dog who knows that
'something is up'.

I did'nt expect Joe to die, for some silly reason. I suppose I thought
that because he had been so very much a part of my life he would stay
on, the grumpy, cantankerous, loving genius that he was

But that is not, to coin a phrase, 'life'. And Joe was after all a mortal
man, though I often doubted that fact at times in the past.

I cant write a letter of 'sympathy'. That would be both irritating
and a waste of your time. You know anyway how much I grieve for
you, and how much you are in my thoughts.

I suppose, in a way, that this should be a letter of reminder: to us
both, of all the good and wonderful things which he brought, in very
different ways, to us both.

A celebration of the happy, extraordinarily happy, times we have all
shared.

I will always remember you washing up coffee mugs in, was it
Markham Street, and me calling you, for the last time ever! Pat.

'I'm NOT Pat' you said fiercely. 'I'm Patricia if you dont mind.' I
did'nt. And we made more coffee for the Cast crouched about in the
little sitting room upstairs.

The tremendous 'ups' and 'downs' of 'The Servant' which we

shared. The wonderful joy when it was a success. Joe often told me, in a rather gentle manner, that my account of the party I gave at the Connaught after the First Night was not exact. But it was. In my mind anyway!

I shall never forget Basil Dearden kneeling on the carpet before Joe and paying him hommage. Sincerely, honestly, meant. What a funny evening it was [. . .]

The time we all went to Venice and got stinking on Bloody Mary's on the Golden Arrow, the days at Taormina on the beach with the Dankworths.

So many things.

And there were other things, less happy, which we shared. The other side of a Joe who could be petty minded at times, and spiteful.

Oh I know about all that. I remember the business in Rome about 'Under The Volcano' . . and found it hard to rid myself of anger and bitter amazement. But I did: in the end. One does!

He had a quite extraordinary capacity for making enemies of those who liked him, and respected him. His behaviour with that tame millionair who offered me five million quid to make 'any film you can think of' was bewildering! I remember that after their first meeting, at which you were probably present, at the Georges V, Joe spent half an hour on the telephone complaining about the service, the drink, and, finally, the blasted Poule au Pot! And days later the millionair, a pleasant enough fellow really, called me to say that he found it impossible to 'get on' with Losey, but that I must not worry about it, because he knew that Losey was a genius. And <u>all</u> genius were rude or difficult!

Nevertheless: we lost five million smackers!

But of all times I suppose that I remember the Early Joe. The tall, exceptionally fine looking American in blue jeans and a jeans-shirt, which we had hardly seen in England at that time, standing about in a bar on some location, in cowboy boots and wearing a red handkerchief knotted at his throat. We had started 'The Sleeping Tiger'.

He was 'Victor Hanbury' then: and Tony and I had a hell of a job to get him alternative accomodation when, at The Ship in Shepperton, where he was staying, he was spotted by Ginger Rogers mother with a scream of horror! I got him smuggled, literally, into an hotel at Windsor. We got him two rooms, one they turned into a private sitting room for him at great effort. And when we proudly took him there, hidden in the back of my car under a rug (can you believe!) he complained bitterly about the noise.

The noise came from a gentle weir in the Thames some distance across the gardens. It was then, I suppose, that I knew I'd got a problem for a friend.

But a friend I had. And a friend, inspite of some pretty hefty hiccups here and there, he stayed. I know that he knew that I respected him: I think that he knew how deeply I loved him too, and that I knew most of his dirty tricks and still did'nt care. He was who he was; and either one left him strictly alone, or one stayed the course. Often hanging on by the eyelashes! I stayed.

Your support, your courage, your innate good manners and good sense, did such a lot to smooth over difficult patches in his life.

You certainly helped greatly to smooth ruffled feathers of pride or risen hackles of anger . . , as well you know.

Without you beside him, whatever the cost it often was for you, Joe could not have survived the onslaughts of fate .. many of which he brought down on his own arrogant head, as we both know. But you were there, thank God! and I know that he loved you, for he told me that often enough, and he was not a desperatly 'loving' man, really.

For myself I know that he enriched my life beyond measure.

He gave me the courage to extend myself in my work: he never told me what to do, but watched closely what I did and asked for more . . extending, demanding, fullfilling me as an actor, helping me to expand and to experiment. And the pleasure was intense: and rewarding; as were the letters which he wrote after each film .. noticing things which I had thought that perhaps he had not seen: but old Joe had seen all, nothing escaped him.

I remember, with constant joy, the day he showed me his Cartier watch from Liz Taylor and his enraged re action when I said that I liked him better in the days when he wore a 'tin one'[.] He knew just what I meant by the remark, and finally, ruefully, he removed the watch and put it into the pocket of that huge house-coat thing he used to wear. I know the watch went back on the moment I left the room! But the one thing I will always, always, remember him for was his blinding courage, his passion for the Cinema and good players and good Crew, and his burning determination to make magic on the screen.

That he did. He has at <u>least</u> four Great Movies to his credit.

They will last longer than any of us, and will be argued about and discussed, long after we have gone our way, and those Movies were made despite every known problem set in his way; health, money, Money Men and all the rest. He won out. Four Great Movies may seem a small sum for such a rich life: but they were Movies which altered the way all Movies were to be made in the future. I think thats a pretty wonderful record: and maybe four is too modest an assumption on my part . . . but it's enough to be going on with.

Clever sod! Shitty bugger! Goodness HOW I shall miss him.

Ever

   Dirk

To Julian Barnes   *Clermont*
                                                      7 July 1984

Julien –

I sat in stupefied awe: not so much at the staggering wealth of vegetable-provision your photograph displays but at the care and attention to the captions![1]

If you tell me that the arrow was bought, ready stick-able, I'll practically never speak to you again.

I have a vision (innacurate?) of you with rule and pencil and tongue hanging out, drawing, then cutting, and finally sticking this veritable work-of-art across the top left hand edge of your very own beetroots. (Alright if you like them: but desperately greedy and in need of 'swelling space' and prodigious amounts of water to glut them.)

It gave, as you will gather, the greatest pleasure.

I have a worrying feeling that perhaps, only perhaps, you have got everything packed a bit close. And 'close' means mildew and mould and aphids. But you know Dartmouth Park better than I do.

I can only speak from my local miseries and over-eagerness to have too much of everything.

Finally I did: and could'nt give away the produce. Lettuce I sold for a half-penny EACH! Before they flew up into spirals of seed.

The watering, the mulching, the manure (a very costly item here where we dont have many horses and fewer cows . . . so it's either pig

---

1. The gardeners were comparing notes; JB had sent a fastidiously annotated photograph of his *potager* in north London.

or goat droppings: both vile and over acid anyway) finally got me down and I chucked it all in after ten exhausting years. Where was once my potager, oh Lord? Where in deed. Indeed, I mean.

A mass of turbulant bramble and broom, ignored by all save the magpies and oriels.

I go now to the market and buy the lot. Cheaper and less tiring.

But dont stop! It is the most marvellous feeling, the first time, to be able to say, smugly, 'from our own garden'.

Then it pales.

I find, to my distress, that many of my London friends are quite certain that everything is grown and culled by my own peasant hand. But since (as) many of them cant tell a strawberry from a cabbage what the hell.

Our summer, such as it has been (it has almost rained since April) is now on the wane. We really count May to July as the Summer months, anything after that is a bonus and the sun is already moving across the terrace so that the shadows fall longer by the time one listens to the BBC World Service. (And a fat lot of good that does one) at 8pm. Most of the summer flowers are failing or over: the roses have puffed up, exploded in the heat, and gone: the pear trees are just beginning to grow yellow, and the wasps are about. And the Attenboroughs scream and squeal in their swimming pool far across, what once was, a peaceful olive grove. Ah well . . .

But thank you for the splendid 'boast-card' view. I am deeply, deeply impressed, and hope that the beans are good when eaten. Probably at their peak while you are chuntering about in wherever it is you are going to have your hol. But with a little butter, a touch of garlic, and a scatter of FRESH parsley they are, as they say, 'a meal by themselves' !

Ever <u>Dirk</u>.

To Norah Smallwood

Clermont
15 July 1984

Norah dearest –

Ten fifteen am and already the hills are hazed in heat and the terrace steps, which are not under the vine, too hot to walk on. NEVER end a sentence <u>withapreposition</u>. I know!

It's the sort of heat that you would not care for: I do not. I feel lethargic and flat, if that is not feeling the same thing, and unable to deal with much.

Although I confess that I have just done a 'large wash', as Lally would say, shirts, pants, underwear, and a pair of cotton slacks. V. difficult to wash I find: and not entirely clean yet. Inspite of my constant scrubbing at the concret sink in the wash-house.

Lady decided to be ill; so she has'nt been for three days or so, and the washing rises like a tide to smother one. Forwood is NOT frightfully good at blowing his nose on one handkerchief-for-a-week.

He blows it once. On a fresh handkerchief. I blanch. Which is more than the handkerchiefs do under my lavish care and the cake of Le Chat white soap.

Enough! They flutter away on the line in the brilliant sun, and if you do not look closely you would be convinced that a spell-binding washerman had been at work. But dont look too closely.

Frankly, it is about time we had a bit of summer. It has been foul almost since April .. and lowering cloud, humid and depressing, has settled over us up here leaving the plain and the far coast-line sparkling in sun.

It is vastly annoying. But, of course, good for the terrace pots, for they have been spared the full heat and flourish. Even the mildew has, in some miraculous way, been spared us. [...] We have still three terraces thigh-high in rank grass because, during May when they should have been cut, it rained ceaselessly and the land became a bog. Now in the intense heat the earth has dried and caked, and the grass is yellow and tangled like a mad-womans hair. Glenda wont mind .. I feel certain .. and there is nothing that we can do until cooler weather comes.

Glenda J. as I told you, arrives on Saturday for a 'crash-out' after a very exhausting run in her five-hour play.[1] So it'll be pleasant; because she wanders about by herself, makes her own coffee when she wants it, and gluts on whatever books she can lay her hands on. She says that for so many years, as a child, she was deprived of any kind of learning, and is now, at forty five, making up for it in a big way. She wanted to know if I had got the Ivy Compton B. book[2] ... and I said

---

1. Eugene O'Neill's *Strange Interlude* at the Duke of York's Theatre.
2. *Secrets of a Woman's Heart: The Later Life of I. Compton-Burnett 1920–1969* by Hilary Spurling (Hodder & Stoughton).

no. It is too big and I'm bored with Ivy Compton B. Glenda was v.
cross. But said she'd not bring it out because it WAS long and she'd
rather talk anyway. Oh dear! However the 'talk' is good [. . .]

I have just spoken to Elizabeth on the telephone, who is busy trying
to collect information for me about our father for the 'thing' I have to
write.[1] To our consternation Mamma destroyed years and years of
photographs and bits-and-pieces. We never realised that she had. The
desk in which was the 'Photograph Drawer' always appeared to look
intact. But it is apparently not. Nearly <u>everything</u> has been destroyed.
I cant think why she did this. Fortunatly my brother carted off a lot
of stuff from my fathers studio after he died. So there is something
left. But early photographs, letters from J.M. Barrie, from Pavlova,
from the Astors, from Munnings and [Augustus] John . . . and many
many others, have all gone. Even a collection of rather splendid
Brangwyn engravings, dedicated to Pa, have dissapeared. Oh woe!
And I have re-read this letter and it is a most disagreeable one! I AM
sorry! Deep in grumbles and protestations!

I think that Sundays have a particular gloom about them: especially
those which follow National Holidays. (Yesterday was the 14th).

We have been pestered by wandering women who clamber up the
hill in quite unsuitable shoes and demand that I sign copies of my
books.

As I am usually hidden up here, poor Forwood takes the brunt.

To suddenly open your eyes from under the shade of the lime-tree,
where you have taken your after-luncheon rest, and stare at a perfectly
strange woman, one yesterday was dressed in a see-through frock with
black underwear clearly on display, is a bit of a shock.

So we have wired up the gates, most inconvenient generally, and sit
here as if beseiged.

I had so much publicity during the Festival .. pages and pages ..
and also I have been on the Television, in French, speaking about my
work (!) and then, recently, about poor Losey .. that there is a sudden
rush, it is the Holiday Season, of Fans. It is as bad as it was all the
years ago when I was a young Film Star with five in Staff to protect
me! And now at sixty three it is the same. Odd.

I went through a huge file of letters yesterday from Dorothy

---

1. Dirk had been commissioned by *The Times* to write an article about Ulric for its
Bicentennial in 1985.

Gordon, (my Mrs X.) It was too hot to work, and so I idled through the years '67 to '69. I found it a strange, moving, business. There are hundreds of letters, and this file is only for part of '67 and half of '68.

I discovered, only yesterday, that she was a direct descendant of Daniel Webster .. which surprised me rather, for I did'nt remember that bit, nor do I remember what D. Webster did, or was! So I looked him up and he was a v.v. important Lawyer and was responsible, in 1842 for defining the border between Canada and the U.S. So there!

I still cant make out exactly WHAT Dorothy's nationality was. She writes with great dislike of the Americans ... and yet claims Webster as her kin, she was Dorothy Webster Gordon, but insists that she has a British-French passport which she renewd every ten years. Refusing to be a 'damned Yankee' ... but what was mostly interesting, apart from the rememberance of a faded love-affair, for that is what it seems, was finding the second chapter of 'Postillion' as written to her on the house letter-paper with virtually no alterations, and just as it stands today in the printed book. I cant, as yet, find Chapter 1. Chapter 2 is simply dated June '67. Which makes it almost exactly ten years before it got published, by sheer fluke! As you remember ...

[...] Patricia Losey has just called to say how happy she was with my 'tribute' to her husband on the TV. It seems to have pleased all kinds of people, those who were closest to him and those who knew him only as one of the great directors of the Cinema. It's frightfully hard to 'do' those interviews ... one speaks for two hours, knowing that only certain pieces will be used to fill, perhaps, a twenty minute piece. I had no idea how it would be used. But I gather it was very well 'edited', and moving, and truthful. So thats a relief. His family, all boys, at least have a video recording of it and me and their father. And I was asked to speak of him because, inspite of the thousands of people who knew him better than I did, I knew him first. And started him off, so to speak. His autobiography,[1] published last month, strangely, in France, is overwhelmingly generous to me. He has written things there, in this fat book, which he never wrote to me! Nor ever said! Nor ever <u>would</u> have said. One is made to feel humble and proud, all at the same time. An odd mix!

---

1. Losey did not write his memoirs, so Dirk probably refers here to *Le Livre de Losey* by Michel Ciment, originally published in Paris in 1979 then revised as *Conversations with Losey* for publication by Methuen – but in 1985.

I wish that you had met him. As one always wishes that the people one loves and respects should. He was so incredibly anti-Class, as he knew it in England, and yet so enjoyed its privileges! His taste in everything, from food to writing, to flowers and people, was impeccable. He read everything, and while he was dying he had poetry read to him day and night by his sons, and a friend whose voice he particularly loved. A man of paradox .. a man of generosity, meanness, cruelty, at times, and profound love.

How fortunate I was.

And what pleasure it would have been to have had you both here on the terrace, white wine in hand (essential to him!) and a 'sparkler' of a question placed, so that you could worry it, and argue it, and spin off into other regions. But alas! Not now .. but you would have enjoyed it!

And I must leave you with this ill-written piece of rubbish. A Sunday letter, thats all. But bringing with it, as you know, my deepest love and loudest appeals that you do NOT go wobbling about on your concret garden among the floribundas, or whatever! Please ..

Your devoted <u>Dirk</u> XOXOXO

To Norah Smallwood   *Clermont*
                                              1 August 1984

Dearest Norah –

It was very naughty of you to telephone last night. I get quite flustered when you do, thinking of all the pennies which are used up on me when Chatto¹ could do with a good belly-full instead. I hardly take anything in, so worried am I ... looking at a metaphorical egg-timer all the while.

Still: you called, and it was splendid to hear you, and to know that you had such a 'scrumptious' time [...] peaches and figs and so on.

Goodness me. There IS a special thing about an English (white) peach .. I dont know why. I who detest fruit in anything but a wine gum (?) do quite like them. We had a tree growing hard against the wall of the house near Hascombe. I fear that the early wasps, or some damned insect, got to them just before we did ... but none the less they were delicious.

---

1. The cat.

If you like peaches.

Here they are, presently, tumbled in great heaps in the market and you just eat them all day, it seems. Or perhaps they preserve them? Anyway, there is what is known as a glut ... and the white ones are super. French even so!

[...] I agreed, to my amazement, to judge (!) a competition for the Mail On Sunday ... along with Fay Weldon and Melvin Bragg and some one else I cant recall. The job, our job, was to consider a first paragraph of a novel written by a reader. One hundred words. Confidentially they expected about 250 entries: instead they got 5.500! And had to weed it all down to a mere 21. So we had to judge the 21. It is amazing, reading the stuff, how much people detest their partners! Almost every 'novel' started with Mark or Jenny (they were given those two names by the Mail to start them off: 'Write an opening paragraph of not more than 100 words about someone called "Mark" and "Jenny") and Mark and Jenny, my dear, killed each other off in almost every piece! Amazing social comment. And they were ALL married.

Not much joy among the lot: but a burning desire to express themselves.

The old adage, 'There is a novel in everyone' seems to be true.

I managed to award two only 9 and a 10 (out of ten marks) but it was tough going. What poor David Hughes (who invented this idea for his paper) had to go through reading over five thousand I cant imagine! Put him off writing for life I should'nt wonder ... and he's had such a whopping success with 'The Pork Butcher'.[1] I just wonder if he has sold anything much. The reviews were breathtaking. Even in 'Country Life'!

I got that out of the way and then had a stab at a portrait of my Pa.[2]

Difficult. It is almost impossible to write a simple story of 2.000 words about a hugely complex, and interesting, man.

I think it's alright. Forwood thought so .. but he's 'family' so might be biased .. and he even approved my punctuation. I took great care!

I asked The Times to send me some information on Pa: stuff that I did not perhaps know, for he was a silent fellow, very reticent.

---

1. Hughes's novel, published by Constable, was based on the massacre at Oradour-sur-Glane.
2. Published the following January as 'The Picture Man' in *The Times: Past Present Future*.

I was amazed at the things which he managed to 'invent'.

The First infra-red camera, the first underwater camera and film, the first lense to photograph movement, without fuzziness or blurring, in the theater thereby changing photography in the theater AND the cinema for all time all over the world!

His first subjects in this field were Thomas Beecham and Pavlova .. both of whome were amazed, and delighted, to see their 'action' in performance for the first time. He also was the first man to use colour photography in the paper, as early as 1931 ... and I'm afraid it all went over our heads as kids and we had no idea of his value.

Nor had The Times (today I mean) until they discovered that it was going to be 200 years old on Jan. 2nd and that my father was of such amazing importance to them.

There is one rather moving photograph which they sent me of Pa being presented with a cheque collected 'from all departments of The Times on his retirement. An amazing amount ..'

Of sixty five pounds!

Even allowing for the fact that in 1957, when he retired, this was worth much more than it is today, it still seems to me pretty wretched.

Mind you: he got an awful lot of ghastly silver junk .. ink-stands and huge cigar boxes and a chalice-thing and God knows what all ... this was all stolen from my sisters house two years ago, plus all Grandfathers good silver ... whacking big candelabras and plates and cutlery ... but the one thing the theives did'nt take was his most treasured possession.

A silver replica of a Tate And Lyle syrup tin. He always kept his pens and pencils on his desk in an old battered original. The Art Department gave it to him when he left. I have it safely here. And keep MY pens and pencils in the original!

What a very uninteresting letter Dirk!

It must be the heat. 88 in the shade and it is not yet noon.

I dont care for this kind of heat at all .. neither, I feel certain, would you. But the sky IS Vermeer blue. For that alone I revel.

I spoke to you, briefly, last evening about my new Pen Friend, Esmond Knight, NO relation to Jill Esmond, that I know of. He has been happily married all his life to the glorious Nora Swinburn[e].

He wrote because he had so enjoyed the three 'ortobios' .. at least Nora read to him, for he was blinded during the war in the Navy.

And STILL works in the theater. His next assignment, at the

Barbican, is a revival of 'The White Devils' ... he is seventy eight[1] ..
I think ... and I have encouraged him to write (he learned touch
typing at St Dunstans) his book. When everyone had given him up,
sightwise as they say, he saw, or Nora saw, in some French paper an
advertisement for an eye-doctor who could cure blindness. Unbeliev-
ing they wrote to him, made an appointment, went to his clinic (in
the marshes near Rye) he had an operation, and two injections of the
special potion the doctor had invented, and when the bandages were
removed from his eyes the first thing that he saw was Nora, by his
bed, holding towards him ... a dandelion. 'By God!' he said, 'Nora!
Thats a dandelion!' He saw, well enough, for the next thirty years. But
an undiagnosed glaucoma had started in his strongest eye, and he is
now totally blind.

But you would never know it! His courage, her courage, are monu-
mental .. and SO English-understated. He may not write anything: I
dont know. But I felt he had to be encouraged, and it will be wonderful
for him for, as a great player of Shakespear, he 'knows the words' ..
and uses them accordingly!

So I've told him that IF he gets anything down on paper I would
ask you to have a look. It would be such a push to him to know that.
Nora, his wife, is eighty two ... goodness, I hope that I have their
courage when I hit that part of time! End of paper ... and BORING
letter.

but never end of love from Dirk XXXXO

12.30 pm.
Wrote all the over-page stuff and went to have a relaxing little glass of
something before luncheon.

Walked to the post box and got your letter and the (one presumes)
cover for poor, miserable, 'VOICES'.[2]

I did'nt know I'd written a book about Mill Hill.

Or Kingston Hill, come to that.

At first I had to laugh, because 'weep I dare not' .. or whatever the
phrase is. But God Almighty!

Is that the best they can do at Triad?

---

1. Esmond Knight was indeed seventy-eight when he played in John Whiting's *The
Devils*, directed by Matthew Warchus, at the Barbican Pit.
2. The paperback edition.

Pinch my own 'idea' and send it reeling into Suburbia?

[. . .] No respectable person would be seen dead reading 'VOICES' on the Tube . . . and I would have grave doubts that any respectable person would buy it . . . it's as nasty as a Girlie Magazine. To be kept in secret in your Macintosh pocket.

Woe is me . . . 'What a fell day is this . .'

Alas! <u>D</u>

Norah Smallwood died on 11 October, leaving a list of friends who would be invited to choose an item from her Estate. When her executor, Dorothy Watson, telephoned Dirk and asked what he would like, he replied: 'I have the whisky glass she always used when she stayed with us in France and that is all the memento I need.'

Dirk was the prime mover behind the 'wrap party' in tribute to Joseph Losey which was held on 19 September at Twickenham Studios.

To Patricia Losey   *Clermont*
                                                    25 September 1984

Patricia –

Well: I'm just about thawed out now. Coming back from a week in London is strangely exhausting, I dont know why.

Probably Heathrow, which never fails to work it's ghastly horror on one, has a lot to do with it!

I think we did alright on Wednesday . . . as you so generously suggested yesterday on the telephone.

It was a happy event, rather than a miserable one, and the feeling of warmth and affection among us all was really contagious . . if that is how you spell it? I think that there is an 'i' missing somewhere, but what the hell.

What made it so particularly good, that evening, was not so much that so many had made the trip, but that there were so many <u>young</u> people there, as well as those of my age: who were young . . . once upon a time.

I thought that was very good. I was particularly touched that the Baker-Boys were there: not that I was ever, what you might call, devoted to Stanley . . . but he was okay: nicer than his wife anyway. But the boys were splendid.

Your own son is'nt that bad, is he?[1] Clever old you .. and the Losey Lot will do very well.

Whatever we all felt, thought, or sensed, happiness rather than gloom was the order of the evening and I am certain that Joe would have almost approved. I say 'almost' because it's as near as I can get to being accurate.

We were all there because we had loved him, admired him, been nourished (theatrically speaking) by him. And everyone spoke of him with such terrifically warm pleasure that he HAD to be a decent bloke underneath all the humph and huff and blowing.

That I loved him, and that you loved him, goes without saying but it was a particularly glowing feeling of delight that I got from all those very different people who had come, many of them, from so far.

No weary Knight bleating from a pulpit: no quotes from John Donne, no singing of 'The Lord Is My Shepherd' . . . none of the crap. Just an end-of-picture-party for a most particular man.

Thats what it was, and how it should have been.

Splendid Miss Bacon,[2] and Theo[3] and all the others who worked so hard must have been well rewarded, I'd think, by the extreme pleasure that work gave to so many.

And they would'nt have done all that without having loved the chap as we did.

So there we are, dearest Patricia. A chapter closed. But not firmly. The memories are evergreen and cant fade, and love, the love which was engendered that evening, must have reached him; wherever he is.

With all my admiration – & love –

<u>Dirk</u>

In October, Hélène Bordes, Maître de Conférences in the Faculty of Letters at Limoges University, had written to Dirk, seeking his approval for a paper she was preparing on his first three volumes of memoirs. Dirk felt it would have no interest for her students, because his books were not published in France – 'they are considered "too local" in appeal!' – and his dialogue did not translate well. He did not wish to be involved in any way with her project but thanked her for the compliment and wished her

---

1. Ghigo Tolusso, PL's son by her previous husband.
2. Victoria Bacon, Losey's last secretary.
3. Theo Cowan, for many years the trusted press agent to both Dirk and Losey.

good luck. A few weeks later she sent him an outline of ' "Peuple" et "Pays" dans l'*Autobiography* de Dirk Bogarde'.

To Hélène Bordes

[Clermont]
Grasse 06
16 December 1984

Chere[1] Mme Bordes –

Thank you so much for your warm and encouraging letter of the 8th December.

I must confess, with my hand on my heart, that I was not able to understand all of it: and I really dont know quite what you are doing with my 'works'.

I cant believe that they are of any importance to a University.

But I am most honoured that you have chosen to use me as your example!

You are sad that you have no bibliography .. well: there is'nt much to offer you. It could never be as complex and important as my filmography ... I have been asked to write for 'The Guardian', 'The Observer' and the London 'Times'. And I have done so: they were not very important pieces, but they were published and proved to me that writing books is easier than journalism!

Various magazines have commissioned me to write, and usually I refuse because they take time from my 'serious' writing. But recently, for example, I was commissioned to write a 'life' of my father who was Art Editor of 'The Times' which celebrates it's 200th Anniversary in January. They have suddenly, almost too late, discovered that Papa was very important to news-papers and made many inventions which are in use today. So the son applauds the father. I found it amusing to do!

My poetry has been published in various literary magazines, and one which I had the temerity to include in 'Snakes And Ladders', 'Steel Cathedrals', has gone into a third anthology of War Poetry!

'Postillion' is now in it's seventeenth edition and the first part of it is now compulsary at the State Schools for Study! <u>Poor children</u>. What

---

1. The lack of clarity in Dirk's handwritten address to HB indicated that he was unsure whether she should be 'Cher' or 'Chere'; it is standardised here as the latter. The accent on the correct form, *Chère*, would always be a mystery to him.

has interested me, and made me happy, is that my writing is now accepted, in England at least, as 'pure prose'. And that is the most important thing to me.

Sadly my writing, the irony, the wit, etcetera, does not translate well into French. We HAVE very different languages indeed, with different meanings altogether. 'Postillion' (in French) was awful! A reve d'enfance or d'enfance reve or something silly.[1] And I think that 'Des Voix Dans Le Jardin' was the nearest good translation ... but it puzzled many of my French readers. The autobiographies, alas, are not translated.

In Greece, South America, America, Finland, Sweden, etc, yes.

But not France. Ah well .. the sixth volume, of romantic-writing, is due to come out, as we say, in France next year. I fear for the translation greatly! It is nearly all dialogue and set in West Los Angeles which is as different to Paris or Limoges as Mars! So what happens I do not know .. in America they hated it! In England it was on the Best Seller lists for weeks and weeks .. but Americans do not like criticism!

Anyway: good luck to you ... and thank you for your courtesy and care.

I hope my work has made YOUR work worth all the trouble you have taken.

A Student at Nice University has just written a thesis on my writings so maybe I am not <u>completely</u> crazy after all! I hope that he is not!

With all good wishes, and thanks,
    Sincerely,
        <u>Dirk Bogarde</u>.

To Kathleen Tynan   *Clermont*
                                              29 December 1984

Kathleen dearest –

[...] I am writing because I nearly did a terrible thing.

Burning a vast box of stuff from the Studio here, old Christmas Cards, gift-wrappings from Ohouah, Queensland, and sundry bits of muck .. including an enormous quantity of cigarette packets (smoked) I NEARLY lost your letter of December 14th.

---

1. *Une Enfance rêvée.*

How it got there I do not know. It wafted away into the long grass just as the flames were about to lick it's tender edges. And I saved it.

So it seems only right that I should apologise personally for being so crass as to allow a letter of yours to mingle with the Fan-Junk from Queensland, and Oregon, and West Cricklewood.

It was jolly nice to have your letter anyway: so many chums seem to have sold up, divorced, left for Bermuda or whatever, that a familiar hand is deeply welcome on a lonely Christmas Eve; when you arrived.

Actually: hand on heart, it was'nt THAT lonely a Christmas.

I lie.

Naturally.

We had a pair of elegant escapees[1] from New York and Jingle Bells who insisted that there should be no reminders of the dreadful day. And there were none. Brilliant sun, cold, ice on the pond, champagne in the flutes, chairs on the terrace, heavy sweaters and someone reading Emerson. Aloud.

So we did sort of obliterate Christmas. Not hard to do on six bottles of Cristal!

She, the lady of the pair, is the highest paid scriptwriter in L.A and manages to remain sane, a lady (in capital letters) and live in Connecticut. He is far too handsome for the Movies of today, struggles hard against 'The Gremlins' or Al Pacino, has given in finally and settled down in Connecticut with the Lady Scriptwriter. All of twenty years his senior, but who the hell's counting if happiness is all?

Anyway, they were fun, and the fearful day faded into a haze of good grub and wine .. we went for a long walk in the mountains along a real Roman road (They dont have them in Connecticut) and crawled in and out of a real neolithic grain store (2.000–4.000 BC. They dont have those in Connecticut either I gather) and came home to tea here with the Lartigues, Jacques is 92 and young with it.

And that was that. Forwood managed the two days very well indeed. His first real 'throwing to the lions' bit for a while. And survived it extremely well. But as long as the guests are'nt bores it's pretty easy, and he forgets that he has'nt read his Guardian.

A little before the Festivities M. Umbrella[2] came down and had a happy day with me here, which was GREATLY releiving and

---

1. Diana Hammond and companion.
2. Anton Troxler, also known for fiscal reasons – and with affection – as 'Elsewhere'.

comforting, so the rest of the crap did'nt really count. I can eat for a year or two at least. Which, you will admit, is useful to know. The only snag is that I have to work. And I'm fast getting out of the habit. I'm as bankable as Atomic Waste in the Movies, but the book-field is okay. So I have to take the hard road. Since I am a novice, and my beloved Norah Smallwood died in October so that my guide and councillor is no more there to batter me, I feel, I confess, rather lost and not a little cold.

I batter away at a new novel ... the autobiography bored me SHITLESS. So I turned that aside, after four regurgitated chapters, and bashed into society (with a capital S) in Sussex. I mean, a family of such vast proportions that I keep having to read and re-read the stuff to remind myself who was who and what colour they had their hair ... it's not EXACTLY Proust. But as far as words and characters are concerned it rings bells! Oh Lor' ...

I was asked to be a soulful monk opposite Robert de N. in some fillum to be made in Brazil.[1] But it sounds to me a real 'toughie', and I'm not into flying about in single engined planes from Colombia to Peru and back. Especially just at this moment 'in time'. So that was set aside. Also it meant fifteen weeks in the jungle, or whatever, and at my age I really prefer a glass tank of wax lilies on a grand piano: and one set.

A far more relaxing way of spending an evening was with Princess Alx. who came down here to celebrate the 150th year of Lord Brough[a]m finding Cannes. I rather think he'd have been better off not doing such a rash thing: however the Consul ordered me to attend a private supper party in the Royal suite and it really was fun, mainly because we were only twelve at table and she is devine, as always. I almost gave her a socking fat kiss when we parted, and she was about to do the same, when protocol slipped between us, thankfully. There is, after all, a limit!

I drove home in a haze of pleasure and a torrential rain storm which had washed away a good deal of the road. Forwood was a little worried sitting on his tod with the roof leaking and the thunder roaring and me lost, so it appeared, for some hours. But I got back, leaving my

---

1. David Puttnam and Sandy Lieberson had asked Dirk if he would co-star with de Niro in Roland Joffé's *The Mission*, with a script by Robert Bolt, to be shot on location in South America. The part, rewritten for a younger actor, was eventually played by Jeremy Irons.

shoes somewhere between Cagnes sur Mer and Le Rouret. It was that kind of storm.

Then there was an enormous hommage to Visconti in Nice one night, and we all got given gold leopards for some reason.[1] But it was fun .. even though I had to make my speech in Frog which always worries me.

So, you see, we manage [. . .]

Off to London for a week or so (if I can buy the Connaught) at the end of Feb. I to do a big TV Show, Forwood to have his check. The Connaught is now so costly (unless your money is in dollars) that I cant swing it longer than a week .. the TV pay for one week, which is'nt bad ... but it adds up to 2.000 quid a week WITHOUT breakfast: but I cant face service flats and hate the Dorchester and why ever not anyway?

I'm getting choked off splitting logs and laying tables and de-freezing some disgusting packet of Cantonese Rice or whatever. So a bit of a spoil is in order.

This then, to wish you happiness and success in this worrying New Year, and to bring you great love from here. Forwood is trailing about down on the lower terraces with his grass machine, otherwise he'd stick his name to this as well as mine .... but, no doubt he'll write you one day!

All love, all safety, and good work . . .

Ever Dirk XXX

P.S. Saw a creepy-sad TV programme here, Hommage to Deitrich. She would not appear (naturally) but spoke by telephone. It was deeply sad and almost exactly as you describe her to be. Petulant, flirty, and a bit pissed. Oh shit .... D

P.P.S. Telephone call from Glenda J. to say she arrives Tuesday. For a week. Back to splitting logs and Cantonese Rice. Double Shit! D

To Hélène Bordes

Clermont
14 February 1985

Dear Madame Bordes

Lord! You say this often enough, so I might as well use it also! I am

---

1. A reference to Visconti's *The Leopard.*

overwhelmed by the amount of work you have had to do, and the great generosity of spirit towards my humble efforts which you show.

I really only wrote the autobiographies because the first one was a success and people, it appeared, wanted me to write more.

So I did!

But I had no idea that I would end up being so beautifully dissected by such <u>careing</u> hands in the University of Lovely Limoges.

If I say 'Thank you' you must forgive me. I have always been told, by Lally! that to say 'Thank you' was 'good manners' and, anyway, the least that one could do. I cant do more because I am far too stupid to understand ALL your writing, and, as I have said, overwhelmed by your interest.

That my works, such as they are, should have given you interest enough to spend so much effort and time, amazes and delights me. It almost manages to explain my own book to myself! How about that? I wrote, as I always write, 'off the cuff' without very much literary pretensions, as you will know .. and I was, at first, worried that writing at all about oneself was a very concieted thing to do. The pronoun 'I' has not been my favourite one.

However Norah Smallwood, my original, glorious, publisher, made me realise that I had, after all, led an extra-ordinary life, as opposed to a quite ordinary one, and that, historically, one day, my comments on the period in which I had lived might be of some value to a researching writer.

We neither of us expected success: just a well done job.

However she lived to see that we had worked together and had made a success of the job at the same time. This pleased her more, I believe, than almost anything she had done in her publishing life ... and it was a remarkable one, with her 'personal' writers such as Iris Murdoch, Lawrens van der Post, Huxley, V.S. Prichart and .. shall I tell you this? PROUST himself! She was the one who got him properly translated into English twice. Thank God, and Norah!

So you see I was in good hands: her pushing paid off, even more than the inspiration and bullying offered me by Mrs X. Alas! both are now dead and I am left with an immense hole in my capabilities, afraid to try anything without their criticism.

Your generosity has done a great deal to throw, as we say, a bridge over that hole of despair. So 'Thank you' is really NOT enough!

Your splendid package arrived only an hour or so ago, so I have not had the time to digest it carefully. I shall do so this evening when the house is still and the chores are done, and then I will write to you again.

One tiny item: 'Derek' is the English for 'Dirk' ... which is Dutch, and which I greatly prefer, although my Mama wanted me to be 'Derek' because it was, she insisted, a French name! Perhaps it was in 1921? I dont know, but I dislike it .. and the other thing, <u>for your eyes only</u>, is that it is quite impossible to obtain a copy of 'Postillion' in French because the lady who published this in Paris was furious with me because I would (COULD) not go on 'Apastrophe'[1] ... so she said that she would send all the unsold books back to me here at Clermont in a truck: or burn them.

Well: they did'nt arrive here, So .... no one can find a copy in French

That, I think, is madness!

Our Simone [Signoret] ... OF COURSE we share her. I love her deeply, and respect her for all her wild, marvel ous, determined ideals ... as well as for her determination to write. We started to write a book for the first time on the same day!

'How far have you got?' she would ask me.

'About fifty pages.' I would reply.

'Pooh! Bof! Me? I have seventy two ...'

It was fun, and we both 'worked'.

[...] The young student from Nice sent me his thesis yesterday.

Okay. An interview, not a thesis at all .. questions and answers, and dull ones at that. Sometime I will be asked an original question and then I will not be able to answer it!

I am so weary when people say that actors cant write. Or should NOT write. Some of us, of course, are idiots. I know that. But many of us are not. If we understand Shakespear, Pinter, Molier, Racine, Webster, Mann, and so on, it does not mean that we may write like them but it DOES mean that we can interpret what they mean, which is more than a critic can, and it would follow that with a deep love, and understanding, of words, one might be able to write a little more than an autograph! Ah well ... This is all for the moment, apart, that is, from the phrase which you so dislike .. 'Thank you'.

---

1. *Apostrophes*, the hugely influential books programme presented on Antenne 2 by Bernard Pivot.

And my most sincere admiration ...
    Dirk Bogarde
       à bientôt

To Hélène Bordes   *Clermont*
                                          19 February 1985

Chere HB –

Before I leave for London and all the things which I must face there, a note (on the terrible typing paper!) to say simply: Yes. Despair was the word I meant and so was bridge.

I thank you for helping me to cross a little easier.

I write like an idiot: re-write and re-write, page after page, so that sometimes I type one page, or even one paragraph, eight, ten, twenty times. And still I am not satisfied. Do you know that feeling?

I am certain that you do.

So that it is crossing a deep pit of despair, dark and hopeless, so that one KNOWS one will never get 'it right' ... and that the way across the pit is dangerous because if one falls, from tiredness or from a lack of criticism and council, or even comfort, one could fall for ever. One HAS to get to the other side of the pit: and your letters and your thesis have provided me with the plank and the rail to go ahead. Simple!

When I say 'only an Honoury degree'[1] you must realise that what I mean is that I have not worked for it: like the teachers and students who really have! I have been given it as an honour, that is to say, for all my works ... but not because I REALLY studied and sweated at my exams and my lectures! Do you understand that? I feel very humble.

But no more! I shall look very strange in my cap and gown, and the journalists, be sure! will laugh a good deal. But I really dont care.

I AM writing now, another part of autobiography, and today I realised that I have written almost the entire story of the fall of Singapore in 1942 ... and it has been written about 6.000 times by far wiser men and it has almost NOTHING to do with my autobiography! How mad one can become. It will all have to go ...

---

1. Dirk had told HB only that he was to be honoured by 'the third oldest university in G.B.'.

or almost all .. for I only got to Singapore AFTER the events about which I have the audacity to write!

So: three days of wasted work. Idiot.

That is why I say that I am stupid! You see ...

'West Of Sunset' is now in livre de poche[1] .. and is this week No.3 on the Best Seller lists ... Norah S. would have been pleased: she saw every word of the book, it was our last together, and although she said that she did not 'really care for the ugly people' she thought it was 'werry, werry, good.' She could never pronounce her 'v's ... but it was high praise indeed!

And now to pack some clothes and get the house ready for my two guardians, young with a baby, who come here and look after the place and feed the dog.

I hope that the baby leaves SOME of the china intact!

I try to remove all that she could reach with her horrible little hands ... but sometimes I'll go and forget something in my hurry.

Ah well ... à bientôt
    DB.

P.S. Wednesday 20th. The Press in England have, just this morning, put out a Press-Report that I am to be awarded an Hon.Dr.Litt. in July. By St Andrew's (Scotland) University.

So now I am free to tell you: and you are the first person I have told! So. A 'Mercie' for everything. C'est pas de tout mal, je crois?
    DB

To Elizabeth Goodings

Clermont
7 March 1985

Dearest LuLu –

Your sweet card with the pensive lady leaning on a telescope with a sailor, is here before me.

It arrived, as you must have seen, at the Connaught eventually .. and now is here on my desk to remind me just how long ago all that week seems!

A long week for me: somehow it was one of stress and worry rather more than worse ones have been: I think that Tote was in a very

---

1. In the UK, of course.

miserable state: he <u>hates</u> that suite because it reminds him of wretched times; so the next time I'll have to change around a bit .. and for some reason he was depressed, and terribly tired all the time.

Stress, of course. And waiting for the results of blood-tests and all the other damned things. Also the fact that he is slowing up distresses him terribly, and of course he is slowing up. I cant pretend, much as I would like to, that he is not. So all in all it was not the most cheerful of weeks even though the final results were satisfactory, and the Parkinson Type of problem has not, they assure him, progressed much since the last visit, if at all.

However: slow he is. And constipated! And it was a drag of a time.

We eventually got back home in fairly good form. He was quite calm about the trip and I managed to carry both bags leaving him only the briefcase and a light packet which had two frocks for the Isoardi child.

I even got a trolley! So that we had no great problem with luggage and he seemed to cheer up very much as soon as we were crossing the Alps and is now, three days later, a different person! He is relaxed, happy, hopping about the kitchen and cooking things. I'm afraid that he so loves this house that nothing else will ever be able to take it's place.

We had a worry, the first day we got back, with a letter from our Tax People here, with the wrong this-and-that. Nothing that couldn't be dealt with eventually, but he was instantly in a fidget and fuss, and got the 'shakes' and so on.

It cleared up the next morning: but it's a hell of a haul really.

I hate it for him because he was always the one who shielded me from the problems of daily life so that I could just get on and do my job .. and now it is me who must do it for him: and I sometimes feel that I'm not terribly good at it! I get so impatient, which, of course, I must not be, thats the very <u>worst</u> thing. But watching him try to put three pears into a plastic bag at Timy's is pretty difficult. I have suggested now that he puts them in one at a time. Which he says he'll try next time he has to buy fruit ... he was trying, as he said, not to be so slow ... but of course was much slower!

However now that we are home he is happy, and has slept well, and gone to the lav easily and is less shakey ... which is strange. We had some other problem, the sort which normally sends him off like a jelly, but for some reason he was perfectly calm and easy, and not a shake in sight.

So I think that home is where we have to stay.

Bendo greeted us with two eyes like enormous blood-oranges!

Just before we left for London I threw his sodding ball into the bramble thicket by error ... it bounced off a tree ... and he tore in to search for it. I heard a sharp squeal of pain, but thought nothing of it really. In the evening his eye was bloodshot ... the day we left it was swollen, I bathed it, left Optrex and stuff for Marie-Christine ... and came to London. But the eye was infected.

So.

The day after we got back off to the Vet. and we waited (we had no sort of appointment) in a room with a crowd of grumpy ladies with cats and little dogs. Anyway we finally got in and it is discovered that he has scratched the eyeball badly with the thorns of a bramble ... SO. Eye baths, six times a day, drops, four times a day, anti-biotic pills three times. I'm getting to be a walking Vet. But the eye is better, and the other eye, which was infected, has almost completely cleared up.

We got back, as I told you on the telephone, to brilliant skies and a hot sun, all the daffodils out down by the pond and the grass a mass of violets and anenomies.

Next day it started to rain and has poured ever since! And it's cold!

So there is no way that I can get to work in the garden, which is now a wreck after the snow and ice and desperatly needs some work done.

But I really DO feel too ancient to cope just at present. So I'll wait the rain out and then have a shot. Slowly!

All the shutters will have to be repainted, the drive has got to be relaid, the oranges and other dead trees cut down and carted away ... and when am I going to have time to get down to my OWN work? Writing is simply impossible just at present, so I'm breaking myself into the routine again by letter writing ... hence this to you.

[... W]e none of us know what is going to happen to us over the years, do we? So it's no good trying to look ahead, everything is mystery, with a big capital M!

[...] I dont suppose that we'll be over before July ... for my St Andrews caper. I hope not anyway ... and I'm not very sure that Tote will come all that way up. He says he will, and wants to ... but we'll see. He managed very well at the TV thing the other night, and I really did'nt think that he would even make it to the Studios. So. We'll see.

Meanwhile I'd better go and feed Bendo, seal this, and split the logs, it's a nasty, raw, evening . . . .

but this comes, as usual, with all my love. Dirk –

To Kathleen Tynan

Clermont
Sunday April 28th. '85.

Kathleen –

[. . .] Devestation was the word for what we all suffered here[1] . . . I am only surprised that T. Richardson[2] was hit. I thought he was all pine and whatnot? Here we lost all the orange and lemons, the olives are leafless and all the palms are dead.

Along the Croisette they look rather like poles: at the airport, Welcome To The Cote d'Azure, they look like old feather dusters . . and are rust red.

That fills you in alright. Yes: Pinter is a different fellow I fear. He and I 'hosted' a party-cum-memorial-Service on a sound stage at Twickenham Studios for Losey last year, and he was very cool, and rather like a lama with disdain. She[3] frightned the shit out of me, an agressivly faux-charming Lady. 'I do SO love your books . . .' Shit! What do you say? 'Thank you, so kind.'

I remember Harold in the days of yore. Timid, because I had questioned him about Lobster Thermidor which continually arrived in the Script of 'The Servant'. I was bewildered, and in awe of the Intellectual Writer. So I picked my way with care.

'Why is it that every rich person in the film only ever eats a Lobster Thermidor?' I asked bravely.

There was a stricken silence from the assembled Cast, Losey and Harold. Who pushed his glasses up his nose, so to speak, and then said in a shaking voice, 'What OTHER meal do the Rich People eat, then?'

---

1. In recent storms.
2. Tony Richardson, director and former husband of Vanessa Redgrave; he had a house in the hills behind St Tropez.
3. Lady Antonia Fraser.

And he did'nt actually know. He and Vivien [Merchant] had been taken to dine by the Oliviers (or someone) and they had been given L. Thermidor. So that is what he imagined all the rich ate.

We substituted the meal for others in the final Script.

But that is who Harold <u>was</u>: once upon a time. And nice with it.

But of course, we all change. And today he must be very, very happy and proud because he has recieved tremendous notices for the new revival of 'Old Times' in London, with Liv Ullman playing, and has been accepted, at last, as The Great British Dramatist. Well: I think that he is. So thats alright. But I do wish that I had'nt lost him so completely!

But news from here? Well: we continue. Went to London for the six-monthly checkup, which was satisfactory [...] London rather haggered and sad, like the elderly women one sees sitting sadly on the benches in the late sun on the Promenade des Anglais. Retired Governesses .. widow ladies .. ageing Gamblers .. There was no one there, in Town, that one cared to see, frankly. Family: thats really all. And to Hatchards for books and Trumpers for haircuts .. and oysters and scallops in white wine and rather too much Moet. Glad to get home; I'm off to St Andrews University in July to receive my Hon. D. Lettres!

Mortar board, gown and hood. All very frightening! I graduate with Manny Shinwell![1] Who is 101. And have to make the acceptance speech for the rest of them. I quake with terror. But have found a splendid Speech written by Colette (!) on her being made a Member of the Belgian Academy[2] .. so I'm paraphrasing that. Cheat.

Forwood will have his checkup at the same time, but I dont think he'll make the trip to St Andrews ... it's a bit too far and he gets rather restless in crowds. A chunk of plastic intestine is a real bore. One wonders how the Pope Copes? He's got YARDS of it. Must be on a liquid diet.

I have sold the film rights to my first novel; Edwige Feuillere is doing 'Cuckoo' in a radio adaptation (in eight parts) of 'Voices In The Garden' for France-Culture, and someone is taking an option on 'West of Sunset' which has done, thank God! extremely well ... and is third

---

1. Lord (Emanuel) Shinwell, pugnacious Labour politician.
2. Colette was elected to Belgium's Académie Royale de Langue et de Littérature Française, as its 'foreign literary member', on 9 March 1935.

on the Best Seller List in the Good Book Guide ... Bruckner first
with 'Hotel du Lac' and that ubiquitious Umberto Whatever with his
Rose Book next,¹ then me. I am constantly amazed.

I have written two thirds of a new novel 'Closing Ranks' and
chucked it! <u>There</u> is a brave gesture! It wont work ... and rather than
flog along on a no-go I've let it slide. I DO think I'm brave!

So now it's a bash at the 4th Vol of 'bio (which sell) .. and although
one might think that there is no mileage left, there is. I think –

I'm thinking of calling it 'REGURGITATION'. But, of course,
will try for something better. If possible.

Forwood is still working on HIS EPIC (Longer than War and
Peace by the sound of it, and far more people too) so one way and
another we are 'occupied'.

The Festival starts next week ... I'm avoiding everything this year
like the plague but will go down to see Losey's final film, which he
had cut and mounted just before he died. It's 'Steaming' .. and Nell
Dunn wrote it from her funny play. I gather it is fine. But Joe and a
comedy are difficult to put together. It is not in Competition, but just
there as an Hommage to the man. All the Top Lot Intellectuals from
Paris descend: I take Patricia. It's at four in the afternoon so it'll be
informal, and jeans; rather than dinner jacket.

[...] Sunday today. The Attenboroughs are down for three long
weeks, he to run his British Film Nonsense at the Damned Festival,
having now cut and edited 'A Chorous Line' ... I've run out of spelling
today.

And I'm pretty short on typing too: sorry.

So. Reverting to Sunday, I'd better go and get some glasses out, for
they will be over for lunch in ten minutes, and I've garliced the lamb
[...]

Is Boaty still alive? I know that she's an Agent: but that does'nt
prove anything, does it?

With devoted love
    <u>Dirk</u>

---

1. Anita Brookner and Umberto *(The Name of the Rose)* Eco.

To Hélène Bordes   *Clermont*
                                                   8 June 1985

Chere Mme La Planche – or? <u>de</u> La Planche?

How hard we writers have to work!

Thank you so very much for the final 'proof' copies, and all your minute corrections!

I am just the same as you. I 'fiddle' and change things about all the time in 'proof', and drive the publishers completely insane.

But ever since I was warned that 'words are not made of India rubber, you know!' I have tried to prove that they <u>are</u>! By fitting letters into spaces and finding new words for old. [The proof] looks <u>extremely</u> professional and important: I feel my head grow larger as I read, and it gives me great pleasure: as you know.

<u>Not</u> that my head is growing larger; but what I read of my modest works.

I was delighted to see again [a photograph of] the pont St Etienne ... how often I used to admire it as I drove south to the country for lunch on Sundays[1] .. to eat delicious food, to gather walnuts, to walk beside a glorious lake whose name I no longer remember. All I DO remember is my love for the Perigord, my intense dislike of the British who seemed to live in every hole and cave, and my distress in Oradour ... to which I went very often· I wonder why I did?

I remember one disgusting English journalist (a woman too) saying with great pride one day 'Oh, we've QUITE taken over the village now, all the French have gone except for the woman who runs the grocers shop. Never hear a word but English: <u>such</u> a comfort.' I hated her deeply.

In Oradour, which I discovered by accident walking in the country near my little hotel while I was working with Resnais, I remember a fair May evening, with a light shower of rain falling, which drenched the lilac bushes in the Doctors garden and filled the still air with a glorious, sad, scent, and made the tram-car lines glisten in the cobbles of the street. No one was there but myself and ... a nightingale! Of such memories are autobiographies born.

[...] Of course you must join the 'voices of the two other needle women', <u>they</u> gave me encouragment, and so do you. Thus you qualify

---

1. During the filming of *Providence*.

Madame La PlanchE! With a big 'E' .. my typing is getting worse
because the mistral blows and I hate it very much .. it disturbs me
and confuses me and irritates me because it is ripping the branches
from the lime-trees and tearing my glorious vine, which has struggled
so hard to be good after the winter. The olives, Thank God! are
recovering .. not all, but most.

The ones in the valley caught it worst; on the top of the hill
here they are NEARLY like they were last year. I am so grateful.
A summer with an orchard of 400 brown olive trees would be
dreadfully miserable.

Your flowers which perished are just as important to you as my
vine and my olives ... so of course you must grieve for them. And
grieve too at the appalling cost of replacing them! I refuse to pay
five francs fifty for a small root of Impatiens! I really do. So the
bed this year is barren .. I am far too mean I suppose. But five
francs fifty for a tiny plant, which will be burned by the mistral
anyway, is too much.

[...] I dread already the advent of St Andrews, and all the bowing
and the kneeling and things which I must do in my cap and gown. I
am certain that I shall forget the 'dance' ... it is so confusing and
complicated and dates back to the fifteenth centuny ... so I MUST
get it right!

A few months ago when they told me I would be so honoured I
thought that it would be fun.

But now that it is really near my heart leaps with panic like a
frightened faun: it is SUCH a long way to go, and to be among
people again and on trains and airplanes ... I am really so rooted
here .. I hate the wrench of leaving. Even to get such a glittering
prize!

I am about to start Chapter eight. If I can find the way to do
so!

Starting is terribly hard I find .. so is stopping: but the exact line
to open a new chapter and catch the readers attention is a brute to get
absolutely right. I sit in a haze stareing into space and look as if I were
in hibernation.

I often wish that I were. Sometimes, when I have read over some
of the other chapters, I loose heart dreadfully ... it is all rubbish,
lacking in style, wit or elegance .. and then, another time, I'll read it
and sit here with a face as smug as a crapeaud! Pleased as pleased .. is

there an 'e' at the end of crapeaud or is there even a 'd'? Heavens! The man has lived in France for nearly twenty years and cant spell 'toad'! But the bakers wife this morning complimented me on my perfect accent.

She was FAR too wise to compliment me on my perfect French!

But I gained courage and sailed down the street to the alimentation with high held head. Madame Roux said I spoke well. So .. what had I to fear? However: it is still difficult to start a Chapter.

I get a lot of letters from English people who have come to live in France from choice, but who find the French difficult to live with.

They ask me how I have managed! I write back, in anger very often, and remind them that they must abandon their Englishness if they are to live here, they have not moved into an empty room! They have moved to a country which was far more civilised before them .. and I remind them that they would still be ambling about in woad and fur if they had not been invaded by William! I equally remind them to remember that France was Occupied, and how dreadful a blow that was to the soul of the country. If they dont know what Occupation means (and they dont) then at least they should try to understand what it meant to their neighbours and feel compassion for the pain and the distress that it caused. Sometimes people write back: and apologise for their stupidity, and say they will look at 'things French' with a different eye from now on.

I may yet get the Leigeon d'Honneur!

At least I do my best to bring the two, very different, countries together. The main trouble with the English is that they have never bothered to learn ANYONE'S language! They always considered that their own was enough all over the world. Well: perhaps in the days of the Empire it was. But there is no longer an Empire .. so it is about time they tried to speak something else! It is, I know, shyness to a great extent .. and they have an in-built certainty that the French detest them.

Maybe they do: I confess I have never found it, except perhaps in Paris; but in Paris the French even hate each other! So it is not a good example. But otherwise I have found kindness and generosity of the spirit, and the fact that one even TRIES to speak the language, however badly, is appreciated greatly. It is a compliment after all to speak the language in the country which you have chosen for your 'own'.

I must leave you. This is an inept, badly typed, badly spelled, letter .. but it is nevertheless sent to you with gratitude and affection.

So make of it what you can, and then tear it up!

A bientôt – <u>DB</u>.

To Paddie Collyer[1]   *Grasse*

                                              19 June 1985

Dear Miss Collyer –

Thank you for your letter of the 8th.

I am sorry that I have not been able to assist you more with your 'problems' over 'VICTIM'.

It was all such a long time ago and so many other films have come between.

Mr Relph[2] (who was not absolutely happy about the subject, especially with the 'final scene', which worried him!) may be able to assist you much more.

In 1961 it was impossible to go 'a lot further', as you suggest!

It was difficult enough to make the film at all: the lawyers who had to read it for libel declared that there was no problem but that they wished that they could wash their mouths out: they found it so distasteful!

So think on that!

It is all recorded, anyway, in my book 'Snakes And Ladders'.

As far as I am aware a great many homosexuals 'resist their instincts', it is not at all unusual, but what you call a 'practicing' type would have been quite unpalatable then as, indeed, he would be now to Family Audiences.

You must remember that the film, in 1961, was made for Commercial Cinema .. it was the first tiny break-through towards films of a more important nature. For that Rank must be thanked. They had the courage to give it a release, even if it was restricted.[3]

---

1. PC was working on an MA thesis, and sought Dirk's help for information about Allied Film Makers, producers of *Victim*. He had replied, telling her as much he could remember and accepting that the film had been a turning point in his career insofar as 'after it I was able to get away from the jolly Doctors and Brave Soldiers ... but not for a long time after'. *The Servant* was a mere two years away.

2. Michael Relph, producer of *Victim*, which was directed by Basil Dearden.

3. Not only by an 'X' Certificate from the British Board of Film Censors.

A great many distributors did NOT want to show it at all.

I well remember that a number of people I knew well were deeply shocked by the subject and would never have set foot in the Cinemas to see it! Bigotry was a major force in those days: you cant blame Rank for restricting the release. I might just add that a number of Distributers did'nt wish to show 'Death In Venice' either!

No American company would have dared to make it, and a very few were brave, their word, enough to screen it in the States.

We have come a long way now .. anything goes. Which is a great pity.

Lord Arran saw the film on TV when he was in the middle of the Wolfenden Business[1] and wrote me a charming letter saying that both he and I could claim to have altered the Law. He was desperately moved by the film (which he had never seen before) and it added power to his elbow: it was exactly what he needed to 'finally convince' the reluctant members to vote as he wished.

From that point of view the film was important: made at a time when films of that kind were NOT popular and the subject matter was simply not acceptable. Ralph and Dearden made a number of films in this manner, about the colour problem, handicapped children and so on. A far cry indeed from Anna Neagle and Mike Wilding ..

The letters which poured in from families, from men, from wives, were heartbreaking. But we had lifted the corner of a veil, and people suddenly realised that they were 'not the only ones' in the world.

All it was was an excellent little thriller with a bit more to it than that! As such it worked beyond our wildest dreams .. but we had to go slowly, and Dearden <u>more</u> than anyone deserves the credit for his honour and bravery and integrity.

Sincerely – <u>Dirk Bogarde</u>

---

1. In fact Lord Arran saw the film many years after Lord Wolfenden's Committee had reported, and only after the Sexual Offences Bill became law in 1967; but he knew of its impact and, to a lesser extent, that of *The Servant*.

To Hélène Bordes

(Postcard) *St Andrews*

4 July 1985

Chere Mme de la Planche –
    C'est fait!
    I am now a Doctor! – & it was a very moving, and ancient, ceremony. The College began life in 1411. –
    So I <u>am</u> honoured. Tonight I have to make a speech[1] to the University – I am <u>VERY</u> terrified!
    Merci!
        <u>DB</u>.

To Lucilla Van den Bogaerde

Clermont

28 July 1985

My dear Cilla –
    Thanks for loving letter and postcard .. boastcard [...] and for thinking of the St Andrews caper.
    All tremendously moving, humbling, and exhausting!
    Cocktail party for eighty Faculty Members and wives (wives by far the worst and noisiest!) and then a dinner at the Principles house for twenty, with me at head of the table. Fairly agonising really, because the flight had been an hour late from London so there was no time to change (I'd, thank God! worn a blazer and dark tie) or to pee. Which was tiresome. But everyone was in tremendous form and most wonderfully kind, except that Academic Life is a bit strange to me even though I have read all my Iris Murdoch etc.
    Next thing, back to the hotel, a vast granit lump overlooking the 18th hole of the Old Course.
    A sitting room with three chairs, a pastel of Honesty and dead asters, a cabinet with ten tarnished golf-trophies and a TV set which did'nt, or I could'nt, work.
    The bedroom was fairly hairey ... enormous; a window ON the 18th bloody hole, sea mists, sea gulls, two divan beds and a wardrobe.
    In the lav. no-where to put anything. A loo beside the window which had a squint, immovable, plastic venetian blind. So that to sit

---

1. Reproduced on the opposite page.

Chancellor,   St. Andrews -   July 4ᵗʰ '85 -

Λ
1   My Lord's,ladies and gentlemen: I bring no feigned modesty with me
    to this 'ancient house of learning."
    It is quite possible that I bring no modesty at all. //
    Humility has it's origin in an awareness of unworthiness,and
2. sometimes,too,in a dazzling awareness of saintliness.
    But where,in my career,could I have found cause for anything but
    astonishment ?
    As an actor I became a writer without noticing the fact,and with
3   only two people suspecting it.A marvellous woman in America whom
    I never met but with whom I corresponded for many years until her
    death,and my first,and beloved,Publisher Norah Smallwood.
    My astonishment is compounded by the fact that I stand before
    you,in this 'hallowed seat of knowledge "as a thoroughly ill-educated
    man.
    All my early life I resisted,with grim determination,any form of
    learning whatsoever: to the suicidal despair of my parents and the
    exhausted hopelessness of my teachers. I found ignorance far less
4   tedious and much more comforting.
    And that ignorance has brought me here tonight. Do you wonder at my astonishment
5   But do not pity me because in my sixty fourth year I am still
    astonished.
    To be astonished is one of the surest ways of NOT growing old too
    quickly.
    I grow wearier every day as I confront my work;more and more
    uncertain as to wheather I should go on with it,I find reassurance
    only in my fears themselves.
6   The writer,or the actor,who looses his self doubt,who gives way as
    he grows old to sudden euphoria,to prolixity,should stop playing.
    or writing,immediatly: the time has come to lower the curtain or to
    put aside the pen. taking
    I am full of self doubt,and even this signal honour which you have
    bestowed upon me does not allay my fears: I shall continue to worry
7   that I have not yet Quite got it all-together.
    But your splendid encouragment and support give me hope;so I shall
    go ahead (biting my nails) determined to do better, and be worthy of your TO
    belief. (other powered by doubt)   to constantly improve,
    On behalf of my distinguished fellow graduands,and myself,I thank you,
    most profoundly.
    The Court of the University,

    DB

Dirk's notes for his speech at St Andrews, inspired by Colette.

or to stand one had to hang the only towel up. I felt rather lost at one A.M after the dinner was over. We'd (my minder and I) left London at two thirty for the three-something flight.

Next morning, in thick mist, off to Thanksgiving .. then the Robing Ceremony which was a bit jolly with everyone pulling themselves into their robes and buttoning up. Mine was rather splendid: not as pretty as Jacquie's[1] wedding dress but nudging it. Black satin with huge sleeves and a million yellow buttons down the front, all covered in silk. Graduation a sort of terror: a procession led by giant silver maces and various heraldic creatures on gold-covered staffs ... and three hundred students to be given their 'scrolls'. I sat in terror .. but really only had to watch what the others did (300 times) to get the dance steps right.

I graduated with a splendid lady from Maine, who had flown in the night before and was eighty years old that morning! Dr Elizabeth Holt .. she is one of the greatest Art Professors in the world ... and then there was a particularly nice Sir James Black (pathologist) who had discovered something vitally valuable to the stopping of internal bleeding and duodenal ulcers ... well worth honouring, I'd have thought ... and then me, for Letters.[2]

A long and fairly shy-making Lauration, during which one had to stand and face the Professor giving it; back to the thousands in the great, ancient (1411) Hall ... and then the bowing and the kneeling and the 'capping', with what remains of John Knox's own cap, and then the 'hooding' when a uniformed gentleman placed a yellow silk hood, or cape, around my shoulders and I was an Hon. Doc.

I must confess it was all very impressive, not at ALL Municipal (like Leeds, Sussex, Bristol etc) and one really did feel, strangely, enobled by the events and the solemnity, hymns and all that.

Then there was a great lunch .. God! the Scots gobble! And very well .. and a Garden Party in the courtyard of St Salvators Hall .. all Strawberries and cream and hundreds of Mums in merangue-hats and Dads in tails .. I skipped this and took my minder, Ros Bowlby,[3] off

---

1. Rupert Van den Bogaerde's first wife.
2. The art historian Dr Holt was also awarded an Hon. D.Litt.; the pharmacologist Sir James Black, an Hon. D.Sc.
3. Formerly of Chatto & Windus.

for a five mile walk along the sands ... which was MUCH nicer.

Then, in the evening all the formality of the Graduation Dinner, at which I had to speak so therefore was too petrified to drink or eat anything set before me ... and after that, sweltering in my robes (we all were) the Graduation Ball in a huge marquee which was as pretty as a Tissot. Fellows in the kilt, girls with tartan sashes in long dresses; very elegant. Breakfast was served at four am ... I'd skipped off at midnight.

I was sad that Ma and Pa were not there: that Norah had died, that my splendid Mrs X in America had skipped off too and that there was no 'family' there to see the Ugly Duckling get his 'hood'.

But there you are. Cant have everything. Tony had to remain in London, which was wretched, but he's not up to that kind of a junket now ... so I was, except for sweet Ros, who came with me to 'mind' me and hold my hand, on my tod.

I would'nt have missed it for anything: and I ask nothing more.

It was nice to be so honoured for writing! Not for acting ... or being a politician or something.

Flew back, in my University tie to which I am now accorded: and got picked up by a young man at the luggage-collection at Heathrow, the first person I even <u>saw</u>, who asked me when I had graduated! He was a St Andrewian himself and had graduated the year before.

I felt quite chuffed!

[...] Tony's checks were satisfactory .. and he has'nt to go back until April .... the longest time he's, we've, been 'off the hook' ... so now it's back here in blinding heat and trying to get a book finished and tables laid and dogs fed and all the mundanities. However it was a good break .. tiring, terribly expensive, alas! but very pleasing.

So were your letters and card ... I do wish that one day we can all meet up again: I cant, nor will I, make plans when one comes to London for the Medicals because everything depends on the results .. and as soon as they are over, <u>if</u> they have proved to be okay .. T. wants to get home .. he cant cope with restaurants or crowds of more than two people and has to be near a familiar Lav! All very tiring and boring .. but God does play odd tricks ... and Parkinsons AND cancer seem to me to be quite a lot for one elderly gent. Ah well.

[...] P.S. Aunt Sadie (94) was NOT present! But I bet there was a lot of switching off of the TV sets in Glasgow; I got the full 'cover'

over a rather grumpy looking Queen opening a supermarket and a wet, and cross, Diana in the Highlands!

Much love
<u>Dirk</u>
XXX

To Audrey Carr[1]   *Clermont*
28 July 1985

Dear Mrs Carr –

Thank you so much for your surprising letter!

I am at a loss as to know why your mother-in-law chose to, as you say, 'hang a film star' in her house!

But I can give you the background to the thing it'self.

It was drawn by my father (a fairly decent painter) and was exhibited at the Royal Academy in, I think, 1958 .. he was very chuffed that he was 'hung'.

I never, personally, liked the thing: indeed it is of me playing Sydney Carton, but we all went up to the Exhibition to honour Papa and, lo and behold! it was sold already.

We did not know to whome, or at least I did not.

It is possible that your mother-in-law knew my father who was, indeed, a charming man, or on the other hand she might have liked the film!

I cant, at this stage in my life, offer any other suggestions.

My fathers name, incidentally, was Ulric van den Bogaerde ... which is why there is a 'U' on the paper and not a 'D'!

Alas! I have no personal memories of a 'great Edwardian lady!' .. but she sounds absolutely splendid and, who knows, she might have gone to the Cinema from time to time if she cared so much for the arts in general.

---

1. Audrey Carr wrote to Dirk about a pencil portrait which had hung in the hall of her mother-in-law Christine Carr's house at Lewes. Confusion attaches to this picture. The study shown at the Academy in May 1958 was bought for 10s 6d and only resurfaced in 2005 when it was sold at auction for £165. The portrait acquired by Christine Carr was almost certainly drawn to improve the likeness, and exhibited by Ulric in August that year at the show he held jointly with Dirk at the Rose and Crown, Fletching.

Anyway: that's the story as far as I know it: ten out of ten to you
for guessing ("'Tis a far, far better thing I do ..')
Dirk Bogarde

To Elizabeth Goodings

Clermont
Sunday 4 August 1985

Dearest LuLu –

Brock[1] is, I rather hope! about to leave for his Boss's house (half a
mile down the road in Opio!).

He's had a good sleep [...] and been swimming all day, and lying
in the sun and really looks nothing like the white-whey-faced youth
who arrived on Friday evening. Absolutely shagged out: whatever he
earns he bloody well deserves it. I've loaded him up with Supponerils[2]
and hollyhock seeds (for Kimbo[3]) and he'll be off presently: after he's
eaten his tea.

Trouble with not smoking is that people eat so much! We demolished a whole bloody chicken at lunch ... I was hoping there would
be a bit left for T. and I for supper tonight. But no.

I only say 'hope' he'll be leaving because although he is splendid
company he does talk rather a lot .. not about himself so much, about
everything. He's very well informed and well read, to my surprise ...
for I thought he wouldn't be into reading books. But apparently he is.
Slowly!

[...] I understand so well your present situation,[4] watching for
(or dreading) the good days and the bad days, the little signs which
mean worry, the restlessness and silences ... T. is TERRIBLY brave
and good about things, and is coping mentally now wonderfully well.
What else to do?

But he dreads, as I do, the time when, for example, his French
Driving Liscence runs out and he has to have a Test for the new one:
and/or sign a form declaring that he has no 'impeding ailment' ...
well: when that comes along I don't know what we'll do. I'm far too

---

1. Brock was involved, as associate producer, on a dramatisation for Yorkshire Television
of Graham Greene's *May We Borrow Your Husband?*. Dirk was to write the screenplay and
play the lead.
2. Presumably a make of *suppositoire*.
3. Brock's wife, Kim.
4. George Goodings had recently been diagnosed with cancer.

old to try and learn driving again .. perhaps I shall have to buy one of those awful chugging buggies old ladies have to go shopping!¹

T. of course has no pain like G. And for that God be thanked. But the slowness, the shaking legs, the slight wobbles now and then distress him dreadfully ... I know this, of course, and we discuss it calmly and coldly. It has to be faced flat on. The moment that Gilles² said it was cancer that was it. Cold, clear headed, no panic. Now: face this. How do we get on with it .. out of it .. how best to deal with things.

We made out. And then bloody Parkinsons on top! And Tote, the active, tall-standing, proud fellow ... oh shit.

We all say 'Why should it be us?' We wonder, 'What have we done to deserve this?' It's silly ... we haven't DONE anything. It just happened to us, that's all ... and we have to take it.

I am not a Goddy person, so cant lay blame or plead for special help! But there are moments ... there are moments ... and the awareness that each day is a new one, each might bring something lovely as well as something wretched ... but that it'll be a new day, does help a bit. You are right; one does see things in a different light, feels in a different way, becomes a different person to some extent. But the strength that was ALWAYS there all the time just waiting to be put to use, comes to the fore.

At least that's how it feels to me.

You probably will see some deterioration .. you might not .. but if you do you must expect it. I have got used to it now ... I see the signs of age, the good days, the bad days, the buttons which wont get buttoned, the paper he cant fold, the table napkin he cant un-fold, the spoon he cant quite get into the saucer ... it's not ALL the time ... but it's there, and it wont ever get better.

So I fold the papers and the napkins and cut the tomato for the salad and button the buttons ... NEVER in front of people ... unless I can do it so no one notices.

It works alright ...

It's just that I must'nt be ill! Thats a bugger .. and worries me more than many other things to which I have, as you will, mercifully

---

1. Dirk claimed that he did not drive because of his involvement in a fatal accident in India during the war; however this has never been corroborated. It is thought more likely that he (a) was, when young, incompetent at the wheel; and (b) enjoyed being chauffeured. Tony, on the other hand, was an accomplished and enthusiastic motorist.

2. Their doctor, Gilles Cabrol.

adjusted. And you'll adjust as well: you'll find it just sort of happens
... you do it subconsciously and remember (as you do) that you have
got your kids about you, and a loving family who will help as much
as they can. It's not as bad as being stuck in a flat, alone, in Brighton
.. with no one at all except the District Nurse.

The ones to be sorry for, if sorry is the inadequate word, are the
victims ... not ourselves. Yet.

I know that whatever happens I have to try and keep this place
going as long as humanly possible because I have almost seen Tote
'die' when he is away from it ... when he's in London it's pretty hellish.
All that matters are the Tests, the results and then he wants to come
immediatly Home. It's pathetically sad, and touching ... so I know
my duty now ... no return to a dear little flattie in London or
somewhere ... we stay here until the last moment. If we are lucky
enough.

It <u>could</u> be 'years', you know. But I doubt it really ... I mean for
you. There are no miracles in medicin, but there <u>are</u> remissions and
there are 'holdings' when things stabalise; do as I do and prepare for
the worst things and then you'll find such relief when things are'nt as
bad as you imagined in those grey hours: there are always hidden
strengths in us ... and the main thing is to guard them and keep them
strong and polished bright. Like swords against adversity.

You'll manage, I am certain that you will; dont over-tax your
emotions with guilts and regrets, too late for those now ... you need
the force of lions, and you cant waste energy fretting about what was
or what could, or might, have been. Remember what was <u>good</u>, what
<u>IS</u> good, and fight for yourself as well as George; but <u>spare</u> yourself.

You, like an actor, are your own instrument. You have to manu-
facture your own guts, courage and love. No one else can do it for
you, and it's bloody tough work. But, if you do it reasonably, dont
fret about, dont dissipate the force, you'll get through the battles. If
this sounds like a lecture it really is'nt supposed to be! I'm trying to
share some of your burden ... not much. I cant do that really so far
away ... but loving you as I do, and giving your bundle a bit of a lift
now and again might, only <u>might</u> mind you! help the load a bit.

I pray so.

It's six o'clock, I really must turf Brock off .. after all his Boss paid
for the fare and has given him a room in the house ... so he'd better
go and do his 'bit' there. At least he wont keep them all awake ALL

night hacking away with that cough … he'll sleep like a log with my Shovvies.

And it's time for my drink, anyway … and then, when the terrace is still again we'll sit in silence and watch the sun sink and wonder if it'll be an egg and a tin of soup or just soup in a tin … you know?

<u>Anything</u> will do: as long as there's no bloody washing up and setting tables … . Basta!

This with all my love, as ever, & for ever
<u>Dirk</u> XOXOXOX

To Elizabeth Goodings   *Clermont*
                                                        9 September 1985

Darling LuLu –

The most extraordinary thing about writing a book is finishing it! It is really just like having a baby, I imagine … only the pregnency is two years (in this case[1] anyway) instead of nine measly months. I feel so absolutely flat and dispirited: there is nothing left in my head at all .. no running-thread of thought, no rumbling about with ideas, no sorting out of dates and facts and selecting and rejecting things.

Condensing sixty-five years of your life into a modest book of some 250 pages aint easy! I have ghastly back-ache, from sitting on this upright kitchen chair for so long .. and a head-ache, probably for the same reason .. I MUST get a decent chair. An Office-type. Upholstered and swivelling .. like the one I had at Adams up in the gallery. Why did I get rid of that? I suppose because it never occurred to me that I'd ever have to earn my living writing.

Having no Norah has'nt helped much either; this is the first book (No. 7!) I've written entirely without her advice; even for 'West of Sunset' she was there to read what I had written, even though she did not edit or correct. She did, as a matter of fact, start off correcting this latest effort, now I remember … because I started it ages ago, set it aside because it bored me … and went on with the novel,[2] as you will remember.

This time last year you were here and read the two, I seem to remember, or what was ready of the two. And I wondered then which

---

1. His fourth volume of autobiography, *Backcloth*.
2. *Closing Ranks*.

to carry on with .. you suggested the autobiography ... and perhaps thats why I went on finally. Sally said, on the telephone today (Sally is my typist you remember) that she found it 'desperately sad ... but NOT depressing!' ... I don't quite know <u>what</u> to make of that ... but you cant alter the facts of life to suit a book ... things happen as they happen and however hard you try to pretend that they DID'NT they bloody well did ... and thats the end of it!

Anyway: thats the lot. I never want to write about ME again! Far too boring and far too limiting really. You simply have to stick to the facts and cant fiddle about with them. Well: <u>too</u> much anyway! Someone said, not long ago in some paper, that all autobiography was really only a novel in the end, and to some extent I suppose that this is true. One re-arranges the facts a bit to save time and space .. and condenses the years into a few lines ... so in effect one IS novelising ones life.

Anyway I hope that I have covered everyone and everything properly: I must admit that writing about the time when T. was in hospital and you and I went off round the Tate and the National and had lunch at little restuarants and Guinness in The Globe brought it all back pretty vividly!

I had, of course, my detailed Diary to help me .. and there it all is in black and white .. so no one can say it is'nt true!

I have'nt been able to mention EVERYONE in my life! How could I? So there might be some grumpy faces when they read the Index! And I have shoved Rupert[1] in among the voices on this terrace, along with Mark and Sarah[2] and Brock ... to leave him [Rupert] out, although he has never been here, seemed unkind and would have made Gareth (B) sad ... because even he hardly gets a mention!

I have seen so <u>little</u> of Gareth and Cilla in my life; is'nt it odd? When you boil it all down we have seldome come together: I mean not like you and I, and George even ... the war made a huge difference there I suppose because G. was six when I went off and twelve or thirteen when I came back[3] which makes a gap [...]

However it's all done, I've called it 'BACKCLOTH' after all: there is a new book coming out quite soon called 'Time and Time Again'[4]

---

1. Gareth's third son.
2. Elizabeth's son and daughter.
3. From Army service.
4. Subtitled *Autobiographies*, by Dan Jacobson (André Deutsch).

. . . so I had to make a change, for that was my original title . . . and 'Aunt Kitty's Room' as you said, did'nt 'feel' right somehow . . .

I have done fourteen full-page drawings (scribbles really) ranging from Lullington to Raffles Hotel in Singapore, and what I THINK I remember Aunt Kitty's room to have looked like in West End Lane!

Tote recognised it immediatly! He said that was EXACTLY how he had thought it would have looked . . so I'm reassured. To an extent.

The cover, if they use it, has a super photograph Tote took of me last year repainting the swimming-hole! Just my back and a roller brush and bucket and half the pool fresh brilliant blue and the other faded and crummy . . . it looks as if I am painting a backcloth; not the Hippo-Pool.

I think they might buy it. They'd be dotty not to.[1]

Now thats enough of that. I wait here fretting away for the final two chapters to arrive properly typed from Sally . . . and then I'm almost sure I'll feel better!

The Atts for dinner last night [. . .] We fed them, naturally, in Attenborough Style. A huge, really big, leek-pie, which Dick had two helpings of, TWO chocolate ice creams with nuts and cream walloped on top, half a round of cheese, lots of bread and butter, figs from the garden and TWO bananas from the greengrocer!

I sat amazed . . . but could say nothing. Sheila had exactly the same, but one vast portion of leek-pie and not two. We had a bottle of wine, they did rather, and then coffee. Tote and I had finished our supper before they had started! Oh! I forgot . . with the Leek-pie they had my tomato salad mixed with fresh basil, sugar and oregano . . . and ate it all. We had made enough for our lunch today. No way.

But they are, when they are alone with us here, very relaxed and obviously, one feels, are very fond of us both. We never dry up for conversation and Dick is very un-pompous. EXACTLY what he is NOT in public life. Strange. He's had a ghastly time with the Americans over his film[2] . . . they have behaved dreadfully badly, as they always do, and summon him back and forth across the Atlantic as if he was an office boy. I dont know how he does it, or why he lets them do it to him . . . and told him so. He agreed that he was too decent and that his British Manners of fair-play and good humour were out of place in Los Angeles. As I know to my cost!

However off they go on Sunday for two weeks . . . to fight the battle again. No wonder, really, that they need so much food. They have to keep their energy going somehow . . . but I do fear the day when he'll explode!

The weather is still very hot, and we sat out until dinner time on

1. They did. The jacket was emblazoned with Tony's snapshot of Dirk at work inside *le bassin*.
2. *A Chorus Line*.

the terrace in flip-flops and tee shirts ... and only went in to eat ...
its cool after the sun has gone behind Indian Hill ... but not too cool
to have to sit indoors with the door shut. We watched a part of 'A Star
Is Born' which someone sent us from the U.S .... I say a 'part' because
it runs for four and a half hours!¹ We just did the 'Born In A Trunk'
piece and it made us all blub ... so ended a pleasant evening. Tote in
very good form, which was wonderful for me. They dont bore him
and they dont tire him ... and they know the form, and if he was
tired they'd slip off easily. It's useful.

[...] The men are here to finish off the mowing: and in all this
heat too ... I cant think what the bill will be. Too much anyway ..
but perhaps I'll sell the book? Who can tell .. I'll have to sell something
else otherwise! [...]

All my love as ever.
Dirk XXOXX

To Kathleen Tynan   *Clermont*
                                              29 September 1985

Dearest Kath –

I have JUST finished my bloody book: and the void has to be filled
somehow [...] I've also finished my first fillum script ... and that
was a lot of jokes!

Graham Green's short story 'May We Borrow Your Husband' ...
which has had five scripts made of it, all failures, I gather. They asked
me to play the Observer, always, as you know, the dullest part in any
book and especially in a Green book ... and I said I would if they
could write the part up .... and of course they could'nt, and I said,
silly fart, 'I'll have a bash then' ... and bashed it off in seven days and
wrote myself the longest, DULLEST, BORINGEST, part ever.

They have accepted the script with alacrity ... and I'm stuck!

But since it all takes place in Antibes I can at least come home of
an evening! Trouble is they cant decide how to pay me: and have
become quite bewildered by the idea that they have two Agents to
deal with!

[...] Weather glorious, as it was when you were here .. and as hot.

---

1. Another of Dirk's exaggerations: Cukor's 1954 musical, starring Judy Garland and James
Mason, runs for three hours.

Which I dont care for .. and it makes it most worrying to know that you are somewhere in the center of [Hurricane] Gloria or whatever it's called.

Golly! I'd hate to be in N.Y during an emergency ... all those swaying buildings and trees flying in Central Park.

I pray you take the greatest care: but of course I wont know until I read it in The Guardian, will I?

We have had a quiet social life since you left: which had to be so because I cant lay tables and wash up and prepare food and write a book. Thats beyond me .. Iris Murdoch can, which irritates me greatly. But she can also write REAL books ... her new one, just out, has had super reviews and the girl who typed her Manuscript said it was dreary-dull and 200.000 words long! Try that for size.

The British Consul[1] came to lunch yesterday with his wife, April (well .. she's very nice with it) and we had a happy enough time. He's young, and what they call 'dynamic' and 'into' the Arts and April is given to wearing cotton frocks with brogues, long hair with flowers wreathed through, like a wan Ophelia, and drinks hot water rather than anything else. Which is easy, of course, but a bit tiresome topping up her cup all afternoon ... or morning.

David Puttnam and Patsey came over and stayed a whole day because they so hated the 'Du Cap' (as the Americans now call the Hotel) and were a glorious bounty. He is FAR too nice to be the Moguel he is![2] I cant understand how it works.

And various others wandered in for meals or drinks and wandered away again.

And now the Season is finally over. The hour went back here last night which is always very unsettling for me ... it means that when it's twelve o'clock by my gut, and a beer is desperately needed, it's only eleven o'clock by my watch .. and I have to hang about for an hour ... maddening.

Perhaps today I'll cheat.

I rather dread the coming month because I have to sit for my portrait by a gentleman called David Tindel[3] .. who is to 'do' me for the National P. Gallery which, as Forwood said dryly, is really joining

---

1. David Gladstone.
2. He was soon to be appointed chairman of Columbia Pictures.
3. The Royal Academician David Tindle.

the Establishment ... however as I am in Who's Who already I see no reason not to hang on the august walls of the N.P.G.

I had to telephone Mr Tindel today in Northamptonshire to ask him how rich he was; because I have to find him local accomodation somewhere ... and as the season is over everything possible has closed down until December ... which leaves a crummy sort of Car-Motel up the road or an elegant, and costly, Auberge four miles away. He said that the N.P.G would give him 'a certain amount of money to cover costs' and when I told him that a taxi to Cannes from the village would set him back thirty quid. ONE WAY. He practically had a seizure.

So I'm going to try and get him into the Motel ... which makes him altogether too near for comfort. But it's all my fault. I should have declined.

He has a nice, roughish, North Country accent .. and is about the same age, I gather, as Hockney ... and paints very well indeed. So maybe we'll get on very well indeed ... although I hate 'sittings' ... the most dreadful torture I can think of at the moment. I cant even drift off into 'plot-thinking' because I have'nt any plots drifting about and my Muse, or whoever she is, has drifted off to the Great Wall of China and shows absolutely no signs of returning for a very long time.

Which is depressing.

And that is two 'driftings' and one 'drift' too many in two lines.

Forwood read the TS of the autobio' the other day, he always very kindly does this chore, to check if there was anything which might be libellous ... and quite enjoyed it but said that he had found one or two split-infinitives.

As I dont KNOW what a split-infinitive is to begin with it makes things a mite uneasy. But I hope Editors will. And do something.

[...] The Auberts'[1] celebrated Brigitts fortieth birthday at some vastly grand hotel in Eze .. naturally we did not go .. Forwood refuses to drive in the dark now ... and the mention of a black tie sends me into a trance of terror. But I did send her forty WHITE roses ... a sign of virginity, I thought ... and as she is heavily married and has two strapping children I thought she'd prefer white to red .. Try and buy a white rose here! They are only grown for wedding 'bowkays' or, lowered voice, childrens funerals.

---

1. Jean-Pierre Aubert and his wife Brigitte.

Anyway, at VAST expense, she got her 40 white roses. And the point. So that saved a lot of driving and sitting down to a ghastly dinner for 300 'personal guests' in Eze. What <u>are</u> 'personal guests' may I ask? I thought that all guests were personal at a birthday party? Perhaps not. I dont know ... and this really is degenerateing into piffle: so I'll stop immediatly. It was simply to say again how truly lovely it was to be with you again, how lovely you looked, and how good you were to lavish wine upon one. And such wine! I only hope you looted it from what Angela Fox, in her forthcoming book, calls 'Richardsons Nit De Duke'.[1] She has taken all her family to the cleaners in this epic .. and most of her friends ... it'll cause quite a little stir come the Spring.

My love to you as ever ..
    Devotedly
        Dirk.

To Hélène Bordes

Clermont
11 December 1985

Chere Hélène –

A note in great haste and I apologise already!

I have been in London for five whole weeks, it feels like five whole years ... while my partner (Forwood) underwent surgery[2] and we had a generally dismal and worrying time. I did not get any mail from home (here) because I could not cope in London with illness AND letters ... so everything was left in a HUGE pile here until my return ... among the pile all your charming little 'butterflies' of thought [...]

My head is bursting with so much mail (and impots!) to take in, plus bills for Electricity, Gas, Water and idiot Fan Letters from Germany (and England too!)

So this can only be a short 'contact' .. We arrived back here last Wednesday night (exhaustedly I watched, <u>with horror,</u> the Louvre![3]) and in the early hours of the morning Forwood began to heamorrage

---

1. Tony Richardson's house was in a hamlet called Le Nid du Duc. In her unsparing memoir, *Slightly Foxed* (Collins), Angela Fox spelled it correctly the first time, and on the next page Ni le Duc.
2. On his prostate.
3. *Le plus grand musée du monde.*

badly. (I dont know if this is the correct spelling. But you will cleverly make out what I mean!) [...]

He is now in a Clinic in Grasse, recovering, and I am trapped in the house (I cant drive you remember?) and the nightmare which I always dreaded has come about ... oh well. Maybe, with luck he'll be back on Friday ... and then starts the long convalescence .. and I cant cook either! God help us all!

The Louvre I found bitterly dissapointing ... that idiot woman did all MY talking! I spent months studying the subject, and we were 'free' and not like School-Teachers ... and suddenly they 'cut' all my work and replace it with some stupid voice of a woman speaking EXACTLY as I did NOT want it to be! I wanted it to be alive and amusing. How else do you make 'stone' come alive for M. Toutlemond I wonder? And then they dubbed me with a terrible voice ... not like mine at all .. and only left in a few of my words ... I was very sad.

I agree with you about Charlotte [Rampling] ... she is very inexperienced[1] .. but we do have a complicity .. and she was <u>so much</u> better in the original work ... they cut her pieces dreadfully too ... we need never have gone to Paris at all!

The next Episode, on the Flemish Masters, they tell me will be better. I wonder? That comes sometime in January, I think .. I dont know or care now. Madnesssssssssss.

[...] The film-adaptation of Graham Greene's short story will start shooting down here, at Cap Ferrat (we have found a hotel which looks like the 'old Riveria' there ... all the others look like shoe-boxes now!) And I shall be acting again for the Television this time, <u>not</u> the Cinema ... my first ever in England.[2] I usually only work for TV in the USA because they pay so much more money and guarentee that the films will NEVER be shown in Europe!

I <u>insist</u> on that. And after the debacle of the Louvre you will understand why.

I am typing so badly because I am out of practice, cold, and very weary with trying to cook for me, the dogs, go to the Clinic in Grasse, and keep myself cheerful in the long, dark evenings ...

Forwood has been my manager since he first 'discovered' me in a

---

1. In documentary work.
2. At least, since 1947.

small theater outside London in 1938[1] and became my Agent. After the six years of war, and one disasterous marriage,[2] he came to look after my affairs because I could not handle them! Now it looks as if I must reverse the role .. and try to understand my business problems. Not easy for a person like me who only ever worked in cotton-wool, cosseted from the problems, so that I could act or write . . . it is very different now. And age does not wait! [. . .] I am what we call Next Of Kin and held responsible . . . which I dont mind at all .. it is not difficult to repay all those years of care, I must return a little which I was given. But this house is so isolated! And I am so awful at cooking (very good at tinned soup!) This depressing little letter is simply to keep in touch . . . I wont be able to write much until everything has settled down and this huge pile of mail has been sorted. To hell with the autogrammes! To hell with the Charities asking for money . . . to hell with it all .. plus the impots!

& forgive this terrible typing –

Ever. <u>D</u>.

To Mary Dodd   *Clermont*
                                                 18 December 1985

Mainie dearest –

I am at a slight loss as to know exactly how you should now be addressed. The Reverand Mrs D . . . or Mrs D simply .. or what?[3]

It does'nt much matter anyway: I'll still write Mrs J. D. on the envelope and etiquette has to go to hell.

I'm writing because Coz gave me your letter, and card, to read, and then went off to bed . . . not BECAUSE of your card and letter; but because he had foolishly thought that he'd have a 'little lay down' on the sofa, rather than, as I insist, he did 'a Churchill', and got into bed. He got into bed.

He's progressing slowly. It's not been easy; but then he only left the bloody Clinic a week ago tomorrow . . . so he's bound to be 'fragile' and a bit wonky .. not in the head (although <u>that</u> counts too!) but in the legs and things . . . he simply wont come to terms with the fact

---

1. They met at Amersham in 1939.
2. To Glynis Johns.
3. MD's husband, James Dodd, had been appointed a non-stipendiary minister.

that he's had TWO op's in less than six weeks .. and lost a fifth of his blood during the gay little hemmorage (sp?) last Thursday at four am. I ASK you! What are you supposed to DO at that hour. It's only three am in London, no Doctor would reply (or did!) and the body is at it's lowest ebb. Mine was. I jolly quickly got pulled together and dealt with things as best I could ... and our good young Doctor in the village pulled on his (v. chic) sweater and jeans and tore up ... and frankly saved your Coz's life ... he had half an hour to 'go'. The bladder was full and about to burst ... (I DO hope you've had Christmas by this time?) When I eventually spoke to our smart Sloan Street Dr he advised that I should force him to drink 'gallons of water, and it'll soon clear.' Had I done so we'd <u>all</u> have clear'd and Coz would have been a gonner. I have to reconsider Doctors ... it's all a bit like 'The Citadel' (too young, you are ... but it was Cronin's best book, and a terrible fuss was caused.)

So now we stumble slowly towards recovery. I hope. I am in the unfortunate position of not being able to drive. So: a taxi every morning (£6 a time!) to do the chores ... and then come back and try to COOK! I've never boiled water! Somehow we manage. Coz now shuffles about with my prepared veg, and pokes the sausages and so on. Apparently, last night, I nearly killed him because I put too much Worcester sauce in the baked potato-cold-minced-lamb. As he is quite incapable of tasting <u>anything</u>, and has been for years, I can only fear that I must have over-done the shaking-of-the-bottle. <u>I</u> found it scrumptious.

But of course I quite like Indian food.

However the urine is running clear, no more clots, so far .. he is not allowed to drive, walk far, or generally move about ... which galls him .. but he's settling for it. What he CANT bear are people ... so no people. It does'nt bother me a fig; but I sometimes feel he'd be better to make an effort, just a little.

We'll give it another week anyhow.

I was desolate, as he was (he wont remember to write to you for ages) about your burgulary ... it's the little things you love most which hurt ... not the object d'art ... Lu, my sister, got ripped off a year ago, and was shattered to bits because one of the things taken was a small, five inch high, Lalique glass Madonna and child which Tote had given her, oh, ages ago, and which she simply treasured, and 'spoke to', as she put it, daily. She did'nt mind a bit that the clocks had gone, the Georgian silver, a bronze of some value, my mothers pearls[;] all she minded was that Lalique glass Madonna. And I DO know how she feels ... take the entire house, but leave me that. 'Course they did'nt ... she fitted into their pockets neatly and went off for 'drug money'.

Golden days here ... odd .. it's like September, and the leaves are yellow and all about the place, but the bees and lizards scuttle and fly, and the birds are far too well fed to bother with my peanut-bag. Yet. It was the same last year [...] blue and gold and South of France ... ten days later we had five inches of snow, the Garage was blocked by a ten foot drift, and the temperature fell to –19 for over a week. So I know what to expect now! Anyway, one makes the most of it .. I honestly dont think that we'll be able to stay on here much longer. Twelve acres to mow, the house rather bigger than I thought, the terror that something might happen suddenly again and that we could'nt make it to the hospital, or even down the track in snow, for example. So where? Probably, with deep reluctance, back to U.K .... have'nt worked it out yet, but when Coz is 'in form' we'll have to have a 'serious talk'.

The thought appalls me! How can I pack all this up alone? Christ!

I start my wretched TV film in mid-Febuary in Beaulieu ... it's only an hour and a half away from here, but I might just as well be working in Cirencester. We'll have to get Guardians and so on .. and Coz will <u>have</u> to come and sit in the hotel and be grumpy. He'll hate it all. But I cant leave him here alone. He cant open a tin even!

Growing old is brutal. I thought that it started gradually. It does not. One AGES gradually and grows-old overnight ... disconcerting.

I am busy correcting the French translation of 'West of Sunset' which is really v. good ... I laughed aloud at my own nonsense! 'BACKCLOTH' comes out in Sept: as I think I told you ... and the film should take me up to the end of March .. after that it is all a puzzlement .. except that I'm getting more offers to write TV scripts (which I resist) and someone wants a book on Provence.

How original can one be? I cant do that either ... because it would mean a long tour about Provence, at least four months .. and that's now out of the question.

The way I type and spell should put anyone off .. I seem to have rather run out of typing, and spelling, today. Perhaps it's because it's almost four in the afternoon and a smudged face, Bendo's, is pressed against the glass door of this studio waiting for his grub ... then the fire to lay and light .. and Coz's tea to cart up ... two bits of cake as well .. and then the evening begins: it is dark by five, but, to cheer him up I remind him that the 21st is the longest [*sic*] day and that after that the sun starts to re-mount. We'll see.

This is a dotty letter .. but it is just to re-assure you that I am in full control of my faculties and think that we'll make it through ... and that the real reason I was 'distraught' the other evening was because I had forgotten to telephone you, <u>as promised,</u> and had taken a sleeping pill! So apologies for that ... I'm really quite cool and brisk.

I bloody well have to be now.

Off I go to feed dog and Coz ... and split logs (HOW I hate it) and lay the fire and close the house and watch the birds come in to roost.

It was a lovely letter of yours, and a pretty (if familiar) (Bethlehem or wherever, Goddy) card .. I sent only a few, to people in the U.S and some local friends ... the Postoffice ladies, the woman who does the washing .. WAIT until she gets a look at Coz's bloody sheets! and so on ... so you'll have to accept this, whenever it arrives, with all my love and blessings for a safe, healthy, and, shall we say, amusing? life as a Vicars wife ... we'll all laugh about it one day, they say, so we might as well start right now!

Devotedly
<u>Dirk</u> OXXXOX

LATER 4.45 pm Fed Bendo, and then decided to take him [for] a walk through the Attenboroughs Gate .. Coz, awaked by the barking, decided to come as well. A very slow, tottery, march with his stick .. but in the last of the light rather beautifull. <u>It</u> was; not Coz ... the first Forsythia out in the hedges and Bendo thieved a nice olive log from the Atts. log-pile for tonights fire. Coz wandered off to make his tea and I've come up to add this ... I don't really know what for! It's as full of news as a washing-up cloth.

<u>D</u> XXX

To Hélène Bordes   *Clermont*
                                                   3 February 1986

Ma chere Planche –

I sit and freeze: even here in the Studio above the woodshed .. and the typewriter has become tiresome with the cold and will not respond; or maybe it's my hands?

[...] I am now rapidly becoming involved in the damned film and will soon be on my way down the hill to Nice, where I will stay until we finish ... sometime in March. It is too difficult to commute from here to there and still be fresh and bright for work! I am, alas! not the young man I once was .... so to the Negresco, or somewhere, and a warm room and a not-too-far journey to the Location. At Cap Estelle ...

I confess I dread it all. The early mornings, the worry about the lines, the constant demands from the actors to change this or that, to increase their parts or to alter a line to 'make it funny'. I shall behave just like Pinter! He refused to even listen to anyone, and sat like a stone image and let the seas break all about him: secure, un-budging, definate. I hope I have the courage!

[...] I am so happy that St Jacques' seems (at this moment) to amuse you .. it is beautifully written in English, and by a, then, very young man ... his work is rare and perfect .. sometimes one has to wait for five or six years for the next book to come out, and it is always worth the wait. Always. Anyway to me. The film in which I 'played' him was called 'Ill Met By Moonlight' (Shakespear!) and it was a true adventure which he underwent in Crete when he captured the German Governor General and brought him off the Island to Malta! He used to dance, sometimes, dressed as a cretian peasant, with the German Officers in their Mess and gently slip a hand-grenade into the pocket of their uniforms ... and run! He was decorated for his gallentry ... and the General he captured grew extremely fond, and admiring, of him and they remained friends until well after the war. A strange, brilliant, funny, erudite young man ... he was difficult to 'capture' on film! But he rather enjoyed my performance ... his only grief was that my 'derrier' was less large than his! He likes his ouzo and wine and

---

1. Dirk had sent HB Patrick Leigh Fermor's *The Violins of Saint-Jacques*, originally published in 1953 by John Murray and lately reissued as a Penguin Classic.

food ... so he did get rather fat .. I used to call him a 'bloated Byron' ... which he thought a compliment .. he is married and lives on a beautiful Island in a house which he and his wife built themselves. He has no children, preferring, rightly, beasts to them!

[...] There is a long piece on me in some chic magazine in Paris called 'Citie' ... I have not seen it and it is bound to be rediculous ... so dont be too cross. I am not the master of what the journalists write ... they do as they please and invent rubbish ... I have learned over the years to be tolerant and remember that we say in English, 'What is in todays paper will be wrapped round the fish tomorrow'. Sometimes it helps.

We have had tempests, snow, hail, fog, ice ... Nice, and it's silly Carnival des Fleurs has been almost destroyed ... and the house here is cold and wet .. not the kind of weather I enjoy de tout! Maybe it'll clear by the time we start work on the coast ... but who can tell?

[...] and now I must leave you .. and commence the learning of my own script! Madness ...

As ever <u>D</u>

To Bob Mahoney and Keith Richardson[1]

Clermont
23 March 1986

My dear Bob & Keith –

A joint Thank You letter: I hope that you will forgive me, there is a stack of mail here, after five weeks away, which looms for attention.

To thank you seems a bit silly: but there it is. I am a bit silly.

But I do thank you for sticking so closely to my script .. for showing me such extreme kindness at all times, for your generosity in many areas (not least in the bottle!) and for your courtesy and understanding towards Forwood .... amazingly better since this new treatment we took on at the Pasteur Institute.

I touch wood, naturally .. it is no great joke to see a man cut down in his prime and left helpless ... and one does not believe in miracles any longer, anyway not at my age.

For my part I am pulling out of a weeks total exhaustion! I crawled to my bed and more or less stayed there .. somehow Television

---

1. Director and producer respectively at Yorkshire Television for *May We Borrow Your Husband?*.

(although it at no time felt like Television to me) is a rather demanding business and the fact that we shot a full Movie, I prefer that term, without any loss of quality at all, in four weeks still rather amazes me.

The Crew were exceptional .. I loved them all and their kindness to me was overwhelming . . . red roses, if you please, in the car on my way home here which nearly un-manned me! I have worked with very many Crews all over the world . . . and found that none were better really.

A few little hic-cups here and there, that wont really show in the end.

Considering that none of them had worked together as a team before and were uncertain about Movies to start with, and the intense discipline required for concentration and so on, still leaves me astonished, and they loved it, that I know, and are terribly proud of their Film.

I know that the Actors finally came round: a difficult start for them mainly because of the weather and a feeling that they were being a bit neglected by 'Teachers Pet'! Understandable .. with the weather we had . . . but they got together finally and I think we worked well as a team.

I am certain that your decision about Charlotte[1] was the right one .. and she will give you a most unusual performance, certainly she was no hardship to work with! Easy as could be and quick to learn .. for my part I hope that 'William'[2] is not too drab and boring .. God knows it's a sod of a part and duller than cotton stockings, but I hope that, together, we have given him some dimension.

I dont know what happened at the Party,[3] finally. I hear from some (NOT from Brock, who is the original clam) that it got a bit hairy towards the finish .. I pray that you will both be aware that whatever happens to wretched 'Peter'[4] must be ambigious . . . and not clearly 'a queer plot'. That would bugger the Greene story and my efforts to script it . . . 'Tony'[5] only ever watches: remember. Thats his kick . . . but he does NOT cart the boy to bed! Do make it clear .. Think of Mrs Whitehouse, or whatever she's called, and all your astonished and uncomfortable fellows at Yorkshire!

---

1. Attenborough, who co-starred.
2. Dirk's role.
3. A 'colourful' scene in the film.
4. The hapless bridegroom, played by Simon Shepherd.
5. The character played by David Yelland.

Incidentally: I hope that you win your battle, if battle it is to be, over the Main Titles ... they should perhaps be warned to take a deckko at my contract before they come up with any odd ideas!

All that is left for you to shoot now, if this reaches you in time, is the Gymkhana ... I wish that I was there with you, but I [am] not into horses and Yorkshire skies .. and I've done my part anyway.

It seems a very long time ago since July, Bob, when you came here with that wretched book and when I agreed to meet you ONLY out of good manners, for I had absolutely NO intention of coming near the bloody subject at that time.

I suppose that I'd had a beer too many too early in the morning!

Anyway: I'm glad that I said 'Yes'.

It is not something I'll try again in a hurry: but one-off aint so bad and, apart from being shit scared every single day from about Christmas onwards, it was fun and good to work again.

But fear, daily fear, plus bronchitis for two weeks of the four, plus a conviction that I would not be able to keep up the pace and that I had, perhaps, lost 'touch' is too much of a strain to maintain at my age.

But thank you both, once again, for making it so pleasant, so easy, and for looking after me so well.

I hope that my own work will be some kind of <u>proper</u> 'Thank You' when you have cut it all together.

<u>Very</u> sincerely
   <u>Dirk</u>.

To Brock Van den Bogaerde   *Clermont*
                                        29 March 1986

My, very, dear Brock –

The dust is settling: by that I mean that my desk is starting to look less like a stall in the Portobello Road and more like a proper, well tended, writers, work-area. I have written hoards of letters to the hoards who wrote letters to me while we were on the 'shoot' .. and now I am faced with more hoards who have had the kindness to send me all manner of gifts and (terrible!) cards for my birthday[1] ... everything from stuffed Koala bears, Kiwi's (I'm hot in Australia and

---

1. His sixty-fifth.

N.Z) and polyester ties in various (appalling) patterns. I am writing on a new machine (your lot buggered up my old beloved somehow, and I have'nt had time to take her into the menders) so any mistakes must be forgiven ... I have a feeling that this one will blow up before long anyway: it's making the oddest noises .. Also it has strange keys like: ç ¿¡¡¯˅˄ and so on .. it's half Frog and half Arab I think.

Who would want to print a ? upside down, thus ¿, only an Australian surely. What this letter is all about, really, is to say to you how enormously proud I was, and am, of you for your behaviour during the filming of your Uncle's little Epic. It is so typical that one leaves the person one loves the most to the end of all the 'Thank You' letters ... in the hope that they will, perhaps, understand that their work was not taken for granted. Yours was not, at any time, on any level.

You behaved impeccably throughout: you gained the respect of the entire Crew, you held the lot of them together quietly and without fuss, you never for one moment let the Uncle/Nephew relationship show, beyond the natural, and deep affection, which you know we have for each other, and you made my job easier to do in consequence.

I have always known, as you must be aware, from the very early days when I grew to know who you were, or to be more accurate, who you MIGHT develop into, that I have had the greatest hopes and respect for you.

One reason why I rather pushed Dad into letting you come to learn French here was to help you to find feathers on your wings rather than just the 'fluff' of adolescence. The training, not at Berlitz, was not easy for you I know .. and there were terrible moments of self-doubt, on your part, sulks, on your part, and impatience on mine. I've kept all your letters .. so I know how painful sometimes your time was here. But, and it's quite a big BUT, I do think that you returned to Chicago with a different slant to life ... and you have maintained that slant; it is standing you in good stead now. You have learned, retained learning, dared, and won! Not bad ...

I am, as you know only too well, a pretty pernickety fellow .. I was trained in a bloody hard school, and sweated blood to get where I got .. I therefore have very little interest in people who dont take their chances, and who dont behave as professionally as I would wish.

There are far too many people running after the bait in this world, and far too many who just make an easy grab for it: but that is not your way, and it is'nt my way: your professionalism stands out a mile, your determination to suceed as 'Brock' is clear to all to see, your determination to learn, to be, if need be, temporarily shoved about in the course of that learning, is evident, and the fact that you are going to get there, right up on top, is as clear as daylight in a dark cavern.

Go on fighting for your beliefs; keep your good manners; (there is NEVER any need to loose them, people think sometimes that one does'nt need Good Manners but they are grotesquely wrong .. it costs nothing to be polite, to smile, to remember someone's name; and you will reap the whole field!) and always remember that, years ago, it almost must seem to you, you did say 'I can do that!' and you have. Remember too that I called you ONE.

You are.

If I bawled you out (I did it deliberatly a couple of times for not letting me know that the Unit had broken: of course I KNEW you'd broken! But a little reminder was needed; give 'em an inch and they'll take a mile .. remember that yourself and NEVER let them do it to you!) it was professional, premeditated, and seperated us as 'relations' and made us more part of the Crew than they actually were aware. Joining a Crew is <u>essential</u>, holding them together the most important thing that can happen on a film .. no matter what. The result of the film can be screwed by the Director finally, but the intent, the careing, the affection, and the gut-breaking work are all up there on the screen somewhere, and it all comes from the top.

So remember <u>that</u> when you get there: it's a tough, sometimes lonely, always exhausting, job ... but it'll be worth it to you all your life.

You are off soon to do the final 'bit'. The film may be a cock-up .. it may fail on a number of levels [...] dont count on a great success .. but do remember whatever becomes of it that you have every reason to be proud of your contribution, you have learned a hell of a lot quickly, you have come a long way, and there is no way that you must retrace your steps .. it's onwards and upwards for you, and no looking back.

I loved working with you: it was all that I had secretly hoped it would be years ago, without ever thinking, for a moment, that we'd actually be there together shareing the Bill!

I'm very proud, very respectful and very grateful.

Always
   <u>Dirk</u>
      XXXXOOXX for Mrs Bognor.

To Hélène Bordes   *Clermont*
                                                26 May 1986

Chere Hélène –

We have a greve at the TRI[1] in Nice. So God knows when this will reach Limoges!

[...] Yes: the Festival is done. Dreadful, as usual .. and not entirely 'correct' either. It was fairly certain that 'LE Mission' would win[2] ... no one sends a film to Cannes, in compitition as well, when it is <u>unfinished</u>, the sound is not correct, the editing not finished (and wont be until September!) so HOW can an unfinished film win the Palmares!! It would NOT if I had been President .. of that I am certain!

I made one award to two elderly men, Powell and Pressburger, who are now both well into their eighties, but who, together for twenty-two years, made some of the most marvellous films we ever had in Britain ... perhaps you never got to see them because they were, the best ones, made during the war.

I did their last film together, down here in Provence (which was supposed to be Crete! And looked like it .. no one guessed, and all my French friends who saw it on TV were so envious that I had been in such a savage and glorious Island! I did NOT dissillusion them by saying that if they had taken their cars from the garage, or caught a bus, they could have had my experience only one and a half hours north of Nice!) Mind you, it was made in 1959[3] ... and this part of Provence had not been ruined by motor-ways, gas stations, ski stations, and terrible apartments!

Anyway: I presented them with a horrible medal and a scroll, and they had a tremendous, and moving, ovation, and all was well. I slipped away out of the back of the dreadful Palais and sped home before anyone knew I had gone.

Apart from that, and three or four old friends who came up to escape the hell of the Croisette, it was a calm two weeks .. and VERY, VERY HOT!

Too hot to work on the land, and too hot to think about writing .. so I just sit like a bundle of old washing ...

---

1. The sorting office.
2. Roland Joffé's film took the Palme d' Or.
3. *Ill Met by Moonlight* was made in 1956 and released the next year.

I am glad that 'fatiguer' made you laugh! In Paris I am considered
very ill-bred when I attempt to speak French, because I just use the
words I have learned in Provence, like, for example, 'Moutonnier'
which no one even knows what it means in the 6th arrondissment!
And I have not spelled that correctly either .. it's too hot.

The film about the Somme in 1916[1] is very daunting. It is, the book,
400 pages long, and the final scenes are those which take place on July
1st .. the first great battle of the Somme when we lost sixty thousand
men dead between 7 in the morning and mid-day! HOW can I write
a film which requires so many bodies in the green corn of the Somme
valley above Serre?

I took my sister, Elizabeth, there some years ago, to show her the
places I knew from books and from people who survived ... it was a
golden evening, the corn was green and tall, the trees had all re-grown,
the land was soft and peaceful ... apparently. But she was horrified!
She said that she could feel the earth still trembling and the noise of
distant guns, and she went back to the car and sat there until I returned
and we drove in silence back to Amiens ... or Albert .. I forget. Albert,
with the Virgin on the cathedral ...[2]

Three days later we were in Normandy! And I went all over my
old places again, trying to remember what had happened where ..
and she HATED all that too, and said it was the most awful
holiday she had ever had; all she could feel was the trembling earth,
the distant guns, and the pain and sadness. I am a horrible brother.
So I took her back to Paris and we had champagne at the Ritz and
that was MUCH better. She even saw Chanel! And that was better
than anything!

I have despaired of my Muse returning from congé .... silly
vâche! So I picked up the novel which I abandoned two years ago
half finished and began to re-read it ... it's really not so bad! I
think I can do something with it ... but not on this silly machine
with it's stupid 'o' and all the ¡¿ and other errors ... for which I
apologise.

So .. no more

---

1. Dirk had been invited by David Puttnam to write a script based on *Covenant with
Death*, a novel by John Harris about the First World War. When it was first published in
1961 by Hutchinson, Dirk, wearing his producer's hat, had commissioned an adaptation
from Keith Waterhouse and Willis Hall, but the project was abandoned.
2. About fifteen miles north-east of Amiens.

[. . .] How funny to have an old carpet for a cat . . . it'll soon grow back, and she'll be as impossible and loving as ever, dont worry, but keep her away from the oven!

Love <u>DB</u>.

To Mary Dodd   *Clermont*
                                                  27 May 1986

Dearest Mainie –

I know that I have'nt written to you for years and years . . . perhaps, even, I owe you a letter! I cant be sure of that. Somehow time speeds along, one gets muddled up with all sorts of little bits of trivia, and worry too of course! and one ends up plodding along doing nothing very much but suddenly finding that the day is over and one has, to all intents and purposes, wasted most of it!

Maddening.

I've been busy with the buke . . correcting proofs. A ghastly business. This time, in a 310 page book, I discovered over 200 errors . . . mostly typographical, but others more serious which altered the meaning of a sentence . . . and some just plain soppy. How can a computer, for that is what the things are printed by, turn the River Thames into the River Thomas! It looks so silly . . and although it is only a difference of two letters what a difference they make . . . . anyway I screamed and beat my fists (metaphorically: of course. I'm too timid to do more than insist. Firmly.) and insisted that the proofs were reprinted before they could possibly be sent out to reviewers etc. This was greeted with a cry of rage from Viking who assured me that 'any reviewer KNOWS that proofs are full of errors; they take that into account.'

I still bleated on, and finally, when their OWN proof readers discovered 50 more errors which I had overlooked, they gave in; reprinted the lot, and the next batch, which arrived a few days ago, had only seven errors. Why, pray, could'nt they have had seven errors in the first place.

So that all kept me busy . . and bug-eyed. And then the photographs came, the ones they had chosen from a vast batch which I supplied . . and I hated some of them and the captions were wrong-spells-wrong and so THEY had to be done over again and all got back to the printer by the 19th of this month which was D. day. Anyway: all done now. And I hope I wont have to see it again until it is bound and covered. Cover not so good. A bit vulgar ... I have asked for it to be toned down a bit in colour .. it's a photograph of me from the back (!) painting out the hippo-pool which Coz took last year, and is quite fun and apposite for the title ... but they have scrunched it up with awful writing and worse colouring, a sort of yellow babies-motion colour, which I have instantly changed to plain white. When in doubt use white ... anyway it's due out in September and I have to come over for the Promo, a hideious week, from the 13th to the 18th ... Coz has to have his 'check' then anyway, so we HAVE to come over, but I shant enjoy my stint, <u>and</u> worrying about him and all. Oh Lor ...

He's off, at the moment, to the Pasteur in Nice to see his rum Professor .. who seems to be making a difference re-Parkinsons, having taken him off the English medicins which, he insisted, we[re] slowly paralysing him ... so far he does SEEM a bit better, less shakey, does up his shoe laces, threads his typewriter ribbon, folds his newspaper and so on ... the only thing is that he is slow ... and finds eating a problem: that is, holding anything on a fork, and cutting things up. Difficult. But, on the other hand, he has been mowing, slowly but well, in blistering heat (we've been in the 80's all month) and seems to manage alright.

[...] It is quite clear to me now that we cant hang on here much longer, and I have put the house on the market, very discreetly, and then, if it sells, the market is what they call 'depressed', we'll come back to England I fear. I think that he wants to be somewhere where he can be looked after .. and at nearly 71' I rather agree. I cant do it AND work .. and work I must.

This, as you will gather, is strictly confidential ... so keep Mum. I'll let you know if and when the time comes ... but another ghastly winter trapped up here with no way in or out wont do .. I cant manage alone!

Meanwhile the month ahead seems rather busy, alas! [...] Russell Harty and a crew of 10 arrive for three days to do a Profile on me to tie in with the book and the film I adapted from Greene's rather silly story, 'May We Borrow Your Husband?' which is due to hit your screens in late October.

It's all a fag, and I worry that it tires Coz ... but I think, in a way, that it is better for him to have some stimulation, even if it is a Telly

---

1. Tony would be seventy-one on 3 October.

Crew from Yorkshire! than just sitting about wondering if he will go to the Lav or not. [...] The Crew will eat up in the village .. but, knowing the chaps, the drink they will consume (from paper cups!) will be prodigeous .. unless of course it rains ... which after a month of amazing heat it is almost bound to do.

Coz just back from Pasteur. His Professor is VERY delighted with him .. and sounded most encouraging: it still does'nt make Coz leap about like a hare ... but it was a good prognosis and must cheer him up a little bit. He goes back on the 7th .. and it seems that the pills are just beginning to balence out: thats the main thing ... they can also, unlike any other pills for Parkinsons, be <u>decreased</u> in time. Maybe, it is not very frequent, it could be so for Coz ... one prays so. The usual British medecin is only <u>increasable</u> ... leading, eventually, to paralysis. I cant think why it has taken so long for us to discover this here, but thank God we did.

Telephone call to say that would I object to the film (M.W.B.Y.H.?) being shown theatrically (in a cinema that is) in the U.S.A, Australia and Canada! I'm delighted .. I'd rather it was a film than a quickly-forgotten TV evening. It could 'take off' like that one about the Laundrette, or the Letter to Brezhnive[1] ... or however he is spelled ... and that would make me very pleased. But it's not certain ... for my first ever adaptation though, it is a pleasing sign. Took me seven tough days to do in eight hour stretches. A very sore bum, but it seems to have worked, they will bring me a Video of it at the end of June when it is quite finished .. I did'nt altogether like the very first assembly, very rough, and not what I had really intended; so they went back to work and got my complaints sorted out ... Coz, who was adored by the entire Crew and the Director .. had a good deal to do with persuading them that I was right and they were wrong.

Very useful chap, your Coz .. parasite-ivy notwithstanding!

Off now to sort the sodding laundry list, pack it in baskets and cart it off to the lady in the village who 'washes'. At a price [...]

And then lay lunch, eat it, wash it up, and sit in a heap again in the heat.

Too hot to mow, so one waits now until seven to begin watering the pots.

---

1. Two recent, low-budget British successes: *My Beautiful Laundrette*, directed by Stephen Frears, and Chris Bernard's *A Letter to Brezhnev*.

By which time, be sure, I'm two glasses of scotch into the wind ....
and dont give a fig for watering, petunias, geraniums, nicotieanas, or
any other plant.

Only me!

With much much love –

    Dirk

        XXX

To Hélène Bordes   *Clermont*
                                                 17 July 1986

Chere Hélène –

I am writing simply because your lovely cards from Metz came this
morning, and I have nothing to do. So I write a note to you, <u>not</u> for
answering, just for 'telling'. If you understand!

[...] I find that the French simply ADORE talking .. more than
even eating, and much more than thinking! I am driven mad sometimes by the ladies in Genty, or Monoprix, who talk and talk and talk
while all you want to do is pay for your pain de son and a bottle of
Haigh!

And on the TV they will debate a TERRIBLE old American film
which has no value <u>at</u> <u>all</u> for DAYS! Tant pis. If it amuses them why
not.

I have nothing to do today because it is one of those awful days
when one simply 'waits'. Forwood had a complete 'check' at the
Clinic in Grasse and they have discovered two spots on his liver.
Plus parkinsons this is too much. So we sit awaiting, nervously, the
commencment of Chemoradio, which is very unpleasant, and pray
that no operation is needed ... but there is a sadness, after 45 years of
his care and council I feel a little bit lost being the Nounou[1] .. and
trying to do all the things which he did for me so well. Contracts,
impots, cheques and etcetera ... leaving me free to be an actor or a
writer. But, in my heart, I feel that those days are over now.

Ah well. I'll hang on here, even though we are an hour from Nice
where he will have to go I imagine, and try to find help somewhere.
The house is too isolated for a woman on her own (too many Arabs

---

1. Nanny.

wandering about at night) and after all people have their own jobs to do: we'll see.

[...] I have also, to try and keep my mind off unpleasant things, started another novel. One MUST occupy the mind and not just sit stareing into space worrying. I like the first chapter (All that I have written as yet!) but have not the Idea where it will go!

So far a man in London with a disasterous marriage and two horrible children, is leaving (amicably) his wife, and on the morning that he does, the mail arrives with a small packet containing an old iron key from his younger brother whome he has not seen for many years and who lives in . . can you believe this! Bargemon-sur-Yves, Var. I had to invent a town or village . . and that is where the rest of the story will take place, because he will go to Bargemon-sur-Yves and find many surprises but NOT his young failure of a brother who has just 'disappeared' into the wilderness for ever.

But the brother has left behind many problems, an un-married wife, a hundred canvasses (paintings) and a child who is a Mongol! After that I dont quite know what happens . . . trust me! But I am playing with a title already which COULD be 'The Jericho Walls' . . . (they fell down, did'nt they?) Well, it could be a symbolic meaning. I dont know . . . I'm muddled, and silly, and worried but I MUST work . . . the September in London business has had to be cancelled, of course . . . I was supposed, on top of all the other things, to have been the first actor to be Awarded[1] by the British Film Institute . . . rather like the French Academy of Film, or whatever it is called.[2] A great honour I am told, but I really need more than honours at the moment, thanks . . .

So there we are: a golden day here, a nephew (and his lady) have left last week, who were adorable and amusing and stayed two weeks instead of two days as originally planned . . . and this was before we had to go to the Clinic for the awful 'check'. Growing old is very, very tiresome, and comes to one so quickly . . . merde!

And with that vulgarity I leave you for another look at Bargemon-sur-Yves. I have to describe it carefully . . . and I am mixing up two real places so that everyone, including me, will be confused.

[...]Dont reply to this. Keep our bond . . . and dont overwork.

---

1. A Fellowship. He would accept one in 1987.
2. La Cinémathèque française.

I'll keep you in touch with progress here, have no fear . . . .
    Love
        <u>Dirk</u>

P.S. I forgot! The Saumur Windmill[1] has been writing almost daily!
On holiday in Quiberon or somewhere. All madness, what AM I to
do, and she thinks that you are 'Adorable'. Prenez garde! <u>D</u>

To Hélène Bordes

(Postcard)   *Clermont*
                                                    23 August 1986

Hélène my dear –
    Thank you for your 'thoughts'. I was glad to have them. Leave here
Sunday 31st .. back, perhaps, end of Sept/early Oct. House sold, I
think, we sign papers on Friday, dog in paradise. (The worst part
really. But it was soon done, one minute, and he is outside the Studio
here where he always sat to wait for me while I worked) and, apart
from the most terrible fires, the worst yesterday, ever, things are more
or less ready to 'go'. The heart-break is over. I am resigned now and
want only to get to London and have things dealt with. Write to me
one day at the Connaught [. . .] but do not expect a reply very
quickly! Thank you again and my love . . .
    as ever
        <u>Dirk</u>

To Susan Owens

(Postcard)   *Clermont*
                                                    28 September 1986

Susan –
    A splendid and funny letter from you waiting for me here yesterday
when I got back. I am so glad that you had such a happy day .. terribly
exhausting but fun! I was not in the LEAST 'ANNOYED' to see
you.[2] I was very happy and, as you must have realised, got you in one

---

1. Another obsessive, this one French.
2. After nine years of correspondence SO and Dirk had finally met, at a signing for
Backcloth in Hatchards.

.. long before you said 'Owens'! But I was deadly frightened by the crowd. I dont mind them sitting in the circle or the stalls but it's a bit scary to have them all round you! You try it!

Got back yesterday after a terrible three weeks of hospitals and 'scanners' and so on, plus the book, and am now, with my sister and brother, packing the place up. Cant manage twelve acres and three floors on my own now. So off to find somewhere smaller and nearer a town .. so I can walk to the shops and the market. Bendo is no more, alas. A <u>terrible</u> step, but it had to be taken .. and it was so quick and he was in my arms anyway and thought it was all a game.

So a new start. Worrying but exciting in a way. I'll let you know where I am, when I know!

In haste, with affection – <u>DB</u> –

To Hélène Bordes
(Postcard)

La Colombe [d'Or]
4 October 1986

Hélène –

All finished yesterday. The house is stripped, keys exchanged (plus cheque!) & I'm here until Tuesday, then London. No house, no car, furniture in store, I feel lost & 'epuisée' – I can hardly walk, a sense of Relief and Sadness – but a new beginning somewhere, sometime. The book No.I on ALL the lists! But I told you that I imagine' –

Love <u>D</u>

To Hélène Bordes

Hotel Lancaster [Paris]
13 November 1986

My dear Hélène –

I am using a borrowed machine, which is probably why there will be more errors than ever. This is the first letter I have had time, or relative peace, to write, so be patient! I am sitting at a little Louis-Quelquechose piece of furniture in the bed room ... it is all rather cramped, with eight suitcases, two machines, overcoats and anoraks, and shoes scattered everywhere. Outside the window there is a pleasant view over a courtyard with a few trees, a blackbird chattering in the

---

1. He did, on an earlier card, in which he described HB as the book's '"fairy" Godmother'.

yellowing leaves and, can you believe it? a <u>real</u> bat swooping above the rooftops ... not Clermont; but better than the Grande Boulevardes ... if I was one floor higher I could even see the egg-shell domes of the Sacre Coeur ... anyway: Paris is Paris and I love it and all the noise and light ... for a little while anyway. I MUST like it, there is no other way out at the moment. I am only allowed to have 92 days in England as a Foreign Resident and I have been using them up very fast with the medical tirridaddle, Scanners, etcetera ... for the moment things seem to be less fearful than they were. Nice got it wrong, I am told, so it was a wise thing to do to clear off and get some sensible advice and no more hysteria ... I think there is a vast difference between Nice and Paris as far as medecine is concerned: but that was my nearest base. So I had to take what was on offer, and what was on offer was not good news.

Being ill, as I once said to you before, in your own tongue is very, very, important indeed! However, it all costs a great deal of money, worry and moving about ... and even though I love Paris, as I do, eating out every day, morning and night, is expensive and <u>boring</u> too ... but there is not much alternative. The hotel restuarant is like a morgue ... and the food awful. One must eat. So ...

The Television play[1] was shown to the Press yesterday in London on a huge screen; not on that terrible box, and recieved a big ovation .. which is pleasing. It will be shown to the public on the 23rd ... and then we shall see what the Press really thought about it. One never can tell with them I fear. 'Backcloth' is in it's fourth edition already and Christmas looms ... and perhaps the TV will help to boost the already excellent sales. No one knows, for certain, in England, that I have left my beloved Clermont ... although there are suspicions, but so far the papers have not got the story. Yet ...

I suppose that when they do find out they'll be round this hotel like flies ... so far I am being very discreet and staying away from Prisunic or Casino! .. I hurry along little streets and do what shopping I must, whiskey, beer, biscuits, etc, at Felix Potin and no one cares.

I have at last unpacked everything, the cupboards are full, I wear a tie and a shirt every day; tres comme il faut after years of old jeans and sweaters, and am trying to adjust to a new life rather late in my life .... next medical check is in London in early January ... if that is

---

1. *May We Borrow Your Husband?*.

satisfactory then I might perhaps take a small appartment here if I can find anything which suits my pocket. We'll see . . . meanwhile my love to you, and apologies for this typing and for the long delay in finding peace, or time, to write to you . . . thank you for your letter which came the other day . . . take care, and be valient too . . I must go and wash, or have a bath perhaps? and then trail off to find a restuarant I can afford and which is <u>quiet</u>. Two of the hardest things to find in Paris. I was spoiled for 18 years by the peace of Clermont . . . the new owners, the Belgians, are apparently doing quite a lot to the place to accomodate their five children. But they have in no way altered the house, thank God . . .

All my love –
<u>Dirk</u>

To Penelope Mortimer   *Hotel Lancaster*
17 January 1987

Dearest Penny-Lopey –
Here's where I am now. Got back from London yesterday with a fat package of mail sent on from Chateauneuf, and your letter of December 11th, sweet heavens . . . Clermont sold up in July; Forwood ill with a cancerous polyp, then Parkinsons, and so on. No need to write more of the story, it's all been bloody.

So since then I have been too-ing and frooing from clinics and Harley Street and Wimpole and the Devonshire and all the other ghastly streets of that ilk. And inbetween 'tests' and 'scanners' have been in the Connaught or here . . . and now, since last week and a clearance, thank God, it's got to be here from now on in. An apartment somewhere, if I can find one that wont completely ruin me.

I am becoming rather institutionalised, if that is how it is spelled, by living in hotels and pressing buttons . . . but it is a limited life and one sits in two modest rooms with eight suitcases and two type-writers overlooking a courtyard, the Sacre Coeur, and an ivy covered wall full of roosting starlings . . . spending a fortune.

Become so entrenched here that the entire staff gave me a drink party on Christmas Eve which moved me greatly, and especially so when the Head Concierge presented me with the two crossed keys of a Night Porter in gold and said I was now 'in the Union'.

But apart from moments like that, it is rather sterile and I find it almost impossible to type, or write, in a bedroom ... with unmade beds and old clothes scattered among the foolscap and envelopes ..

I have a novel in hand, but have done nothing to it since the troubles started in the summer. It sits resentfully beside me, and I have rather lost interest ... one day I'll pull myself together. One day .. God knows when.

In the packing up of Clermont I came across a complete file of your letters from many addresses and lands, and have guarded them jealously .. perhaps, one day, you'd like them back? At present they are in store somewhere in Cannes. But one day ... they were super to read and so funny. Never read the Queen Mum book,[1] but know that she is NOT all chuckles and merangues. I expect you were dead on the nail, you usually are, and that always makes people unhappy, silly farts.

I got a huge packet, this time in London, from Viking with ALL the reviews for my last effort (Backcloth) which are rather hilarious to read after so many months. It came out in September, and I went and flogged it all over the place ... read a few reviews and shrugged .. as well I might, as we were selling a cool 39.000 up to December. But reading this lot of bunk was fun. So contradictory ... the provincial press super and understanding of the work, the London Press, so sophisticated that they bust with spite, furious that I played 'my hand too near my chest', whatever that really means ... but which was EXACTLY what I meant to do .. so they complain, and forgot to read between the lines. Suppose that might have happened to the Queen Mum book. The British simply hate being criticised for any- thing but <u>love</u> tearing others apart, from the French to poor sodding Prince Edward and on ... oh well.

Thats enough for now .. I'm trying to catch up on this packet of mail and not to loose old freinds. There was no time, ever, to send out change of adress cards, for I have NO adress yet, and most people think I'm still in Provence. Well: now you know better!

From your affectionat – <u>Dirk</u>

---

1. PM's *Queen Elizabeth: A Life of the Queen Mother* (Viking, 1986) had proved controversial.

To Laurence Harbottle   *Hotel Lancaster*
                                             3 February 1987

My dear Laurence –

After a great deal of heart-searching and head scratching I have, at last, come to terms with the problems which beset us and submit a 'plan' for your, I hope, approval.

I have signed to do a film[1] for BBC TV which will commence shooting on March 31st and end sometime about May 15th. I shall come over to London some days ahead of the start-date, on the 8th March to be exact, for I still have 30 days of this fiscal year in hand, and when 'shooting' is completed should have about 50 in hand of the new period.

During the time I shall be in London it is my intention to try and find somewhere to live, and to move myself, once and for all, back to the U.K.

We have had a pretty reasonable try at trying to find something here in Paris which would provide us with a new existance, but it really is not going to work. The cost of a moderate apartment is very high, and if I hired a live-in 'bonne' as I should have to, her wages would cost as much as the rent of the entire flat! Social Security takes care of that, without her food or keep! So that's out.

Paris is lonely if you have no friends, and although we HAVE a few who are pleasant and loving, no one wants to live in peoples pockets so to speak, and at our ages, 72 and 66 I honestly feel it wiser to get back home and try again among friends and family and in a language which I can speak.

There is always the constant nagging worry that a Doctor may be needed, and I frankly dont want to have to go through the miseries of last year again.

I know that this is going to mean a pretty hefty sacrifice financially, but, frankly, this style of living, in an hotel, simply cant go on any longer; the money just swirls away, and I'll have to face up to the facts, unpleasant though they may be and, with your help, try and make them as palatable as possible.

I think that this quite long period of time should give us a breathing space to get something worked out now that I have really made a

---

1. *The Vision* (see below, 21 March 1987).

decision. I am sorry that I have havered about for so long, but the decision has not been easy to make.

[. . .] I have no idea what sort of income I can expect to live on: which is a worry. We have been spending here at the most absurd rate, even though we have both done our very best to economise . . . I dont even eat a breakfast! But at least a third of my French fortune has gone, and I owe tax on the TV film I did for Yorkshire last spring: so there will be a chunk taken from what is left.

However perhaps in the weeks that I am in London we can have some kind of discussion together and try and resolve things once and for all.

This letter is merely to alert you to the decision I have made, and to help you prepare the ground a bit on my behalf.

Sorry to be so tiresome and to have been so indefinate in the past, but one simply has to try things out for oneself, and if they dont work try something else.

Thats what I'm doing now: wish me luck!

With very warmest wishes,
     <u>Dirk</u>

To Penelope Mortimer   *Hotel Lancaster*
                                      17 February 1987

My dear Penelope –

At the grave risk of boring you witless I am once again writing. This time to say that I finally finished the Q.M book and simply had to write and say how terrifically I'd enjoyed (and admired) it.

Christ knows how you managed to wade through all the stuff which you obviously HAD to, and how you managed to make your little 'notes' so that you could remind your reader from time to time where he was.

I cant help feeling [. . .] that you must be damned near the facts, and the picture you paint, for use of a better phrase, of that miserable family is tremendous.

<u>What</u> an unhappy lot they are.

No wonder the Queen looks so grumpy and slouchy at times . . . she's actually quite fun when you meet her privatly, but the fun goes out the window at the drop of a hat. Or whatever.

And as for the Consort: Christ. He's as jolly as an open coffin.

I think that it is a masterly book, and, as always with your own brand of 'riting' it is wonderfully readable and races along, a thing which is rare in a biography of this kind. But you dont clutter. Super!

A thing en passant .. when David was being buried[1] I saw a bit of Frog Newsreel which we did NOT see in London, of the Ladies draped in black standing together in a huddle like partridges. The D. of Windsor at the back. She was far from 'at ease' and, at one moment pulled anxiously at the Queens sleeve who suddenly turned on her with a scowl which would have sent me back to Boston there and then. The dislike was so intense that it <u>shimmered</u> off the screen. The Queen Mum knew all that happened but merely stood stock still looking the other way. I felt that afternoon tea that day was going to be tough. Even the French commentary caught it's breath .. and all one heard was a whispered gasp.

Anyway: I've had a marvellous time, and thank you.

I'm off to London in a few days to start work on a rather good TV play .. so I'll have to start packing in a minute .. it's snowing again. What do they SEE in Paris? Certainly winter aint fun ...

Have you finished your book? Dont answer .. retorical question. (SP?)

And thanks again .. with infinate love ..

Dirk –

---

1. The funeral of the Duke of Windsor on 5 June 1972.

II

THE LONDON YEARS

D irk and Tony rented a house in Chelsea from the actor – and, later, Oscar-winning screenwriter – Julian Fellowes, who lived in the basement.

To Hélène Bordes
(Postcard)

15 Moore Street
21 March 1987

Hélène –

A very pretty little house built in 1820 .. with a very small, but green, garden and a lot of cats plus two blackbirds! But we are off to the miseries of Cardiff (an industrial estate) for the film[1] in two or three days, and I shall be there, except for a weekend now and again back here, until the end of May. [...] I have been in various clinics having Radio and so on on my lungs .. all clear but I have a viral-infection and cough all the night, which is exhausting and irritating! Age! Lord ..

Today London is like Lovely Limoges .. wet, grey, silent and dreary, but the fire is warm and the house welcoming so I do not complain. I'll write from Cardiff when I can .. I have to work EVERY DAY! What a fool I am.

Love DB –

---

1. In April Dirk went on location to Cardiff with Lee Remick, Eileen Atkins and Helena Bonham Carter for the BBC Television production of William Nicholson's *The Vision*. Eileen Atkins played the wife; Helena Bonham Carter, their daughter. The story was so downbeat that they called themselves 'The Glums'.

To Hélène Bordes

(Postcard)   *Colombe d'Or*
                                                  2 June 1987

Here for 2/5 days to see the INSTITUTE PASTEUR DOCTORS FOR
FORWOOD AND SETTLE MY AFFAIRS. I <u>HATE</u> TO BE BACK.
SO MANY MEMORIES AND SCENTS!
   Love DB

To Hélène Bordes

(Postcard)   *15 Moore Street*
                                                14 July 1987

The Quatorze! Hot, hot in London, and no air. I am sticky and
miserable. You with summer bronchitis .. me with a very bad liver
attack! I have been drinking too much from sad despair. Where to
live? How to live? The prices here are crazy .. and every day I go to
look at another awful house at mad prices .. maybe after the summer
it will be easier. I cant settle to write, maddeningly, and have little in
the way of concentration .. I read, and wander about, and lay the
table, and wash up, and wander about, or just sit! Not very good for
the soul you will agree .. but I feel now the full weight of the flight
from France and my heart aches terribly. The furniture is all in England
so is the bank account, so the break has been made. But I still have
my Carte de Residence! So I cheer up a very little when I think of
that: at least until 1994!
   Be of good heart, I think of you too .. but I am not in a writing
mood, as you can see .. but there <u>is</u> all my strong affection still ..
   & love <u>Dirk</u>.

To Hélène Bordes

                                                15 Moore Street
                                                21 August 1987

Belle Hélène! –
   [...] I was so happy to get your card [...] another year of holiday
passed and the summer hurries towards the awful autumn and the
falling of the leaves which I really DO detest!
   A sign, I am certain, of ageing. Ah well ... My Ageing!

Here in London we stifle in a temperature of 30°! Can you believe it? The English certainly can not .. and hate it.

So do I. My bedroom is under the roof and it's like trying to sleep in an oven. I have been, as you will know, in Calcutta, Java, Singapore, and many other places but they are not a bit different to dreadful London in unaccustomed heat. One sweats miserably and there is no air and I grumble. I lie on my bed and try to read: it is not comfortable. The perspiration runs under my chin and dribbles onto my chest, and into my eyes and everywhere .. and I look at my fat tummy (I do not smoke since March 1st .. so I have put on DISGUSTING weight) and wonder what is happening to me.

Now: 'Backcloth', in paperback, has been No. 4 on the Best Seller list for six weeks. One giddy week it was No. 1! At the airports it is No.1 in non fiction ... a clever decision of my publishers to put it out for the Holiday Season.

So now I will be read from Malaga to Malta and I know I have been spotted in Bar sur Loup and St Tropez! I am, of course, very happy ... the book has worked better than the others even though the Press was not so kind to it, and said it was 'dull and dissapointing ..' Obviously from the letters I get, the reading public do not share that view.

I stopped there for a moment because a great storm has hit the city. The sky is black the thunder roars and the lightning rips into the darkness of the rooms. Maybe it'll be cooler after? I do hope so.

The family in the house opposite my 'Office' here are French and the daughter has just hurried out, her head in a coat, to find their cat. Which is sitting in MY dining room down below! Cats! They are so indifferent to our love for them. I will call from the window and tell the girl ... pardonnez moi ...

She was very relieved. And said that she had seen me on Tv last night. True. And very dull I was!

The other piece of news which is good, or which feels good for all is not certain yet, is that I have found a house.

A farmhouse built in 1707 in the old village of Kensington which is now, as you know, massive, but the house is small, white, with no garden, just a little patio with pots at the back .. inside the vibrations feel good, as they should in an old house which has seen generations of people come and go. It is simple, modest, and faces north onto a garden which belongs to the Carmelite Convent (so it is all green) and south onto a big Studio and a lovely ancient tree and roofs ... it is simple, very quiet and was VERY V E R Y expensive! God! But the furniture from Clermont will fit, it is all the right period .. and although I will have to sell off many many pictures (I had too many anyway) the few I really love will look very well in Queen Anne House (it's name.) We are supposed to exchange contracts on Monday ... and they promise to move out on the 30th Sept .. so I SHOULD be able to move in in the first week of October which will be exactly one year since I left Clermont to the days!

But I cross my fingers. I expect something will go wrong, it is almost sure to do so.

I can not tell you what awful places I have had to look at. Flats where one would die a day after moving in from sheer sadness ... houses full of damp, misery, children, and the feeling of divorce! Awful .. At the least this little house feels well and happy and quite seemed to like me. Alors ... on verra ..

The storm has stopped, the light comes back, the cat is wandering below in the garden avoiding, very delicately, the puddles of water. I must leave you and continue with my 3.000 word piece for the Sunday Times Travel section on ... The Riveria!

Off I go [...]

Love comme toujours
    <u>Dirk</u>.

Dirk and Tony moved to the house in Duke's Lane at the end of September.

To Hélène Bordes
(Postcard)   *Queen Anne House*
                                            12 November 1987

The patient[1] is ill. Everything suddenly blew up about 3 weeks ago. More Clinics, more 'tests', more 'Scanners' & this time it is, alas, positive. I have been too busy to even think or write, but loved your long letter & card today. We carry on – what else? I'll write when I get a desk! All love. <u>DB</u>.

Four days after sending the above card, Dirk suffered a mild stroke at home. Reports were carried in newspapers abroad as well as in Britain.

---

1. Tony's cancer had returned.

To Hélène Bordes

(Postcard)   *[Queen Anne House]*
8 December 1987

Hélène dear –

All is well, chere amie – I am lame and still a bit wobbley as you can see – but we will get strong once this AWFUL Christmas is over! Love to you as always – & happiness & peace in 1988 –

With love <u>Dirk</u>

After the stroke, and with Tony in increasingly poor health, Gareth Van den Bogaerde and his family rallied to the cause. Rupert and his wife Jacquie, a trained nurse, had moved in to Queen Anne House for a while.

To Gareth and Lucilla Van den Bogaerde   Queen Anne House
27 January 1988

My dearest Cilla & Gareth –

I am only too well aware that I have never really PROPERLY thanked you both for your wonderful, and quite unstinting, kindness, generosity and love during the last three months.

I will try to do so now.

The shadows seem to be lifting, at least from my head, and I am able (look at this!) to type again . . it's taken it's time but it is happening. [. . .] I have an Office built . . carpets laid, shuffled about and got one or two things dealt with, mail sorted, drawers cleared, books stacked. So on. I'm <u>trying</u> to break through again . . it's been far too long. Which is why I never did more than thank you in the most perfunctionary way.

My heart wanted to say more; I just lacked the energy somehow.

My typing as you can see is all to hell . . . I'm getting the letters muddled up . . dislexia perhaps? Who can tell . . or just that this is the first letter I have attempted since early November, or late November or wherever it was.

But it's only to say how wonderful you both were . . and how tremendously kind and calming you were inspite of the sacrifices which I know you had to make in your own life-style to accomodate two elderly gents in trouble.

Both you, and your extraordinary family, swamped this place with love and security just when it felt arid and cast-off.

Leaving Clermont was, for both Tote and myself, an amputation rather than a severence . . . killing Bendo a sort of suicide . . something which we'll take a time to get over.

But thanks entirely to you this house now seems not so hopeless, so unfreindly, so alien . . . Rupert, Brock, Kimbo and Jackie and Ulric (and Alice on the telephone!) have given the place a luster it never had before.

With your love and care I think we might even make it!

I dare not look at the future . . who dares I wonder . . but for the forseeable future, anyway, thank you all . . . thank you both: I know that you will say, 'Well, thats what families are for' and so they are. But you gave more than just immediate family affection, you gave something so cherishable and rare that I shall never, how ever hard I try, be able to repay you, nor make you realise how deeply grateful I am to you all.

And thats quite enough. I shall start sounding soppier than I even am.

For the errors in typing, my apologies . . . but there are no errors in my words of love and gratitude.

Always
    <u>Dirk</u>.

To Olga Horstig-Primuz[1]   *Queen Anne House*
                                               27 January 1988

Excuse the errors – I have not
typed since November! <u>D</u>

Most loved Olga –

I am very well aware that it is a long time ago that you wrote to tell me, or telephoned as well, to say that you were leaving the Office. I should have sent you flowers: a golden pen . . . maybe an apple tree in blossom . . . I did none of these things and I did'nt even write to you or telephone.

---

1. OH-P, Dirk's agent in Paris, had retired. While Dirk lived in France, they would speak by telephone on Sunday mornings. Only now did a correspondence develop.

I have excuses, of course. What good Actor has not!

Depression was the main one, and a complete lack of any kind of incentive: I was still, it seems, in my state of post-shock-after-the-stroke and nothing was anygood that I did, nor did I do anything. But I sat all day and read the papers or just sat. Stareing at nothing. Not my usual form at all. I have always been a fairly active person, eager to hurry about and do this or that. I have NEVER just done nothing at all! Which is why I have never taken a holiday unless I could avoid it; to sit on a beach in the sun, or under an umbrella, with a little swim now and again, or a sip of wine, is my idea of total hell on earth.

But the stroke, and it <u>was</u> mild, laid me completely out.

The last two years have been a terrible strain I fear [. . .] I suffered a big loss and I miss France every single day of my life. I always will. But there is no way back now.

And so . . . grieving for my lost country, France, for the peace and beauty of Clermont, for the life that once I had, rather drained me and I could not put a pen to paper, or even lift a telephone to send you a telegram, to tell you how deeply I shall miss you and how utterly different the world I knew is, now that you are no longer fully active.

I miss you enormously: I miss our little chats on Sunday about this or that . . . nothing important, but just a familiar holding together which I enjoyed greatly.

Cannes, Paris, all France, will not be the same now that you are no longer in that curious old office which I loved so much even though I did not often see you there. But from the early 'fifties until last year I knew that, not so far away, you were sitting behind your desk ready to surprise me with a new Client or an old, and loved, one! And that you were near to come and have a drink at the Lancaster, or to have a luncheon in the garden, your handbag full of clippings from . . . oh, Figaro, Paris Match, Variety . . anything.

Never mind. Both our lives have altered.

I shall always remember our meeting with B.B and Cloun .. or Clown[1] in English .. remember you dragging an excited little Vera[2] to meet me when we came over for the 'Servant' . . . the evening you came up to meet a rather strange, leggy, creature called Rampling!

---

1. Bardot – Dirk's co-star in *Doctor at Sea* – and her dog.
2. OH-P's daughter.

I never spoke enough French for you: I was useless in so many ways as a client, but we <u>did</u> do one thing together which I shall cherish all my life. We did 'Providence' ... and that was a good thing. Thank you for your love, your care, your sweetness at all times ... for the happy days we spent together at Clermont ... once with your Mamma, remember? and the time we had at Festivals in France and Italy.

What a good time it was! How <u>lucky</u> we have been! No one will enjoy it more than we did, will they? Nothing will ever be quite the same again. Tant pis. I LOVE you quand meme ...

Your devoted Dirk – XX

To Ulric Van den Bogaerde
Queen Anne House
5 February 1988

My dear Ulric –

Your letter of the 20th January just got here this morning. What did you do? WALK to the mail-box? Anyway: it was good to have it even though your news did sound a bit depressed, rather than depressing ... You are going through a really foul period of time.[1] I knew it well and detested it .. I could'nt fart in a blanket, for Heavens sake! I was the total despair of my beloved and careing parents, and got shoved from one school to another, one Tutor to another, and finally ended up in a Technical College in Glasgow where I rotted away quietly all day (Did I know a thing about H2SO4, Bunsen Burners, the effect of copper filings on sulphuric acid? Did I? And what is more did I care?) and went to the ice-rink in the evening with a cousin who loved a goal keeper in the Canadien Ice Hockey Team.

Not me.

So it was not my time either. But, honestly, dont give up all hope .. you are a very bright fellow, personable, clever (I know that. I can tell.) and very intelligent ... the fact that you dont seem to be able to put it all together just yet should'nt get you into a state of despair and hopelessness. It all takes time. Not immediate. Something, or someone, will suddenly grab you and it'll all shake down. I am quite certain.

What you HAVE to do is keep reading. Not Beano but real reading. And keep writing ... write anything, write rubbish ... write a daily

---

1. Gareth and Lucilla's son was seventeen and at school.

analasys (cant spell it) of yourself. Whatever you do keep on <u>expressing</u>
yourself, and keep very alert. Maybe Florence will help to jog you into
some sort of awareness ... maybe you'll want to read a bit more about
the city, it's history, the art it has to offer, the type of life that goes on
there and has gone on there for simply hundreds of years with very
little change .. I mean, allowing for motor cars, disco's, and Tourists
and all the crap of this ugly centuary. Anyway: we'll see.

But as long as you <u>become</u> someone, not just a dollop of humanity,
as long as you remain aware, careing, interested and, above all, curious,
I am certain that your life will be fullfilling and rewarding.

I never watch my old schlock on the TV, it's too small, the screen
I mean, and the fact that I never get a penny piece in residuals so
pisses me off that I just turn my back.

Sucks to them.

But I DID watch the 'Servant' and quite enjoyed it again after 25
years or so .. The Blue Lamp was on too late for 'ickle me' ... so I
missed that. I get shouted at in the street now of course. I'm amazed,
literally, that they recognise me after so long ... but people do. Funny,
I have'nt at this mo. got any photographs, I burned the lot during the
move from France .. but as soon as another sodding German Fan
sends me a packet for signing, I'll snitch one[1] [...]

Now: there we are. I hate this machine ... it's different from my
old faithful [...] and the bloody 'I'' and 'O' are in different places.
Oh well.

Be of good heart, courage, and dont be hopeless: that leads to
helplessness and thats VERY boring indeed!

You are better than that!

Love <u>Dirk</u>.

To Hélène Bordes
(Postcard)

Queen Anne House
12 February 1988

Chere Hélène –

Thank you, my dear, for the cards and the messages of courage they
contained! I was in need of them, I assure you. Courage has mounted
high again. Yesterday was the Big Cancer examination for the Patient

---

1. For a friend of UVdB.

and the chemiotherepy is working! The tumor has been, they said, 'considerably reduced'. A tremendous bit of luck and fortune .. so we continue. Everyone very happy because this is entirely an expiriment. The pills come from Japan and are not in use normally in Europe. We are guinea-pigs .. tant pis[1] if it works. So now the future is less appalling for the moment, and the builders are hard at work making me shelves for my books and desks for this machine .. and one day, who can tell? I may get back to my work again. I have a big piece in the Sunday Times on Sunday next about the Riveria![2] I'll send you a copy next week. My only piece of work for two years. Oufff .. thank you again for your hand across the sea, the 'plank' is always there. A good feeling!

My love <u>Dirk</u>

To Nerine Selwood
(Postcard)   *Queen Anne House*
                                              18 March 1988

Dear Nair –

In haste in reply to your letter recieved today [...] Alas! Tony has cancer AND Parkinsons and side effects from the chemio therepy. He's also had a v. bad fall in the street and cut his face and broken his teeth, so life is pretty well a buggers muddle. I am still having phisiotherepy for my right leg, everything else still works thank God! .. but I am lame and with all the housework and cooking (I cant!) to try and do, life is a problem to say the least.

This week is full of dentists, the cancer specialist and later on in the week the occulist who is to perform a small operation with laser to heal a burst artery in T's left eye. If you had told me that all this would be my lot at 67 I very much doubt that I'd have bothered! [...] Anyway. Have a good day on the 28th .. I shall do my best to forget it.[3]

Love. Dirk –

---

1. He means *mieux*, of course.
2. 'Impressions in the Sand' (14 February).
3. Dirk laboured under the impression that they shared a birthday. NS was born four days before Dirk.

To Hélène Bordes
(Postcard)   *Queen Anne House*
                                                      30 April 1988

Chere Hélène –

Thank you for your sweet letter which gave me great pleasure today.
I needed it because, alas, The Patient and I have lost the battle. Day and
night nursing by two nice girls, and not very long to go. It is a strain, but
at least I am able to sleep again, and apart from feeding the nurses, and
him, my work is not difficult. The loneliness will be when it comes. It
was a good fight, valient, determined, but the good Lord has decided
that He will be the winner. Mal chance . . . one day, I promise, I'll write
that LONG letter. For the moment I wait only . . . .

My love & thanks. <u>Dirk XXX</u>

Anthony Forwood died at home on 18th May at the age of seventy-two.

To Hélène Bordes
(Postcard)   *Queen Anne House*
                                                      21 May 1988

Hélène my dear –

My Patient died peacefully in his sleep on Wednesday morning. I
was with him but he was unaware thank God.

Now I must try to begin to live again: and alone.

The house is very empty without him.

And my life also.

Thank you for your card, it gave me great comfort.

All my love <u>Dirk</u>.

To Susan Owens
(Postcard)   *Queen Anne House*
                                                      3 June 1988

I was saddened to get your letter with all it's wretched news.[1] Mine is
pretty bloody too. Mr F. died ten days ago and the pain is starting

---

1. SO's husband had had a series of strokes and she was told he did not have long to live.
He died in August 1989.

right in now. I cant write more or longer, there is no sort of incentive and I have so much to clear up, not least all his papers and clothes and etc. Not fun. And after fifty years (minus seven for the war) you feel a bit lost. Being alone is one thing being on your own and lonely quite another. It does'nt hit you during the weeks of nursing and care, but then that is all done [and] the silence is deafening. Family and chums have been wonderful. But there is still that terrible emptiness when you shut the front door and they've gone.

I'll get better, they tell me, but no one can quite say exactly how long it takes. For ever I'd think. At least you have your children. I made a big mistake .. so dont expect any signals for a while.

DB –

Putting this house on the market today! Move off to a small flat in Chelsea, with a Porter at the door so I can just lock-up and go – <u>DB</u>

To Julian Barnes
(Postcard)   *Queen Anne House*
                                                  11 June 1988

Julian –

How comforting was your letter; how chuffed T. would have been, he always felt so fearfully inadequet intellectually, as he insisted and nothing I could say or do would ever convince him that people actually did like him MUCH better than me! He never learned, the silly fellow. I realise, from the letters which have come since he died, just how much he was liked and respected, and that the balance between Sweet and Sour, if you like, he and I that is,[1] was rather good. Anyway we had a terrific fifty years together and nothing can take any part of that away. The last five years were hell. But then one has to pay it seems. Sod it.

<u>D</u>

To Mark Goodings and Judy Roberts[2]   *Queen Anne House*
                                                  14 June 1988

My dear Mark & Judy –

Thank you so much for your invitation to the nuptials. How

---

1. Emphatically in that order.
2. Elizabeth's son and his fiancée had asked Dirk to their wedding.

splendid for you both and how I wish that I could be present.

But it is not to be: I tried a first trip out on Tuesday just to see if I could face the world again and found that I'm not quite ready for all that just yet.

But I shall be very much with you in spirit, and I wish you both a wonderfully long and happy life together: it is, after all, something about which I know quite a bit!

Be happy, be courageous, gracious and loving and give way when essential to do so and you'll make it work in this shoddy world.

Above all share things together, that is a very important part of the relationship, and discuss before you have a fight or a slanging match!

Great happiness and a long life together.

With much love

<u>Dirk</u>

To Nerine Selwood   *Queen Anne House*
                                                 18 July 1988

Dear Nair –

Thank you so much for your letter which I got on Friday . . . much better than those incomprehensible things from Telecom or the Gas People which leave me helpless with worry!

I have managed to destroy 45 years of T's letters and files and bundle off his clothes to Oxfam. Always a distressing business . . but now the place is empty of his presence, and I must start off all over again.

To this end I have sold this house, at a profit, and move into a titchy pent-house with a terrace facing south over a beautiful garden ten minutes walk from Sloan Square. I cant bear this area, full of nig-nogs and punks and gobs of bubble gum all over the pavements. So I'm off at the end of the month. Another move within nine months is impossible to contemplate, but I'll have to have a bash and Lu says she'll come up and stay with me while I sort myself out. I have'nt even unpacked the books from the <u>last</u> move yet so at least they are still in their containers!

She, Lu, has been a brick, we have managed to console each other very well,[1] and she wanders up from time to time and spends a couple

---

1. Elizabeth's husband, George, had died on 15 February.

of days here and we sit and read and lay tables and shop in M&S . . .
it's company for us both.

One day perhaps you and I could manage a meeting. God knows
when . . . but, honestly, I dont want to remember the past, and have
'a natter about the NADS and the old days'. As far as I am concerned
they are distant history and I have no rememberance, and wish none,
of that time. So much, you must realise, has happened to me over the
years, so many new faces, new experiences, new directions, that all I
can do is look ahead to whatever the future has in store for me. I have
written my books about the past, burned all my papers and diaries,
and cleared my decks so to speak. Now it's full steam ahead and there
is no time for reminiscencing about a dead time . . it's all in the distant,
forgotten, past. Can you under stand this possibly cruel, but quite
unintentionally so, attitude? I really cant go back, and I frankly have
no interest in doing so. We really have'nt very much to speak of
together, we have both gone such different paths and they will never
cross again as once they did: we are too old for that now, and 'memory
lane' is somewhere I dont want to linger in!

However, a card now and again, a letter, and we keep in touch, that
is as much as one can expect at present. There is so much still to do,
and so little time in which to do it . . . I'll let you know where I move
to and when, if I have the strength left!

As ever

Dirk.

To Hélène Bordes
(Postcard)
                                                            [Queen Anne House]
                                                            18 August 1988

My dear:

Thank you for writing [. . .] I am still in the same house! The
young people who 'bought' it got posted, suddenly, to San Franscisco,
so No Sale. Merde! Excuse me . . . however I sold it again a day later
to two exceptionally pleasant people who paid more money!

But the lawyers and etc are taking so long on the contract for my
flat that I fear I shall spend the winter in Hyde Park . . I think, if
things DO work correctly, that I shall be able to get into the flat at
least in the first week of September. Almost exactly a year that I moved
in here. Ah me! My electric machine has broken down, so in fury I

went & bought this simple, idiots, machine which works manuelly ... but at least I can type and I am so bewildered by computers and all things mechanical ... I go to lunch today with my Lit. Agent to show her half a book I found I had written years ago at Clermont and never published .. letters to my wonderful Mrs X. After so many years I think they have a value. I wonder? She will read them today, or the next, and tell me! I am slowly coming back to life!

Love D. X

On 9 September Dirk moved into a flat on the third floor (fourth storey) of 2 Cadogan Gardens in Chelsea.

To Penelope Mortimer

Cadogan Gardens
25 September 1988

Penny-lopey – love –

Joy and delight, first off. Delight to have your letter [...] I am sitting in my little (titchy) Penthouse. An inflated word for a small cabin stuck on top of an Edwardian mansion. I had thought that it was very probably 'Nannies Quarters', but in the recent wind realised that I swung about and creaked like a galleon. Oh well. It cost an arm and the proverbial leg (what DO they cost I ask myself?) but I'm in. A far cry from the farm and even from the 1710 nonsense I bought, and thankfully sold to buy this, off Ken Church Street. NEVER venture there. Most awful place [... with] neighbours who wrote, very kindly, and pushed the letters under the front door, saying 'Can we do your shopping?' and (This was the dottiest and most unusual) 'Please dont grieve.'

Now come on. You either grieve or you dont. After fifty years it is a kind of loss. And I cant help looking grumpy anyway. I'm so preoccupied with all manner of tiddly little things.

How many pennies to the pound? What does a florin represent now .. where can I get a typewriter that WERKS? I dont want one which corrects all my errors, scolds me with bells, and fucks up my margins ... and has a list of instructions in incomprehensible Jap-Eng. Fuck it.

Anyway. Joy and delight. And the joy is that you wrote: before leaving the 'quaint' (not my word. The Agents') house I destroyed, as I had to, forty eight years of Forwoods files and etcetera ... he was the

Business Head until the arrival of Parkinsons and then Cancer put paid to all that nonsense ... so I heaved stuff off to the shredder in sacks. Bank statements going back to 1962, old contracts for films long forgotten, letters from the dead.

All gone. Until the University of Boston wrote imploring me to sell them my archives! I ask you. So all the MS were dug out of the shredder, all the most lovely letters, I dont mean 'from the dead', not only those, but lots from the loving living. By which I mean a trillion of yours! All safely in Boston, all sealed until well after we are dead. But what <u>supreme</u> letters you wrote to me, what splendours they were and still are. From, I dont know, Holland Park would it be? Or Belsize Park .. one of those places, through the miseries of Yaddo and on .. and then spasmodic silences .. but splendid letters. I think that I wrote to you from Paris last? Cant remember, it's all a hideious blurr now ... and the last five years were fucking awful honestly. Never mind. It's over, that part, and I start again. Odd how tough you suddenly find yourself to be. For a time.

I have two thirds of a book, sold to Viking, and am slowly coming up out of the deep-freeze, and this is my very first letter in my new, titchy, little study. A view north with no distraction beyond the parapet, and a plastic desk and this manuel, manuel? typewriter. Hence errors and etc. But it at least does'nt speak to me or wring bells. It does'nt work, either – 66 quid at Rymans – oh well . . . .

Please lets have lunch in October. Oh please. Shyness CANT be anything to do with us, for Christs sake .. we know each other far too well. Say what you cant eat, I dont go to M&S now, too far away and I cant walk it ... so it's grub from Partridges in Sloan Street. (Where else, pray) and you can choose whatever you like but COME. After the 9th. I have a to-do with Princess Anne then. Attenborough [...] has arranged a New Award For Acheivement[1] and I have to be the fall-guy ... a <u>dreadful</u> kind of This Is Your Life. I ask you.

Love, EVER, <u>D</u>.

---

1. The Princess Royal, as President of BAFTA, was to present Dirk with its inaugural Tribute Award for his outstanding contribution to the Cinema.

To Eileen Atkins *Cadogan Gardens*
4 October 1988

Eilleen dear –

Forgive this dainty card: all I could find to thank you for 'NEXT SEASON'[1] ... which I am rather longing to read, because I am stuck in the sugary land of Joyce Grenfell.[2] I cant be doing with her Christian Science nonsense, (in the middle of a total war!) or her overt snobbery .. nicely meant but snobbery.

Just saw today in the paper that they have opened a new Holiday Inn in, guess where? SWINDON! That'll be a load of fun. Do remember it next time you go down the M4 to do some location. Ghastly evening yesterday at a script conference for this dotty BAFTA thing on Sunday. Unspeakable dialogue most of it inaccurate, and we all sat round a board room table being bored and being served bits of dead chicken and wilted salad by a sullen lady who clearly wanted to go home as much as I did. I got to bed at 1.30 .. rather pissed, and cant remember what we decided to do or not to do. Oh dear.

I wrote what I thought was an ironic little piece for the Indipendant[3] last week and have been delueged (no 'e') with more than 700 letters from sodden lady readers. Sodden because they were all so saddened by my 'unhappiness' ... I did'nt know it had shown! Was'nt meant to ... anyway they all offer me 'peace and solitude' in places as far apart as Bath, Alloa, Hastings, Dartmoor and Cork ... golly! I shall have to write and thank them all: so I'd better end this. But thanks again and all love ..

Dirk – XXX

To Dilys Powell *Cadogan Gardens*
17 October 1988

Dilys dear –

How good to have your note. I'd love to lunch with you .. cold cuts, something terribly simple, I eat like a sparrow ... but can it

---

1. A novel by the director Michael Blakemore, first published in the UK in 1969 by Weidenfeld & Nicolson.
2. *Darling Ma: Letters to Her Mother, 1932–1944*, edited by James Roose-Evans (Hodder & Stoughton).
3. 'A half-life in World's End' *(The Independent*, 19 September 1988).

be after November 11th? I've got myself caught up in a memorial thingummy for Armistice Day ... reading Saki at the National. And I quake.

The Celebration[1] was utter hell. They always are. Keeping Sir R.A off the stage was the hardest part, but I managed by doing it all myself. People were wonderous kind and loving and I was very nearly brought to a blub by the ovation, standing! at the end. The foul Press said it was five mins. But I rather think I got it stopped by three. However: not bad. And lots of chums came from distant places, [Jean] Simmons from Los Angeles, [James] Fox from Sydney, and so on ... all in all gratifying but potty, and terrifying. I HATE a black tie ... I always look like a Maltese waiter.

I do hope that you are stronger now: crawling up your stairs. Goodness. I have NONE here. It's a sort of one story box on the top of an Edwardian house ... and none the worse for that. From my bed I can look into the sitting room.

There is a certain comfort in that, and in the fact that I have already collected two pair of wood pigeons, two blackbird, one pair of Magpies and one pair Rooks! How is that for getting a feel of the country in a secluded, and unused, London garden square?

So lunch soon ... I'll write when the Thing is over. I am never certain about the rehearsals ...

With overpowering love –
     Dirk

To Penelope Mortimer

Cadogan Gardens
29 October 1988

My dearest P –

And, of course, you wont get this until Tuesday. But it is to say what a splendid evening I had.[2] Really.

I know that you were wincing with shame and all those Mortimer Agonies (quite unwarrented, as usual) but I was facinated to be able to watch a fillum which had absolutely nothing what ever to do with

---

1. The BAFTA award ceremony was considered by most of those present to have been a disaster, with Dirk at his least gracious. Lord Attenborough – at the time Sir Richard and the Academy's vice-president – would later remember the evening as 'a nightmare'.
2. Dirk had been on an extremely rare visit to the cinema, taken by PM to see her adaptation of Galsworthy's *A Summer Story*, directed by Piers Haggard.

me. No responsibilities. And that is usually what happens when I go to the flicks. Responsibility. Either my work as an actor, as a writer or to the Cast and the ruddy Director ... and how often I have heaved with fury when the prop men have used enough smoke in a cottage chimney to rival Battersea Power Station at full blast.

Yesterday I merely thought, 'Silly farts. Is the kitchen on fire?'

No: there ARE things wrong with the film. Director, I'm afraid; not ANYTHING wrong with the script I hasten to add, and the performances as we agreed are very uneaven, the music too bloody lush, and the crowds all a bit tidy and clean and all. If only Visconti had got hold of them!

But there was another part of it all which pleased me so, the evening I mean; first time in years I had gone to a cinema .. first time I'd tried sitting with this still-slightly-wonky leg ... first time I'd gone out, as it were, 'on my own' ... and given that my hostess was you whome I love anyway, and that I had a smashing ride in a super motor with Terry Someone and a delicious, relaxed and paid-for supper with all the whisky I could require, I mean, really, what more could I ask.

Everything worked very, very well. Even the girl beside me in the cinema offered me her Malteaser. Was'nt that pleasing? I scowled at her of course. I always do. Terror lurks not very far beneath this apparently cool façade. I'm as cool as a microwave oven really.

But thank you.

Now lets have no more grovelling [...] the film is done and over and whatever it's faults they are not yours, and I had a really lovely evening. I'm not going to say thanks again: even you will get bored.

With love, always,
   <u>Dirk</u>.

To Penelope Mortimer

Cadogan Gardens
10 November 1988

Dearest Penelope

What I should be doing is having a bash at my bit on the Holocaust for the Tellygraf. I just cant face it somehow ... maybe tomorrow I'll feel lighter of touch and mind. But three fat books all about those who survived have rather dented my brain.

[. . .] Nicholas,[1] darling or not, pays me rather well: and I do find it a form of therepy actually. I have'nt written a thing for two years . . . and the thought of getting down to it again depresses me greatly. But Nicholas offered a sort of branch over my sluggish stream of despair and I had a grab and got hauled up a bit. Not much: but a bit. And it's better.

Having to do something when all incentive is lost is quite good for the soul. Or whatever. And, oddly, I quite enjoy doing it . . . I got very funny feed-back from the O'Brian Bit[2] . . . and that is rewarding too.

I think that the Vita/Harold thing[3] might be a bit dreary for you, as you clearly dont seem to care for them. I could'nt take him but did quite admire her . . . but I'm a bit stuffed with all that Dyke-Runaway and silly old Violet and the rest. I think it would be a terrible penance, and they are bound to play Anthony Andrews and Jane Seymour in the thing.

There is absolutely nothing that I LONG to do . . . I would like to do something with H. Bonham Carter who played my child in a recent play on TV and was super to work with . . . we want, desperatly, to be Dad and Daughter again . . . but cant think of anything. And Charlotte Rampling and I were almost off with Vita's 'No Signposts In The Sea'[4] only the lady producer was such a cunt and the adaptation impossible. Everything turns to dross when I get near. I wonder why? And Glenda and I tried for a year to get 'Buried Alive' off the ground but could'nt get the lolly. Amazing.

I must walk up to the doctors now and order my Soneryl for the week-end I'm running out. He wont give me more than fifty at a time for fear that I'll gobble them all up and skip over. Silly fart. Little does he know that all that is taken care of anyway. Neat little packets from Parig[i][5] . . . still, it's excercise for the leg, to walk up the street I mean,

---

1. Shakespeare – Literary Editor of the *Daily Telegraph*, who earlier in the year had 'recruited' Dirk as one of its book reviewers. The timing was impeccable, and Shakespeare was swiftly promoted from a mere branch-offerer to 'Plank', the second in Dirk's life. The present assignment was a trio of books about the persecution by the Nazis of the Jews.
2. Dirk had reviewed Edna O'Brien's *The High Road* (Weidenfeld & Nicolson).
3. PM had been asked to adapt *Portrait of a Marriage* (Weidenfeld & Nicolson, 1973), Nigel Nicolson's study of Harold Nicolson and Vita Sackville-West.
4. Vita Sackville-West's 1961 novel, published by Michael Joseph.
5. On 3 July 1996 Viking Penguin would present Dirk with an inscribed pill-box to mark one million sales of his books under their imprints. He said: 'I shall keep my suicide pills in it.' His hosts were unsure whether or not he was joking.

and his secretary thinks I'm quite lovely. So I'll boost my ego modestly and mail this, which comes with a stack of love to your sodden garden and you ..

Always

Dirk

On 14 November Dirk took part in an Armistice Festival event at the National Theatre, reading from the short stories of Saki (H. H. Munro), with Barbara Leigh-Hunt, Tim Pigott-Smith and Zoë Wanamaker.

To Dilys Powell

Cadogan Gardens
24 November 1988

Dilys my dear –

I sent off the 'piece' to Mr Perry[1] a day or so ago: I dont know if it's what he wanted or not, and he has'nt yet called me back. So perhaps it was'nt any good.

I was terrifically honoured to have been asked to write for you, and I only hope that I got the thing right ... difficult stuff, one is so afraid of 'gushing' and doing a sort of R. Attenborough. All that darling and adorable and so on: not my style.

I'd love to lunch with you ... no reason for you to trail over here to me and, anyway, I cant cook an egg even ... I subsist largely on frozen delights from the local mini-Harrods[2] in Sloan Street. But it's alright. So, yes please, let us make a date at your house, but SIMPLE. I eat little and a glass of white wine will do for me really. Dont even need the grub.

At the moment I am wrestling my way through a book, writing it I mean, which I have to deliver to my publisher on December 30th. I shake with terror for I am so out of practice and pages stay blank and white and evil. And empty. Gosh, it's awful. So as soon as I am in reasonable shape, by which I mean, when I can, more or less, see the end in sight and be able to relax and take a morning off, I'll let you know. Will that be alright?

At the moment of writing this I am coping with builders putting

---

1. Dirk wrote the Introduction to *The Golden Screen: Fifty Years of Films* (Pavilion/Michael Joseph, 1989), a collection of DP's reviews, edited by George Perry.
2. Partridges of Sloane Street.

up book shelves for my much depleted library. I have had to rid myself
of so much now that I'm in a one bedroom flat .. perhaps just as well,
I was not travelling light, as they say, and the junk that has accumulated
over the years was awesome. Most of it has gone now, and I am
reduced to the bare necessities and one or two sentimental pieces.

The Saki readings which I did with Zoe Wannamaker and Tim
Piggot Smith at the Olivier were fun. In a terrifying way. First time
on a real stage for 32 years! But they seemed to delight in Saki, who
was unfamiliar to them, apparently, and the Olivier was packed to the
gunnels .. good.

But I dont really think it is worth all the hassel, that acting lark,
and anyway no one asks me now to do anything, so there is no point
in fretting. I'll carry on with this writing business, it does pay a <u>little</u>
and it also helps to keep ones mind a little more alert than usual.

Mine, my dear, seems to have gone into hibernation.

I'll write to you as soon as I get the present 'block' unblocked ..
and we'll have a meal at your place. I do rather long to see you
again ...

With much devoted love, as ever –
   <u>Dirk</u>

To Bee Gilbert   *Cadogan Gardens*
                                              18 February 1989

Sno my love –

You are, I gather, due home in a sec. So this ought to be waiting
for you: but knowing this ghastly country I'd very much doubt it. Is'nt
it utter hell?

Loved your letter, sad about your financial straits, mine will be just
as jolly when they twig I'm here, and happy that you found a Tote
Note, they are quite rare I gather and people collect them rather.

So thats got rid of that. Now then; about the fillum ... well the
answer is, reluctantly, no.[1] I hate 'Evenings' but quite like 'Matinees'
and do them constantly. But getting to and from in an evening is too
costly now .. renting cars and etc. I cant sit about waiting for taxi's
for fear of the dreaded cry 'Were'nt you Dirk Bogarde?' which assails
me daily ... unless I dress, as I do now, in trodden shoes and my old

---

1. BG had invited Dirk to a première.

anorak from home which is, by this time, crawling with greasy-lice. I am seldome recognised like that. But in a decent bit of gear it's hellish. And, in anycase, I have'nt got a D.J. I gave mine to Save The Children and they got a thousand quid for it. Lucky children in the Sudan. What was the matter with me? I loathe children, especially under ten (they should, from birth, be stuffed with dates and garlic and slowly turned on a spit) [. . .]

To reply to your final question, yes, indeed, I come out to play, matinees only of course, I have finished my new book (Viking!) which is called 'A Particular Friendship' (edited letters to a lady I never met who lived in the U.S (reluctantly) and who was dying of cancer and to whome I wrote from '67 until '73 . . . v. sad.) and now I live in a sort of Portakabin on the roof of an Edwardian maison in this elegant garden square, with a terrace and blackbirds, woodpigeon, magpies and a thrush, and a bedroom and a titchy office and a wok! Bought it last week and have started Chinese cooking in self defence against frozen gunge and smoked salmon and pasta. I'm not certain if I'll manage, but I must try. I cant cook an egg . . . Tote did all that. But I'm having a whack and if it is not Connaught it [is] better than out-of-date Paki-Stuff.

I keep on cooking for six, which is dotty. But it is so difficult to scale things down for one.

Reading this over it seems that I bought the apartment a week ago, but you are so clever you'll twig that it was the G.T.C wok.[1]

[. . .] Call me, or I'll call you perhaps, after the 20th . . and we'll meet. I do an excellent cold lunch. Try.

I am doing David Jacobs stint (for fun) on Radio 2,[2] but apart from that I have almost renounced the cinema and the theatre. Except for my Saki readings, which are easy, and fun, to do. And only on Sundays.

End of page – but not end of love from <u>D</u> XXXX.

I assume Sarah-Jane Holm[3] is one of yours? Sarah-Jane sounds like an American brand of fudge. Wont one name do? [. . .] Love you – D

---

1. The General Trading Company, then in Sloane Street.
2. A chance encounter with the presenter of the station's lunchtime-music programme had resulted in Dirk standing in as 'holiday relief'.
3. The actress daughter of Ian Holm and his first wife, Lynne Shaw.

To Dilys Powell

Dearest Dilys –

Of course I have not forgotten our 'modest meal'. You are a bit dotty really.

All you have to do is tell me when it's convenient for you .. and your Lady-Cook. I dont give a fig about the dog, but am terribly glad that you love him and were wrong about the other and never loving another and etc. All that silliness we go through.

I loved doing the Intro for your book, just hope that it is good enough .. Perry is good at his job, a glutton, and possibly quite an intellectual. But. I had a horried time trying to get him to do a reasonable script for that awful BAFTA Business; it was utterly impossible and, finally, I ad libbed the whole evening.

However he appears to hold no grudge [...] I'm doing whatever [he] wants me to do .. merely, my beloved Dilys, because I consider it a signal honour to have been asked.

So shut up and stop grovelling ... you KNOW how much I love you.

Reviewing, yes, not very well, but good therepy at a difficult time.

Cant act because the Casting Directors all think that I am very aged, with white hair, a limp (always a stick!) or whatever. I get SO angry when they ask to see a 'Vidio' of my 'last work'. Christ Almighty ... but I did fill the Olivier Theater with my reading from Saki .. and I go off on tour in April, no, sorry, May ... with the show.

It's fun .. and does'nt mean a whole whack ... just Sunday nights.

We have sold out the Yvonne Arnau Theater[1] within one hour and a half for the first Perf. on May 7th. So SOMEONE seems to reckon me!

The book is finished at last. Ready for first week in September.

It's alright, I think [...] not very long but they paid me enough money to keep this little flat going for a bit. I pray. She'd[2] be glad, for she so much wanted them to be published ... so now I have, but only a short amount. Letters, I think, unless they are brilliant, can be a bit

---

1. The theatre in Guildford named after Dirk's unofficial godmother, Yvonne Arnaud. He delivered a poem by Christopher Fry at its opening in 1965.
2. Dorothy Gordon.

of a bore. And mine are not brilliant. Amusing, perhaps, light, and loving but they aint Intellectual!

I have very much got used to living alone at last ... went through a boring patch, half a bottle, or more, of whiskey per night and THE most awful hangovers ... but it was needed. I got 'flu and had ten long days in bed all by myself, crawling to the lav, unable to eat anything, and simply drinking bottles of Evian water. Cured myself and wondered why on earth I'd had so little courage that I drank so as not to think. Silly, silly. All better now, and I rather dread being asked to go anywhere ... I rather like where I am and have even taught myself how to cook. (Could'nt boil water six months ago.) Now have a Wok .. and create AMAZING chinese dishes. Well: I like them, so who cares?

Glenda J. and I May, only May, do another revival (TV or Film) of 'Chalk Garden' with Helena Bonham Carter, John G. and Lauren Bacall .. it could be fun? We'll see ... anyway, I'll go and post this and hope that you get it and that we'll meet for a modest, and it MUST be, lunch ... or shall I bring you some sandwiches from Partridges? Terribly good .. and easy to eat. Unless ones 'plate' is loose ... oh Lor' ...

With profound love as ever.

Dirk

To Brock Van den Bogaerde

Cadogan Gardens
20 May 1989

My dear Brock –

It was tremendously kind of you to drop in on Wednesday evening. I was feeling just a bit 'saggy'.

Perhaps you knew, perhaps you did not, (for we did not speak of it) that it was the eve of Tote's death. The anniversary, if you can call it that, of the worst days of my life.

So you can imagine that just being with you, and knowing how very deeply Tote had loved you, and all that you stood for, as indeed do I, made a curious feeling of 'bond' again. I felt not so much a sense of loss as, in an odd way, a sense of having made the year and got through it.

There were times, and you may have guessed, when I was perfectly ready to fuck off ... but it seemed such a damned cowardly thing to do, and Tote would have been really angry, and I felt that, after 49 years, I had been extremely lucky and should give thanks ... rather than sulk and take a bottle of pills. I had them ready.

But the marvellous thing was that it seemed to me that you were, very quietly keeping 'an eye on the bloke'. Perhaps you were'nt .. but the feeling gave me great courage. The times when you dropped in for a beer and a bit of gossip restored, time and time again, a rather shakey existance. One I really did'nt want, and one which I could not see myself enduring all alone.

You helped me over that hurdle often.

For that, and so much more, thank you.

When I said, the other evening as you were leaving, that you were all I had got left now, I did, actually mean it.

No blackmail intended here, a simple statement of fact.

Perhaps because in many ways we are rather alike (in being shits?) under the skin, perhaps because of the strange early days we shared at Clermont, and the days later when you came to Berlitz .. I dont know what it was, but it has remained and will do so.

You are very much a part of the life I was given to share with Tote and, like a hidden thorn under the finger nail, so to speak, you stay. I am immensely proud of you: respect you above all else, and love you very much indeed.

Thank you for the care, for the courage you have offered me.

I know, now, that I can manage what may lie ahead because you have carried the lamp and shown me, in an odd way, that I'll manage the path, lonely or not ... I'll do it. And I'll do it for you.

We are, after all, Bogaerdes, and that aint to be sneezed at.

Remember the motto we hold, 'Ever green'[1] .... Why not?

With gratitude & love always
  <u>Dirk</u>

To Alain de Pauw   *Cadogan Gardens*
                                        8 June 1989

Cher Alain –

Helas! I have forgotten almost all my French, so this will have to

---

1. The Van den Bogaerde family, whose name means 'of, or from, the orchards', have the motto 'Semper viridis'.

be in English which Christine will have to translate. Alain, <u>thank you</u>. It was a wonderful, if moving, surprise to have the magazine.[1]

So strange to see, once again, so many familiar things which I never expected to set eyes on again, nor wished to, for that part of life is over for me.

But I am charmed, ravished, and jealous all at once! You have made the house (YOUR house, not mine now) so beautiful . . it is clear and un-cluttered and warm and loved: that is clear to see. And the pool is ravishing!

I was amazed to see the tiny tree in the front lawn, on the edge of the wall almost, which I planted as a seedling years ago. It is, if it is the same one, huge now. I often wondered if I had put him in the wrong place. But he looks splendid right infront of the view. I call him 'he' always because he was a baby from the big cypress outside the old dove-house and laundry-room . . . I planted him when we moved in in 1969 . . . he was then over thirty years old, and the first 'baby' he had I stuck down on the wall.

In the long room, as we called it, you will find, under the arch at the far end by the kitchen-fireplace, a strange blue and black tile which I had set into the floor. I dont think that I ever told you what it was, did I? I stole it from the very top step of the old Rhul Hotel[2] in Nice under the eye of a cross policeman! I told him, because he thought I was crazy, that at some time every crowned head had once trodden on that tile . . . and that from it you could re-create the entire floor of the hotel . . . it is a pattern tile. So he let me keep it, and when we were digging up the earth floor and laying the tiles, old ones I had found, I set him in. Voila!

Truly, Clermont is gloriously beautiful now, and I am so wonderfully happy, as I was the first day that we met, that you and Christine had it.

For I knew that your love for it was as great as mine.

I am now in a modest flat with a wide terrace, a view over great trees and a private garden, with just enough furniture and room for one person.

I sold the house I bought, thank God! to two very rich Americans

---

1. The de Pauws had sent an article by Christine's journalist sister, with new photographs of Clermont.
2. The Ruhl is now a casino.

... and thus was able to afford this flat in the Snob Area of Sloan Square and Knightsbridge which is fine by me, because I can walk everywhere I need.

Loneliness, of course, is the cruellest blow. But that has to be coped with.

Sold all my furniture, well: nearly all ... and all the paintings I had ... so it was funny to see the Georgian round table still in the cockpit at Clermont .. George II ... the wood at anyrate ... and the Italian chairs ... which I wish I had brought here! They would have fitted the flat wonderfully, but not the house.

Again, thank you both.

[...] Be happy there this summer: I will think of you, and look at the pictures often. You were wonderfully kind to think of me.

With warmest wishes and love to you both ...

Always
Dirk

P.S. I shall be working on a film with Tavernier[1] in Sanary in September/October but, have no fear, I will NOT come near Grasse. Too painful still –

To David Frankham   *Cadogan Gardens*
                                        14 July 1989

David my friend –

Super good to have your letter: I regret to tell you that the 'Telegraph' has now become 2 papers![2] One Saturday and one on Sunday, and I never quite know when I'll be printed. I have done a hell of a lot from Hellman (no pun –) to Capote, now on the Goldwyn book,[3] very funny and AWEFUL [...] and did a lengthy review for the

1. Dirk was to play the 'title role' in Bertrand Tavernier's *Daddy Nostalgie*, written by the director's ex-wife, Colo O'Hagan, and co-starring Jane Birkin and Odette Laure.
2. Not exactly. Various departments in the *Daily Telegraph*, including Books, were fused with their counterparts in its Sunday sister. For the three years during which this ill-starred attempt to create a 'seven-day newspaper' was in operation Dirk and some of his fellow reviewers appeared in the pages of both titles.
3. Having dealt with *Lilly: Reminiscences of Lillian Hellman* by Peter Feibleman (Chatto & Windus) and *Capote: A Biography* by Gerald Clarke (Cardinal paperback; Hamish Hamilton, 1988), Dirk was now tackling *Goldwyn: A Biography* by A. Scott Berg (Hamish Hamilton).

new book on Carrington[1] (Strachey's wife.[2] Lytton I mean.) which caused a bit of a flutter and a lot of mail.

When I say aweful above, I merely mean that the La La Situation[3] is, was, well still is, aweful. So evil and crooked, and the little shivers of fear still run up and down ones spine. I have had my share, as you know, of the visciousness from Head Office ... it was even nastier with Goldwyn. God!

I am typing badly because I am jammed full of anti-biotics on account of teeth. While Tony was so desperatly ill it was impossible for me to think of being unwell myself, so I have let things lapse too long, and now reap the whirlwind [...]

This country: honestly. I wish I could go back to France but darent risk another move. Three in 18 months practically killed me. Anyway DID give me a stroke. Thats okay now; I'll never be able to Stride Over The Downs again, but, frankly, at my age, I dont give a fuck.

As long as I can get to the off-market and get my whisky I'll manage.

The Saki readings became boring. One evening on stage, sitting waiting for my que, I suddenly thought, 'Sod this. I'm bored rigid and it'll be the same tomorrow, and I hate hotel-in-the-Provinces-Life and want to go home to London.' So I did just that!

We played to packed houses nightly, it was decent pay, but we all agreed that it was, frankly, pretty dreary after the first euphoria had worn off. Readings are NOT like a play. You just read. Dull.

So I packed that in and am off home to France to do a film for Tavernier in September. He's written it especially for me, so I could hardly refuse.

He made 'The Lacemaker', 'Around Midnight' and 'Judge And the Assasin' and 'Sunday In The Country' etc. I don't know if they hit L.A or Calif. or even the U.S. But he's choc a block with Awards and I think he's terrific. So. After 12 years I return to the Cinema. Rather a drag, but about time I got up off my ass, arse, and got to work. I have a new book coming out in September here, wont allow it to be printed in the U.S or for that matter, any of my books. The Critics are anti-British, say I'm anti-Semetic, and dont write 'gutsy' books. So sod them. This is an edited collection of some of the letters which I

1. *Carrington: A Life of Dora Carrington 1893–1932* by Gretchen Gerzina (John Murray).
2. No – but indisputably his love.
3. Hollywood.

wrote to Mrs X, my unknown saviour in Connecticut. It's fairly slim, a decent cover, Snowdon photograph of ageing writer, and it's very sad. It is Viking's Book For The Fall non-fiction. So that is decent. As soon as I have done the promotion, a signing at Hatchards and one at Heffers in Cambridge and a Questions and Answer evening at the National (theatre not cinema) I go straight to France. To Bandol, near Marseilles ... which in September, should be alright. If my teeth get mended!

All in all I am TRYING to come to terms with a full-life, as they call it, but it aint easy and the worst thing is the loneliness, and as I am not a bit gregarious I suffer in utter silence from Friday evening until Monday.

My fault entirely. But I hate social life now; done it all and been there.

Just been interviewed for a vast Bio on Judy G, by the guy who did the Capote book.[1] Very nice, and took two days chatting and asking .. he's NOT about to bash her, the opposite ... but, sadly, it always comes down to pills and the potions. I gather Liza [Minnelli] has'nt done too well from the Warhol book[2] .. silly child. She is utterly distant now as far as I am concerned, because, she says, I'll be angry with her for 'screwing up the chances'. She's right.

I'm off .. thanks for the letter. Hope the CBS was'nt too awful, hope the loot helps, and I admire you for being able to contemplate Another move!

As ever Dirk —

To Bertrand Tavernier   Cadogan Gardens
                                              19 July 1989

My dear Bertrand —
    Thank you so much for the 'new' script.[3]
    I have read it with care ... it is difficult for me to fully understand the French after two years away! It seems to be much better than the first one, and there are some very moving moments.

---

1. Gerald Clarke (see p. 446), whose *Get Happy: The Life of Judy Garland* would be published in 2000 by Little, Brown.
2. *The Andy Warhol Diaries* edited by Pat Hackett (Simon & Schuster).
3. Of *Daddy Nostalgie*.

I regret that I am NOT thin and gaunt, I'm rather plump!

But I dont want to be as old as the Papa in 'Sunday In The Country',[1] so perhaps it's just as well.

I pray that you do not expect me to play the role speaking French? I always understood that Daddy would speak English to his daughter whenever possible. I simply could not manage to learn a role in a foreign accent now: it is too long since I left France, and it's difficult enough for me to act, for God's sake, let alone act in a different tongue.

I would never be able to use the 'nuance' which I need: but we will see how things are with the English script. You can always dubb me for France.

Tell me, when you can, if you want me to supply costume .. it'll mean extra luggage .. and perhaps Daddy does'nt need much in the way of clothes.

I too am very, very proud to work with you; after all I have refused to do a film for almost 12 years, preferring to concentrate on my books than to work with 'second class' directors! So you may find me rusty, but I <u>will</u> do my best.

With grateful thanks, my love in abundance to Jane [Birkin], and warmest regards as ever to you . . . .

Ever

<u>Dirk</u>

To Eileen Atkins   *Cadogan Gardens*
                                                        21 August 1989

Glum[2] dearest –

Oh dearie me! Your v. glum card arrived and I dont quite know where you are, so will send this to the waterside and hope that Bill,[3] or a cat or something, might send it to wherever you are struggling.[4] [. . .]

I'm about to leap into action, in a VERY glum way, for the book

---

1. Played by Louis Ducreux.
2. See note 1, p. 419.
3. William Shepherd, who married EA in 1978.
4. EA was on a pre-West End tour with Paul Scofield and Alec McCowen in Jeffrey Archer's *Exclusive*, a so-called Fleet Street 'drama' and the theatrical equivalent of a traffic accident – disagreeable for participant and spectator alike.

and then for the film with Tavernier in France. I rather dread that. I have'nt made a film, per say (is that how you spell it? I dont know) since 1978 ... which is altogether too long ago. I am not afeared of forgetting 'the acting' but it will be the first time I have travelled away on my own for over forty years! There's a thought. And what to do hanging about every weekend alone? Oh well ...

I have had a v. jolly time with teeth. Whole lower jaw infected by a desease called septecimia ... so ALL my teeth except four stumps left in the front, were yanked out, and a splendid new half moon of teeth glued onto the said stumps. Filed down to sort-of pins. All this took rather longer to do than to tell. Went into the chair at 2 pm and crawled out, with a battered face, at 6 pm. I felt very brave indeed. And was rather amazed that I had <u>new</u> teeth and no septecimia any longer.

It may amuse you to know, should you wish to indulge yourself in the same kind of activity, that it cost £7.000. There. At the Devonshire Clinic I was assured that a top and bottom, done the same way, would set me back £35.000. Ring-a-bloody-ding. Anyway I now can chew. I can smile without cupping my hand over my fangs and so on. I let things go too far while Tony was so ill ... and too far they finally went. It is a silly, silly, thing to do. Dont. Had the flat painted out. My salary at the Telegraph doubled per Review, 25.000 copies of my new book had to be reprinted because of one line which 'could' have been defamatory[1] ... so that has been jolly, and generally done fuck bugger all. Seen a bit of Chatty Bags Angela,[2] whose new book has been rather a worry to her sons .. and their wives, but thats Angela .. and bought myself a lot of new frocks from Aquescutum, or whatever they call themselves, which cost a lot but I had not had a new suit since '81 and now that I have put on a STONE in weight something had to be done. I now have new dresses and feel better. I dont know that I LOOK any better, but who cares. I am going to be fat and eccentric and they'll all have to lump it.

I'm doing a platform at the Littleton with my buke. I cant imagine why or what I must do. Read bits, I gather, and answer questions. It

---

1. A reference in *A Particular Friendship* to Christopher Thynne had been thought, incorrectly, by his mother, Daphne Fielding, to be libellous.
2. Angela Fox, widow of Robin, whose second volume of autobiography, *Completely Foxed*, had just been published by HarperCollins.

all seems to me very silly indeed, but it's rather lonely not having you up river, so there is no reason to sit about here waiting for you to return to the Playhouse, or wherever, with P. word perfect.

Rex. H[arrison] is doing the revival of 'The Circle' with Glynis Johns and Stewart Grainger. He said he thought he'd made a 'bit of a cock up'. I reckon he's right there . .

Great love <u>D</u>.

Dirk returned to the South of France at the end of September, to begin work on Daddy Nostalgie. *He was there for five weeks.*

To Eileen Atkins
(Postcard)
Hotel Ile Rousse
Bandol
7 October 1989

THE MISTRAL (GHASTLY WIND 100 MPH) BLEW IN THIS A.M. BRINGING YOUR SAD/FUNNY LETTER [...] YOU HAVE NOT LOST A SCRAP BY DOING THE PIECE. AND, ANYWAY, YOU STILL HAVE OLD HAG V.W[1] TO HANG ONTO WHEN YOU FEEL YOU ARE DROWNING. FILMING IS ALL VERY WELL BUT. 6.45AM TO 7.PM IS PUSHING IT A BIT. AND PLAYING IN FROG UTTERLY TERRIFYING. BIRKIN A DREAMCHILD (OF 40!) AND TAVERNIER SMASHING. AS HE WRITES ME LETTERS TO SAY THAT I AM THE GOLDEN HAIRED BOY I CANT COMPLAIN. AFTER 12 YEARS AWAY I SEEM TO HAVE IT ALL STILL IN PLACE. V. ODD! DAY OFF TODAY AND TOMORROW. Oh God! EATING ALONE IN CRYSTAL PALACE, SCRIPT AGAINST THE CRUET, IS WEIRD AND I GLUE MYSELF TO THE TV AND SWITCH CHANNELS ALL NIGHT. AWFUL JUNK. I DO MISS SLOAN SQUARE. TALK ABOUT GLUM AND GRUMBLE. BACK VIA CANNES-NICE. IT'LL BE A BIT RUM TO GO THERE AGAIN. I <u>DO</u> LOVE YOU. GLUMMER THAN GLUM.

---

1. *Exclusive* had expired. EA had triumphed earlier in a one-woman show adapted by its director Patrick Garland from Virginia Woolf's *A Room of One's Own*.

To Hélène Bordes   *Cadogan Gardens*
                                                    6 November 1989

Hélène ma cherie – (familiar!)

Home at last. Happy in a way, sad to leave my dear France, glad the film is finished, and is good I believe, and happy, happy, to get your 'cards' this morning.

What hellish little creatures some women are! How awful for you to be so troubled by such an idiot.[1] There seem to be so many lonely, lost, silly creatures in the world ... and here it is the same, especially after the book-signings which I had to do. Cambridge, Oxford, London ... mad women who brought flowers, letters, gifts of abominable shapes and sizes, ties, socks, handkerchiefs ... oh dear! The sadness and the irritation in the middle of intense work. Signing as I did, 700–800 books in two hours is intense – or is for me. And trying not to be impolite. But sometimes ..... the idiots win.

London incredibly dirty after France. Cold also, a brilliant sun a bitter wind. I go shopping for my modest needs: people glad to see me back, brown and a bit fat. Beer at the Cantine I fear with the équip[2] ... my stomache, not my face so much. Tavernier on the phone last night to say that he has seen all the work now in Paris on a good screen and with proper sound. In Bandol it was in some awful little cinema and the screen was too small for the film and the sound did'nt work. So.

Forgive my typing. I had my injection for grippe on Friday and yesterday I felt a little strange! Alright today but very tired from re-action.

I miss the people of the équip. They were so AMAZINGLY kind to me, every single one. On the last Friday in Bandol I had a big farewell party for everyone (fifty, plus wives and some children) at the Pullman. I took all the salon, chairs, canapes, etcetera and we had 17 bottles of champagne, 3 of Scotch and Gin and lots to eat. It cost F.7.500 and was worth every sou. Kindness and affection and respect are wonderful gifts to recieve, you will agree? I miss them ... tant pis ...

[...] During the filming at Cannes we had to drive up into the

---

1. The 'Saumur Windmill' (see 17 July 1986) had again been pestering HB.
2. An attempt at *équipe* (crew).

hills to do a scene or two. I was in dread that we were getting near Clermont.

At Valbonne, thank God, we turned away and I did not look up into the familiar mountains. I could not bear to. It was bad enough at the airport at Nice . . . so familiar for so many years. From 1948 when it was a little shed with a green grass field and honesuckle round the wall of the Departure Lounge until the last few years with so much travelling to London for scans and doctors and so on . . . . time lost, time forgotten . . I am getting old and mournful. Silly!

Now someone, pleasant, arrives for lunch . . . a fish pie I have planned, and fruit and good French cheese and French bread. I have a good local shop not far away owned by a charming couple from Bordeaux with their two boys who work very hard. It is ALMOST like being at home . . . . and we speak French together. Which was useful for me in the film, because although I play an English man living in Bandol I do have a French wife who refuses to speak to me in English! So . . . . I had some very difficult moments as you will imagine . . .

Now. I must lay my table and get on with my boring jobs: I leave you as always with my love and affection and bon courage . . .

& come to London one day? It would be So lovely if you did –
Ever Dirk

P.S. Birkin, by the way, adorable – & marvellous to work with. D

To Dilys Powell   *Cadogan Gardens*
                                                  26 January 1990

Dearest Dilys –

You are dreadful. I saw you at luncheon only a week or two ago. Well; before I was bedded,[1] but I have'nt been forgetful of you.

Or has time sped along? Probably. Anyway . . . Paris is over and done.[2] Quite hellish journeys both ways, people, searches, general hassle and at Paris the idiot from the Production who came to meet me lost the car in the Underground Parking at Charles de Gaulle for

---

1. With flu.
2. Dirk had written an additional scene for *Daddy Nostalgie*, which had been shot at a studio in Paris.

ONE HOUR, and then found that he'd lost the bloody ticket for it. So we were another hour with forms and screams and French Invective flying. And an hour in Sunday traffic into town, and Tavernier waiting for me patiently in the Lancaster. Three hours late. God. Work next day alright, the new, extra, scene, played well. I wrote it in bed with flu and made it much better generally. He feels confident of the film, and is clearly very happy but it IS desperatly sad ... and perhaps that wont be such a good idea. Marcel Ophuls who saw the first final cut (without my extra scene) said that my work surpassed anything I had done in Death In Venice. And that I was 'amazingly courageous' to play the role so 'honestly'. I think that by that he meant without make up of any kind and my balding head and beer belly showing! But, after all, I was playing my own age, the father of Mlle Birkin and wife[1] to the adorable, but no longer young, Odette Laure (theatre). Never mind. It seems I have not lost my knack after twelve years. Goodness. But as Bertrand T. said at dinner on Sunday 'Good wine is meant to mature for years. And it looks better covered with dust and cobwebs'. I do see what he means. But one is shocked slightly.

Desperatly saddened yesterday by news of Ava [Gardner]'s death. She was an adorable and loyal friend for so many years. Sad, lonely, and wretchedly ill with cancer, of course, and shingles and God knows what. Refused to stop smoking and drinking and stayed quietly in Ennismore Gardens with her beloved corgies. Wretched, wretched cruelty. I have done my piece (on Tavernier) for the new Sunday Indipendant[2] .. and they seem pleased. I hope that I will be, and that Bertrand wont be angry. He should'nt be: it's a paeon (sp?) of praise for him.

It seems to me that I am now a journalist rather than an actor or a real-writer. But I'm off to Hay on Wye for some book Festival in May, a luncheon in my honour! Madness ... and then I am doing Questions and Answers to students at Guildford University, and THEN I do the narration (as Galsworthy) for Channel 4's[3] version for Radio of the 'Forsyte Saga' and after that, my dear, I am running a few master Classes for the young at the National.

So. You cant say I'm not trying to spread my past good fortune!

---

1 . No, husband.
2 . 'Take three, in splendid CinemaScope' (*Independent on Sunday*, 28 January 1990).
3 . BBC Radio 4.

May I telephone and suggest a lunch chez vous after the next week [...] I'll call.
    Devotedly
     Dirk

P.S. Tavernier has refused to have the film entered for Cannes.[1] Thank God! It'll be out end of April.

To Hélène Bordes   *[Cadogan Gardens]*
                                            28 January 1990
                                                Sunday.

Cher, cher, Hélène –
    Can you believe your luck! I have bought another 'new' typewriter. This one is a little easier to use than the other brute. But it still corrects, and erases, and rings bells and terrifies me.
    [...] I am just back from Paris: one day to do an extra scene which Tavernier wanted me to write. (No payment naturally!) We worked in a dirty shed, sitting in an old Renault-car at a supposed Service Café on the road from Cannes to Bandol. Too complicated to explain it to you, but that is what had to happen. And because I have had this terrible flu and been in bed for eight days, and trapped in the flat for yet another eight to avoid temperature changes, I was forbidden to work outside at night on the Perepherique, or however it is spelled, and so this awful old studio, north of Neuilly, was discovered and we worked there. All was well, and I flew back to London that evening at 8.30pm. Dont believe that a trip between London and Paris is only 40 minutes. It is. In the air. On the land it takes, altogether, six hours! Three to get to, and from, airports, the security searches are intense, not that I mind that, but it is the crowd, the smell, the noise ... awful.
    I had two wonderful hours to myself in Paris. In the morning before we started work at ten thirty. I went immediatly to my nearest Casino, or Felix Potin, to try and get my favourite Tripes a la mode de Caen. Difficult on a Monday morning. But I got some frozen in a packet which looks alright. I shall try my first tomorrow. What an excitement.

---

1. Tavernier would change his mind.

Then some eau de toilette (Givenchey. Monsieur Giv.) which costs half the price in Paris in comparison to London, and some good music on compact discs, and a large Munster cheese. Idiotic. But the smells and the textures remind me so much of Clermont. Paris was glorious on Sunday night when I arrived. Light, laughter, crowds, no dirt, the City looking amazingly beautiful (they have cleaned the Arc. It looks as if it was carved from butter.) Amazing. Glorious. I felt so much at ease and happy. The Lancaster to welcome me, Marie Therese at the telephone .. she's been there for forty years, ever since I first went there. We embraced with tears. She and I seemed, apart from one waiter, Gilles, to be the very last of the Old Brigade. Ah me ...

What is happening to the world, as far as weather is concerned!

No rain here either. Sun, a cold wind; on Thursday a real hurricane killing people and destroying 3.000,000 trees. Million that should be. Frightening up here on my roof, but I was safe. There was a crash as the people below me had all their windows blown out. Just like in the Blitz. But I survived; a good piece in our Big paper which I wrote for them about the Tavernier film ... I go to a Literary Luncheon in my honour in Wales in May, lecture to the Students at Guildford University, will take some Master Classes in acting at the National Theater and have a half-book ready which Viking will use as their Fiction No. 1 for ..... 1991! When I shall be 70. Oh dear God. If I am lucky.

So you see, I try to keep alert and active .. I dont think that I shall try another film. This one was my first for 13 years.

And enough is enough, Five am Calls are not for me a mon age!

[...] I must go out now to mail this and some others. I did a programme on the radio last month[1] and simply spoke, in passing, about euthenasia and how, after Forwood, my brother in law, and another close friend, all of whome died hideiously, I agreed with it completely. I have had a sack of sad letters asking me to help. Life is precious, but terrible at the same time.

All my love – <u>D</u> XXX

---

1. *Desert Island Discs* (Radio 4, 31 December 1989).

To Susan Pink
(Card)   *Cadogan Gardens*
                                                7 March 1990

Oh! The agony!¹ Your magic hammer almost killed me – I cant think
why. However I did all the rest of the BBC work standing & sort-off
sitting – on a V. high chair. And not a flick of pain. Odd? But after 36
solid hours of talk I was far too tired to come in on Tuesday – But
will see you next Tuesday as usual. Leg works SPLENDIDLY. I'll
just have to type standing up.
    Bugger.
    Love. <u>D.B.</u>

To Dilys Powell   *Cadogan Gardens*
                                               9th May 1990
                                               <u>*At four o'clock*</u>

Darling Dilys –
    I have just got in from lunching with you. And, as I came up in the
lift, (I live in what was Lily Langtree's maids-rooms. Converted. To
be sure.) the telephone was ringing and stopped, naturally, just as I
inserted my key into the door.
    So now I'll never know who tried to call me. No one ever does:
really. So I'm curious. But I did so enjoy being with you: this is NOT
a thank you letter it is, rather, an apology-letter. For I always seem to
be yelling at you and hardly ever give you a chance to speak. Quietly,
elegantly, you go about the business of eating and drinking and I'm
still bawling away about Euthanasia or some other quite unsuitable
subject.
    You are deeply patient. But I DO love being with you.
    What is so silly, after so many years, is that I am still shy of you. I
know that you have accorded me great intimacy: I am aware of that.
I am equally terrified of overstepping the mark, so to speak, and
therefore feel dreadfully inadequet. Like my spelling. I am not quite
altogether.
    The wonderous thing is that the instant one speaks of the Cinema

---

1. SP, Dirk's physiotherapist, had administered further treatment on the leg weakened by
his stroke. His card is reproduced overleaf.

2 Cad. Gdns.
7.3.90

Oh! Ye agony! Your magic hammer almost killed me — I can't think why. However I did all the rest of the BBC work Standing + Sorry — of sitting — on a V. high Chair. And not a fleck of

pain. Odd? — But after 3½ Solid hours of [took] [I was] far too Tired to come in on Tuesday — But will see you next Tuesday as usual. Leg works SPLENDIDLY. I'll just have to type standing up. Bugger.

Love. DB.

v. high chair.

you are instantly alive and alert. The eyes flash fire, your hair spreads like a childs in the wind, you are re-vived from the mundane things of life and the Cinema is your 'fix'. I know that. I recognise that. [...] But I fear to bore. One can, God knows.

Probably thats why the Masterclass business is such fun! I am asked terrific questions. What lenses, when a cut was made, and why, who had to use an Idiot Board, how an effect was achieved, did I really do the stunts on such and such (yes. I did.) did I hate Rhodesia, when we shot 'Simba' there, and were the Mau Mau really in such a strong position. Yes they were. But I never went NEAR Rhodesia or Kenya or wherever it was, that was an elderly Double (well: he was at least forty and had white hair ..) so I could'nt hate the place. The nearest I got to Kenya on that epic was Studio E. at Pinewood with a lot of withered bamboo and Virginia Mckenna in a head scarf. You know. Film. I revelled. Perhaps thats the only real time that I come alive. Sometimes, in this last film with Bertrand, I used to sit under a tree outside the little villa which we were shooting in, and I would say to myself, aloud, really quite aloud, 'Yes. <u>This</u> is the thing I really want. This is when I am at the utmost peak of happiness and awareness. Sitting here waiting to be called to perform. To "be" someone I have totally invented'. To find a new dimension, to enter it, to give that dimension Life, if one can do such a thing, and to make someone in an audience perhaps in Tokio, maybe in Southgate or Northampton or even Munich or Fairbanks, move and say 'I know that feeling. I have done that, said that, felt that. How does <u>he</u> know?'

I suddenly realise, sitting here writing to you, that during ALL my acting life I have NEVER, except for a very few occasions, left the Set. I have always stayed there; sitting in my chair, some way from the action .. but there, I have never been far away. I feed on the atmosphere, on the sights, the smell, the sound, of a film being got ready.

Is'nt it strange how the best senses all begin with an 'S'?

Perhaps that is how I learned, for no one ever really taught me except a rude, and right, Cameraman who, watching me thoughtfully while we changed magazines, said 'You know? I just wonder how the fuck you have lasted.'[1]

I had made ten films ... either I hit him, walked off in a fury, or asked him what I should do. I did that last thing: and Bob Thompson told me. From the amount of frames per second through the gate, to the difference between a 75, a 5 or a 20 lense. He told me what the boom was for, never to speak when I shut a door, set down a glass, lifted a prop of any kind, how to avoid the dolly-tracks, pause if I

---

1. H. A. R. (Bob) Thomson, camera operator on several of Dirk's films for Box and Thomas, confirmed that he did explain the tools and tricks of his trade, but would never have spoken in that way to someone of Dirk's eminence.

heard a distant plane or an extranious sound approaching .. how to
'use' the pause [...]

And I have wittered on. I hate to bore you when we are together
for such a short time. You must tell me next time when to shut up. I
will. Because this damned machine has taken life unto it'self and is
behaving outrageously.

I loved being with you. I'll write, in detail, after Cannes ... if there
IS an after Cannes. There must be?

All my love
     Dirk XXX

Dirk flew to Nice for the screening of Daddy Nostalgie *at the Cannes
Film Festival, where it was, after all, an official French entry.*

To Bertrand Tavernier

Cadogan Gardens
Wednesday afternoon.
16th May 1990

My dear Bertrand –

I will confess to you now that there were times, in the eleven years
I have waited for you, that I felt sure I would never work again, and
that if I did it would be a bit-part in some dull little English comedy.
I never quite reached despair but I was very, very, conscious of the fact
that the last film I made, in 1977 was with Fassbinder and was called
'Despair'! Not very comforting.

But on Monday evening I knew that the wait had not been in vain,
that you had sought me out, and that we had worked together on
something of infinate value. I am so immensley proud.

I was too full in my heart that evening to tell you what I wanted
to: perhaps too involved, certainly too emotional to say anything that
would have made sense at that time and in that awful villa. But now
that I am safely back in my flat, away from all the excitement, I can
say to you that I LOVE your film.

I was, as you will imagine, surprised and delighted by the version
you have crafted. I was smashed by Jane and her impact .. by Odette,
and was pleased that I had not let you all down and that I had not
forgotten the lessons I had been taught by Micky Powell, Joe, Luchino,
Dearden, Resnais and all the others who taught me about the cinema.

I am so deeply proud of the film: I am <u>so</u> proud to be a part of it, and I was tremendously moved all the way through and truthfully began to forget, quite soon into the story, that I had anything to do with it!

I suppose there are a few moments when the story languishes a very little bit; I heard one or two criticisms of it .. but no more and I could not possibly tell you where they were or, more importantly, how to cut them. For my part it seems to me very much your film.

The kind of film you make, bearing your own style and it is wonderfully satisfying. You must have felt that the other evening with that enormous audience, with the waves of affection and respect which were swamping us all.

They LOVED your work. Cannes is NOT a kind town in the Festival, but the affection and respect we were shown overwhelmed me, I hope that it gave you intense pleasure. Thank you for letting me join you, for your infinate kindness and consideration, for your awareness that I tried to work for you, and the film, with all my heart .. you gave me such confidence, such a feeling of safety, that I felt certain I could not fail you and I pray that I have not.

We will see what the critics and the others say of us, but even if they are not particularly good, or even if they rave, I know that we have made a quite beautiful film together, all of us, and that as one paper said, it is a glorious epitaph to your father .. it is also a most beautiful dedication to a magic-man, Micky.[1]

For that, for so much more besides, my thanks, and my devoted love and respect.

If you need a door-handle, a coffee cup, a pin or a pine tree in your next movie please, I beg of you, send for me? Okay?

I am still walking on air, remembering scenes, cuts, the music, Jane, Odette, and you .. and your laughter.

I am no longer alone. Thank you ...

With devotion

 <u>Dirk.</u>

---

1. BT dedicated *Daddy Nostalgie* to Michael Powell – Dirk's director on *Ill Met by Moonlight* – who had recently died.

To Dilys Powell   *Cadogan Gardens*
                                      18 May 1990

Darling –

I only wrote the p.c in haste so that you would know as soon as possible how things had gone for us. Because I know that you were interested. Todays 'Times'[1] has filled me with joy. I walked to the greengrocers on air! Idiot.

But after 11 years away from the cinema one was a little bit worried that I might have lost the edge, or, worse still, picked up some easy tricks. Nothing to fear. Neither was true. The evening was amazing. I suppose there were only about 500 people outside the Palais; maybe 1.000. Police, photographers and the usual tra la la .. BUT Birkin and I got such an overwhelming reception from the crowd yelling 'Jane! Deerk!' that she went white with surprise and amazement. It took us ten minutes to get to the top of the staircase, with three stops for photographers, and backward waves to the crowd below. My little Agent who had come with me as a sort-of minder, and who had resoloutly never set foot at the Festival was lost to sight behind us and yelled out 'Whats happening!' and I yelled back 'A miracle! Enjoy it Jonathan[2] .. it may never happen again!'

In the theater the whole audience rose to applaud as we walked down to our seats. The film was followed in utter silence. Not a cough, a whisper, only very soft sobbing! At the end, just as the picture faded and BEFORE 'Fin' appeared, the whole place rose as one and applauded until it became embarressing! That is why I feel that it was a triumph. And why we were all, Tavernier, Jane and myself, <u>really</u> overwhelmed. Consider: a modest picture with three players. In a small, tatty, bourgeoise, villa. Cinemascope, brilliantly used, and in which nothing-very-much-happens. Except that EVERYTHING people experience does. This was clear to an audience if not to that idiot Walker in the Standard who complained that it was unbearably slow and dull, and cliché. ... well: Johnson[3] in 'The Times' got the point. So did all the European Press. Not ONE British person was present at the Conference, which lasted for an hour and a half.

---

1. A report from the Cannes Festival by David Robinson.
2. Altaras, who in the mid-1980s had taken over Dirk's representation for theatrical work.
3. Robinson.

Unusual[1] if you are not Munroe or Brando! But no member of the British Isles. Odd. Sad. And irritating.

Perhaps, because the film is the French entry and in French for the most part, they felt it was not their business. But, surely, the Cinema is every critic's business? Anyway there it is .. it was a super evening and the descent down the staircase was even better than the ascent! How they yelled and cheered. Tears were not far away, I assure you. I had come back .. and the wait of eleven years to do something really worth while was worth it. Tavernier is the most adorable of men. I am SO proud for him. He was so quietly overwhelmed. And, a most endearing moment, the film, on a seperate screen all alone in it's majesty, is dedicated to ... Michael Powell. I thought that was pretty decent. It made it fullcircle for me, too, for the very last time I was in that sal[l]e I presented Powell with the highest honour the French can bestow on a film-maker. He was 82 then .. and fiercly proud of getting it. As I was giving it to him. We wont win anything I bet:[2] but it does'nt matter .. we won the hearts of a very tough audience completely .. and although I look ghastly (real cinema-verity!) it's a better performance than 'Venice' and more complete, because it is not hacked about in the editing, than 'Despair'. It's a much better way to end than that!

At length, to amuse and comfort you, for me! No nightmares .. I cant THINK what I was doing in the middle of the night. Do you? And I talk so much I never notice your silences. Perhaps I bore?

Oh Lord . . . .

My love dearest –

Dirk XXXX

To Bertrand Tavernier   *Cadogan Gardens*
                                           18 July 1990

Bertrand –

Your letter has given me infinate pleasure. I have been talking about you all bloody week!

To 'Premier' and 'L'Express' and, yesterday for five long hours, to a guy called John Halpern (?) [Heilpern] for Vogue, New York.

---

1. i.e. to have a press conference at such length.
2. An accurate prediction.

Apparently our film is 'terrific' and you and I will be the rage of New York. I'll believe that when the time comes .. if it does!

But, clearly, the film has made an impact. I am so glad for you .. you took the risk with me. I pray it works.

[. . .] Nunnaly Johnson[1] was a glorious man: I adored him. We made one terrible film (which he wrote very well but could'nt direct) in Rome and southern Calabria. It was originally called 'La Sposa Bella' and it starred, originally also, Montgomery Clift and Ava Gardner, Joseph Cotton, Aldo [Fabrizi] and Vittorio de Sica plus Enrico Maria Salerno. They replaced Clift (insurance would'nt take him on) with me.

Well: a big shock for Ava and for Nunnaly .. I arrived from L.A the day before shooting. All was delight! Ava and I loved each other instantly, like Birkin and me .. and Nunnaly. We shot for veritie ... she wore no make up, one awful old dress, it was good. After three weeks MGM saw the first set of rushes, had hysterics, ordered the whole 3 weeks to be reshot with Ava dressed by Valentina, shoes by Ferragamo, make-up ta ta ta ta. We all gave in and did as we were told and the film was a disaster. And, as far as I know, was only ever shown on TV late at night. Nunnaly once said to a Press Conference in Rome. 'Dirk is a very strange guy. I have ruined his career with this picture and he still likes me!'

I did too. So did we all. But he was not a Studio Man and just died when they insisted on glamour. It was, after all, a film about the Civil War in Spain. We were all rather good .. but not dressed by Valentina and Ferragamo and so on. Nunnaly tried to live in London for a while, wrote scripts but nothing much else. He was a wonderful, civilised, man. I still remember him with great affection.

[. . .] The Harmer[2] story sounds a marvellous idea: I dont quite know what you have in mind. Remember, cher amie .. that Micky Balcons daughter, Jill, is still very much alive, and his grandson, Dan Day Lewis is very much in evidence. Mad, but brilliant they say. So you would have to fictionalise the whole thing, and I am not too sure that I am not now far too old to play either of them! Or would be by

---

1. Nunnally Johnson, a friend of Losey and fellow-refugee from the McCarthy witch-hunt, directed *The Angel Wore Red* (1961). The film did receive a theatrical release in the UK.

2. BT had the idea of making a film about Robert Hamer, writer and director of the Ealing classic *Kind Hearts and Coronets*, who died in 1963 at the age of fifty-two.

the time we could get ready to shoot anything. The idea of playing an idealist who is thawarted by the Studio-Setup and driven to drink and death intrigues me greatly. I watched it happen to Bob, he was a sweet, brilliant, funny man, as perhaps you know. I saw it happen to Lewis Milestone, and, eventually, to Cukor. The cruelty and the visciousness was absolute. They had no chance to exist.

It breaks my heart that Huston made such a mess of 'Under The Volcano', the only film I have ever longed to make[1] .. and nearly did three times, once with the Mexicans, once with Cukor who backed out, and once with Losey who, eventually, dumped me and went with Burton. It never got made ... until the Huston debacle which we saw in Cannes at 'our' Festival.

But the destruction of an idealist has always facinated me.

I am too old for Volcano and anyway it's done now, but cant we think of something to do together before I have to play Santa Clause?

[...] I miss you. I still have a pile of interviews to do for you and for France. They are already beginning to call us Les Aimants ... and I do see why!

[... T]hank you for 'Hunted'.[2] It arrived this morning. Enfin!

Now all I have to do is go and buy a Video! All my old tapes were the other thing, BTA or whatever it is called. I cant face the idea of chucking them away, on the other hand transferring 150 tapes to VHS will be expensive. So far 'Hunted' is my only VHS version .. but I have, as yet, no where to play it.

We'll see what happens.

Happiness and love ..

As ever

<u>Dirk</u>

To Pat Kavanagh   *Cadogan Gardens*
                                                        18 July 1990

Patricia my dear –

There can be nothing worse, I am certain, than a whining author except a whining actor. Disaster strikes when the two are combined!

---

1. Apart, of course, from an abandoned 1958 project in which he was to play T. E. Lawrence.
2. BT was a great admirer of this early (1952) film of Dirk's.

Which, frankly, is why I have never really tried deliberatly to disturb you in the 'turning of a sock' .. I have never truthfully felt that I actually 'belonged' somehow.

Apart from loss, which is always devestating when quite unexpected, the gradual decline of ones powers, both physical and mental, is an ugly additive. And when that decline encompasses one's work, that is to say what one actually does for a living, however modest, then everything slithers into despond. Hence frog in muddy pond.[1]

Which is where I was. Am, I feel, clambering back to the bank very slowly, but no longer huddled in sludge simpering with misery, rage and, undeniable, frustration of the soul!

The cinema in the shape of Tavernier has wrought a minor, very minor, miracle after twelve fallow years, and now writes to say that he wants to work with me again and will I agree? Can we discuss doing something together and from scratch. That was a splendid lift this morning ... and alongside that letter, from Ullapool of all places where he presently is sitting by the sea, is yours.

So it's a good morning for cheer. For a re-habilitation into the area of self-confidence and belief in ones self. I had completely lost that. Utter, despairingly, wonderingly, hoplessly. Gorn .. as they say. Hence frog and mud metaphor (?)

But thank you.

No. Indeed, there will never be another Tony nor will there ever be another Norah! Impossible. Norah was critic, teacher, bully, vain of me, and determined to FORCE me. I needed that then. She set me on the rail .. but she's gone, Tony has gone, and the rail is still there.

I just dont quite know how to get back on again. I will. Never doubt me. I merely doubt myself .. a different matter. And once I am certain that I can manage I bloody well will. You'll see.

It's just that I felt a terrific lack of spur .. of a feeling of interest .. going it alone is something everyone has to cope with, and it can be managed. But a bit of a push, a tiny shove in a direction to take, a feeling of enthuasism perhaps .. do rather help.

I felt a loss of that terribly. But now, well, last Sunday even, I felt the prick of a spur when I saw that I had got onto the list again, not bad I said aloud .. thats good. 4th on one 9th on another. And a

---

1. PK had written a sinew-stiffening letter after Dirk told her he was, creatively, like a frog in mud.

not-altogether satisfactory book. Read the reviews? I did.

But, you see, no one <u>told</u> me. I got no feed back from Wrights Lane[1] of any kind. And of course dont expect it when I see the huge deficite on my Returns. I really did think that perhaps I'd cover most of my advance. But not so. And that really screwd me up. I plodded off to the BBC to do my Start The Week .. flogged the book as best I could, but there was no one there from the firm. No one even <u>knew</u> that I had done it I suppose? [...]

However I stray from my path. As usual. Your letter gave me great heart. I will continue. Just let me get the maggoty books on poor Garbo[2] out of the way (God! They are dire) for the Telegraph and then I'll bash on. I can, and I will .. 'Fade To Black'[3] will emerge. I have a shape. All I have to do is write the bugger.

[...] Thank you, dear Pat, for patience and for sense and for help. And, above all, for believing.

With love –

   <u>Dirk</u>

P.S. Maria my Colombian Lady Who Cleans has just said. 'Me see you Piccadilly yesterday eveningtime.'

I demurred politely. I was doing an interview for Vogue N.Y.

'No' said Maria. 'One shop. You very, very big. And all this book. Many many books. Peoples laughing. Very happy. Big, bigger than the Christus ..'

Okay. I'll buy that. Hatchards[4] one supposes? Good old shop. <u>D</u>.

To Ulric Van den Bogaerde   *Cadogan Gardens*
                                               2 August 1990

Most dear Nephew –

What delight today, at luncheon, to discover your fat, not to say bulging, letter which arrived by the second post. A breathless scrutiny assured me that you were A. Well, B. that I now have yet another

---

1. Then Penguin's headquarters.
2. *Garbo: Her Story* by Antoni Gronowicz (Viking) and *The Legend of Greta Garbo* by Peter Haining (W. H. Allen).
3. A projected volume of autobiography, set aside in favour of the novel, *Jericho*.
4. Since the launching of *Postillion*, the bookshop had championed vigorously all Dirk's books.

grand-nephew[1] (Brock has already sired a foul little thing called Leo. Leo and Moses. Christ! A better double-bill I have not heard of. Playing bones? Or jews-harps?) [...]

I am busy with the French Press. They arrive every Monday morning from Paris at 11 am .. and depart, exactly,[2] at 1.30am. Very civilised and nice, and only want to discuss the film and etc. The sort of conversations which you would enjoy .. and they are, male and female, all Young.

Film, now called 'These Foolish Things' in English .. they really could not take Daddy Nostalgi here .. as I knew they would not .... opens in Paris on the 11th Sept .. on the evening of the 10th I have to go to a huge retrospective of my work at the Cinematheque, they are doing about twenty-five clips from my early films which the French have never seen! Including clips from Doctor At Sea in which they will see an 18 year old ravisher called B. Bardot. First time around!

I rather dread it all, but everything is being paid for, and I have my old suite at the Lancaster. So I should worry. Did I tell you that I have had ALL, repeat ALL, my teeth removed? Wonderous. Implants and a flashing smile again without fear of abscesses or bad breath!

I honestly dont know why I did'nt have it done years ago. Too damned expensive I suppose. But it's worth it. I suppose having a twenty year old smile in a face like an armidillo is a bit silly; but very nice and comfortable. And, so far, no one has commented.

I have been doing my Masterclasses at the Olivier, Old Vic and at the Guildhall .. great fun if a bit tireing. Three hours on yer feet with bouncing questions is a bit tough, but worth doing. I shall take it on again after holidays in November .. fit in between exams .. I really do like being with the young who WANT to learn. The only sad thing, and it really is bloody sad, is that none of them, as far as I can see so far, have a hope in hell. The old saying is cruelly true: You've either got it, or you've HAD it. But one carries on with them .. why not?

Two of my girls sleep in an empty car by Waterloo Bridge. If they can do that then I reckon I can spare them three hours of my time.

I am really typing very badly today. I hate this daft machine which rings bells and screams and tries to correct my spelling. But they no

---

1. Rupert Van den Bogaerde's baby son was christened Moses. Ulric, who was working in Le Boulou, near Perpignan, had enclosed photographs of the new arrival.
2. Not quite.

With Princess Anne during BAFTA's tribute at the Odeon Leicester Square on 9 October 1988 – for most of those present, a night to forget.

'I like 'em in my hand' – alone on stage, and connecting, during happier times in the early 1990s.

A comeback and a swansong: with Bertrand 'The Genius' Tavernier and Jane Birkin in 1989, on the set of *Daddy Nostalgie* (*These Foolish Things*).

With Sir Peter Ustinov and the 'eager, quick, relaxed' Jacques Chirac, at the French Institute, Kensington, 15 May 1996.

(Below) Hélène Bordes, whose analysis of Dirk's memoirs convinced him he was being taken seriously as a writer.

Dominique Lambilliotte, whose persistence bore fruit.

Christine and Alain de Pauw, who bought Clermont from Dirk and kept him *au courant* with developments.

A Jane Bown study of John Osborne, otherwise 'Cpl 22524901' or simply '225'.

'Mr and Mrs Glum' – with Eileen Atkins in *The Vision*.

'He IS a comfort' – Bacchus, a gift many years earlier from Xan and Daphne Fielding, installed safely on the balcony at Cadogan Gardens.

Preparing to talk about the Holocaust to the pupils of King's School, Rochester, in May 1992.

'I cheer up a very little when I think of that' – the *Carte de séjour* which Dirk kept in his wallet until his death, seven years after its expiry.

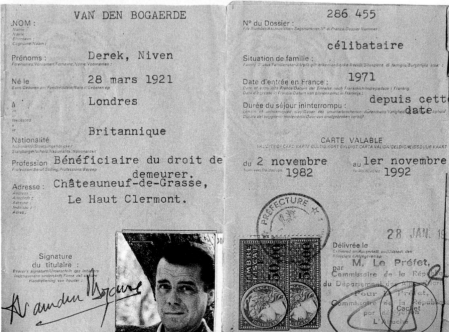

NOM : VAN DEN BOGAERDE
Name :
Eltername :
Cognome/Naam :

Prénoms : Derek, Niven
Forenames/Vornamen/Forname/Nome/Voornamen :

Né le 28 mars 1921
Born/Geboren am/Foeddasdate/Nato il Geboren op

à Londres
in
te/cested
le

Nationalité Britannique
Nationality/Staatsangehörigkeit/
Staatsburgerforhold/Nazionalita/Nationaliteit

Profession Bénéficiaire du droit de
Profession/Beruf/Stilling/Professione/Beroep demeurer.

Adresse : Châteauneuf-de-Grasse,
Address :
Anschrift : Le Haut Clermont.
Adresse :
Indirizzo :
Adres :

Signature
du titulaire :
Bearer's signature/Unterschrift des Inhabers
Indehaverens underskrift/Firma del titolare
Handtekening van houder :

N° du Dossier : 286 455
File Number/Aktenzeichen/Sagsnummer/N° di Pratica/Dossier Nummer :

célibataire
Situation de famille :
Family Status/Familienstand/Ægteskabelig-/Situazione di famiglia/Burgerlijke staat :

Date d'entrée en France : 1971
Date of entry into France/Datum der Einreise nach Frankreich/Indrejsedato i Frankrig
Date d'ingresso in Francia/Datum van binnenkomst in Frankrijk :

Durée du séjour ininterrompu : depuis cette
Length of uninterrupted stay/Dauer des ununterbrochenen Aufenthalts/Varighed date
Durate del soggiorno ininterrotto/Duur van onafgebroken verblijf :

CARTE VALABLE
VALIDITE OF CARD/KARTE GÜLTIG/KORT GYLDIGT/CARTA VALIDA/GELDIGHEIDSDUUR KAART

du 2 novembre au 1er novembre
from/vom/fra/dal/van 1982 *to/bis/til/al/tot* 1992

28 JAN. 19

Délivrée le
Delivered on/Ausgestellt am/Udstedt den
Rilasciata il/Afgegeven op

M. Le Préfet,
par
Commissaire de la Rép
du Département des A
Pour Préfet,
Commissaire de la Républ
par délé
L'Attaché

The last big interview, filmed in the summer of 1991 and transmitted as *Dirk Bogarde – By Myself* the following January, shortly after the announcement of his knighthood. Photographed by its director, Paul Joyce.

The artist as subject (1): stages in David Tindle's realisation of the National Portrait Gallery's commission, for which he spent four days at Clermont in April 1986. His pencil drawing was shown and sold at the Royal Academy Summer Exhibition in 1988; the painted 'pre-study', at a London art fair in 2007. The finished canvas was among a small selection lent by the NPG to 10 Downing Street early in Tony Blair's tenure as Prime Minister.

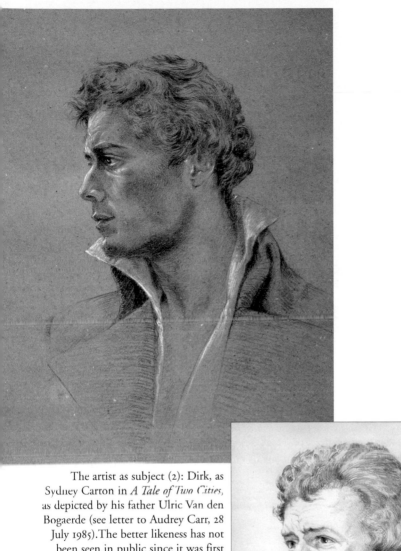

The artist as subject (2): Dirk, as Sydney Carton in *A Tale of Two Cities*, as depicted by his father Ulric Van den Bogaerde (see letter to Audrey Carr, 28 July 1985). The better likeness has not been seen in public since it was first exhibited in 1958.

Tableau for Sybil Burton (see letter to Eileen Atkins, 3 May 1991). The figure seated in the middle of the front row was not, despite speculation in recent years, Picasso, but a passer-by unknown to any of the principals. (Left to right, standing) Donald Pickering, Alma Cogan (the stunt's organiser), Stanley Baker, Graham Usher, Murray Drucker, (partially hidden) Burt Shevelove, Gerd Larsen, Donald MacLeary, Tony; (seated) 'Boaty' Boatwright, Dirk, The Man Off The Street, Sara Harrison, Noel Harrison. The identity of the book and the relevance of the doll have defied the memory of the surviving participants.

'We had a terrific fifty years together and nothing can take any part of that away.'

longer make gods-honour-bang-bang machines. We all have to be so damned clever. Which I am not [...] Also we are in soaring temperatures of 35° and London is pretty bloody. People fainting everywhere and squealing about the Heat. Idiots. We are not allowed to water gardens or lawns and there are mutterings about rationing water soon. Apparently each time you have a shit it takes over two gallons to flush it down the pipes into the, crumbling, sewers. All great fun. It's even getting hard to buy Evian or Volvic. Except that I am Teachers Pet at the grocers and am assured that I'll be alright. I mean, really! What are we all coming to? Brock in for a beer last night and brought a mass of my old Videos having had them transferred from BETAMAX to VHS for my new machine. Rather wistfully I looked at a long documentary about my house in the Alpes Maritimes . . the last one I agreed to do in the terrible summer of '86. How pretty it all was. And how certain it all seemed! No such luck. Anyway. Nice memories as well. It was just seeing the dogs again which stung a bit.

[. . .] Next time you write I suggest that you use letter paper rather than cardboard sheets. Cheaper. And someone ripped off one of your rather fancy stamps. I wonder which one it was? The 2.30 ones were all intact. Honestly, you cant leave a fag-end in an ash tray in this benighted city.

Much love . . .
　　Your ageing Uncle
　　Dirk.
　　　OXXO

P.S. Thanks for the snaps of the Child. They have been sent on to the Natural History Museum for their archives. A missing link is ALWAYS vastly interesting to them.

Jack ('Tony') Jones died on 12 October.

To Christopher Whittaker[1]

Cadogan Gardens
16 October 1990

Dear Christopher Whittaker –
　　It was very good of you to write and give me the news of Jack's death.

---

1. CW had shared the last years of Jack Jones's life.

They are not easy letters to write, as I well know, but it is so much better to find out that way than from the Deaths Columns.

We very much lost touch after the war; but he was a brave and valient sailor . . . and was much respected.

He had, as you are very well aware, a pretty wretched war .. the wounding never healed, and he was constantly in pain but seldome complained.

Alas! the vine gets barer .. thank you so much for writing and please accept my heartfelt sympathy.

Very sincerely
    Dirk

To John Osborne   *Cadogan Gardens*
                                               24 October 1990

Dear John –

Do you, I wonder, remember as acutely as I do that very wet Sunday when you and M.U.[1] walked up from the Green Line Bus stop in Little Chalfont and, sodden as a pair of seals, you changed clothes, got fed, and handed me the script (type-script) of 'LOOK BACK IN ANGER'? Remember that? I know that you had the laplander slippers from the cover of 'A.B.C.O.P',[2] and you said so. All that preamble simply to remind you that, even though we do not see each other now, we have known each other for a very long time.

And since when.

Your letter today has given me the greatest possible pleasure.[3] To be judged by ones Peers is always a rather worrying business, but to be judged with such care and encouragment verges on sheer hysteria of delight! I am terrificaly glad that you liked the Independant bit. It has, of course, been greatly misunderstood as a sort-of cry of loneliness and despair. Which, to some extent, it possibly was. Or the sub-text was. But it really WAS supposed to amuse! Those things actually happened to me in my first year in this daft town. Those people, as

---

1. Mary Ure, JO's then wife.
2. JO's first volume of memoirs, *A Better Class of Person: An Autobiography 1929–1956* (Faber & Faber, 1981).
3. JO had written to congratulate Dirk on his article, 'A Short Walk from Harrods' (*Independent on Sunday*, 30 September).

you must know, really did exist .. and in consequence the telephone does'nt even ring on weekdays!¹

But I had hoped that it would have amused people rather than got them so sad that they have offered me caravans on sites from Salcombe (with a view of the bay and resident caretaker on the site ..) to Dunoon. People have offered to read to me, write to me, take me [for] walks in Kensington Gardens or, are you ready, the Yorkshire Dales (Peaceful, bliss, REAL people. Not grotesques like London ..).

I do not complain, you understand. Merely fret that people will read things in a different light.

I packed up acting for twelve years in order to try and develope another string to my bow. I really did foolishly think that my life was finally settled in the farm (small holding) in Provence, and that I would never have to leave. I never wanted to. Hence junking the Movies. Idiot fellow. At sixty seven I had to start out all over again. One manages. I went back to the cinema (In France, With Tavernier) and had a whopping success. Gratifying after so many years away!

I think it opens here in Feb. We'll see. But before that another book has to be delivered somehow. I'm at Chapter 7. It's agony. I cant write in this town. However; never look back and never look down lest you fall.

One day, perhaps, before I am raddled to death, you and I might be able to get together and do something? It's about time you know. I admire you greatly; I always have. And you write whopping things for actors to do. I dont mean like the recent bash at 'L.B.I.A.'² that was disgraceful I thought frankly. Never mind .. rummage about and see if you could find something. Not a Theater Piece. Cant cope with that now. Next time you come up to honour Oscar³ try and remember that I am four hundred yards away. In Lily Langtry's Laundry.

And it would be terrific to see you again.

<u>Dont</u> nudge my basket in Partridges⁴ ... come and eat instead?

Ever, with respect and affection.

<u>Dirk</u>

---

1. Dirk had observed: 'The telephone hardly ever rings. Sometimes it doesn't make a sound for days. And never between Friday afternoon and Monday afternoon.'
2. A 1989 revival of *Look Back in Anger*, starring Kenneth Branagh and Emma Thompson, at the Lyric.
3. When in London, JO stayed at the Cadogan Hotel, where Wilde was arrested in 1895.
4. JO said that Dirk should not feel constrained to reply to his letter: 'I may nudge you with my basket in Partridges one day ...'

To Dilys Powell   *Cadogan Gardens*
                                                  15 November 1990

Dearest Dilys –

Oh dearie me! I know that you are going to think that I have quite forgotten you? Not at all. My silence has been imposed by a number of irritating, worrying at times, items.

Well: to start with. 'Flu. Not desperatly badly but quite bad enough. Caught, of course, from my students during Workshop at the Guildhall. I realised, sitting like a toad in a circle of 34 young people, that thirty of them were reeking with the bloody germs. Red of nose, coughs, barking like seals: Nothing to do but carry on and try to make them understand the difference between a 5 lense and a 75 lense . . . . not altogether certain of the difference myself now. Technics alter.

But I got through two sessions of three hours and got, in consequence, 'flu. Bed ridden for a day and a night, miserable and coughing for a week. No work done, no letters written, hence silence.

I was unable to go and be capped and gowned at the bloody Guildhall for services to the Arts (!) which was almost a relief. Imagine the horror of the luncheon which preeceded it! My co-graduand was one Vivien Ellis (music)[1] who at 87 is irritable and concieted in equal amounts. So he had the day to himself while I coughed gobbits in the Kleenex. Then: what then? Oh. A dear chum[2] of many years, since '47, called about some piece I'd written in a paper and I said 'Have you got 'flu, you sound wretched' and she said no it was not 'flu, but she had an appointment, on National Health, for her first Bariem (a?) meal at St Thomas on December 18th. This sounded grim. She was unable to swallow. In pain. So. I got her into private care, she was dealt with in FIVE days. Into the Cromwell . . operation for cancer, and telephoned me on Monday evening from her private room to thank me and say that she was sure that now all would be well. But she died next day.

When I was told, by a brother of hers, I heard myself saying idiotically that she could'nt be dead because I had spoken to her the evening before. So are bad scripts written!

---

1. Vivian Ellis, composer of the recently revived *Mr Cinders* and its featured song, 'Spread a Little Happiness'.
2. Anne Leon – the 'Annie' after whom Dirk had named his parrot.

But the worst part was the bill. Can you believe a private room at the Cromwell, without the surgeon and all that, cost £8.500?

The total bill amounted to 12,700. Which I do not possess in this country. However, after a morning of suicidal despair about being over-generous and loving to someone outside the family (as my sister was later to point out!) Viking telephoned to say that they had bought my new novel ... anyway the half I had by that time written, for a very decent sum. It is not a Sean-Connery-Amount, to be sure, but it got me out of the mire at the Cromwell! So you do see, I hope, that I have been fairly distracted. And that £8.500 was for FIVE days only. The poor lamb [...] only lasted five days. Golly whiz. Now I am back on my feet, almost, and trying to sort out the mail .. and your dear card was among it all ... and hence this letter. I really do find that looking after the tax, the rates, the lawyers letters and so on is a bit of a chore. Spoiled, of course, for fifty years, or there abouts, it was all done for me. All I had to do was the acting part. Easy as falling off a log. Or, in some cases, a roof.

'Daddy N.' is now re-titled, thank God, 'These Foolish Things' which is slightly better. It was NOT a big success in Paris. Too sad, about two elderly people with a middle aged daughter ... and everyone applauded and wept but told their friends not to go. Big hit in Italy and in Switzerland and, for the first time in my life, I won Best Actor at the International Critics Festival in Spain. We open here in Feb .. and at the London Festival on Sunday. I shall keep well away from it all.

I have planted out the window boxes with winter things .. and am just able enough to have a meal for someone tomorrow who wants to dramatise a piece I wrote for The Independent. I DID suggest that I might quite like to do it myself. . But he says he has some ideas and can we meet. So ... ham and salad and how to dramatise my piece. Hence silence!

I hope this has filled you in? Anyway – Love, & love <u>Dirk</u>

To Alain de Pauw   *Cadogan Gardens*
                                                       7 January 1991

Cher Alain

How good of you to write once more. To keep me in 'touch' with Clermont. Naturally I envy you greatly to know that you are still there and that it still gives you peace and shelter, as indeed it once did me.

I spent my first Christmas and New Year absolutely on my own!

The first time in 70 years!

I thought that I should try it ... just the once .. to see if I could manage it, and I did. I apparently had a far better time than most of my family and my friends! People had terrible rows, got stuck in traffic or snow, were bitten by dogs, got flu, were burned by the fire (logs falling from a too-big fire) and God knows what else. More marriages seem to founder at Christmas than at any other time .. but then in the idiotic UK the wretched holiday lasts three weeks! Only today do people crawl back to their offices .. can you believe it?

And so, with a probable war ahead, let me wish you and Christine and your family safety, above all peace, and health in this New Year.

And again, my most sincere thanks for your thought of me ..

As ever

<u>Dirk</u>

To Julie Harris   *Cadogan Gardens*
                                            18 February 1991

Julie dear –

[...] Darling: frankly No. I wont be at your party at the Garrick.

I honestly dont see any reason to celebrate the fact that one has reached seventy![1] Why? It is'nt the end of the line for God's sake .. lots of time ahead, and lots and lots of things to do.

I, for my part, will have nothing whatever to do with <u>my</u> birthday if and when I hit the mark! Balls ... it's like any other old birthday, best forgotten, it only makes one FEEL old ... the day before one is 69 the day after 70. So whats the big deal, it's all a matter of calanders and that sort of nonsense.

Anyway, love, I would not know anyone there, save for you and Mu[2] I expect, and I NEVER do the Evenings, only ever Matinees .. I was forced to hand Natasha Richardson a prize at some ghastly 'do'[3] and did so only because I adore her and it was her first award and I

---

1. JH, Oscar-winning costume designer for *Darling*, was born the day before Dirk.
2. Muriel Pavlow, Dirk's co-star in *Doctor in the House*.
3. The London Evening Standard Awards, at which she was honoured as Best Actress for *The Comfort of Strangers*.

have known her since she was, well ... BEFORE .. she was born. Never again.

I dont expect you to forgive my refusal, it is not because I dont value you and your freindship, it's just that it's not my scene, not reclusive, just selective.

Celebrating a birthday in that manner seems a bit daft to me.[1]

Now eighty is something else. That is REALLY a landmark ... I know a lot of people who retire at seventy five! And move to France or Spain or go off to China and walk along the Wall!

There is a lot of life left, darling. Promise you.

Love
    Dirk

To Kensington and Chelsea Borough Council   *Cadogan Gardens*
6 February 1991

Planning application/listed building application.
DPS/DCS/GA/TP/90/2180/2182. 49 Kings Road.

Dear Mr French[2] –

I write to protest, very strongly, about the apparent decision to install a branch of McDonalds hamburger, take-away on the above site.

It will completely wreck a well-loved Conservation Area, cause intense distress to those who live in the area, plus dirt, pollution and added noise.

The Kings Road, which I have known all my life, has steadily declined into a Down-Market area. The arrival of a McDonalds will finally bring about a feeling of total desolation to this sad street.

I beg of you to use your good offices to try and alleviate this Conservation disaster .. we managed in Paris and other Continental cities where the take-away's were jammed into areas of particular historic and national attraction.

---

1. Instead he sent JH an immense bunch of roses.
2. Michael French, then Director of Planning Services at the Council. McDonald's were opening a branch on the site of what had once been the White Hart pub, later the Chelsea Drug Store, and had applied to make several additions, including a large canopy bearing its yellow logo.

Even though much of the Kings Road is now squalid and dirty, the prospect of Royal Avenue to the Hospital is STILL one of our jewels. Can you do something to help preserve this?

Your help in this worrying matter would be most gratefully appreciated by us all who live in the borough.[1]

Very sincerely,
Dirk Bogarde.

To Olga Horstig-Primuz   *Cadogan Gardens*
                                                14 March 1991

Darling Olga –

As I write this poor Jane is down the road, not very far from here, in the church for the burial of her beloved Pappie.[2] Nothing I fear will hurt her as much as this, for she absolutely adored him, and nothing that I can think of will heal her grief. Neither Jacques, Charlotte or Lulu[3] ... It is desperately sad. I did not go to the funeral because I dislike them[,] funerals, and also because I am not a part of that very big, rather distinguished family.

And they are ALL a bit cuckoo!

But afterwards I will be here to help her, if I can.

I am typing this so that you may understand it easier! What is this about your 'view getting worse' as you say? I am in the same boat ma belle! I have to wear glasses to peel potatos! And now that I have learned (amazingly) to cook .. and enjoy it! ... I wear glasses all the time. Except at public functions like the Variety Club Award, or the Evening Standard (our only evening newspaper) awards. They are all on TV so I dont wear my glasses. I'm about to be 70 in a day or two but that is of no consequence. The next ten years are the test!

'Daddy Nostalgie' (title changed here to 'These Foolish Things') will open here at the top, top, cinema, the Mayfair Curzon, as soon as 'Mr Et Mme Bridge'[4] come off ... very boring. That is the film

1. Although it was one of many from local residents, including Patricia Losey, Dirk's appeal was to no avail. On his archive copy of the letter, he added: 'Macdonalds won.'
2. David Birkin, husband of Judy Campbell. Serge Gainsbourg, with whom Jane Birkin lived for twelve years, had died on 2 March.
3. Jacques Doillon, with whom Jane Birkin now lived; her daughter by Gainsbourg; and her daughter by Doillon.
4. *Mr & Mrs Bridge*, directed by James Ivory.

with Joanne and Paul Newman. I have'nt seen it but have been told that it is 'stultifing'. Not a good indication! It had wonderful reviews from all the critics, but who wants to go and see two elderly Americans regretting their lives and wondering what a bidet is for?

On the other hand, who wants to see an ageing Daddy dying with his miserable daughter and boring wife living in Bandol!

Merde . . . .

'Jericho' will not be published until next spring. England is SO slow . . . and this afternoon my editor from Viking arrives to start the cutting and re-arrangement. This is the part I hate. They like the book but say that it is a little slow here and there . . . so. I wrote very hard for five months. 86.350 words. Pas mal? I like it . . it is set in the Var so that I could keep in touch with my beloved France and it brings me close to Clermont just to write about the flowers which were growing in April/May. It is so strange how quickly I forget my garden and the work I had to do there. Age, I suppose?

NEXT DAY.

A full day yesterday: I had to start the Editing of my book [. . .] I was very afraid that they would ask me to cut a great deal. I wrote far too much; but they only want small cuts and one or two 'scenes' extended. So that is alright. I am VERY relieved. I have lived with the book for two years . . actually I started it in '86 just before we discovered the bad news about Tony. So it was set aside. Anyway; now it is done. Today my niece and her husband for lunch . . ouf! and then tomorrow Thomas, my 'adopted' grandson, of Tony's, comes to lunch. He asks for my 'special'. A chicken in the bricque with eight <u>bulbs</u> of garlic and six lemons, stuffed with wild mushrooms. I admit I do it rather well, and it is easy and came from a recipe we got in Chateauneuf.[1]

Apparently there was a re-peat of the Visconti show on Antenne 2 . . I have had a lot of mail congratulating me on speaking French so well. I feel very ashamed! But, somehow, I seem to speak better now that I am in London . . idiotic, but true. Or perhaps the years have finally got ripe. Like a good Camembert? You think it possible?

No news from Jane today or yesterday and nothing in the papers. She is very little known here and Gainsboroug not at all . . except for

---

1. As O H-P noted in the margin: '*Bonne recette*'.

that idiotic song.¹ Ah well .. we are different countries twenty miles apart. I must go and lay my table for lunch [...] All my love always ..

Ever

    <u>Dirk</u> XXOX

I was awarded a special prize, by the Variety Club, for my 'World Wide Contribution to International Cinema'! Finney won Best Actor, Natasha Richardson (Daughter of Vanessa Redgrave) Best Actress. Nonsense, but fun!

To Nicholas Shakespeare   *Cadogan Gardens*
                                         21 April 1991

Nicholas –

Of course I was very saddened when I heard that you were about to slide out of the Editors Chair.²

But I absolutely understand, and agree, that you should.

After all books have to be written so that they can be read. Simple.

I'm really only writing to say a rather belated 'Thank you'.

It is a thank-you which might seem trivial but which was, to me, very important that I convey. Because, quite honestly, I am not absolutely certain where I would have been today had you not come to see me in that foul little house in Kensington three years ago. You did, without knowing it, pull me back from a chasm so black, so deep, that all could very well have ended in ashes for me.

Or, frankly, a pill-bottle.

It was, that evening, a pretty bloody time. I had learned earlier in the day, that cancer had reached the lymph-glands in my patient, and that it was simply a question of time.

I suppose that I should have called and asked you to cancell your meeting with me, but, for some strange reason, I did not do so.

I did'nt exactly know how to cope, where to go, what to do, how to adjust. Fifty years companionship was about to end; a whole future

---

1. Jane Birkin and Serge Gainsbourg had an international hit with his composition 'Je t'aime ... moi non plus'.
2. NS had announced that he was standing down as Literary Editor of both the *Daily* and *Sunday Telegraph*.

so comfortably planned had hideiously, and suddenly, come to an end, and I was frankly a stranger in an alien land after twenty two years abroad. Radiently, happily, glowing, wonderously, abroad. Never to return. Idiot me.

And then, that sorry evening, you arrived. Doctors had come and gone, the patient dozed. I, in despair, had to work out what to do.

And you arrived with a plank, and hand-rail, to help me across the chasm.[1] It may seem odd to you that being asked to review books for the Telegraph can reach such a giddy height of meaning.

But that is what happened. Instead of packing it all in, as I very likely would have done when the fuss was over, I suddenly found a perfectly good reason for 'going on'. You offered me that.

So for that incredible boost to courage, moral, and belief in self, I must say 'Thank you'. And having done that, causing you a wincing embarressment . . (SP?) I'll let it go.

But thats how it was. For my new belief in self, for my get on with it, and start all over again . . for that at least.

Thanks.

Ever

<u>Dirk</u>

To Penelope Mortimer   *Cadogan Gardens*
                                                            29 April 1991

Penelope –

Perhaps this will find it's way to your trembling hands among the beastly builders and the debris and the STUFF.[2]

If I had not had a stroke (due to moving at an advanced age) I'd have pissed off back to France after Forwood died. But simply could'nt face another move.

Willesden sounds alright. Not sure about P. O'Tool.[3] Terrific bore, rather a good actor. Once. But if you have a garden and grandchildren (all South facing?) [. . .] then you are wiser than moaning in the peat and mire of the Post Office.

---

1. An account of how NS first 'threw a plank across the ravine' was written by him in *The Daily Telegraph* on 2 October 1993 and reprinted in *For the Time Being*.

2. PM had forsaken the country for north-west London, to be near her family.

3. PM's discovery that Peter O'Toole was a neighbour proved a boon when friends asked: '*Willesden?*'

If there was peat and mire? There usually is. I was up to elbows in both yesterday on my titchy balcony. Changing the earth in pots (what a fucking chore THAT is four flights up) and planting my Lavateria (SP?) and a whole flock of dancing, nodding, violas. It all looks v. pretty and smells super.

Wallflowers. You see. Odd, is'nt it, how once one has had a garden it is almost the most impossible thing to give up. I know I have to have a sort of litter-box .. anything where I can see light and breath the air. And plant a pot.

[...] What is this Mac Classic?[1] Never heard of it. Should I? I could'nt wind up my Hornby train. Would that count against me?

The only thing is, it looks a bit soulless. But then so, I suppose, does this electric job. Took me months to find something simple enough to use.

My old Smith Corona, strong as an ox, and travelled the world (Literally) finally blew a gaskett, or whatever they do, and died.

I managed to get this through a kind editor at the Telegraph (for whome I review books) who told me to go to W.H. Smith in Notting Hill Gate where they had SERIOUSLY simple typewriters. Hence this year .. or yeer[2] .. thing.

I did the whole of 'JERICHO' on it. 86.533 words exactly. Finally I mean. According to my [...] typist in Hitchin. She has a vast machine which does everything. Including count. Cant spell, neither can she (Nor me) but it does amazing things like, if you want to change a characters name two thirds of the way into the epic, all that you have to do is press a button ONCE and you get 'Abrahams' changed to 'Aronovich' in a flash.

I do reckon thats good.

[...] Yup. Saw first episode of 'Marriage'[3] .. was v. impressed. Then the awfulness of the acting and direction took hold and I squirmed out of the 2nd. Sorry.

Not your fault .. but those lump un-ladies [sic] and that DIRE Harold!

---

1. PM had written to Dirk on an Apple Mac computer.
2. This 'ere.
3. PM's adaptation for the BBC of *Portrait of a Marriage*, with Janet McTeer, David Haig and Cathryn Harrison.

Poor Nicholson .. he was a wet, that was true, but not wringing-wet.

We'll talk about that one day. It's one of the reasons I wont do TV.

My new film, with Tavernier, opens at the Curzon next month. We are the RAGE and toast, of New York. Words like 'unforgettable', 'magnificent' 'triumphant' and 'unmissable on all points' sound pretty to the ear and look lovely in print. After 12 years away! I DO hope this finds you in the pink . . . as it leaves me. For the moment ..

My love D̲ XXXXX

To Wallace S. Watson
Cadogan Gardens
2 May 1991

Dear Professor Watson –

I was facinated to get the packet of mail[1] from you today. [... and] amazed to find the copies of the private letters which I had written to Fassbinder after all these years. Amazed for two reasons: that he had bothered to keep them, and that they had surfaced in Pittsburg!

The advice I offered him in these letters still holds good today, the great sadness of 'DESPAIR' is that he, finally destroyed a marvellous movie.

Willfully, I sometimes think.

The letter of 24th September '77 was written shortly after I had returned home from Paris after having dubbed the final cut. Not a lot .. but pieces here and there. The cut-version staggered me. It was so amazingly good, so tremendously sad and, this is important, so wryly FUNNY!

The film was selected, as it stood, for Cannes and for the German Entry in the following year. May.

Between September of 1977 and May of 1978 Reiner took his scissors and tore the film to shreds. When I arrived in Cannes for the Press Show the splendid cameraman, Michel (SP?) Balhaus [Michael Ballhaus], with a hint of tears in his eyes, said not to attend the

---

1. Wallace Steadman Watson, of Duquesne University in Pittsburgh, had written for permission to use Dirk's correspondence with Fassbinder in a study of the latter's life and work, and in a scholarly article. These duly appeared as *Understanding Rainer Werner Fassbinder: Film as Private and Public Art* (University of South Carolina Press, 1996) and 'The Bitter Tears of RWF' *(Sight and Sound,* July 1992).

screening. Reiner was locked in his room, impossible to talk to, and far worse he had destroyed the film. I went, with Andrea [Ferréol], it was after all our duty to do so, and the warning was correct. The film was a mess. Scenes were transposed, cut, elimin[a]ted, and all, or nearly all, of Andrea's performance was ruined. The comedy, and there had been valuable comedy, had gone. So too had many other 'set pieces'.

I was pretty shattered. There was still a sort of movie .. but not the movie I had last seen in Paris in black and white.

Reiner was, finally, persuaded to attend the Press Conference and behaved impossibly .. replying to questions rudely, arrogantly, stupidly. We could not save the film or him. He was dressed in leather pants, bikers-boots, a battered black felt hat with a hole in it, a sagging, filthy, black tee-shirt full of tears and rents. It was a tragic, stubborn, farewell. I never saw him after that. I was not angry: just wretched. So much had gone, so much had been ruined.

So much for pills and potions and 'the wrong kind of friends'. He had plenty of those. But he was, I assure you, one of the, if not THE, most exciting young director I had ever met or worked with. He knew more about movement and the camera, about light and about sound than even Visconti ... and he knew it all!

He was humble (with me) exciting to work for, breathlessly inventive.

Thinking that the first scene in the movie would be played between Andrea and I in the sitting room of our flat ... comfortably dressed with our glasses of 'goggle moggle' was a grave mistake. We did it, as it now stands, all over the apartment and mostly lying flat on the floor while Andrea was stripped!

Not at all my idea .. or that of Mr Stoppard!

Stoppard was brought onto the film, according to Reiner (and he may have been fibbing) simply because he, Reiner, wanted a 'real English adaptation of [Nabokov].' He had seen Stoppards work, knew his use of English was eccentric but excellent and he wanted, above all things, for his first big International Movie to work with a real adaptation. Not a hack job by some secretary who might 'know English pretty well.' He wanted a clear, understandable, script in correct English.

Translations of European films are often done by English-Speaking-American voice-coaches .. so there is always a problem! Reiner knew what he wanted to do with the Nabakov story: he did not want it written for him particularly.

However Stoppard was summonsed, I gather they got on pretty well, and finally a very interesting, but confused and dense, script was produced.

At this point Stoppard was not really very aware that the cinema is visual as an Art Form! So he tended to over-write and, for Reiner, over-embellish.

The 'puns' for which he is so famous meant absolutely zilch to Fassbinder. I had to explain them in detail to him. No easy matter. He would consider in silence, sucking on his moustache, and then say 'It's schoolboy stuff, right?' and throw it out. This was a constant problem, and it irritated him all the time. If anything in the script became too complicated he'd say 'Another Stoppard "pun". God! The English!'

It was difficult to save poor Tom Stoppard from destruction.

Reiner's impatience was a dangerous sign: his boredome threshold was very, very short. When I first saw the final cut in Paris, and we did the dubbing, I called Tom and told him that I considered he'd get a bit of a shock when he saw his work but that he'd be very proud finally. He was not at all proud.

In an angry letter to me, he complimented ME on my work but said that the film was 'a disaster, a lemon, a ruin . .'

And so it was from where he sat.

I have described the day at my house in Provence when we all met to iron out the 'bumps' in the script. Tom re-wrote pages, threw new ideas around, and whole new scenes. Reiner, as I have indicated in 'An Orderly Man', lay prone in the cool of my drawing-room reading motor-magazines. He did not attend at all. He KNEW what he wanted to make, and how, and that was enough. He was just waiting for us all to finish struggling and get on with the beer.

I did not want to hurt Stoppard: he was a very good friend during all the problems, and I respected him greatly as a theater-writer.

After the showing of the film he saw in London he never contacted me again.[1] Reiner stayed away from the Crew Party on the last night of shooting in a small hotel near Luneberg, on the then-Wall. I knew he would not be able to face the farewell . . . emotionally he was very

---

1. Untrue, as we have seen.

soft once you had got to his gut, and he was amazed, and delighted, by Andrea and myself because we were both professional actors of much experience and he had never worked with others than his 'gang' who were keen, but amateur. Except for the marvellous Bernard Wickie[1] . . . He [Fassbinder] shoved a letter under my bedroom door while I was down in the hotel bar hosting the party in his place. The letter, for reasons of copyright, I had to use in 'Orderly Man' as if it was a dialogue scene between us. Not so. His dialogue is his letter . . and this letter is with all my other stuff in Boston University under the care of the good Dr Gottlieb.

Reiner had killed himself, by this time; I did'nt know how to contact his mother, and used his letter as best I could. But that is what he wrote.

Had he lived, even though he deliberatly or in madness (and that was possible on some of the stuff he took) ruined 'DESPAIR', I know that I would <u>walk</u> to wherever he was, to work with him again. So, I know, would Andrea Ferriol . . whose wonderful performance he had so cruelly mutilated. We simply knew 'genius' when it was around. And you dont get to work with them so often.

He and I worked together brilliantly. I knew, just from a look, what he wanted, we hardly ever spoke . . just did the job. I sometimes got behind the bad-times with the pills and the 'gang' . . and I know that I had his respect and, for what it is worth, his total confidence and love. Andrea and I held him together at times, when the pressure from his friends got too heavy.

Certainly use the letters. Apologies for the errors and all the (sic) bits![2] I type so badly . . and spell dreadfully. Having witnessed the ruin of what had been, in my opinion, my very best performance, I left the screen for 13 years.

Tavernier brought me back. I could'nt be more delighted! I did NOT want my 50 year old career to end on 'DESPAIR'!

Very Sincerely
<u>Dirk Bogarde</u>

---

1. Bernhard Wicki, who played Orlovius.
2. Inevitably WW's transcription contained many of them.

To Eileen Atkins   *Cadogan Gardens*
                                                          3 May 1991

Darling G¹ –

Fear ye not! I am not starting a correspondance course, done that
thanks, but I got your splendid letter this am, and having written a
mass of tosh (well: not really. Quite good really, about Fassbinder for
some professor at Duquesne University who is doing a vast book on
the fellow and wants to use some letters I wrote to him during the
filming. Him being Fassbinder. Got it?) well . . . anyway. Having done
that I thought I'd write back to you (<u>no</u> answer required, I'll see you
shortly I hope . .) to say that I was very touched that you had plodded
off to the old Paris² to see my movie. We open here at the Curzon in
a weeks time. I dread the UK press. They are so bloody to me, I
suppose because I pissed off for 22 years and worked abroad? I cant
THINK why they call me 'bitter'. Christ!

I know what you mean about Odette [Laure] in the fillum. She is,
as it happens, younger than me, and has almost never been in a film.
She is strictly Theater.

I adored her. We had no common tongue, I mean, I could speak
Frog to her and she could just about say, 'I tink I okay big boy, You
tink?'. And we fell apart laughing, because her English was learned
during the Liberation!

But Tavernier cast her before me   so I had to match up. See?
Anyway I loved her for her total committment to the project and no
fart-arsing about.

She had a little bower of a dressing room in the ruined villa in
which we 'shot', and Jane and I shared a room next to the lav. Only
one . . with a green plastic curtain. Opening into our room. So. When
anyone went to have a piddle, (for something more we left, naturally)
but with a piddle we all sang and hummed and it was perfectly alright
until the thing got blocked and we were stuck with a smell that only
the Kurds can appreciate. But that is how we made the movie. I
LOVE it that way. The Hollywood way doesnt work for me I fear.
But no matter, it wont have to.

I imagine how hellish it must be for you with no air-conditioner,

1. Glum.
2. The Paris Theater (cinema) in New York.

but think of the hugeness of your success![1] [. . .] It really is so splendid. I hug myself; for you.

Here, when you get home, it's much the same as it always was only a bit more gloomy than when you left. The recession is grim: but the Rich are still with us, and so that must be alright. I suppose.

I found, the other day, an aged copy of The Sun! Stuck in a drawer behind a lot of screws and nails and electric light bulbs. Dated May '65 . . and with a huge spread about a party I gave for Sybil (Burton) Christopher the night before she sailed for N.Y and left U.K for ever. The cast list was amazing! I took over a new club called the Ab Lib[2] . . . and closed it . . because of the noise we all made until six am and breakfast. It was for Syb's chums to say farewell. I had stipulated to her, on the telephone, a supper party at the Connaught for twelve or so.[3] She thought I meant something QUITE different and invited ALL her chums who were around, which came to 300. NOT INCLUDING all members of the London Ballet . . or whatever it was called[4] in those days.

But the point of all this is simply to say that one of the 'rocketting stars' who were present was Miss Jean Marsh![5] And I never knew or remembered!

I feel so guilty . . golly. But it was a considerable time ago. [. . .]

Tonight I am off to rehearsal for 'Saki', to 'do' the music cues! We open in Bath next Sunday: George Fearon is doing music . . . not my idea but old Piggot Smith who is producing the show for his Compass Company . . . he's as nervous as a child bride, and taking everything MUCH MUCH too seriously.

I have suggested tunes that Mr Fearon might use. Edwardian stuff, like Floradora, The Belle of New York, The Arcadians . . so on. I am so old I know them. No one else did! So one begins to know about

1. EA was the toast of New York for her performance as Virginia Woolf in *A Room of One's Own*.

2. The Ad Lib, in Leicester Place, London W1. The party took place on 18 September 1964.

3. Dirk and Tony planned this extravagant social highlight with precision. It involved, on the previous day, the sitting for a portrait photograph by a group including Dirk, Tony, Stanley Baker, Noel Harrison and another of the party's prime movers, the singer Alma Cogan.

4. The Royal Ballet.

5. Jean Marsh and EA created the television series *Upstairs, Downstairs* and *The House of Eliott*.

being 70. I dont, for a moment, consider <u>you</u> to be among the aged!! No, not that. It's just that you are a clever lady and you might perhaps KNOW those things. I felt such a loon whistling stuff to an amazed, bewildered, group. Never mind.

Yah. Helena sort of managed Press-wise here.[1] Not over generous. They were kind to Mel G. not so kind to Close ... but they do seem to think that the British own bloody Shakespeare and that no one can do him except them.

I've seen so much BAD acting since I got back to the UK that I now keep out of the way. I cant wrestle with my conscience watching Judy Dench or Prunella Scales at it. Oh dear! Your best mates. Sorry .. but really ... it is all very Cottage Industry Stuff to me. Like the Stonehenge Woollen Industry, which you ARE too young to know about. It is marvellous that you have gone 'away' to work ... as I did. To broaden the horizons ... actors must, I feel. As indeed so must writers. We are so much richer for that trip. Even if we do, as I know you do, rather ache for the river,[2] Bill, the cats and trolling about in the garden now that May (bloody so far) is here. But still: we got away.

Had lunch yesterday, at her house, with Dilys Powell. 89, my dear, deaf as a post but still writing and as bright as a button. Or a very sharp knife. I do so envy people who really adore their work. It's so stimulating. I had been sent for to talk about screen-acting to one of her protégés ... a pleasant, dull, fellow who is a Top Producer for Welsh TV. Which <u>should</u> have put me off. What can you say to a Welsh TV Producer? Nothing he'll understand, thats for sure. I talked myself into a writhen log. The food was inedible anyway .. so I talked on. God knows about what. You simply cant define acting! It happens or it does'nt. Piggot Smith says that I am a 'behaviourist' (Whatever that means. Do you know?) but I do know that he's a Real Actor. And that it shows!

Chinese family, very noisy, have moved into the flat below. Shouts and cries and high chitter-chatter from the women. They are from Singapore. I DO wish they would go back there. At the moment they are having a terrible row in their bed-room, under mine, and she is

---

1. Franco Zeffirelli's film of *Hamlet*, starring Mel Gibson, with Glenn Close and, as Ophelia, Helena Bonham Carter.
2. Thames, beside which EA and her husband lived.

screeching. She's covered in Cartier and Chanel. Oh Lor ... I had
better stop this and go to the photo-copy shop and do my things for
the Professor in Pittsburg. I am now so aged that I am about the
only living relic who remembers Losey, Cukor, Visconti and, now,
Fassbinder.

I wish they paid me.

My balcony ablaze with wallflowers, violas in profusion, the rose in
fat bud, the hostas brilliant, a brave fuschia has opened a nervous
flower .. it is a mass of bees, and you'd imagine you were in the
Cotswolds.

Except with the Chinese below and Peter Jones opposite you know
bloody well you aint.

Come home soon ... enjoy what is left of N.Y, and remember that
you are greatly missed but enormously loved ...

Did I say anything pleasant about Miss Collins last time? In the
Cowards?[1] Forget it. Erase. She's terrible. I have now watched three
... all dire .. except one burst of excellence from your chum Miss
Phillips in 'Astonished Heart' but the rest, tragically, is crap. How you
can turn Coward into dust and ashes and 'Dynasty' is amazing. It all
depends, darling, on your Director!

With endless love
Dirk XXXOXX

Forgive errors. I think faster than I can type. – OR the other way
round –

To Olga Horstig-Primuz   *Cadogan Gardens*
                                           22 May 1991

Olga darling –

Well: first of all forgive me for being so late in my reply to your
sweet note .. a feeling of sadness and irritation there I could feel! As I
wrote in my card, Rosay[2] was not the only one to discover the bore of
getting elderly ... it is wretched, and even if you think I am a little bit

---

1. Joan Collins was leading the cast in a BBC production of Noël Coward's sequence of
six playlets, *Tonight at 8.30*. Dirk had earlier judged her performance in *Hands Across the
Sea* as 'very good'. Siân Phillips co-starred in one episode.
2. Françoise Rosay, who appeared with Dirk in *Quartet* (1948).

like a petit poussain compared to you, you are wrong! I am forced to realise that the things I used to take for granted are now only 'loaned' to me for my life-time, and that they wear out eventually. Teeth for one, eyes for another, legs, ma belle, for another! It is never ending ... but one goes on, because one must and, anyway, there are compensations. I am told!

The film has opened in London to very good reviews .. some marvellous .. all good but one or two rather idiotic. The main Critics were all in Cannes, so we had to put up with the second-stringers. Most of them report football matches as far as I can see. I am still considered to be 'light weight' and the 'pretty young Doctor'. I shall NEVER live those early films down. Seems so silly .. but the younger critics still blame me. They also think that Tavernier is 'arty', and quite miss the point of his work. We are so seperate, France and England, in our likes and dislikes. It amazes me that a mere twenty two miles can make so great a difference. But, alas, it does. The English live on an island. [A]nd it shows badly: they are so insular! God! Anything you say in criticism is screamed at by the Press. I have had a terrible time since I got back here with the cheap papers. But I managed, at a big Award ceremony which was televised, to say my piece uninterrupted!

I told them that they were out of touch with reality when they said that I lived in a basement, alone, a recluse, broke and drinking two bottles of whisky a day! It was apparent that I was not ... there were 500 people present, and when I said that I was NOT a recluse, that I had not retired, but that I was bloody selective! they 500 rose to their feet and gave me a standing ovation! I was very pleased. But you can imagine the cheap Press the next day. I got rubbished well and truly. But I dont think that it mattered because more people had seen me on the TV than buy the cheap papers! So .. I have managed to fight them and so far, touch wood, I have won. But they wait for any mistake or failure. God! I hate them.

[...] The show that I do on 'SAKI' has been a great success [...] it is very nice to hear applause again! The whole company, six of them plus the pianist/Composer, come this evening for sandwiches and Frascati .. we are to discuss last week, and I feel certain that they will try to persuade me to take the show on for a long run. I shall remain firm. They can replace me if they like .. but the idea of working every night in the summer in a theatre appalls me! So ...

I imagine that you know that Capucine[1] had a very long, and discreet affair with a cousin of the Queens. Nicholas Phillips? He was found dead in his car a few months ago .. suicide of course, but thankfully the Coroner refused to pass that verdict and simply said that there was no proof that he had intended to take his life. The cheap papers re-printed the Capucine business and said that she had 'originally been a man'! I ask you . . . . You will realise how low we have got in this country. Thankfully people simply no longer believe what is in the cheap press now.

[. . .] I think that you perhaps knew that I did the narration, as John Galsworthy, for the BBC doing the 'Forsyte Chronicles'. All the nine volumes! It took 25 weeks, of an hour a time, on Saturdays. I did the entire narration, alone, in a small studio in 3 days! Not bad! I did 850 tapes and only had to do two retakes .. and not my fault, simply the pieces were too long. It has been a huge success. Now they are selling the cassett of 9 of them. A little money for me. 'Voices In The Garden' is now on cassett .. read extremely well by a very good man called Andrew Sachs. It runs eleven hours. Very good for blind people or people who cant hold a book. Lots of those about!

The summer has come at last .. and a London summer can be lovely. My little terrace here is full of flowers and looks very good indeed. It is hard work, because I have to cart everything, like rubbish and old earth, down to the big garden four floors below. I look such an idiot carrying buckets along Sloan Street full of earth to dump in the garden! But what else to do with the stuff I wonder? Anyway, sitting out with my drink in the evening sun, surrounded by geraniums and nicotiana and my fuchias almost reminds me of Clermont.

Tony died three years ago last Saturday. How the time goes!

[. . .] Now: enough .. I will take this to the post and buy the evening paper and have a rest until the Gang arrive for food and drink. I'm not lonely!

All my love, Courage! – Dirk XXX

---

1. Capucine, the French actress and former model born Germaine Lefebvre, who co-starred with Dirk in *Song Without End*, had committed suicide in Lausanne on 17 March the previous year. Nicholas Phillips, a direct descendant of Pushkin, was a distant relative of the Duke of Edinburgh.

To Alice Van den Bogaerde[1]   *Cadogan Gardens*
                                              3 August 1991

Alice!

Quelle surprise! What a splendid one. I had no idea that you could use a pen. Let alone write correctly, and spell!

Amazing! I wonder what on earth reminded you that perhaps, only just perhaps, I'd be chuffed to get a letter from you in Paris?

Never mind. Fear not 'Uncle', something did, and it was most enjoyable to get . . . your letter I mean . . and to know, above all, that you like where you are and seem, cross fingers, to be breaking new ground.

It's very difficult to convince people of your age that living in Wandsworth, Fulham, or the better parts of Worlds End is not really living at all. Terribly important for you to get away from that sort of background for a while, and see how it is elsewhere.

I am, as you know, devoted to France and always will be. Brock and Rupe have promised to get my ashes (when I'm gone) across and then scatter me somewhere. I dont insist on Provence, I wont know will I? and I have told them both that Calais will do at a pinch. Even out over the station. I really dont mind . . . I just feel better about it to know that, one way or another, I shall go back.

I dont adore the Parisiens . . but I dont dislike them as much as most English people do. They dont like each other, you must remember, and they are very, very, selective . . . but they are a courageous lot, sharp, clever as paint, and they wont put up with anything that is really naff. That is left to the petit bourgeoise to do . . and there are a great many of them around. The Parisiens, and the French in general, are not like us. They are'nt chatty over the garden fence and they dont rely on cups of tea to calm everything from a nervous breakdown to a wedding celebration. They dont 'join', like we do . . . . they are very reserved, deeply conscious of 'family' and privacy, unlike us, and they dont actually bother about what other people think of them. I dont think that they are so much <u>hostile</u> as <u>indifferent</u>. Think of it. You may find the men 'pretentious' and sometimes 'sickening', although you dont specify how. But they really are a bit brighter than the average Hooray

---

1. Gareth and Lucilla's daughter, then aged eighteen; sister to Ulric and half-sister to Brock and Rupert. She had been studying in Paris.

Harry, Henry, or Harriet over here. Every fellow has the same feeling towards a pretty girl, and you are not an exception there, and flirting and showing off have to come into it. Better that than be totally ignored!

I have just re-read your letter and noted the date, and realised that my surprise letter was probably engendered by Paris Match last week.[1] I do hope that seeing me slammed as a homo has not upset you? It is actually quite untrue anyway .. and what about the ones who <u>are</u> and dont get onto the elegant list! Wow! Naturally my copy here had all the relevant pages removed at Customs .. so it was due entirely to my French chums who telephoned. I quite forgot you might read it or be embarrassed. Sorry. But not, this time, my fault lovie.

I have just finished, yesterday, a three-day 'shoot' for Channel 4 all about my life and career.[2] Very boring indeed, but I decided to do it rather than let them do it without me. That way I do have a little controll over what goes on. I know that the family wince or have the vapours everytime I open my mouth on the Telly or the radio . . . but they can rest assured they hardly come into things . . . no one gets a mention really .. and I am dead darling about them all.

But I know how they fuss. Auntie Lulu particularly!

[. . .] Brock drops in from time to time for a beer. He's a very loyal chap [. . .] Came to dinner one night and I cooked him a really decent dinner. I have learned, not before time, to cook! It amazes me .. but it is worth the effort.

[. . . G]reat love to you, keep well and be extremely happy and <u>enjoy</u> yourself . . . it all goes so damned quickly, you'd not believe.

Thanks for writing, it was super ..

Great love

<u>Uncle Dirk</u>

---

1. A war of words between the English and the French had been launched the previous November by *The Sun* with a headline addressed to the President of the European Commission: 'UP YOURS DELORS'. A recent salvo from the French Prime Minister, Edith Cresson, who was quoted variously as saying that all, most, or one in four Englishmen are homosexual, prompted *Paris Match* to publish a humorous article by Jean Cau, 'Les Anglais "homos"'. This was illustrated with photographs of Boy George, Oscar Wilde, Somerset Maugham, Noël Coward, Guy Burgess, Anthony Blunt, Jimmy Somerville, Lawrence of Arabia, Freddy (*sic*) Mercury, David Hockney and Dirk. As the last three were not even mentioned in the text, Dirk could feel justifiably aggrieved, if only at the magazine's gratuitousness.
2. *Dirk Bogarde – By Myself*, a Lucida Production, directed by Paul Joyce.

To Hélène Bordes   *Cadogan Gardens*
                                                      5 August 1991

Hélène ma belle –

Your lovely letter arrived two mornings ago when I was just on my way to the Studio to begin 'shooting' a two day Documentary, the LAST!, on my Life and Times. I did one final one in 1986 when I had to leave France. This is from the start of my career, my life even, up until today. With my last film .. Tavernier's, and my last or newest, novel, Jericho. I was cross, worried, and wearing very formal clothes. Hermes tie, most discreet, dark suit, white shirt. I even had washed my hair the night before, unusual ... I HATE washing my hair and all the tra-la-la afterwards. I have hair like a Japanese doll. Fine, dead straight, it blows in the wind like silk. And the bald parts show .. and I then have to glue it all together with something terrible in a spray-can ... So your letter made me happy, and I carried it in my pocket for the rest of the film! Madness. But perhaps it brought me luck?

Your adventures sound awful [...] Illness, or imagined illness (comme Moliere!) is terribly difficult to handle, especially if one is what we call the 'care-er' .. the one who has to look after, help and cheer. Ah! I know. I have become the Vice President of a thing here in the UK called Voulantary Euthanasia. I wrote a long piece for a paper pleading for people to have the right to die with dignity,[1] IF THEY REQUESTED IT, AND IF DEATH WAS INEVITABLE BUT AGONIZING. Naturally this has caused a fuss. But a good fuss! The Society, V.E.S, recieved 10.000 letters of support in the first four months of this year. We have an 'advanced warning' form or, better to understand, a 'Living Will' which merely states how we wish to be assisted out of pain or, worse, a vegetable-state. To be signed ONLY when we are well and in our right minds, and to be revoked at any time. It is merely something to alert our Doctors, and something, which we hope, will make their actions legal. I have so many lectures ahead I could spin! And, of course, so many furious people, of all Religions, who hate me! But I know that I am right to try and help get this law brought to legality. I have agreed to talk in the House Of Commons! if they demand. I dont care. I have seen appalling pain

---

1. 'Pleading for the valley of the reaper' (*The Sunday Telegraph*, 22 April) and 'The right to die with dignity' (*The Daily Telegraph*, 16 July).

and distress in death, both in Normandy when I was young, and later
in my life, and people constantly write begging me to help them. I
will!

'Jericho' is all finished and is being corrected. My Copy Editor had
only 12 questions out of 86.000 words! One was 'Is Valbonne spelt
correctly?' It was, and 'What is a Hoti?' He knows now! So that was a
relief .. and I finished the cover, which is quite good I think, an
'impression' of my imaginary 'Jericho', with terrible rocks and lovely
olive groves ... I have abandoned the idea of another memoir. The
reason being that everything seemed to be so sad after Clermont.
Death, destruction of all my dogs, posessions sold, my stroke, and
finally a solitary life five floors up in the middle of a city I really dont
love among people who, now, feel strange to me! So .. it's gone. I do
not believe that negativity is a pleasant product! And in my corridor I
was always so curious, opening the doors along the way, that I never
realised how many things there were to do there! Walls to paint, boxes
to open, many, many little things instead of pushing into doors and
wondering what to find. I am too old for adventures now. I am very
happy to be settled painting my walls and changing my mind! Easy!
So I will start to work again on a novel in the autumn, when the
evenings get longer and it is dark and cold all day. For the moment I
lecture here and there, read for the Blind, books on Compact Disc or
Tape (Backcloth next. I have just finished 'A Particular Friendship'
and it is'nt bad. I was rather tearful at the end! My dear! What conceit!)
and, of course, occasionally the BBC for poetry readings, or the 'Saki'
show which has proved to be very popular indeed.

Guess what! I have learned, finally, to C O O K! I love it! I was very
shy to start with, my hands shook, I spilled the olive oil over the recipe
book, I cut my fingers peeling the garlic and chopping the onions ...
but I have done it at last. I can now cook, without too much fear, my
rissotto Milanase, or my one with fungi or porcini (delicious) and my
Navarin printanier est tellement formidable! I do not speak of my
poulet avec 70 gousse d'ail! Fantastic.

It does take a very long time to peel 70 gousse. <u>New</u> garlic. But it
is devine!

I am very much like you: I believe in doing as much as I can while
I still can. What good is sitting alone in my room? Or reading? Or
not dareing to do something new and exciting and useful? If you are
wanted go!

As you are doing with the American trip. Wonderful! Absolutely right .. how good of you, and how good FOR you. Plenty of time later to sit and knit .. and when we do get to that stage, you and I (although I dont think I could learn to knit!) we will have plenty of things to remember with pleasure.

[...] I gather, from friends in Paris on the telephone, that there is something disagreeable attributed to me in Paris Match. But what can I do? It is, of course, untrue, but I cant possibly afford to take legal action against such a gigantic publishing house. Tant pis. It has been banned in Great Britain so I imagine it must be really ugly. However ... dont believe it, whatever you do .. and remember me with affection as I ALWAYS remember you ..

With all my love & [four hearts] of fondness –

Dirk

To Alain de Pauw   *Cadogan Gardens*
                                                 22 August 1991

Cher Alain –

My deepest apologies for not having written to thank you for such a magnificent present!

Clermont all before my eyes in glowing colour! So little changed that I had a lump in my throat, and yet so changed, so beautifully changed, that I was filled with joy to know how wonderfully that magic house was being cherished.

You and Christine have done all the things I promised myself that I would one day do when I had enough money!

The potager was always a 'disaster area', now it is ravishing, most beautifully sited, un obtrusive and very, very nescessary!

The one thing I had never considered was a donkey or an ass (?) from Corsica! A splendid idea.

Forwood and I spent all summer mowing the terraces and the grass, stacking and burning in the winter .. terrified of fire.

For quite a long time, I confess, I was unable to look at any photos of the place .. especially those taken before we started work, and during the happier days, from '68 until the end of the unhappy 80's. But very gradually, as time has deadened my heart, I have started to be able to come to terms that one life is over for ever and another, not as beautiful but fairly comfortable, has begun.

These wonderful pictures today have pricked my eyes with tears, I do admit, but not wrenched my heart completely.

They are proof that your love and care have enriched it .. and for that, as you know, I will always be deeply grateful.

If one still night, when the moon is high, you think that you see a shadow moving among the olives just below the little terrace, or sitting under the big olive over the pond, say 'Bon soir!'

It will be me.

With affection and gratitude ..

Ever <u>Dirk</u>

To Lee Langley[1]   *Cadogan Gardens*
                                            9 September 1991

Lee, love –

I have'nt written to you only because I knew that the script I read was not, what they choose to call, 'Final'. And so I thought it wiser to wait a little longer. Anyway, like you, I was, I suppose I AM, very leary about it ever being made. Should 'leary' be 'leery' [?] I rather think so. Mrs O'Leary's cow destroyed Chicago. Right?[2]

I thought you had done a mammoth job of 'Voices'. I refused ever to touch it, rightly I think. Equally I refused to play in it. I had my own vision of Archie-Charlie and it did'nt actually match with that of our UK producers.

Who, frankly, were'nt really au fait with the kind of language they used.

I offered to take them to Badminton or Chatsworth or some other little place, just to hear how that kind of English is spoken.

But no. Straight back to Mill Hill and Hendon, so I packed it in.

What you have done is quite splendid. No book is EVER like the film, that would be nonsense. As you know very well a writer offers only a suggestion, others can pick it up, or over. And, as is normal, a different thing is born.

I did'nt know that Marcus was going to be English. Super that he

---

1. LL wrote the screenplay for the adaptation of *Voices in the Garden*, starring Joss Ackland, Anouk Aimée and Samuel West.
2. A cow belonging to a Mrs O'Leary was reputed to have kicked over a lantern, thus starting the great Chicago fire of 9 October 1871.

is, and I have checked on him[1] since my Agents 'Stand By For Possible Action' and he is very, very highly considered. And you have given him a smashing part, so he'd better take the chance! I only worry, vaguely, about Anouk. I have known her very very well ever since she was sixteen. Even hid her in a dustbin when the cops were after her because her 'papers' were out of date and the fellow she loved so desperatly was a bit late on his film. Heigh ho!

I worked with her on a disaster called 'Justine'. She pissed off and left us floundering for the final three weeks: we used a double and 'out takes' to get through and neither Cukor or I ever forgave her. Nor did Mr Durrel, as I recall! She is a bit capricious .. but delicious .. and tiresome.

I half forgave her a few years ago at Cannes. What point is there in being angry about a long-dead film?

But my 'Cuckoo' she aint! Never mind. Let us all hope that your stirling work and my modest basic stuff will, in some measure, survive ... I DO admire you, and I am most tremendously grateful.

All we can do is sit back and wait, I suppose?

'Jericho', the new effort, surfaces in March. I hope. They are SO slow in the UK .. they have had it corrected and all, plus cover design, since February!

Blimy ... proofs due on the 12th.

Super about Mark Shivas.[2] Not an easy guy, you must feel rather smug! I would! Great good luck, lovie ... for us both!

I'm off to buy a new typewriter. This bugger has lost it's 'O' and it's 'P' and you can imagine how tiresome that is ... so forgive errors .. and accept my loving, and grateful, thanks ...

Ever, with love,
    <u>Dirk</u>

To Penelope Mortimer   *Cadogan Gardens*
                                          12 September 1991

We seem to no longer address each other. So –

I must learn to type. Properly, I mean. Like pressing the button which gets I instead of i. Maddening.

---

1. Samuel West.
2. BBC Television's then Head of Drama had rung to congratulate LL on her script.

[. . .] I think I am tired today: I was talking, hardly lecturing really, 300 boys at Tonbridge. On the Holacaust. And Hate. Just simple Hate.[1]

Rather an amazing business. I did'nt think that I would be able to talk, frankly, about Bergen-Belsen . . . or Treblinka etc. I failed pretty badly in '86 when I tried on a film that R. Hartey did on me. Blubbed. Shameful. But, I suppose, because I have got old now and time has hazed memory, acute memory, I managed yesterday. For one solid hour.

Not a sound. Not the proverbial pin-drop. At the end they all stood up and applauded. The Head said, later, that no one, not even Leonard Cheshire, had moved so many people so deeply! I tell you this in all privacy . . I was exhausted, but tremendously stimulated somehow.

I offered no answers. I asked THEM why the hatred we all see today was so manifest, and warned them that they, not I, would see a repeat of the awfulness which I had seen at twenty four and that they must be aware of it, and try to stop it. For their own sakes and for their children. I dont know what good it did: I do know that some of them were blubbing, very quietly. So I think I got it over.

Their Vicar, Rector, whatever the hell he is, was there. Trying not to be, but I spotted him with that dog-collar. And hit hard at God . . the only thing I allowed the poor sods to keep was faith in themselves!

I told them, catagorically, that there was no such thing as God . . and that they would be on their own, the only thing that would save them was themselves and their own good sense.

I dont think he quite knew what to do: I was VERY reasonable. If you believe in the Immaculate Conception how can you believe in a God who did'nt turn up at Auchswitz or Belsen or Mauthausen?

Oh bugger it. I got a smashing letter this am from the Masters, and that set me up for the day. Until my 'proofs' of 'JERICHO' arrived. God! Viking aint Chatto in 1975 . . . so tatty, mean, squashed. The very last, key, line of my sodding book is printed on the top of the last page . . all alone! One line one page. Am I mad, or are they?

[. . .] On Monday, if all goes well, and I bet it wont, they start to

<hr>

1. Dirk had reviewed four titles under the heading 'How Could Such Hatred Exist?' (*Daily Telegraph*, 10 August). Such was the response that he wrote a follow-up article, 'No Answer to the Sorrow and the Pity' (5 September). History teachers at independent schools had taken note.

shoot on my book 'Voices In The Garden'. With Anouk Aimee playing Diana Cooper. Well: MY version of Diana Cooper. The only thing they have actually kept are some of the names and the title. Movies ARE mad.

Lee Langley, who adapted it as I told you I think, wrote a sweet note prodding my reluctant heart to take pen and write and thank her for her work. It is not her fault that nothing is the same. That the idiot Producers dont think that the Upper Classes 'speak like that today'.

I drift in a haze of despair. Thats why one thinks how splendid it would be if you <u>did</u> do Hons and Rebels[1] because I know that you know how they were/are. But who, my darling, can SPEAK like that now?

I watch that filthy Telly to get into the 'feel' of things. And the only feel I get is one of utter frustration and futility; and hatred against the lower-orders who demand mediocraty (SP?) and GET IT!

The Titmus thing[2] has to be seen to be believed. Astonishing. It would be (apart from one young woman who is far too good for them) JUST acceptable on the Civic Center Stage in Stockport, done by the local Drama Group. And as for the 'The House Of Elliot' words totally fail me. I am breathless with horror, shock, surprise, and, finally, disbelief. I hear myself saying, aloud, 'I dont believe this. I really dont quite believe this, do you?' And there is only me to reply. And I say: 'No. No I dont. I <u>dont</u> believe it.' and a good time is had by all. God!

So do write. You say projects and no pennies. Well get on with a damn project for Heavens sake . . . you handle dialogue so beautifully, you are so economic, there are no cliche's, you are wise, funny, and often sharply bitter. But ALL OF IT is so good! So 'sayable' . . . actors do actually <u>dream</u> of getting that sort of script. Some actors anyway.

Miss H. [Katharine Hepburn] could, as I have written elsewhere, read a script like a musical score. No fool she. She knew. If you go through her writers they were all marvellous WRITERS! She damned well knew . . so did Spencer [Tracy].

Holding a piece of Pinter in your hand gives one the same comfort and security as a thick glove in artic winter. You know you'll get there,

---

1. Jessica Mitford's autobiography (Gollancz, 1960).
2. An adaptation for Thames Television by John Mortimer of his own novel, *Titmuss Regained*.

somewhere, in an electryfying turmoil of doubt and despair, but total sureness of the written word. Never alter a semi colon. Never need to.

Just get the moves right. And, of course, the Mind.

Thats all.

You can write that way. I dont mean Pinter, for God's sake .. and maybe now [. . .] he's gone to bits. I hear so. But he did write like an angel.

I must stop enjoying myself here. I have another fifty three letters to deal with appropos the Holacaust piece and the follow up I had to do. That makes it over 300 now. Terribly sweet, kind, helpful letters .. all offering to help me in my quest for an answer to 'Why?' the hatred. And, of course, they cant answer any better than I can.

Some, of my age, now confess that they too were in Belsen, one has written '.. we were among the first through the gates of Belsen and the sight that met our eyes was terrible. When the war finished I put it mentally behind me. But in the last few years my mind has repeatedly gone back to Belsen, memories which come back sharper than things which have happened recently. Another thing now is I wake up at three am in the morning and try as I might those memories return to the same place. Old age I suppose. But like you I still ask "Why?". Forgive me for taking up your busy time . . .'

So. I have to reply.

What a dreadful letter, Well: you should'nt have sent me an eight foot plant that wont 'tolerate a cold climate'.[1] Idiot girl . . .

Head full of self. Sorry. Find a theme? Try .. oh! do ..

   D.

To Penelope Mortimer   Cadogan Gardens
                                            19.9.91

So – you fucking asked! You get!

It's going to be yonks and yonks before we see this kind of a date again. They tell me. I dont much care, moi meme, but it seems to have a certain significance for the young. As I no longer can claim to be in that league I give not a fig. Figgy-fig-fig.

Finished my proofs. Always, after the very first book, a fearful let-down. This is a wretched little effort. Decently written but dull.

---

1. PM had given Dirk a melianthus for his balcony.

The cover is 'pretty' and I did it myself. Quite like the feeling that Graham S[utherland]. is somewhere floating about and probably still saying .. 'Oh dear! Dont put EVERYTHING into the cover. Let the reader imagine a few bits here and there.'

I ignored him then: at 17. and still appear to at 70. What chance has a teecher-got? I do know how to spell that: it amused me to write it so.

Alarm at stinky old autumn indeed. How one detests it. I am swaddled in nylon ropes, cradles, and noisy workmen all flashing Builders Bums at every window. They pray, as I do, that they'll be finished in a week or less .. so that they can flee to East Germany (if you please) where they work and make a fortune working for Dutch and German millionairs. Dont ask me doing what. I did'nt ask. But a 'grand a week aint bad' .. it aint indeed.

So I have not concentrated very deeply .. even on the proofs .. but did enjoy your letter and the flurry of questions and queries.

[...] I dont think all TV is as dead-end as you [do]. For the Dirty Unwashed yes: but 'T.M.D'[1] was written for Channel 4 ... and got shoved out as a film in the States by a sort of fluke. Someone saw it and had a bash with it and it raced away. So then they dared it here. See?

I am mad about Juliet S[tevenson]. she is dotty and totally marvellous and was daft enough to come to a couple of my Workshops at the Vic. I must say the humility, with the other lesser mortals, was refreshing.

[...] You ask where you can find me in 'your experience'. Blimy! I dont know. I dont know what your experience is. All I do know is that you have been a bit off-kilter about me from the first, amazing, meeting at home. With two kinds of present, because you were uncertain about which to give me, and both turned out to be wrong. You are a noodle-doddle.

From the point of being a character I can be The Servant as easily as I can be Stephen (Accident) or Von Aschenbach. Also I am wildly loved as Simon Sparrow. A fairly wide range, I'd have thought? And what about 'Max' in 'The Night Porter' and 'Gabriel' in 'Modesty Blaize' or 'Blase'? However you spell it it was a fuck-up. But I had fun

---

1. *Truly, Madly, Deeply,* written and directed by Anthony Minghella, starring Juliet Stevenson and Alan Rickman.

and took the Movie. So really, darling girl, I cant tell you more about me than that. If, for example, I DO get to do 'No Mans Land' for the BBC, and if Harold does decide to direct it, even if he does NOT, I will play 'Spooner'. Sandles, woolen socks and Mill Hill Accent. Why not?

Now that I have reached Old Mens Estate I <u>do</u> decline certain roles as unsuitable. I can, alas! no longer yearn for the love of a lady .. well, not decently. And, anyway, I've done that in 'May We Borrow Your Husband?' (My adaptation. I dont think Greene meant it MY way!)

And I am not desperate to play really old fellows. I mean white hair and stick brigade. OR landed-gentry-wistfully-sinking. A cheap cocky braggert? An elderly wide-boy, a Kray? A loving, tender, Dales-Doctor. Christ! It's an endless list. I dont always have to wear a tie and look like a cocker spaniel!

In order of your anxiety-questions.

I am as content as a clam. If they are content. Anyway, content. I have come to terms with catastrophe at least, and tucked it all away very neatly into the compost of my life. I have absolutely no fear whatsoever. About anything. Except, I suppose, cancer or one of those things. Senile dementia ... but I'll come to terms with those, I reckon.

If you can come to terms with Senile Dementia?

As I am Vice President of the Voulantry Euthanisa Society, and now lecture on it to irate, pleased, agreeing, disagreeing, cross, calm, women in the National Council of Women of G.B (or something like that) and lecture to 15–18 year olds at Tonbridge and Kings College and, I think next week [...] Rochester (Kings School) on, of all things, the Holocaust, as I am also a founder member of BACUP,[1] the organization which helps people with cancer, and their families, to come to 'terms' with it ... as I read for the blind, for the R.[N.]I.B .. and give Workshops at the Vic and Guildhall, write for the Telegraph each Saturday .. there abouts .. and do Platforms at the National every now and again, I really dont feel that I can complain about a lack of things to do! Honestly! I am making use of my life in the only way I can, that is by helping people one way or another without being soppy and pious. I am about the most irreverant fellow you could meet.

But I <u>do</u> love people, and they seem to quite like me. It's comforting.

---

1 . Now Cancerbackup.

I prefer myself at all times to being bored by one kind person or one ego-busting-actor (ress), I have a large family of Young, to whome I am always available IF NEEDED. Otherwise I stay away. Firmly.

[...] I have a lot of friends, I stay away from most of the time, because I do honestly prefer solitude, and I am never lonely.

Alone. Yes. There <u>are</u> sagging week-ends ... no telephone; but if it rings I quake for fear of boredome, or an accident somewhere.

I actually like me better than I like some others. There are, as you must be aware, a few glorious exceptions to this rule. You are one of them, Robert Fox and Natasha others, my adopted grandson[1] of 18, two young you wont know. She was my PA during my years at Chatto, he is a Bowlby of the Norfolk branch, in fine arts with capital letters, I am God father to their first born,[2] on whome I slight[ly] dote in a potty way ... and I am devoted to my Swiss chap[3] [...] And his beautiful wife Elizabeth ... so there you are. A sort of background? Surely?

It did not just 'happen' to me. Arriving back here with a dying man, pretending that he was'nt, buying a house here, realising my roots had been torn up at 66 ... finding that leaving Provence, France, was not a severance but an amputation .. all that, plus death and fifty years of friendship bumping down a too-small staircase in a body-bag and a swiping stroke on top, did not make anything easy.

The Press sniped. The tabloids shrilled. I crept about my daily tasks, eating, shopping, buying my beer, managing my money, cashing a cheque, in a haze of fear and a terror of shyness.

At first I only went out in the very early mornings, was pretty pissed by noon, slept that awful sleep all afternoon, watched TV and, sometimes, bought the Standard from Europa Foods across the street. Not far to go; no one to recognise one.

And then, as the healing almost started, someone on the Telegraph asked me to review a book. I had never done such a thing before.[4] I could just about make a cup of tea .... but I tried. And I won. And I now have a contract with them and almost no time to do all the things I have to do! And I simply LOVE going out now; in the streets I mean, I love people liking me, asking me about .. oh, Euthanasia ..

---

1. Thomas Forwood.
2. Romilly Bowlby.
3. Anton Troxler.
4. He had, but seldom.

the Holocaust .. or my books. Thanking me for things I had not
realised I had done. Gifts I did not realise I had offered. Amazing! I
am so wonderfully happy that I know I'll get clobbered, deserve to,
but enjoy it while I can.

You must understand that this was gradual. You either give in or
bash back .. adjust or go under. For the savagery of terminal cancer
AND Parkinsons, for the despair of a foul death and it's suffering, I
feel I have to bash on to honour the sacrifice.

However daft that may seem, that is what I am trying to do.

Probably come un-stuck. Especially with the Euthanasia thing ..
but I'll fight on until I can fight no longer. And if kids of 15, 16, 17,
18, WANT me to tell them about Belsen, about the Holocaust, about
the building of Mauthausen, about hate. Then I will do it willingly.
And do.

A letter this morning, one among some 350 I have had, says, in
part, 'I was asked to give a short talk to our local PROBIS (?)[1] about
the place (Belsen). Like you I could not finish, broke down in tears,
and had to sit down, as I thought, ashamed. I was told that my
behaviour brought to those listening the whole horror of what I had
witnessed. I was so very grateful when I read your article to know that
others suffered as I did.'

He signs his name and, in brackets, (Formerly A.D.H. 2nd Army.
Lt. Col. RAMC.)

And there are lots more like that: so I do feel I am not just a wimpy
actor signing letters to demand Democracy In Russia a good ten days
AFTER the fucking coup!

Know what I mean?

If all this sounds utterly nauseating, and I bet it does, it is just to
TRY to give you some idea of what I am.

So there you are. I think I have answered all the questions you pose?

No reserve, no suspicion, no need to stay intact or hide. I am me.
Wide out in the open. The only thing about which I DO have a
feeling of guilt, and it is not that strong, is that a short time after I got
back on my feet, moved into this flat, took a deep breath and knocked
off the booze, I was pounced upon by my old contemporaries. Some
rich, some famous, all hideiously boring, narrow, dull, and marking
time into a pit.

---

1. Probus – the clubs for retired businessmen and professionals.

I have dropped them <u>all</u>, Deliberatly, and without giving them any real reason. Any reason at all. Dont want 'em. Useless. They drain me .. I have far more to give others and younger ones. And if the tide runs out for me and I am left bereft in a chair, then that'll be fine. I am very fond of me, as I have told you, and I get on well with me. I make me laugh .. make me shudder at the waste of good food when I cook a meal for six because I cant work out how to modify the recipe for two .. I know I'm a twat. But who cares? People quite like that .. and I just like being kissed by the girls in the shops. Why not? I like people to smile at me, even though they dont address me, I like smiling back, and I love taxi drivers who yell out at me in the street, 'Okay, Dirk? Look great for your age mate ..'

Yeah. I like that.

Will that do? Impassioned answers impassioned. Okay? If you never write again I'd <u>really</u> understand! And still love you!

<u>D</u> XXX

PM replied, saying she was not entirely convinced by Dirk's 'Pollyanna' image. She was exploring the possibility of writing a screenplay for him, based on his reaction to Tony's death, as described in the previous letter.

To Penelope Mortimer

Cadogan Gardens
24 September 1991

Bloody hell, you are difficult. I TOLD you that you would find my letter nausiating, people like you, those who see everything in dusk-tones, would. I AM a sort of Pollyanna .. and after years of just keeping away from people on account of millions came to me to watch my cavorting, living a secluded life in my small-holding, contented and really not much in the public eye, I suddenly got shoved into FULL LIFE with no protection and in a Foreign Land.

After a time of, shall we say reflection?, I decided that having had one stroke and not much liking the effects, I could very well have another, had to live in filthy UK .. had to live in London .. cant drive, killed a clutch of people with a car, so never again[1] .. where better to be than where I started off at 16 as a Student at Chelsea Poly?

---

1. See 4 August 1985, note 1.

Parents had been students there too. And the Slade. I felt 'right' in the area. Coming to terms was difficult. To terms with walking quite unprotected in streets jammed with curious people.

'I think it is. Look!'

'You ask him. Go on. He cant bite you?'

'<u>Were</u> you Dirk Bogarde?'

'Left France, have you?'

'I remember your face but not the name? Humphry someone ..'

I ducked into my anorak and tried to walk, as I told you, only at dusk or just when shops had opened. Fewer people. No standing with curious, autograph hunting, housewives in lines at the Check Outs.

Sainsbury's, Tesco, Waitrose were soon abandoned. People followed one.

'He's buying tinned tomatos.'

'Thinner than I imagined.'

'Smaller.'

'And balding ... see?'

'Pity. But after fifty, you know ..'

'Could you sign this? Not for me, for my neice, grandmother, wife, son, sister, baby-sitter, cousin Agnes, Eileen, with two e's please, Anne with an "e" .....'

No one, ever, in France behaved like this. Not even in Paris .. unless they were British. I felt, all the time, as if my cock was hanging out of my pants: I hunched my shoulders, wore a Purdy cap, scuttled (as far as I could scuttle with a wonky leg) and my doctor thought that it might be 'obesessional'. Might it? I'd never had an obsession before, save for lizards, frogs, birds, and those kinds of things.

So I decided to either go mad or face up to it.

I faced up to it. Took off the cap .. walk INTO the Check out .. smile at everyone because they SMILE at me! Memory jogs them .. of some time in which I must have figured in their private lives somewhere .. at any age from 10 to seventy. I have, after all, four generations of 'Fans'.

My films are always on TV on Sunday. I am counted as a friend.

Okay. I'll settle for that. It is far better than hiding in this flat wondering what to do, how to die gracefully.

What else?

Now, something you will find difficult, I embrace being 'public' .. I just ADORE kissing Angie, Maureen, Isobel at Lees in Cale Street

.. and Miss Gloucester (because she lives there) and Anne in GTC
... if they laugh, because I am there, I am chuffed rotten. And they
do!

Motto. If you are scared of the sea dont go near it. I am presently
swimming, crawl perhaps? to Long Island, anywhere .. I like
swimming.

RAGE. Yes. You make the general error of thinking that RAGE
has to be manifest, that one shouts and screams, bury's one's head
sobbing with what you call 'fury'. Balls. RAGE is sometimes inside.
Heard of a Rage To Live?

You react to one puny sentence in my letter about fifty years and
body-bags on a too small stair-case. Natural enough, it was the only
bit of reasonable sentence-construction in the whole thing. And gave
you your knee-jerk.

But RAGE did'nt remotely come NEAR the thing.

Acceptance, humility, fear of 'what now', relief that three years of
almost un-endurable suspense, of desperate distress physically, of loss
but relief that it was over. Knowing is so much better, I promise you,
than wondering: and hope is pretty hollow when it leaves. But never,
at any time, RAGE. I now use your words.

No sense of <u>injustice</u>. Why? Belsen was injust NOT the staircase ..

Helplessness, yes. To a point. But one is forced by distress and need
to rally. No <u>fury</u>. At all. Why? It happens; we are born to die. From
the first heaving yell.

When Anna, the Night Nurse, and I tried to turn the patient he
said, and I could only hear by putting my head against his chest and
'took' the vibrations, 'If you did this to a dog they'd arrest you'.

Right. He was being 'jokey'. But he was right. Which is why I am
now the Vice President of V.E.S ... and sticking my neck out against
Catholics and British Manners and Members of the BMA. IN public.

But no Rage. I had the most wonderous fifty years of my life. So
did my partner. WE both knew that we'd have to pay. And did. Okay?

But never RAGE, <u>fury</u>, <u>bafflement</u>.

I am not appalled. If 'a faint whirring grabbed' you, great. Go
ahead!

I do suggest that you perhaps try to read the books that some of
your mates, and I do count myself as one, write. You rather grandly
say: 'I read very little, particularly of people I know.'

Well sod that old girl. You DONT know me! Thats the rub .. for you, not me. I have come to terms with my life, I only have an active ten years reasonably left. Christ! Why waste them? Eh?

[...] I have just written to Radio Drama. TV [sic] and refused, politely, their kind offer to write a play, or a series, for them. I have quoted the things I watched for homework. 'Tittmuss', 'House of Elliot', 'Trainer'[1] and some dire thing, they adored, which starred my (once) deeply respected Tom Courtney.[2] Impossible to believe any of them. Lowest-Common-Watcher. I'd rather stay with my Telegraph Readers. At least they write back intelligently. I'm off to do a bit of Auschwitch again: then there is RAGE. Then, my love. I am not sure that I can do it for Radio 4 .. they ask .. but talking to kiddies makes it easier/tougher. When they blub you know your rage was not misplaced. Will that do? Hope that you are not vexed that I shoved R. Fox the Handle?[3] [...] It's only a nudge of course. But he's bright, clever, and very sharp. Also his track record is amazing, and his wife[4] is to die [for] she is so adorable, tough, beautiful and can act! Wow!

Love

<u>D</u>.

To Penelope Mortimer   _Cadogan Gardens_
                                                  26 October 1991

Never lost a child at the Science Place.[5]

But frequently longed to do so. Hateful memories of pressing buttons to illuminate things or make steam-pistons work.

And then the questions after.

'This Week'[6] was a total waste of time, I thought. And I was pissed off that so much time and money was spent and everything shoved into a half hour of negativity.

A pile of letters, naturally, today. Enclosing booklets in bad print

---

1. A BBC series with a racing background.
2. _Redemption_ (BBC).
3. An adaptation by PM of Irene Handl's 1965 novel, _The Sioux_ (Longman).
4. Natasha Richardson.
5. PM had taken a ten-year-old to the Science Museum and lost him momentarily in the throng around Japanese Robots.
6. Dirk had taken part in a _This Week_ programme (ITV) on euthanasia.

called 'AWAKE!' or 'THE SHINING ROAD'. (To god, of course. Silly.) and all of them missing the point entirely.

Is the UK simply stuffed with ladies who 'walk with the Lord' and think I'll be better off if I did?

Seems so to me.

I wonder what they'll do with someone in their arms trying to tear their eyes out? In howling pain?

A woman in Cale Street asked me if I minded her jumping the queue at the greengrocers on account of she only had twenty minutes to do her shopping because her husband's 'dose of Morphine' would wear off and 'he'll try to chew the electric light cable again: 'I'v moved the lamp away from his bedside .. but you never know ..'

And, another lady, in Lennox Gardens, had promised to shoot her husband in the back somewhere on the south Downs, which they both knew from childhood and loved, when his pain became quite intolerable. It was 'hopeless now because the pain is so great that I cant get him out of bed, let alone drive him down to Firle ..'

Things like that, apart from personal rememberances, give one a degree of what you call 'conviction'.

The word that you have to remember is the one you use to me. 'Vololuntary'.

There is nothing hysterical about it: and no one can POSSIBLY kill Granny in her flat so that the 'children can have a place to live'.

But one was not given time to explain that the other night.

Never mind.

I am reading away like anything.[1] It takes a hell of a long time to do. Half a book has, so far, taken five hours. But I am quite enjoying 'me'.

More on Monday and half Tuesday. After that I really must get on with my next. God! I am such a dreadful work-avoider you cant imagine.

M. Major[2] flourishes wildely. A real plant now .. glory be to goodness.

White fly still on my fox-gloves; I long for the cold, hate this daft warm-muggy-flu-dark-at-four existance.

With a real winter you can believe in a Spring.

---

1. He was recording *Backcloth* for the RNIB.
2. The melianthus PM had given him, not the then Prime Minister.

Get yourself to W.H. Smith soonest. They are selling excellent little electric typewriters like this. For only 69.99.

And they really DO work.

Love <u>D</u>.

To John Osborne   *Cadogan Gardens*
                                             8 November 1991

My dear John –

What a good fellow you are! Just as I was about to start the washing-up your splendid book[1] arrived.

I was pretty chuffed, as you must know.

I enclose the review I did last week.[2] I got you early from the good John Sandoe (or no 'e'?)[3] and, as you will see was ravished anew by your writing. Goodness me, how I admire you and your work.

I have read all the reviews, or anyway the reviews so far published, with wry amusement. They are terrific really: just carping, as usual.

I simply dont understand this country and it's journals and it's journalists. I know how much you love it, and rightly (for you) but I miss my 'home' most dreadfully. I suppose that after 21 years of bucolic life in an athmosphere of serenity and earth, water, stone and air . . . that I would.

Cadogan Gardens is okay. Excellent in some ways, but it aint like my farm . .

Never mind. Now and again a huge wind blows me into sense and awareness and you have done it this time!

Still: we all have to start off again somehow, and it's just got to be faced. Washing up with a ten thousand metre mountain just beyond the window above the sink is a little different to washing up with a fat Fillipino lady scraping out her saucepans just across the well above my present sink. But one copes!

Next time you are at Oscars Dive call me? [. . .] and come up and have something to drink or eat. Whatever . . .

I'm just up the road, as you know . . I go to do all my TV crap in

---

1. *Almost a Gentleman: An Autobiography – Volume II 1955–1966* (Faber & Faber).
2. Choosing *Almost a Gentleman* as his Book of the Year *(Daily Telegraph*, 23 November), Dirk described it as a 'towering, magisterial, epic hurricane of a book' and 'A complete triumph'.
3. Right first time.

the Langtry Room¹ frequently. The flat is too small, and anyway private.

Again thank you, and I'll not bleat on about 'ALMOST'. You must know what total delight, admiration and joy it has given me, and will give me again . . .

Ever, from a long time ago . .

Yours,

Dirk

To Susan Owens   *Cadogan Gardens*
                                              9 November 1991
                                              Saturday –

Dear S.O.

It's four fifteen and just getting dark. I really cant get used to this daft UK business of 'turning back the clock'. Sod it!

[. . .] I have just walked down the Kings Road (wanted to get a new CD of Gershwin. Its £22, and they had'nt got it. Just as well for me.) and the amount of humanity streaming along that road is amazing. Where do they all come from? Where do they go to? What have they to spend? Do they realize how tacky they look in their tights and Doc Martins? Or lacey stockings with Trainers AND shorts, plus HAT!

I have never seen so many utterly plain people in all my life. And all drifting along like zombies. The stink of cheap fat frying, bottled coffee, Big Mac's bulging everywhere. Oh dear!

[. . .] Yesterday I did a TV interview about Ralph Thomas, who directed all the 'Doctor' films as well as some of the others, like 'Two Cities' .. boring, but I could'nt get out of it. And on Thursday I was on, of all things, 'Woman's Hour' talking about my Cancer Charity . . . so it's all hustle and bustle which quite suites me as long as I can keep my own pace.

[. . .] They started shooting on 'Voices In The Garden' in the S. of France at the beginning of October. I reckon it'll be finished by now. But it was quite a pleasant surprise coming, as it did, just before Christmas and just before I have to pay a hell of a packet for the re-painting and re-pointing of this bloody great house. We, the Tenants,

---

1. At the Cadogan Hotel ('Oscar's').

have all been screwd silly. It happens once every six years .. so I reckon next time around someone else will have to pay MY whack!

But for weeks now, since July, end of, I have had Builders Bums stuck on cradles at every window .. and I've been making mugs of tea and coffee like some old drab in the W.I ... but it keeps the chaps in kind fashion and they merit it I reckon .. swinging about like apes five floors up.

This Week was cut to ribbons, but it has caused a terrific response .. and we have had 10.000 letters of enquirey since the beginning of the year. Amazing. There are a lot of people who want help .. and who feel comfortable with the Advance Directive. It is legal, but it all depends on your Doc. You, ideally, should give a copy to your next of kin .. one to your Lawyers .. as well as your doctor. 3 in all. And get it witnessed by 2 witnesses. I suggest NOT members of your family .. because that can cause problems later sometimes .. just get 2 friends who have nothing to gain from your death to sign. I did that. Easier, and tidy.

[... V.E.S. will] send you the Living Will (Advance Directive) and all the info. you need. I think when you see it and read it you will see just how sensible it is. That poor family with the boy at Hillsborough[1] is enough to break your heart. And there are TWO families like that still.

It is now almost really dark ... I think I'll trail off and light the lights, settle down with a book, and have a read until Scotch-Time.

Look after yourself, dont despair .. and battle on. There is still a lot to do in life, as I am finding out!

Ever
DB.

To Philip Hoare   *Cadogan Gardens*
                                                      1 December 1991

Dear Philip Hoare –
Thank you for your letter of the 28th.[2]

---

1. Tony Bland, an eighteen-year-old supporter of Liverpool FC, had been in a persistent vegetative state since the disaster at Hillsborough football ground on 15 April 1989. In March 1993 he would become the first patient to have his life-support system withdrawn under legal sanction.
2. PH was researching his *Noël Coward: A Biography* (Sinclair-Stevenson, 1995).

I hasten to reply before the onslaught of Christmas Cards.

Noël Coward was very angry, in a totally un-violent way! when I left the Theater for the Cinema.

He had seen the First Night of a play I did at the New Lindsey Club Theater, was overwhelmed by us all, and got it moved into the West End.[1] He was passionate about the theater, and that had better be understood from the start. The Cinema in his eyes (in mine also at the time) was a 'piffling business. You dont have to act, it's all technicians'.

He was wrong, of course, but that is how most theater people felt, and to some extent still do feel, about film-playing.

His anger, mild though it was, was really a 'reproof' .. I had just come out of a six year, quite tough, war. I was, as he said, 'new blood' and the theater was screaming out for new blood.

'Every old tabby with a varicose vein has been playing the Juvenile since '39. We need new guts, a new breath, new wind.'

Well: he did'nt quite know what that was himself, frankly .. he could'nt write the sort of stuff the 'new blood' needed after six years of knocking off Germans and Italians!

He wrote a play 'Peace In Our Time' and included a decent part for all of us (7) who were in the Lindsey Play. I had by that time, that is to say when he was ready to let us see his script, signed a contract with a film company called Wessex. They were under the Rank Umbrella.

He was seriously angry that I turned down the role which he had very especially written for me. I never read it, but was told, by him, in the most intense detail what it was all about. I privately thought it was pretty frightful. But did not say so.

When I told him about Wessex he was, I think, more astounded really than angry that I could actually, after six years away, turn down his play. Written, the part, especially for me. I explained that after six weary years on a Captains Pay .. and in debt anyway to the Army (who had apparently over-paid me at some time) that the security of the Cinema was very comforting and inticing.

He eventually, reluctantly, saw my point. He was sad, but understanding. 'It was bound to happen.' was all he could finally say.

---

1. Not entirely accurate, but a fair indication of Coward's enthusiasm for *Power Without Glory* and its young company.

We had made it quite clear between us, at a very early supper at the Savoy Grill one night early in the run of the play, that I did not share his predilictions. He was immensely graceful and no more was ever said .. apart from one smiled, regretful word. 'Pity'.

He was very tough about THE VORTEX[1] .. we had to be word perfect after the first (agonizing) read-through. Remember only he and John G. had had a bash at Nicky before. I was not about to do a replica of them. This he sensed at the read-through. I think he was alarmed. Never said so, just went off to Jamacia and sent me a telegram on the first night which simply said 'Dont Worry Dear Boy It All Depends On You'.

My notices, I seem to remember, were mixed. Some excellent and some, from elder critics who remembered (or pretended to) his perf. disaster. The cast, made up of many of his friends, cant have made him totally comfortable in Jamacia. We had a great success anyway .. even though Isobel Jeans (playing Florence) glued her wig on every night after the first one during which I SHOOK it off her!

We got a standing ovation (rare in those days) but she refused to do it again, or have it done, because, as she said, 'I frequently have very adorable friends in front. They would be terribly distressed.'

We finished the run .. successfully .. but I never heard from Noël again until he suddenly arrived one day at my house in the country, quite unexpectedly, for tea. There were a crowd of chums and family down. He was enchanting and enchanted them ... we did not refer to the play.

Years later I did 'Blythe Spirit' for CBS TV in New York with a quite wonderful cast.[2] He was in Jamacia. And remained mute.

So I dont suppose that my Charles Condamine had pleased him.

But, after 1946 he had lost his way. A whole new world of players had arrived and what he had always apparently wanted, new blood, new guts, and a crowd of young players to take over from the 'old tabbies' he pretended to despise but for whome, alas, he still wrote copiously.

His time was over and it bewildered him greatly.

---

1. Dirk played Nicky Lancaster – the part in which Coward had made his name – at the Lyric Hammersmith in 1952.
2. A further reference to the 1966 NBC production with Ruth Gordon, Rosemary Harris and Rachel Roberts.

I last saw him in his last play.[1] Dined with him afterwards in his
rented house, or flat. He was ill, clearly, frightened of death; worried
about his performance. Had I liked it? Had the American part worked?
Was it moving? (It was hideiously moving. He had been helped to his
feet at one agonizing moment.) Did I feel that there was a film in any
one of the plays?

We parted comfortably, affectiontly, I think that he liked me and I
know that he was almost surprised that I liked him.

It was very, very difficult not to. I never pretend, and this I think
intrigued him, and more than that, comforted him.

But we never discussed my performances in HIS works. He was
passionate about some of my film stuff. But we left the theater where
it belonged for me.

On the back boiler.

Yes he was a hard taskmaster, but he was also a genius . .

I was one of the most fortunate of mortals in that I was allowed to
work for him, be accepted by him, be amazed by him . . and on one
simply amazing evening at my house, have him play to Judy Garland,
and sing with her, his entire repertoir (SP?) for two unforgettable
hours. Alas! no tape recorder. A blinding, glorious, Heart Stopping!
performance from them.

Thats all I know.

Goodness! How lucky I was. How rich I am!

Sincerely[2]

  Dirk Bogarde

Sorry about typing & spelling and all the 'amazings'. DB.

To Dilys Powell   *Cadogan Gardens*
                                                   1 December 1991

Dilys dearest –

Feel deprived no longer! I aim to come to your table immediatly I
am summonsed . . . so that, rather unfairly, leaves the ball in your
court.

Apart from having to wait in all bloody day for the man who will

1. *Suite in Three Keys: A Trilogy* (1966).
2. A knowledgeable insider says: 'There is more romance in this letter than in *Peter Pan*.'

'help you with your washing-machine' (and who NEVER comes) my days are dullish.

I have just had my contract with the Daily Telegraph renewed for the third year, and at a bit, not much but a bit, more money. Which makes me feel, quite erroniously, more like a writer than I did.

Bertrand Tavernier wrote last week to say he 'longs to work together again' and have I thought about his idea for a film based on What Happened To Ealing Studios? I have thought. But dont really know what did happen, apart from the fact that [Michael] Balcon hated all his successes because they were 'vulgar and un-British' and pined to make lots of 'Passports To Pimlico's'. But I cant see this making a film.

Can you? Even his daughter wont discuss what Really Happened.

So I feel that we wont get much out of that subject.

Joanne Woodward wrote yesterday and said wistfully, 'Will we ever get to work together?' and I had to write back and say that even if they re-made 'On Golden Pond' she and I, being un-bankable, would never get the parts. And anyway; I cant swim. Nevertheless I wrote the news to Tavernier. You never know what can happen by planting a little acorn. Or, at least, seed.

I have watched the two hourly programmes which I have filmed for Channel 4. To my dismay I was not appalled.

It is not a discussion, just me talking to camera (five hours in fact, two for the 'cut') about my work and film acting in general.

It's quite funny. And quite instructive I think.

It goes out in January, over two weeks, on a Saturday night.

We'll see.

I pulled out of the 'Saki' show finally . . . it really was not quite up to snuff. And I seemed to be carrying the show so that if I did'nt make the performance, because of a cold, flu or the dreaded bronchitis the theater would empty. Too much responsibility . . . I think Alan Bates took over. He'd be alright. A pleasing voice.

I have just sent in my Christmas Offer[1] to the Telegraph, plus a

---

1. 'Puddings and presents but no Santa Claus' (*The Daily Telegraph*, 21 December), an extract from his work-in-progress, *Great Meadow*. The drawing, a remembrance of Lullington, was one of Dirk's extremely rare commissions. His renewed interest in what was originally titled 'Lally' – a further 'evocation' of the childhood recalled in the first part of *Postillion* – had been prompted in late 1990 by a request from the *Telegraph Magazine* for a Christmas short story of 7–8,000 words, for which they would pay £15,000. 'I mean,'

large illustration! I must be mad. Or they are ... and now I just have one trio of books (on Evacuees!)[1] to deal with and then I can get down to my new book. A fictional-autobiographical extension to 'Postillion' which most people seem to like the best. And it's fairly easy to do now that I have licked the trick of going back to being eleven or ten. Anyway: the person I was in 1929–30. History!

I do hope you are completely flu less .. and love you dearly .. D

To Penelope Mortimer   *Cadogan Gardens*
                                                          31 December 1991

Penelope –

The last day of a fairly perplexing, but not awful, year for me. I write to you now because I got your letter this am and also a Knight-hood.[2] Both were pleasing. The Knighthood expected (sort-of.) I angered the Queen M. by my portrayal of bloody Browning in the Attenborough Epic and the cries of outrage could be heard from Clarence House and Glamis.[3] Really it was a kind of 'off with his head', and the Queen cut me dead at a Royal Line up[4] .. so, one way and another I felt they might, as they have done in the past, have drawn a line through the family name. Which would have incensed my Pa who never thought anything good could come of 'being a theatrical'. Anyway, I'm writing because you asked me to, and also to say how good it was to have your humble-grovel-fatuous .. (third attempt) note.

[...] Dont, for God's sake, be totally crushed by events.[5] It seems sometimes to me as if you are. And I dont KNOW what the events were. Merely hazard sliding guesses and feel wretched. Sticking your hands into the earth does heal: but not all of the body, and not ALL of the soul.

---

he told Pat Kavanagh, 'who would not be interested in £15.000?' The abandoned piece from his bottom-drawer was not quite what the newspaper had in mind, but its re-emergence encouraged him towards working it up to book length.

1. Reduced to a pair: *They Tied a Label on My Coat* by Hilda Hollingsworth (Virago) and A *Time for Love* by Shirley Anne Field (Bantam Press).

2. Dirk had been created Knight Bachelor in the New Year Honours.

3. Browning had been a member of the Royal Household.

4. There is no corroboration of this.

5. PM was working on a second volume of autobiography.

Do get above the murk. You'll perish otherwise .. and the clear spring which supplied your fountain with so much glory will become polluted by bitterness and/or hoplessness. And that is monstrous of you. Self destruct?

Write what you remember, pain and all; when I was starting, timidly, to attempt my first (I've done five) vol. of autobio., I remember whining to K. Tynan, who was being patient and driving at the same time, that I did'nt know how to eliminate libel. He just said 'Write it all down. Someone else will deal with the libel.' I did. And they did. And there you are.

Do likewise, as they say. When I say 'tact' I mean, I suppose, discretion .. a gentle form. [...] Dont bother about sticking knives in wounds. Have a jolly good pick away at the scabs. Under a scab, have you noticed? the flesh is often pink, shining, and clean. Altogether lovely and secure, hidden under the ugly crust which kept on 'catching' in your 'woollies'. Understand?

Your Christmas sounds rather woeful. [Mine] was wonderously selfish. Alone entirely .. boudin blanc (Harrods) with mashed and sprouts just as I always had them for Christmas lunch in the halcyon days. The big dinner came later at nine-ish.

This trip it was a comforting tin of Baxters and a certain amount of Scotch. Could'nt have been happier. Apart from those fucking choirs, Holy Night, White Christmas and Jungle Bells. God!

I suddenly discover that I have used up my last piece of typing paper, so I'll clear off and mail this, hope springs eternal with me .. and buy a quire or whatever it is I need. I'm in the middle of a book and it's got to be In House by March.

Happy, constructive, brave, New Year . . . be sensible about yourself, you deserve you. Enjoy it a bit. Could'nt you?

Ever

<u>Dirk</u>
   XXXX

The interview for Channel 4, Dirk Bogarde – By Myself, *was transmitted in two hour-long episodes on 11 and 18 January.*

To Gareth Van den Bogaerde   *Cadogan Gardens*
                                                 23 January 1992

My dear Gareth –

I am typing this for only one reason: that you should be able to read it and not try to decipher my hideious handwriting, made far worse than usual after replying to a great pile of mail.

Your letter has given me such infinate pleasure, it would be difficult for you perhaps to understand.

I am always aware, and terrified, that when I appear on TV or even the Radio, I shall offend someone. I see The Family wincing in distress and saying helplessly, 'Why did he have to say that?' . . . so it was with great trepidation that I accepted, as a final performance, the TV thing I have so recently done. Well: it was shot in August, but shown last week.

I insisted that it would be done entirely by myself . . . hence the title .. that there would be no questions, only guide-words like 'Losey' or 'Dearden' or 'Lead into Forwood', that sort of thing. So in fact I would be doing a sort of A.J.P. Taylor lecture. Did you ever see him? Historian, splendid, never used a script or referred to a note. It IS possible .. and because you are in complete control you know there wont be a left-fielder suddenly, like Parkinson, Wogan, (I refuse to even read his letters!) or poor old Russel Harty and the rest. I insisted on vetting all the footage (five hours of film) and made only two modest cuts. They agreed, and I think they realise that you can do an interview without an Interviewer nodding his head in a close-up! Anyway; it was done, and thank you for your generosity.

As far as I am concerned thats it. No more to be said now. Not quite sure what happens to the remaining three hours. Interesting point.

And thank you for your sweetness about the Knighthood. All nonsense I suppose, but people in the street seem to like it. I tried, very hard, to get out of it, [w]as councilled to 'think it over for three days and give a favourable answer on Monday by 10 am.' I had a pretty bloody week-end. No one to talk to. One is forbidden to even speak of it .. to wife, husband, parent .. anyone. And then I finally thought, the hell with it. There is only one other Knight

of the Cinema and thats Chaplin.[1] So I said yes. And was ill with
terror for two long months .. more. However the worst is still to
come: I shall enjoy it only because it is giving Lu such inordinate
joy! And Lally keeps half a bottle of sherry by the TV to celebrate!
God knows what. Never mind. Daddy would have been amused.
He made me promise, faithfully, that I would never accept a political
award, or purchase one, or one for a charitable business. I promised.
And I dont think that I have broken the promise because this was
offered for my service to the Cinema and also, which is rather nice,
for being a good ambassador for my country while abroad! Odd
that. But I did my best I admit. Especially after Heysell[2] and one
or two other bits like the Falklands . . . .

[. . .] I am so grateful for your good wishes: I am glad that you are
happy about it. I'm getting used to it now. It is good that I never
changed my name to Niven! Can you imagine NOT being a Bogaerde?

Always my love, & my admiration – your devoted brother –
Dirk

To Patricia Kavanagh   *Cadogan Gardens*
                                                   24 January 1992

Patricia dear –

Here is the first part (I anticipate only two) of 'GREAT
MEADOW'. Much of which you have read before[3] .. but it has been
tidied up and I made a few changes here and there.

I did, I think, tell you once that it was a bit like eating four melted
Mars Bars all at once. And you, with inordinant wit and perspecacity,
(? SP for both) said that 'some people like that Dirk'. So now you can
have a belter yourself.

There can be illustrations .. I can do some .. my Pa has done a
very pretty (thats the word. He was a rather 'pretty' painter in the '30s)

---

1. Dirk evidently meant Knight of the Screen – and on it, rather than (a) behind it like
Lean, Hitchcock, Balcon and Korda; and (b) both on and behind, like Chaplin and
Attenborough – although the last was honoured for much more than merely his work in
the Cinema. Even so Dirk overlooked Stanley Baker, who likewise worked mainly in films.
2. The disaster on 29 May 1985 at the Heysel stadium in Brussels, when hooliganism by
supporters of Liverpool Football Club resulted in thirty-nine deaths, mainly fans of the
Italian club Juventus.
3. Under its original working title of 'Lally' or 'Lallie'.

view in oils of Great Meadow .. and it would make a splendid cover if anyone wanted it.

But perhaps no one will. I still have the feeling, inspite of your good lady who reads for Kiddies that it was too sophisticated, that it would be a good kids book. Roald made a killing by talking about bodily functions and so on. Maybe not. But for the vast majority of my readers who read to each other in bed with the cocoa or by the fireside with a modest glass of Dry Fly Sherry this sort of thing is, <u>alas</u>, what they really like. I know from the response to the first book and from anything that I write for the Telegraph which has the least link with 'then'. The mail after 'A Night To Remember'[1] STILL arrives. I think we all survived after Arnhem! Amazing ...

Anyway .. this is it. I start Part 2 tomorrow (Saturday). Unless you cry 'Halt!' Then [sic] I shall carry on.

Love – <u>Dirk</u>

To Harold Pinter   *Cadogan Gardens*
                                                           30 January 1992

Harold –

Very much to my astonishment we finished the recording[2] yesterday at, exactly, 13.32 .. give or take a second.

I cant imagine what it sounds like: how we played it.

You will be the judge.

This, really, simply to thank you for such a wonderous part .. I did not, as I told you, see J.G .. and did not have his 'voice in my ear' so perhaps it is not what you would have wished.

All I know is that I was ravished by such words.

Each was like savouring one pure spoon of caviar.

By that I mean no onion, egg, tabasco, tra la la .. simple, joyous words.

It was the first time for me to play such a part. Once I came near perfection (word-wise) with D. Mercer and Resnais .. but with this it

1. A reminiscence of concerts during the winter of 1944–5 *(Sunday Telegraph,* 12 January 1992).

2. Of HP's *No Man's Land* for Radio 3. Dirk played Spooner, the character created by Gielgud for the National Theatre. Michael Hordern took the role of Hirst, played originally by Ralph Richardson. The director was, as always intended *(pace* Dirk, p. 418), Janet Whitaker.

WAS total joy. Never played a 'Spooner' before, and probably I never will. So, simply, Ta.

I forgot to tell you: Jimmy Wax[1] and I 'Passed Out' together at Sandhurst. Side by side we were; marching up the white steps of that extraordinary building behind a Royal on a white horse, which, just as Jimmy and I (heading the line) reached the top step deficated grandly.

He was a dear friend, and remained so ... seemed oddly fitting to be working on his dedication.

With tremendous admiration –
   & love
    <u>Dirk</u>

To Penelope Mortimer   *Cadogan Gardens*
                                         5 February 1992

Penelope –

Well then. I simply dont know what you do about the Pinter Piece.[2] Rather difficult [. . .] But he is a difficult fellow, I mean, he has altered so much as a person since I knew him in the early sixties.

But then I suppose we are all different? He just seems differenter.

I did my stint in that hideious basement in Portland Place .. no air, wrenched my pectoral (dont laugh) by pulling open those sodding bronze doors, and in consequence was in great pain for the whole recording and am only now JUST able to reach to the colander.

Well: you dont know where that is. No matter. It hurts. And I am told it must be rested. Thankfully I no longer mastubate.

But Harold came to the First Reading. We all, of course, read as if we were reading the words of 'Nearer My God To Thee' on that ship.

But he seemed jolly enough; replaced three commas and one adverb.

Important, as it turned out, and mis-typed by a lady at the BBC.

To my terror I am bidden to dine with him and Antonia (!) and some 'extremely amusing woman you will like' at a restuarant he'll tell me of later in this week. Oh well [. . .]

---

1. HP's agent from 1946 to 1983, and dedicatee of *No Man's Land*. Dirk's account of their passing-out is extravagantly elaborated.
2. A section of PM's memoirs-in-progress, relating to *The Pumpkin Eater*. See 1 December 1971, note 1.

But, yes, I am occupied. In buying my sister frocks and gloves and hat and thermals (what if it's snowing?) for the dubbing-caper on the 13 ... and arranging lunch and supper and all the tra la la that seems to be part and parcle of this Family Treat. No treat for me, I assure you, And I am wearing a simple black frock and a decent plain tie and thats IT. No top-hat and spangles. I only wear costume in costume parts.

I THINK my present opus has been accepted by Viking for Christmas. I want it for a stocking-filler. I reckon I'll make a bit of loot from it because it is so yuckky and full of 'nostalgia' and Virol and paraffin lamps and all that to-do. We'll see. I think the Blue-Rinses will heave with horror at 'JERICHO' ... all that bondage ... so this will get me back onto an even keel.

[...] I am glad that your new Agent seems sensible. Mine is. But reasonable, which is not always wise with giants like Viking. But I do NOT complain over much.

Now piss off, girl. I must get back to the 'Thank You For Your Very Kind Letter' bit. Thousands (it seems) since the K.C.B or whatever it is.[1] By the way, your mammoth plant, cut to the ground as you saw, is a mass of little green shoots. I'm in for trouble it would seem.

And did you know? We gain three minutes light every evening!
Wow!

Love <u>D</u> XXX

To Hélène Bordes   *Cadogan Gardens*
                                                      22 February 1992

Chere Planche –

Your letter came today, and I write immediatly to say how relieved I am that 'JERICHO' was acceptable.

NOT an easy story for my elderly readers! They will be very shocked I fear, but AIDS, or SIDA, is still almost un-mentionable in this country and I decided that no one had written a Detective Story about it, so I would!

My Doctor, who advised me medically, was very curious to know about the 'ugly' side of life. I told him that I really did'nt know a thing

---

1. Knight Bachelor.

about it!! I had never been into a Club like the Poisson, and as you will see, I did not describe it because I can not!

All imagination, and, naturally, reading the newspapers ... but otherwise it is all faux. As faux as Bagremon, Sur-Yves! WHERE did that name come from? Hommage, perhaps, to my old friend Montand?

It is published here on the 16th of March, and then I do the Big Ouf! Touring the North, Glasgow, Edinborough, Manchester even Dublin .. to talk about the book et moi meme: bien sur!

I hate to do this, but one has to now in the recession .. alas.

But the really exciting news is that my next book will be published in October! A memoir of childhood continuing the 'Summer' part of 'Postillion' which so many seem to have liked more than any of the others, really. So this one, 'GREAT MEADOW', is almost finished, has been bought, and so I will have TWO books printed this year for Viking, and five altogether! If you include 3 re-prints.

Pal mal? Pas mal de tour, cher Planche ...

On Wednesday I have to submit to jornalists and photographer from Paris who will come to my apartment for a piece in Figaro Madame .. I would never allow a British Press person NEAR the flat ... so you will see how much I still respect and love my France.

I hope I'm not wrong!

The Palace tra-la-la was great fun last week. It was very impressive, I managed to kneel for the sword, and really quite enjoyed it!

The Palace is not Versailles ... much later .. but impressive as all those Royal Houses are. Gilt, crimson, vast corridors, huge salons, all the Kings and Queens watching from enormous paintings .. tapestries and chandeliers, the Household Cavalry, the Guards, the Ghurkas, and the Queen in a simple silk frock, one rope of pearls, a small clip on her shoulder, very charming, expert and amused. I bowed for her to place my insignia round my neck and then was truly one of her Knights Bachelor .. for services to the Arts.

How Papa would have smiled. I never passed one exam, was always the bottom of the class, failed even six months of intense Tutoring, and was finally allowed to go to Art School. Well: there is hope for some idiots after all! I am a Knight of G.B .. I am a Commandeur of my beloved France .. and altogether, when I finally finish 'MEADOW' I will have written ten books. Something must be wrong?

And yes: now I am Sir Dirk .. on my envelopes and in my cheque-book .. The evening before the Ceremony, the concierge called up to my suite at the Connaught and said: 'Oh. Sir Dirk ... I have a Mr Bogaerde in the hall ..' and for a moment I thought it was me! But I quickly realised that it was my brother and his wife who had come to dine, and that I would never be just 'Mr' ever again!

That, I think, sums it all up perfectly ..

With my love, and my gratitude for your affection ..

Always

Dirk XX

To John Osborne   *Cadogan Gardens*
                                              18 June 1992

My dear 22524901. (Disbanded)[1]

Anguish prompts me to invade your 'Sleepy Hollow' in the hills of Salop. Anguish reading todays 'Spectator'.[2] You APPEAR to be leaving us all? You simply can not contemplate anything so churlish and unkind.

Do, please, reconsider. What else will you do pray? Another play? Too early, is'nt it, for another autobio .. although, as you know, I absolutely long for it ... so what else will you do, apart from being bloody to your wife and opening another bottle and some daft Local Fayre near Shrewsbury.

Oh do come back! Forget the foulness of the Press .. I know it is almost impossible .. I come out in hives if I merely see the word 'BOG' or 'DICK'.[3] Reel away, I do, with beating heart. HOW I loath them. The 'piece' did jolly well. You cant possibly see it in that light I know, but, it got tremendous 'spacc', as they said in Beverly Hills, remember, and it was very seriously considered and the critics,

---

1. Dirk and JO had taken to addressing each other by an Army serial number – in JO's case, mischievously, as he never served in the Forces. Noël Coward began a 1930 letter to T. E. Lawrence, otherwise 338171 Aircraftsman Shaw: 'Dear 338171, (May I call you 338?)'. An amused Lawrence obliged.

2. JO's *Déjàvu* had opened at the Comedy Theatre to supportive, if unenthusiastic, reviews. A heatwave was no help to the box office, and the play, his first for sixteen years, would close in seven weeks. In a diary for *The Spectator* (20 June) he lamented his error on submitting to interviews, and wrote: 'No more plays, no more journalism for me.'

3. Evidently a reference to the appearance of his name, misspelled or otherwise, in print.

as Visconti always said, are Eunichs, they cant create ... it frustrates them.

Your filthy Female Interviewers are so familiar to me. 'Have you any friends?' or 'Are you in love with anyone?' or, worse, 'Have you no love to give?'. Christ. I've had them all.

You are far too rare and wonderous a creature to be dunted by the crassness of them. Long, long after they have been shovelled into tastefull, or tasteless, plastic urns your books, particularly your books, will still be bound in leather.

I did'nt contact you at Oscars, because I am only too well aware of the stresses and strains of 'before the play' ... and when I did get brave and call you'd flitted.

But you were constantly in my thoughts. Not that it did the least good ... nevertheless ...

So reconsider, please. If it is an idle threat fair enough. If you actually mean it I'll have you reduced to the ranks from which you rose and, worse than that, you'll be required to do ten rounds of the Parade Ground in Full Marching Order, at Slow March Tempo to selections from 'High Society'.

That'll teach you, you impudent fellow ... what nonsense.

I shall have to cancel my order ..

No. 267237.[1]

For the final stage of what he would one day describe as his 'Anthracite Years' in Glasgow, Dirk had lodged – even found refuge – in King's Park with John ('Uncle York') and Hester McClellan and their two children, Nickie and Forrest. Aunt Hester (née Niven) was the third of Margaret Van den Bogaerde's four sisters. Still living in his native Scotland, Forrest had been diffident about making contact with Dirk at the time of the St Andrews degree ceremony, but wrote when the knighthood was announced and, later, sent a copy of his autobiographical novel, Then a Soldier *(Book Guild, 1991). Now he enclosed a further work.*

---

1. Dirk had his own number wrong: it was 269237.

To Forrest McClellan   *Cadogan Gardens*
                                          6 July 1992

Forrest –

A facinating, if depressing!, collection of stories[1] from you today.
Naturally I was far too curious not to read them almost right away.
Especially the Aunt Sadie parts and the references to your father! [. . .]
The awful gentility of it all almost suffocated me again today at seventy
one as it did then, when I was a child and, later, a miserable child and
adolescent. Thank God for Aunt Hester. She knew, without a word
ever being said, how unhappy I was and how awful the situation was
in Springfield Terrace (Crescent?) Bishopbriggs.[2]

Years ago, when I was first born, Aunt Sadie longed, and tried, to
get legal rights over me because she was quite convinced that my
mother was incapable of bringing me up. There was a desperate battle
between them, and, on one occasion I can remember being fought
over, physically, and Aunt Sadie, in her despair, wrenching my arm
and dislocating it! All hell broke out in sobs and tears and apologies
and so on.

Anyway, thank God, I stayed with Mama. I was always told, later
in life, that Uncle Murray was unable to have children and that this
was discovered very early in their marriage and was the cause of much
distress and hostility. I think, frankly, that it did have an awful bearing
on their marriage. She was determined that she had married 'beneath'
her. She accused Hester of the same error!

My life with them was far FAR worse than anything I wrote in my
book. The scars that the time there, three years, burned into me never
healed. But, and this I have said before and repeat, without those
awful years of bigotry and loneliness I would never have got through
life.

Those years made me strong, determined to save myself, and to get
away from all that was 'dainty' 'false' and 'genteel' and, no need to put
a fine point on it, cruel. Uncle Murray was deadly cruel. He falsified
my school reports, censored my letters home every week, watched me

---

1. FM had sent a copy of his privately published set of family vignettes, *Some of My Aunts and Uncles*.
2. For his first two years at Allan Glen's School, Dirk stayed with his mother's eldest surviving sister, Sarah (Sadie), and her husband William Murray at 42 Springfield Square – the period captured with spectacular harshness in *Postillion*.

with curious intensity when I took my weekly bath, and although my parents were paying them pretty well a weekly wage for my board and lodging, he made certain that I accounted for every penny I was allowed by my parents for my 'Saturday Pennies'. I spent most of my time quite alone in their 'front room' because the boys I knew at school were either, in his opinion, 'rough and common' or 'dirtying your aunts carpets'.

Frankly, and I can hardly blame them in a small masonette, they wanted me out and back home, in the first miserable year. We all learn, too late, that things are not as easy as they seem with a boy of 13 and ill with homesickness. Hester, on the other hand, and Aunt Nona,[1] got a pretty good idea of things [...]

My father so detested them all that he refused to set foot in poor Scotland ever again after his first journey with my mother after he married her.[2] The visit home was a disaster. My mother was glittering, gay, jolly, and painted her nails. She also danced and drank rather a lot! Aunt Sadie was deeply shocked; and furious that her friends all found 'Madge' such fun. Naturally they would stuck up in the suburbs of Glasgow. When I had to be removed from the Murrays (I wrote the famous, desperate, post card from Queen Street Station which Murray discovered me writing and made me mail) it was your beloved Mama who took me in, causing more bad feeling within the family at the time, because I still had a final year to go at the school and it was considered, by Dr Steel,[3] 'very unwise to move him away at this stage'.

Quite frankly Aunt Hester was glad of the money. Life was ANY-THING but easy in Kings Park. Goodness, how kind she was. How we ganged up on York when he had his 'huffs' .. how careful I was laying out the table for his weekly Bridge parties. How they managed with me I'll never know. But they did, somehow ...

[...] I dont, honestly, think that my reportage was 'vengful' in my book. I did my best to explain that it was mostly MY fault. The absolute impossibility of the two very different temprements joining or even understanding each other. Hopeless; they did their best, I did my best, but we were never going to make it work. Except when he went off to Ireland .. then Sadie was a quite different person. Almost

---

1. Agnes, youngest of Margaret's four sisters.
2. Ulric broke that vow when he took Dirk to Glasgow in 1934.
3. James Steel, headmaster of Allan Glen's.

jolly, always smart and trim, and ready to do something exciting! Like going to the cinema or to hear the Orpheus Choir, or some thing . . she was a very different person.

Anyway: that time is all over and gone. They were part of a lost age. Brave, genteel, always hard up but ever proud.

Jimmy[1] was another thing. You have caught him well. My Mama got him his big break with the 600 Group, he used to come and stay with us in the country with his very 'good pal' Hugh Heather . . and Other Uncles . . . but he jolly well knew that being with the Murrays was to be the death of us all. He was wonderfully kind: gave me small gifts of money, a scarf, a shirt sometimes. Always rich and elegant and adored by the family. I speak, of course, of the early 'thirties. I never knew him in the later years. Or Nona, come to that . . . and apart from Sadie and Willie,[2] whome I saw for a meal when I was in Glasgow with some play, I never saw any of them again . . . goodness me.

Thanks for writing anyway. It was really strange to find out 'What Happened Afterwards' and how extremely good and patient you were during all those years. They must have cherished you greatly . . . I am only sad that Hester did'nt live to see you rewarded academically, she so desperatly wanted it for both of you. It was the dream she held closest to her heart all her life. I know that for a fact . . . And you both rewarded her!

I'll finish this rigmarole now . . . with great affection, ever . .

Your Cousin

Dirk

To John Coldstream   *Cadogan Gardens*
                                                    17 August 1992

My dear John –

I am truly sorry: I really cant deal with this chap.[3] I am a simple (in all senses of the word) man . . and I am, to a large extent fairly logical.

I cant make this effort out. It is, in my opinion, over-written, pretensious, poetic, illogical and incomprehensible.

---

1. Youngest of Margaret's four brothers, who worked for a time as a salesman for an engineering firm.
2. The eldest brother.
3. JC, Nicholas Shakespeare's successor as Literary Editor of the *Daily Telegraph*, had sent Michael Ondaatje's novel *The English Patient* (Bloomsbury) for possible review.

It would be quite wrong for me to attempt to review it, I have no doubt whatsoever that it will win all the prizes.[1] It's that kind of book, but I defy any 'ordinary' reader, and I count myself as one of that ungainly group, to carry on to the end without longing to chuck the thing at the wall.

It is a book written by someone who obviously adores the English language but who does'nt know it as a 'mother tongue'.[2]

It dazzles with cleverness and research. But unless you get a real cock-stand from de-fusing bombs, unless you can really believe in someone so appalingly burned that he looks like a tar-baby but is still capable of quoting, chirpily, chunks of Herodotous and manages to exist on morphine . . unless, in fact, you can suspend belief on a very high level, then this fails utterly.

Sure, he's done his homework (too much) sure he knows his mines and his Classics. He does'nt know much about the Human Heart or the people about whome he writes. And the moment that impossible 'Kip'[3] enters stage left all belief vanishes.

A most irritating Sunday! Irritation with myself for my ignorance, irritation with the pretensiousness, irritation that I am not capable of 'reading' Kandinksi or Jason Pollock. This fellow is the literary equivalent of those two painters. And that sinks me.

With humble apologies. I did think, after two chapters, that perhaps I MIGHT make it . . . foolish fellow.

Yours
    <u>Dirk</u>

To Penelope Mortimer   *Cadogan Gardens*
                                            15 December 1992

Penelope –

A relief to get your letter. I did not write or telephone for fear of disturbing you. Or whatever. I am so very relieved that the book[4] is 'finished or otherwise' (whatever that might mean) but more to the point that <u>you</u> appear to be alright.

---

1. Dirk was prescient. It shared the 1992 Booker Prize with Barry Unsworth's *Sacred Hunger* (Hamish Hamilton).
2. Ondaatje, born in Sri Lanka, lived in Toronto.
3. A Sikh sapper.
4. *About Time Too* (see DB to Daphne Fielding, p. 543).

Of course use anything you consider useful from my letters .. they were sent to you anyway. I cant really believe there is anything 'funny and good' to use, but I have'nt seen them since writing them! I am locked half way through my FINAL auto. Difficult. I have destroyed one half already (I bought myself a shredder from Rymans. Glorious fun!) so I will be late for the dead-line in Feb. Sold already .. thats the third book sold this year. Do I swank?

You betcha ..

Anyway I am no longer an actor I now write only. The 16 shows I did all over the UK were a glorious realisation that people actually read what I wrote and liked me anyway. Tears and love. Sickening if you did'nt realise it was true. I have stopped, prudently, at the top . . . no more now.

But I still would love to see you when this daft business is over .. in the New Year? You write … meanwhile all my love .. I seem to think, probably quite wrongly, that I pushed you to get this book written that day in your garden?

If so I'm proud, if not so, I'm thrilled that you have done it!

The bloody M. whatever, is feet high. It must be the growing season in S. Africa, or Beth Chatto' 'spelled' it. It's glorious. And no frost.

Yet.

Great love –

D XX

To Mary Dodd   *Cadogan Gardens*
                                                  23 February 1993

Mainie my dear –

Your letter has moved me greatly.[2] I wanted to write this to you rather than just telephone. But I have had to wait for various bits and pieces, rather like you!, to go away or be dealt with before I could properly sit down and concentrate.

Lu has been with me for the week-end, I took her home yesterday,

1. The plant PM gave Dirk had been supplied by the celebrated gardener.
2. Dirk had sent MD a proof of *A Short Walk from Harrods*, saying: 'I do rather feel like those ladies who quite firmly reject the child they have been nourishing within for nine months! I dont want it published. I feel it is a fearful infringement of my life .. and, indeed, Tote's.'

she had read the MS which had shattered her but, like you, she offered no criticism. Just wept!

I am so deeply grateful to you for the care and trouble which you have taken to read, and consider, the book. Because of your re-action and also because Lu's so agreed with yours, I have told Viking to go ahead. I had, as you know, grave doubts about it all.

My main terror was that I might have sullied, in some way, the wealth of those years which I was permitted to spend with Tote.

Capatalise, I think is the word I want. But I really did'nt think of that while I was writing. And I was on the thing for eighteen months as you know! I tried, very hard, to keep as calm, clear, and uncluttered as possible ... because I have to remember that it is to be read by strangers. Sometimes hostile strangers at that. I did'nt want in any way to spoil what was for me the most perfect relationship of my life. The sheer 'goodness' of Tote had to be preserved at all costs. I pray that I have done that. You so much as suggest that I have.

It is a tribute to him. I know that he would have been very embarressed if he had ever thought that he was considered so highly, and with so much affection and respect: as well as love. For love it was .. is.

All the events took place, I have naturally disguised place names and the names of the people. I am not in the Mayle[1] pitch.

Otherwise, this, is how it was. I was not ready to try and write dispassionatly really. It took a lot of courage and a lot of diciplin. And it was exceptionally painful. I finished on the 4th of this month feeling relief but, the next day, discovered a gigantic cold-spot on my lip, an agonizing back, and a deep longing to sleep for years!

I had not realised that 18 months of 'going back' could be so very disturbing. All the time I have been wondering if I could have done better .. NOT left the hill, kept, somehow, going up there. But finally Tote's own fear of 'being ill in a foreign language' convinced me that we simply had to close up the shop. So, for better or for the worst, that is what happened. I feel that what he had to contend with, and always with such grace and good humour, had to be honoured.

If that is not too silly a word? He was as brave as could be, as strong and un-complaining as you could imagine. His main worry was how I would be able to cope. Naturally! So I was determined not to let him

---

1. Peter, author of *A Year in Provence* and *Toujours Provence*.

down, and I honestly, hand on heart, dont think I did.

Hope not.

Your help has been invaluable. Really and truly. For had you felt the least twing of distress over any matter of taste or behaviour I know that you would have told me so. Equally with Lu; I begged her to say if I had erred, or caused her distress.

She assured me not [...] She just was appalled that so many quite dreadful things happened in such a short time. Nothing seemed to go right .. and nothing did! [...]

We have, or rather I have, added a short piece at the very end of the book about re-discovering your book, JERICHO,[1] in the office on the day I got back from filming in France. It is essential really. I dont know why I dropped it .. but I wanted to end on an Up Note .. and the film seemed to be the right one. Fanny Blake (My Editor) said that JERICHO was every bit as important to me, she thought, because from it I gained confidence to write on, and then go on stage and 'do' the Concerts. I think she's probably right. Anyway: it's there, just before the very last lines. I DO think it was fortunate to hear a recording of an Operetta of Offenbachs' with that splendid last line!

'If you cant have what you love, you must love what you have.'

Very, very true.

Thank you darling girl ... I feel braver now that I have your views, and indeed your approbation ... the Editors, the Publicity, all the others at Viking dont really count for me. They did'nt know 'lote .. with the exception of Fanny Blake, who did and adored him. But they have all been wonderfully patient and have not pushed me into publishing at all. Until you and Lu had read it .. and no one could be closer or wiser than you two .. I held off. They understood. I wrote today to say it was all alright. I'd take the can. As my agent, Pat Kavanagh, rightly said, 'Dirk! After all that, surely you have grown another carapace?'

I suppose I will?

Thank you again. I treasure your letter ... it is more helpful than you could ever imagine.

With my profound love & gratitude.

  Ever,

    Dirk XXXOOO

---

1. Jericho was dedicated to MD 'with endless love for Thursday teas'.

To Daphne Fielding   *Cadogan Gardens*
                                        5 May 1993

Dearest Field –

I should be doing one of three urgent things: I should be planting out my vile little pansies .. and then watering the buggers, I should be scurrying on with Chapter 2 of the sequel (!) to 'JERICHO', I should be filing the Statements from Lloyds Bank, and I should be finishing off an imagined view of the Piazza San' Marco which I have scribbled for some bloody Charity. Instead I write to you in reply to your lovely letter of last week. I do thank you. You seem to be getting back into form again .. and that is good news, handwriting same old elegant loops and swoops, Basildon Bond yet!

Easter was loathesome, and as if that was not enough I got back from Italy just intime to have May Day .. Christ! And it was howling with rain and bitter wind and I'd just left Milan the day before in blazing sunshine and bright Italian skies. How GOOD it was to be back! How wise I was to accept the chance to do the 'promotion' of 'JERICHO' in Italian. My first foreign promo. and my first time back in Italy for over twenty years! And it was exactly the same. Not a thing had changed. Apart, that is from the waiters and bar men and conciergies in the Hassler. But I was treated like a Prince. They were so wonderfully kind and loving, and I honestly felt that I had only just driven down the road from dotty Villa Bertie to get the London papers. But of course I had'nt.

Frankly I was alarmed to go entirely on my own. So I didnt. I took a very nice girl from my Publishers called Nicki[1] who was bright, clever, and had never set foot in Rome before. But I feared that I'd fall over, get a rush of blood to the head, limp everywhere, and feel exhausted and faint with terror.

Quite, my dear, the reverse! I simply adored the whole four days .. it was the best fun. Not a wheeze of asthma, not a hobble, not a moment of doubt. I just lay back, worked my ass off with interviews and TV, and was put up in the old Hassler with a view down the Steps, in Rome, and in the Principe de Savoya[2] in Milan .. with a glorious room and a view over a Fun Fair called Luna Park.

---

1. Nicki Kennedy, of the Intercontinental Literary Agency.
2. Principe di Savoia.

However there was double-glazing to the room. So that was alright!
Mind you I never left the hotels, except to dine, and then by super
Mercedes, and never even trod on a pavement in Rome .. there simply
was'nt time.

We started at eight every morning, four interviews (together) each
hour, until eight in the evening. Remember: the Italians work late!
And hard ... but everytime I felt weariness overcome me someone
handed me a flute of Krug and I very soon recovered all my strength!
What was splendid was that none of this splendour cost me a thing. I
just hope that Longanesi, my very grand publishers, sells some books.
Certainly the reviews were favourable, and I got plasted all over Italy
in two top TV shows .. (which terrified me.) Except I had a marvellous
translator, a girl, who works normally in Brussels for the Common
Market people. So she does instant translation ... you just chatter
away and she translates there and then, quite brilliantly. She was called
Olga, was as black as a chimney and came from Putney! But she was
quite marvellous .. four fluent languages and she was only about
twenty five or so.

So that took the fear out of the job. One program was an hour and
a half long, at 'peak time' and devoted ENTIRELY to books and
writers! Can you imagine that happening here in the UK? The other
programme was a sort of Chat Show but composed, that evening
when I did it, of Doctors, Surgeons, and Consultants! How the hell,
I wondered desperatly, will I fit into this! I was Special Guest and left
to the last, which was useful, because, with Olga's help, I could
understand the dialogues .. so I was able to pitch in as Vice President
UK of Voulantry Euthanasia, and one of the Vice Presidents of
B.A.C.U.P .. my cancer charity. So that was all very fortunate ...
thank goodness I paid some heed to being a 'Pollyanna' inspite of
some jeers here!

I went, with my 'Team' from the Publishers, down to Bologanaisi
in Piazza del Popolo[1] for supper. Although the patron, who was
marvellous and kind, had retired, his son now about forty, had taken
over and I got the best table and great affection .. and not a picture
on the wall, not a chair, table, curtain, nothing at all had changed! It
was so odd, twenty something years older, to be in the very same
setting as once I had been as a younger man. I liked it enormously ...

---

1. Dal Bolognese, in the Piazza del Popolo.

and the grub! Well .. need you ask .. all the spring vegetables, the baby lamb, the kid, the freshly made tortolini, ravioli, brains in butter, zucchini, figs and tiny attichokes .. it made Nicki fall spell bound! And the next night, on the roof at the Hassler I showd her Rome at night and she just burst into tears. No noise, just quiet tears spilling down her face. I told her I had done exactly the same thing on <u>my</u> first night looking down on Rome. So that was rather nice for me to be able to hand on cherished memories to a younger person who would, one day I knew, count that as one of HER cherished memories. So sometimes there is a pleasure in growing old. Not often, I know, but just sometimes . . . .

I have now been asked to go to Athens in October .. but I dont think I'll go .. 'A Short Walk . .' is published then. It would be tiresome to miss that here, although I am certain to be slagged off . . . never mind. It would be cowardly to duck out and chuck it all. 'Great Meadow' goes out, read by me, in Whitsun Week at 8.45 am BBC .. it's a very important 'slot' I gather. It's in the Whitsun Recess .. but why that makes it important I dont know. Do all the Politicians listen in then? Or what? 'Jericho' is a Book At Bedtime in June-July. Read by me . . . I would'nt let anyone else do it. I'm recording an abridged version of 'A Short Walk . .' on Wednsday. This is on cassette, as 'GREAT MEADOW' is, for private sale.[1]

A new venture of Penguin! Rather a good idea. Talking Books are becoming very popular now. Not just for the blind but all over. So that all helps the coffers a bit.

Oh dear, yes [. . .] I seem to be forever dipping into my pocket.[2] It's so damned difficult. I appear, to the world at large, to be without responsibilities! No wife, no children, and so I have to spread myself a bit all round [. . .] Lally needs a bit of help .. not to mention Thomas, my adopted grandson! Now at University on a grant of £50 a week. What in the name of God can you do with that? So Uncle <u>has</u> to work .. which is really just as well. I'd be really in a pickle if I hadnt got something to do . . . and I do rather like my Scotch at six!

[. . .] I was watering a hanging geranium, just before starting this letter, it's in a pretty terracotta wall-pot just above Bacchus's[3] head! So

---

1. Another Dirkism: he means 'on commercial sale to the public'.
2. Dirk responds empathetically to DF's account of difficulties in her family.
3. The stone figure given many years earlier to Dirk and Tony by DF and her husband Xan.

instead of wine, his libation, which he does'nt altogether care for, is a
mix of water, earth, peat and Growmore! He sports a narrow brown
moustache . . . I better go and wipe it off. It'll be dry now. Then I'll
look out something to eat for supper. No lovely Hassler grub here . .
or Bologanasie goodies . . . I really MUST try a rissoto on Saturday.
Tide comes up from Sussex for her monthly spoil . . . just three days
[. . .] I cook her delicious things . . and Nicki bought me a huge packet
of dried porcini mushrooms in Rome as a prezzie . . I'll use them in
my rissoto . . . juicing up, I leave you, with love and hugs . .

As ever, dearest Field – D XXXOOO

To Penelope Mortimer   *Cadogan Gardens*
                                          9 June 1993

Penelope –
   Well: alright then. Sulk if you want to . . or whimper away that we
are, or have, 'drifted'.
   What a soppy word. I certainly dont feel drifty . . not at all . . I am
still your friend and always will be. I dont drift. I remain prudent and
dont intrude. Alright? 'Little Boys Should Be Seen . .' and all that
stuff. The fact that ever since I started out as an actor I have denied
that edict (is it one?) and never stopped drawing attention to myself
in every disgusting way is neither here nor there.
   Broken all the rules dear. Audrey Hepburn and I once compared
notes and burrowed in our mutual shame.
   But I have not drifted. You may have . . often have in fact. Dont
you remember? You used to get weary of one, and just dribble away
. . it was absolutely understood. Understandable. After Laddo or Ludo
or wherever it was,[1] there was a singing silence. One did'nt hear a
sound for years. And then muffled ones from a Post Office . . and then
more silence mixed up with gardening hints . . . and then little siren
calls from Cricklewood.
   And to the pictures, yet! No. We have'nt drifted. It's the normal
course.
   And sadly, really sadly, I dont do 'evenings' now, only 'matinees'.
   I am usually sodden with drink (That is a VAST EXAG-
GERATION, but I liked the phrase) by seven o clock, and, apart

---

1. Yaddo, the writers' colony.

from that I am to be found correcting a MS. Now that I am a writer
and no longer act, nor ever will, I practice hard and daily.

My auto out Oct. 7th … when is yours? Collision course? Fun.

I'm on a novel now .. sequel to the last because people rather liked
the Downs Syndrome child and the wayward nine year old.

I am going to dump the D.S one, too much trouble, and the
wayward one is about to be ten (easier to cope with dialogue wise).
The trouble is that I tend to haunt the school queue hurrying to and
from Hill House,[1] trying to guess height and age.

I'll be arrested ere long ..

Sorry about the 29th .. a rain check? And my melianthus is cut
hard back every November (black flies and white!) and flourishes
madly in a fearfully pretty terracotta classic pot which cost £45. So
you are tended with loving care daily … I ruffle your feathers and lift
your skirts (signs of black fly) and drench copiously with libations of
Gromore.

Drifting? Drifted?

Tosh.

With my love
    Dirk

Just back from Hay.[2]

That was huge fun! D

To Daphne Fielding

Cadogan Gardens
13 September 1993

Dearest darling one –

Oh what a groan of relief when your fat little missive arrived this
morning. I was a titchy bit worried .. but I do fidget rather, and then
realised that you'd probably be a bit busy what with Summer and all.
Not that there was much summer, really. But I thought you'd be a bit
Social. Well: more social than usual. I mean I have taken it on board
that you cant dash about and that you have to have a minder, and all
.. knew that. But, you know, sometimes one lets time slip past so
quickly, and then the weeks become months. Nearly did call you

---

1. The nearby boys' private school.
2. The Literary Festival.

actually. Paddy [Leigh Fermor] was in Town for an 'op. I saw it in the paper. He was at Sister Agnes (Edward VII) so I called and he said to come and see him so I did. With some 'splits' of Bollinger, and he was prone on his poor back, but jolly with it. He wanted, on some wild impulse, to telephone you from his bed and we'd all have a gay old chat. But, knowing your situation, I stayed his eager hand and said that perhaps we should'nt call. Just on spec. out of the blue and all that. He [...] shuffled off back to Greece shortly afterwards. He wrote a sweet note of Thanks, and said it really was'nt much fun haveing op's at his age, and that he felt distinctly woozy and hoped he'd make the trip. I gather that he must have? There was an angry letter from him in the Spectator about something. Cant remember what. But a long, furious, Paddy Thing.

You know?

Now .. I have finished 'A Short Walk From Harrods'. It comes out next month. An extract in the 'Saturday Telegraph' and a long promotional tour to follow. Leeds (!) Norwich, Eastbourne Brussels Antwerp .. and so on. I'm buying myself a new frock for the occasion. Now that I am up to all these 'Shows' I have to look proper. No open neck shirts and Literary-Style-Jeans and blousons for moi. Hacketts and Hermes. Very expensive but worth while. With my face steadily dissolving into sags and wattles, wearing a decent suit and good shoes does rather take the beady eyes off ones deficiencies. I am collecting a mass. Alas!

I'll send you off a copy when I go into the Office (Viking) on Wed. I dont know what you'll think of it: I cut out most of the really bad bits but people still groan and weep and say how-awful. But it was, it always is, is'nt it? However, I have tried to amuse the reader as well. You will, doubtless, tell me! Did you hear me reading 'Great Meadow'?

Rather early of a morning. During the Recess (apparently peak time) it was very popular thank God, and lots of Elegant Ladies in the Cadogans cried out to me in the street; was'nt that nice? I am glad you liked 'JERICHO' ... very well abridged, I thought, he's a nice old chap[1] ... (Younger than me!) and looks rather like a Don. Probably is. He does all my bukes. I am now '¾' of the way into the sequel! 'A Period of Adjustment', I am finding it rather fun, difficult to do, to write a seperate book with already established characters. Each book

---

1. Mark Handsley.

has to 'stand on it's own' so to speak. But it does keep me close to my beloved France. Well: our part of it anyway. The Var, and Garde and a bit of the Alpes Maritime. Trouble is, I find that I forget, or am slowly beginning to, so many once familiar things. And it is only six years ago that I had to come back with Tote. Five since I've lived in this appartment. Amazing . . .

A busyish time for me, this summer. People come over from the States, so that means lunches and so on .. and Tide comes up every month now to have a three day 'spoil'. Which means long chatter on the lines of ' . . . and do you remember the awful mole-skin travelling rug that Mummy WOULD wrap round herself when the hood was down? And how simply AWFUL it was when you almost cut off your index finger with the axe trying to open MY money box . . .' Well: my dear. You can imagine. Senility calls us. However [. . .] she's enjoying being a widow with champagne and little bottles of Floris scent.

My brothers' middle son Rupert, who lives near Perpignon, had a quite ghastly experience this summer. His wife was declared clinically mad, schizo .. and was locked up in a very nice place. They could'nt keep her there indefinatly, and stuffed her with pills and a strict routine, and let her go. One morning (they have two adorable boys neither of them spoken to by her for two years!) she ran barefoot from the house, got in the car, drove away. No papers, no money, nothing. A fearful crash on the road to Narbonne .. she, wounded but walking, was helped to a house where she knelt on the ground and begged the farmer to shoot her because she was mad and wicked and would harm her children if he did not. A good French farmer, he called the police, but she had scarpered into the hills. And has not been seen since! Rupert arrested under suspicion (at the start) the police searched every leaf and blade of grass, my poor bro' rushed to his son, I ransacked my bank, we all did what we could and we ALL said 'This does'nt happen to people like us! It's the sort of thing you read in the tabloids!'. Silly asses. It <u>has</u> happned to us. So. Rupert is now at liberty, has appealed on TV asking for help, huge rewards offered for info. Silence. And this was in early May. The police, and the Army (!) say we must wait until the Hunting Season starts. Someone will probably find her. For the moment that is that. Wow. As they say.[1]

---

1. The full story is told by Rupert Van den Bogaerde, writing as Rupert Bogarde, in *Daybreak into Darkness* (Macmillan, 2002).

[. . .] Really! Ones families . . what a problem they turn out to be. I thought I'd be safe from all that. But not at all. I'm the only one who is earning lolly. Naturally enough . . . and like you I am constantly being sought for advice by the children who dont want 'Mum and Pa to know . .' Useful, tiring, but at least one is wanted. I think?

I liked the Partridge[1] very much indeed. Read all her books . . did'nt care for some of the early stuff. 'Pacifists War' and so on, but I have never cared for Pacifists much. Even though I am sure they have a point! Has'nt ever worked, mind you. Hence Bosnia et al. Now wallowing, no other word will do, in Nancy M's letters. 'Love From Nancy'[2] . . they are so good and funny . . . must be read in little gulps. Not taken all together.

[. . .] Glad you liked the ladies on your card. I rather thought you might . . very elegant and lean, just like you! Bon chic, bon genre! Red boots notwithstanding. I'm off to make myself some risotto and then go to Hacketts for a fitting. Then hunt through books for suitable 'pieces' to read to the Belgians on the 1st. Thank you for you[r] acres of love poppies and daisies . . . moon ones . . . and this comes with great ropes of sweet peas and honeysuckle to drape around your slender body . .

Always all my love . .
Your devoted
Dirk xxxx

P.S. Stood behind F. Partridge at the check-out in – Partridges! Doughty Lady indeed! D.

To Daphne Fielding   SW3
                    19 October 1993

Dearest Daph/Field –

I have been banging about doing Book Promotion; all kinds of places from Cheltenham to Leeds. Ghastly nerves to start with, always, but as soon as I hit the stage I'm fine. And Audiences are SO good and loving and make it all appear effortless! Then, after I have read a

---

1. *Other People: Diaries 1963–66* by Frances Partridge (HarperCollins).
2. *Love from Nancy: The Letters of Nancy Mitford,* edited by Charlotte Mosley (Hodder & Stoughton).

few bits and pieces and answered all the questions which they pose (usually this takes 1 to 2 hours) I settle down and sign books for them. As I now have 11 in paperback this can take AGES! But it's good for sales. Not Margaret Thatcher Stuff, but not bad .. and I jumped to No 2 on the Best Seller List in the first week. I'll probably drop now that she is published,[1] and Terry-Awful-Waite[2] was No 1. I cant think why? He makes me feel utterly creepy. Odd.

So your loving and lovely letter went unanswered but not un appreciated because you know how much I value your opinion. Especially as you were so close for so long. I am happy that people who knew and loved him [Tony] have said as you have said, that I have set him down on paper just as he was. I suppose, after all those years, I should have known his 'voice' but it is not the same thing as writing it down and bringing him alive again. I think, hope and pray, that I did that.

The reviews have been enormously gratifying .. not one snide or beastly one. At least, YET! There is still time, alas.

[...] I have been waiting for a man to come and do the 'grouting' on my terrace ... the recent rains have started to see[p] through the cracks in the tiles into the sitting room of the German lady in the flat below. She's been very polite about it, but wants to know, 'Pleeze, ven I ken put paint to my ceilink?' I have to tell her to wait for the British Worker to arrive when he says he will, and she sighs a heavy sigh because [...] she knows the British Worker as well as I do. Anyway: he's arrived now. An hour late .. and gone to park his van.

So that'll be another hour I suppose.

I have to go and be guest of Honour at a very big gathering at the RAC Club tomorrow. The Booksellers Association have invited me! I am chuffed with delight. They actually chose me as their Guest of Honour instead of M. Thatcher! I have to speak to them about the wickedness (in my view) of the probable imposition of VAT on books! The Press will be present .. so I have to watch my step. I dont at all approve of writers/actors involving themselves in politics, but on this occasion I feel that my career is being threatened along with a great many other people .. and all the un-told hundreds of young who

---

1. *The Downing Street Years 1979–90* (HarperCollins).
2. Terry Waite's *Taken on Trust* (Hodder & Stoughton) had been published the previous month.

WANT to write. And all this quite apart from the terrible price it will put on learning. Will they tax school books? How do they define what a school book IS? I had to read Scott at school . . . some kids now read Jane Austin today: some even read me for GSCE or whatever that stands for (GCSE? Does that look better? I dont know) . . I just know that £15.95[1] is too much for most people today . . . so with VAT on top of that it'll be 'night night darling' to us all.

As soon as this Promotion business is over I can get down to my book again, the sequel to 'JERICHO' . . . it's rather fun to write in a sort of ghastly way. I find that my people have rather taken me over and do exactly, and precisely, what they want. I just have to write it all down. I decided that my hero, William, was in danger of becoming very dull and unattractive. So I arranged for him to meet, unexpectedly, a lady from Louisiana called Loulou de Terrehaute. And she rapes him! It so shattered my beloved (young) Editor who was reading the last pages on the Tube to work, that she went red in the face and was quite shattered to think that someone might read it over her shoulder. I asked if she had found it offensive? Perhaps I'd better trim it a bit? But she screeched, and said 'No! Dont touch it . . it's amazing . .' I have fearful thoughts of her rather worthy, but quite pretty, young husband being tied up to the four-poster tomorrow!

So . . . I have dipped my fingers into violent sex. I'm amazed that I even knew how . . . golly whiz . . .

Tomorrow is the speech to the Booksellers, then a couple of trips about the place and I end up in Eastbourne, all sold out, and then do a final evening at the Olivier in November. Also sold out!

Then back to work . . . . I have finished Nancy M. (all I could bear to read. I chucked it when she started to get ill. Had quite enough of all that, thanks.) and started on the autobiography of my mate Penelope Mortimer.[2] Once married to John Mortimer. I rather pushed her to write this because, two years ago, she was terribly low and could not think of what to do . . she'd also had a nasty op. for lung cancer . . I thought that to bash away at her autobiography (she'd already done one half some years ago) would be amusing and good for her.

Well. I'm not easily shocked but, God almighty, I really got a fright

1. The recommended retail price of *A Short Walk from Harrods* was £15.99.
2. *About Time Too: 1940–1978*, published by Weidenfeld & Nicolson simultaneously with a reissue of *About Time: Autobiography 1918–1939* (Allen Lane, 1979).

when I read her epic. Due out in a few days time and she'll be hung
or hanged. It is the cruellest book I think I have ever read about a
failed marriage. She spares no one. Neither herself or, above all, her
wretched ex-husband, John. It is shattering. I heard myself say, aloud,
'Oh no! No you <u>cant</u> write that down ..' but .... she has.

Silly of her. It's a revenge thing I suppose, and she claims that she
and John are now both old and not easily hurt. Much! It's the children
I am sorry for ... the spite and cruelty are really too much .. I dont
at all reccomend it to you. Clever, brilliant writing, but far far too
personal. How odd that someone who is sensitive as a writer should
be so hideiously insensitive about her own life. I do get fussed and
saddned. I had a bit of a struggle composing my letter of 'thanks' to
her. But the critics will have a field day next week ... unless I am very
much mistaken: and I think not.

The sun is fading, the air chilling ... it's been the most lovely day
in London, a sort of Provence/Var day .. clear sky, aching blue, still
and hot in the sun. <u>How</u> I miss what you call our 'lost fairylands'.

Bacchus got moved about today while the chap was grouting. God!
He's so heavy! But there he stands, eating his bunch of grapes and
stareing through the October trees towards Peter Jones. He IS a
comfort.

I must seal this, correct it first,[1] then troll over to the post box
across Sloane Street. You might get it tomorrow morning if I catch
the five o clock post.

It comes, anyway, with acres and acres of lush love .. as always ..
Your very devoted chum
<u>Dirk XXXX</u>

To Brian McFarlane[2]   *Cadogan Gardens*
                                                 29 October 1993

Dear Brian –

I am writing this in a gap between plumber and the builder!
Somewhere a pipe is leaking and no one quite knows where. Somewhere under the fitted-carpet.

---

1. *Sic!* Dirk made a desultory eleven amendments.
2. BM had interviewed Dirk for *Sixty Voices* (British Film Institute, 1992; revised in 1997
as *An Autobiography of British Cinema*, published by Methuen).

I give up. And hasten to use the time away from my proper work by replying to your kind letter of the 23rd.

How amusing that you have seen 'Singer' AND 'Libel'. I really do think that the latter was the most awful tosh ... it felt like it at the time and it was, if you please, 'a replacement movie'[1] for the destroyed 'Lawrence Of Arabia' called, at that time, 'Ross'.

I still dont know why it was cancelled at the last moment ... two weeks from shooting in the desert! I only knew that we had to find a new project quickly and to use the Crew we had already hired.

'Libel' was ready, had been discarded, got re-written fifty times and finally got made. No one was happy. But Olivia [de Havilland] secured MGM money and so we had to 'go' for the thing. I had to wash my hair daily on account of the silver paint in my hair, and the make-up for No 3 or 9 or whatever he was called,[2] took four hours to apply, and ages to shoot because I had to change and go back onto the same set as quite another person. It was all chaos and I cant be sure that anyway one ever saw it! It was adapted from an old play written, and hugely successful, in 1922[3] ... I was a year old. So you can tell how it creaks!

'Singer' WOULD have been alright except for the idiot casting of Mills as my, and Mylene's,[4] dream-boat! I ask you! Originally was to be Paul Newman .. but he rightly turned it down. Then I refused Burton, then with only one picture to do with Fox who offered him 'cheap' for £25 000. They wanted shot of him. I did'nt want a failed Star and said 'No'. He later got shoved into 'Cleopatra' when [Peter] Finch quit ... But when I knew it was to be Mills I got into the leather gear and camped it silly. In desperation. We sold ten thousand pairs of leather pants in the first month of it's release in London alone!

I recently took part in a documentary (four part) for Channel 4 TV called 'Hollywood-UK' .. which was goodish. About the British Cinema from '50–66. I did'nt have much to do ... but there were good clips from Darling and The Servant and so on ... and too much on that daft Terence Stamp who really could'nt act his way out of a

---

1. But not the first: Anthony Asquith's production of *The Doctor's Dilemma* started shooting in May 1958, about six weeks after his Lawrence project was abandoned. He and Dirk began work on *Libel* in February 1959.
2. 'Number Fifteen', the third of Dirk's roles in a plot that defies brief summary.
3. Edward Wooll's play was first performed in 1935.
4. John Mills and Mylène Demongeot, Dirk's co-stars in *The Singer Not the Song*.

paper bag [. . .] However it covered the period and many of the films about which you are writing. They were interesting years.

[. . .] 'Great Meadow' has been on the B/S list for some weeks in p/b .. and I recorded it for the BBC ... which was fun. It was the easiest book I have ever written but the hardest to convince my Publishers it was worth printing! Luckily I prevailed, and they agreed and it has been a big success. TWO books on the b/s list in the same weeks is rather a pleasant feeling. I am very glad that I have totally pulled out of the Movies and acting all together. I dislike the Cinema today so much ... and most of the people in it! Never even go to a Movie and hardly ever watch TV ... it's a forgotten time for me. No. Never went to Africa for 'Simba'. I was cast long after they did the second unit casting! The double was eight foot tall with white hair and was a hunter! God knows how we managed ... if we did!

Remember nothing whatever about Boxes Company Of Youth.[1] Dont think it survived longer than the dreadful Charm School.

I think it must be about time for you to revisit the UK .. and pick a few more brains here. Not many people are interested in the Old Movies .. we keep on bleating about the New British Cinema, only there is'nt one! The British have never learned the Star System .. and they never will. For a while Pinewood tried to imitate Hollywood with disasterous results ... but it simply is'nt the British Way.

The French do it far better ...

I think by the noises that the plumbers have found the leak or whatever .. so I'll finish this off and go to the mail.

Best wishes to you and your wife, and write again soon ..

Until next time ..

Ever

<u>Dirk</u>

---

1. As BM records in *The Encyclopedia of British Film* (Methuen, 2003; revised 2005), the Company of Youth was established by Sydney Box to groom young actors and actresses for stardom. When he joined the Rank Organisation in 1947 'he took the Company with him and it metamorphosed into the derided Rank Charm School'.

To Simon Hopkinson   *Cadogan Gardens*
                                                  25 November 1993

Dear Simon –

I know that you wont believe this: it's too silly and obvious. But it is absolutely fact. When I got back last night,[1] read the bundle of Dotty Fans and tore the wrappings from countless packets of Maynards Winegums, Keep Faith With Jesus Books and requests for signed photographs, all collected from the National, I opened your package and cried aloud: 'I've got it!'

For weeks I have tried to get that book.[2] From Dillons, to Smiths, to Sandoe … no luck. And there, in my weary hands, was my long sought treasure, from you, after a splendid supper!

I know it sounds improbable. But it's true, and thank you.

From 1954 until I finished 'Death In Venice' in 1970 I always had the top right hand corner table at Harry's.

His (Son, not Papa) brother-in-law was my (brilliant) dentist when I lived in Rome. During the work on 'Death' (eight months) I got to my table when able. For a steamed sole and boiled potato.

The kindness in that place, the 'piping hots' as we called them on winter nights at the bar, the belonging, although one really was'nt a Glamorous Film Star, engenderd was wonderous. I had a house out on Guidecca … with a half hectar of garden onto the lagoon … .

Thank you for my supper, for the warmth, for the kindness .. and thank you for my book. I treasure it … I wont be able to remotely cope but I'll try!

I do apologise, I have to say, for being rather on a High … after the Show I suppose I get over-loquacious, and J.B always makes me feel stupid … not his fault! Mine!

But thank you –
    <u>Dirk</u>

---

1. Following a Platform performance at the National Theatre, Dirk had dined with Pat Kavanagh and her husband Julian Barnes at SH's renowned restaurant, Bibendum.
2. *The Harry's Bar Cookbook: Recipes and Reminiscences from the World-famous Venice Restaurant and Bar* by Arrigo Cipriani (Bantam, 1991).

To Brian McFarlane   *Cadogan Gardens*
                                              26 November 1993

Dear Brian –

Good to hear from you .. you appear to be as busy as I am! Or impendingly .. to judge from your next summer schedule.

I finished my Tour, thank God, on Wednesday night at the Olivier. A S/R/O performance which was fine, and they enjoyed it but I very suddenly began to realise that I was going down with a throat of major proportions! Everyone here has Beijing flu .. and I was certain I was about to go under as well. However it did'nt show, and I signed books afterwards for what seemed eternity but was really only about an hour and a half (the 'performance' runs two hours, usually) so I got through all that and then had to go to dinner with my female Agent (Literary) and her husband and friends. Business and bloody. The throat raged during the night and today I croak about .. with another lunch to endure in an hours time at the Connaught!

I wail on.

'Walk' has sold 30.000 copies since October 9th .. not bad .. and is now in third edition [...] and I am just on the penultimate chapter of 'A PERIOD OF ADJUSTMENT' ... delivery date 31st January, so I'll probably do it. They asked, my publishers, when the NEXT one was due and what I would be writing about!

Christ!

I shall go back to autobiography ... plenty of stuff left .. and it seems to me that it sells better than fiction. People just love to think that they actually know you! Madness ... But I have a few choice bits in my head about various Critics here .. some now dead .. others not so dead but should be .. and bits and pieces of stuff which can go to make up a sort of 'BACKCLOTH' type of book. Esseys joined together. We'll see.

One thing I cant contemplate is sitting on my butt doing bugger all! Not my style ... I was amused to know that you were dealing with 'So Long At The Fair'. I had a terrible battle to get that role! Rank were determined that I was 'working class only' or 'spiv' and 'thug' or IRA terrorist .. so it was a quantum leap to play a pleasant, if dull, English Aristocrat! Jean [Simmons] and [I] became very close in the working time .. and Rank jumped on that for Exploitation .. Will They Marry? I nearly did propose, her Mama was terribly anxious that we should marry because she feared (with reason!) that her daughter was being besotted by Stewart Granger. She was. And married him and not me. But Rank got their Exploitation stuff and 'So Long' was well and truly launched!

The 'show', since you ask, consists of me by myself. A lectern, a chair, and empty stage, tabs up, one spotlight, and a hand-bag (Carpet bag to be accurate) of selected books ... some mine, others ranging from Belloc, to Keats, Gore Vidal and God Knows Who Else. A rag-bag .. with bits of Victorian poetry chucked in for fun. It works well .. and after about a half hour, forty minutes, I then deliver myself up for Questions. On any subject, and any matter. Thats the hard part!

And by far the most interesting for me. I answer anything as truthfully as possible. Thats the gimmick if you like. And people appear to find that a quite irrisistable thing; and they grow bolder and braver as more people ask things which can, and do, range from Do You Agree with Single Parent Families, Did you have a very 'private' relationship with J. Garland, A. Gardner, etc .. to How can I get information on Voulantry Euthanasia and what do you do about a 'stroke' patient ... amazing things come zinging across the stage! Sometimes I'm there for two hours .. once, Edinburgh, three with NO interval! If they had an interval they'd never come back .. or else come back emboldened by booze .. and I like 'em in my hand!

But I am thinking of packing it in. It is such a business, travelling to and from like a parcle. Norwich one week, Chester the next, Leeds and so on ... I feel that at my age (I shall be 73 in March!) I can take it easier by just letting the books speak for themselves! The new one will be my twelfth. A decent amount, round figure, to stop and consider ..

Forgive my spelling, you are aware that I cant. And with this incipient throat nagging away I am more aware of <u>that</u> than my a's and b's and c's!

Anyway .. I must go off and change for lunch ... let me know how things go on with your Large Grant! One of the questions I am ALWAYS asked is what has become of the British Film Industry? What indeed! I always bring the house down when I deplore Mike Leighs films about abortions and people sleeping in cardboard boxes all over Waterloo Station, and long for the return of elegance, style and Myrna Loy! They yell with agreement .. and the sad fact is that we dont have anyone in the UK left who knows what style is .. or elegance .. or grace .. or how potent 'implied' sex can be, rather than close-ups of bare bottoms and people shoving their tongues down each others throats! Of either sex!

And that reminds me, throat, that it's time to pack this up ..

With best wishes

Ever

Dirk

To Eileen Atkins   *Cadogan Gardens*
                                                        4 December 1993

Eileen dearest –

With all your troubles and tribulations you were more than angelic to write as you have.[1] Thank you.

Words, written words, do linger longer than spoken ones .. and I have lingered over yours this morning with infinate pleasure and comfort.

It was a bit of a bugger to write with no notes or diaries .. and the subject, so to speak, was pretty wretched. I had to read the whole thing, unabridged, for Audio Books a couple of weeks ago and was devestated! Odd ... speaking the words which had been spoken; trying to re-phrase voices from the past in the village ... hospital-songs and so on .. got to me. As they say. Quite silly. But I did a decent job.

Darling: you and Bill did more to help me at a particularly tough time than anyone else. Frankly. I did'nt feel that it was correct to burden my friends with my problems. Something that I had to sort out. But as actors SOMETIMES do, you and I seemed to have a 'coming together', a fluidity of mind and work and your kindness to me all through that glum little saga was inspirational. I knew that Tony was for the chop, but I was determined that he'd not know for as long as I could play the game of 'pretend'. And appear, to him, that all was normal. In that game you colluded with me wonderfully .. and my gratitude knows no bounds. Really. And then after, on those Sundays with Bill and the cats and people coming in and lunch and all ... I began to heal. There was no pressure, no nervousness.

---

1. EA had written to say that *A Short Walk from Harrods* was 'a gem and will be wonderfully cathartic for anyone who has lost someone close to them or indeed lost a way of life'.

Do you know that I actually stayed away from some chums, for a time, for fear they might think I would ask for a job! Christ! How potty can you be? Very, is the answer to that.

So please believe me when I say that you and Bill really did help me to sort myself out by myself. Which is simply what I had to do ..
Cardiff' was a nightmare, frankly, but because you chucked yourself so wholly into the thing, because working together was so relieving and sure, I got on with the 'pretending' and it almost came true!

I cant thank you and Bill enough.

The other evening, capering about on stage at the Olivier to a mass of loving people (with a Wendy Windmill person translating for the deaf. Try that for size!) I did feel that, perhaps, at 73 I had just got through the murk .. and was back into the sun. A good feeling.

But thank you for your letter . . . and for your help .. and for being my friend. I do, really, love you very much indeed . . .

Always – Dirk XOXO

To Brian McFarlane

Cadogan Gardens
19 January 1994

Dear Brian –

Thanks for your long letter .. I am just about clear from Volume No. 12 (Adjustment) which I delivered last month and am now trying to cope with the cover. I do all my own covers because I am, frankly, better than their lot!

I am sad that 'Short Walk' is so horribly delayed.[2] It amazes me how hopeless the British are at business. No gumption at all [...] You'd think they could shove a couple of crates over by air to Sydney, Melbourne and so on. Madness. It, the book, is about what happened when a slight ache became what our beloved village doctor euphamistically said was just a 'touch of Parkinsons' ... when I knew that you could not have just a 'touch' of the dreadful desease. Then Cancer struck, and then the world fell in and I was forced, because of my managers illness, to come back to the UK. And, so far, I am still here! It is, I am told, very sad indeed and people use boxes of Kleenex while they read! Enough already! It has a hopeful ending ... and 'A Period

---

1. The filming of *The Vision* in 1987.
2. In being distributed to Australia.

Of Adjustment', now finished, is the sequel to 'JERICHO' [...]
Now the cover .. and then the next book. I am no longer under
Contract to Rank ... but to Viking! MUCH better. I might try and
have a 'go' at the Critic-Book, we'll see ... cant make a whole book
out of the buggers but it'll make a chapter, that I am certain about.
They are venal here. Pretty bad in the States too ... but then ALL
Britain is awful to me I find.

They are petty minded, mean, spiteful, arrogant, fearful and terrified of anything they think 'foreign' or 'unusual' .... it's all based on
loss of Empire, of course. As well as loss of football powess and
practically every other loss. Cinema included. We are a nation of smug
hypocritics ... and I see no possible change in my life time.

If this tunnel to France really does work, we might see some
amazing disturbance to the smug, complaicency ... but so far the
British feel it is an un-natural thing and not to be considered
seriously at all. I think that because they still have'nt got their
railway working at this end .. and dont know where to put it ...
they long to remain an Island. You can get from anywhere in
Europe now to Calais in a very short time. Until you hit the
Channel ... and then it takes you as long to get to London as it
does to get from Budapest to Calais! Amazing.

When I was a school boy it was Kathleen Hepburn, Claudette
Colbert, Gary Cooper, William Powell, Myrna Loy .. and so on. I
never bothered with British pictures. Tom Walls, Jack Hulbert, and
so on .. they were Servant Girl fodder we thought! And I still dont
give a fig for British Films today. They are'nt real, somehow .. with
Losey it was quite different .. but we never, of course, were Servant
Girl Fodder! There is a startling, brilliant, biography[1] out next week
about him. I am too close, and too involved in it, to review it .. but
wrote a portrait in the Daily Telegraph last Saturday.[2] Caused a minor
stir.

Just wait until they get the book! It is cruel, biased rather, but, alas
a portrait of incredible power. It's called Joseph Losey. The sub-title is
'A Revenge On Life'.* And thats what it is. His widow is hysterical,
with reason, and his son comes to lunch today ... so I'd better get the
table laid.

---

1. David Caute's *Joseph Losey: A Revenge on Life* (Faber & Faber).
2. 'A Genius in Love with Vulgarity' *(Daily Telegraph,* 15 January 1994).

All good wishes for what remains of this year ... and thank you
again for your letter ...

In haste!

<u>Dirk</u>

*P.S. I suggested Dilys P. to review in my place. She accepted – its due
on Saturday. She's 92! <u>D</u>

To David Frankham   *Cadogan Gardens*
                                                       29 March 1994

David, dear fellow –

As birthdays go it was really very good indeed! Your letter arrived
ON the day .. and some 200 other cards from my Readers. They
simply send the letters to 'A Short Walk From Harrods' and they
arrive. To my shock. Most have to be answered. Good P.R work! So
the cost of stamps gets frantic attention from me.

[...] I did'nt get rid of the bloody Labique's[1] ... I only broke down
their door once. After 12 solid hours of practice. Imagine! Those
flouncing bitches clanging away at two pianos without a break! Jeasus
... then when the other people realised that I had complained in rage
they all started complaining and finally they were FORCED to leave
by universal consent. Two giant cranes arrived one morning (Sunday)
big enough to lift a chunk of the Santa Monica Freeway and carted
their fart-arseing pianos off to Switzerland. I now have a plump lady
from the Germany Embassey .. and she does'nt even play a jews-harp.

Well. She would'nt, would she? Really ...

[...] The 'quake'[2] was not a lot of fun I gather. I had chums who
lost a lot and not just cracked swimming pools ... but people do seem
to cope eventually. I LOATH 'quakes' .. I have been in two minor
ones and hope never to have the misfortune of being under, or near,
the Beverly Wilshire Hotel when the next one comes along. Unlikely,
but you never can tell. I am now going to cease this .. and start on
the cards. You ARE a good fellow. Anything you want to ask about

---

1. The concert pianists Katia and Marielle Labèque had been living, with their twin grand
pianos, on the first floor of Dirk's block.
2. An earthquake had struck California in January, killing sixty and making 25,000
homeless.

'HARRODS' I will answer with delight. It has obviously been vastly helpful to a great many people. For that I am deeply grateful .. it makes ones life really worth while and useful! All was not lost!

Ever

Dirk

To John Osborne   *Cadogan Gardens*
                                       19 April 1994

From 269237 –

No, dear Corporal, you are'nt a bit mad.

Yes, it was Amersham. On the hill to be exact. And it was all a hell of a long time ago, and I have not, as you realise, forgotten.[1]

Scalded, I was, by those words. 'Look Back ..' I mean – Elevated, lifted beyond the rubies. Dashed by bloody Earl St John (Boss, then, at Rank) to pieces the week later. But we tried.

Yes too [. . .] my funny Mai Zetterling . . . she was gloriously wanton .. filthy feet every night on that bloody bed.[2] And not always astonishingly un-smelly. Goodness! Her feet were filthy because she spent much of her time barefoot. (One of those ladies. With silver teaspoons as a necklace. And a wandering hand between ones thighs . . .) But she was a good girl. Really.

I last saw her in France. She lived in a sort of goat-shed up a hill, with a pretty (queer) husband and wore lots of leather, and muslin blouses. Smoked like Etna, and was plump and still, oddly enough, Mai.

Then we lost track. She said she'd not like my 'life style .. to[o] po-faced for me. I am a gypsey!' And I felt that her's, with all the goats and the queer husband who 'wrote books', might not be exactly mine. So.

And then the wretched obit. a couple of weeks ago,[3] and one feels ones age.

I loved all of your oeuvre. I love your writing. Your sheer simplicity and blazing audacity. I would have said more and more but was stuck

---

1. Reviewing JO's *Damn You, England: Collected Prose* (Faber & Faber) for the *Daily Telegraph* (16 April), Dirk wrote of their first meeting, when JO brought him a copy of *Look Back in Anger* for consideration by the Rank hierarchy.

2. In *Point of Departure.*

3. Mai Zetterling had died on 17 March.

with '850 words, maximum'. So had to cut it short. I could have been funny (with your stories of playing him) about Shaw. God! That odious Dubedat! I spent three weeks learning the speech to the Doctors, and when I had mastered it I went to Puffin Asquith (Directing) and made him sit and listen to me. Gave a jolly decent perf. He sat imobile. 'Well?' he said sweetly. 'It does'nt make any fucking sense, Puffin!' He shook his head sadly and said, 'Oh my darling Boy, it never has. Not for over eighty years!' But we shot it anyway.

Sort of. Not very funny, really, but I imagine that it was at the time.

This just to thank you, Corporal, for your hand-of-cards[1] and your thanks. Absolutely no need.

Cherished is. And cherished is what your friendship, your work, your amazing splendour in writing, is to me.

Thank you . .

<u>Dirk</u>

To John Osborne   *Cadogan Gardens*
                                       16 May 1994

Dearest Corporal – 229

I reel with delight/horror at your batch of cards. Why do you plague me with perfectly hideous stamps? Surely Salop can do a titchy bit better than that? So far they have not hit Sloany Strasser. Unless I am just using up old stock. Which is how I feel today. I have had the builders and decorators in for twelve days. Imagine the expense! The misery! I have <u>three</u> rooms . . in one of which I presently crouch smothered in books (displaced) china (displaced) piles of unopened mail . . also displaced, and I am miserable beyond endurance. I am amazed that Bragg even knows who I am. He has always been singularly surly when I graced his BBC Thing.[2] Mr Waugh[3] is nice. On the tellyphone anyway, but rather pleads for bits for his magger. Keith

---

1. Postcards of thanks for Dirk's review.

2. Melvyn (now Lord) Bragg presented *Start the Week* on Radio 4. Dirk had more than once been a guest on the programme.

3. Auberon Waugh, editor of *Literary Review*, famous for persuading the great and the good to write for a pittance.

I well remember of old. He adapted, with Willis,[1] 'George Dillon' which I managed to secure for a few months. It was'nt bad as far as I remember. But was a no-no for Rank, ABC and everyone else.

I do hope you got a bit of loot from that transaction? I remember I paid the boys a lot of lolly to write it. They came to a nervous lunch in my posh-palace (It was a bit showy-offy I admit. 42 rooms . . .) and scuttled off to write your piece. I was so frightened of them, the New Young Men, and they were so terrified about being served by a real Butler in white jacket with a silver platter an all, that nothing very convincing was ever going to come out of poor old 'Dillon'. And, as far as I remember, did'nt.

But I did try. It was the only John OSBURNE I could afford. And of course it was 'flawed' as they say . . . you shared the billing I mean. Not pure, [—[2]], J.O. . . . never mind! I did have a shot. Bad luck.

This fucking machine has what is euphamistically called a memory. I dont need it to have a memory. Just to type and not flash lights [at] me and warn me that I have mis-spelled. Jesus! I KNOW that! And I <u>can</u> remember. Well. Most things. Not all. No. I give you that. But most. Essentials, like my address, the price of the evening paper, the name of the girl in Tesco who does'nt sneer and calls me 'SUR'. I'm not that gaga yet. Just feel it.

I read you avidly in the Speccy. And am DELIGHTED that at last people are being nicer to you. About time too. Of course you will find it is something to do with generosity-of-spirit as one grows older. Suddenly they realise, these clever dicks, that there is nothing new and exciting about and that they are in serious danger of missing the trolly at last! Golly! They only now have discovered Hugh Grant (or whatever his name is) and are fussed and put-out that America decided that 'Four Marriages . .'[3] was fun and real and not about Out-Of-Work-Plumbers living under the M4 Fly Over. If you have read the shrug-ging, carping, 'silly little film' stuff they have un-blocked their turgid little minds to swill about, you'd quickly realise how LUCKY you and I have been with the shits! I loath and detest them far more than

---

1. Keith Waterhouse and Willis Hall, whose film script of JO's *Epitaph for George Dillon* was commissioned by Dirk in the early 1960s. An alternative version of the lunch at Drummer's Yard, in the presence of Capucine, is given memorably by Hall in *Dirk Bogarde: The Authorised Biography*.
2. Indecipherable – part of an insertion by hand.
3. *Four Weddings and a Funeral*, directed by Mike Newell.

you ever did . . . and I do read your buks. I am not writing very sensibly on account of Frank (wallpapering) who is singing 'You ARE My Sunshine' for the fiftieth time, and George (hanging a picture-light) singing 'I Belong To Glasgow' for the millionth time. I am beginning to go spare in the head.

I dont think I'd care very much for the Derby Business[1] . . all those horses and huge hats and silly faces . . and I really would not expect you to give me a tingle if you ever did get to Oscars pad. A far too fraught week, and I'd be the one to cause you distress, not you me. I'd be the most awful let down because I really AM dreadfully DULL and ill-read and un-social.

Lets just remain as we are. You cherished beyond anything . . and I your old Army Mate . . . I am busy with a new oeuvre.[2] Picking up mates from the past now dead, alas! It is, can you believe, quite funny. Because they have gone, and apart from their middle-aged children, there is no one to distress. I speak of long-forgotten Colonels, Corporals, Privates . . not Actors and such. The Corporals and Colonels were much funnier. I dont think I remember a really funny actor after Rex [Harrison] and Coral B[rowne] . . . . oh dear! But how lucky to have had them. I MUST stop Frank from another stanza, Chorous, of 'Sunshine'. You see? Tu voir! I can no longer spell . . . I am riven with angst and the stink of wall-paper glue . . but I do send you deepest love and affection. Give my love to the Long Mynde . . I climbed it many a weary time. In full pack and gaiters. Goodness me yes . . . and the Stepier (Stepper?) Stones? and a cherry brandy (dareing) on a freezing afternoon at the Lyggon Arms.[3]

Ever – 269.

To John Osborne

Cadogan Gardens
26 May 1994

Dear 225 –

Rain. Blackness. Misery for three weeks, but the builders have gone. Gone, and left the sodding lift buggered up. You cant 'call' it, there is

---

1. The annual excursion to Epsom organised by the Garrick Club, of which JO was a member.

2. It would become *Cleared for Take-Off.*

3. Sundry landmarks near JO's Shropshire home, as remembered from Dirk's Army training; although the Lygon Arms is in Gloucestershire.

a fuse. So the whole building loath me because the thing is stranded on my floor and I'm on the top, He! He! He! Only I dont feel like that really. It's tough to clamber up five fucking flights with two baskets of goodies and a bunch of flowers plus six nicotiana plants to stick out during this awful Holiday ahead. I bought some Rowantrees Fruit Pastilles, which eases the rage.

I loved your slew of cards .. terrifically good to know that you realise how much you are respected, and loved, by your Peers and, now at last, the Viscious Press.

They have, the Press, pricked you often enough, found themselves proved wrong about everything they said, and now have come to heel. Silly, ghastly, sods.

Unless you actually need the money DONT join them. My Pa, a journalist all his life, was so shamed by what he called 'the fouling' of his profession by the new un-couth that he removed 'Occupation' from his new Passport! At the age of seventy six. I was amused. No longer. I'd rather say I cleaned the shit house than was a 'journalist'. We have both, you and I, met those deceptive little girls with SW1 or SW3 or Chalfont St Giles' accents who seem so pleasing and shit on you from a great height a day or two later. Sad really. Because they need one, one does'nt, (unless just starting and callow) need them! And there are one or two Worthy Ones. Not the cruddy Lynn Barbers and Julie Burchills . . . sneering and fearful and LOCAL! God, so local! But there are a couple who were good, clever, useful even .. but they seem to be swamped now. Barber writes about squirrels and lamp shades (for some reason) and Burchill writes about spleen. She'd not be very good in Time Out now. They are better, ruder, younger, and, without comparisons but learning. Enough. Basta.

I am battering away at the Bakers Dozen of a book. Autobio. They say they sell better than novels; which is boring, because you have to stick to facts.

This new effort is a series of essays remembering a vast range of people (from my first 'mucker'[1]) in the Army, in Normandy in fact, (there is, by the way, never a sexual connatation in the word 'mucker'. It is something hard to explain, and far harder to explain to women. And it aint that god-awful American word, Bonding) to Ingrid B. and Losey and even Kathleen Tynan with whome I have always had a close

---

1. Flt Lt Christopher Greaves.

relationship inspite of the fact that Ken <u>detested</u> me and all that I was. It did'nt bother us! Odd. But gathering all these people together makes one realise, in this silly little office looking out onto a wet Cadogan Street, just how fortunate one has been in life. Anyway: I have. With the very few chums I have had, saved up, and still have. You, for example, speak of trust in your slew of cards. I have never doubted yours for me or mine for you. It is just a fact. Same with Robert F[ox]. A different, younger, chum. But we trust each other. I have, in a modest way, taken over from Robin ... it is tremendously rewarding for me. I only hope it has helped, or been useful, to him. And there are others. I have NO old friends. Well: a couple. But I had to junk them when I got back to the UK for fear of being gobbled up and destroyed. God! They are SO boring sitting waiting to die. I mean, of course <u>I</u> will one day .... but not before I have done everything I want to do. Dont be amazed that people are starting to 'look kindly' on you! They just missed out at the beginning.

I did'nt.

I have always known what true greatness was, and I have always known that you had it in you. So did Graham Sutherland, Henry Moore, Dilys Powell, even Rex Harrison etc, all sorts of odds and sods. Greatness is not given lightly .. not always recognised in a lifetime. Hold on to yours: it's rare; practically un-discovered, and quite the most wonderous thing one can be given.

Lucky old you.

Sorry about the typing .. but at least, if you wish to, you can almost read it!

Love to the Long Mynd –

Ever

Dirk

To John Osborne   *London –*
                                   21 June. '94 (Raining, of course)

Dear 225 (Cpl)

Your splendid, undated, letter flopped onto my mat this am along with a plea to 'Save The Children' (Why the hell should I?) and a card from some firm in Bond Street offering me a 50% cut in their latest furs. Honestly.

But your letter gave me huge pleasure. I have shingles, can you believe, and am sad and miserable and itch and will be in this condition for at least another fucking month. So it's not exactly conducive to a tip tap at the typewriter. I drag about whining softly and read bits of books. Do you know what I mean? Bits. Not whole, proper books. Bits.

Lack of concentration I suppose.

People, in the shops say 'Oh! You look so well . .' little realising the agony I suffer, and that High Bloodpressure is the reason for my ruddy good health. Aint life a bitch?

And you taking 'leave' in the middle of the Big Race![1] Poor H.[2] must fret terribly. I mean, I would. Anyway you got back to Oscars, and that was a relief.

I dont know when you wrote this missive so can only conjecture when you went to the Palace.[3] You DO mean The Palace? Not the one in the Kings Road or on Brighton Pier? What a lark . . . I mean if it was the proper Palace. Rather pleasant in the private quarters, rather awful elsewhere. I think the most terrifying thing I have ever witnessed was the sign at the top of the Grand Staircase which we climbed to get annointed, or whatever it is. It bluntly said Last Gentlemans Lavatory. So you knew that if you missed it it was dribble dribble for two sodding hours . . . more if the Hong Kong Police were being given gongs.

And they were.

Yes: I know that I have the brain of a newt, but Gods Honour I do find it frantically difficult to get a book to actually READ. A jolly good read. I have told J. Coldstream (To whome you do owe a book, by the way, you agreed to review something on Merrick.[4] He's waiting in anguish.) that I wanted 'out' from reviewing. I simply get lost in the welter of 'good writing' and do find it absurdly difficult to like anything. I avoid Ms Brookner, even in the street. I'm trying hard with Hilary Mantell at the moment . . and had a tiny look at the new Julia Blackburn, and Coldstream sent me Andrew Sinclair and I itch more than ever.[5]

---

1. JO had been taken ill – or, as he told Dirk, 'had one of my QUEER TURNS' – at the Derby.
2. JO's wife, Helen.
3. The Osbornes had been invited to a reception at Buckingham Palace.
4. Howard Kissel's *David Merrick: The Abominable Showman* (Applause, NY, 1993).
5. Anita Brookner's *A Private View* (Jonathan Cape); Hilary Mantel's *A Change of Climate*

I am sick to death of aboriginies .. Chatwin did them splendidly but thats enough .. and I dont actually go a huge bundle [on] the Blacks in Seth Efrica; so I have two bum-books here. The Sinclair, with a quite revoltingly common, really common, cover might be possible ... but I am hesitant. I just wish someone would write something I could'nt bear to put down. My last essaies (SP?) in that direction were you and A. Clark.[1] Un-putdownable and greedy-for-more stuff.

But woe is me. All this Brookner, Mantell, Trollop (Aga)[2] stuff swamps me. I did'nt terribly care for Potter. Was deeply embarrassed by what I saw of the Bragg Braggadacio[3] .. I had actually seen all that up close for myself. I saw no point in making a public spectacle of the business. One way, I suppose, of getting your play on? I did'nt care for a lot of his stuff .. 'Singing Detective' was fun, but after that it was showing off because he knew what fuck meant.

He got involved, briefly, with Losey [...] and I begged him, Losey, to re-consider. Pinter was not, I said, Potter.[4]

No way.

V. Common indeed to turn the page, but I have a gentleman coming to lunch and am in a sort of mild 'state' .. you'll have to put up with me.

I am terrifically glad that all manner of people are taking the road to 'blue remembered'.[5] I cant see why you consider it less than your due. You have NEVER been out of fashion, as you say .. never been set aside and forgotten. Your blistering truth has seen to that .. and the Speccy Bits are read avidly. I know that. And no one on God's earth could confuse you with Sir (Jesus!) T. Rice ... I mean who is he? I dont think I could whistle a single thing he's wrote .. can I? And Derek Whatever ... camping about as a Detective Monk![6] Shit ... I

(Viking); Julia Blackburn's *Daisy Bates in the Desert* (Secker & Warburg); Andrew Sinclair's *In Love and Anger* (Sinclair-Stevenson).

1. Alan Clark, whose *Diaries* (Weidenfeld & Nicolson, 1993) had been a triumph.
2. Joanna Trollope, whose work had been identified as pioneering a new genre, the 'Aga Saga'.
3. Channel 4 had screened an interview by Melvyn Bragg with Dennis Potter shortly after the dramatist had been diagnosed with cancer and given a few months to live.
4. The other way round, but we take the point.
5. JO had been visited at his house on the Welsh border by several MPs and journalists. *Blue Remembered Hills* was a 1979 Dennis Potter television play.
6. Sir Tim Rice and Sir Derek Jacobi.

have instructed my lot (Viking) and everyone else I can lay a hand on, NEVER to use my idiotic knighting. I feel so cheap after years and years of trying to get my name known as a <u>player</u>.

It <u>is</u> in Europe .. but here I am less than the worst TV Host-Show-Chap.

Boring ... but I really do prefer being Mr B ... and that is how I am known in the street and the greengrocer or fishmonger ..

'Kept four really lovely scallops for you Mr B ..' shouted across Cale Street gives me infinate pleasure .. We are all, I suppose, snobs of differing sorts. I just did'nt want to be lumbered up with some of these hideious Knights. But I was assured that it would be 'a terrible slight to the PM ... you are his personal choice. Give it a weeks thought .. ?' so I did. Idiot.

[...] I'm off to Manchester (Library or Royal Exchange? I never can recall. It's in the round[1] and was great fun last year ..) then, of all places, Woking who have a new 900 seater Theater (I wont play less!) and then somewhere north, and ending at the Olivier again.

And that'll be that. I do try and flog the goods ... it's harder to write the fuckers.

All great love to you ... did you watch any, or all of D day[2] on the Telly? I was trapped in bed, so lay there for two days blubbing ... what a cunt.

Dont fall about again .. but if you do, try and do it somewhere calm, and not near energetic gentlemen (?) in Wimbledon.[3]

Your very affectionate
   & respectful –
   ~~225~~
No! Thats <u>You!</u>
   I'm 269.

4.15 pm P.S. Gentleman gone, done the washing up, feel filleted and dull, and it is raining and I'm glad I loathe tennis, so will mail this, get the Evening Standard, and crawl off to bed.

---

1. The Royal Exchange Theatre.
2. The fiftieth anniversary of D-Day.
3. Sport was never Dirk's strongest point – its locations even less so.

To Jill Melford   *Cadogan Gardens*
                                                     29 July 1994

Maudie – oh! my love –

I got a letter from that fearful [–] this am saying 'let's be friends'
and she'd like to help me in my campagne to try to stop the building
of a road across the prettiest part of Sussex. Never mind! YOUR
disgusting card, naked-ape-on-beach-at-sunset, arrived at the same
time. So I feel better. Or betterish.

I think I'll put this all down in numbers? Okay? You really HAVE
been away too long. <u>So. No. 1.</u> Yes, ta. Shingles almost all gone. There
are two fucking scabs which wont fall off. Got it? Most tiresome.
When I whined to my Doctor last week he assured me that my attack
was 'medium'. His most recent patient was literally smothered in
blisters and screaming with pain. And she was just ten years old. So I
shut up. At least, as he pointed out, I had not yet asked him for Death
Pills. Apparently it is quite common. I must admit I was ready, at one
time, for the things. I have never in my life been so depressed and
suicidal ... and you actually DO know me! But with this unaccustomed heat, and it has been in the upper 30's .. (that is nudging the
nineties in old fashioned speech) it has [been], <u>is still,</u> difficult to bear.
So, Angel, dont bother to have them. Shingles.

No.2. I have been fairly sotto, naturally, so apart from a huge
luncheon party for Boaty at Bibendum (where I sipped away at the
Evian and made nervous attempts NOT to faint with the heat [...])
and one other lunch, I have remained within the building. Apart from
a very jolly morning when, dressed ONLY in my underpants and
shirt, no shoes, I took the elevator [...] to the hallway below to
collect the Sunday papers. As I slid past my floor I said, aloud and
sadly, 'Oh! Fuck! I've done it. Locked myself out. Keys in pants
pocket.' So. What to do? Sloane Street on an early Sunday morning?
No money, no Filofax .. no bugger all, but bare, bare, little feet. So
along I troll to Partridges. Well: where else? I know that they bake all
Saturday/Sunday night.

Knocked frantically. Was let in amidst huge laughter, and we called
999. I begged the very clinical lady not to send round a HUGE fire
engine with ladders and blue lamps (it was still only about eight am)
and she said where was I? and what was my name? and when it was
all given she simpered with sweetness and said had I seen myself on

TV the night before (and the night before that, frankly. A two part documentary) and anyway before I could get back bare-foot the engine had arrived, and pulled up noiselessly and no blue lamps and five quite ravishing young firemen who thought it was all the 'gas' of the week! They assured me that they'd just come off a 'job' in Leytonstone, twenty story block, huge fire, all 'spades', forty badly burned and 'one silly fart got so fucking hysterical she just jumped from the thirtieth [*sic*] floor and cut herself in two on the balcony railings below. What a fucking mess!'

They were as jolly as clockwork clowns, and since they could only work IN the lift (it was the front door) we all sat about in the hall reading the Sunday papers until the two of them forced the lock. It took them forty five minutes. And they ripped open the door to do it. Great.

Laughing and joking, my particulars were taken down, date, time, place, and it was pointed out that a 'modest Call Out', was £180, to discourage the Yuppie piss-pots in the area, but I was certainly not a Yuppie, so could I give them my date of birth? I did, with relief . . I did'nt care how aged I was. But what was marvellous was that I did'nt have to pay a farthing because I was, 'Well over the age, Dirk . . well over . .' So they all got a tenner apice and I was left with an open door. Until Tuesday. They dont actually repair the damage. Never mind. I now wear two sodding keys on a vastly expensive chain round my neck AT ALL TIMES. If we ever do meet again and you think that I am bowed down with sadness or some ghastly form of arthritis, remember: it's two heavy keys only. So far.

The heat here has, really, been marvellous and too much all at the same time. I mean, you sort of expect it in Palm Beach or Cannes . . but not in Cadogan Gardens. Sweating away at night is hell. I am barefoot from morn to night, and so are all the peasants in the street. If it ever occurred to you that the British Middle Class were UGLY UGLY you were absolutely right. Come and see them wobbling along Sloane Street, The Fulham Road, the Kings Road, or slumping about at those hideious little pavement cafe's we suddenly invent. Christ! There is no one pretty alive here . . . they are all sickeningly plain, fat, ill-dressed, and junk-fed. But, I suppose, so are the Americans? A terrible woman, with ghastly teen-aged son wearing a sort of divided skirt with a baseball cap and a tee-shirt covered with 'Free O. Sullivan!' on it, asked me how to get to Harrods. I told her, and could'nt resist saying that it was a very long walk, and that if the young man with her was also going, they would'nt be admitted. <u>She</u> was in a sagging bra, sneakers, and patterned shorts. She asked, quite politely if Harrods was 'like Buckingham Palace?' or some place. Was'nt it just a <u>store</u>? Like Bloomingdales? And I had to say No, not quite. They have regulations. And she said that the Americans had Fought For Democracy and she was going up to Harrods. Which she did. I could'nt blame her really, but they are a dreadful lot. So are we, I gather, in Greece and Italy ... oh well ... [...] A lady below, Flat No 2, has ripped it all out and re-furbished it to a most alarming degree. Quite splendid if it was on the top with a view, but it's the one on the right, facing the street and north, and is hell!

She is, presently, asking £300.000. Wow.

[...] Stella[1] and I continue our incestious affair. She cooks for me (impossible) nasty little crème brulé things, and I give her bits, aching with garlic which make her eyes water and force her to say, 'Well dear. You DO like spicy food. I make do with a leaf of bay ...' So you can imagine how we cook! She sews brilliantly, irons marvellously, and leaves the Jiff in the most impossible places. But we get on terribly well and I love her, and she said last week that she only wished that she had had 'this sort of life forty years ago. I'd have been a much happier woman!' So I did'nt say anything and went on typing. Well .... what else?

And thats it. My family well, squabbling, the usual. The heat goes on, I went by car, with Brock (who was invited) to Daphne Baths-Fielding birthday lunch which Alexander Bath[2] gave for her at Longleat. Only thirty of us, her 'most loved friends'. She was ninety! Brock and I were the only two commoners present. All the Dukes and Duchesses of G.B were crammed into Bishop Kents' Library .. and Alexander, naturally, had a Mexican Peasant Band playing all morning and hitting sticks and bongo-drums and dancing bare foot. <u>All through</u> lunch. When Daphne sweetly and sadly, said 'Alexander! I cant hear a single word my guests say to me!' He just beamed and said 'Fuckin' bad luck Mum!' .. and that was that. It was a long, hot, journey on the M4 ... Like shingles, I dont think [I'll] bother to do it again!

Too hot & sweaty to write more – but <u>do</u> come home soon?

Love. <u>D</u>. XOX

---

1. Dirk's latest housekeeper.
2. Alexander Thynne, 7th Marquess of Bath, and DF's eldest son.

To David Frankham   *Cadogan Gardens*
                                                              26 August 1994

Dear David –

It really was splendid to get such a huge letter from you! Apart from your hideious adventures with steak, and selling up AGAIN (Will the boy never settle?) it was all about me. Which, of course I enjoy disgracefully. To start with (we'll come to the steak in a minute) I had an absolute ball doing the 'Widow'.[1] It seemed such a potty thing to do .. but, after all, if Glyndebourne ask you, you would be foolish, and churlish, to refuse! We did four shows in the awful Festival Hall .. and one supreme one in the vast (5,000 seater) new concert hall in Birmingham. That was a riot. We sold out months in advance and it felt like it. But EMI did'nt record there. They felt it would'nt 'take off'. So when we got to London, trailing clouds of glory and appeals for a repeat, or repeats, they decided to mike the thing. But, quite properly, NOT the commentary. Which is why I am off mike! I understood this perfectly, and it was all arranged easily. BUT. The show is not long enough without a commentary, either for the disc or for the Concert Hall ... so they re-instated me, to my dismay .. I had not 'voiced' for CD. There is a marginal difference.

Anyway it was a wild success as you probably gather. The Princess Alexandra and sundry small Royals all trolled in in T shirts and jeans (It was a hot night, informal, and they did'nt want to alert our disgusting and dangerous press). Mr and Mrs Major snuck in too .. and various, what we all call here, 'Luvvies' of varying caliber.

I must say that standing in the middle of a very big orchestra, with a huge chorous (SP?) was at first un-nerving to say the least. And Franz[2] was cold and very distant .. he did NOT approve of Stoppard or me interrupting his musicians. But, five minutes in, I saw him leaning in the podium laughing .. so was Felicity[3] and so was Tom .. and from there on in we all played <u>together</u>! Hugely delightful.

Franz has handed in his resignation and leaves, next year, to take

---

1. In July 1993 Dirk had given the narration, written by Tom Stoppard, at four concert performances of *The Merry Widow* by Glyndebourne Festival Opera in Birmingham and London. A recording had now been released as a double-CD (EMI 5 55152 2).
2. Franz Welser-Möst, who conducted the London Philharmonic Orchestra and the Glyndebourne Chorus.
3. Dame Felicity Lott.

over Zurich. The London Critics have flayed him alive .. too young ... to Austrian .. to everything negative. Now that he is leaving they are appalled and grovelling and had 'discovered' him in the 'Widow'! I ask you! I hope he does piss off, he's terribly nice and brilliant I think. He's a child .. and slim and pretty and that can NOT be forgiven by our mealy-mouthed critics who expect every conductor to look like Beecham ... ah well ..

Funny that you could find 'Daddy'. I think it is one of Taverniers best films and I am very glad I chose to 'go out' on that.

Otherwise I might have ended up like [Jack] Nicholson or [Kevin] Costner who are now (here) being turned against! Typical.

All my dialogue with Jane was ad-libbed and written by me! Need you ask ... the original dialogue was ghastly. Full of 'Pussykins' and 'Pattykins' and 'Daddy's little angel'. He was written, originally, as a much older man. So I switched that and made him a bit of a shit. More fun that way ... we did the famous car scene months later after the rough-cut. In a parked car, with black velvets and some 'rain' sprinkled on the windscreen. The film lacked a punch. So I was forced to write the scene, in bed here with flu! and fly to Paris and do it months later <u>inside</u> because I had a temperature of 102. Amazing what you can get up to in fillums!

[...] I am now on another bit of Bio ... just using up things I did'nt dwell on last six times! It's working title is 'Cleared For Take-Off' but I might change that later. Viking like it, the book so far , , so we'll see. Glad you saw the 'Damned' again. I'd love to see it ... it really was based entirely on fact. [...]

The locations, and the great house, were all for real ... thats why it cost so much money. I got cut to shreds but was given DIV as a consolation prize so I dont complain. Forget Listz ... I dont even mention it in my Concerts. <u>All</u> recorded, by the way, but I dont want them released. They belong to the National anyway really:[1] and run two to three hours[2] [...]

I am shocked beyond belief that you choked! I nearly did in a chic resturant called Bibendum, but managed to cope ... Emlyn Williams'

---

1. Since the early 1990s the National Theatre has kept in its Archive a recording of all Platform performances on its various stages.
2. Dirk's 'concerts' tended to last about ninety to a hundred minutes; the book-signings afterwards were known to exceed that.

funny wife, Molly, did'nt. She croaked at the Ivy on a piece of . . . . .
steak! So watch it . . keep to expensive gruel.

[. . .] I have to go, next month, to be Host at the Best Young
European Musician Award.[1] Very prestigeious . . and Princess D. will
be there, if she's not in the bin, then it's the Olivier to open the Tour
of the book [. . .] I think I will make this the last one. I have, after
all, twelve books to my credit, and I really, at seventy four, dont feel
like proving ANYTHING!

I've been rather ill since May with a bad bout of shingles which, in
turn, led to a peculiar heart problem. Not at all pleasing. It has been
specialists and so on and massive pills and inhalers at GIGANTIC
cost . . . getting better now otherwise you'd have had to do with a post
card! But to be able to walk . . . and breath . . again is marvellous. And
I HAD to get better because everywhere, even the Olivier, is S.R.O.
You really cant 'pull' the National!

I must go now and get some work done. Thanks again . . dont buy
the book. I'll send you one as soon as Bank Holiday (Monday) is
over.

Be careful how you masticate . . .

Ever

   Dirk.

To David Frankham   *Cadogan Gardens*
                                             31 October 1994

Dear David –

Halloween! But thank God we dont do a thing about that in
England.[2] The Scots and Irish go potty . . we sort of hang about until
November 5th and burn Guy Fawkes instead. [. . .] My ageing body
has been going through hell since May and shingles . . . that was a six
month stint and left me, when it finally did leave me, only a month
or so ago, with a 'fluttering heart'. The bloody thing was out of kilter
and raced along like a mad clock. Exhausting, sometimes frightening,
very depressing as well! I kept on wondering if this was IT. Like the
Big One in L.A.

Mercifully we got it under some kind of control with filthy pills

1. The National Power World Piano Competition.
2. Those were the days!

which gave me TRIPLE vision . . . however I had the Tour to do, and did it. Very tiring. But ultimatly successful [. . .] Sold lots of books, which is the idea, did a whacking S.R.O at the Olivier and collapsed with fucking flu! I ask you!

I finished the last anti-biotics yesterday and am now a weak, shaking, old man, and loathing the sights of Christmas which, can you believe it, are already on show in Peter Jones, Harrods and etc . . . it is all so hideious, expensive and as you know OUR holiday here lasts from the 24th until the end of the first week of January. No wonder we are in the shit. Really: no wonder.

The book has done well . . . Best Seller lists in the first four weeks, and then slid about a bit . . . but there is a terrific amount against me. Alan Bennets super book,[1] to start with. [. . . Viking] are v. happy, and I don't exactly feel sad. But the 'sex' in 'Period' has fussed some of my steady readers! So I think some will shy away from the thing. They only like autobiography 'all about YOU and your house.' See? Oh well . . . another on the way, and Viking have taken it. Thank God. It gives me something to do in the winter days . . and by Golly! They are long here as you may remember. However I have been the happy posessor of TWO books at the same time in the Lists. Gratifying. Although, of course, I am not known in the Literary World. Far too grand for me, and I manage to avoid them at all costs. So bloody precious and silly. I had enough of that when I was an actor . . I am SOOOOO glad I'm out of that scene! If you could see what they are doing to K. Branagh and his missus and his Frankenstien[2] . . . . it opens in L.A first (wisely) which enrages the British. But they did'nt give a toss for Four Weddings . . . and loathed Romantic Summer[3] (or whatever it was. The one with old Blowright and the other ladies in an Italian villa in 1920) . . so Branagh is wise. All made here, all English Technicians, all English players (save de Nero) and a Hollywood opening with the P. of W. in attendance. And we are sullen with fury and have put him, and her, through unutterable hell in the Press. I dont think you have ever seen a real Tabloid, have you? They did not exist when you lived here. They were comic papers in comparison to

1. Dirk's *A Period of Adjustment* faced competition from, among other new titles, Bennett's *Writing Home* (Faber & Faber).

2. Branagh directed *Mary Shelley's Frankenstein*, in which he starred with his then inamorata, Helena Bonham Carter, and Robert de Niro.

3. Presumably *Enchanted April*, directed by Mike Newell.

even the worst you can summon in the U.S. I did a big show, European
Pianist of the Year (Young, All under thirty) at the Festival Hall. When
I say I did it, I mean that I introduced it. Princess D. is patron, and
actually arrived! When I came to introduce her the whole Festival
Hall exploded with delight. She ADORES all that. Worse than
Garland! I must say she is radiently lovely, clever, a bitch, and knows
exactly how to play the house. Poor Charles, a really decent man,
has'nt a chance in hell with her. [. . .] Enough gossip.

But that evening at the Festival Hall there must have been three
hundred photographers on ladders, standing round the stage door
from ten in the morning, waiting. And she was'nt due until 6.45 that
evening! It's all madness. No mention, <u>at all</u>, of the pianists, or the kid
who won (Russian, from Tashkent, 21, and brilliant[1]) or the reason
for her presence. Just headlines, '<u>Is she sad?</u>' '<u>Wearing Last Years Dress</u>'
or '<u>Business As Usual In Split Family</u>'.

It really makes me feel ill. I wish I was fit enough to crash off and
go back to France. Writing about it is the only way I can keep close
to it now.

[. . . M]ost reviewers now dislike the fact that I get on the List,
have written twelve successful books, and Sell Out at every theater I
go to. They never, therefore, give you a pat on the back and deliberatly,
as this Sunday, avoid any mention of one at all! Quite clever to
mention everyone, but me, reviewing Death In Venice! I dont honestly
care, but realise that I am now set-aside quite happily. Anyway, the
really good news is that the specialist (how I detest Harley Street!) on
Friday said 'Want to hear the good news? You wont have to have an
Op. It's sorted itself out on the tablets.' Which left me weak with
antibiotics and delight. The Op. in question is not huge fun. They
stop your heart for a moment or two and then re-jig it. Or something.
Not mad about the idea. However, so far, all is well.

'Cast A Dark Shadow' sometimes surfaces here at the N.F.T .. but
rarely .. and it really was'nt a bad little film. I have been watching
quite a lot of TV now that I have suffered a temporary (cross fingers)
strickening! I never do normally, but have been rather forced this trip.
Caught up on some really weird old films .. not of mine .. of all sorts,
and seen a few that I missed years ago. I have a gigantic (for the size
of my flat) Bang and Olfsen thing. Super, and splendid for selected

---

1 . The nineteen-year-old Yevgeny (Eugene) Mursky, from Uzbekistan.

Videos ... awful for crooked politicians, you can see the hairs in their nostrils quivering with fear! Very off putting.

[...] Now I must get down to some readers mail ... I get a lot at this time of the year. New book, Tour ended. One woman wrote the other day and said that she had sobbed all the way through 'Harrods' so that her husband had to take the book away from her. She found it so distressing to read about 'your darling dogs' .. I ask you! The end of a friendship, fifty years, terminal cancer, the loss of my farm, a stroke ... and all she sobbed about were the sodding dogs! <u>They</u> were lucky. Did'nt know a thing. Are'nt people odd? I have had a mass of letters all saying the same thing: 'how <u>terrible</u> for you to have to kill your <u>sweet</u> Bendo' or whoever. Shit-aroo ...

Off now. Rain raging down, leaves falling like playing cards, drains swelling and spilling ... ah well! Tomorrow is November ...

Thanks for clippings –

& letter

<u>Dirk.</u>

To Helen Osborne   *Cadogan Gardens*
                       2 February 1995

Helen dear –

You were'nt supposed to write back.' I said so specifically. However you ignored me and I'm glad.

I was devoted to him, as I hope he knew. The strange thing is that I dont remember that we ever met again, after that initial amazing treck he made up the drive in pouring rain with 'Look Back' sodden in his hand. But we seem never to have eased away. Laterly we had huge fun with daft letters, and post-cards (boast-cards really!) and I was always promised a 'tingle' when you arrived at 'Oscar Wilde'.

Never mind. Thats how our friendship was .. uncluttered.

I wanted so much to come up with Robert and Edward,[2] but I'd have been a problem to them ... I have to pee every so often on long journeys by car, and that irritates everyone. Especially on the motor way. But I did want to be there. Very much indeed.

<u>Dont</u> get soppy. I know you wont. Those foul idiots will keep your

---

1. John Osborne had died on Christmas Eve.
2. Fox, who had offered to take Dirk to Osborne's funeral in Shropshire.

bile rising, cringing Wesker and Crighton.[1] Christ! How the ravens collect. Not even good big vultures. Just ugly black creatures.

We have'nt met, you and I, since (I think) Tunisia![2] In that house on the beach one dark night. So do give me a 'tingle' if you want to, and come up here and have a drink. I'm only yards away from Oscar.

My love, and courage to you . . .

Ever

Dirk.

At John Osborne's Memorial Service in London on 2 June, Dirk read from Jeremy Taylor's Holy Dying. *A notice outside St Giles-in-the-Fields declared that the following would not be admitted: 'Fu Manchu' (Sir Peter Hall), Nicholas de Jongh, theatre critic of the* Evening Standard, *Albert Finney and 'The Bard of Hay on Wye' (Arnold Wesker).*

To Helen Osborne   *Cadogan Gardens*
                                           3 June 1995

Helen dear –

Gosh. I bet you are whacked. I hope you are in some safe haven and being cossetted (SP?) or just ignored as you might wish.

It was a very splendid day, and you behaved quite marvellously.

It is'nt at all easy. But perhaps the overwhelming sense of love and affection and, perhaps above all, respect, that filled that pretty little church might have comforted you? I pray that it did.

It was all so beautifully, I said to Roberto [Fox] 'seamlessly', ordered and so moving without being at all maudling or soppy.

I hope you were pleased. At least about that part . .

I pissed off sharpish because I had to write an Appreciation, can you believe, for my beloved Dilys Powell who has, I have just been informed, died an hour ago. So I barely got myself sorted out . .

Good job you dont get champagne at Memorial Services. I'd have been well away. Thank you Helen dear. I know the road you walk, been that way not so long ago. It's not a lot of fun: but if you are

---

1. Arnold Wesker and Anthony Creighton, who had commented disobligingly following Osborne's death.
2. HO, then Helen Dawson and working for *The Observer*, had visited the location of *Justine* in 1968.

tough-minded, as you and I both are, it is possible to heal. Well, after a while. And in a 'sort of' way. It'll come, promise you. Meanwhile we never got to have our drink: perhaps we can do that when things are not so pressing and wretched and everything.

I'm pretty well always here, and if you are at Oscars it's a short walk . . . just holler . . .

With my love and admiration . .

Ever <u>Dirk</u> X

To Jill Melford   *Cadogan Gardens*
                                          24 August 1995

Dearest Maud –

I hope you are not in a mental home. I am very near that state. I got your lovely card with the seagrapes . . and cant really reply at length because I am whacked, and YES! I have been in 'the middle of a chapter'. So I'll do a sort of resume in one-line moments of delight.

I burst a vein in my 'good leg' and am in consequence swollen up and in a degree of discomfort. I mean, I cant really walk. Well: I got to the Bank this morning. Basta. No one cares, they all smile knowingly and mutter about my age. I hate the lot of them. My sister [. . .] said that when it happened to her her foot went blue. Had mine? I said blueish. She said it wont go for at least six months.

[. . .] I have started another book (what else do I do? Now I cant even walk to the gents Department at P.J?) and there has been a titchy little booklet, four inches by four, sixty pages, sixty pence, to celebrate the 60th year of Penguin. We are all, well most of us, are on the list. I am proud to say that my effort, little scraps called 'From Le Pigeonnier' (bits of Harrods) is right up there with Auralius, Paglia,[1] Woolf and Plato. I sold 100.000 copies in the first two weeks. No one cares of course, I am 'film star', but at least I did make the listings. Could'nt not with that haul. I dont get much in the way of Royalties . . . not expected . . I was happy to be included in the exhalted list.

[. . .] My beloved old (92) chum Daph wrote today . . '. . the things I have loved most in my long and lucky life have been Reading, Riding, Rejoicing, and Rogering. In that order. All that now remains

---

1. Marcus Aurelius and Camille Paglia.

is Reading'. Dont you think thats pretty game? Her eyesight is now on the blink and blindness threatens. Oh dear, oh dear.

We have, for 28 days, sweltered under a cloudless sky. Glorious for you and I but disaster for the British. They all behave as if the Second Coming was being announced. Perhaps it is? Gardens have dried up, lawns are brown, trees shedding leaves, and water is being rationed here and there. Not London.

It's not hotter, and as nasty really, as New York in August. And as humid. But the British wilt and jam the roads and beaches and complain and HAVE TO BE the MOST UN-CHIC people on the streets. If you could see the floppy shorts, the brown socks and sandles, the shapeless florals, the red necks and arms, the sweat under those arms, the STENCH of them at the check-out ... SHIT!

It's cooler today .. 75°. But on Monday it was 96° in the hall here and all the lemons in the 'decorative' bowl on the table shrivelled up like marbles.

I did too ... sleeping at night was horried. Is horried. Wet throat and rumpled bed. But I dont whine away like the others, even if my Milk Tray has melted into a solid block of squidgy, nasty, oozing nuts and stuff. Ugh.

Stella is very well, she says her basement flat is cool, and if she did'nt come to work for me she'd do away with herself. 'Whats the point in me otherwise? I'd have no one to care for and no one would care for me.' So I did'nt sack her. Finding the Jif IN my bed is tiresome. But I just lift it out. No fuss.

We had VJ day. Ages of it. I kept reeling back with shock to think that I was ancient as the old sods marching. I am too. It was all very well done and very moving in it's descretion. No [...] Vera Lynn or that capering capon Sir Cliff [Richard] ... just the bands and ENORMOUS crowds. Never seen so many .. the Queen almost human for once, and standing for over two hours as everything marched past from Prince Phillip (!) to a scatter of 1939 taxies .... but it was a good day. Thank God it's all over now. Until the next lot.

It's frankly been too hot to go anywhere much. Have'nt set foot in the Connaught or Bibendum for over two months ... I hate the tourists .. most of all the Japanese. They, incidentally, fled on VJ day, I really cant blame them, the hate was palpable. But I have to record

tomorrow, in a small and air conditioned studio, off Shepherds Bush. A selection of bits from all the Bios on filming. Should'nt take long. I did the WHOLE of Death In Venice, a literal translation from the German by a professor at Oxford,[1] in a day and a bit. Did'nt understand a word, dear. Not a word. Nor did they in the control room. We even had a crib-sheet to help us pronounce the words in English! I ask you. It'll rock Pinner and Sidcup to the very foundations. I'm going out to lunch with Simon [Hopkinson] at Bibendum. He asked me to join an elegant luncheon party. Why not? It's for free.

[. . .] Someone asked me the other day why I did'nt pack it in and have 'a lovely holiday' . . . I wondered vaguely where the lolly would come from if I did!

[. . .] just <u>you</u> come home.

And soon!

Your devoted mate

Dirk XXX

To Christine de Pauw   *Cadogan Gardens*
12. Mars.'96

Chere Christine –

Thank you for your charming letter, which brought back so many (too many!) memories. At least the photographs did.

It is clear that you and Alain have worked a miracle at the house, and it must be large enough, now, for all the family! Do you remember the very first day you saw it, and decided to buy it, that you also were a little worried 'about where all the children' would sleep? You, or was it Alain, said 'Oh! we'll put them on shelves.' So perhaps that['s] what you did!

But please, and <u>do</u> understand gently what I say, please dont send me any more photographs. Every time I see Clermont it breaks my heart.

I love what you have done, and admire your good taste, but it is still full of 'phantomes' for me. So many years of 'remembering', so many people on the terrace, so many dogs (You must have found some!) and such a very different life to this I now live, saddens me. I try to forget, but I suppose at 75 (which now I am!) one seems to

---

1. David Luke.

remember more. I am just so happy that it belongs to you: I pray you will remain happy and contented there.

Dear Christine, thank you, and very
much love . . . .
Dirk X

To Susan Owens
(Postcard)   *Cadogan Gardens*
                                                    1 April 1996

Dearest S.O.

It[1] was a very strange day! 375 cards & letters – and more flowers than a Jewish funeral. They now start to stink! Off to the sink & Fairy Liquid!

Thank you & love DB

Dominique Lambilliotte, a Parisienne who had worked in publishing, began writing to Dirk after she had read, and been much moved by, A Short Walk from Harrods *in 1995. His initial and characteristically cautious replies, on postcards, developed with this letter into what became his final, all-too-brief 'particular friendship'.*

To Dominique Lambilliotte   *[Cadogan Gardens]*
                                        Good Friday. [5th] April. '96

How can I chide you! Apart from the fact that you are persistant, and one usually has to give in to that! Like flood water . . . I was ravished by the book.[2] Thank you.

Of course it made me wildly nostalgic and, to some extent, sad .. I knew it so well ... from the first moment that I stepped into the terrace through the great door I was lost in delight. It never changed. And that must have been 1950–51 I suppose. We had no money. The 'allowance' was £25 for whatever one did. No Hotel du Cap! No lunch at the Colombe either. A drink at a table and Titine suggesting that one stayed for lunch. I told her it was

---

1. His seventy-fifth birthday.
2. *La Colombe d'Or at Saint Paul de Vence* by Martine Buchet; photographs by Prosper Assouline (Editions Assouline, 1993).

impossible, she suggested with enormous logic (French) that we ordered the hors d'ouvre ... that would make a perfect lunch for three and not cost much .. and we did, and I never stayed anywhere else all the time I travelled in France. When she died I took a big pot of pink (all that I could buy) flowers of some kind, and placed them on her white tombe in the churchyard. I visited her always, until I had to leave. The kindness of the Roux family to me was extraordinary. I was gradually 'absorbed' into it. A glorious feeling. Friends, not 'Clients'. I imagine they are the same today. But I have never gone back, and never will. Finish is finish.

So it was pleasurable to see the pool again and remember how we all helped dig it out of the cabbage-patch of the house next door! And the painting! The arrival of that particular green instead of hideious turquoise was greeted with horror by most, with delight by those who had done it so brilliantly.

For that, thank you.

You might not have liked the Asquith Diaries ... but I am sad about the corrected version (?) of 'Chips', he was SO loathsome ... it must have taken a lot of editing, a lot, a lot .... what a pity! Actually the Gladwyn Diaries (Jebb)[1] was amusing in it's snobbery. But she was not a fool and, I'm told, a good Ambassadress. We had need of one after the Coopers[2] ...

I should, respectfully, drop the word 'sneering' from your extensive vocabulary. It is something I have never done and I detest it in others. So must you.

'Victim' was courageous. I was noted for that! Idiots .. it was a very dull little film which I perked up with a good scene between the husband and wife when I admitted to wanting the boy in question.

It caused a HUGE shock in the UK .. got the film banned in the US and brought me sacks of thankful Fan Letters. The contrary to what they all believed would happen. I was determined to break the Fan-Worship thing I'd got into. It did that, but a more adult one came in. They are now my 'Readers' .. because after 'Victim' I was gradually taken seriously, thank God!

---

1. DL had read *A Particular Friendship*, in which Dirk mentioned the published diaries of both Lady Cynthia Asquith and Sir Henry 'Chips' Channon. She had also been given those of Cynthia Gladwyn, wife of Gladwyn Jebb, Ambassador to Paris 1954–60.
2. Duff and Diana Cooper.

I dont think that I care a great deal for Fiona Shaw[1] .. rather a lot
of noise. Unlike today. Brilliant sun, cool wind, London gloriously
dead. Where DO they all go? The airports are busting .. off to some
hideious Canary Island.

Some weeks ago, the end of January to be exact, I suddenly felt a
bit strange .. I was putting in my cuff-links ready to go to some
wedding. So I went to bed and stayed there for a week. Odd. I was
perfectly happy, I read a great deal, ate nothing, had my scotch at six
and a beer at noon. And slept. My 'bonne'[2] (who died yesterday of
cancer .. what a world ...) made me dreadful creme camarels (for
nourishment) and I just sat, or lay. Happy, as I say, but helpless.

Finally I got my Dr to come round one evening, and he said nothing
was physically wrong but (he knows me for years . . . twelve or fourteen)
I might have had a mild breakdown. Some days before the wedding I
was off to attend, my Editor, Fanny, was sacked with no reason, by
the American Boss of Viking. His excuse was that she did not put
enough 'in put into the Firm'. She was wrenched away from me, in
the middle of a difficult book, and banished. I was expected to stay. I
have been their top best seller for eight years. Since I joined them. I
think that loosing her was the final straw. I lost my land in France,
my whole life there; there was a hideious period in Paris trying to find
somewhere to live, back to London (hateing, hateing) cancer and the
awful Parkinsons, and finally this flat and total, relieved in a way,
solitude. Everyone said how courageous I'd been! (Again this word)
to start a new existance and write. I wrote successfully, with Fanny to
guide me as Editor, until that dreadful day at the end of January. She
was sacked two days before Christmas. She has three small boys [...]
Tough. This saga, the Dr thought finally 'found me out'. The strength
I had tried to keep was taken by the simple removal of my Editor.
Does this make any sense to you? It does, in a strange way, to me. All
is well now. Fanny was permitted (can you believe the vileness) to
remain and 'edit you from home', but it did'nt work. I hated it. I
wanted to get back into the House. So I sacked Fanny! She had cleared
off to Hanoi on a trip ... and I have new editors, and am back in the
House which is what I absolutely need. Security. I am a Company

---

1. Fiona Shaw was playing the title role in the National Theatre production of *Richard
II*, which had toured to Paris.
2. Stella, Dirk's *bonne à tout faire*.

Man ... from the Army (six $\frac{1}{2}$ years) to the Rank Film people, (18 years) to Chatto and Windus and finally to Viking. And so one goes on fighting. I have picked up my pen again, in a metaphorical manner, and the book[1] has lurched ahead.

My very best birthday present was a letter from Viking to say that I had sold OVER a million copies of my 12 books in paperback and that was very rare. I agree. I only got them all in Penguin (they bought all the earlier titles) six years ago. So over a million in six years gives me joy. It pleased them too ... as indeed it should.

So that was how I drifted into my seventy fifth year. If I am secretive that was the one thing I could not hide ... but I refused TV and Radio and all the tra la la that goes on .. but could'nt dodge the flowers and cards ... after 250 I gave up counting and binned the lot. They go to be recycled somewhere. A comforting thought.

Now you see what persistance gets you. I do not apologise .. it is a Holiday and I cant be bothered to pick up the book again.

Could'nt write you an admonishing card because my handwriting has gone crazy ... thats a bore. That is, I fear, the result of a small, tiny, stroke? Ah well ... you have to expect that .. I'm an old man now!

With thanks for nostalgie –
    <u>DB</u>.

To Dominique Lambilliotte   *[Cadogan Gardens]*
                                              Good Friday. No.2[2]
                                              30 April 1996

The last day of April. Lilac everywhere, tulips in the window boxes, leaves starting on the trees .... and I have been spared to see another spring! Amazing. On Sunday I had to go down to the studios where I started my career in early '48. A curious feeling. I was required to unveil a plaque to a series of funny (?) films I had made there from '50 to '70.[3] I took no part in the latter ones, I had long since backed off. But I was the one to open the curtains. A gruesome experience.

---

1. *Closing Ranks.*
2. Not exactly, but it was another Bank Holiday weekend.
3. The British Comedy Society had initiated a commemoration of the 'Doctor' films at Pinewood.

Everyone was there either dying on their feet or dead already, or pretending to be 'young'. Which is objectionable.

I was looking in a mirror really! People who had been jolly and young with a future apparently before them, with whom I worked and drank were all there in elastic stockings and carrying sticks!

I felt humbled and horrified. I knew then that I was now 'old' .. the newspapers, which I avoid like dandelion wine, call me 'Veteran'.

I dont know which is worse. But inside, inside you see, I know that I am <u>really</u> sixteen. And the image which the mirror portrays does not in the least match the image of 'me' which I prance about with before entering a room or taking my seat in a restaurant. Hell! [. . .] On May 15th I go to meet 'our' President. Poor man will be in London for some official reason. The French Consul has invited five or six 'French-English' to meet him. For a 'cup of tea'! at the Consulate. I am delighted to go ... the last President I met was De Gaulle in '45 and he was'nt the President. Then came the others and amazing Claude Pompidou, and I had to leave during Mitterand's office. He liked me in 'Death In Venice' I gather: which is probably why I received my promotion to Commandeur. I'm more proud of this than ANY-THING I have.

Is'nt that strange.

I am struggling with this wretched book ... it has a worrying theme which slightly worries Viking/Penguin. The forced repatriation of the Cossacks and White Russians to the Russians across the river Duro in Austria. In 1945. We valient British promised to repatriate them to Italy. We cheated and sent them home. Home! My God! They were all instantly massacred. A not delicious story. It will upset a lot of idiots who are 'proud to be Brit.' This ugly word, 'Brit', was coined while I lived abroad. It shocked me when I heard it first. In, can you guess? Monte Carlo, when I opened a theater there for Princess Grace. I was called 'a brit', Edwige Feuillier (SP?) was the 'frog' and Vivica Lindfors an 'Eyetye'.[1] Oh the elegance . . . . . . (Dots. What else?)

Yes: I found another 'bonne' [Lily]. Nice little child (I think) black as a witches cat, comes from Abyssinia . Or somewhere about. Maybe Somalia. Works hard, speaks perfect English, and is jolly. She is fairly lost about what I do. Writing is not something that comes easily to her imagination I feel. It does'nt come easily to mine either.

---

1. He meant Valentina Cortese, not Viveca Lindfors.

I should talk.

But for the moment the house (I refuse to call it a flat) is together. My shirts are perfectly ironed, collars just so, cuffs stiff and correct. As I spend most of my days dressed as I dressed at home, open neck shirt, torn jeans (shorts were too dangerous when I had to use the huge German hay cutters ... stones got chucked about and cut the flesh) and flip flops or filthy sneakers. I find it hard to adjust.

When I first got here, on my own, I was advised, by a number of polite people, that 'in this area (tres Snob) it is usual to wear a tie and proper shoes. This is not Piccadilly you know ...' The reproach was gentle, but it was there. And after I got knighted the pressure grew. I refused politely, which is why, when I do wear a suit and go to dine there is a smattering of sarcastic applause .... they know that I <u>have</u> the costume. Just too lazy to wear it. Funny old lot.

I do not know why you seem to find what you need to know about my works in, of all things! The Economist! I have never seen a copy of the paper ... I take The Spectator ... and I have never heard that I was ever mentioned in the thing. I am not, as you must realise, at all accepted here as a 'writer'. They almost dont recognise me as an actor .. or ex-actor, since I defected to Foreign Parts. Visconti, Resnais, Fassbinder et al, are not at all 'correct' in the UK.

It drives me frankly mad. And to have to live as an ignored creature is irritating. Audiences and Readers follow me with adoration. Too much so. Sometimes. But Critics and the Literary World smile very gently and pat my head. Sometimes.

So to appear in The Economist amazes me. However it will be some time before this book appears. If I ever get around to finishing it, that is to say. I begin to be bored with it .... it rather irritates me.

So. Maybe there will be another Good Friday and I can give you a time when you should hasten down to your Giggling-Boys[1] and ask for a copy. But dont count on it ....

I'd better get back to work ...

<u>DB</u>

---

1. Enthusiastic admirers of Dirk's work were based at the Paris outpost of W. H. Smith and at Galignani in the rue de Rivoli.

To Dominique Lambilliotte

Cadogan Gardens
4 June 1996
Good Friday 3.

Chere Dominique –

It must be a sign of madness that I send you this personal paper. Probably it is. However I finally finished the last word of the book on Saturday 1st, and am still lightheaded. I have yet to get my typist to 'do' it and send it to the big Boss[1] who is flying to N.Y on Friday, and Chicago the Friday after, and I might have to wait a week extra for a result. While she (another she!) comes together from her jet lag. So it is imperative that she gets it to read in peace on the flight (far more peaceful than her office I assure you) and can make a decision. I have a feeling that just perhaps she may wince a bit ... the final chapter ends in an orgy of sado-~~machoism~~ SP?, <u>and</u> the brutality, although remembered through the filter of years, of what we did to 70.000 men women and children when we yeilded to the Russians and the Yalta-Agreement. It was not pleasant. And I have had a job trying to steer my way between libel (the case against the two officers, accuser and deny-er still continues!) and melodrama.

British soldiers using bayonets (not to kill: okay, but ..) against children and women is hardly acceptable. And hardly known about to this day. Like the Jews in Drancy .... and Petain ... and the Frog police. So much has been conveniently forgotten ... and I was only 24 at the time. However ...

So, having no one to think about <u>constantly</u>, no 'Loveday' no 'India' no 'May' or 'Bob' ... takes a bit of getting used to after almost two or more [years] ... well: more. I started the thing in 1982 ... and it was thought to be 'too soon'. So it's hung around until the trial was over.

So now they, who have lived with me and lived a vivid life, are now no more. Useless puppets in the attic of my mind. Sad.

And this machine has finally broken down. It no longer will reverse. Like me in a waltz.

I found M. Chirac most impressive.[2] Eager, quick, relaxed and so MUCH better and more alive than anything we can offer. It was a

---

1. Clare Alexander.
2. At the Institut Français in South Kensington, not the Consulate as Dirk thought initially.

huge breath of fresh air. Here was a Leader. Here, indeed, was France
... whatever else a Governed country. WE really are hopeless ... if I
had not had that stroke I'd have been back in a flash after Forwood
died. I dont belong here now, I was away too long, I dont 'fit in' here.
I have no friends to speak of, and spend my time alone in my own
company, which I much, much prefer. And I have a very pretty house,
I cant bear to call it a 'flat', in which to indulge myself. Chirac may
be all sorts of a shit: but he is at least positive!

And speaks, I imagine, perfectly 'a la mode' ... ours does'nt.

Ustinov, Rampling, Huppert and I were the representatives of the
UK-French Brigade. I floundered badly at first. Not a single word of
French could I utter! Not a word! I was in agony ... but very gradually
my courage returned and very gradually I tried the water. I managed.

You will never know how glorious it was to hear French all round
me.

[...] Our hooligans have returned from ... where? .. cant remember. Ah! Hong Kong, where they were beaten at football and they
then got drunk and wrecked the plane: in flight. It really is amazing
how angry and frustrated the British Young are. No war to clean them
out .....

I am going to do one final concert for something called The Last
Word. It's rather boring. I agreed to do it in December, June seemed
so far off. Now it's next week. I shall read to them .. and answer
questions. We are sold out. I always am. The ageing residuals of my
Film Audiences. Very nice and loving. And they dont destroy airplanes
in full flight.

I have been asked to do the 'Diary' for The Spectator. Not the
Economist. I like the Spectator, it's rather less 'intellectual'. Otherwise
I am sure I'd not have been asked. I can do it whenever I like, so I am
not tied to a weekly deadline. Which I normally have been when
reviewing.

Now I am off. I have to draw a map, or plan, of the setting of the
last book. Where the House is, the orchard, the Home Farm, the
stream etc etc ... if it works out I may suggest it for the cover. Or the
fly-leaf?

If she likes what she reads flying on her broomstick to New
York ...

That is your ration ... sorry about the errors and the machine.

I wonder where I can buy a new machine? One that does'nt frighten my wits out of me. People always say, Ah! You MUST get a Word Processor ... but I can hardly open a tin of sardines, let alone use a machine with buttons to press and green letters everywhere. And, in any case, they can always be read as mechanical. Or electrical.

No effort has been taken ... Dont care for that ...

Voila –

DB.

To Dominique Lambilliotte

Cadogan Gardens
28 June 1996
Good Friday 5th.[1]

Dominique –

'It must be a sign of madness ..' means just that.

I NEVER capitulate to ladies since the death of Mrs X ages ago.

So, I suppose I went raving mad and wrote to you .. which gives me infinite pleasure. You must understand that although you have a firm idea of who I am, I am probably much nastier! I have one other friend in France. A Professor at Limoges.[2] I love her very much. We write as often as we can be bothered to. It's that sort of relationship. She braved the journey and came to Paris when I was staying once at the Lancaster. Brought me a tin of cèpes in oil. I forgot them for so long that they turned into brown glue. She has now lost her whole family, is deeply religeous (which I am not) and goes giving very complex lectures to Students everywhere. In the U.S at the moment I think. But she has no illusions about me .. having met me in the Lancaster (what HAS happened there?) she got a pretty clear idea of who, what, I was! I call her my plank .. planche. Once I had a very bad attack of writers-block and she, strangely, managed to break it.

She, as it were, threw a plank across my ravine.

All that sort of nonsense.

I have sent the MS off to my publisher. No response yet. I dont think they will like it much. Or at all! It is not entirely about the exchange of the Cossacks. Thats a tiny part, but I had to read a thousand papers to digest it all. They, the publishers, are giving me a party (God help me!) on the 3rd to celebrate the fact that I have sold

---

1. Unsurprisingly, the mathematics had gone awry. This was Dirk's fourth letter to DL.
2. Hélène Bordes.

over one million copies of my works in six years in Penguin. Apparently only the writers we call 'Airport Junk' sell so many. Oh well. No intellectual am I: I dont really mind. I meet less boring people that way. I did a show (one of my readings) for the National [Royal] Geographical Society last week. They usually have Professors or Very Clever People who discuss the heavens, or just space, or the effect of copper on zinc. That sort of thing. God only knows what I was doing there. But I sold out (800 +) and we all had a very jolly time. No one else has EVER sold out at the Institute before. Well: are you facinated by 'space' or the effect of copper on zinc stuff? At lunchtime? However it was a triumph, and I enjoyed myself and every one else did too. So. Modest? Non – pas de tout – pas moi. We are a benighted nation here. We lost at football[1] (thank the Lord) the papers were so viciously anti-German that it seemed as if we were fighting a war again, not just playing a game. The nation was terribly shocked. Our age, who had endured the war, were angrier than the youth who had'nt an idea. But the blatent spreading of hatred against ALL foreigners by the Tabloids is monstrous, and worrying. WE are gradually being taken over by Japan, you, and Germany .. and very few of Tout Le Mond have the least idea. Craven idiots.

Even if you have doubts about Chirac you should be glad that you do not suffer our despair over Major! Actually that day was fun, but we ALL spoke English! There you are! Rampling was very shocked to hear how incomprehensible Huppert had become ... Ustinov bumbled away, as usual. I have known him since we were sixteen!

Going back to this xenophobia business: I reviewed four books on the Holocaust some time ago, for my paper (Telegraph) I headed the piece WHY? meaning why did these hideious things happen ... and it was the first time in my life that I ever had 'Hate Mail'. It is a very, very disagreeable feeling. Always written in red or green ink .. always anti-semetic, violently so, and screaming 'Jew Lover' or 'Jew Boy' at me as many times as possible .. with chunks of the Bible underlined in red and green ink. For good measure. I was appalled. So was the paper.

A good, conservative, almost dull, paper hiding such hatred. Goodness.

---

1. In the semi-finals of the UEFA European Championship, held in the UK, Germany had beaten England on penalties.

You just never know, do you?

[...] By the way, I have, today, decided NOT to do the piece in the old Spectator. Something is going wrong there, and I dont much like it .. good people are leaving quietly. So I dont think I'll join the team that exists. Un-subscribe yourself immediatly! Oh. I re-read your letter. I read bits from my own work at 'The Last Word'. Bits which readers seem to appreciate greatly, and which, for some reason, make them weep silently! I think that the 'blurb' on the hardback of 'Short Walk' is particularly thought provoking.

Also an Auden poem, 'Tell Me The Truth About Love' which I read quite sickeningly well! Then some Belloc, for laughter, and a piece of old rubbish by Alice Meynil[1] which I used to read aloud to my brother soldiers in our hut during the first weeks of 'Call Up'. Most of them, to my shock, were illiterate. I used to help them to write to their mothers and sisters and, of course, wives and mistresses ... or girl-friends as we would have it in those far away days. I was amazed that even though there was such illiteracy among them, their vocabulary was astonishing! I dont suppose many of the girl-friends knew what the hell Albert, John, or Dennis, was talking about ... even if they could read ... but we sent them off, they signed their names after I had read the stuff over to them. Some in masculin tears even ... ah, well ... not many made it back. I have never heard that any of them did, and only ever got one Question (I take Questions at the end) from one of the men who had been with me in Yorkshire (I think) and remembered and said how happy he was to say thank you at last. His wife was beside him! She beamed and the audience, at that concert, 1.300, applauded.

The telephone rang just then. Viking have accepted my MS and like it and the title, 'Closing Ranks'. Thank God for that. Two years slog. They think it is a somber book. They are damned right ... and want just 'one or two tiny cuts and trims ... nothing serious' .. we'll see!

So that is 14 books altogether. I rather hated having 13 .. a sort of Bakers Dozen. Unsatisfactory, it irritated me greatly. But now all is done and I am completely empty. Vide. Is this what it is like having a baby? Well ... I have a large family, at rather a mature age!

So. That is all. I hope you can read this ... I keep the old machine,

---

1. The poet Alice Meynell.

I detest all that green lettering flying about on a screen ... I loose contact with my reader that way. This way is laborious but far better and, apres tout, personal. I hope you agree ...

Dirk

To Dominique Lambilliotte   *Cadogan Gardens*
                                                 25 July 1996

Dominique –

I hasten to reply to your salmon-questionair.

I have been rather mucked about recently. It has been discovered that I have two blocked arteries in either leg and an operation is the only way out. I detest hospitals, especially after the grim weeks of the stroke, but I fear that the pain now stops me even going to our local Hediard or Fauchon,[1] which I live in and have loved for eight years. (The ONLY place I can get a decent camembert, or my A La Perruche (sucre de canne) and various other delights which keep me in a French habit) and that is only a few steps away. So .. I'll have to go in at the start of the Fall .... when my doctor (doctor to the Royal Household and adorable)[2] returns from his holiday in Sousse.

It's a bloody bore. But I am editing fast (very little as I was assured), bits and pieces, a sweet, tough, Editor, and I am re-writing a couple of pieces (which will change the ending greatly) and wont have that to fuss me.

I mean, of course, I have ONE artery in each leg. Not several!

The party of 'celebration' was elegantly done. My 'Team', even the mail girls, and large portraits of myself all over the walls, with huge 'Congratulations' on them. Then there was a presentation of a modest, but enchanting, snuff or pill-box in gilt and enamel with the details beautifully written and the date. It was very touching and good of them. Then we all (twelve of us) went to a delicious restaurant and I was so moved etc that I could'nt eat a morsel but drank a deal of champagne and agreed that the new book would be published, and ready to be published, by March. So .. (God it is so hot today! I drip over this machine.) The next thing that faced me was the National

---

1. Dirk was comparing two great Parisian purveyors of fine foods with Partridges in Sloane Street.
2. Dirk would dedicate *Closing Ranks* to Peter Wheeler, saying 'Without whom ...'.

Geographical Society business, which was packed out, adult, and rather fun to do. I have just changed the cartridge in this elderly machine. Not very well. Anyway, that is the sum total of my summer adventures. Apart from the awful Wellington Hospital built by, and for, Arabs and the only doctor who can do the delicate X Ray and injections for the veins works there. It is like a Holiday Inn in St Etienne, crammed with vast rich Arab ladies in total black with gold bits dangling and Chanel Shoes peering out under their chadors .... marble, rosewood, great bowls of flowers, richness beyond dreams. They made me pay my cheque BEFORE I had even removed my tie ... maybe not St Etienne? Perhaps somewhere ruined by the blight on the South near Jean les Pins somewhere .... anyway, <u>awful</u>.

I am so sorry about the Spectator. I just suddenly got a feeling that things there have changed and not for the better and that my name would not enhance it's chances. I have not been forgiven here for my 'popular' films in the 40's and 50s .. for my 'foreign name' and worst of all for leaving the UK to 'avoid taxes'. It was NEVER for that reason .. but they loathe the real reason far more. My feeling for France and all things French. Un-allowable. Odd [...]

I have been reviewed patronisingly. And brutally by women authors. Is'nt it odd? I dont know any of them. Never reviewed them either. But I have stopped doing that for good .. I told the truth, as I saw it, delighted the readers and enraged the writers. All too small a world, so I pulled out. I only began writing at home for the simple reason that the days in winter were short, the evenings long, and after the logs had been split, the sheep seen to, the mowers covered, the hay gathered (for fear of fire) there was nothing to do. So I wrote. Having sold 'in excess of one million' I consider myself very fortunate.

Yes: indeed I got your p.c view of your pretty terraces ... the mail has been all over the place and the strikes continue spasmodically. We never quite know when they'll hit us. And now the Metro has joined them ... it's July, the place is crammed with Americans and Japanese, the heat is quite dreadful and the IRA chuck their bomb[s] about like apple cores.

I dont understand any of it. Except that I wont fly again! And I shant go NEAR Atlanta after last nights caper.[1]

[...] I get so many letters from young people who wonder how I

---

1. A bomb had exploded in the host city for the Olympic Games.

have survived, how I am so honest and brutal with myself (!) and can I advise them? Well: I cant really, I try to ease their burden by writing, in hand, a short card of encouragement ... one letter which arrived this morning ended ... 'Your lack of confidence is your strength. Where did you find the courage to show it? PLEASE keep talking and writing.' I cant understand this really, the poor fellow (it IS a fellow) is in a bad way I fear ... being forced to write to a stranger or a writer cant be easy, can it? And how the hell do I reply? I'll think of that later.

[...] I am horrified to think that you have bought all those video's. Bertrand Tavernier did that on a London trip and was astonished when I removed his bulging plastic sack at the Connaught and gave it to the Porter. You are not allowed to carry umbrellas, sacks, or anything like a camera or a telephone. That is absolutely forbidden. And ladies can <u>now</u> wear trouser suits so long as they match! It is wonderfully, and correctly, Victorian ... Edwardian really. De Gaulle used it as his H.Q during the war so the restaurant is one of, if not THE, best in London. Michel Bourd[a]in runs a superbe kitchen ... why have I wandered? Ah yes! Your video's. You know I have never seen any of them .. there is a new story which I read for Reed International, same ones who did 'Death In Venice'. It's charming. Called 'A House In Flanders' by Michael Jenkins.[1] I loved it when I read it, and gave it a rave review and accepted instantly when I was asked to read it. See if you can find it with your boys-team!

I stopped there to listen to the radio News. Another bomb in Spain at a tourist site, and the Atlanta games are to continue inspite of the blast yesterday ... the Americans are so hysterical, poor dears. I remember that when the Gulf War broke out London emptied, you could'nt get a seat on any flight to the U.S.A .. but any table you wanted at the Savoy, the Connaught, L'Escargot, and etc ... hotels were empty in a trice.

This is a mammoth letter about nothing ... but it may be added to the pile you are accumulating in lavender under your bed. Or wherever you keep your mail. I must get on with the rewrites .. and wash my arms. I stick to the papers on my desk. It is most disagreeable .... to end, I am so happy that you have found a private happiness ..

---

1. Published by Souvenir Press, 1992; Dirk's reading was released on cassette by Reed Audio.

one must have courage always, I think that is what I shall write to my
mournful young writers. NEVER give up the fight ... after all I only
started writing for something to do in the long evenings and I have
sold in excess of a million! At seventy five that HAS to be courage.

Or idiocy?

Ever DB

To Helen Osborne   *Cadogan Gardens*
                                                       27 August 1996

Helen –

I have had a bloody sort of summer. Not swank. Fact. I have to go
and have my legs dealt with at Edward VII .. the arteries have, what
they cheerfully call, 'furred up'. I cant begin to tell you how painful it
is. So since I can no longer walk, even across to Europa Foods in Sloan
Strasser, I sit here in a heap and batter away at this. I'm perfectly
comfortable: unless I walk. Fuck.

Loved your (slightly) incomprehensible letter, which made me feel,
once again, how much I miss your laughter. Never mind. If I am
legless when next you come you can push me about in a chair. That'll
be the day. Would'nt J.O be AMAZED! Dainty little me.

Robert [Fox] sent me a copy of his fillum[1] on tape ... and was a
tiny bit worried that I had nothing to say about it when he last called.
Merely because I had'nt even looked at it. Was'nt it rotten of me?
Problem was that I could'nt work the bloody machine-thing .. but
dont tell him that. I whinnied on about Editing the book (I was, and
it's sold and all wrapped up) because they want it for March .. so I
had to be quick. See? Then off to the Wellington I sped to be dealt
with by a terribly nice Arab gent (he was. Actually) who is the only
man in London who does the operation. Shoving needles into your
groin and watching how the colours race (or dont) through your veins.

Mine did'nt. All that much. But I scarpered from that place because
the Sister, Lourdes Marie Louise (Do you believe?) said I must lie flat
for six hours after the operation, and I MIGHT be kept in overnight
which would cost me another £480 quid. So when she was'nt looking
I called my car and fled. When we got to Selfridges (on the journey)

---

1. *A Month by the Lake*, directed by John Irvin, starring Vanessa Redgrave and Edward
Fox.

my driver asked if I was bleeding? I said no. And we got back here, un-bloody, by six of the clock, with an Evening Standard and a triple Scotch. They asked me for the cheque before I'd even taken off my tie, and then offered me the menue (I chose steamed plaice) and then got wheeled down to X.ray. I cant tell you the fuck-up it all was. But then you must sort of know that route anyway .. well: sort of.

Anyway. Roberts fillum. Well. Yesterday being the Bank Holiday and not a soul alive, I put it on and managed to get it working. It really was rather a long time since I'd been sent it. It was rather a long film. Too. Apart from the staggering Miss V. who could make a menue from Macdonalds sound magical and looked more beautiful than I can tell ... there was'nt much else to see. And Ed. has got to go to a dentist and lower his voice. I was'nt quite certain who, or what, he was playing. Far too short for V ... which was a bit cruel of Robert .. but nepotism[1] is never good, do you think? I was staggered at the sight of Alida Valli ... I remember the glory of her so well .. and evenings with Losey and that School all sitting about in the Roman heat. How glorious she was. How naughty ...

Ghastly Sheridan Morley HAS done his book. Lawyers have been assured it is a 'picture book' .... due in October.[2] I long to sue him .. I did sue the last fucker who tried a 'picture book'[3] and sent the money to the Marsden. So lets try the dreadful Morely ... poor Larry O![4] One is never safe. Never. David Caute carved Losey into segments. All ugly ... oh dear ...

All my love – Dirk XXXX

---

1. Vanessa Redgrave had been Robert Fox's mother-in-law, through his marriage to Natasha Richardson.
2. In May HO had warned Dirk of rumours that Sheridan Morley was at work on a book about him. On learning this, Dirk found himself 'unable to eat any of the lunch I'd carefully prepared. Peas, new spuds, scallops.' *Dirk Bogarde: Rank Outsider* was duly published by Bloomsbury. Dirk did not sue. Indeed he informed the author that it 'could have been worse I suppose' – in the circumstances, high praise.
3. *Dirk Bogarde: The Complete Career Illustrated* by Robert Tanitch (Ebury Press, 1988). The book was withdrawn while a passage about *Song Without End* was reprinted; and Dirk's 'damages' of £2,500 went to BACUP.
4. Roger Lewis's imminent biography, *The Real Life of Laurence Olivier* (Century), was attracting attention.

To Dominique Lambilliotte   *Cadogan Gardens*
                                            3 September 1996

D –

No. I have not gone into hospital yet.

Everyone is on holiday .. all the medical world that is to say. The Proles are back. Their wretched children litter the streets and scream and fight and are generally repellant. Why is it that we, the English, have become so foul? Viscious, loud, swigging from cans in the street, chewing gum and spitting it out in disgusting lumps that avoiding is essential, but very difficult for one like me, hobbling about like something out of Grimm clutching my black cane. Ah me ... I really do thank God that my Papa is no longer about to be humiliated, he'd have had a seizure at the street behaviour and, more than that, at the general behaviour of people in the streets all around him. This area, once so elegant and peopled by what we called the 'Gentry' is sadly sliding into decline. It looks alright, very attractive, but the quality of the people who are moving into the flats which are being hacked out of the great mansions (like mine, I confess!) fill up with BMW's and the younger glitterati who are almost as awful as they are across the river! God! What a snob I am today .. well: I am.

This house belonged to Lilly Langtry .. she had a special door for the King, when he was Wales .. it still has his feathers carved above it. The house stood in a pleasant garden (still does) and was secret. Secret enough for Langtry anyway ... then they began to build on the fields all around her .. and the house, once called The Bridge House, became No. 2 .. and the garden was called Cadogan (after the ruthless but quite jolly Lord who owned all the land, and still does!) Gardens and so the rot started. It is an area of huge mansions, each one different from it's neighbour, wonderfully built ... and I live in the attics and what was once the Laundry and the Drying Yards is, are, now my sitting room and balcony.

It's a little bit like Parc de Monceau. My garden, I mean: huge trees and birds, silence, and NO children. Its four floors below me, of course, but that makes it all the more attractive .. and only at week-ends do the Young come in with their pic-nic baskets and rugs and hurl caution to the wind and take off (practically) all their clothes. You have to have a key to get in ... which keeps the worst of the world outside. It's very nice.

I've never been down there! I much prefer the privacy of my terrace and to look down at the world below.

Telephone at that exact moment to say that I am expected at the Hospital 'for your Op, on the 18th ..' So now I know and I am really very relieved. It is so wretched hobbling along as if I were a hundred, and to be in such pain. I get to the stage when I almost weep, helplessly, and that would not do! Especially as people will nod and smile at me in the street, or try to congratulate me on 'Great Meadow' when I actually feel very far from that heavenly place! However .. let us get on with the business.

Reverting to a question you ask in your last letter. I WAS published, and well, in France by Albin Michel .. who did a splendid edition of 'Une Aimable Occupation' and latterly by Acropole. I was taken-up by a rather mad, but clever, woman called Hortense Chabrier .. she got the sack, for some reason, and I refused to do 'Apostrophe' simply because I was too scared of my French, the Owner (forgotten who at Acropole .. very unpleasant man) said he'd return to me the ENTIRE First Print. I told him to do so. And he did. Two camionettes arrived at the house and I directed them to a local quarry where they dumped the lot. I gave the surprised men a reasonable pour-boir and never saw any of them, books or men or Publisher again. So.

Perhaps I was absurd to be so timid .. but I detest TV and was far too frail in my French at that time. Signoret did it and was terrified! And she was a froggy. Anyway, I have been published almost everywhere else. Even in Japan! Always in Italy, in Germany never (I am not kind to the Germans and do refer to Belsen and so on ..) Finland, Greece, and so on ... nothing of great value. I dont make a fortune out of them, they pay very small amounts for 'foreign' books. I was sad about France .. because I was modestly beginning to do well with Chabrier ... and I liked her. But I did NOT enjoy sitting in Printemps beside a woman demonstrating potato-peelers. That was sheer agony: another of the Acropole gentleman's ideas .. I was pushed about Paris like a monkey on a barrel. I dont regret the quarry ... But I do like it when I get letters from some Long House in Borneo .. (from a missionary or someone) or perhaps from a soldier in the last Gulf war (we seem to be on the edge of another one today. Oh God ..) reading me in his tank. That I find most moving .. that someone can shove me into his pocket and take me into his battle, or else read me by the lamp light in the Long House with rats in the roof, so far away. I find it immensly rewarding.

I have had to re-write a chunk of 'Closing Ranks' because my new Editor [Clare Alexander], who is adorable and is the Publishing Manager as well, seemed distinctly uneasy about my S/M husband and wife. She did'nt say so, but just winced when she got to the sex. So I rewrote it, because she correctly felt that my white-haired ladies in country towns (who make up a great proportion of my English readers, alas) would have a seizure in the local Library.

So now they have a tidy, less explicit, and frankly better, version.

[...] But my white haired ladies are a problem. Sometimes at the Concerts I view their packed ranks with alarm. And wonder wistfully if I am writing books or planting cotton! So many beaming white heads. A harvest to die for ... ah me. Incidentally I refuse to be published in America also! They will try to Edit me, re-arrange things. It drives me mad. Also they think that my work is too bland. And it worries them that I have retired from the movies. What, they demand, can they 'hang my books on? You dont have a hook ..' So now, in the States, if you really want to read me you have to go via Ottawa or Vancouver and have them shipped in. Madness.

Oh yes! 'Victim', the gender-bender film, I made in 1961, was a desperate effort to kill the 'matinée idol' roles. It did too! And I wrote the key scenes ... just to make certain it was all stated. First time ever on a TV, or any other, screen. It was BANNED for years in the States! We showd it last night as the Film Of The Day on the main channel. But it was on [...] too late for me. I was fast asleep, but once again it had wonderful reviews. I remember when I was asked to take over from the original actor who refused it finally because it would 'prejudice his chances of a Knighthood' that Capucine, who was staying with me, asked plaintivly Why the English thought that nothing went on below their chins? My father said he agreed with her, but wished I'd do a 'really juicy piece of Trollop' instead. Perhaps I should have done? But no. No. It got rid of all those wistful little fellows I'd been playing for years ... for ever!

Dont clean your teeth tonight with shaving foam, although the Christian Dior is rather pleasant ....

Love

<u>D</u>.

Dirk was admitted on 18 September to the King Edward VII Hospital for Officers, where surgeons performed an angioplasty to ease his circulation problems. The operation was successful, but on the 20th he suffered a severe stroke, resulting in serious handicap. Henceforth his correspondence was restricted almost exclusively to brief notes, dictated occasionally to a secretary but more often to Brock and to a friend, the photographer Gabrielle Crawford. Dominique Lambilliotte received a number of these, in addition to one at Christmas 1996, written fully by Dirk, in which he described the stroke as '8 on the RICHTER SCALE!'.

To Olga Horstig-Primuz
(Dictated, but signed)   *Cadogan Gardens*
7 January 1997

Dearest Olga,

Happy New Year. I am now back in my flat, even though I am in a wheelchair which will be my fate for some time to come! I have no use in my left side but have just about managed to correct my speech. It was a very surprising shock in September and I was in intensive care for two weeks. However I am trying now, with therapy and a nurse day and night in the flat. Rather restricting. I might just have well got married after all!

Much love, as ever

Dirk XXXX

To Olga Horstig-Primuz
(Dictated, but signed)   *Cadogan Gardens*
16 November 1997

Dearest Olga,

I am amazed by your news of your pacemaker. I had no idea you were in hospital – anyway I hope everything is alright now. I have been taken off Prozac and am much better myself – I lost so much weight I looked like an El Greco Saint! – but with no saintly feelings at all! Either. The weight is going on and I nearly have my left leg – so we 'walk' every day and I feel much more optimistic. My new book (a collection of all my book reviews of the past three years)[1] will be published in June – I will send a copy.

[...] I'll sign off by wishing you a very happy Christmas and say that I'm back off into hospital for Christmas at my own request. Believe it or not, I do want a rest from this wheelchair and all the telephone calls – I do dread being left alone in this flat for the five days the English take to enjoy themselves.

The nurses are off – one to Ireland one to India, so I'll go into hospital and avoid all the problems.

I wish you love – as ever and for always.

Your loving –

<u>Dirk</u> XXX

To John and Rebecca Harrison[2]
(Postcard)

Cadogan Gardens
30 November 1997

HAD A STROKE – HENCE DICTATED.

How splendid to get your letter about DG. I loved her very much. I expect you've got her Vauxhall Mirror her closest confidant – she told it all her sadnesses and all her grief. She never spoke of anyone at Yale – and in all the years & all the letters, I knew only of Carol[3] – whose permission I had for the letters. I know she had good friends at the University but she was forbidden to tell anyone about me! It was a kind of love affair without the carnality – strange but true.

Best wishes

<u>Sir Dirk Bogarde.</u>

Although he would not walk again, and never wrote more than a sentence or two by hand, Dirk continued to produce an occasional book review and to sign the cards he dictated. When he died on 8 May 1999 he was in the best spirits since his stroke in 1996. His ashes were scattered at his beloved Clermont.

---

1. *For the Time Being* comprised not only his book reviews from 1988 to 1996 but also other pieces of his journalism from that period and before.
2. The Harrisons were friends of the late Dorothy Gordon.
3. Dorothy Gordon's daughter.

DIRK'S OUT-TAKES

A selection of remarks from letters which did not make the 'final cut'.

'... being in love has two sides to it; one of complete and bewildering beauty, and the other of angry pain and soul tearing misery.' (to Elizabeth Van den Bogaerde 20/10/45)

On von Aschenbach, seven weeks after completing the role in *Death in Venice*: 'I had no idea that I had got so tremendously involved with the man. Strange. I miss him terribly [. .] and his wandering spirit, now that I no longer need him, is floating about all over me.' (to Kathleen Tynan 24/9/70)

'After all love is thicker than blood.' (to Joseph Losey 25/11/70)

'I'm really DREADFULLY DULL. How I ever got to be the age I am God alone knows . . . . and he must have been looking out for me somewhere along those thorny little paths we laughingly call the roads of life.' (to Penelope Mortimer 12/1/72)

On his father beset by power-cuts: ' . . . he was as cheerful as an Air Raid Warden.' (to Penelope Mortimer 17/2/72)

On himself, following a severe bout of gastric illness: 'I have a sort of tortoise head grafted onto a long pale endive-body.' (to Penelope Mortimer 28/2/72)

'But I dont think that I have a troubled mind, darling. Or a troubled heart. Not really so. I have a heart that is constantly troubled FOR people I love who seem to be sad or worried or not tranquil . . . and to whome I can do no more than warm, or touch, or put out silent hands . . .' (to Penelope Mortimer 28/2/72)

On not having a proper swimming-pool: 'I never was frightfully keen on being all that clean anyway.' (to Ann Skinner 4/3/72)

On being informed that Dorothy Gordon had died: 'I felt rather empty and wretched. A habit of love suddenly whipped away like a dusty rug from under ones feet.' (to Penelope Mortimer 21/5/72)

On Annie Fargue: 'Pretty. Gorgeous yet. Funny. And sharp as a box of knives.' (to Penelope Mortimer 30/9/73)

'After fifty three the face does'nt suit youth anymore. It all sort of falls in .. like a melting Walls Ice Cream with Chocolate ...' (to Penelope Mortimer 30/9/73)

On not wishing to fly at short notice to New York: 'I am, fearfully, a timid animal, and prefer the small hole I have made for myself up here on the hill.' (to Lucilla Van den Bogaerde 5/10/74)

On his mother: 'It really is terrible. I have no filial love left there.' (to Lucilla Van den Bogaerde 5/10/74)

On the script for Losey's *The Romantic Englishwoman*: ' ... as witty as a strangled baby.' (to Penelope Mortimer 10/6/75)

On Alain Resnais: 'He's as naughty as a Victorian Nursery.' (to Penelope Mortimer 26/6/75)

'... a bit of a shove is all one really needs to get on sometimes.' (to John Charlton 7/9/75)

On his spelling and punctuation: 'I just "bash" along I fear, and things get left behind rather.' (to John Charlton 7/9/75)

On agents: 'I prefer dull honesty to evil Whizz-Kids. I know both.' (to Edward Thompson 25/1/76)

'I dont actually dig Method Actresses. It turns them into Virgins however much they get fucked.' (to Penelope Mortimer 14/5/76)

On working with the leading directors in European cinema: 'Odd how I seem to be collecting the Intellectuals when my own, intellect, is that of a newt.' (to Kathleen Tynan 4/11/76)

On Noël Coward: 'Not only was he the funniest man in the world [...] but he was also quite the most kind, generous and good. And thats saying a lot. No shafts of cruelty ... malice a bit, but malice properly used in the stew of life can be fun ... no evil, ever, respect and love constantly. He was a rum fellow. And deeply missed.' (to Kathleen Tynan 6/12/76)

'All I can say is that I am deeply grateful for those glorious, carefree, Bath Oliver Days ... they will never come back. And no one will ever have them again.' (to Nerine Selwood 18/3/77)

'... super to be rewarded, but even better to reward.' (to Brock Van den Bogaerde 29/6/77)

On submitting short stories to magazines: 'All mine came back like roosting starlings.' (to Nerine Selwood 9/8/77)

On needing inspiration in order to write: 'One just has to sweat things out until that damned Muse trolls past again dragging a trolly full of ideas.' (to Norah Smallwood 10/11/77)

On *Snakes and Ladders*: ' ... all the people IN the book moved me on in life ... the people NOT in did not.' (to Norah Smallwood 28/1/78)

On reaching chapter nine of *A Gentle Occupation*: 'I'v got the lot of them on an airoplane and have a serious desire to crash it. Immediatly. With NO survivors.' (to Norah Smallwood 1/2/79)

On a thank-you letter from Princess Alexandra, who visited Clermont: 'She really does want to come back. She thinks I have a simply "lovely Lav."!' (to Norah Smallwood 27/7/79)

'I could no more fly to Australia than I could Hang-Glide.' (to Norah Smallwood 6/8/79)

'I think that writing is very difficult indeed [...] I really do. Not, perhaps, as mentally exhausting as the Cinema (done properly!) but jolly nearly so.' (to Norah Smallwood 12/8/79)

On Iris Murdoch's Booker Prize-winning novel, *The Sea, The Sea*: 'I think it is an altogether "common" book.' (to Norah Smallwood 12/8/79)

On his performance in *Permission to Kill*: 'I look like a cross between a turtle and Boris Karlof[f] in "The Mummy".' (to David Frankham 22/8/79)

'The vine has been stripped of grapes .. enough for 200 bottles of rosé. Which Daily Lady and her husband are about to start treading. One swift look at her feet and one stays with ones beer . . .' (to Norah Smallwood 27/10/79)

On the writing process: 'Sometimes, if you passed the studio door here, you'd think that I was in need of a doctor or a strait-jacket: talking to myself, playing the scenes . . yelling oaths at the typewriter.' (to Norah Smallwood 21/11/79)

On John Gielgud's *An Actor and His Time* (Sidgwick & Jackson): ' . . . what a pity that he always takes poor advice. Still, he may make a penny or two to help re-gild the pavilion which he inhabits and looks, to me, like a Hollywood version of Versailles. Done cheap.' (to Norah Smallwood 27/11/79)

'Fanny Craddock is a tiresome virago. But well intentioned as far as I am concerned.' (to Norah Smallwood 27/11/79)

On dieting: 'Better be round and jolly than thin and dead.' (to Susan Owens 29/12/79)

On Cannes during the 1980 Film Festival: 'it's full of everyone you dont want to know or even remember . . . all looking older, uglier, meaner and fatter.' (to David Frankham 5/6/80)

'Bad manners I'll not have from anyone.' (to David Frankham, 18/8/80)

'How I HATE picking olives. I always thought it was a rather Biblical thing to do; that you swung about in the sun with a bottle of wine and a straw hat and shovelled the little black berries into sacks . . . not a bit of it. Hands and knees, crawling among the prickles and last years long grass, if I have been idle enough not to cut it earlier . . . fingers frozen in the early frost, and knees wet from the bogs . . . and it takes hours to fill half a bucket, because you have to pick each one up individually and have a look at it to see the voles or rats have'nt bitten off half.' (to Susan Owens 25/11/80)

'I am always nervous of people who "teach" writing or painting or even acting. Much is theory. And much is rubbish. If the rules are STRICTLY adheared to the "soul" goes out of the work.' (to Nerine Selwood 24/2/81)

On his writing: 'I dont know what the hell I am doing half the time: I just sit at this machine and write. Could'nt tell you HOW! It happens.' (to Nerine Selwood 24/2/81)

'I am so sick of the British idea that every Frenchman wears a beret, smokes a Gitane, and walks about with a long loaf. They've come a long way since those days . . . further even than we have.' (to Norah Smallwood (1/3/81)

'I'm happiest in the silence I must confess . . but that makes one deadly dull!' (to Nerine Selwood 8/6/81)

'Actually I detest Autumn colours. Those beastly golds and russet tints . . . the angry purple of Michaelmas da[i]sies . . . and I DETEST all dahlias.' (to Norah Smallwood 1/8/81)

On Anthony Burgess's *Earthly Powers*: '. . . it is a very good "read" . . and he is wonderfully over informative on everything from God to the back streets of Nice!' (to Norah Smallwood 1/8/81)

'The one thing you have to remember about Americans in Business is that they only call you when they want you. Otherwise your dead.' (to David Frankham 19/8/81)

'I write because I have the time and it gives me pleasure to reach you. For no other reason.' (to Norah Smallwood 29/8/81)

'It's a rum world, Publishing . . . almost as silly, I sometimes feel, as the Cinema.' (to Norah Smallwood 29/8/81)

'We are moths; we actors.' (to Norah Smallwood 29/8/81)

'I have a very unfair advantage over more brilliant and experienced writers: my Film Name. But I <u>do</u> try to sort that one out . . . it's something I cant help anymore than I can help the fact that I'm getting badly thin on top!' (to Norah Smallwood 12/9/81)

'. . . divorced from my Film work, I am really not at all an interesting creature. Not even, alas! to myself . . .' (to Norah Smallwood 3/12/81)

On a visit to Clermont by John Fowles: 'We spent a good deal of it crawling about on hands and knees seeking Orchis. He found, to my relief, a patch of Fly, a second patch of Bee, and a whole orchard, one could say, of a pink orchis with a deeply unpleasing smell. He was overcome with delight. . . . sniffing away like a truffle-hound. More a Botanist than a Master writer. But enormously warm, shaggy, kind and humble. I like him very much.' (to Norah Smallwood 12/3/82)

'I should have been educated, really. I might have done awfully well . . .' (to Norah Smallwood 20/5/82)

On the problems of leaving Clermont to make a film: 'One really is caught in a web here: a web I love very much, but a web for all that.' (to Norah Smallwood 20/5/82)

'I spend more time at this machine than I do in bed!' (to Nerine Selwood 16/8/82)

On Tony's convalescence: 'We have up days and down days and I am as attentive as a wheeling hawk.' (to Norah Smallwood 20/4/83)

On his white hydrangea: ' . . . a vision of enormous blooms, fat as a housekeepers cat and twice as pretty . . .' (to Norah Smallwood 20/7/83)

'I made my money out of the houses I bought, did up, and sold rather than from the Movies!' (to David Frankham 18/9/83)

On his grown-up young relatives: 'I was NEVER like that at twenty five! Green as a frog was I, and still am.' (to Kathleeen Tynan 15/10/83)

On the translation of *Voices in the Garden*: 'Why does French read so ravishingly I wonder? It seems to me a far better book than my original!' (to Kathleen Tynan 15/10/83)

On his 1983 Christmas card: ' . . . it is as un-festive as a foaling mare.' (to Norah Smallwood 8/12/83)

On being described by his new publisher as 'An author at the height of his powers': 'When I read this out to Forwood he only asked if I'd prefer mashed or plain boiled potatoes with the tripe a la mode . . . which goes to show how seriously I am taken in this house.' (to Norah Smallwood 8/12/83)

On his dog, Labo: 'He really was an Italian-Fellow all the way through: which is probably why Visconti so loved him. A shaggy twin. Arrogant, selfish, glorious. And most ungrateful.' (to Norah Smallwood 29/2/84)

On his movies being rerun by television: ' . . . in the days when we made those films we really did'nt believe that TV was anything but a Rich Mans Toy . . . we never expected it to crush us!' (to Susan Owens 4/2/84)

'. . . I dont look like the bloody "Spanish Gardner" any more . . .' (to Susan Owens 4/2/84)

'I have always thought that good dialogue can DESCRIBE A PLACE far better than a writer.' (to Mary Dodd 7/6/84)

On the exhibits in the Musée Picasso, Antibes: 'I find that they interest me as much as the paintings on the side of a childs cot.' (to Norah Smallwood 21/6/84)

'[America] is more surprising and odd than Europe, and yet it is Europe displaced.' (to David Frankham 27/6/84)

'Books dont make your fortune, and I have'nt made a Fillum since Adam was a boy!' (to Susan Owens 9/8/84)

On productions in England of *The Cherry Orchard*: '. . . while it has always been "worthy", and very often beautifully played, it is about as Russian and volatile as a Mars Bar!' (to Humphrey Jenkins 20/8/84)

'Comedy is FAR harder to play than tragedy: if you can master comedy correctly you can literally play anything you like.' (to Humphrey Jenkins 20/8/84)

'. . . you are one of those rare people who can move mountains and divert rivers.' (to Susan Owens 9/9/84)

'The main trouble with me is that I have a very limited intellect and not a great deal of experience. Well: a limited (again) experience of a limited existance, if that makes any sense. It does to me, which is very depressing!' (to Pat Kavanagh, 29/10/84)

On appearing on television chat shows: 'I am not a rich man, and although it is a form of simple prostitution it does allow me to join kith and kin for free.' (to Humphrey Jenkins 27/3/85)

On being awarded an Honorary Doctorate of Letters at St Andrews University: ' . . . anything is possible to achieve if you are determined . . . even if you cant spell, punctuate, add up or have ANY educational benifits whatever: like me. I was the despair of countless headmasters, apart from my poor father and mother, and now I cant tell any of them that it was alright in the end. Fate!' (to Susan Owens 29/3/85)

'Life is <u>not</u> all rose and gold, I can assure you!' (to Jack Jones 2/4/85)

'. . . I have always tried to bring good-taste and some degree of elegance, if possible, to the written words I have set down.' (to Hélène Bordes 10/5/85)

On Norah Smallwood: 'She was a titan! Nothing could escape her brilliant eye or the furious correcting of her right hand and pencil!' (to Hélène Bordes 10/5/85)

On receiving his Hon. D.Litt at St Andrews University: 'It was, without question, the most important day of my adult life I suppose .. apart from war, that is.' (to Hélène Bordes 9/7/85)

On the first draft of his script for *May We Borrow Your Husband?*: 'As you will see: I dont quite know how to type a TV (or a film) script, even though I have read millions.' (to Bob Mahoney 9/8/85)

On completing *Backcloth*: 'The void is terrible .. as if I had had twins!' (to Hélène Bordes 23/9/85)

On France: ' . . . for some of us it is "under our skin" just as we are "in our skins" when we live here.' (to Hélène Bordes 23/9/85)

On not being disturbed while watching films on television: 'Fact is that I get so damned hooked on a Movie that I dont come out of the trance until the final credits!' (to Brock and Kim Van den Bogaerde 13/7/86)

'It is much too difficult to deal with illness in a foreign-language . . .'. (to Hélène Bordes (7/8/86)

On being unable to drive: 'I never knew such a little thing would alter my life!' (to Hélène Bordes 7/8/86)

On his co-star in *May We Borrow Your Husband?*: 'She's quite marvellous, works brilliantly, had never seen a camera in her life and comes off the screen like a bomb. Her name is Charlotte Attenborough!' (to David Frankham 23/8/86)

'I have no wish to surrender my French residency and I love France far too much to abandon her.' (to Hélène Bordes 13/10/86)

On life at the Hotel Lancaster: '... shareing two rooms with Forwood is a little like having a Hippopotamus in the house.' (to Olive Dodds 9/12/86)

On returning to the bestseller chart: 'I am cheered, a little, to see that I am back on the BS List today even though I'm No. 10 ... but better than a slap in the belly with a dead cod.' (to Pat Kavanagh 6/9/87)

On his sister's loss of her husband: 'We never had an idea, did we, in the careless summer days of our childhood that we would, both of us, be called on to answer for all the joy we were getting then.' (to Elizabeth Goodings 21/2/88)

'... after all my reading public like to "pry".' (to Pat Kavanagh 22/8/88)

'I begin to sound like Jeffrey Archer. I only wish I could write his tripe.' (to Pat Kavanagh 22/8/88)

On life after the loss of Tony: 'At least I do now know the difference between 'Alone' and "Lonely" which I had'nt fully understood before!' (to Dilys Powell 27/9/88)

On Bruce Chatwin's novel *Utz:* 'It's as spare as a grocers bill.' (to Nicholas Shakespeare 12/12/88)

On not attending the funeral of a friend: 'I declined to go, because I prefer to aid the living rather than the dead.' (to Hélène Bordes 12/10/90)

On the perception of him by the tabloid press: 'I am supposed to live in a basement flat, in the dark, drinking whisky all day because I am forgotten and alone and broke. I ask you! I feel a frightful fraud at the Connaught!' (to Dilys Powell 14/4/91)

On *These Foolish Things:* 'It's taken me years to get the art of concealing art properly adjusted to my work. Now I think, think, I have done it .. and I can pack it in and get on with my books.' (to Dilys Powell 27/5/91)

'I am a good listner. When I allow anyone else to speak.' (to Penelope Mortimer 29/8/91)

'Everyone seems to be into Lesbians today .. and very odd fellers.' (to Penelope Mortimer 29/8/91)

'I am not a raging-bull type actor. I might have different sorts of rage but not giant. I am wispier .. not a toughie.' (to Penelope Mortimer 9/9/91)

On the Holocaust and the prospect of it happening again: 'We are evil essentially. It is a dreadful thought but tragically true.' (to Graeme Wright, editor of *Wisden Cricketers' Almanack* 20/9/91)

'Jealousy has ten heads.' (to John Osborne 14/11/91)

On seeing in the *Daily Telegraph* a photograph of himself and Elizabeth, taken immediately before his Investiture at Buckingham Palace: 'Christ. It's bad enough being like a turtle without having to see it all in vivid Technicolour, Panavision, and, almost, Steriophonic Sound!' (to John Coldstream 20/2/92)

'[N]ever intrude. Never be rude.' (to Penelope Mortimer 7/9/92)

On a signing session in Chester: 'Lots of jolly chat, lots of books sold, kindness spilling like sunlight.' (to Penelope Mortimer 6/10/92)

'As Colette said .. to grow old is to cease to be amazed! I am <u>constantly</u> amazed!' (to Hélène Bordes 8/10/92)

On Alexis Smith: 'Mind you, she'd go to the opening of an eye ....'. (to David Frankham 8/6/93)

On being guest of honour at the annual dinner of the British Society of Cinematographers: 'It seems that photographers age, get fat, get bald, get thin, quicker than the rest of us! Difficult, because I have not yet, touch wood gone white.' (to Brian McFarlane 2/4/94)

'I know that I appear to be a bit too direct sometimes. It has been known to seriously distress some people: but I CAN be tactful when I feel, and know, that tact is needed. I would'nt have got this far unless I had.' (to Rupert Van den Bogaerde 18/8/94)

'Life is a fucker sometimes, and if you try to hide it all, the wounds and cuts and bruises, something else will give and we-all-fall-down.' (to Rupert Van den Bogaerde 18/8/94)

'There are more tacky little Knights stuttering about than midges in summer.' (to David Frankham 11/1/95)

On giving up his Platform performances, or 'concerts': 'Being all alone on a vast stage with just four or five books for two hours is too much of a strain now. I used to love the love!' (to Olga Horstig-Primuz 19/7/95)

'After all I only started to write to fill in those long evenings after the lamps were lit. Provence gets dark about 3.30 up in the hills. I felt that pulling a rug was indecent somehow. So wrote instead. Funny how life can alter things . . .'. (to Helen Osborne, 23/5/96)

. . . and his direct answer to a direct question:

'"Tell me," you ask "How many things do you hate?"
   Oh! How difficult . . . really not so many. Certainly mimosa, an ugly flower which comes from an ugly country, vipers because they bite, Germans because they kill, the Japanese because I knew them in '45 and they are worse than vipers and Germans put together . . . I hate frelons [hornets], for the same reason that I hate vipers, I hate tinned spaghetti; chlorine in the drinking water; bigotry (although I think that I must be one myself!); the mistral, because it destroys my plants and trees and weeks of back-breaking work in moments, snow and ice; a broken finger nail in wool; the slaughter of cattle and sheep, chickens in battery farms, tea without sugar, English boiled cabbage (they put one cabbage into a barrel of water with soda, to make it green, and boil it for a week!) flying; going to America, stupidity in people, (so much about!) damp bread, walking with bare feet in muddy, or sandy water (I once trod on a broken bottle as a child at the seaside and have never forgotten that!), being TOO happy: because unhappiness is almost certain to follow! And so on . . , trivia . . . I can tell you better what I LOVE! Boudin blanc! Boudin noir! Tripes a la mode de Caen . . . ALL Chinese food and oysters, caviar and champagne, Concorde, elegance, good manners, kindness, effort, and the local lady who keeps the goat herd down the lane! And much, much more! Including long letters . . . .'. (to Hélène Bordes 5/10/85)

ACKNOWLEDGEMENTS

'Vol 2 is horridly difficult,' Dirk wrote to Dilys Powell when he was completing *Snakes and Ladders*; '... it is the leaving out of people which I find so difficult ... selection is frightfully tiresome and hurtful, of course, to people who tear out to read the index and find, angrily, that they are not included when they all "did so much" for me. Oh bugger! Perhaps I'd be better employed with a novel.' The present book is, in its way, 'Vol 2' of what has come to be known as The Dirk Bogarde Project and while I hope the selection is neither tiresome nor hurtful, it has been at times agonising. The *salon des refusés*, as is clear from the long list of names below, has become a crowded space. But this is the inevitable consequence of the decision to treat Dirk's correspondence from the second half of his adult life as a complement to, and quite often variant on, his memoirs.

Many of these names are common to the equivalent roll-call in the biography. Most who helped with my research extended their generosity to the loan of any letters and cards from Dirk that they had kept. In one or two cases – and despite extensive searches in attics, on bookshelves and among other secreted treasures – the quarry eluded their owners. However, there was compensation, for me at least, in the emergence of important items from sources that I had not previously tapped.

My principal debt, as always, is to the Van den Bogaerde family, who for the best part of eight years have continued to give their unqualified support, even though there has been the potential for their privacy to be placed in jeopardy, and even when the resolution of individual members has been tested. Their names are given individually at the front of this book. The Forwood family, too, has shown further kindness and understanding to the author-as-editor. Others to whom I am especially grateful for substantial and significant loans are: Dame Eileen Atkins, John Beech, Hélène Bordes, Véra de Ladoucette, Alain and Christine de Pauw, Mary Dodd, David Frankham, Bee Gilbert and Sir Ian Holm, Dominique Lambilliotte, Charles Lind, Patricia Losey, Brian McFarlane, Susan Owens, Ivor Powell, Ann Skinner, Bertrand Tavernier, Roxana and Matthew Tynan, the late Helen Osborne, and the late Nerine Selwood.

As with the biography, this volume would not have progressed beyond the initial glimmer of hope without the authorisation of Dirk's estate, in the person of his nephew Brock; the commitment of my publisher and editor Ion Trewin, with his assistant Bea Hemming; and the encouragement of Dirk's – and my – agent Pat Kavanagh. Constantly in the background, with his sagacity and valued friendship, has been Laurence Harbottle. So, too, with his mastery of Dirk's on-line archive, has Christian Sandino-Taylor. In the final stages of what the film world knows as 'pre-production' I was once again fortunate enough to be guided, first, by Maddie Mogford of Reynolds Porter Chamberlain; then by Linden Lawson, nonpareil among copy editors; and by Jane Birkett, who faced a uniquely daunting set of proofs. If there are inadvertent omissions from these final pages, they are the fault of the editor and certainly not of Douglas Matthews, indexer extraordinary. In its look and feel I count this book as a true companion to the biography, and for that I thank Helen Ewing, Georgie Widdrington and Natasha Webber, as well as others at Weidenfeld and Nicolson who, when faced with a second mighty typescript from the same source, did not insist on a reduction in production values.

And finally . . . Since the summer of 2000, when I was commissioned to write Dirk's Life, my wife Sue could be excused for thinking that 'there are three of us in this marriage'. Fortunately, she too knew him – and has been the essence of forgiveness.

*   *   *

Access to letters held in public collections was granted by kind permission of the following:

The Academy of Motion Picture Arts and Sciences, Beverly Hills – for correspondence to George Cukor

The British Film Institute, Special Collections – Joseph and Patricia Losey

The British Library – Dilys Powell; Harold Pinter

The Brotherton Library, University of Leeds – Norah Smallwood

Fondazione Istituto Gramsci, Rome – Luchino Visconti

The Harry Ransom Center, University of Texas at Austin – Tom Stoppard; Julian Barnes and Patricia Kavanagh

The Howard Gotlieb Archival Research Center, University of Boston – Penelope Mortimer; Peters Fraser and Dunlop (pfd); and the sole surviving letter to Dorothy Gordon

The Roald Dahl Museum and Story Centre – Roald Dahl and Patricia Neal

The University of Reading, Special Collections – Random House, including letters to Norah Smallwood and John Charlton

For further personal loans (identified in bold), for granting permission as the executors of an estate, for opening doors and drawers at institutions, for wizardry with digital scanners, and for general enthusiasm I am also indebted to:

Judith Aller, Jonathan Altaras, Jamie Andrews, Verity Andrews, Jenny Arthur,

Lady Annunziata Asquith, Lord and Lady Attenborough, **Julian Barnes**, Phillippa Bassett, **Neville Beale**, Kathy Beilby, Fanny Blake, **Ronald Blythe**, **Helena Bonham Carter**, Giovanna Bosman, Michael Bott, Penny Breia, David Bristow, Natasha Brook, Ian Buruma, John Byrne, **James Cairncross**, Kate Calloway, Sandra Caron, **Audrey Carr**, Chichester Reference Library, Anne Clarke, **Paddie Collyer**, **Mark Daniel**, **Lady Daubeny**, Caterina d'Amico, Christiaan De Forche, **Deborah**, **Duchess of Devonshire**, Jonathan Diamond, **Bryan Forbes**, Joan Foster, Sarah Fowles, **Carol Gordon**, **Sue Grantley**, Tom Graves, John Greaves, Stacey Greenfield, Dominic Gregory;

Barbara Hall, **Harbottle & Lewis**, Clare Harington, Kathleen Harnack, **Julie Harris**, Noel Harrison, **Rebecca and the late John Harrison**, Val Hennessy, **Philip Hoare**, **Ellen ('Lally') Holt**, **Simon Hopkinson**, Justin Hunt, **Lord (Jeremy) Hutchinson QC**, Professor Russell Jackson, Aidan Jamison, **Humphrey Jenkins**, J. C. Johnson, **Paul Joyce**, **Julie Kavanagh**, Nicki Kennedy, **Kensington and Chelsea Borough Council**, Elizabeth King, **Tony Lacey**, **Lee Langley**, Ruth Leon, **the late Jean Lion**, Mercedes López-Baralt, **Juliane Lorenz**, **Joanna Lumley**, Anna McCorquodale, **Bob Mahoney** and **Keith Richardson**, Nadine Malfait, Nicoletta Mannino, Jean Mason, Nicholas Mays, **Jill Melford**, Janet Moat, **John Moffatt**, **L. Robert Morris**, Jeremy Mortimer, **the late Joan Mulcaster**;

Sean D. Noel, **Robert L Palmer**, **Penguin Group**, **Peters Fraser & Dunlop (pfd)**, **Susan Pink**, **Tina Pointing**, **Stan Procter**, **Random House Group**, Michael Richardson, **Sheila Rickards**, Caryl Roberts, **Peter Rogers**, **Maj.-Gen. Richard Rohmer**, **Renate Rooney**, **Leonard and Roxanne Rosoman**, Joanne Rule, Arnold Schulkes, Jean Selfe, **Nicholas Shakespeare**, David Sharp, Christopher Sheppard, the late Ned Sherrin, **Barbara Siek**, Caroline Simmonds, Mark Smith (Whitby's Photo-Video Ltd), Norman Stone, Saskia Stoop, David Tindle, **University of Bristol Library Special Collections**, **Michel** and **Régine van der Haert**, **Dorothy Watson**, **Professor Wallace S. Watson**, Don Weekes, Kenneth Westwood, Josie Whibley, Janet Whitaker, **the late Christopher Whittaker**, Sir David Williams, Liz Williams, **Kathleen Withersby**, **Susan Wooldridge**, **Geoffrey Woolley**, **Graeme Wright**, **Agnes Zwickl**.

JC

INDEX

Page numbers in **bold** indicate the first page of a letter to a correspondent (and extracts in 'Dirk's Out-takes' on pages 597–607)

Writings by Dirk Bogarde (DB) appear under title; works by others under author's name

Accident (film), 34, 36, 38, 46n, 98 & n, 303, 332
Ackerley, Joe Randolph: *My Father and Myself,* 120
Ackland, Joss, 496n
Acropole (French publishers), 593
Acton, Sir Harold: *More Memoirs of an Aesthete,* 67 & n
Adam's Farm, Sussex, 29–30, 31, 246n
Adams, John Bodkin, 62
After Noon Plus (TV show), 261n
Agate, James, 217
Agutter, Jenny, 213, 217, 233
Ahmet (Arab gardener), 68, 133
Aimée, Anouk, 37, 496–7, 499
Aitken, Maria, 315
Albin Michel (French publishers), 593
Aldiss, Brian: *A Soldier Erect,* 67 & n
Alexander, Clare, 582 & n, 594
Alexandra, Princess, 228–9, 358, 566, 600
All About Eve (film), 93
All That Jazz (film), 253
Allan Glen's School, Glasgow, 527n
Allen, Woody, 233
Allied Film Makers, 372n
Altaras, Jonathan, 462
Ambazac: Château de Mont-Mery, 150n
Amis, Martin, 1
Amsterdam, 155, 255
Anderson, Lindsay, 99n
Anderson, Michael, 88n
Anderson, Robert, 279
Andersson, Bibi, 169
Andresen, Björn, 56n
Andrews, Anthony, 438
Angel, Daniel M., 56
Angel Wore Red, The (film), 464n
Anne, Princess Royal, 434
Another Country (film), 339

Anouilh, Jean: *Point of Departure,* 135 & n
Antonino (gardener), 30, 33
Apocalypse Now (film), 233 & n
Apostrophes (French TV programme), 361 & n, 593
Archer, Jeffrey, Baron, 605; *Exclusive,* 449n
Arena (TV documentary of DB), 11
Arkin, Alan, 145
Arnaud, Yvonne, 101, 442n
Arne, Peter, 151
Arnhem, battle of (1944), 135, 145, 154
Arran, Arthur Kattendyke Archibald Gore, 8th Earl of ('Boofy'), 373 & n
Ashcroft, Dame Peggy, 332n
Ashton, Sir Frederick, 283
Asquith, Anthony ('Puffin'), 38, 96 & n, 545n, 555
Asquith, Lady Cynthia: diaries, 377 & n
Assassination of Trotsky, The (film), 58n, 67, 73, 74n, 81, *At Long Last Love* (film), 130n
Atkins, Dame Eileen, **435, 449, 451, 485, 550**; films with DB, 419n; on tour in Archer's *Exclusive,* 449n; in Virginia Woolf's *A Room of One's Own,* 486n
Attenborough, Charlotte, 397 & n, 604
Attenborough, Sir David, 274
Attenborough, Richard, Baron: Arnhem film (*A Bridge Too Far*), 11, 135, 150n, 154, 157, 190–1; DB entertains in France, 72, 309, 385; occupies neighbouring house in France, 85, 224, 345; DB records favourite music for, 101n; Brock's view of, 200; founds Beaver Films, 224n; and DB's *A Gentle Occupation,* 234; films *Gandhi,* 234, 237, 309; and DB's cassette readings, 235; house burgled, 294n; criticised by Rushdie, 311 & n; at 1985 Cannes Film Festival, 368; film of *A Chorus Line,* 368, 385; arranges BAFTA award to DB, 434 & n, 435, 436 & n; honours, 520n

Attenborough, Sheila, Lady *see* Sim, Sheila
Attlee, Clement, 1st Earl, 332
Aubert, Brigitte, 388
Aubert, Jean-Pierre, 214 & n, 388
Auden, W.H.: 'Tell Me The Truth About Love',
    586
Australia, 255

Bacall, Lauren, 169, 443
Backcloth (DB): writing, 312 & n, 368, 382n,
    383, 604; publication, 393, 403–4, 408n, 410,
    412, 421; recorded version, 494, 509n;
    structure, 548
Bacon, Victoria, 354
BACUP (now Cancerbackup), 502 & n, 535
BAFTA (British Academy of Film and
    Television Arts): Awards, (1981), 274;
    inaugural Tribute Award to DB (1988),
    434–6, 442
Bagnold, Enid (Lady Jones): *Autobiography*, 335
Bailey, David, 35, 283
Baillie, Dame Isobel, 201
Baker, Sir Stanley, 38, 50, 152 & n, 353, 486n,
    520n
Balcon, Jill, 464, 516
Balcon, Sir Michael, 516, 520n
Ballhaus, Michael, 481
Bandol, France, 448, 452, 455
Banks, Evangeline, 234n
Barber, Lynn, 558
Bardot, Brigitte, 120, 425 & n, 468
Barnes, Julian, **344, 430**; as TV critic, 327 &
    n, 329; DB dines with, 547 & n; *Metroland*,
    328 & n
Barron, Zelda, 215 & n
Barrymore, Ethel, 130
Bates, Sir Alan, 42, 64–5, 69 & n, 73, 115, 213n,
    217, 516
Bath, Alexander Thynne, 7th Marquess of,
    565 & n
Bavaria Films, 182, 185
Baxter, Keith, 46 & n
'Bay of the Little Lost Sheep, The' (DB; article),
    232n, 236n
Beaton, Cecil: *Self Portrait with Friends*,
    263 & n
Beatty, Warren, 34
Beck, Reginald, 194
Beecham, Sir Thomas, 351
Beel House, 66n
Bell, Rosalind *see* Bowlby, Rosalind
Belloc, Hilaire, 586
Ben-Hur (1910 film), 95
Bendo (dog), 225–6, 228, 230, 236, 286, 291,
    293, 295, 309, 331, 365–6, 394, 408; death,
    409
Benn, Tony (Anthony Wedgwood Benn), 282

Bennett & Druet (architects), 310n
Bennett, Alan: *Writing Home*, 569 & n
Bennett, Arnold: *Buried Alive*, 302 & n, 302,
    307
Bennett, Caroline (Penelope Mortimer's
    daughter), 305n
Bennett, John, 305n
Bennett, Margot, 100n
Berenson, Marisa, 134, 136
Berg, A. Scott: *Goldwyn: A Biography*, 446n
Berger, Helmut, 37, 70, 112n
Bergman, Ingmar, 132
Bergman, Ingrid, 99, 233, 558
Bernard, Chris, 405n
Bertil, Prince of Sweden, 228
Besch, Joseph, 49n
Betti, Ugo: *Summertime* (play), 221n
Betts, Sally: as DB's typist, 9, 145, 201, 320, 383,
    385, 480
Beyond Good and Evil (film), 113n
Bilbow, Tony, 314n
Birkin, Andrew, 276 & n, 303, 308 & n
Birkin, David, 476n
Birkin, Jane, 446n, 449, 451, 453–4, 460–2,
    476 & n, 477–8 & n, 567
Birthday Party, The (film), 46
Bissett, Jacqueline, 267n, 339
Black, Sir James, 376
Black, Karen, 338
Blackburn, Julia: *Daisy Bates in the Desert*,
    560 & n
Blackwood, Lady Caroline, 220
Blake, Fanny, 329 & n, 533, 578
Blakemore, Michael: *Next Season*, 435
Bland, Tony, 512n
Bloom, Claire, 100n
Blue Lamp, The (film), 66n, 427
Blunt, Anthony, 224n
Boatwright, Alice Lee, 252 & n, 254, 368, 563
Bogaerde, Alice Van den (Gareth's daughter),
    491; telephones DB, 424
Bogaerde, Brock Van den (Gareth's son), **172,
    398, 443, 599, 604**; stays with DB in
    France, 137, 139–40, 195–202, 379, 381–2;
    sickness, 159; enrols at Dance Centre,
    London, 174n; attends Berlitz language
    school in Cannes, 195–6, 198n, 399; in USA,
    208; as associate producer of dramatisation
    of Graham Greene's *May We Borrow Your
    Husband?*, 379n, 397–400; helps DB settle
    into Queen Anne House, 424; visits DB in
    Cadogan Gardens, 443, 469, 492; son, 468;
    and DB's wish to have ashes scattered in
    France, 491; at Daphne Fielding's birthday
    lunch, 565; DB dictates late letters to, 595
Bogaerde, Elizabeth Van den (DB's sister) *see*
    Goodings, (Margaret) Elizabeth

Bogaerde, Gareth Van den (DB's brother), **198,** **423, 519;** reconciliation with DB, 137; moves to Chicago, 159–61, 195; and mother's death and funeral, 249; DB sees little of, 383; in DB's autobiographies, 383; helps DB after stroke, 423; visits DB in London, 525

Bogaerde, Jacqueline Van den (Rupert's first wife), 376, 423–4, 540

Bogaerde, Kim Van den (Brock's wife), **604;** DB sends seeds to, 379; visits DB in Kensington, 424

Bogaerde, Leo Van den (Brock's son), 468

Bogaerde, Lucilla Van den (Gareth's wife), **159, 168, 198, 374, 423, 598;** DB sees little of, 383; visits DB, 137, 525

Bogaerde, Margaret Van den (DB's mother): visits DB at Clermont, 55, 93; and husband's funeral, 97; marriage and children, 103; in nursing home, 103, 105–6, 142; and publication of DB's *Postillion,* 169; DB visits in England, 214, 236, 248, 249–50; death, 248, 250–1; in DB's memoirs, 282; destroys records and photographs of husband, 347; behaviour, 528; DB's attitude to, 598

Bogaerde, Moses Van den (DB's grand-nephew), 468

Bogaerde, Rupert Van den (Gareth's son), **606;** in DB's autobiography, 383; visits DB, 423–4; and DB's wish to have ashes scattered in France, 491; wife's mental breakdown and disappearance, 540; *Daybreak into Darkness* (by 'Rupert Bogarde'), 540n

Bogaerde, Ulric Gontron Jules Van den (DB's father): in France with DB, 55, 68, 93, 147; death, 96–8, 142; and DB's *Postillion,* 165; in DB's memoirs, 282; DB writes on for *Times* bicentennial, 347 & n, 350 n, 355; retirement presentations from *Times,* 351; pencil portrait of DB, 378n; painting of Great Meadow, 520–1; dislikes Murrays in Glasgow, 528; dislikes new journalists, 558

Bogaerde, Ulric Van den (Gareth/Lucilla's son), **426, 467;** boyhood, 170; visits DB, 424

Bogarde, Sir Dirk: as writer, 1–9, 126–7, 140, 145, 162, 180–1, 188–9, 202, 209–11, 218, 220, 224, 227, 232, 236–7, 239–40, 254, 255, 276, 281–2, 285, 287, 306, 326, 358, 362–3, 368–70, 382–3, 386, 403, 407, 569, 578–9, 593–4, 599, 600, 601; style and spelling, 2, 8–9, 598; sexuality, 492, 495, 514; resides on Continent, 4, 27, 162–3; reading, 9–10, 31, 64, 67, 120, 197–8, 222, 242, 245, 248, 277, 283, 331–2; political incorrectness, 10; life in Italy, 27–33; pet dogs, 28–9, 63, 64, 71, 76, 84, 92, 101–2, 107–8, 174, 204, 223, 225–6, 228, 230, 236, 286, 291, 293, 295, 309, 331, 365–6, 394, 408, 424; hepatitis, 34n;

gardening, 36, 58, 107, 129, 158–9, 181, 209, 225, 241, 249–50, 295, 310, 317, 324, 330–1, 344–5, 480, 490; earnings, 63; dental problems, 49, 66, 213, 447, 450, 468; gives up smoking, 67; plans to write memoir, 77; drinking, 99, 537; records favourite music for Capital Radio, 101–2; visits to London, 105–7, 214, 236, 274–6, 290, 299, 307, 308, 310–11, 319, 330, 363–4, 367, 383, 389; appearances on Russell Harty's TV show, 125n, 126, 141, 163; suffers from flu and abscess, 125; military service, 180 & n; employs voice coach, 203; diet, 209; cassette recordings of books, 234 & n, 248n; bronchitis, 236; dress, 243–4, 271; pestered by Bromley correspondent, 259–60 & n; receives hate-tape from England, 260–2; returns to screen acting, 264–73, 447–56, 460–1, 466, 471, 484; paintings and drawings, 270, 378n, 384; buys gun as protection, 294–5; French honours, 299 & n, 304, 326, 580; receives fan mail for books, 226, 236, 306–7; given award at Cannes Film Festival, 311; presents TV documentary from Louvre, 317–18, 324–5, 389–90; as President of Jury at Cannes Film Festival (1984), 326, 334–5, 337–40, 347; acquires Patricia Kavanagh as new literary agent, 327; judges *Mail on Sunday* literary competition, 350; Hélène Bordes writes study of, 354–6; on first name, 361; honorary doctorate from St Andrews, 362–3, 365, 367, 374–7, 603–4; pencil portrait by father, 378 & n; non-driving, 379–80 & n, 390, 392, 604; Tindle portrait of, 387 & n, awarded British Film Institute Fellowship, 407 & n; leaves Clermont, 408–11, 424; financial concerns, 413–14; rents house in Chelsea, 419; puts on weight, 421, 450; buys house in Duke's Lane, Kensington, 421–2; suffers stroke, 422–3, 425, 447, 479, 583; and Tony's death, 429–31, 433–4, 605; sells Queen Anne House, 430–2; moves to flat in Cadogan Gardens, 433; inaugural Tribute Award from BAFTA, 434 & n; sells papers to University of Boston, 434; book reviewing for *Telegraph,* 438 & n, 446–7 & n, 498n, 503, 510, 516–17, 529n, 552, 554n, 560; medication, 438; learns to cook, 441, 443, 476, 492, 494; stands in for David Jacobs' radio music programme, 441 & n; disgruntlement with England, 447, 542, 585, 592; conducts master classes, 454, 456, 458, 468, 472; on *Desert Island Discs,* 456 & n; supports euthanasia, 456–7, 493–4, 502–3, 508n, 509, 512, 535; physiotherapy on leg, 457 & n; in Cannes for screening of *Daddy Nostalgie,* 460–3; feels loss of creativity,

Bogarde, Sir Dirk—*contd*
466–7; French present retrospective of films,
468; honoured at Guildhall, 472; pays for
Anne Leon's private medical treatment,
472–3; Variety Club award, 478; gives
farewell party for Sybil Burton, 486; on effect
of ageing, 488–9; narrates Galsworthy's
Forsyte Saga for BBC, 490; autobiographical
TV programme, 492 & n, 493, 516, 518–19;
religious scepticism, 498; views and
campaigning in later years, 500–4; roles in
later years, 501–2; knighthood, 517, 519–20,
524; childhood in Glasgow, 526–9; solo
readings and talks, 548–9, 562, 567; shingles,
560, 563, 568; locked out of flat, 563–4; gives
narration for *The Merry Widow*, 566 & n;
heart problem, 568–70; bursts vein in leg,
573; poetry readings, 586; operation
(angioplasty), 587, 590, 593, 595; suffers
severe stroke (1996), 595; death, 596; out-
takes, 597–607; on hate- and love-objects,
607
Bogdanovich, Peter, 130, 153
Bolt, Robert, 340n, 358n
Boluda, Eduardo and Antonia, 27–30, 32–3,
36, 39, 45, 53, 55–6, 81n
Bonham Carter, Helena, 419n, 438, 443, 487,
569n
Booksellers Association, 542–3
Bordes, Hélène ('the Plank'), **355, 359, 362,
369, 374, 389, 395, 401, 406, 408, 409,
419, 420, 422, 423, 427, 429, 432, 452,
455, 493, 523, 604, 605, 606, 607**;
correspondence with DB, 7, 584; writes
study of DB's autobiographical writings,
354–5, 360, 369; pestered by correspondent,
408, 452
Boston, University of: acquires DB's papers,
434, 484
Bounty, The (film), 340
Bourdain, Michel, 589
Bowie, David, 312
Bowlby, Nicholas, 276, 503
Bowlby, Romilly, 503n
Bowlby, Rosalind (*née* Bell), 276n, 376–7,
503
Box, Betty, 42 & n, 45, 49,115, 217, 546
Box, Sydney, 546 & n
Bragg, Melvyn, Baron, 350, 555 & n, 561
Branagh, Kenneth, 471n, 569 & n
Brecht, Bertolt: *The Life of Galileo*, 35n, 95n,
131
Breen, Joseph: US Production Code, 328
Bridge Too Far, A (film), 11, 135, 145, 150n, 154–5,
179, 190–1, 197n
Brien, Alan, 158n
British Broadcasting Corporation (BBC):

homage to DB, 151; *see also* individual
programmes
British Comedy Society, 579n
British Film Institute: awards Fellowship to
DB, 407 & n
Bromley (Kent): correspondent pesters DB,
259–60 & n
Bronson, Charles, 145
Brook, Peter, 289
Brookner, Anita: *Hotel du Lac*, 368; *A Private
View*, 560 & n
Brooks, Louise, 275
Brooks, Richard, 266–7 & n
Brougham, Henry, Baron, 358
Browne, Coral, 557
Browning, Lieut.-General Sir Frederick ('Boy'),
11, 154 & n, 190, 197n, 517 & n
Brynner, Yul, 96
Buchet, Martine: *La Colombe d'Or at Saint
Paul de Vence*, 576 & n
Buckle, Richard, 263n
Bullitt (film), 267
Burchill, Julie, 558
Burgess, Anthony, 1, 232–3 & n; *Earthly Powers*,
283, 601
Buried Alive (cancelled TV film), 302n, 307n,
438
Burke, Alfred, 192n
Burstyn, Ellen, 132–3, 144, 146, 147–8, 152, 156
Burton, Richard, 38, 47 & n, 63, 74n, 94, 464,
545
Byrne, John, 12

Cabrol, Gilles, 380
Cadogan Gardens, Chelsea, 433, 592
Caine Sir Michael, 115n, 141, 145, 155, 207
Cairncross, James, **192**
Cal (film), 339
Calder-Marshall, Anna, 134, 136
Callil, Carmen, 286n
Campbell, Judy, 476n
Campbell, Mrs Patrick, 8
Campbell, Patrick (Lord Glenavy), 293
Camus, Albert: *l'Etranger*, 48 & n
Canby, Vincent, 167 & n
Candy (dog), 28, 34, 124 &n
Cannes, 67; Film Festival, 68n, 111, 117, 130–1,
212–13, 220, 233, 251, 253, 309, 310–11, 326,
334–5, 337–40, 347, 368, 401, 460–3, 600
Capital Radio, 101n, 235
Capote, Truman, 446
Capucine (born Germaine Lefebvre), 88, 213,
490 & n, 556n, 594
Cardinale, Claudia, 237
Cariou, Len, 156n
Caroline, Princess of Monaco, 288
Carr, Audrey, **378**

Carr, Christine, 378n
Carrington, Dora, 447 & n
Carson, Hunter, 338
Cast a Dark Shadow (film), 570
Cau, Jean: 'Les Anglais "homos"', 492n
Caute, David: *Joseph Losey: A Revenge on Life*, 552, 591
Cavani, Liliana, 35n, 96, 98, 100–1, 104–5, 111–12, 113 & n, 114, 124, 130, 235
Chabrier, Hortense, 329, 593
Chalk Garden, The (proposed film), 443
Chamberlain, Neville, 301
Chamberlain, Richard, 72n
Chamberlin, Powell & Bon (architects), 310n
Channon, Sir Henry ('Chips'): diaries, 577 & n
Chaplin, Sir Charles, 270, 520
Charles, Prince of Wales, 38n, 190, 201, 280n, 569–70
Charlie and the Chocolate Factory (film), 280n
Charlie's Angels (TV programme), 207n
Charlton, John, **126, 598**; and DB's writing, 10, 126, 172, 229; takes holiday, 293; suggests title for DB's book, 295n
Chat, Le (film), 68n
Châteauneuf de Grasse *see* Haut Clermont, Le
Chatto, Beth, 531 & n
Chatto, Rosalind, 74 & n
Chatto & Windus (publishers): publish DB, 140, 159, 162–3, 166, 206, 220, 258–9, 277, 316; troubles at, 286n; Norah Smallwood leaves, 327
Chatwin, Bruce, 561; *Utz*, 601
Chekhov, Anton: *The Cherry Orchard*, 289, 603
Chelsea: DB and Tony rent house in, 419; *see also* Cadogan Gardens
Cheshire, Leonard, Baron, 498
Chess, Mary, 247
Chirac, Jacques, 580, 582, 585
Chorus Line, A (film), 368, 385n
Christie, Julie, 34, 50, 117, 136, 152n, 217
Christopher, Sybil (*earlier* Burton), 486
Churchill, Sir Winston, 332
Ciment, Michel: *Conversations with Losey* (*earlier* Le Livre de Losey), 348n
Cinecittà, 45
Cipriani, Arrigo: *The Harry's Bar Cookbook*, 547 & n
Clark, Alan: *Diaries*, 561 & n
Clark, Kenneth, Baron, 317, 325
Clarke, Gerald: *Capote: A Biography*, 446n; *Get Happy: The Life of Judy Garland*, 448 & n
Clayton, Jack, 60, 61, 78, 130, 153n
Cleared for Take-Off (DB), 557–8 & n, 567
Cleopatra (film), 545
Clift, Montgomery, 464
Clockwork Orange, A (film), 83

Close, Glenn, 487
Closing Ranks (DB; novel), 329, 368, 382n, 579 & n, 580, 587 & n, 594
Cochrane, Peter, 231 & n
Cogan, Alma, 486n
Cohen, Nat, 167& n
Colbert, Claudette, 51
Coldstream, John, **529, 606**; as literary editor of *Daily Telegraph*, 529n, 560
Colegate, Isabel: *The Shooting Party*, 277
Colette, 367, 606
Collins, Joan, 212n, 488
Collyer, Paddie, **372**
Columbia (film corporation), 58
Company of Youth, 546 & n
Compton-Burnett, Dame Ivy, 346–7
Connery, Sir Sean, 69, 135 & n, 145, 155, 266n
Conran, Shirley: *Lace*, 321
Conti, Tom, 245
Conversation Piece (film), 112n
Cooper, Sir Alfred Duff, 245, 577
Cooper, Lady Diana, 242, 499 577; *Autobiography*, 245 & n
Cooper, Gary, 207
Coppola, Francis Ford, 233n
Cortese, Valentina, 288, 580n
Costner, Kevin, 567
Cotten, Joseph, 464
Courtenay, Sir Tom, 90 & n, 217, 290 & n, 508
Covington, Julie, 217
Cowan, Theo, 354
Coward, Sir Noël, 127, 139, 333, 488, 513–15, 575n, 598; *Blithe Spirit*, 514; *Suite in Three Keys*, 514n, *The Vortex*, 514
Cox, Lionel, 299n
Cox, Nerine *see* Selwood, Nerine
Cradock, Fanny, 600
Craig, Wendy, 49
Crawford, Gabrielle, 595
Creighton, Anthony, 572 & n
Cresson, Edith, 492n
Croft, Peggy, 4
Cronin, A.J.: *The Citadel*, 392
Crowley, Mart, 254 & n
Cukor, George, **200**; and film of *Justine*, 37, 497; DB films with, 143; in DB's *Snakes and Ladders*, 206; and *A Star Is Born*, 386n; decline, 464
Cuore di cane (film), 128 & n
Cusack, Cyril, 35 & n, 95

D-Day landings (1944), 4, 337, 562
Daddy Nostalgie (*These Foolish Things*; film), 446n, 450, 451, 453n, 460–3, 468, 473, 476, 481, 489, 567, 605

Dahl, Roald, **265, 279,280, 284**; DB plays in
    The Patricia Neal Story, 264, 270–3; writing,
    289, 521; on gardening, 321; *Danny the
    Champion of the World*, 280 & n
Dahl, Tessa, 273
Daily Telegraph, The: DB reviews and writes
    for, 438 & n, 446–7 & n, 498n, 503, 510,
    516–17, 529n, 552, 554n, 560
Daisy (dog), 63, 64, 71, 76, 84, 92, 101–2, 108,
    174, 204; death, 223
Dam Busters, The (film), 88
Damiani, Damiano, 41 & n, 45
Damned, The (*La caduta degli dei*;
    Götterdämmerung; film), 27, 37, 40, 44,
    59–60
Dance, Charles, 332n
Danjoux, Marie and Henri, 81 & n, 82–3, 91,
    99, 241 & n
Dankworth, Sir John, 342
Darling (film), 7, 42n, 216n, 545
Dartmouth College, 43n
Daubeny, Molly, Lady, **289**
Davie, Michael, 242n
Davies, Andrew: *Rose*, 274n
Davies, Pamela, 126 & n
Davis, Bette, 7, 78–9, 81–2, 87, 92, 93n, 138–9
Dawson, Beatrice ('Bumble'), 36 & n
Day of the Locust, The (film), 132n, 136n
Day-Lewis, Daniel, 464
Dearden, Basil, 66n, 342, 372n, 373
Death in Venice (film): DB plays Aschenbach
    in, 40–4, 52–6, 63, 81, 122, 130, 547, 597;
    shooting, 44, 49; Losey and, 47; screened,
    58, 70, 73, 172, 373; wins award for Visconti,
    68n; Visconti justifies making, 105; shown
    on TV, 290
Dee, Simon, 45
de Havilland, Olivia, 545
de Jongh, Nicholas, 572
Delfont, Bernard, Baron, 167 & n, 233 & n
Delon, Alain, 37, 74n, 94
Delors, Jacques, 492n
Demongeot, Mylène, 545
Dench, Dame Judi, 487
Denham, Maurice, 274
de Niro, Robert, 569 & n
Desert Island Discs (radio programme), 456n
Despair (film), 168, 170, 175, 182–5, 194–6,
    202n, 205, 227, 234, 460, 481–4
Devils, The (film), 72n
Devonshire, Deborah, Duchess of, 278
Diana, Princess of Wales (*née* Spencer), 280n,
    378, 568, 570
Dietrich, Marlene, 324, 359
Dillon, Carmen, 69
Dirk Bogarde – By Myself (TV programme),
    492 & n, 493, 516, 518–19

Diversion No.2 (revue), 192
Doctor's Dilemma, The (film), 96n, 545n
Dodd, James, 391n
Dodd, Mary (*née* Forwood), **391, 403, 531, 603**
Dodds, Olive, **605**
Doel, Frank, 6
Doillon, Jacques, 476 & n
Doillon, Lou, 476 & n
Doll's House, A (film), 100
Donald, James, 193
Donaldson, Frances, Lady: *Edward VIII*,
    145 & n
Donaldson, Roger, 340n
Donen, Stanley, 340
Don't Look Now (film), 117, 152n
Dosai, Istvan, 339n
Dotrice, Roy, 175 & n; daughters (Karen,
    Michele and Yvette), 217
Douglas, Kirk, 253
Drabble, Margaret, 92
Drummer's Yard, near Beaconsfield, 11
Ducreux, Louis, 449n
Dullea, Keir, 100n
du Maurier, Daphne (Lady Browning), 154 &
    n, 190
Dunn, Nell: *Steaming*, 368
Dunnock, Mildred, 272
Durrell, Gerald, 87
Durrell, Lawrence, 255, 497; *Justine*, 265
Dylan, Bob, 134

Eastwood, Clint, 42n
Eco, Umberto, 368 & n
Economist, The (journal), 581, 583
Ekberg, Anita, 202 & n
Elizabeth II, Queen, 378, 414, 574
Elizabeth the Queen Mother, 412, 414–15, 517
Elliott, Denholm, 244n, 274
Ellis, Vivian, 472
Enchanted April (film), 569
Esther Waters (film), 4, 192n
E.T. (film) 309
Etranger, l' (*Lo straniero*; film), 48 & n
European Pianist of the Year *see* National Power
    World Piano Competition
Evans, Dame Edith, 43, 273
Evans, Maurice, 113
Evening News, 244
Everett, Rupert, 339n

Fabrizi, Aldo, 464
Falk, Rossella, 38–9
Falkender, Marcia, Baroness, 139n
Fargue, Annie, 598
Farrow, Mia, 34, 35n, 153n
Fassbinder, Rainer Werner, **175, 194**; directs
    Despair, 168, 173, 174–6, 178, 182–4, 190, 227,

460; pessimism, 175–8; relations with DB, 183, 190; reputation and expertise, 191, 196, 234–5; DB describes to Wallace S. Watson, 482–5; death, 484

Fawcett-Majors, Farrah, 207 & n

Fearon, George, 486

Feibleman, Peter: *Lilly: Reminiscences of Lillian Hellman*, 446n

Fellini, Federico, 54, 95, 196

Fellini's Roma (film), 95

Fellowes, Julian, 419

Fells, Dorothy, 4

Fermor, Sir Patrick Leigh: DB plays in *Ill Met By Moonlight*, 395–6; DB visits in hospital in London, 539; *The Violins of Saint-Jacques*, 395 & n

Ferréol, Andréa, 168, 176, 183–4, 190, 194, 203, 482–4

Ferrer, José, 49 & n, 56

Feuillère, Edwige, 288, 367, 580

Field, Shirley Anne: *A Time for Love*, 517n

Fielding, Daphne, **534, 538, 541**; visits DB, 134, 136, 139; believes passage in *A Particular Friendship* libellous, 450n; birthday lunch, 565; on reading, 573–4

Fighting Cock, The (army newspaper), 4

Figures in a Landscape (film), 48 & n, 59

Finch, Peter, 72n, 545

Finney, Albert, 89n, 339 & n, 478, 572

Firth, Colin, 339n

Fixer, The (film), 31n, 62n, 63 & n, 111, 155, 302n

Fonda, Henry, 96

Fonda, Jane, 100n

Fontanne, Lynn, 201

Foot, Michael, 282 & n

For the Time Being: Collected Journalism (DB), 479n, 596 & n

Forbes, Bryan, **223**; and *The Madwoman of Chaillot*, 37 & n; *Familiar Strangers*, 224n

Foreman, Carl, 96 & n

Forsyth, Bruce, 216

Forwood, Anthony (Ernest Lytton Langton Forwood): keeps diary, 1; relations with DB, 3, 85, 390–1, 406, 466; resides on Continent, 4, 27; in Labaro (Italy) with DB, 32; motor cars and driving, 39, 49, 57, 70, 379, 380n, 388; in Venice with DB, 50; moves to le Haut Clermont with DB, 53; cyst, 61; and DB's refusing film parts, 70, 100; domestic and gardening activities, 82–3, 85, 110, 157, 169, 257, 318, 322; accompanies DB from Dover, 123 & n; friendship with Brock Van den Bogaerde, 137; on Jack Jones, 141; drawing, 148; in Paris with DB, 152, 325; aunt visits in France, 161; in Berlin with DB, 190; abscess on tooth, 214; compiles index

for DB's *Snakes and Ladders*, 214; and death of Daisy (dog), 223; flu, 237; writing, 237, 368; reads Millar book, 242; arthritic foot, 254; helps bury Labo (dog), 264; in thunderstorm, 281; Parkinson's disease, 240–1, 299n, 302, 364, 380, 404–5, 406, 428; witnesses snake attack on toad, 296; cancer, 308 & n, 310n, 380, 406, 420, 422, 426–8, 550; convalesces, 310, 602; and DB's award at Cannes Film Festival, 311; sadness at leaving Clermont, 317; watches *Jewel in the Crown*, 332; noseblowing, 346; approves of DB's article on father, 350; entertains in France, 357; ageing and deterioration, 364–5, 377, 380; misses DB's honorary doctorate at St Andrews, 367, 377; on DB's drawing, 384; photograph of DB used as book cover, 385, 405; and Attenboroughs, 386; reads typscript of DB's *Backcloth*, 388; prostate operation and convalescence, 389–93, 396; and prospective return to England, 393; and filming of *May We Borrow Your Husband?*, 405; leaves Clermont, 424; death, 429–31, 433–4, 443–4, 456, 490, 605; letter willing, 440; at Sybil Burton's farewell party, 486n; in DB's *A Short Walk from Harrods*, 531–3, 542, 550–1; and DB's literary qualities, 602

Forwood, Gareth, 36 & n, 72, 98 & n, 127n, 192–3

Forwood, Leslie Langton, 61–2

Forwood, Thomas, 127n, 477, 503 & n, 536

Forwood, Véronique, 127n

Fosse, Bob, 253

Four Weddings and a Funeral (film), 556, 569

Fowles, John, 601

Fox, Angela, 45, 450; *Slightly Foxed*, 389 & n; *Completely Foxed*, 450 & n

Fox, Edward, 334, 571, 590n, 591n

Fox, James, 50 & n, 57n, 334n, 436; *Comeback*, 334n

Fox, Robert, 503, 508, 559, 571–2, 590–1 & n

Fox, Robin, 40 & n, 45, 50, 559

Foyles luncheons, 264, 333

France: political situation, 207, 284, 304, 311; DB's devotion to, 371, 491, 524, 583, 588, 604; *see also* Haut Clermont, Le; Paris

Frankel, Cyril, 125n

Frankenheimer, John, 31n, 62 & n, 70, 100, 157

Frankham, David, **266, 446, 553, 566, 568, 599, 600, 602, 603, 604, 606**; correspondence with DB, 7

Frankovich, Mike, 58

Fraser, Lady Antonia, 366 & n, 522

Frears, Stephen, 405n

French, Michael, 475

Freud, Lucian, 278

Friedkin, William, 46n

Fry, Christopher, 442n

Gabin, Jean, 68
Gainsbourg, Charlotte, 476 & n
Gainsbourg, Serge, 476n, 477–8 & n
Galileo (film and play), 35 & n, 95 & n, 131 &
    n, 132n
Galsworthy, John: The Forsyte Saga, 450, 490;
    A Summer Story, 436n
Gandhi (film), 234, 237, 309, 311n
Garbo, Greta, 129, 324, 467
Gardner, Ava, 125n, 128, 129–30, 454, 464
Garland, Judy, 86 & n, 206, 214, 278, 386n,
    448, 515
Garland, Patrick, 100n, 451n
Garnett, David: Lady into Fox, 96
Garrick Club, 557n
Gassman, Vittorio, 309
Gaulle, Charles de, 580, 589
Gavin, Brigadier-General James, 155n
Geeves, Val, 4
'Genius in Love with Vulgarity, A' (DB;
    newspaper article), 552 & n
Gentle Occupation, A (DB; novel): title, 229–30;
    writing, 218, 220, 222 & n, 224, 231, 233–4,
    239, 599; publication and reception, 235–6,
    238, 251–2; launch and promotion, 244, 248,
    264n; corrections and editing, 230, 234, 251;
    foreign translations, 269–70, 593
Gerzina, Gretchen: Carrington, 447 & n
Gibson, Mel, 487
Gide, André: The Immoralist, 118 & n
Gielgud, Sir John, 77, 144, 146–7, 150–1, 156,
    181, 204, 207, 208, 258, 443, 514, 521n; An
    Actor and His Time, 600; Stage Directions,
    77n
Gilbert, Bee (Bridget), 61, 70, 75, 82, 99, 108,
    154, 302, 307, 440; correspondence with
    DB, 6; and Ian Holm, 6, 100, 157, 276 & n
Girardot, Annie, 120
Giraudoux, Jean: The Madwoman of Chaillot,
    37n
Gladstone, David and April, 387 & n
Gladwyn, Cynthia, Lady, 577 & n
Glasgow: DB's childhood in, 526–9
Glyndebourne Festival Opera, 566 & n
Go-Between, The (film), 34, 38, 50, 55n, 67n,
    68–9
Godwin-Austen, Robert, 246–7 & n
Goetz, William and Edith, 114 & n
Gogh, Vincent van, 135
Goldman, William, 155
Goldwyn, Samuel, 446
Goodings, (Margaret) Elizabeth Marie (née
    Van den Bogaerde; DB's sister; 'Lu'; 'Lulu'),
    147, 150, 164, 363, 379, 382, 597, 605;
    letters from DB, 3; stays at Haut Clermont,

146–50, 156, 173–4, 225, 229, 230, 232; DB
    gives Postillion to, 163–6; and mother's death
    and funeral, 249; and DB's article on father
    for Times bicentennial, 347 & n; and
    husband's cancer, 379–81; burgled, 392–3;
    visits Somme battlefield with DB, 402;
    husband's death, 431 & n, 605; and DB's
    knighthood and investiture, 520, 523, 606;
    reads DB's Short Walk from Harrods, 531–3;
    visits DB in Chelsea, 537, 540
Goodings, George (Elizabeth's husband), 146,
    156, 173–4, 232, 379n, 381, 383, 605; death,
    431n
Goodings, Judy (née Roberts; Mark's wife), 430
Goodings, Mark, 430; injured in fight, 98;
    appearance, 152 & n; in DB's
    autobiography, 383
Goodings, Sarah, 383
Gordon, Carol, 596
Gordon, Dorothy Webster ('Mrs X'), 27;
    correspondence and relations with DG, 5–6,
    10, 77, 98, 118–19, 211, 305, 347–8, 433, 441–2,
    448, 596 & n; DB never meets, 87, 92;
    death, 118–19, 584, 598 ; South African
    correspondent enquires about, 318; in An
    Orderly Man, 294 & n
Gordon, Ruth, 514n
Gotlieb, Howard, 484
Grace, Princess of Monaco, 288, 580
Grade, Lew, Baron, 233 & n
Grand, Elaine, 261n
Granger, Stewart, 451, 549
Grant, Cary, 207
Grant, Hugh, 556
Grasse see Haut Clermont, Le
Great Gatsby, The (film), 153 & n
Great Meadow (DB): Jeremy Hutchinson and,
    185n; writing, 265 & n, 516n, 524; DB
    submits to Kavanagh, 520; DB reads on
    BBC radio, 536, 539; success, 546
Greaves, Flt Lt Christopher, 558 & n
Greene, Graham, 238 & n, 239; Dr Fischer of
    Geneva, 244n, 251 & n; May We Borrow Your
    Husband?, 379n, 386, 390, 396n, 397–8, 404,
    502
Grenfell, Joyce: Darling Ma: Letters to Her
    Mother, 1932–1944, 435 & n
Gribble, Bernard, 268
Griem, Helmut, 41, 90
Griese, Irma, 94
Gronowicz, Antoni: Garbo: Her Story,
    467 & n
Guard, Dominic ('Leo'), 57n, 69
Guardian Travel Supplement, 232
Guildford: Yvonne Arnaud Theatre, 442 & n
Guinness, Sir Alec, 193, 207, 245
Guinness, Matthew, 193

Guinness, Merula, Lady, 193

Hackett, General Sir John: *I Was a Stranger*, 197 & n
Hackett, Pat: *The Andy Warhol Diaries*, 448 & n
Hackman, Gene, 145, 155
Haggard, Piers, 436n
Haig, David, 480n
Haining, Peter: *The Legend of Greta Garbo*, 467 & n
'Half-life in World's End, A' (DB; newspaper article), 435 & n
Hall, Sir Peter, 221 & n, 226, 333–4, 572
Hall, Willis, 11, 402n, 556 & n
Hamer, Robert, 464 & n
Hamlet (Zeffirelli film), 487n
Hammond, Diana, 357n
Handl, Irene: *The Sioux*, 508 & n
Handsley, Mark, 539 & n
Hanff, Helene: *84 Charing Cross Road*, 6
Harbottle, Laurence, 413; on DB's extreme Bromley fan, 259n
Harris, John: *Covenant with Death*, 402n
Harris, Julie, 474
Harris, Rosemary, 514n
Harrison, Cathryn, 480n
Harrison, John and Rebecca, 596
Harrison, Noel, 486n
Harrison, Sir Rex, 99 & n, 138, 188–9, 451, 557, 559
Hartley, L.P.: *The Go-Between*, 34, 50
Harty, Russell, 125n, 126, 141, 163, 165, 322, 498, 519
Harvey, Anthony, 42 & n, 264n, 266, 267–8, 279
Harwood, Ronald: *The Dresser*, 290n
Hatchards (bookshop), Piccadilly, 467
Haut Clermont, Le, Châteauneuf de Grasse: DB purchases, 40–1, 43–4; life at, 54–6, 58, 71–2, 75–6, 81, 85, 99, 105, 110, 123, 127, 201, 365–6; visitors, 55, 75–6, 110, 161, 228–9, 230–1, 251–3, 285; refurnishing, 236, 240; affected by earthquake, 259; DB puts on market, 317, 404; DB sells and leaves, 408–11, 424, 494; de Pauws occupy and alter, 445, 495, 575
Healey, Denis, Baron, 162 & n, 163
Hearst, William Randolph, 32
Heat and Dust (film), 309
Heilpern, John, 463
Heinemann Educational Books, 77
Hellman, Lillian, 446
Hemingway, Ernest, 208
Hepburn, Audrey, 537
Hepburn, Katharine, 499
Heysel stadium, Brussels, 520 & n

Higgins, John, 285
Hillsborough football ground disaster, 512 & n
Hinxman, Margaret: *The Films of Dirk Bogarde* (with Susan d'Arcy), 7; interviews DB, 44, 46n, 62n
Hiscock, Eric, 278n
Histoire d'O, L' (film), 128 & n, 130, 138
Hitchcock, Sir Alfred, 520n
Hoare, Philip, 512; *Noël Coward: A Biography*, 512n
Hobson, Sir Harold, 158 & n, 217
Hodges, Mike, 302n
Holden, Edith: *The Country Diary of an Edwardian Lady*, 206 & n
Holland, 156
Hollingsworth, Hilda: *They Tied a Label on My Coat*, 517n
Hollywood-UK (TV documentary), 545
Holm, Sir Ian, 61, 70, 75, 82; relations with Bee Gilbert, 6, 100, 157; on poverty, 63; in Budapest, 64, 302n; buys house in Kent, 70n; visits DB in France, 73, 83n; film reviewed, 109; plays J.M. Barrie, 216; occupies London premises, 308
Holm, Sarah-Jane, 441
Holocaust: DB writes and lectures on, 498, 500, 502, 504
Holt, Elizabeth, 376
homosexuality: legal repression, 3; DB on representation in *Victim*, 372–3, 577, 594; in England, 492n
Hopkins, Sir Anthony, 191n, 340n
Hopkinson, Simon, 547; DB lunches with, 575
Hordern, Sir Michael, 521n
Horstig-Primuz, Olga, 424, 476, 488, 595, 607; at Cannes Film Festival, 311
Horstig-Primuz, Véra, 425
Hough, Richard: *Edwina*, 332n
'How Could Such Hatred Exist?' (DB; newspaper review), 498n
Howard, Brian, 246n, 247
Hughes, David, 91n, 350; *The Pork Butcher*, 350
Hughes, Thomas: *Tom Brown's Schooldays*, 84 & n
Hulbert, Jack, 552
Hunted (film), 464
Huppert, Isabelle, 338, 583, 585
Huston, John, 89n, 339–40, 464
Huston, Ricki, 30 & n
Hutchinson, Jeremy, Baron, 185
Hutton, Michael Clayton: *Power Without Glory* (play), 513n

I Could Go On Singing (film), 86 & n
Ill Met By Moonlight (film), 395–6, 401n
'Impressions in the Sand' (DB; newspaper article), 428 & n

Independent on Sunday, 454
IRA: bombing in London, 292–3 & n
Irons, Jeremy, 358n
Irvin, John, 590n
Isoardi, Marc and Bruna, 291n, 295
Isoardi, Marie-Christine, 291, 364–5
Italy: earthquake (1980), 259; *Jericho* published and promoted in, 534–5; *see also* Labaro; Rome
Ivory, James, 309n, 476n

Jackson, Glenda: in *Sunday, Bloody Sunday*, 72n; directed by Ken Russell, 72 & n; in *The Romantic Englishwoman*, 115 & n, 141; in *The Patricia Neal Story*, 264–6, 268–9, 273, 284, 287, 303; DB admires, 268, 273; plays in *Rose* in New York, 274; cast with DB in *Buried Alive*, 302 & n, 303; at Cannes Film Festival, 309; visits DB in France, 346–7, 359; in *The Chalk Garden*, 443
Jacobi, Sir Derek, 561 & n
Jacobs, David, 441
Jacobson, Dan: *Time and Time Again: Autobiographies*, 383n
Jaeckin, Just, 128
Jamaica: DB writes on, 232 & n
Jarre, Jean-Michel, **218**; lunch with DB, 298
Jeans, Isabel, 514
Jenkins, Humphrey, **603**; and Newick Amateur Dramatic Society, 299n
Jenkins, Sir Michael: *A House in Flanders*, 589
Jericho (DB; novel): writing, 407, 467, 477, 480, 493–4; publication, 497, 524; printing and proofing, 498, 500–1; reception, 523–4; promotional tour, 524; dedicated to Mary Dodd, 533; sequel (*A Period of Adjustment*), 534, 543, 551–2; published in Italy, 534–5; broadcast on BBC, 536, 539
Joe Allen (of Covent Garden), 254 & n
Joffé, Roland, 358n, 401n
John, Sir Elton, 195, 231
Johns, Glynis, 98n, 391n, 451
Johnson, Nunnally, 464 & n
Jones, John Francis ('Jack'; 'Tony'), **141, 251, 604**; DB corresponds with, 3; death, 469–70
Joyce, Paul, 492n
Juggernaut (film), 109n
Justine (film), 7, 37, 42, 202n, 265, 497, 572n

Kael, Pauline, 167 & n, 181, 204
Kagemusha (film), 253n
Kandinsky, Wassily, 530
Kaniewska, Marek, 339n
Karina, Anna, 37
Katz, Norman, 54 & n, 57
Kavanagh, Patricia, **327, 465, 520, 603, 605**;

as DB's literary agent, 327–8, 516n, 533; DB dines with, 547n
Kendal, Felicity, 217
Kendall, Kay, 87, 101, 188–9, 206, 214, 217, 228
Keneally, Thomas: *Schindler's Ark*, 320
Kennedy, Edward, 36n
Kennedy, Nicki, 534–7
Kensington: DB buys house (Queen Anne House, Duke's Lane), 421, 430–3
Kensington and Chelsea Borough Council, **475**
Kent State University, 52n
Kind Hearts and Coronets (film), 464n
King and Country (film), 37, 56n, 90n, 290n
Kissel, Howard: *David Merrick: The Abominable Showman*, 560 & n
Knef, Hildegard: *The Gift Horse*, 77 & n
Knievel, Evel, 121
Knife in the Water (film), 36
Knight, Esmond, 351–2
Knopf (US publishers), 236, 238, 258
Kopechne, Mary Jo, 36n
Korda, Sir Alexander, 520n
Kozintsev, Grigori, 77 & n
Kroll, Jack, 234n
Kurosawa, Akira, 253

Labaro, near Rome: Villa Berti, 27, 29, 32, 43, 46
Labèque, Katia and Marielle, 553 & n
Labo (dog), 54n, 63, 71, 84, 101, 108–9, 174, 223, 602; death, 263–4
'Lady' *see* Martinez, Mme
Laine, Dame Clementine Dinah (Cleo), 342
'Lally' *see* Searle, Ellen
Lambert, Gavin: *On Cukor*, 201 & n
Lambilliotte, Dominique, **576, 579, 582, 584, 587, 592**; correspondence with DB, 576, 584
Lancaster, Burt, 112n
Landa, Alfredo, 340 & n
Lane, Allen (publisher), 327
Lang, Jack, 299n
Langley, Lee, **496**; screen adaptation of *Voices in the Garden*, 496–7, 499
Langtry, Lillie, 457, 471, 592
Larkin, Philip, 10
Lartigue, Jacques Henri and Florette, 241, 357
La Rue, Danny, 139
László, Philip de, 89
Lattuada, Alberto, 128n
Laure, Odette, 446n, 454, 460–1, 485
Laurentiis, Dino de, 45, 154 & n
Lavery, Hugh, 193 & n
'Lawrence of Arabia' (abandoned film; later play, 'Ross'), 464n, 545
Lawrence, T.E., 525n
Layton and Johnston (singers), 87 & n

Lean, Sir David, 520n
Le Carré, John: *Smiley's People*, 251 & n
Lees-Milne, James, 210 & n, 211; *Harold Nicolson: A Biography*, 277n, 331–2
Lehmann, Rosamond: *The Weather in the Streets*, 31
Leigh, Mike, 549
Leigh-Hunt, Barbara, 439
Leighton, Margaret, 67, 69
Lenya, Lotte, 103
Leon, Anne, 472 & n
Leon, Sir John *see* Standing, John
Leopard, The (film), 37n, 359n
Lessing, Doris, 1
Lester, Richard, 109n
Letter to Brezhnev, A (film), 405 & n
Levin, Bernard, 182, 217
Lewis, Roger: *The Real Life of Laurence Olivier*, 591 & n
Lewis, Rosa, 242
Lewis, Wyndham, 248
Libel (film), 38, 96, 545
Lieberson, Sandy, 358n
Lillian, Princess, wife of Prince Bertil, 228
Lily (DB's housekeeper), 580
Lindfors, Viveca, 580
Lion, Jacques, 246n
Lion, Jean, **246**
Lion in Winter, The (film), 421n
Little Night Music, A (film), 156
Logan's Run (film), 207n
Lom, Herbert, 233
Loncraine, Richard, 244n
London: DB visits from France, 105–7, 214, 236, 274–6, 290, 299, 307, 308, 310–11, 319, 330, 363, 367, 383, 389; DB seeks house in, 308, 312, 317, 413, 420; DB rents house in (Moore Street, Chelsea), 419; *see also* Cadogan Gardens; Chelsea; Kensington
Longanesi (Italian publishers), 535
Loren, Sophia, 309
Loschetter, Léon, 82n, 150
Loschetter, Thomas, 82
Losey, Joseph, **32, 36, 40, 43, 46, 50, 58, 66, 68, 74, 95, 111, 115, 116, 124, 597**; relations with DB, 7, 27, 46–8, 60, 74, 81–2, 89–90, 94–5, 124, 153, 558; DB works with, 27, 63, 130, 196, 303; as visiting Professor at Dartmouth College, 43n; wins Palme d'Or at Cannes (1971), 68; and prospect of directing Bette Davis, 81; directs *A Doll's House*, 100; films in 1975 Cannes Festival, 130–2; in DB's *Snakes and Ladders*, 206, 214; and Dennis Potter's *Blade on the Feather*, 244 & n; death and tribute, 341–4; character, 348–9; memoir on, 348 & n; 'wrap party' for, 353–4; and *The Servant*, 366; final film

(Steaming), 368; and proposed film of *Under the Volcano*, 464; Caute's biography of, 552, 591; qualities, 552; and Dennis Potter, 561
Losey, Patricia, **43, 55, 68, 124, 341, 353**; correspondence with DB, 7, 39; DB's regard for, 34, 38, 49–50, 74, 89; and DB's attitude to husband, 95; thanks DB for TV tribute to husband, 348; attends Cannes homage to husband, 368; appeals against McDonald's in Chelsea, 476n; and Caute's biography of husband, 552
Lott, Dame Felicity, 566
Lourdes Marie Louise, Sister, 590
Löwitsch, Klaus, 184, 194
Lowry, Malcolm: *Under the Volcano*, 89n, 162n
Loy, Myrna, 549
Lucan, Richard John Bingham, 7th Earl, and Veronica, Countess of, 138
Ludwig II, King of Bavaria, 70
Luke, David, 575 & n
Lullington Court, Sussex, 186–7
Lumley, Joanna, **315**; and Dirk's Foyle's luncheon, 334n
Lynch, John, 339n
Lyndon, Victor, 50 & n
Lynn, Dame Vera, 574
Lyrics for Lovers (DB's record), 89n, 282

McClellan, Forrest, **527**; *Some of My Aunts and Uncles*, 527n; *Then a Soldier*, 526
McClellan, Hester (*née* Niven), 526–7
McClellan, John ('Uncle York'), 526
McClellan, Nickie, 526
MacCorkindale, Simon, 217
McGowen, Alec, 449n
McDowell, Malcolm, 48n, 83, 99–100, 207
McEwen, Ian: *The Cement Garden*, 303n
McFarlane, Brian, **544, 548, 551, 606**; *An Autobiography of British Cinema* (earlier *Sixty Voices*), 544n; *The Encyclopedia of British Film*, 546n
McKenna, Virgina, 459
Mackenzie, Sir Compton: *My Life and Times*, 337 & n
McQueen, Steve, 135 & n, 267n
McTeer, Janet, 480n
Magee, Patrick, 46n
Mahler, Gustav, 44, 48, 53–4
Mahoney, Bob, **396, 604**
Mail on Sunday, The, 350
Major, Sir John, 566, 585
Major, Norma, Lady, 566
Majors, Lee, 207n
Malcolm, Derek, 158
Malik, Art, 332n
Malraux, Florence (Resnais' wife), 138
Manchester: Royal Exchange Theatre, 562

Mangano, Silvana, 154 & n
Mann, Roderick, 109
Mann, Thomas: *Death in Venice*, 44, 49n, 52–3, 54, 122, 575
Mansfield, Katherine, 326
Mantel, Hilary: *A Change of Climate*, 560 & n
Marais, Jean, 141
Marcus Aurelius Antoninus, Roman Emperor, 573
Markandaya, Kamala: *The Golden Honeycomb*, 198 & n
Martinez, Mme ('Lady'), 149 & n, 169, 198, 222, 241–2, 260, 264, 291, 297, 346
Mary Shelley's Frankenstein (film), 569 & n
Mason, James, 386n
Mastroianni, Marcello, 48n
Maugham, Syrie, 236 & n
May We Borrow Your Husband (TV film), 379n, 386, 390, 395, 396n, 397–8, 404–5, 410, 502, 604
Mayle, Peter, 532
Melford, Jill, **563, 573**
Mercer, David, 132n, 138 & n, 143–6, 153, 156, 170, 208, 226, 521
Merchant, Vivien, 367
Merry Christmas Mr Lawrence (film), 312 & n
Merry Widow, The (operetta), 52n, 566
Meyer, Russ, 212n
Meynell, Alice, 586
Midler, Bette, 216
Mikhalkov-Kontchalovski, Andrei, 213n
Miles, Sarah, 57 & n
Milestone, Lewis, 465
Millar, George: *Road to Resistance*, 242
Miller, Arthur, 83; *The Archbishop's Ceiling*, 169 & n
Mills, Sir John, 62, 126 & n, 545
Minghella, Anthony, 501n
Minnelli, Liza, 309, 448
Minney, R.J.: '*Puffin' Asquith*, 38n
Minx, Dieter, 176
Mirren, Dame Helen, 217, 339–40
Mission, The (film), 358n, 401
Mitchell, Julian, 339n
Mitchell, Yvonne, 193
Mitford, Jessica: *Hons and Rebels*, 499
Mitford, Nancy, 272; *Frederick the Great*, 64n; *Love from Nancy: The Letters* (ed. Charlotte Mosley), 541n, 543
Mitterrand, François, 284n, 304, 580
Modesty Blaise (film), 46, 125n
Monaco: Théâtre des Beaux-Arts, 288, 580
Montagu of Beaulieu, Edward, 3rd Baron, 3
Montand, Yves, 36, 49, 267
Month by the Lake, A (film), 590 & n
Moore, Henry, 559
Morahan, Christopher, 332n

Moravia, Alberto, 130
More, Kenneth, 63, 268; *More or Less*, 215 & n
Moreau, Jeanne, 81, 138
Morgan, Michèle, 309, 311
Morley, Christopher: *Thunder on the Left*, 50
Morley, Sheridan: *Dirk Bogarde: Rank Outsider*, 591 & n
Mortimer, John, 120n, 544; *Clinging to the Wreckage*, 292; *Titmuss Regained*, 499 & n
Mortimer, Penelope, **78, 80, 89, 91, 93, 96, 101, 117, 120, 137, 152, 219, 309, 411, 415, 433, 436, 437, 479, 497, 500, 505, 508, 517, 522, 530, 537, 597, 598, 605, 606**; correspondence with DB, 7, 8, 9, 304–5; offers to write script for Bette Davis, 78; teaching at Yaddo, New York State, 118n, 537 & n; injured in motoring accident, 137; takes DB to cinema to see *A Summer Story*, 436n; moves to Willesden, 479 & n; adapts Nicolson's *Portrait of a Marriage* for TV, 438 & n, 480–1; proposes writing play on DB's reaction to Tony's death, 505; writes autobiography, 517 & n, 522n, 543–4; *About Time: Autobiography 1918–1939*, 543n; *About Time Too: 1940–1978*, 543 & n; *Daddy's Gone A-Hunting*, 80, 87; *The Home*, 90n; *Long Distance*, 119–20 & n; 'A Love Story', 122 & n; *The Pumpkin Eater*, 78 & n, 80,522n; *Queen Elizabeth: A Life of the Queen Mother*, 412, 414–15
Mosley, Nicholas, 58 & n, 74, 331–2
Mountbatten, Admiral Louis, 1st Earl, 332
Mountbatten, Edwina, Countess, 332
Mr & Mrs Bridge (film), 476
Munro, H.H. ('Saki'), 439–40, 442, 447, 489, 494, 516
Murdoch, Dame Iris, 374, 387; *The Sea, The Sea*, 599
Murdoch, Rupert, 283n
Murray, Arthur, 83n
Murray, Sarah (*née* Niven; DB's aunt; 'Sadie'), 165–6 & n, 200n, 377, 527–9
Murray, William, 165n, 200n, 527–8 & n
Murry, John Middleton, 326
Mursky, Yevgeny, 570n
Music Lovers, The (film), 72n
My Beautiful Laundrette (film), 405 & n

Nabokov, Vladimir: *Despair*, 168, 175n, 176, 184, 188, 482; *Lolita*, 203
National Film Theatre: John Player lectures, 62 & n, 86; DB's interview with Bilbow at, 314n
National Power World Piano Competition, 568 & n, 570
National Theatre, London: Armistice Festival event (1988), 439–40

Neagle, Dame Anna, 373
Neal, Patricia, **265**; film on, 264, 272–3, 284
Neame, Ronald, 73, 86 & n
Nelson, John, 166
Nesbitt, Cathleen, 201
New Yorker, The (magazine), 121
Newell, Mike, 556, 569n
Newick Amateur Dramatic Society, 299n
Newman, Nanette, 224n
Newman, Paul, 135 & n, 477, 545
Niblo, Fred, 95n
Nicholas and Alexandra (film), 83 & n
Nichols, Dandy, 46 & n
Nicholson, Jack, 567
Nicholson, William: *The Vision*, 419n
Nicolson, Sir Harold, 209, 210n, 245, 277, 331, 438, 480
Nicolson, Nigel: *Mary Curzon*, 193 & n; *Portrait of a Marriage*, 438 & n, 480 & n
Nietzsche, Friedrich, 113 & n, 130
Night Porter, The (film), 96, 100, 104–5, 109–10, 111–12, 114, 117, 124 & n, 130, 138, 315
'Night to Remember, A' (DB; newspaper article), 521
Niro, Robert de, 358
Niven, David, 127, 140
Niven, James (Jimmy; DB's uncle), 529
Niven, Neil Munro ('Roey'; DB's uncle), 165–6 & n
Niven, Sarah (DB's aunt) *see* Murray, Sarah
Niven, William (DB's uncle), 529
Nixon, Richard M., 118 & n
'No Answer to the Sorrow and the Pity' (DB; newspaper article), 498n
Nore (house), Godalming, 246–8

O Lucky Man! (film), 99
O'Brien, Edna: *The High Road*, 438
O'Connor, Pat, 339n
Oh! What a Lovely War (film), 38, 40
O'Hagan, Colo, 446n
Olga (translator), 535
Olivier, Laurence, Baron, 145, 227 & n, 258, 591 & n
Ondaatje, Michael: *The English Patient*, 529n, 530n
O'Neal, Ryan, 155 & n
O'Neill, Eugene: *Strange Interlude*, 346n
Ophuls, Marcel, 454
Oradour-sur-Glane, 148 & n, 350n, 369
Oranmore and Browne, Oonagh, Lady, 139
Orderly Man, An (DB): writing, 5, 274, 276, 281–2, 287, 298; book jacket, 298 & n; publication, 302; authenticity, 306; on concentration camps, 320; popularity, 328; on Fassbinder, 483–4

Osborne, Helen (*née* Dawson), **571, 572, 590, 607**; and husband's illness, 560 & n
Osborne, John, **470, 510, 525, 554, 555, 557, 559, 606**; death and memorial service, 571–3 & n; *Almost a Gentleman*, 510n, 511; *A Better Class of Person*, 470; *Damn You, England*, 554n; *Déjàvu*, 525n; *Epitaph for George Dillon*, 556 & n; *Look Back in Anger*, 470–1, 554n
Oshima, Nagisa, 312n
O'Toole, Peter, 56, 63, 479 & n
Our Mother's House (film), 153n, 214n
Owens, Susan, **204, 299, 314, 408, 429, 511, 576, 600, 603, 604**; illness, 7, 204; DB meets, 408 & n; husband suffers stroke, 313–14; husband's death, 429n

Pacino, Al, 207, 357
Page, Anthony, 279
Paglia, Camille, 573
Paris: DB visits, 109, 152, 154, 317, 324–5, 410–11, 455–6, 468; Louvre, 317, 324–5, 389–90
Paris Match (magazine), 492 & n, 495
Paris, Texas (film), 338, 340
Parker, Joy, 105, 107
Parkinson, Sir Michael, 519
Parsons, Ian, 292
Particular Friendship, A (DB), 6, 8, 10, 12, 27, 211 & n, 433, 441–2, 447–8, 450n, 494
Partridge, Frances, 541; *Other People: Diaries 1963–66*, 541 & n
Partridges (Sloane Street grocers), 439 & n, 443, 469, 471, 541, 587n
Patricia Neal Story, The (film), 264n, 265n, 267–8, 272–3, 278–9, 284, 287, 303
Pauw, Alain de, **444, 473, 495**; improvements to Haut Clermont, 445, 495, 575
Pauw, Christine de, **575**; occupies Haut Clermont, 445, 495
Pavlova, Anna, 351
Pavlow, Muriel, 474 & n
Payne, Humfry, 106n
Pearson, John: *Façades*, 222n
Peckinpah, Sam, 105 & n
Penguin (publishers) *see* Viking Penguin
Percy (film), 83, 108n
Percy's Progress (film), 108
Period of Adjustment, A (DB), 538, 539–40, 543, 548, 551–2, 569 & n
Permission to Kill (film), 125n, 128, 141, 143n, 599
Perry, George (ed.): *The Golden Screen: Fifty Years of Films*, 439 & n, 442
Philby, Kim, 96
Philip, Prince, Duke of Edinburgh, 415, 490n, 574

Phillips, Arlene, 174n
Phillips, Leslie, 63
Phillips, Nicholas, 490 & n
Phillips, Siân, 488
'Picture Man, The' (DB; article on father), 350n
Pigott-Smith, Tim, 332n, 439–40, 486
Pinewood Studios, 459, 546
Pink, Susan, **457**
Pinter, Harold, **521**; writes script for *Accident*, 34; and Losey, 43; DB reads to Alexis Smith, 113; adapts Proust, 116n, 153; DB defends, 217; relations with DB, 366–7; reputation, 367; behaviour, 395, 522; DB praises writing, 499–500; directing, 502; Penelope Mortimer and, 522–3; *Betrayal*, 217; *The Birthday Party*, 46 & n; *No Man's Land*, 502, 521n; *Old Times*, 113 & n, 367
Pitt-Rivers, Michael, 3
Pivot, Bernard, 361n
Plath, Sylvia, 303n
Plato, 573
'Pleading for the valley of the reaper' (DB; newspaper article), 493n
Pleasence, Donald, 244n
Plon (French publishers), 236
Plowright, Joan (Lady Olivier), 258, 569
Plumb, Blossom, 147–8 & n
Plus grand musée du monde, Le (TV documentary), 324n, 389–90 & n
Point of Departure (play), 91n, 552n
Pollock, Jackson, 530
Polo, Richard, 254n
Pompidou, Claude, 580
Postillion Struck by Lightning, A (DB): writing, 5–6, 140n; publication and reception, 156, 162–4, 169, 171–2, 179, 185n, 197, 221n, 226, 228, 243; success and foreign translations, 355–6; French versions lost, 361; on childhood in Glasgow, 527n, 528
Potter, Dennis, 561; *Blade on the Feather*, 244 & n
Powell, Dilys, **51, 104, 106, 127, 129, 131, 143, 146, 157, 167, 178, 180, 204, 326, 333, 435, 439, 442, 453, 457, 462, 472, 515, 605;** correspondence with DB, 7, 12, 51; at Delhi Festival (1974–5), 127 & n; DB writes appreciation on retirement, 157; reviews DB's *Postillion*, 178; acquires cat, 182; previews movies for *Sunday Times* in retirement, 327n; collection of reviews published, 439n; DB lunches with, 487; reviews Caute's biography of Losey, 553; DB praises, 559; *An Affair of the Heart*, 335
Powell, Michael, 401, 461 & n, 463
Power, Tyrone, 207
Pressburger, Emeric, 401

Priestley, J.B., 52 & n
Prince, Hal, 156n
'Private Dirk Bogarde, The' (TV documentary), 11
Private Eye: attacks Norah Smallwood, 286n
Probus (clubs), 504 & n
Procter and Gamble (company), 284n
Prouse, Derek, 127 & n
Proust, Marcel: *Remembrance of Things Past (A la recherche du temps perdu)*, 42, 45, 95n, 116n, 153
Provence: DB invited to write on, 255, 393
Providence (film), 132, 138 & n, 143–6, 152–4, 156, 158–9, 166–7, 179, 181, 191, 204n, 208, 369n, 426
Public Lending Right, 328n
'Puddings and presents but no Santa Claus' (DB; newspaper extract), 516n
Puttnam, David, Baron, 358n, 387, 402n
Puttnam, Patricia Mary, Lady, 387

Quartet (film), 488
Quayle, Sir Anthony, 46 & n
Quinn, Anthony, 45

Rabal, Francisco, 340 & n
Rampling, Charlotte: with DB in *The Night Porter*, 96, 100, 105, 109–10, 112, 124; physique and qualities, 134, 136; marriage to Jarre, 218n, 298; DB entertains, 298; makes TV documentary on Louvre with DB, 324–5, 390; DB on first meeting, 425; proposed for Vita Sackville-West's *No Signposts in the Sea*, 438; at London reception for Jacques Chirac, 583, 585
Rank Charm School, 546n
Rank Organisation: DB works for, 4, 27
Rattigan, Sir Terence, 123; *A Bequest to the Nation*, 63n, 65
Réage, Pauline (pseud.): *l'Histoire d'O*, 128 & n
Rebecca (proposed film remake), 152n
Redford, Robert, 135 & n, 145, 153n
Redgrave, Sir Michael, 87
Redgrave, Vanessa, 50 & n, 72n, 234, 366n, 478, 590n, 591 & n
Reed International (Reed Audio), 589n
Reed, Oliver, 72n
Relph, Michael, 372–3 & n
Remick, Lee, 419n
Resnais, Alain: relations with DB, 7, 138, 153, 181; views, 35; DB films with, 40, 57, 132–4, 143–6, 153, 156, 159, 167, 179, 191, 369, 521; and Gielgud, 204–5; and 'Mon Oncle d'Amérique', 205, 253n; reads DB's published memoirs, 226, 235; incomprehensibility, 245; at 1980 Cannes Film Festival, 253; DB on, 598

Rhodes, Zandra, 275
Rice, Sir Tim, 561 & n
Richard, Sir Cliff, 574
Richardson, Keith, **396**
Richardson, Natasha, 474–5, 478, 503, 508 & n, 591n
Richardson, Sir Ralph, 43, 521n
Richardson, Tony, 366 & n, 389
Rickman, Alan, 501n
'Right to die with dignity, The' (DB; newspaper article), 493n
Roberts, Judy see Goodings, Judy
Roberts, Rachel, 514n
Robinson, David, 158, 462n
Rocco and His Brothers (film), 37n, 114
Rock, Phillip: *The Passing Bells*, 227–9
Roeg, Nicolas, 152 & n
Romantic Englishwoman, The (film), 113n, 115, 126n, 131 & n, 132, 141, 598
Rome, 89, 97–8
Roper, Lanning, 225 & n
Rosay, Françoise, 488
Rosoman, Leonard, 222–3; *The Wave, Amagansett* (painting), 214 & n
Rotunno, Giuseppe, 95 & n
Roud, Richard, 44 & n
Roux family, 112 & n, 577
Royal Geographical Society, 585, 587–8
Rushdie, Sir Salman, 311
Russell, Ken, 72n, 89
Russell, Leonard, 131n
Russell, Michael, 245n
Ryan, Cornelius, 213n
Ryan, Kathryn Morgan, 213 & n
Ryan, Maureen, 30–1
Rylands, George ('Dadie'), 204

Sachs, Andrew, 490
Sackville-West, Vita, 277, 438 & n; *No Signposts in the Sea*, 438
St Andrews University: awards honorary doctorate to DB, 362–3, 365, 367, 370, 374–7, 603, 604
St John, Earl, 554
Saki see Munro, H.H.
Salerno, Enrico Maria, 464
Sandoe, John (bookshop), 510
Sansom, William: *Proust and His World*, 117 & n
Santos Inocentes, Los (film), 340n
Sarne, Mike, 64n
Sassard, Jacqueline, 69
Scales, Prunella, 487
Scargill, Arthur, 337
Schaffner, Franklin, 83n
Schauberger, Dagmar, 180
Schell, Maximilian, 73

Schicle, Egon, 168 & n
Schiller, Lawrence (Larry), 267 & n, 279–80
Schindler, Oskar, 320, 326
Schlesinger, John, 42, 61, 72, 132, 136, 153, 233
Schneider, Romy, 68–9, 70, 74n, 90, 94
Schulkes, Arnold, 42, 73, 155
Scofield, Paul, 449n
Scott, Paul: *The Jewel in the Crown*, 332 & n
Sea Shall Not Have Them, The (film), 88n
Searle, Ellen (*later* Holt; 'Lally'): in DB's *Postillion*, 140 & n, 148–9, 163, 164–5, 169, 229, 516n; DB's money gifts to, 148–9, 536; and DB's knighthood, 520
Sebastian (film), 42
Secret Ceremony (film), 35, 114
Selwood, Nerine (*née* Cox), **299, 428, 431, 599, 600, 602**; DB corresponds with, 3
Senso (film), 114
Serpent, The (film), 96–7, 116, 128n
Servadio, Gaia: *Luchino Visconti: A Biography*, 323
Servant, The (film), 34n, 38, 49, 57n, 86, 114, 126, 141, 366, 371n, 423, 427, 545
Sexual Offences Act (1967), 373n
Seymour, Jane, 438
Seyrig, Delphine, 120, 303
Shaffer, Anthony: *Sleuth*, 46 & n
Shaffer, Sir Peter, 46
Shakespeare, Nicholas, **478, 605**; as literary editor of *Daily Telegraph*, 438n
Shaw, Fiona, 578
Shaw, George Bernard, 8
Shaw, Robert, 38, 46n, 48n
Shepherd, Simon, 397n
Shepherd, William (Bill), 449, 550–1
Sherriff, R.C.: *Journey's End*, 300–1
Shinwell, Emanuel, Baron, 367 & n
Shivas, Mark, 497
'Short Walk from Harrods, A' (DB; newspaper article), 470n
Short Walk from Harrods, A (DB), 531 & n, 532–3, 536, 538–9, 542–3 & n, 548, 550–1, 571, 576
Sica, Vittorio de, 464
Signoret, Simone, 36, 39, 43, 49, 67, 81, 112, 125, 213, 267, 361, 593; *La nostalgie n'est plus ce qu'elle était*, 221 & n
Sim, Sheila (Lady Attenborough): in France, 85; photograph used on jacket of *An Orderly Man*, 294 & n; DB entertains, 385
Simba (film), 314, 459, 546
Simmons, Jean, 266 & n, 328, 436, 548–9
Simon, John, 167 & n
Sinclair, Andrew: *In Love and Anger*, 561 & n
Singer Not the Song, The (film), 545
Sitwell family, 222

Skinner, Ann, **40, 71, 189, 195, 215, 233, 597**;
    correspondence with DB, 6, 9
Skolimowski, Jerzy, 213 & n
Sleeping Tiger, The (film), 112n, 342
Smallwood, Norah, **163, 171, 188, 197, 209,
    221, 222, 225, 228, 230, 238, 240, 243, 248,
    255, 259, 260, 263, 270, 276, 281, 286,
    290, 294, 295, 310, 316, 319, 321, 330, 335,
    345, 349, 599, 600, 601, 602, 603**; and
    DB's writing, 1, 6, 7, 126, 180–1, 188–9, 360,
    382, 466, 604; death, 7, 353, 358; relations
    with DB, 6, 163, 258, 293, 305–6, 316; DB
    dedicates *A Gentle Occupation* to, 232; visits
    DB in France, 251, 285; attacked in *Private
    Eye*, 286n; deposed at Chatto, 292; in DB's
    An Orderly Man, 294; visits USA, 316n, 318;
    farewell party, 322; leaves Chatto, 327; knee
    operation, 330n
Smith, Alexis, 112–12, 233, 606
Smith, Dodie: *Dear Octopus*, 158
Smith, Jean Kennedy, 36 & n
Snakes and Ladders (DB): working titles, 156 &
    n, 172 & n, 201n; writing, 206; publication
    and reception, 211, 213–16, 243; index, 214,
    215; Peter Hall praises, 221n; French edition,
    222n; readership, 226–7, 228; DB records on
    cassette, 234 & n; and biography of
    Visconti, 323
Snowdon, Antony Armstrong-Jones, 1st Earl
    of, 274–5
So Long at the Fair (film), 327–8, 548–9
Somme, battle of the (1916), 402
Sondheim, Stephen, 156n, 161
Song Without End (film), 114n, 202n, 490n,
    591n
Spanish Gardener, The (film), 147, 603
Spark, Dame Muriel: *Loitering with Intent*, 283,
    287
Spectator, The (journal), 525, 581, 583, 586, 588
Speer, Albert: *Inside the Third Reich*, 64n
Spielberg, Steven, 309n
Sposa bella, La (film), 464
Sprigge, Elizabeth: *Sybil Thorndike Casson*, 77n
Spurling, Hilary: *Secrets of a Woman's Heart*,
    346n
Stamp, Terence, 115, 545, Standing, John (Sir
    John Leon), 193 & n
Star Is Born, A (film), 386
Start the Week (radio programme), 467n, 555n
Steaming (film), 368
Steegmuller, Francis: *Cocteau*, 67n
Stella (DB's housekeeper), 565 & n, 574,
    578 & n
Stephens, Sir Robert, 156 & n
Stevenson, Juliet, 501 & n
Stoppard, Miriam, 185
Stoppard, Sir Tom, **170, 174, 182, 202**; DB

meets, 168; film version of *Despair*, 174, 190,
    194, 482–3; writes narration for *The Merry
    Widow*, 566n; *Every Good Boy Deserves
    Favour*, 182n; *Travesties*, 170 & n
Strachey, Lytton, 447
Straw Dogs (film), 105n
Stribling, Melissa (Melissa Dearden), 66 & n
Strick, Joseph, 202n
Stritch, Elaine, 144, 156
Stud, The (film), 212
Summer Story, A (film), 436n
Sun, The (newspaper), 492n
Sunday, Bloody Sunday (film), 72 & n
Sunday in the Country (film), 447, 449
Sunday Telegraph, The, 446n, 539
Sunday Times, The, 157; industrial dispute,
    283 & n
Sutherland, Donald, 136 & n, 152
Sutherland, Graham, 275, 501, 559
Sutherland, Kathleen, 275
Suzman, Janet, 83n
Swanson, Gloria, 274
Sydow, Max von, 128 & n

Tafler, Sydney, 46 & n
Tale of Two Cities, A (film) 378, 511, Tanitch,
    Robert: *Dirk Bogarde: The Complete Career
    Illustrated*, 591 & n
Tauber, Richard, 185
Tavernier, Bertrand, **448, 460, 463**;
    correspondence with DB, 7; directs DB,
    447–56, 459, 466, 471, 481, 484–5, 489, 493;
    and success of *Daddy Nostalgie* at Cannes
    Festival, 462–3; suggests new film with DB,
    516; visits London, 589; *Daddy Nostalgie*,
    446 & n, 447–50
Taylor, A.J.P., 519
Taylor, Dame Elizabeth (Richard Burton's
    wife), 35n, 81, 156 & n, 343
Taylor, Jeremy: 'Holy Dying', 572
Telegraph Magazine, 516n
Thames Television, 320
Thatcher, Margaret, Baroness, 282; *The
    Downing Street Years 1979–90*, 542 & n
That's Entertainment (film compilation), 130
Theroux, Paul, 232–2 & n
These Foolish Things (film) *see Daddy Nostalgie*
This Is Your Life (TV programme), 49
This Week (TV programme), 508 & n, 512
Thomas, Ralph, 42 & n, 45, 49, 217, 511
Thompson, Edward, **74, 598**; encourages DB
    to write, 74–5
Thompson, Emma, 471n
Thomson, H.A.R. (Bob), 451 & n
Thorndike, Dame Sybil, 77
Thorne, Anthony, 328
Thulin, Ingrid, 41

Thynne, Christopher, 450n
Time of Your Life, The (proposed film), 41n
Times, The: industrial dispute, 283 & n; DB
    writes on father for bicentennial (1985),
    347 & 9, 350–1, 355
Tindle, David, 387–8
Tobias, Oliver, 212n
Todd, Sir Ian, 310–11
Todd, Richard, 88 & n
Tollitt, Tina, 7, 277–8
Tolstoy, Count Nikolai: *Victims of Yalta*,
    210 & n
Tolusso, Ghigo, 354n
Tonbridge School, 498
Topol, Chaim, 131, 132
Tracy, Spencer, 499
Tree, Penelope, 36
Trefusis, Violet, 276, 438
Trevor–Roper, Hugh (Baron Dacre), 88 & n
'Trick or Treat' (film project), 144n
Trintignant, Jean-Louis, 36
Trollope, Joanna, 561 & n
Troxler, Anton, 357 & n, 503 & n
Troxler, Elisabeth, 503
Truly, Madly, Deeply (TV film), 501 & n
Turing, Alan, 3
Tynan, Kathleen, **133, 144, 205, 212, 235, 252,
    257, 273, 287, 324, 338, 356, 366, 597,
    598, 599, 602;** correspondence with DB, 7;
    article on DB in *Vogue*, 59–61, 65, 134n;
    friendship with DB, 62, 88, 134; and DB's
    recording of favourite music, 101; DB
    proof-reads for, 212; and Kenneth's death,
    257–8; book on Kenneth, 297; visits DB in
    France, 297; relations with DB, 558–9;
    Agatha, 202, 205 & n, 209, 212, 214, *The
    Summer Aeroplane*, 134 & n
Tynan, Kenneth: dress, 62; disbelieves DB's
    account of Belsen, 88; on DB's hesitation
    over writing, 126; and Mai Zetterling, 135 &
    n; and French politics, 207; manner, 217;
    death, 257–8; on Louise Brooks, 275 & n;
    Kathleen's book on, 297; advises DB on
    libel question, 518; dislikes DB, 559

Ullmann, Liv, 132, 367
Under the Volcano (film), 89, 162, 169, 339, 342,
    464
United States of America: DB's view of, 160,
    173, 603, 607; DB's book promotion tour,
    238; DB films in, 267–9
University College School, 8
Updike, John, 1
'Upon This Rock' (documentary), 43n
Ure, Mary, 470
Urquhart, Major-General Robert, 155n
Ustinov, Sir Peter, 214, 254, 583, 585

Valli, Alida, 591
van der Post, Sir Laurens, 337; *The Seed and the
    Sower*, 312n
Variety Club: makes award to DB, 478
Venice, 41, 45, 48–52; Harry's Bar, 547
Verneuil, Henri, 96
Victim (film), 66n, 372–3, 577, 594
Vidal, Gore, 96; *Myra Breckinridge*, 64n
Vidor, Charles, 202n
Vienna, 127–9
Viking Penguin (publishers), 327, 329, 403,
    438n, 441, 448, 456, 467, 477, 498, 523–4,
    533, 552, 569, 579
Villalobos, Reynaldo, 267n
Vincent the Dutchman (film), 135 & n
Visconti, Luchino, **53, 59, 65;** relations with
    DB, 7, 95, 316; DB films with, 27, 40–1, 44,
    130, 179, 196; and *The Damned*, 36–7; and
    Death in Venice, 40–1, 48, 51, 53–4, 56, 59–61,
    105, 122, 172; and DB's rented house in
    Venice, 51; upset by Kathleen Tynan's *Vogue*
    article, 59–61, 65, 134; wins award at Cannes
    (1971), 68 & n; film of Ludwig of Bavaria,
    101; on Proust, 116; in DB's published
    memoirs, 206, 214, 235; biographies of,
    322–3; homage event, 359
Vision, The (TV film), 413n, 419n, 551n
Visions of Eight – The Strongest (film), 135n
Vitti, Monica, 120
Vogue (magazine), 59, 65, 133–4
Voices in the Garden (DB; novel): title, 239n;
    writing, 237, 244, 250, 254, 255; published in
    USA, 258; reception, 278n, 283–7, 241, 289,
    304, 324; promotion, 284n; submitted for
    1981 Booker Prize, 286n; French translation,
    324, 329, 602; publication, 352–3; broadcast
    in France, 367; as cassette, 490; film version,
    496–7 & n, 499, 511
Volonté, Gian Maria, 42 & n
Voltaire, François Marie Arouet, 11
Voluntary Euthanasia Society, 493, 502, 507,
    512, 535

Wagner, Robert, 254
Waite, Terence (Terry): *Taken on Trust*,
    542 & n
Walker, Alexander, 94–5, 104, 462
Wall, Max, 175 & n
Wallis, Sir Barnes, 88 & n
Wallis, Hal, 47
Walls, Tom, 552
Wanamaker, Zoë, 439–40
Warchus, Matthew, 352n
Warner Brothers, 38, 51, 53, 56, 73, 99, 234
Warner, David, 144, 156
Waterhouse, Keith, 11, 402n, 555–6n
Watson, Dorothy, 353

Watson, Wallace Steadman, **481**;
  Understanding Rainer Werner Fassbinder,
  481n
Waugh, Auberon, 555 & n
Waugh, Evelyn, 123, 237, 239; *Diaries 1911–1965,*
  242
Wax, Jimmy, 522 & n
Webster, Daniel, 348
Weldon, Fay, 350
Welles, Orson, 43
Welser-Möst, Franz, 566–7 & n
Wenders, Wim, 338–9
Wesker, Sir Arnold, 572 & n
Wessex Films, 513
West, Samuel, 496n
West of Sunset (DB; novel), 295, 307–8, 327,
  330n, 338, 363, 367–8, 382, 393
Wharton, William: *Birdy,* 222
Wheeler, Peter, 587n
White, Patrick: *The Eye of the Storm,* 105
Whitehorn, Katharine, 213
Whitehouse, Mary, 110, 397
Whiting, John: *The Devils,* 352 & n
Whittaker, Christopher, **469**
Wicki, Bernhard, 484
Wien Film, 143 & n
Wild Bunch, The (film), 105n
Wilde, Oscar, 471
Wildeblood, Peter, 3
Wilding, Michael, 373
Williams, Edy, 212 & n
Williams, Emlyn, 175 & n
Williams, Molly, 568

Willis, Connie, 190
Wilson, Harold, Baron, 109 & n, 152n, 311
Wilson, Mary, Lady, 139n
Windsor, Edward, Duke of (David), 415 & n
Windsor, Wallis, Duchess of, 415
Winner, Michael, 218
Wiseman, Thomas, 113 & n
Witt, Peter, 74
Wogan, Sir Terence (Terry), 519
Wolfenden Report, 373 & n
Woman in Question, The (film), 96n
Woman's Hour (radio programme), 511
Wood, Natalie, 254; death, 288 & n
Woodward, Joanne, 477, 516
Wooldridge, Susan, 332n
Woolf, James, 78 & n
Woolf, Virginia, 222, 573; *A Room of One's Own:*
  stage adaptation, 451n, 486n
Wooll, Edward: *Libel,* 545n
Wright, Graeme, **606**
Wrong Is Right (film), 266n

Yaddo, New York State (writers' colony), 118n,
  124, 537 & n
Yates, Peter, 267n
Yelland, David, 397n
Yom Kippur War (1973), 102, 125, 128, 142n
York, Michael, 37, 100, 207 & n, 213, 217, 233
Young, Freddie, 129 & n
Young Winston (film), 73n

Zetterling, Mai, 91 & n, 135, 554
Zurlini, Valerio, 125 & n